Perspectives on American Politics

Perspectives on American Politics

FIFTH EDITION

William Lasser

Clemson University

Houghton Mifflin Company

Boston   New York

Executive Publisher: Patricia A. Coryell
Publisher: Suzanne Jeans
Senior Sponsoring Editor: Traci Mueller
Executive Marketing Manager: Nicola Poser
Development Editor: Christina Lembo
Associate Project Editor: Kristen Truncellito
Senior Art and Design Coordinator: Jill Haber
Cover Design Director: Tony Saizon
Senior Photo Editor: Jennifer Meyer Dare
Composition Buyer: Chuck Dutton
New Title Project Manager: Susan Brooks-Peltier
Editorial Assistant: Tiffany Hill
Marketing Associate: Karen E. Mulvey

Cover image: © Sampson Williams/SuperStock

Printed in the U.S.A.

Library of Congress Control Number: 2006940954

Instructor's examination copy
    ISBN-10: 0-618-83394-3
    ISBN-13: 978-0-618-83394-8

For orders, use student text ISBNs
    ISBN-10: 0-618-71915-6
    ISBN-13: 978-0-618-71915-0

23456789-CRS-11 10 09 08 07

To Susan J. S. Lasser, with love

Contents

*searching for truth. . . . The defense also claimed the mantle of truth
and accused the prosecution of placing barriers in its path. And
throughout the trial, the pundits observed that neither side was really
interested in truth, only in winning. They were right—and wrong."*

*The Government's power to censor the press was abolished so that the
press would remain forever free to censure the Government."*

Readings by Perspective

Foundations

American Politics Today

Issue and Controversy

🔐 View from the Inside

Federalist Papers

Supreme Court Decisions

Preface

The classic questions of American politics have rarely seemed so relevant to the central issues of our time than in the years since September 11, 2001. How much power should be vested in the President of the United States, and how much should rest with Congress and the courts? To what extent should the fundamental guarantees of the Bill of Rights be sacrificed in the interest of fighting the war on terror? Is America's federal system adequate to deal with the vital problems facing the nation in the twenty-first century? And can America afford to pay for an increasingly expensive foreign and military policy while dealing at the same time with pressing social and economic concerns at home?

Like its predecessors, the fifth edition of *Perspectives on American Politics* focuses on the new realities of life in America within the context of questions of long-standing concern to students and professors of American government. As in all previous editions, a central feature of this reader is the emphasis on examining American politics from several key viewpoints. Every chapter is organized around four essential perspectives—Foundations, American Politics Today, Issue and Controversy, and View from the Inside. Every selection has been chosen for its ability to inform, educate, and engage undergraduate students.

The Purpose of This Reader

My goal in *Perspectives on American Politics* has been to develop a collection of readings that is clearly organized, that can be easily integrated into an American government course and actually help in teaching the course, and that will hold the students' (and professor's) attention by presenting a wide variety of viewpoints, writing styles, and approaches. Above all, I have endeavored to create a reader that shows students just why I—and all other professors of American government—find this subject so meaningful and important.

The challenge in compiling an American government reader is to maintain structure and coherence without sacrificing the extraordinary eclecticism that marks the enormous body of writings about American government. The solution incorporated here is to begin each chapter with certain key questions in mind and then to present a set of readings designed to provide various perspectives on those questions. This approach allows students to focus on a manageable number of critical issues, while at the same time giving them a variety of perspectives on those issues. All of the readings, however diverse they might be, revolve around the central chapter questions and thus maintain a clear and cohesive relationship with each other and with the readings in earlier and later chapters.

Another key goal has been to produce a reader that professors and students alike will find easy to use. The thirteen chapters of this book correspond to the most frequently assigned chapters of most American government textbooks, so they should fit neatly into any standard syllabus. Furthermore, many of the chapter and reading questions can serve as essay assignments, and the selections can be used as a starting point for class discussions of controversial or important issues.

The Fifth Edition

In preparing the fifth edition, I carefully scrutinized each selection for readability, usefulness, and timeliness. The following features are particularly worth noting:

◆ *Four essential perspectives in each chapter.* To make this reader easy to use and to provide a consistent chapter structure, each chapter contains one or more selections under each of the following headings: Foundations, American Politics Today, Issue and Controversy, and View from the Inside. These perspectives make it easy for professors to include or exclude specific material and make it easy for students to find their way around the book. At the same time, however, these perspectives are diverse enough to give students a wide range of vantage points on American politics. These four perspectives appear in the same order in every chapter.

◆ *Selections reflecting dramatic recent developments in American politics.* In addition to the elections of 2004 and 2006, these new developments include continuing debates over affirmative action; the re-emergence of divided government (for the moment, at least), with Republican control of the presidency balanced by Democratic control of Congress; and renewed debate, in the wake of the highly unpopular Iraq War, over whether the United States should act unilaterally or multilaterally in foreign policy and how, and how much, to check and balance presidential power.

The Perspectives

All of the readings are grouped into four perspectives that are presented in every chapter in the order listed here:

◆ **Foundations.** The first perspective presents a classic work in American politics, an important theoretical reading, or a seminal work in American political science. Examples include selections from the *Federalist Papers*; important Supreme Court decisions, such as *Brown* v. *Board of Education* and *Marbury* v. *Madison*; and excerpts from works such as John Stuart Mill's *On Liberty* and E. E. Schattschneider's *The Scope and Bias of the Pressure System*.

◆ **American Politics Today.** The second perspective provides a snapshot of the current state of American politics. This section often comprises works by political scientists and others who do not merely describe the current state of affairs, but seek to analyze and understand it. Examples include a thought-provoking article on what might happen if the Supreme Court reverses *Roe* v. *Wade*, an analysis of the 2006 midterm elections, and a look at the long-term problems in funding Social Security and Medicare.

♦ **Issue and Controversy.** New to the fifth edition are selections in every chapter focusing on current or long-standing controversial issues. In some cases these selections include a pair of readings, in a debate format; in others, a single article presents a thoughtful overview. These selections are designed to promote discussion and debate, either informally or through structured class exercises. Examples include the alleged existence of media bias; a defense of the Electoral College; and an exchange of views on the legitimacy of the Senate filibuster.

♦ **View from the Inside.** This popular perspective from earlier editions appears in every chapter. These readings provide an inside view of American politics and government. In addition to insider accounts of September 11 and the 2004 election, I have included a profile of freshman Senator Barack Obama; an article on the first same-sex marriages in Massachusetts; and the story of a novice lawyer who argued his own case in the United States Supreme Court.

Pedagogy

Like earlier editions, the fifth edition of *Perspectives on American Politics* includes pedagogical devices designed to make life easier for students and professors alike. These include chapter and section introductions and questions that orient students to the key themes, promote critical thinking, and make essential background information available. The questions can also be used by students for review purposes and by instructors for generating class discussion. Outlines for difficult readings, such as the *Federalist Papers*, provide some help to students approaching these works for the first time. Finally, I have provided a separate Instructor's Resource Manual, which features teaching hints for each chapter and each selection, ideas for assignments and class discussions, additional readings, and Internet links.

Some Technical Notes

I have used several standard conventions throughout the text. The omission of large amounts of material is indicated by centered bullets (• • •); smaller omissions are indicated by ellipses (. . .). In general, I have not corrected antique spellings, nor have I modified older styles of punctuation or capitalization. I have eliminated virtually all footnotes; readers who are interested in source notes and other references should go directly to the originals. Where necessary, I have inserted explanatory or additional matter within brackets. For the sake of clarity, I have frequently shortened selection titles, and in some cases I have modified them substantially.

An Apology, More or Less

No anthology can contain everything. Undoubtedly, there will be some who are dismayed or scandalized at the omission or inclusion of a particular article, case, or essay. To some extent, the fifth edition reflects the criticisms, compliments, or suggestions offered by particular readers. All such communications are welcome and appreciated.

Acknowledgments

I am grateful for the advice and assistance of editors, colleagues, and friends both in the preparation of the original manuscript and in the revisions for the fifth edition. I would particularly like to thank Christina Lembo at Houghton Mifflin, who guided me through the preparation of the fifth edition from start to finish, and Nancy Benjamin, who turned the manuscript into a book. It has been a great comfort to be able to rely on their advice and expertise.

My colleagues at Clemson and elsewhere have provided suggestions regarding what to include in the book, both in this and in previous editions. I would particularly like to thank Joe Stewart, R. Shep Melnick, Laura Olson, Marty Slann, Robert Vipond, Adam Warber, and Dave Woodard. A number of others read and critiqued various parts of this manuscript and gave many helpful suggestions, including Charles J. Finocchiaro, University at Buffalo, SUNY; Mitchel Gerber, Southeast Missouri State University; Matthew Wilson, Southern Methodist University; and college-level preparatory instructors Jason Colin Scott, Naples High School (Naples, FL), and Tiffani Walker, Harker Heights High School (Harker Heights, TX). Kelly Jones provided valuable research assistance. Many other users have provided useful comments over the years, and this fifth edition reflects many of their suggestions.

Finally, I thank my children, Max Hoffman and Adina Rose. Their very existence is a constant reminder of what really matters. Above all, I thank my wife, Susan J. S. Lasser, who after twenty-eight years, two children, and five editions remains a source of inspiration. As with the earlier editions, this remains, with love and gratitude, her book.

W. L.

Perspectives on
American Politics

Chapter 1

The Constitution

The United States Constitution forms the basis of the American political system. Despite extraordinary changes in the American economy and in the nation's role and responsibilities in the world, the Constitution remains essentially the same document as written in Philadelphia in the summer of 1787. Over the years, several amendments have made it more inclusive and extended the "blessings of liberty" to previously excluded groups, including blacks and women. At the same time, countless decisions of the United States Supreme Court have altered the nuances and interpretations of the original text. Still, the original document and the political philosophy that lies behind it are well worth studying.

The political philosophy of the Constitution is largely that of the Federalists, its primary supporters. The Federalists were less than a political party; they were a loosely organized group of individuals who shared a commitment to the proposed Constitution and the ideas it represented. Because they won and because they counted among their number such leading figures as Alexander Hamilton and James Madison, the Federalists are far better known than their opponents, who went by the unfortunately negative-sounding name "Antifederalists." To understand the Federalists and their political philosophy, however, it is essential to understand the views and opinions of the opposition.

Chapter 1 begins by presenting the major ideas of the Federalists and Antifederalists (selections 1.1 through 1.5). It then provides a modern example—drawn from the debates over the meaning of the Second Amendment—suggesting that the ideas of the Founding Generation still have relevance today (selection 1.6). It concludes with a selection that asks "Is the Constitution Democratic?" (selection 1.7) and with an inside view of the final days of the Constitutional Convention of 1787 (selection 1.8).

Chapter Questions

1. In what senses are the Federalists properly described as "aristocrats" and the Antifederalists as "democrats"? Consider both the social standing of the two groups and their ideas about politics.
2. Did the Federalists believe in democracy? What evidence is there that they did? That they did not? How can these two views be reconciled?

3. Were the Antifederalists correct in at least some of their charges against the Constitution? Which of their complaints look more reasonable after two hundred years? Which look less so?

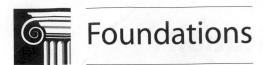 # Foundations

There is no better way to understand the political philosophy of the Federalists than to read the *Federalist Papers*. Originally a selection of newspaper columns written during the debate over the ratification of the Constitution in New York State, the *Federalist Papers* are a compendium of eighty-five essays explaining, defending, and elaborating on the proposed Constitution. The *Federalist*, as it is known, is widely regarded as the definitive statement of the Federalists' views on the Constitution and thus is a frequent reference point for those (federal judges, for example) who seek to know the intent of those who wrote the Constitution. The essays that make up the *Federalist* were written by three prominent proponents of the Constitution: John Jay, Alexander Hamilton, and James Madison. Following the style of the day, the articles were signed by the pseudonym Publius, a name that perhaps sought to imply that the authors spoke for the public interest.

Federalist No. 10, written by James Madison, is concerned with the problem of factions. Frequently, it appears in a textbook chapter on interest groups, and it might profitably be reread along with the selections in Chapter 6. Its greater importance, however, lies in Publius's discussion of human nature and representative government. Publius believes that in a free society, there will soon arise factions, or groups of individuals motivated by a common interest or passion adverse to the interests of other citizens or to the public interest. These factions arise because individuals are free to think for themselves about "religion . . . government, and many other points" and because they have different abilities for acquiring property. Once factions arise, it is in the nature of human beings that they will attempt to use the government to advance their own interests, even at the expense of others. In a pure democracy, the majority faction will pursue its own interest at the expense of the minority, with the result that rational government is impossible. The solution is to construct a representative government covering a large area, so that each representative will represent many diverse interests, and no one faction will be able to dominate.

Notice the consequences of Publius's theory: representative government is not merely a means of approximating a direct democracy but an improvement on it, and representatives are expected not merely to echo the interests of their constituents but to refine and filter those interests and balance them against the interests of others and against the public interest.

In *Federalist* Nos. 47–51, James Madison lays out his theory of the separation of powers. Contrary to the assumption of most other Americans, Madison did not believe that legislative, executive, and judicial power should be rigidly constrained, each to its own branch of government. In fact, *Federalist* No. 47 was written explicitly to challenge the assumption that the separation of powers means that the three departments of government "ought to have no *partial agency* in, or no *control* over, the acts of each other." Quite the opposite is true, in Madison's opinion: each branch should be given a share of the others' powers. It is only if "the *whole* power of one department is exercised by the same hands which possess the *whole* power of another department" that liberty is threatened.

Having demonstrated that the separation of powers does not demand a strict separation of functions, Madison then lays out the psychological basis for the separation of powers. Put simply, human beings are not angels; they are and will always be ambitious and power hungry. The only security against such individuals (and politicians are especially likely to possess such qualities) is to make sure that ambition checks ambition. By dividing power among ambitious people and then making them compete for power among themselves, liberty is protected.

All of this may be a sad commentary on human nature, as Madison suggests, but "what is government itself but the greatest of all reflections on human nature?" Madison's political theory here tracks the Scottish economist Adam Smith's theory of capitalism: we rely on the baker for bread not on the assumption that the baker will want to feed his fellow human beings but on his personal desire for money. Similarly, Madison relies for the protection of liberty not on politicians' love of the people but on their desire to protect their own power.

Also included here is a selection from the Antifederalists, who opposed the Constitution. That they lost their battle does not mean that their arguments were without merit. The Antifederalists were in general educated and intelligent men whose ideas on politics presented a viable alternative to that presented by the Federalists. In fact, the Antifederalists' views typically represented the conventional eighteenth-century wisdom as compared to the much more innovative—and therefore controversial—ideas of the Federalists.

The Antifederalists produced no such book as the *Federalist Papers*. Their writings were diverse, uncoordinated, and of uneven quality. One example—the report of the minority of the Pennsylvania ratifying convention of 1787—is given in this section. This report presents one of the most systematic statements of the Antifederalists' arguments. Notice in particular the minority's fearful and suspicious tone—justifiable, considering the way they were treated by the majority—along with their objections to a large republic; the mixing of legislative, executive, and judicial power; the lack of limits to federal authority over the states; and the absence of a bill of rights.

Other selections from the *Federalist Papers* are contained in Chapters 2, 9, 10, and 12.

Questions

1. What is a faction? Why are majority factions more dangerous than minority factions, according to Madison?
2. According to Madison, what advantages does a large republic have over a smaller one? How might the Antifederalists respond to Madison's position?
3. How does Madison respond to the Antifederalists' charge that the Constitution impermissibly blends executive, legislative, and judicial power? Why, in Madison's view, is it necessary to blend the three types of power?
4. Compare and contrast the Federalists' and Antifederalists' views on human nature. Pay particular attention to Madison's argument in *Federalist* No. 51.

1.1 *Federalist* No. 10 (1787)

James Madison

Outline

I. Republican governments are prone to the disease of *factions*; protecting against factions is critical to the success of any design for republican government.

II. Definition of faction.

III. The problem of factions can be cured by removing the causes of factions or by controlling their effects.

  A. It is impractical and unwise to try to remove the causes of factions; they are "sown in the nature of man."

  B. Therefore factions must be controlled.

   1. Minority factions can be controlled by the principle of majority rule.

   2. Minority factions can be controlled by creating a large republic and by creating a system of representation to "refine and enlarge" the views of the public.

Among the numerous advantages promised by a well-constructed Union, none deserves to be more accurately developed than its tendency to break and control the violence of faction. The friend of popular governments never finds himself so much alarmed for their character and fate as when he contemplates their propensity to this dangerous vice. He will not fail, therefore, to set a due value on any plan which, without violating the principles to which he is attached, provides a proper cure for it. The instability, injustice, and confusion introduced into the public councils have, in truth, been the mortal diseases under which popular governments have everywhere perished, as they continue to be the favorite and fruitful topics from which the adversaries to liberty derive their most specious declamations. The valuable improvements made by the American constitutions on the popular models, both ancient and modern, cannot certainly be too much admired; but it would be an unwarrantable partiality to contend that they have as effectually obviated the danger on this side, as was wished and expected. Complaints are everywhere heard from our most considerate and virtuous citizens, equally the friends of public and private faith and of public and personal liberty, that our governments are too unstable, that the public good is disregarded in the conflicts of rival parties, and that measures are too often decided, not according to the rules of justice and the rights of the minor party, but by the superior force of an interested and overbearing majority. However anxiously we may wish that these complaints had no foundation, the evidence of known facts will not permit us to deny that they are in some degree true. It will be found, indeed, on a candid review of our situation, that some of the distresses under which we labor have been erroneously charged on the operation of our governments; but it will be found, at the same time, that other causes will not alone account for many of our heaviest misfortunes; and, particularly, for that prevailing and increasing distrust of public engagements and alarm for private rights which are echoed from one end of the continent to the other. These must be chiefly, if not wholly, effects of the unsteadiness and injustice with which a factious spirit has tainted our public administration.

By a faction I understand a number of citizens, whether amounting to a majority or minority of the whole, who are united and actuated by some common impulse of passion, or of interest, adverse to the rights of other citizens, or to the permanent and aggregate interests of the community.

There are two methods of curing the mischiefs of faction: the one, by removing its causes; the other, by controlling its effects.

There are again two methods of removing the causes of faction: the one, by destroying the liberty which is essential to its existence; the other, by giving to every citizen the same opinions, the same passions, and the same interests.

It could never be more truly said than of the first remedy that it was worse than the disease. Liberty is to faction what air is to fire, an aliment without which it instantly expires. But it could not be a less folly to abolish liberty, which is essential to political life, because it nourishes faction than it would be to wish the annihilation of air, which is essential to animal life, because it imparts to fire its destructive agency.

The second expedient is as impracticable as the first would be unwise. As long as the reason of man continues fallible, and he is at liberty to exercise it, different opinions will be formed. As long as the connection subsists between his reason and his self-love, his opinions and his passions will have a reciprocal influence on each other; and the former will be objects to which the latter will attach themselves. The diversity in the faculties of men, from which the rights of property originate, is not less an insuperable obstacle to a uniformity of interests. The protection of these faculties is the first object of government. From the protection of different and unequal faculties of acquiring property, the possession of different degrees and kinds of property immediately results; and from the influence of these on the sentiments and views of the respective proprietors ensues a division of the society into different interests and parties.

The latent causes of faction are thus sown in the nature of man; and we see them everywhere brought into different degrees of activity, according to the different circumstances of civil society. A zeal for different opinions concerning religion, concerning government, and many other points, as well of speculation as of practice; an attachment to different leaders ambitiously contending for preeminence and power; or to persons of other descriptions whose fortunes have been interesting to the human passions, have, in turn, divided mankind into parties, inflamed them with mutual animosity, and rendered them much more disposed to vex and oppress each other than to cooperate for their common good. So strong is this propensity of mankind to fall into mutual animosities that where no substantial occasion presents itself the most frivolous and fanciful distinctions have been sufficient to kindle their unfriendly passions and excite their most violent conflicts. But the most common and durable source of factions has been the various and unequal distribution of property. Those who hold and those who are without property have ever formed distinct interests in society. Those who are creditors, and those who are debtors, fall under a like discrimination. A landed interest, a manufacturing interest, a mercantile interest, a moneyed interest, with many lesser interests, grow up of necessity in civilized nations, and divide them into different classes, actuated by different sentiments and views. The regulation of these various and interfering interests forms the principal task of modern legislation and involves the spirit of party and faction in the necessary and ordinary operations of government.

No man is allowed to be a judge in his own cause, because his interest would certainly bias his judgment, and, not improbably, corrupt his integrity. With equal, nay with greater reason, a body of men are unfit to be both judges and parties at the same time; yet what are many of the most important acts of legislation but so many judicial determinations, not indeed concerning the rights of single persons, but concerning the rights of large bodies of citizens? And what are the different classes of legislators but advocates and parties to the causes which they determine? Is a law proposed concerning private debts? It is a question to which the creditors are parties on one side and the debtors on the other. Justice ought to hold the balance between them. Yet the parties are, and must be, themselves the judges; and the most numerous party, or in other words, the most powerful faction must be expected to prevail. Shall domestic manufacturers be encouraged, and in what degree, by restrictions on foreign manufacturers? are questions which would be differently decided by the landed and the manufacturing classes, and probably by neither with a sole regard to justice and the public good. The apportionment of taxes on the various descriptions of property is an act which seems to require the most exact impartiality; yet there is, perhaps, no legislative act in which greater opportunity and temptation are given to a predominant party to trample on the rules of justice. Every shilling with which they overburden the inferior number is a shilling saved to their own pockets.

It is in vain to say that enlightened statesmen will be able to adjust these clashing interests and render them all subservient to the public good. Enlightened statesmen will not always be at the helm. Nor, in many cases, can such an adjustment be made at all without taking into view indirect and remote considerations, which will rarely prevail over the immediate interest which one party may find in disregarding the rights of another or the good of the whole.

The inference to which we are brought is that the *causes* of faction cannot be removed and that relief is only to be sought in the means of controlling its *effects*.

If a faction consists of less than a majority, relief is supplied by the republican principle, which enables the majority to defeat its sinister views by regular vote. It may clog the administration, it may convulse the society; but it will be unable to execute and mask its violence under the forms of the Constitution. When a majority is included in a faction, the form of popular government, on the other hand, enables it to sacrifice to its ruling passion or interest both the public good and the rights of other citizens. To secure the public good and private rights against the danger of such a faction, and at the same time to preserve the spirit and the form of popular government, is then the great object to which our inquiries are directed. Let me add that it is the great desideratum by which alone this form of government can be rescued from the opprobrium under which it has so long labored and be recommended to the esteem and adoption of mankind.

By what means is this object attainable? Evidently by one of two only. Either the existence of the same passion or interest in a majority at the same time must be prevented, or the majority, having such coexistent passion or interest, must be rendered, by their number and local situation, unable to concert and carry into effect schemes of oppression. If the impulse and the opportunity be suffered to coincide, we well know that neither moral nor religious motives can be relied on as an adequate control. They are not found to be such on the injustice and violence of individuals, and lose their efficacy in proportion to the number combined together, that is, in proportion as their efficacy becomes needful.

From this view of the subject it may be concluded that a pure democracy, by which I mean a society consisting of a small number of citizens, who assemble and administer the government in person, can admit of no cure for the mischiefs of faction. A common passion or interest will, in almost every case, be felt by a majority of the whole; a communication and concert results from the form of government itself; and there is nothing to check the inducements to sacrifice the weaker party or an obnoxious individual. Hence it is that such democracies have ever been spectacles of turbulence and contention; have ever been found incompatible with personal security or the rights of property; and have in general been as short in their lives as they have been violent in their deaths. Theoretic politicians, who have patronized this species of government, have erroneously supposed that by reducing mankind to a perfect equality in their political rights, they would at the same time be perfectly equalized and assimilated in their possessions, their opinions, and their passions.

A republic, by which I mean a government in which the scheme of representation takes place, opens a different prospect and promises the cure for which we are seeking. Let us examine the points in which it varies from pure democracy, and we shall comprehend both the nature of the cure and the efficacy which it must derive from the Union.

The two great points of difference between a democracy and a republic are: first, the delegation of the government, in the latter, to a small number of citizens elected by the rest; secondly, the greater number of citizens and greater sphere of country over which the latter may be extended.

The effect of the first difference is, on the one hand, to refine and enlarge the public views by passing them through the medium of a chosen body of citizens, whose wisdom may best discern the true interest of their country and whose patriotism and love of justice will be least likely to sacrifice it to temporary or partial considerations. Under such a regulation it may well happen that the public voice, pronounced by the representatives of the people, will be more consonant to the public good than if pronounced by the people themselves, convened for the purpose. On the other hand, the effect may be inverted. Men of factious tempers, of local prejudices, or of sinister designs, may, by intrigue, by corruption, or by other means, first obtain the suffrages, and then betray the interests of the people. The question resulting is, whether small or extensive republics are most favorable to the election of proper guardians of the public weal; and it is clearly decided in favor of the latter by two obvious considerations.

In the first place it is to be remarked that however small the republic may be the representatives must be raised to a certain number in order to guard against the cabals of a few; and that however large it may be they must be limited to a certain number in order to guard against the confusion of a multitude. Hence, the number of representatives in the two cases not being in proportion to that of the constituents, and being proportionally greatest in the small republic, it follows that if the proportion of fit characters be not less in the large than in the small republic, the former will present a greater option, and consequently a greater probability of a fit choice.

In the next place, as each representative will be chosen by a greater number of citizens in the large than in the small republic, it will be more difficult for unworthy candidates to practise with success the vicious arts by which elections are too often carried; and the suffrages of the people being more free, will be more likely to center on men who possess the most attractive merit and the most diffusive and established characters.

It must be confessed that in this, as in most other cases, there is a mean, on both sides of which inconveniences will be found to lie. By enlarging too much the number of electors, you render the representative too little acquainted with all their local circumstances and lesser interests; as by reducing it too much, you render him unduly attached to these, and too little fit to comprehend and pursue great and national objects. The federal Constitution forms a happy combination in this respect; the great and aggregate interests being referred to the national, the local and particular to the State legislatures.

The other point of difference is the greater number of citizens and extent of territory which may be brought within the compass of republican than of democratic government; and it is this circumstance principally which renders factious combinations less to be dreaded in the former than in the latter. The smaller the society, the fewer probably will be the distinct parties and interests composing it; the fewer the distinct parties and interests, the more frequently will a majority be found of the same party; and the smaller the number of individuals composing a majority, and the smaller the compass within which they are placed, the more easily will they concert and execute their plans of oppression. Extend the sphere and you take in a greater variety of parties and interests; you make it less probable that a majority of the whole will have a common motive to invade the rights of other citizens; or if such a common motive exists, it will be more difficult for all who feel it to discover their own strength and to act in unison with each other. Besides other impediments, it may be remarked that, where there is a consciousness of unjust or dishonorable purposes, communication is always checked by distrust in proportion to the number whose concurrence is necessary.

Hence, it clearly appears that the same advantage which a republic has over a democracy in controlling the effects of faction is enjoyed by a large over a small republic—is enjoyed by the Union over the States composing it. Does this advantage consist in the substitution of representatives whose enlightened views and virtuous sentiments render them superior to local prejudices and to schemes of injustice? It will not be denied that the representation of the Union will be most likely to possess these requisite endowments. Does it consist in the greater security afforded by a greater variety of parties, against the event of any one party being able to outnumber and oppress the rest? In an equal degree does the increased variety of parties comprised within the Union increase this security. Does it, in fine, consist in the greater obstacles opposed to the concert and accomplishment of the secret wishes of an unjust and interested majority? Here again the extent of the Union gives it the most palpable advantage.

The influence of factious leaders may kindle a flame within their particular States but will be unable to spread a general conflagration through the other States. A religious sect may degenerate into a political faction in a part of the Confederacy; but the variety of sects dispersed over the entire face of it must secure the national councils against any danger from that source. A rage for paper money, for an abolition of debts, for an equal division of property, or for any other improper or wicked project, will be less apt to pervade the whole body of the Union than a particular member of it, in the same proportion as such a malady is more likely to taint a particular county or district than an entire State.

In the extent and proper structure of the Union, therefore, we behold a republican remedy for the diseases most incident to republican government. And according to the degree of pleasure and pride we feel in being republicans ought to be our zeal in cherishing the spirit and supporting the character of federalists. ■

1.2 *Federalist* No. 47 (1787)

James Madison

Outline

I. The charge that the Constitution violates the separation of powers principle is based on a misinterpretation of the separation of powers.

  A. The Constitution is consistent with Montesquieu's view of the separation of powers.

    1. Montesquieu's view based on the British Constitution.

    2. Discussion of Montesquieu's theory.

  B. The Constitution is consistent with the implementation of the separation of powers in the constitutions of the several states.

. . . One of the principal objections inculcated by the more respectable adversaries to the Constitution is its supposed violation of the political maxim that the legislative, executive, and judiciary departments ought to be separate and distinct. In the structure of the federal government no regard, it is said, seems to have been paid to this essential precaution in favor of liberty. The several departments of power are distributed and blended in such a manner as at once to destroy all symmetry and beauty of form, and to expose some of the essential parts of the edifice to the danger of being crushed by the disproportionate weight of other parts.

No political truth is certainly of greater intrinsic value, or is stamped with the authority of more enlightened patrons of liberty than that on which the objection is founded. The accumulation of all powers, legislative, executive, and judiciary, in the same hands, whether of one, a few, or many, and whether hereditary, self-appointed, or elective, may justly be pronounced the very definition of tyranny. Were the federal Constitution, therefore, really chargeable with this accumulation of power, or with a mixture of powers, having a dangerous tendency to such an accumulation, no further arguments would be necessary to inspire a universal reprobation of the system. I persuade myself, however, that it will be made apparent to everyone that the charge cannot be supported, and that the maxim on which it relies has been totally misconceived and misapplied. In order to form correct ideas on this important subject it will be proper to investigate the sense in which the preservation of liberty requires that the three great departments of power should be separate and distinct.

The oracle who is always consulted and cited on this subject is the celebrated Montesquieu. If he be not the author of this invaluable precept in the science of politics, he has the merit at least of displaying and recommending it most effectually to the attention of mankind. Let us endeavor, in the first place, to ascertain his meaning on this point.

The British Constitution was to Montesquieu what Homer has been to the didactic writers on epic poetry. As the latter have considered the work of the immortal bard as the perfect model from which the principles and rules of the epic art were to be drawn, and by which all similar works were to be judged, so this great political critic appears to have viewed the Constitution of England as the standard, or to use his own expression, as the mirror of political liberty; and to have delivered, in the form of elementary truths, the several characteristic principles of that particular system. That we may be sure, then, not to mistake his meaning in this case, let us recur to the source from which the maxim was drawn.

On the slightest view of the British Constitution, we must perceive that the legislative, executive, and judiciary departments are by no means totally separate and distinct from each other. The executive magistrate forms an integral part of the legislative authority. He alone has the prerogative of making treaties with foreign sovereigns which, when made, have, under certain limitations, the force of legislative acts. All the members of the judiciary department are appointed by him, can be removed by him on the address of the two Houses of Parliament, and form, when he pleases to consult them, one of his constitutional councils. One branch of the legislative department forms also a great constitutional council to the executive chief, as, on another hand, it is the sole depositary of judicial power in cases of impeachment, and is invested with the supreme appellate jurisdiction in all other cases. The judges, again, are so far connected with the legislative department as often to attend and participate in its deliberations, though not admitted to a legislative vote.

From these facts, by which Montesquieu was guided, it may clearly be inferred that in saying "There can be no liberty where the legislative and executive powers are united in the same person, or body of magistrates," or, "if the power of judging be not separated from the legislative and executive powers," he did not mean that these departments ought to have no *partial agency* in, or no *control* over, the acts of each other. His meaning, as his own words import, and still more conclusively as illustrated by the example in his eye, can amount to no more than this, that where the *whole* power of one department is exercised by the same hands which possess the *whole* power of another department, the fundamental principles of a free constitution are subverted. This would have been the case in the constitution examined by him, if the king, who is the sole executive magistrate, had possessed also the complete legislative power, or the supreme administration of justice; or if the entire legislative body had possessed the supreme judiciary, or the supreme executive authority. This, however, is not among the vices of that constitution. The magistrate in whom the whole executive power resides cannot of himself make a law, though he can put a negative on every law; nor administer justice in person, though he has the appointment of those who do administer it. The judges can exercise no executive prerogative, though they are shoots from the executive stock; nor any legislative function, though they may be advised by the legislative councils. The entire legislature can perform no judiciary act, though by the joint act of two of its branches the judges may be removed from their offices, and though one of its branches is possessed of the judicial power in the last resort. The entire legislature, again, can exercise no executive prerogative, though one of its branches constitutes the supreme executive magistracy, and another, on the impeachment of a third, can try and condemn all the subordinate officers in the executive department.

The reasons on which Montesquieu grounds his maxim are a further demonstration of his meaning. "When the legislative and executive powers are united in the same person or body," says he, "there can be no liberty, because apprehensions may arise lest *the same* monarch or senate should *enact* tyrannical laws to *execute* them in a tyrannical manner." Again: "Were the power of judging joined with the legislative, the life and liberty of the subject would be exposed to arbitrary control, for *the judge* would then be *the legislator*. Were it joined to the executive power, *the judge* might behave with all the violence of *an oppressor*." Some of these reasons are more fully explained in other passages; but briefly stated as they are here they sufficiently establish the meaning which we have put on this celebrated maxim of this celebrated author.

If we look into the constitutions of the several States we find that, notwithstanding the emphatical and, in some instances, the unqualified terms in which this axiom has been laid down, there is not a single instance in which the several departments of power have been kept absolutely separate and distinct. New Hampshire, whose constitution was the last formed, seems to have been fully aware of the impossibility and inexpediency of avoiding any mixture whatever of these departments, and has qualified the doctrine by declaring "that the legislative, executive, and judiciary powers ought to be kept as separate from, and independent of, each other *as the nature of a free government will admit; or as is consistent with that chain of connection that binds the whole fabric of the constitution in one indissoluble bond of unity and amity.*" Her constitution accordingly mixes these departments in several respects. The Senate, which is a branch of the legislative department, is also a judicial tribunal for the trial of impeachments; The President, who is the head of the executive department, is the presiding member also of the Senate; and, besides an equal vote in all cases, has a casting vote in case of a tie. The executive head is himself eventually elective every year by the legislative department, and his council is every year chosen by and from the members of the same department. Several of the officers of state are also appointed by the legislature. And the members of the judiciary department are appointed by the executive department.

The constitution of Massachusetts has observed a sufficient though less pointed caution in expressing this fundamental article of liberty. It declares "that the legislative department shall never exercise the executive and judicial powers, or either of them; the executive shall never exercise the legislative and judicial powers, or either of them; the judicial shall never exercise the legislative and executive powers, or either of them." This declaration corresponds precisely with the doctrine of Montesquieu, as it has been explained, and is not in a single point violated by the plan of the convention. It goes no farther than to prohibit any one of the entire departments from exercising the powers of another department. In the very Constitution to which it is prefixed, a partial mixture of powers has been admitted. The executive magistrate has a qualified negative on the legislative body, and the Senate, which is a part of the legislature, is a court of impeachment for members both of the executive and judiciary departments. The members of the judiciary department, again, are appointable by the executive department, and removable by the same authority on the address of the two legislative branches. Lastly, a number of the officers of government are annually appointed by the legislative department. As the appointment to offices, particularly executive offices, is in its nature an executive function, the compilers of the Constitution have, in this last point at least, violated the rule established by themselves. . . . [Publius next reviews other state constitutions.]

In citing these cases, in which the legislative, executive, and judiciary departments have not been kept totally separate and distinct, I wish not to be regarded as an advocate for the particular organizations of the several State governments. I am fully aware that among the many excellent principles which they exemplify they carry strong marks of the haste, and still stronger of the inexperience, under which they were framed. It is but too obvious that in some instances the fundamental principle under consideration has been violated by too great a mixture, and even an actual consolidation of the different powers; and that in no instance has a competent provision been made for maintaining in practice the separation delineated on paper. What I have wished to evince is that the charge brought against the proposed Constitution of violating the sacred maxim of free government is warranted neither by the real meaning annexed to that maxim by its author, nor by the sense in which it has hitherto been understood in America. This interesting subject will be resumed in the ensuing paper. ∎

1.3 *Federalist* No. 48 (1787)

James Madison

Outline

I. The separation of powers requires that the three departments be connected and blended, giving each control over the others.

   A. Encroaching nature of political power.

   B. Inadequacy of "parchment (or paper) barriers."

II. Preeminent danger of legislative power makes it necessary to give the other two branches some control.

I t was shown in the last paper that the political apothegm there examined does not require that the legislative, executive, and judiciary departments should be wholly unconnected with each other. I shall undertake, in the next place, to show that unless these departments be so far connected and blended as to give to each a constitutional control over the others, the degree of separation which the maxim requires, as essential to a free government, can never in practice be duly maintained.

It is agreed on all sides that the powers properly belonging to one of the departments ought not to be directly and completely administered by either of the other departments. It is equally evident that none of them ought to possess, directly or indirectly, an overruling influence over the others in the administration of their respective powers. It will not be denied that power is of an encroaching nature and that it ought to be effectually restrained from passing the limits assigned to it. After discriminating, therefore, in theory, the several classes of power, as they may in their nature be legislative, executive, or judiciary, the next and most difficult task is to provide some practical security for each, against the invasion of the others. What this security ought to be is the great problem to be solved.

Will it be sufficient to mark, with precision, the boundaries of these departments in the constitution of the government, and to trust to these parchment barriers against the encroaching spirit of power? This is the security which appears to have been principally relied on by the compilers of most of the American constitutions. But experience assures us that the efficacy of the provision has been greatly overrated; and that some more adequate defense is indispensably necessary for the more feeble against the more powerful members of the government. The legislative department is everywhere extending the sphere of its activity and drawing all power into its impetuous vortex.

The founders of our republics have so much merit for the wisdom which they have displayed that no task can be less pleasing than that of pointing out the errors into which they have fallen. A respect for truth, however, obliges us to remark that they seem never for a moment to have turned their eyes from the danger, to liberty, from the overgrown and all-grasping prerogative of an hereditary magistrate, supported and fortified by an hereditary branch of the legislative authority. They seem never to have recollected the danger from legislative usurpations, which, by assembling all power in the same hands, must lead to the same tyranny as is threatened by executive usurpations.

In a government where numerous and extensive prerogatives are placed in the hands of an hereditary monarch, the executive department is very justly regarded as the source of danger, and watched with all the jealousy which a zeal for liberty ought to inspire. In a democracy, where a multitude of people exercise in person the legislative functions and are continually exposed, by their incapacity for regular deliberation and concerted measures, to the ambitious intrigues of their executive magistrates, tyranny may well be apprehended, on some favorable emergency, to start up in the same quarter. But in a representative republic where the executive magistracy is carefully limited, both in the extent and the duration of its power; and where the legislative power is exercised by an assembly, which is inspired by a supposed influence over the people with an intrepid confidence in its own strength; which is sufficiently numerous to feel all the passions which actuate a multitude, yet not so numerous as to be incapable of pursuing the objects of its passions by means which reason prescribes; it is against the enterprising ambition of this department that the people ought to indulge all their jealousy and exhaust all their precautions.

The legislative department derives a superiority in our governments from other circumstances. Its constitutional powers being at once more extensive, and less susceptible of precise limits, it can, with the greater facility, mask, under complicated and indirect measures, the encroachments which it makes on the co-ordinate departments. It is not unfrequently a question of real nicety in legislative bodies whether the operation of a particular measure will, or will not, extend beyond the legislative sphere. On the other side, the executive power being restrained within a narrower compass and being more simple in its nature, and the judiciary being described by landmarks still less uncertain, projects of usurpation by either of these departments would immediately betray and defeat themselves. Nor is this all; as the legislative department alone has access to the pockets of the people, and has in some constitutions full discretion, and in all a prevailing influence, over the pecuniary rewards of those who fill the other departments, a dependence is thus created in the latter, which gives still greater facility to encroachments of the former. . . .

The conclusion which I am warranted in drawing from these observations is that a mere demarcation on parchment of the constitutional limits of the several departments is not a sufficient guard against those encroachments which lead to a tyrannical concentration of all the powers of government in the same hands. ∎

1.4 *Federalist* No. 51 (1787)

James Madison

Outline

I. Maintaining the separation of powers in practice requires giving each branch the means of checking the others.

   A. Members of one branch should not appoint members of the other branches, but an exception is made in the case of the judiciary.

   B. Members of one branch should not be dependent on the other branches for pay and perks.

   C. Above all, each branch must have the *means* and the *motive* to check and balance the others.

   D. Overwhelming power of the legislature requires dividing it into two parts and strengthening the executive branch.

II. Protection of liberty further enhanced by dividing power between the national and state governments and by diluting the influence of majority factions.

T o what expedient, then, shall we finally resort, for maintaining in practice the necessary partition of power among the several departments as laid down in the Constitution? The only answer that can be given is that as all these exterior provisions are found to be inadequate the defect must be supplied by so contriving the interior structure of the government as that its several constituent parts may, by their mutual relations, be the means of keeping each other in their proper places. Without presuming to undertake a full development of this important idea I will hazard a few general observations which may perhaps place it in a clearer light, and enable us to form a more correct judgment of the principles and structure of the government planned by the convention.

In order to lay a due foundation for that separate and distinct exercise of the different powers of government, which to a certain extent is admitted on all hands to be essential to the preservation of liberty, it is evident that each department should have a will of its own; and consequently should be so constituted that the members of each should have as little agency as possible in the appointment of the members of the others. Were this principle rigorously adhered to, it would require that all the appointments for the supreme executive, legislative, and judiciary magistracies should be drawn from the same fountain of authority, the people, through channels having no communication whatever with one another. Perhaps such a plan of constructing the several departments would be less difficult in practice than it may in contemplation appear. Some difficulties, however, and some additional expense would attend the execution of it. Some deviations, therefore, from the principle must be admitted. In the constitution of the judiciary department in particular, it might be inexpedient to insist rigorously on the principle: first, because peculiar qualifications being essential in the members, the primary consideration ought to be to select that mode of choice which best secures these qualifications; second, because the permanent tenure by which the appointments are held in that department must soon destroy all sense of dependence on the authority conferring them.

It is equally evident that the members of each department should be as little dependent as possible on those of the others for the emoluments annexed to their offices. Were the executive magistrate, or the judges, not independent of the legislature in this particular, their independence in every other would be merely nominal.

But the great security against a gradual concentration of the several powers in the same department consists in giving to those who administer each department the necessary constitutional means and personal motives to resist encroachments of the others. The provision for defense must in this, as in all other cases, be made commensurate to the danger of attack. Ambition must be made to counteract ambition. The interest of the man must be connected with the constitutional rights of the place. It may be a reflection on human nature that such devices should be necessary to control the abuses of government. But what is government itself but the greatest of all reflections on human nature? If men were angels, no government would be necessary. If angels were to govern men, neither external nor internal controls on government would be necessary. In framing a government which is to be administered by men over men, the great difficulty lies in this: you must first enable the government to control the governed; and in the next place oblige it to control itself. A dependence on the people is, no doubt, the primary control on the government; but experience has taught mankind the necessity of auxiliary precautions.

This policy of supplying, by opposite and rival interests, the defect of better motives, might be traced through the whole system of human affairs, private as well as public. We see it particularly displayed in all the subordinate distributions of power, where the constant aim is to divide and arrange the several offices in such a manner as that each may be a check on the other—that the private interest of every individual may be a sentinel over the public rights. These inventions of prudence cannot be less requisite in the distribution of the supreme powers of the State.

But it is not possible to give to each department an equal power of self-defense. In republican government, the legislative authority necessarily predominates. The remedy for this inconveniency is to divide the legislature into different branches; and to render them, by different modes of election and different principles of action, as little connected with each other as the nature of their common functions and their common dependence on the society will admit. It may even be necessary to guard against dangerous encroachments by still further precautions. As the weight of the legislative authority requires that it should be thus divided, the weakness of the executive may require, on the other hand, that it should be fortified. An absolute negative on the legislature appears, at first view, to be the natural defense with which the executive magistrate should be armed. But perhaps it would be neither altogether safe nor alone sufficient. On ordinary occasions it might not be exerted with the requisite firmness, and on extraordinary occasions it might be perfidiously abused. May not this defect of an absolute negative be supplied by some qualified connection between this weaker department and the weaker branch of the stronger department, by which the latter may be led to support the constitutional rights of the former, without being too much detached from the rights of its own department?

If the principles on which these observations are founded be just, as I persuade myself they are, and they be applied as a criterion to the several State constitutions, and to the federal Constitution, it will be found that if the latter does not perfectly correspond with them, the former are infinitely less able to bear such a test.

There are, moreover, two considerations particularly applicable to the federal system of America, which place that system in a very interesting point of view.

First. In a single republic, all the power surrendered by the people is submitted to the administration of a single government; and the usurpations are guarded against by a division of the government into distinct and separate departments. In the compound republic of America, the power surrendered by the people is first divided between two distinct governments, and then the portion allotted to each subdivided among distinct and separate departments. Hence a double security arises to the rights of the people. The different governments will control each other, at the same time that each will be controlled by itself.

Second. It is of great importance in a republic not only to guard the society against the oppression of its rulers, but to guard one part of the society against the injustice of the other part. Different interests necessarily exist in different classes of citizens. If a majority be united by a common interest, the rights of the minority will be insecure. There are but two methods of providing against this evil: the one by creating a will in the community independent of the majority— that is, of the society itself; the other, by comprehending in the society so many separate descriptions of citizens as will render an unjust combination of a majority of the whole very improbable, if not impracticable. The first method prevails in all governments possessing an hereditary or self-appointed authority. This, at best, is but a precarious security; because a power independent of the society may as well espouse the unjust views of the major as the rightful interests of the minor party, and may possibly be turned against both parties. The second method will be exemplified in the federal republic of the United States. Whilst all authority in it will be derived from and dependent on the society, the society itself will be broken into so many parts, interests and classes of citizens, that the rights of individuals, or of the minority, will be in little danger from interested combinations of the majority. In a free government the security for civil rights must be the same as that for religious rights. It consists in the one case in the multiplicity of interests, and in the other in the multiplicity of sects. The degree of security in both cases will depend on the number of interests and sects; and this may be presumed to depend on the extent of country and number of people comprehended under the same government. This view of the subject must particularly recommend a proper federal system to all the sincere and considerate friends of republican government, since it shows that in exact proportion as the territory of the Union may be formed into more circumscribed Confederacies, or States, oppressive combinations of a majority will be facilitated; the best security, under the republican forms, for the rights of every class of citizen, will be diminished; and consequently the stability and independence of some member of the government, the only other security, must be proportionally increased. Justice is the end of government. It is the end of civil society. It ever has been and ever will be pursued until it be obtained, or until liberty be lost in the pursuit. In a society under the forms of which the stronger faction can readily unite and oppress the weaker, anarchy may as truly be said to reign as in a state of nature, where the weaker individual is not secured against the violence of the stronger; and as, in the latter state, even the stronger individuals are prompted, by the uncertainty of their condition, to submit to a government which may protect the weak as well as themselves; so, in the former state, will the more powerful factions or parties be gradually induced, by a like motive, to wish for a government which will protect all parties, the weaker as well as the more powerful. It can be little doubted that if the State of Rhode Island was separated from the Confederacy and left to itself, the insecurity of rights under the popular form of government within such narrow limits would be displayed by such reiterated oppressions of factious majorities that some power altogether independent of the people would soon be called for by the voice of the very factions whose misrule had proved the necessity of it. In the extended republic of the United States, and among the great variety of interests, parties, and sects which it embraces, a coalition of a majority of the whole society could seldom take place on any other principles than those of justice and the general good; whilst there being thus less danger to a minor from the will of a major party, there must be less pretext, also, to provide for the security of the former, by introducing into the government a will not dependent on the latter, or, in other words, a will independent of the society itself. It is no less certain than it is important, notwithstanding the contrary opinions which have been entertained, that the larger the society, provided it lie within a practicable sphere, the more duly capable it will be of self-government. And happily for the *republican cause*, the practicable sphere may be carried to a very great extent by a judicious modification and mixture of the *federal principle*. ■

1.5 The Address and Reasons of Dissent of the Minority of the Convention of Pennsylvania to Their Constituents (1788)

• • •

[W]e entered on the examination of the proposed [constitution] and found it to be such as we could not adopt, without, as we conceived, surrendering up your dearest rights. We offered our objections to the convention, and opposed those parts of the plan, which, in our opinion, would be injurious to you, in the best manner we were able; and closed our arguments by offering the following propositions to the convention.

1. The right of conscience shall be held inviolable; and neither the legislative, executive nor judicial powers of the United States shall have authority to alter, abrogate, or infringe any part of the constitution of the several states, which provide for the preservation of liberty in matters of religion.

2. That in controversies respecting property, and in suits between man and man, trial by jury shall remain as heretofore, as well in the federal courts, as in those of the several states.

3. That in all capital and criminal prosecutions, a man has a right to demand the cause and nature of his accusation, as well in the federal courts, as in those of the several states; to be heard by himself and his counsel; to be confronted with the accusers and witnesses; to call for evidence in his favor, and a speedy trial by an impartial jury of his vicinage, without whose unanimous consent, he cannot be found guilty, nor can he be compelled to give evidence against himself; and that no man be deprived of his liberty, except by the law of the land or the judgment of his peers.

4. That excessive bail ought not to be required, nor excessive fines imposed, nor cruel nor unusual punishments inflicted.

5. That warrants unsupported by evidence, whereby any officer or messenger may be commanded or required to search suspected places, or to seize any person or persons, his or their property, not particularly described, are grievous and oppressive, and shall not be granted either by the magistrates of the federal government or others.

6. That the people have a right to the freedom of speech, of writing and publishing their sentiments, therefore, the freedom of the press shall not be restrained by any law of the United States.

7. That the people have a right to bear arms for the defence of themselves and their own state, or the United States, or for the purpose of killing game; and no law shall be passed for disarming the people or any of them, unless for crimes committed, or real danger of public injury from individuals; and as standing armies in the time of peace are dangerous to liberty, they ought not to be kept up; and that the military shall be kept under strict subordination to and be governed by the civil powers.

8. The inhabitants of the several states shall have liberty to fowl and hunt in seasonable times, on the lands they hold, and on all other lands in the United States not inclosed, and in like manner to fish in all navigable waters, and others not private property, without being restrained therein by any laws to be passed by the legislature of the United States.

9. That no law shall be passed to restrain the legislatures of the several states from enacting laws for imposing taxes, except imposts and duties on goods imported or exported, and that no taxes, except imposts and duties upon goods imported and exported, and postage on letters shall be levied by the authority of Congress.

10. That the house of representatives be properly increased in number; that elections shall remain free; that the several states shall have power to regulate the elections for senators and representatives, without being controuled either directly or indirectly by any interference on the part of the Congress; and that elections of representatives be annual.

11. That the power of organizing, arming and disciplining the militia (the manner of disciplining the militia to be prescribed by Congress) remain with the individual states, and that Congress shall not have authority to call or march any of the militia out of their own state, without the consent of such state, and for such length of time only as such state shall agree.

That the sovereignty, freedom and independency of the several states shall be retained, and every power, jurisdiction and right which is not by this constitution expressly delegated to the United States in Congress assembled.

12. That the legislative, executive, and judicial powers be kept separate; and to this end that a constitutional council be appointed, to advise and assist the president, who shall be responsible for the advice they give, hereby the senators would be relieved from almost constant attendance; and also that the judges be made completely independent.

13. That no treaty which shall be directly opposed to the existing laws of the United States in Congress assembled, shall be valid until such laws shall be repealed, or made conformable to such treaty; neither shall any treaties be valid which are in contradiction to the constitution of the United States, or the constitutions of the several states.

14. That the judiciary power of the United States shall be confined to cases affecting ambassadors, other public ministers and consuls; to cases of admiralty and maritime jurisdiction; to controversies to which the United States shall be a party; to controversies between two or more states—between a state and citizens of different states—between citizens claiming lands under grants of different states; and between a state or the citizen thereof and foreign states, and in criminal cases, to such only as are expressly enumerated in the constitution, and that the United States in Congress assembled, shall not have power to enact laws, which shall alter the laws of descents and distribution of the effects of deceased persons, the titles of lands or goods, or the regulation of contracts in the individual states.

After reading these propositions, we declared our willingness to agree to the plan, provided it was so amended as to meet these propositions, or something similar to them; and finally moved the convention to adjourn, to give the people of Pennsylvania time to consider the subject, and determine for themselves; but these were all rejected, and the final vote was taken, when our duty to you induced us to vote against the proposed plan, and to decline signing the ratification of the same.

During the discussion we met with many insults, and some personal abuse; we were not even treated with decency, during the sitting of the convention, by the persons in the gallery of the house; however, we flatter ourselves that in contending for the preservation of those invaluable rights you have thought proper to commit to our charge, we acted with a spirit becoming freemen, and being desirous that you might know the principles which actuated our conduct, and being prohibited from inserting our reasons of dissent on the minutes of the convention, we have subjoined them for your consideration, as to you alone we are accountable. It remains with you whether you will think those inestimable privileges, which you have so ably contended for, should be sacrificed at the shrine of despotism, or whether you mean to contend for them with the same spirit that has so often baffled the attempts of an aristocratic faction, to rivet the shackles of slavery on you and your unborn posterity.

Our objections are comprised under three general heads of dissent, viz.

We dissent, first, because it is the opinion of the most celebrated writers on government, and confirmed by uniform experience, that a very extensive territory cannot be governed on the principles of freedom, otherwise than by a confederation of republics, possessing all the powers of internal government; but united in the management of their general, and foreign concerns.

• • •

We dissent, secondly, because the powers vested in Congress by this constitution, must necessarily annihilate and absorb the legislative, executive, and judicial powers of the several states, and produce from their ruins one consolidated government, which from the nature of things will be *an iron handed despotism*, as nothing short of the supremacy of despotic sway could connect and govern these United States under one government.

• • •

. . . We dissent, Thirdly, Because if it were practicable to govern so extensive a territory as these United States includes, on the plan of a consolidated government, consistent with the principles of liberty and the happiness of the people, yet the construction of this constitution is not calculated to attain the object, for independent of the nature of the case, it would of itself, necessarily, produce a despotism, and that not by the usual gradations, but with the celerity that has hitherto only attended revolutions effected by the sword.

To establish the truth of this position, a cursory investigation of the principles and form of this constitution will suffice.

The first consideration that this review suggests, is the omission of a BILL of RIGHTS, ascertaining and fundamentally establishing those unalienable and personal rights of men, without the full, free, and secure enjoyment of which there can be no liberty, and over which it is not necessary for a good government to have the controul. The principal of which are the rights of conscience, personal liberty by the clear and unequivocal establishment of the writ of *habeas corpus*, jury trial in criminal and civil cases, by an impartial jury of the vicinage or county, with the common-law proceedings, for the safety of the accused in criminal prosecutions; and the liberty of the press, that scourge of tyrants, and the grand bulwark of every other liberty and privilege; the stipulations heretofore made in favor of them in the state constitutions, are entirely superceded by this constitution.

● ● ●

We will now bring the legislature under this constitution to the test of the foregoing principles, which will demonstrate, that it is deficient in every essential quality of a just and safe representation.

The house of representatives is to consist of 65 members; that is one for about every 50,000 inhabitants, to be chosen every two years. Thirty-three members will form a quorum for doing business; and 17 of these, being the majority, determine the sense of the house.

The senate, the other constituent branch of the legislature, consists of 26 members being *two* from each state, appointed by their legislatures every six years—fourteen senators make a quorum; the majority of whom, eight, determines the sense of that body; except in judging on impeachments, or in making treaties, or in expelling a member, when two thirds of the senators present, must concur.

The president is to have the controul over the enacting of laws, so far as to make the concurrence of *two* thirds of the representatives and senators present necessary, if he should object to the laws.

Thus it appears that the liberties, happiness, interests, and great concerns of the whole United States, may be dependent upon the integrity, virtue, wisdom, and knowledge of 25 or 26 men—How unadequate and unsafe a representation! Inadequate, because the sense and views of 3 or 4 millions of people diffused over so extensive a territory comprising such various climates, products, habits, interests, and opinions, cannot be collected in so small a body; and besides, it is not a fair and equal representation of the people even in proportion to its number, for the smallest state has as much weight in the senate as the largest, and from the smallness of the number to be chosen for both branches of the legislature; and from the mode of election and appointment, which is under the controul of Congress; and from the nature of the thing, men of the most elevated rank in life, will alone be chosen. The other orders in the society, such as farmers, traders, and mechanics, who all ought to have a competent number of their best informed men in the legislature, will be totally unrepresented.

The representation is unsafe, because in the exercise of such great powers and trusts, it is so exposed to corruption and undue influence, by the gift of the numerous places of honor and emoluments at the disposal of the executive; by the arts and address of the great and designing; and by direct bribery.

The representation is moreover inadequate and unsafe, because of the long terms for which it is appointed, and the mode of its appointment, by which Congress may not only controul the choice of the people, but may so manage as to divest the people of this fundamental right, and become self-elected.

The number of members in the house of representatives *may* be increased to one for every 30,000 inhabitants. But when we consider, that this cannot be done without the consent of the senate, who from their share in the legislative, in the executive, and judicial departments, and permanency of appointment, will be the great efficient body in this government, and whose weight and predominancy would be abridged by an increase of the representatives, we are persuaded that this is a circumstance that cannot be expected. On the contrary, the number of representatives will probably be continued at 65, although the population of the country may swell to treble what it now is; unless a revolution should effect a change.

• • •

The next consideration that the constitution presents, is the undue and dangerous mixture of the powers of government; the same body possessing legislative, executive, and judicial powers. The senate is a constituent branch of the legislature, it has judicial power in judging on impeachments, and in this case unites in some measure the characters of judge and party, as all the principal officers are appointed by the president-general, with the concurrence of the senate and therefore they derive their offices in part from the senate. This may bias the judgments of the senators and tend to screen great delinquents from punishment. And the senate has, moreover, various and great executive powers, viz. in concurrence with the president-general, they form treaties with foreign nations, that may controul and abrogate the constitutions and laws of the several states. Indeed, there is no power, privilege or liberty of the state governments, or of the people, but what may be affected by virtue of this power. For all treaties, made by them, are to be the "supreme law of the land, any thing in the constitution or laws of any state, to the contrary notwithstanding."

And this great power may be exercised by the president and 10 senators (being two-thirds of 14, which is a quorum of that body). What an inducement would this offer to the ministers of foreign powers to compass by bribery *such concessions* as could not otherwise be obtained. It is the unvaried usage of all free states, whenever treaties interfere with the positive laws of the land, to make the intervention of the legislature necessary to give them operation. This became necessary, and was afforded by the parliament of Great-Britain. In consequence of the late commercial treaty between that kingdom and France—As the senate judges on impeachments, who is to try the members of the senate for the abuse of this power! And none of the great appointments to office can be made without the consent of the senate.

Such various, extensive, and important powers combined in one body of men, are inconsistent with all freedom; the celebrated Montesquieu tells us, that "when the legislative and executive powers are united in the same person, or in the same body or magistrates, there can be no liberty, because apprehensions may arise, lest the same monarch or *senate* should enact tyrannical laws, to execute them in a tyrannical manner."

"Again, there is no liberty, if the power of judging be not separated from the legislative and executive powers. Were it joined with the legislative, the life and liberty of the subject would be exposed to arbitrary controul; for the judge would then be legislator. Were it joined to the executive power, the judge might behave with all the violence of an oppressor. There would be an end of every thing, were the same man, or the same body of the nobles, or of the people, to exercise those three powers; that of enacting laws; that of executing the public resolutions; and that of judging the crimes or differences of individuals."

The president-general is dangerously connected with the senate; his coincidence with the views of the ruling junto in that body, is made essential to his weight and importance in the government, which will destroy all independency and purity in the executive department, and having the power of pardoning without the concurrence of a council, he may skreen from punishment the most treasonable attempts that may be made on the liberties of the people, when instigated by his coadjutors in the senate. Instead of this dangerous and improper mixture of the executive with the legislative and judicial, the supreme executive powers ought to have been placed in the president, with a small independent council, made personally responsible for every appointment to office or other act, by having their opinions recorded; and that without the concurrence of the majority of the quorum of this council, the president should not be capable of taking any step.

• • •

From the foregoing investigation, it appears that the Congress under this constitution will not possess the confidence of the people, which is an essential requisite in a good government; for unless the laws command the confidence and respect of the great body of the people, so as to induce them to support them, when called on by the civil magistrate, they must be executed by the aid of a numerous standing army, which would be inconsistent with every idea of liberty; for the same force that may be employed to compel obedience to good laws, might and probably would be used to wrest from the people their constitutional liberties. The framers of this constitution appear to have been aware of this great deficiency; to have been sensible that no dependence could be placed on the people for their support; but on the contrary, that the government must be executed by force. They have therefore made a provision for this purpose in a permanent STANDING ARMY, and a MILITIA that may be subjected to as strict discipline and government.

• • •

As this government will not enjoy the confidence of the people, but be executed by force, it will be a very expensive and burthensome government. The standing army must be numerous, and as a further support, it will be the policy of this government to multiply officers in every department: judges, collectors, tax gatherers, excisemen and the whole host of revenue officers will swarm over the land, devouring the hard earnings of the industrious. Like the locusts of old, impoverishing and desolating all before them.

We have not noticed the smaller, nor many of the considerable blemishes, but have confined our objections to the great and essential defects; the main pillars of the constitution; which we have shewn to be inconsistent with the liberty and happiness of the people, as its establishment will annihilate the state governments, and produce one consolidated government that will eventually and speedily issue in the supremacy of despotism. ■

 # American Politics Today

Because the Supreme Court plays such a key role in interpreting the United States Constitution (see Chapter 12), constitutional debates in the United States can quickly become mired in legal details and technicalities. The debate over the Second Amendment—which protects the right of the people to "keep and bear arms"—is in this regard the exception that proves the rule. Because the Court has been largely silent on the meaning and application of the Second Amendment, both supporters and opponents of gun control make arguments that more closely reflect the debates of the Founding Generation than the thinking of modern justices. As the legal scholar Wendy Kaminer points out, the Second Amendment debate brings out "the fundamental tension between republicanism and individualism" in the American constitutional system.

Questions

1. What are the meanings of "republicanism" and "individualism," particularly in the context of the Second Amendment debate?
2. What are the strongest points in favor of those who argue that the Second Amendment should be interpreted to guarantee the right *of the individual* to keep and bear arms? What are the strongest points in favor of those who argue that the amendment protects the right *of the people* to bear arms collectively?

1.6 Second Thoughts on the Second Amendment (1996)

Wendy Kaminer

D ebates about gun ownership and gun control are driven more by values and ideology than by pragmatism—and hardly at all by the existing empirical research, which is complex and inconclusive. . . . As for legal debates about

From Wendy Kaminer, "Second Thoughts on the Second Amendment," *The Atlantic Monthly* (March 1996), Volume 277, pp. 32–45—abridged. A longer version of this article first appeared in *The Atlantic Monthly*, March 1995. Copyright Wendy Kaminer. Reprinted with permission.

the existence of constitutional rights, empirical data is irrelevant, or at best peripheral. But the paucity of proof that gun controls lessen crime is particularly galling to people who believe that they have a fundamental right to bear arms. In theory, at least, we restrict constitutional rights only when the costs of exercising them seem unbearably high. In fact we argue continually about what those costs are: Does violence in the media cause violence in real life? Did the release of the Pentagon Papers endanger the national security? Does hate speech constitute discrimination? In the debate about firearms, however, we can't even agree on the principles that should govern restrictions on guns, because we can't agree about the right to own them.

How could we, given the importance of the competing values at stake—public safety and the right of self-defense—and the opacity of the constitutional text? The awkwardly drafted Second Amendment doesn't quite make itself clear: "A well regulated Militia, being necessary to the security of a free State, the right of the people to keep and bear Arms, shall not be infringed." Is the reference to a militia a limitation on the right to bear arms or merely an explanation of an armed citizenry's role in a government by consent? There is little dispute that one purpose of the Second Amendment was to ensure that the people would be able to resist a central government should it ever devolve into despotism. But there is little agreement about what that capacity for resistance was meant to entail—armed citizens acting under the auspices of state militias or armed citizens able to organize and act on their own. And there is virtually no consensus about the constitutional right to own a gun in the interests of individual self-defense against crime, rather than communal defense against tyranny. Is defense of the state, and of the common good, the *raison d'être* of the Second Amendment or merely one use of it?

The Supreme Court has never answered these fundamental questions about the constitutional uses of guns. It has paid scant attention to the Second Amendment, providing little guidance in the gun-control debate. Two frequently cited late-nineteenth-century cases relating to the Second Amendment were more about federalism than about the right to bear arms. *Presser* v. *Illinois*, decided in 1886, involved a challenge to a state law prohibiting private citizens from organizing their own military units and parades. The Court held that the Second Amendment was a limitation on federal, not state, power, reflecting the prevailing view (now discredited) that the Bill of Rights in general applied only to the federal government, not to the states. (A hundred years ago the Court did not apply the First Amendment to the states either.) *Presser* followed *U.S.* v. *Cruikshank*, which held that the federal government could not protect people from private infringement of their rights to assemble and bear arms. *Cruikshank*, decided in 1876, invalidated the federal convictions of participants in the lynching of two black men. This ruling, essentially concerned with limiting federal police power, is virtually irrelevant to Second Amendment debates today, although it has been cited to support the proposition that an oppressed minority has a compelling need (or a natural right) to bear arms in self-defense.

The most significant Supreme Court decision on the Second Amendment was *U.S.* v. *Miller* (1939), a less-than-definitive holding now cited approvingly by both sides in the gun-control debate. *Miller* involved a prosecution under the 1934 National Firearms Act. Jack Miller and his accomplice had been convicted of transporting an unregistered shotgun of less than regulation length across state lines. In striking down their Second Amendment claim and upholding their conviction, the Court noted that no evidence had been presented that a shotgun was in fact a militia weapon, providing no factual basis for a Second Amendment claim. This ruling implies that the Second Amendment could protect the right to bear arms suitable for a militia.

Advocates of gun control or prohibition like the *Miller* case because it makes the right to bear arms dependent on at least the possibility of service in a militia. They cite the Court's declaration that the Second Amendment was obviously intended to "assure the continuation and render possible the effectiveness" of state militias; they place less emphasis on the Court's apparent willingness to permit private citizens to possess military weapons. Citing *Miller*, a dealer at a gun show told me that the Second Amendment protects the ownership of only such devices as machine guns, Stingers, and grenade throwers. But advocates of gun ownership don't generally emphasize this awkward implication of *U.S. v. Miller* any more than their opponents do: it could lead to prohibitions on handguns. They like the *Miller* decision because it delves into the history of the Second Amendment and stresses that for the framers, the militia "comprised all males physically capable of acting in concert for the common defense."

This view of the militia as an inchoate citizens' army, not a standing body of professionals, is central to the claim that the Second Amendment protects the rights of individual civilians, not simply the right of states to organize and arm militias. And, in fact, fear and loathing of standing armies did underlie the Second Amendment, which was at least partly intended to ensure that states would be able to call up citizens in defense against a tyrannical central government. (Like the Bill of Rights in general, the Second Amendment was partly a response to concerns about federal abuses of power.) James Madison, the author of the Second Amendment, invoked in *The Federalist Papers* the potential force of a citizen militia as a guarantee against a federal military coup.

> Let a regular army, fully equal to the resources of the country, be formed; and let it be entirely at the devotion of the federal government: still it would not be going too far to say that the State governments with the people on their side would be able to repel the danger. . . . To [the regular army] would be opposed a militia amounting to near half a million of citizens with arms in their hands, officered by men chosen from among themselves, fighting for their common liberties and united and conducted by governments possessing their affection and confidence. It may well be doubted whether a militia thus circumstanced could ever be conquered by such a proportion of regular troops. Those who are best acquainted with the late successful resistance of this country against the British arms will be most inclined to deny the possibility of it. Besides the advantage of being armed, which the Americans possess over the people of almost every other nation, the existence of subordinate governments, to which the people are attached and by which the militia officers are appointed, forms a barrier against the enterprises of ambition, more insurmountable than any which a simple government of any form can admit of.

This passage is enthusiastically cited by advocates of the right to bear arms, because it supports their notion of the militia as the body of people, privately armed; but it's also cited by their opponents, because it suggests that the militia is activated and "conducted" by the states, and it stresses that citizens are "attached" to their local governments. The militia envisioned by Madison is not simply a "collection of unorganized, privately armed citizens," Dennis Henigan, a handgun-control advocate, has argued.

That Madison's reflections on the militia and the Supreme Court's holding in *U.S.* v. *Miller* can be cited with some accuracy by both sides in the debate testifies to the hybrid nature of Second Amendment rights. The Second Amendment presumes (as did the framers) that private citizens will possess private arms; Madison referred offhandedly to "the advantage of being armed, which the Americans possess." But Madison also implied that the right to bear arms is based in the obligation of citizens to band together as a militia to defend the common good, as opposed to the prerogative of citizens to take up arms individually in pursuit of self-interest and happiness.

The tension at the heart of the Second Amendment, which makes it so difficult to construe, is the tension between republicanism and liberal individualism. (To put it very simply, republicanism calls for the subordination of individual interests to the public good; liberalism focuses on protecting individuals against popular conceptions of the good.) A growing body of scholarly literature on the Second Amendment locates the right to bear arms in republican theories of governance. In a 1989 article in the *Yale Law Journal* that helped animate the Second Amendment debate, the University of Texas law professor Sanford Levinson argued that the Second Amendment confers an individual right to bear arms so that, in the republican tradition, armed citizens might rise up against an oppressive state. Wendy Brown, a professor of women's studies at the University of California at Santa Cruz, and David C. Williams, a law professor at Cornell University, have questioned the validity of a republican right to bear arms in a society that lacks the republican virtue of being willing to put communal interests first. Pro-gun activists don't generally acknowledge the challenge posed by republicanism to the individualist culture that many gun owners inhabit. They embrace republican justifications for gun ownership, stressing the use of arms in defending the community, at the same time that they stress the importance of guns in protecting individual autonomy.

Advocates of the right to bear arms often insist that the Second Amendment is rooted in both collective and individual rights of self-defense—against political oppression and crime—without recognizing how those rights conflict. The republican right to resist oppression is the right of the majority, or the people, not the right of a small religious cult in Waco, Texas, or of a few survivalist tax protesters in Idaho. The members of these groups have individual rights against the government, state and federal. (Both the American Civil Liberties Union and the NRA protested the government's actions in Waco and its attack on the survivalist Randy Weaver and his family.) But refuseniks and refugees from society are not republicans. They do not constitute the citizen militia envisioned by the framers, any more than they stand for the American community; indeed, they stand against it—withdrawing from the body politic, asserting their rights to alienation and anomie or membership in exclusionary alternative communities of their own. Republicanism can't logically be invoked in the service of libertarianism. It elevates civic virtue over individualism, consensus over dissent.

Nor can social-contract theory be readily invoked in support of a right to arm yourself in a war against street crime, despite the claims of some gun-ownership advocates. The right or power to engage in punishment or retribution is precisely what is given up when you enter an ordered civil society. The loss of self-help remedies is the price of the social contract. "God hath certainly appointed Government to restrain the partiality and violence of Men," John Locke wrote. A person may always defend his or her life when threatened, but only when there is no chance to appeal to the law. If a man points his sword at me and demands my purse, Locke explained, I may kill him. But if he steals my purse by stealth and then raises a sword to defend it, I may not use force to get it back. "My Life not being in danger, I may have the *benefit of appealing* to the Law, and have Reparation for my 100£ that way."

Locke was drawing a line between self-defense and vigilantism which many gun owners would no doubt respect. Others would point to the inability of the criminal-justice system to avenge crimes and provide reparation to victims, and thus they would assert a right to engage in self-help. Social-contract theory, however, might suggest that if the government is no longer able to provide order, or justice, the remedy is not vigilantism but revolution; the utter failure of law enforcement is a fundamental breach of trust. And, in fact, there are large pockets of disaffected citizens who do not trust the government to protect them or to provide impartial justice, and who might be persuaded to rise up against it, as evidenced by the disorder that followed the 1992 acquittal of police officers who assaulted Rodney King. Was Los Angeles the scene of a riot or of an uprising?

Injustice, and the sense of oppression it spawns, are often matters of perspective—particularly today, when claims of political victimization abound and there is little consensus on the demands of public welfare. We use the term "oppression" promiscuously, to describe any instance of discrimination. In this climate of grievance and hyperbole, many acts of violence are politicized. How do we decide whether an insurrection is just? Don Kates observes that the Second Amendment doesn't exactly confer the right to resist. He says, "It gives you a right to win."

The prospect of armed resistance, however, is probably irrelevant to much public support for gun ownership, which reflects a fear of crime more than a fear or loathing of government. People don't buy guns in order to overthrow or even to thwart the government; in the belief that the police can't protect them, people buy guns to protect themselves and their families. Recognizing this, the NRA appeals to fear of crime, particularly crime against women. ("Choose to refuse to be a victim," NRA ads proclaim, showing a woman and her daughter alone in a desolate parking lot at night.) And it has countered demands for tougher gun controls not with radical individualist appeals for insurrection but with statist appeals for tougher anti-crime laws, notably stringent mandatory-minimum sentences and parole reform. There is considerable precedent for the NRA's appeal to state authority: founded after the Civil War, with the mission of teaching soldiers to shoot straight, in its early years the NRA was closely tied to the military and dependent on government largesse; until recently it drew considerable moral support from the police. Today, however, statist anti-crime campaigns are mainly matters of politics for the NRA and for gun advocates in general; laws mandating tough sentences for the criminal use of firearms defuse demands for firearm controls. Personal liberty—meaning the liberty to own guns and use them against the government if necessary—is these people's passion.

Gun advocates are apt to be extravagantly libertarian when the right to own guns is at stake. At heart many are insurrectionists—at least, they need to feel prepared. Nothing arouses their anger more, I've found, than challenges to the belief that private gun ownership is an essential check on political oppression. . . .

. . . "Using a national epidemic of crime and violence as their justification, media pundits and collectivist politicians are aggressively campaigning to disarm private citizens and strengthen federal law enforcement powers," proclaims a special edition of *The New American*, a magazine on sale at gun shows. After gun control, the editors suggest, the greatest threat to individual liberty is the Clinton plan for providing local police departments with federal assistance. "Is it possible that some of those who are advocating a disarmed populace and a centralized police system have totalitarian designs in mind? It is worth noting that this is exactly what happened in many countries during this century."

This can be dismissed as ravings on the fringe, but it captures in crazed form the hostility toward a powerful central government which inspired the adoption of the Second Amendment right to bear arms 200 years ago and fuels support for it today. Advocates of First Amendment rights, who believe firmly that free speech is both a moral imperative and an instrument of democratic governance, should understand the passion of Second Amendment claims.

They should be sympathetic as well to the more dispassionate constitutional arguments of gun owners. Civil libertarians who believe that the Bill of Rights in general protects individuals have a hard time explaining why the Second Amendment protects only groups. They have a hard time reconciling their opposition to prohibitions of problematic behavior, such as drug abuse, with their support for the prohibition of guns. (Liberals tend to demonize guns and gun owners the way conservatives tend to demonize drugs and pornography and the people who use them.) In asserting that the Second Amendment provides no individual right to bear arms or that the right provided is anachronistic and not worth its cost, civil libertarians place themselves in the awkward position of denying the existence of a constitutional right because they don't value its exercise.

The civil-libertarian principles at issue in the gun debate are made clear by the arguments of First Amendment and Second Amendment advocates, which are strikingly similar—as are the arguments their opponents use. Pornography rapes, some feminists say. Words oppress, according to advocates of censoring hate speech. "Words Kill," declared a Planned Parenthood ad following the abortion-clinic shootings in Brookline, Massachusetts, last year. And all you can say in response is "Words don't kill people; people kill people." To an anti-libertarian, the literature sold at gun shows may seem as dangerous as the guns; at a recent gun show I bought *Incendiaries*, an army manual on unconventional warfare; *Exotic Weapons: An Access Book*; *Gunrunning for Fun and Profit*; and *Vigilante Handbook*, which tells me how to harass, torture, and assassinate people. Should any of this material be censored? If it were, it would be sold on the black market; and the remedy for bad speech is good speech, First Amendment devotees point out. According to Second Amendment supporters, gun-control laws affect only law-abiding gun owners, and the best defense against armed criminals is armed victims; the remedy for the bad use of guns in violent crime is the good use of guns in self-defense.

Of course, guns do seem a bit more dangerous than books, and apart from a few anti-pornography feminists, most of us would rather be accosted by a man with a video than a man with a gun. But none of our constitutional rights are absolute. Recognizing that the Second Amendment confers an individual right to bear arms would not immunize guns from regulation; it would require that the government establish a necessity, not just a desire, to regulate. The majority of gun owners, Don Kates suggests, would be amenable to gun controls, such as waiting periods and even licensing and training requirements, if they didn't perceive them as preludes to prohibition. The irony of the Second Amendment debate is that acknowledging an individual right to bear arms might facilitate gun control more than denying it ever could.

But it will not facilitate civic engagement or the community that Americans are exhorted to seek. The civil-libertarian defense of Second Amendment rights is not a republican one. It does not derive the individual right to bear arms from republican notions of the militia; instead it relies on traditional liberal views of personal autonomy. It is a communitarian nightmare. If the war against crime has replaced the Cold War in popular culture, a private storehouse of guns has replaced the fallout shelter in the psyche of Americans who feel besieged. Increasingly barricaded, mistrustful of their neighbors, they've sacrificed virtue to fear. ∎

 # Issue and Controversy

For generations, Americans have debated whether the original Constitution is sufficiently true to democratic principles. The Constitution of 1787 has been criticized (among other things) for its acceptance of slavery; for not protecting the rights of minorities and women; for giving too little power to the common people, and too much to the wealthy and well-connected; and for giving the federal judiciary the ability to frustrate the will of the people through judicial review. At times these criticisms have resulted in significant changes to the American political system—some by formal amendment, others by constitutional interpretation. Still more changes—including the development of political parties—have taken place outside the constitutional framework altogether.

In this selection, political scientist Robert A. Dahl examines the Constitution of 1787 and concludes that the original plan of government, although innovative and forward-looking for its time, contained serious democratic deficiencies. Even so, he suggests that the legitimacy of the Constitution "ought to derive solely from its utility as an instrument of democratic government—nothing more, nothing less."

Questions

1. How valid are Dahl's criticisms of the original Constitution? Do the deficiencies of the original document detract from its legitimacy as the foundation stone of the American political system?

2. Does the modern Constitution—as amended, reinterpreted, and adapted to the realities of modern life—correct the democratic deficiencies of the original document? What arguments support or undermine the claim that the modern Constitution remains undemocratic?

1.7 Is the Constitution Democratic? (2001)

Robert A. Dahl

Wise as the Framers were, they were necessarily limited by their profound ignorance.

I say this with no disrespect, for like many others I believe that among the Framers were many men of exceptional talent and public virtue. Indeed, I regard James Madison as our greatest political scientist and his generation of political leaders as perhaps our most richly endowed with wisdom, public virtue, and devotion to lives of public service. In the months and weeks before the Constitutional Convention assembled "on Monday the 14th of May, A.D. 1787. [*sic*] and in the eleventh year of the independence of the United States of America, at the State-House in the city of Philadelphia," Madison studied the best sources as carefully as a top student preparing for a major exam. But even James Madison could not foresee the future of the American republic, nor could he draw on knowledge that might be gained from later experiences with democracy in America and elsewhere.

• • •

Among the important aspects of an unforeseeable future, four broad historical developments would yield some potential knowledge that the Framers necessarily lacked and that, had they possessed it, might well have led them to a different constitutional design.

First, a peaceful democratic revolution was soon to alter fundamentally the conditions under which their constitutional system would function.

Second, partly in response to that continuing revolution, new democratic political institutions would fundamentally alter and reconstruct the framework they had so carefully designed.

Third, when democratization unfolded in Europe and in other English-speaking countries during the two centuries to come, constitutional arrangements would arise that were radically different from the American system. Within a generation or two, even the British constitution would bear little resemblance to the one the Framers knew—or thought they knew—and in many respects admired and hoped to imitate.

Fourth, ideas and beliefs about what democracy requires, and thus what a democratic republic requires, would continue to evolve down to the present day and

---

probably beyond. Both in the way we understand the meaning of "democracy" and in the practices and institutions we regard as necessary to it, democracy is not a static system. Democratic ideas and institutions as they unfolded in the two centuries after the American Constitutional Convention would go far beyond the conceptions of the Framers and would even transcend the views of such early democrats as Jefferson and Madison, who helped to initiate moves toward a more democratic republic. . . .

The Framers were not only limited by, so to speak, their inevitable ignorance. They were also crucially limited by the opportunities available to them.

We can be profoundly grateful for one crucial restriction: the Framers were limited to considering only a *republican* form of government. They were constrained not only by their own belief in the superiority of a republican government over all others but also by their conviction that the high value they placed on republicanism was overwhelmingly shared by American citizens in all the states. Whatever else the Framers might be free to do, they well knew that they could not possibly propose a monarchy or a government ruled by an aristocracy. As the Massachusetts delegate Elbridge Gerry put it, "There was not a one-thousand part of our fellow citizens who were not against every approach toward monarchy." The only delegate who was recorded by Madison as looking with favor on monarchy was Alexander Hamilton, whose injudicious expression of support for that heartily unpopular institution may have greatly reduced his influence at the Convention, as it was to haunt him later. Hardly more acceptable was an adaptation of aristocratic ideas to an American constitution. During the deliberations about the Senate, Gouverneur Morris of Pennsylvania explored the possibility of drawing its members from an American equivalent of the British aristocracy. But it soon became obvious that the delegates could not agree on just who these American aristocrats might be, and in any case they well knew that the overwhelming bulk of American citizens would simply not tolerate such a government.

A second immovable limit was the existence of the thirteen states, with still more states to come. A constitutional solution that would be available in most of the countries that were to develop into mature and stable democracies—a unitary system with exclusive sovereignty lodged in the central government, as in Britain and Sweden, for example—was simply out of the question. The need for a federal rather than a unitary republic was therefore not justified by a principle adduced from general historical experience, much less from political theory. It was just a self-evident fact. If Americans were to be united in a single country, it was obvious to all that a federal or confederal system was inescapable. Whether the states would remain as fundamental constituents was therefore never a serious issue at the Convention; the only contested question was just how much autonomy, if any, they would yield to the central government.

The delegates had to confront still another stubborn limit: the need to engage in fundamental compromises in order to secure agreement on any constitution at all. The necessity for compromise and the opportunities this gave for coalitions and logrolling meant that the Constitution could not possibly reflect a coherent, unified theory of government. Compromises were necessary because, like the country at large, members of the convention held different views on some very basic issues.

Slavery. One, of course, was the future of slavery. Most of the delegates from the five southern states were adamantly opposed to any constitutional provision that might endanger the institution. Although the delegates from the other seven states were hardly of one mind about slavery, it was perfectly obvious to them that the only condition on which coexistence would be acceptable to the delegates from the southern states would be the preservation of slavery. Consequently, if these delegates wanted a federal constitution they would have to yield, no matter what their beliefs about slavery. And so they did. Although some delegates who signed the final document abhorred slavery, they nevertheless accepted its continuation as the price of a stronger federal government.

Representation in the Senate. Another conflict of views that could not be settled without a one-sided compromise resulted from the adamant refusal of the delegates from the small states to accept any constitution that did not provide for equal representation in the Senate. . . .

Faced with the refusal of the small states to accept anything less . . . [the] opponents of equal representation finally accepted compromise of principle as the price of a constitution. The solution of equal representation was not, then, a product of constitutional theory, high principle, or grand design. It was nothing more than a practical outcome of a hard bargain that its opponents finally agreed to in order to achieve a constitution. . . .

Undemocratic Elements in the Framers' Constitution

It was within these limits, then, that the Framers constructed the Constitution. Not surprisingly, it fell far short of the requirements that later generations would find necessary and desirable in a democratic republic. Judged from later, more democratic perspectives, the Constitution of the Framers contained at least seven important shortcomings.

Slavery. First, it neither forbade slavery nor empowered Congress to do so. In fact, the compromise on slavery not only denied Congress the effective power to prohibit the importation of slaves before 1808 but it gave constitutional sanction to one of the most morally objectionable byproducts of a morally repulsive institution: the Fugitive Slave laws, according to which a slave who managed to escape to a free state had to be returned to the slaveholder, whose property the slave remained. That it took three-quarters of a century and a sanguinary civil war before slavery was abolished should at the least make us doubt whether the document of the Framers ought to be regarded as holy writ.

Suffrage. Second, the constitution failed to guarantee the right of suffrage, leaving the qualifications of suffrage to the states. It implicitly left in place the exclusion of half the population—women—as well as African Americans and Native Americans. As we know, it took a century and a half before women were constitutionally guaranteed the right to vote, and nearly two centuries before a president and Congress could overcome the effective veto of a minority of states in order to pass legislation intended to guarantee the voting rights of African Americans.

Election of the president. Third, the executive power was vested in a president whose selection, according to the intentions and design of the Framers, was to be insulated from both popular majorities and congressional control. . . . The Framers' main design for achieving that purpose—a body of presidential electors composed of men of exceptional wisdom and virtue who would choose the chief executive unswayed by popular opinion—was almost immediately cast into the dustbin of history by leaders sympathetic with the growing democratic impulses of the American people, among them James Madison himself. Probably nothing the Framers did illustrates more sharply their inability to foresee the shape that politics would assume in a democratic republic. . . .

Choosing senators. Fourth, senators were to be chosen not by the people but by the state legislatures, for a term of six years. Although this arrangement fell short of the ambitions of delegates like Gouverneur Morris who wanted to construct an aristocratic upper house, it would help to ensure that senators would be less responsive to popular majorities and perhaps more sensitive to the needs of property holders. Members of the Senate would thus serve as a check on the Representatives, who were all subject to popular elections every two years.

Equal representation in the Senate. The attempt to create a Senate that would be a republican version of the aristocratic House of Lords was derailed, as we have seen, by a prolonged and bitter dispute over an entirely different question: Should the states be equally represented in Congress or should members of both houses be allocated according to population? This question not only gave rise to one of the most disruptive issues of the Convention, but it resulted in a fifth undemocratic feature of the constitution. As a consequence of the famous—or from a democratic point of view, infamous—"Connecticut Compromise" each state was, as we have seen, awarded the same number of senators, without respect to population. Although this arrangement failed to protect the fundamental rights and interests of the most deprived minorities, some strategically placed and highly privileged minorities—slaveholders, for example—gained disproportionate power over government polices at the expense of less privileged minorities. . . .

Judicial power. Sixth, the constitution of the Framers failed to limit the powers of the judiciary to declare as unconstitutional laws that had been properly passed by Congress and signed by the president. What the delegates intended in the way of judicial review will remain forever unclear; probably many delegates were unclear in their own minds, and to the extent that they discussed the question at all, they were not in full agreement. But probably a majority accepted the view that the federal courts should rule on the constitutionality of state and federal laws in cases brought before them. Nevertheless, it is likely that a substantial majority intended that federal judges should not participate in making government laws and policies, a responsibility that clearly belonged not to the judiciary but to the legislative branch. Their opposition to any policy-making role for the judiciary is strongly indicated by their response to a proposal in the Virginia Plan that "the Executive and a convenient number of the National Judiciary, ought to compose a council of revision" empowered to veto acts of the National Legislature. Though this provision was vigorously defended by Madison and Mason, it was voted down, 6 states to 3.

A judicial veto is one thing; judicial legislation is quite another. Whatever some of the delegates may have thought about the advisability of justices sharing with the executive the authority to veto laws passed by Congress, I am fairly certain that none would have given the slightest support to a proposal that judges should themselves have the power to legislate, to make national policy. However, the up-shot of their work was that in the guise of reviewing the constitutionality of state and congressional actions or inactions, the federal judiciary would later engage in what in some instances could only be called judicial policy-making—or, if you like, judicial legislation.

Congressional power. Finally, the powers of Congress were limited in ways that could, and at times did, prevent the federal government from regulating or con-trolling the economy by means that all modern democratic governments have adopted. Without the power to tax incomes, for example, fiscal policy, not to say measures like Social Security, would be impossible. And regulatory actions—over railroad rates, air safety, food and drugs, banking, minimum wages, and many other policies—had no clear constitutional authorization. Although it would be anachronistic to charge the Framers with lack of foresight in these matters, unless the constitution could be altered by amendment or by heroic reinterpretation of its provisions—presumably by what I have just called judicial legislation—it would prevent representatives of later majorities from adopting the policies they be-lieved were necessary to achieve efficiency, fairness, and security in a complex post-agrarian society.

Enlightened as the Framers' constitution may have been by the standards of the eighteenth century, future generations with more democratic aspirations would find some of its undemocratic features objectionable—and even unacceptable. The public expression of these growing democratic aspirations was not long in coming.

● ● ●

I have little doubt that if the American Constitutional Convention had been held . . . [in later years], a very different constitution would have emerged from the deliberations—although, I hasten to add, we can never know what shape that con-stitution might have taken. We can be reasonably sure, however, that the dele-gates would have attempted to provide more support for, and fewer barriers to, a democratic republic.

As to the undemocratic features of the constitution created in 1787, let me sug-gest four conclusions.

First, the aspects of the constitution that are most defective from a democratic point of view do not necessarily all reflect the intentions of the Framers, insofar as we may surmise them. Though the flaws are traceable to their handiwork, they are in some cases flaws resulting from the inability of these superbly talented crafts-men to foresee how their carefully crafted instrument of government would work under the changing conditions that were to follow—and most of all, under the im-pact of the democratic revolution in which Americans were, and I hope still are, engaged.

Second, some of the undemocratic aspects of the original design also resulted from the logrolling and compromises that were necessary to achieve agreement. The Framers were not philosophers searching for a description of an ideal system. Nor—and we may be forever grateful to them for this—were they philosopher kings entrusted with the power to rule. They were practical men, eager to achieve a stronger national government, and as practical men they made compromises. Would the country have been better off if they had refused to do so? I doubt it. But in any case, they did compromise, and even today the constitution bears the results of some of their concessions. . . .

Third, undemocratic aspects that were more or less deliberately built into the constitution overestimated the dangers of popular majorities—American popular majorities, at any rate—and underestimated the strength of the developing democratic commitment among Americans. As a result, in order to adapt the original framework more closely to the requirements of the emerging democratic republic, with the passage of time some of these aspects of the original constitution were changed, sometimes by amendment, sometimes, as with political parties, by new institutions and practices.

Finally, though the defects seem to me serious and may grow even more serious with time, Americans are not much predisposed to consider another constitution, nor is it clear what alternative arrangements would serve them better.

As a result, the beliefs of Americans in the legitimacy of their constitution will remain, I think, in constant tension with their beliefs in the legitimacy of democracy.

For my part, I believe that the legitimacy of the constitution ought to derive solely from its utility as an instrument of democratic government—nothing more, nothing less. . . . ■

 # View from the Inside

The final days of the Constitutional Convention of 1787 provided moments of celebration and disappointment, hope and fear, satisfaction and concern. Historian Carol Berkin's account emphasizes not only the last-minute compromises that marked the end of the convention, but also the individual attitudes of the key figures behind the United States Constitution.

Questions

1. What concerns or deficiencies were the convention's last-minute compromises designed to address? Why were some delegates still unwilling to sign the final document?
2. "From such an assembly can a perfect production be expected?" asked Benjamin Franklin in his speech on the last day of the convention. In what ways was the convention imperfect, according to Franklin? Why nonetheless did he consider the Constitution worthy of adoption?

1.8   A Brilliant Solution (2003)

Carol Berkin

Like most Philadelphia days in the summer of 1787, September 12 dawned hot and muggy. Wigs had already begun to droop, collars to sag, and perspiration to form in small beads on the foreheads of the delegates as they made their way to Independence Hall that morning. But an observer might have noted a sprightliness in the steps of some and an air of anticipation, even wary optimism, on the faces of many that had not been seen since the opening days of the convention. For on this Wednesday in September, the Committee on Style was scheduled to report the final draft of what the delegates called "the plan." The only question of importance was whether the convention would endorse that plan.

Never burdened by false modesty, committee member Gouverneur Morris boasted that he had played the major role in preparing this final draft of the Constitution. Writing to a friend several years later, he declared that the Constitution "was written by the Fingers which wrote this letter." Decades later Madison would confirm that "The *finish* given to the style and arrangement of the Constitution fairly belongs to the pen of Mr. Morris." But even without Madison's supporting testimony, no one who knew Morris's remarkable command of language would challenge his claim. For the document the committee presented to the convention bore all the hallmarks of Morris's literary style. Awkward phrasing and stilted language had been transformed, and crisp sentences had replaced overly wordy ones. "Having rejected redundant and equivocal Terms," Morris explained, he had made the text "as clear as our Language would permit." He had taken the twenty-three articles and combined them into seven, gathering together all the decisions on the legislature, the executive, and the judiciary in such a way as to finally make the form of the new government clear. He had reworked the preamble, giving it an emotional force that had been sorely lacking in earlier drafts. In his revision Morris captured perfectly the nationalist vision of a supreme central government capable of knitting together a sprawling country and of overcoming the petty divisions among its competitive states. Where once the preamble spoke for "We the people of the States of New Hampshire, Massachusetts, Rhode-Island and Providence Plantations, Connecticut, New-York, New-Jersey, Pennsylvania, Maryland, Virginia, North-Carolina, South-Carolina, and Georgia," it now spoke simply but powerfully for "We, the people of the United States." And where once the preamble did no more than declare that the Constitution that followed was ordained, declared, and established by the people of these thirteen states, now Morris gave a full accounting of the new government's purpose. The people of the United States had ordained and established this government, he wrote, "in order to form a more perfect union, to establish justice, insure domestic tranquility, provide for the common defence, promote the general welfare, and secure the blessings of liberty to ourselves and our posterity. . . ." Embedded in this list of national goals were the corrections to the many laws in the Articles of Confederation that men like Alexander Hamilton, James Madison, and George Washington had feared would be fatal to the young and newly independent America.

• • •

For the delegates, no rationale or justification for the Constitution and its contents was necessary. Each man in the room could conjure up, if he wished, the bitter battles, the acrimonious debates, the hesitant, probing discussions, the compromises, and the concessions that went into almost every section of the seven articles in this document. They knew how perilously close to dissolution the convention had been during the struggle over proportional representation in Congress, and they knew how convoluted their reasoning had often been on the election of the president. They could admire the skill with which the Committee on Style had erased all traces of disagreement and confusion, but their greatest admiration, no doubt, was reserved for the committee's ability to shroud all signs of anxiety about the distribution of power, all fears that loopholes remained to let tyranny come creeping or rushing in, all foreboding that they could not, had not, anticipated and averted every opportunity for corruption and conspiracy.

The rest of the world, however, knew nothing of the process by which the Constitution had come to be. The veil of secrecy had not been pierced during the months of deliberation, and although newspaper editors might have spread unfounded rumors or made unsubstantiated charges and private citizens might have conjectured and offered unsolicited advice, everyone outside Independence Hall had remained in the dark about the convention's deliberations and their outcome. When the Constitution was made public, its definitive tone might prove to be both its strength and its weakness. The delegates might be glad that the document bore no traces of their own fallibilities and foibles, but the American public could easily mistake this for arrogance or a lack of sympathy for local problems, traditions, or interests. Perhaps more importantly, local citizens might suspect their own delegates of selling out their interests.

Fortunately, the veteran politicians of the Committee on Style anticipated the problem. They included a letter along with the Constitution, addressed to the Confederation Congress but intended to gain the sympathy, or at least the understanding, of constituents back home. At the heart of this letter, written in Gouverneur Morris's hand, was an analogy between the familiar Lockean social contract and the union of the states. Just as "all Individuals entering into society must give up a share of liberty to preserve the rest," so, too, each state had to give up some share of its sovereignty to enter the Union. Deciding what rights, and how much sovereignty, each state had to surrender was, of course, the most difficult and delicate of tasks, made even more difficult because of the widespread differences among the states as to "situation, extent, habits, and particular interests." The potential for conflict, though great, was held in check by the delegates' unswerving attention to their larger goal, "our prosperity, felicity, safety, perhaps our national existence." This focus on the good of the nation insured that state delegations were less rigid on small matters and more willing to make concessions as they participated in the give-and-take of the convention. The delegates did not expect any state to be fully satisfied with the results, but they were confident that "each will doubtless consider that had her interest alone been consulted, the consequences might have been particularly disagreeable or injurious to others. . . ." The letter was the committee's gift to their fellow delegates—a preemptive strike against the local critics they would have to face when they returned home.

After reading the letter to the convention, Dr. William Samuel Johnson declared the committee's report complete. It seemed a moment to relish, but the delegates, being who they were, immediately began to propose last-minute additions and changes. All that afternoon, and the following day, and the next, they bickered over wording, rehashed issues in a desultory fashion, and voted down most of the motions anyone proposed. When George Mason, daily more disillusioned by the convention's work, rose to protest the absence of a bill of rights in the Constitution, the delegates allowed him only the briefest discussion of the issue. Since every state constitution contained such a list of guaranteed rights, an overwhelming majority saw a national bill of rights as redundant. When the vote came, not a single state supported Mason's proposal for a committee to draft a bill of rights. Benjamin Franklin and James Madison fared no better. Franklin's proposal to add canal building to the list of congressional powers was defeated; immediately afterward Madison's proposal for a national university met the same fate. The following day a last-minute scramble to increase the representation of both North Carolina and the absent Rhode Island proved futile.

Some changes were made, of course. Among them, the number needed to override the presidential veto was reduced from three-quarters to two-thirds of Congress. The decision came after a curt exchange between George Mason and Gouverneur Morris, two men who were now barely civil to one another despite their genteel training. Franklin, still concerned about the dangerous mix of "avarice and ambition," persuaded the delegates to add a restriction, at the end of Article 2, section 1, paragraph 7, that the president could not receive "any other emolument" than his salary during his term of office.

In the final day of debate, Roger Sherman asked the convention to consider, once again, the vulnerability of the states in the face of the powerful national government they had created. Sherman, who with William Paterson was the most consistent guardian of states' rights, laid out a dark scenario of a majority of states mobilizing the powers of the national government to victimize other states. To help prevent the majority from doing "things fatal to particular States," Sherman urged that the Constitution expressly forbid the passage of any amendment that deprived a state of its equality in the Senate. The convention voted down Sherman's proposal, but Gouverneur Morris recognized the anxiety that Sherman had revived in delegates from smaller states and proposed that Article 5 include the proviso "that no State, without its consent, shall be deprived of its equal suffrage in the Senate." Morris's motion passed without debate and without dissenting vote.

The desire to make corrections, additions, and deletions seemed spent. Yet the delegates sensed that a perfect accord had not been reached. Few delegates were surprised when Edmund Randolph rose to declare that he could not endorse the Constitution. The power the convention had given to Congress, Randolph said, was too indefinite, too dangerous. He appealed to the delegates to submit the Constitution to state conventions, so that they could suggest amendments and revisions, and then to hold a second "general Convention" that could be guided by these suggestions as they produced a final draft of a constitution. Unless these additional steps were taken, it pained him to say that he could not put his name on the document.

Randolph's decision saddened many, but it came as no surprise to those who had followed his slow, steady alienation over the summer. The man who had presented the Virginia Plan had never been the kind of committed nationalist that its author, James Madison, had been. He came to the convention convinced that the Confederation was too weak and that its deficiencies threatened the stability of the nation. But the alternative government the convention proposed did more than shore up the central government. It siphoned away many of the powers of the states and, in Randolph's mind, created a powerful congress as dangerous to the nation's stability as the weak one had been. Edmund Randolph could not sign the Constitution—but he did not close out the possibility of supporting its ratification by his home state of Virginia.

George Mason's defection, which quickly followed Randolph's, was also expected. Mason had made little effort to hide his dissatisfaction with the convention's refusal to condemn slavery and its rejection of a bill of rights. He denounced the Constitution in words far harsher than Randolph's, predicting that the government the delegates proposed was certain to end either in monarchy or in a tyrannical aristocracy. "This Constitution," he said, "has been formed without the knowledge or idea of the people." Only a second convention would allow the people's voice to be heard. He would not sign this Constitution, he declared, and he would not support its ratification by Virginia.

The third and final open refusal came from Elbridge Gerry, who reeled off a long list of defects in the Constitution. He objected, among other things, to the length of the senators' term of office, to the power of the House of Representatives to conceal their journals, to Congress members' control over their own salaries, to underrepresentation of his home state in the House, and to the necessary-and-proper clause. Only the guarantee of a second convention would satisfy him.

A second convention? Impossible, said Charles Pinckney, and, more than that, useless. The state conventions would produce a thousand conflicting demands and suggestions, and the delegates to the national convention, bound to represent the will of their states, would have no grounds for agreement and no room for compromise. "Conventions," he said, "are serious things, and ought not to be repeated." A man with more humor than Pinckney might have added that conventions were too exhausting and time-consuming to be repeated.

When the vote on calling for a second convention came, Madison recorded that "all the States answered—no." When the vote to agree to the Constitution, as amended, followed, Madison recorded, "All the States, ay." And so it was done; the Constitution was ordered to be engrossed and the convention adjourned for the day.

On Monday, September 17, sixteen weeks after the convention began, the delegates gathered to hear the secretary, Major William Jackson, read the engrossed Constitution. When he was done, Benjamin Franklin rose, a speech in his hands. Once again the elderly doctor called upon James Wilson to read his words for him. "Mr. President," Wilson began, as he read aloud the wry but judicious thoughts of a man who had—as he himself observed—lived long enough to have a different perspective on things than many of his younger colleagues in the room that day. "I confess there are several parts of this constitution which I do not at present approve, but I am not sure I shall never approve them. . . . [T]he older I grow, the more apt I am to doubt my own judgment, and to pay more respect to the judgment of others. Most men indeed as well as most sects in Religion, think themselves in possession of all truth, and that wherever others differ from them it is so far error." Despite the seriousness of the occasion and the gravity of his argument, Franklin could not resist illustrating his point with an account of a comic exchange between two French sisters. The tale, no doubt, lost something in the telling by the far-stodgier James Wilson.

Franklin continued, moving to the heart of the matter. "I agree to this Constitution with all its faults, if they are such," he said, "because I think a general Government necessary for us, and there is no form of Government but what may be a blessing to the people if well administered." Unlike Gerry and Mason, Franklin believed that the government would be well administered for many years. Unlike most of the delegates who spoke of the innate corruption of officeholders, Franklin believed that despotism, when it came, would be the result of the innate corruption of the people themselves. The character of the government, in short, mirrored the character of the people. This did not mean that Franklin had unquestioning faith in the political elite. There was little point in calling a second convention, he argued, for these men would be no less burdened by their prejudices, passions, errors of opinion, local interests, and selfish views as the delegates to this convention had been. "From such an assembly can a perfect production be expected?"

Perfection could not be achieved, in Franklin's view, no matter how many conventions were called. And this was why the work of the delegates gathered in Philadelphia was so admirable. They had produced a near-perfect system of government that Franklin was confident would "astonish our enemies, who are waiting with confidence to hear that our councils are confounded like those of the Builders of Babel," and that "our States are on the point of separation, only to meet hereafter for the purpose of cutting one another's throats." Franklin urged unanimous support of this astonishingly near-perfect constitution, not only here in Independence Hall but when delegates returned home to report to their constituents. "I hope," he continued, "for our own sakes as a part of the people, and for the sake of posterity, we shall act heartily and unanimously in recommending this Constitution (if approved by Congress & confirmed by the Conventions) wherever our influence may extend." Let any who, like me, still have objections to some part of the Constitution, he added, "doubt a little of his own infallibility" and put his name to the document.

Franklin ended his remarkable speech with a motion that the Constitution be signed by everyone present, although the endorsement would read "Done in Convention by the unanimous consent of the States present the 17th. Of Sepr. &c— In Witness whereof we have hereunto subscribed our names." The endorsement had been carefully worded not by the good doctor himself but by his friend, the crafty Gouverneur Morris. By calling for the consent of the states rather than the delegates, a few individual dissenters would not jeopardize the appearance of unanimity.

Franklin's motion should have climaxed the convention's deliberations, but, true to form, the logical flow of discussion was abruptly interrupted. Immediately after Wilson finished reading Franklin's speech, Nathaniel Gorham seized the opportunity to propose one last amendment to the Constitution. Gorham asked that the ratio of congressional representatives be changed from one for every forty thousand to one for every thirty thousand people in each state. The resulting increase, Gorham argued, would lessen popular objections to the Constitution. Remarkably, it was the presiding officer, George Washington, who rose to put the question to a vote. Washington felt it necessary to explain his sudden, active participation in the debates. Up until this moment, he had felt his position in the president's chair required his silence; but now he felt equally compelled to speak his mind. He favored this proposal that would expand membership in the House of Representatives and thus provide greater security for the rights and interests of the people. It would give, he concluded, "much satisfaction to see it adopted." Whatever the views of the delegates, no one wished to deny General Washington this satisfaction. The motion carried, unanimously.

Edmund Randolph brought the convention back to the primary business at hand. He was sorry to disappoint Dr. Franklin, but he could not add his name to the venerable names that would endorse the Constitution's "wisdom and its worth." He refused to sign, he now said, because the Constitution was doomed to failure. It would not be ratified by nine states, of that he was certain. Although Gouverneur Morris declared he was content to see the majority of each state delegation sign the Constitution, Alexander Hamilton pressed the individual delegates to set aside their doubts and criticisms and make the endorsement genuinely unanimous. He reminded the convention—if it needed reminding—that no one's ideas were more at odds with the particular plan of government that appeared in the Constitution than his own, but in a choice between anarchy and political convulsion on one side and the "chance of good" on the other, what man could refuse to support the convention's handiwork?

Despite Hamilton's appeal, Randolph and Gerry stood firm. Randolph admitted that his refusal might be the most awful step of his life, but because it was dictated by conscience, he could not alter his course. Gerry, too, confessed how painful his decision was. Yet he believed the nation stood on the brink of civil war, a war that in his home state of Massachusetts pitted followers of democracy ("the worst . . . of all political evils") against supporters of aristocracy. The Constitution would do nothing to prevent this war; indeed, in its present form, it would fan the fires of discord. He could not sign the Constitution and thus pledge to abide by it. He must remain free to take any action he thought might alleviate the conflict within his state. Gerry's genuine anguish did not diminish his egotism; he closed with an accusation that Dr. Franklin's comments were leveled directly at him and his fellow dissenters.

When the vote was taken on Franklin's suggestion that the states unanimously endorse the Constitution, ten states said "aye"; South Carolina's delegation was divided. There was only one piece of business remaining: whether to destroy the records of the convention's proceedings or preserve them? The choice hinged on what would best serve the interests of the delegates. No one wanted the records made public, but destroying them would leave the delegates without any means of defending their actions against false accusations. Better to place them in the custody of the president, they decided, hidden from the public eye but accessible if needed.

There was nothing left to do but sign the Constitution. The New Hampshire delegates, last to arrive at the convention, were first to put their names to the document. When Delaware's turn came, George Read signed for the ailing and absent John Dickinson. Luther Martin, who had said nothing of his intentions, left without signing, as did fellow delegate John Mercer, raising the number of delegates who refused to endorse the Constitution but not endangering the unanimity of the states. Alexander Hamilton was New York's sole delegate to sign; John Lansing and Robert Yates had departed for good in early July. Nine supporters had been called away, either on Confederation business or to manage personal affairs. Thus, the signatures of Oliver Ellsworth of Connecticut, Caleb Strong of Massachusetts, William Few and William Houstoun of Georgia, William Houston of New Jersey, and Dr. James McClurg and George Wythe of Virginia were missing from the Constitution. As Georgia, the last delegation, rose to sign, Benjamin Franklin could be heard to say that during the long months of debate, he had often wondered whether the sun painted on the back of Washington's chair was rising or setting. "Now at length," he said with obvious relief, "I have the happiness to know that it is a rising and not a setting Sun." With that, the convention dissolved itself by an adjournment sine die. . . .

That evening the delegates joined members of the Pennsylvania assembly for a farewell dinner at the City Tavern. While the determinedly uncouth Luther Martin may not have been missed at the table, the delegates probably regretted the absence of John Dickinson, who had gone home to Delaware, hoping to recover from the illness that had plagued him throughout the summer. Gentleman that he was, Dickinson had entrusted a bank bill to George Read to help cover the expenses of the festivities that evening. After a hearty meal and several rounds of toasts, the men cordially parted company. Like George Washington, many must have "retired to meditate on the momentous work, which had been executed, after not less than five, for a large part of the time six, and sometimes seven hours' sitting every day . . . for more than four months." And like Washington, most delegates knew that a second round of political battle was about to begin. ∎

Chapter 2

Federalism

The idea of dividing political power between a central government and its component parts while preserving both elements was one of the great innovations of American political thought. In the eighteenth century, the accepted wisdom was that sovereignty—that is, the ultimate political power in a community—could not be divided. In a confederation, either the states would have to retain sovereignty, authorizing the national government to take on only certain specific tasks with the approval of all the states, or the states would lose their power and identity and be swallowed up into one great whole. There was, according to this line of thought, no middle ground.

Throughout the constitutional debate of the 1780s, the Antifederalists clung to this traditional point of view. The Articles of Confederation, after all, were just that: a confederation of fully sovereign states that came together in a league, much like a modern alliance, for certain limited purposes. The Articles began, in fact, "We the . . . Delegates of the States." The Antifederalists conceded that the Articles needed modification, but they resisted attempts to strengthen the national government too much, fearing that it would become a threat to the sovereignty of the states.

The Federalists' great contribution was the creation of a new conception of federalism. Under this theory, ultimate sovereignty rested in the people; they delegated some of their sovereignty to the national government and some to the states, and retained some for themselves. Within their respective spheres of authority, both the states and the national government were supreme.

The Antifederalists' charge that such a system could not work—that power, inevitably, must flow either to the states or to the national government—was dismissed out of hand by the Federalists. Nevertheless, in the more than two hundred years since the ratification of the Constitution, power has clearly shifted from the states to the national government. This shift of power began in the early days of the Republic, when Congress claimed broad powers to regulate commerce and encourage economic expansion. It accelerated in the late 1800s and early 1900s as the national government expanded its regulation of railroads and other national industries, established a national banking system, and began to enforce the provisions of the Bill of Rights against the states. But the most dramatic expansion of national power came during and after the New Deal of the 1930s, when Washington took on a wide range of new responsibilities in regulating the national economy. After a brief effort to block these programs on constitutional grounds, the Supreme Court reversed itself, upholding New Deal programs across the board. By the

1960s, the Court's decisions led many scholars to conclude that there were no real constitutional limitations on the powers of the national government.

The 1960s and 1970s also saw a dramatic increase in the amount and scope of federal grants to the states. Along with federal money came increased federal influence on the states. Federal highway money, for example, was conditioned on the states' compliance with a national speed limit and a legal drinking age of twenty-one. In general, the Supreme Court upheld these indirect applications of national power.

By the 1970s and 1980s, however, critics of national power began to score points with their efforts to restrain the role of the national government and return power to the states. Supporters of this "new federalism" urged the national government to give the states money with few or no strings attached; to refrain from "unfunded mandates," which impose costly requirements on the states without reimbursement; and, in general, to scale back the breadth and scope of its regulatory activities. These efforts to shift the long-term balance of power away from the national government took on new momentum after the Republican party gained control of Congress in the 1990s. More recently, however, the momentum of this federalism "counterrevolution" appears to have faded.

Throughout the centuries, a major player in the struggle between the national government and the states has been the U.S. Supreme Court. Early on, the Court made a series of critical decisions—the most important of which was *McCulloch* v. *Maryland* (1819)—establishing itself as the key arbiter between the national government and the states and laying the foundation for a broad expansion of national power. In modern times, the Court has generally upheld the national government's power to regulate broad policy areas, including the economy and the environment, though in very recent years the justices have shown at least some willingness to restrain Congress and the president in the name of federalism. But given that the Court is and always has been a component part of the national government, it is not surprising that, over the long haul, the Court has tended to side with Washington rather than with the states.

The readings in this chapter begin with two selections presenting early views on federalism (selections 2.1 and 2.2). Next comes a review of important recent developments in state and local politics (selection 2.3) and a debate over the significance of the modern Supreme Court's decisions on constitutional federalism (selections 2.4 and 2.5). The chapter concludes with a close examination of the interplay between local, state, and federal officials during the Hurricane Katrina crisis in September 2005 (selection 2.6).

Chapter Questions

1. What is the meaning of "dual federalism"? How does the theory of dual federalism differ from traditional understandings of the nature of sovereignty?
2. How does federalism in practice differ from federalism in theory? Is there a difference between the national government's theoretical power over the states and the relationship, in practice, between the national government and the states?
3. What are the advantages and disadvantages of a federal system of government?

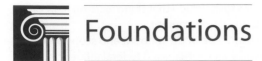 # Foundations

One of the key differences of opinion between the Federalists and the Antifederalists, as their names imply, was over the question of federalism. The Antifederalists, as the political scientist Herbert Storing explains in selection 2.1, objected to the Constitution above all because they feared that it would concentrate power in the national government at the expense of the states. Rather than throw away the Articles of Confederation and start over with the Constitution, the Antifederalists advocated merely modifying and updating the Articles, leaving sovereignty in the states. The Federalists, by contrast, viewed the weakness of the national government as the principal problem with the Articles of Confederation and urged that its powers and responsibilities be significantly expanded.

In *Federalist* No. 45, James Madison (author of the *Federalist Papers* with John Jay and Alexander Hamilton) makes the argument that the national government will never threaten the sovereignty or authority of the states. Just beneath the surface, however, Madison's tilt toward a strong national government becomes clear. All prior confederacies have perished because the central government was too weak, he writes in No. 45; moreover, "as far as the sovereignty of the States cannot be reconciled to the happiness of the people," he declares, "let the former be sacrificed to the latter."

Madison's argument that the "powers delegated by the proposed Constitution to the federal government are few and defined," while "those which are to remain in the State governments are numerous and indefinite" is still formally true. All actions of the national government must be justified with reference to a specific provision of the Constitution granting that power (see the Constitution, Article I, section 8). By contrast, the states possess broadly defined "police" powers—that is, powers to regulate the public health, safety, welfare, and morals.

The powers of the national government may be limited in theory, but in practice the Supreme Court has interpreted the Constitution's grants of power in broad terms. The key case was *McCulloch* v. *Maryland* (1819), which held that the Constitution gave Congress sweeping powers and broad discretion to choose how to carry out those powers. Although on occasion the Court has deviated from this principle, in general it has followed the logic of *McCulloch* and refused to interfere with congressional attempts to assert national authority.

Thus Madison's argument in *Federalist* No. 45 that "the State governments will have the advantage of the federal government . . . [in] the disposition and faculty of resisting and frustrating the measures of the other" has been disproved by history. In any event, Madison's emphasis in No. 45 on the importance of a strong national government makes one wonder whether the argument was made seriously in the first place.

Although the Antifederalists lost the debate over the Constitution, it would be unfair to dismiss their views as narrow-minded, unsophisticated, or incorrect. As you read the selections in this section, remember that the Antifederalists were not merely "against" the Constitution; like the Federalists, they had strong beliefs and political principles and a coherent way of looking at politics.

Questions

1. How did the Antifederalists define federalism? What did they view as the major threat posed by the new "federalism" of the United States Constitution?
2. What are the reasons Madison gives for his argument that the states would be able to resist the encroachments of the national government—just as the members of earlier confederations were able to do?
3. Why do you think that threats to the supremacy of the federal government have been largely unsuccessful?

2.1 What the Antifederalists Were For (1981)

Herbert Storing

Far from straying from the principles of the American Revolution, as some of the Federalists accused them of doing, the Anti-Federalists saw themselves as the true defenders of those principles. "I am fearful," said Patrick Henry, "I have lived long enough to become an old fashioned fellow: Perhaps an invincible attachment to the dearest rights of man, may, in these refined enlightened days, be deemed *old fashioned*: If so, I am contented to be so: I say, the time has been, when every pore of my heart beat for American liberty, and which, I believe, had a counterpart in the breast of every true American." The Anti-Federalists argued, as some historians have argued since, that the Articles of Confederation were the constitutional embodiment of the principles on which the Revolution was based:

> Sir, I venerate the spirit with which every thing was done at the trying time in which the Confederation was formed. America had then a sufficiency of this virtue to resolve to resist perhaps the first nation in the universe, even unto bloodshed. What was her aim? Equal liberty and safety. What ideas had she of this equal liberty? Read them in her Articles of Confederation.

The innovators were impatient to change this "most excellent constitution," which was "sent like a blessing from heaven," for a constitution "essentially differing from the principles of the revolution, and from freedom," and thus destructive of the whole basis of the American community. "Instead of repairing the old and venerable fabrick, which sheltered the United States, from the dreadful and cruel storms of a tyrannical British ministry, they built a stately palace after their own fancies. . . ."

The principal characteristic of that "venerable fabrick" was its federalism: the Articles of Confederation established a league of sovereign and independent states

---

Herbert Storing, *What the Antifederalists Were For*, 1981, pp. 9–14. Reprinted by permission of the publisher, The University of Chicago Press.

whose representatives met in congress to deal with a limited range of common concerns in a system that relied heavily on voluntary cooperation. Federalism means that the states are primary, that they are equal, and that they possess the main weight of political power. The defense of the federal character of the American union was the most prominent article of Anti-Federalist conservative doctrine. While some of the other concerns were intrinsically more fundamental, the question of federalism was central and thus merits fuller discussion here, as it did in that debate.

To begin with an apparently small terminological problem, if the Constitution was opposed because it was anti-federal how did the opponents come to be called Anti-Federalists? They usually denied, in fact, that the name was either apt or just, and seldom used it themselves. They were, they often claimed, the true federalists. Some of them seemed to think that their proper name had been filched, while their backs were turned, as it were, by the pro-Constitution party, which refused to give it back; and versions of this explanation have been repeated by historians. Unquestionably the Federalists saw the advantage of a label that would suggest that those who opposed the Constitution also opposed such a manifestly good thing as federalism. But what has not been sufficiently understood is that the term "federal" had acquired a specific ambiguity that enabled the Federalists not merely to take but to keep the name.

One of the perennial issues under the Articles of Confederation involved the degree to which the general government—or the instrumentality of the federation per se—was to be supported or its capacity to act strengthened. In this context one was "federal" or "anti-federal" according to his willingness or unwillingness to strengthen or support the institutions of the federation. This was James Wilson's meaning when he spoke of the "fœderal disposition and character" of Pennsylvania. It was Patrick Henry's meaning when he said that, in rejecting the Constitution, New Hampshire and Rhode Island "have refused to become federal." It was the meaning of the New York Assembly when in responding coolly to the recommendations of the Annapolis Convention it nevertheless insisted on its "truly federal" disposition. This usage had thoroughly penetrated political discussion in the United States. In the straightforward explanation of Anti-Federalist George Bryan, "The name of Federalists, or Federal men, grew up at New York and in the eastern states, some time before the calling of the Convention, to denominate such as were attached to the general support of the United States, in opposition to those who preferred local and particular advantages. . . ." Later, according to Bryan, "this name was taken possession of by those who were in favor of the new federal government, as they called it, and opposers were called Anti-Federalists." Recognizing the pre-1787 usage, Jackson Turner Main tries, like Bryan, to preserve the spirit of Federalist larceny by suggesting that during the several years before 1787 "the men who wanted a strong national government, who might more properly be called 'nationalists,' began to appropriate the term 'federal' for themselves" and to apply the term "antifederal" to those hostile to the measures of Congress and thus presumably unpatriotic. But there was nothing exceptional or improper in the use of the term "federal" in this way; the shift in meaning was less an "appropriation" than a natural extension of the language, which the Federalists fully exploited.

The point of substance is that the Federalists had a legitimate *claim* to their name and therefore to their name for their opponents. Whether they had a better claim than their opponents cannot be answered on the basis of mere linguistic usage but only by considering the arguments. When, during the years of the Confederation, one was called a "federal man," his attachment to the principles of federalism was not at issue; that was taken for granted, and the point was that he was a man who (given this federal system) favored strengthening the "federal" or general authority. The ambiguity arose because strengthening the federal *authority* could be carried so far as to undermine the federal *principle*; and that was precisely what the Anti-Federalists claimed their opponents were doing. Thus *The Impartial Examiner* argued that, despite the "sound of names" on which the advocates of the Constitution "build their fame," it is the opponents who act "on the broader scale of true *fœderal principles*." They desire "a continuance of each distinct sovereignty—and are anxious for such a degree of energy in the general government, as will cement the union in the strongest manner." It was possible (or so the Anti-Federalists believed) to be a federalist in the sense of favoring a strong agency of the federation and, at the same time, to be a federalist in the sense of adhering to the principle of league of independent states. In the name of federalism in the former sense, it was claimed, the proponents of the Constitution had abandoned federalism in the latter (and fundamental) sense.

The Anti-Federalists stood, then, for federalism in opposition to what they called the consolidating tendency and intention of the Constitution—the tendency to establish one complete national government, which would destroy or undermine the states. They feared the implications of language like Washington's reference, in transmitting the Constitution to Congress, to the need for "the consolidation of our Union." They saw ominous intentions in Publius' opinion that "a NATION, without a NATIONAL GOVERNMENT, is, in my view, an awful spectacle." They resented and denied suggestions that "we must forget our local habits and attachments" and "be reduced to one faith and one government." They saw in the new Constitution a government with authority extending "to every case that is of the least importance" and capable of acting (preeminently in the crucial case of taxation) at discretion and independently of any agency but its own. Instead of thus destroying the federal character of the Union, "the leading feature of every amendment" of the Articles of Confederation ought to be, as Yates and Lansing expressed it, "the preservation of the individual states, in their uncontrouled constitutional rights, and . . . in reserving these, a mode might have been devised of granting to the confederacy, the monies arising from a general system of revenue; the power of regulating commerce, and enforcing the observance of foreign treaties, and other necessary matters of less moment."

A few of the Anti-Federalists were not sure, it is true, that consolidation would be so bad, if it were really feasible. James Monroe went so far as to say that "to collect the citizens of America, who have fought and bled together, by whose joint and common efforts they have been raised to the comparatively happy and exalted theatre on which they now stand; to lay aside all those jarring interests and discordant principles, which state legislatures if they do not create, certainly foment and increase, arrange them under one government and make them one people, is an idea not only elevated and sublime, but equally benevolent and humane." And, on the other hand, most of the Federalists agreed or professed to agree that consolidation was undesirable. Fisher Ames, defending the Constitution in Massachusetts, spoke the language of many Federalists when he insisted that "too much provision cannot be made against a consolidation. The state governments represent the wishes, and feelings, and local interests of the people. They are the safeguard and ornament of the Constitution; they will protract the period of our liberties; they will afford a shelter against the abuse of power, and will be the natural avengers of our violated rights." Indeed, expressions of rather strict federal principles were not uncommon on the Federalist side, although they were often perfunctory or shallow.

Perhaps the most conciliatory Federalist defense of federalism, and not accidentally one of the least satisfactory in principle, was contained in a line of argument put forward by James Wilson and some others to the effect that, just as individuals have to give up some of their natural rights to civil government to secure peaceful enjoyment of civil rights, so states must give up some of theirs to federal government in order to secure peaceful enjoyment of federal liberties. But the analogy of civil liberty and federal liberty concedes the basic Anti-Federal contentions, and Wilson did not consistently adhere to it. As each individual has one vote in civil society, for example, so each state ought, on this analogy, to have one vote in federal society. As the preservation of the rights of individuals is the object of civil society, so the preservation of the rights of states (not individuals) ought to be the object of federal society. But these are Anti-Federal conclusions. Thus, when Agrippa assessed the proposed Constitution from the point of view of the interests of Massachusetts, he did so on *principled* ground, the same ground that properly leads any man to consider the civil society of which he is or may become a member, not exclusively but first and last, from the point of view of his interest in his life, liberty, and property. Wilson, on the other hand, argued for the priority of the general interest of the Union over the particular interests of the states. And this position is not defensible—as Wilson's own argument sufficiently demonstrates—on the basis of the federal liberty–civil liberty analogy.

The more characteristic Federalist position was to deny that the choice lay between confederation and consolidation and to contend that in fact the Constitution provided a new form, partly national and partly federal. This was Publius' argument in *The Federalist*, no. 39. It was Madison's argument in the Virginia ratifying convention. And it was the usual argument of James Wilson himself, who emphasized the strictly limited powers of the general government and the essential part to be played in it by the states. The Anti-Federalists objected that all such arguments foundered on the impossibility of dual sovereignty. "It is a solecism in politics for two coordinate sovereignties to exist together. . . ." A mixture may exist for a time, but it will inevitably tend in one direction or the other, subjecting the country in the meantime to "all the horrors of a divided sovereignty." Luther Martin agreed with Madison that the new Constitution presented a novel mixture of federal and national elements; but he found it "just so much federal in appearance as to give its advocates in some measure, an opportunity of passing it as such upon the unsuspecting multitude, before they had time and opportunity to examine it, and yet so predominantly national as to put it in the power of its movers, whenever the machine shall be set agoing, to strike out every part that has the appearance of being federal, and to render it wholly and entirely a national government."

The first words of the preamble sufficiently declare the anti-federal (in the strict sense) character of the Constitution, Patrick Henry thought; and his objection thundered over the Virginia convention sitting in Richmond:

> [W]hat right had they to say, *We the People?* My political curiosity, exclusive of my anxious solicitude for the public welfare, leads me to ask, who authorised them to speak the language of, *We, the People*, instead of *We, the States?* States are the characteristics, and the soul of a confederation. If the States be not the agents of this compact, it must be one great consolidated National Government of the people of all the States.

The clearest minds among the Federalists agreed that states are the soul of a confederacy. That is what is wrong with confederacies: "The fundamental principle of the old Confederation is defective; we must totally eradicate and discard this principle before we can expect an efficient government."

Here lies the main significance of the mode of ratification in the proposed Constitution. The new procedure—ratification by special state conventions rather than by Congress and the state legislatures and provision that the Constitution shall be established on ratification of nine states (as between them), rather than all thirteen states as required under the Articles of Confederation—was not merely illegal; it struck at the heart of the old Confederation. It denied, as Federalists like Hamilton openly admitted, the very basis of legality under the Articles of Confederation. The requirement in the Articles of Confederation for unanimous consent of the states to constitutional changes rested on the assumption that the states are the basic political entities, permanently associated indeed, but associated entirely at the will and in the interest of each of the several states. Even if it were granted that government under the Articles had collapsed (which most Anti-Federalists did not grant), there was no justification for abandoning the principles of state equality and unanimous consent to fundamental constitutional change. As William Paterson had put it in the Philadelphia Convention,

> If we argue the matter on the supposition that no Confederacy at present exists, it cannot be denied that all the States stand on the footing of equal sovereignty. All therefore must concur before any can be bound. . . . If we argue on the fact that a federal compact actually exists, and consult the articles of it we still find an equal Sovereignty to be the basis of it.

Whether in the Articles of Confederation or outside, the essential principle of American union was the equality of the states. As Luther Martin had argued in Philadelphia, "the separation from G. B. placed the 13 States in a state of nature towards each other; [and] they would have remained in that state till this time, but for the confederation. . . ."

The provision for ratifying the Constitution rested, in the main, on the contrary assumption that the American states are not several political wholes, associated together according to their several wills and for the sake of their several interests, but are, and always were from the moment of their separation from the King of England, parts of one whole. Thus constitutional change is the business of the people, not of the state legislatures, though the people act in (or through) their states.

As one nation divided into several states, moreover, constitutional change is to be decided, not by unanimous consent of separate and equal entities, but by the major part of a single whole—an extraordinary majority because of the importance of the question. The Federalists contended that the colonies declared their independence not individually but unitedly, and that they had never been independent of one another. And the implication of this view is that the foundation of government in the United States is the interest of the nation and not the interests of the states. "The Union is essential to our being as a nation. The pillars that prop it are crumbling to powder," said Fisher Ames, staggering through a metaphorical forest. "The Union is the vital sap that nourishes the tree." The Articles of Confederation, in this view, were a defective instrument of a preexisting union. The congressional resolution calling for the Philadelphia Convention had described a means—"for the sole and express purpose of revising the Articles of Confederation"—and an end—to "render the federal constitution adequate to the exigencies of Government & the preservation of the Union." If there was any conflict, the means ought to be sacrificed to the end. The duty of the Philadelphia Convention and the members of the ratifying conventions was to take their bearings, not from the defective means, but from the great end, the preservation and well-being of the Union. ■

2.2 *Federalist* No. 45 (1788)

James Madison

Outline

I. Importance of increasing the powers of the national government at the expense of the states.

II. Historical weakness of central governments in confederacies.

    A. Ancient times.

    B. Feudal times.

III. Advantages of the states in their relations with the national government.

    A. States as constituent and essential parts of the national government.

    B. Relatively small size of the national government.

    C. Few and defined powers of the national government.

    D. Advantages of the states in times of peace.

IV. Conclusion: Constitution as invigorating the powers of the national government more than adding to them.

• • •

The adversaries to the plan of the convention, instead of considering in the first place what degree of power was absolutely necessary for the purposes of the federal government, have exhausted themselves in a secondary inquiry into the possible consequences of the proposed degree of power to the governments of the particular States. But if the Union, as has been shown, be essential to the security of the people of America against foreign danger; if it be essential to their security against contentions and wars among the different States; if it be essential to guard them against those violent and oppressive factions which embitter the blessings of liberty and against those military establishments which must gradually poison its very fountain; if, in a word, the Union be essential to the happiness of the people of America, is it not preposterous to urge as an objection to a government, without which the objects of the Union cannot be attained, that such a government may derogate from the importance of the governments of the individual States? Was, then, the American Revolution effected, was the American Confederacy formed, was the precious blood of thousands spilt, and the hard-earned substance of millions lavished, not that the people of America should enjoy peace, liberty, and safety, but that the governments of the individual States, that particular municipal establishments, might enjoy a certain extent of power and be arrayed with certain dignities and attributes of sovereignty? We have heard of the impious doctrine in the old world, that the people were made for kings, not kings for the people. Is the same doctrine to be revived in the new, in another shape—that the solid happiness of the people is to be sacrificed to the views of political institutions of a different form? It is too early for politicians to presume on our forgetting that the public good, the real welfare of the great body of the people, is the supreme object to be pursued; and that no form of government whatever has any other value than as it may be fitted for the attainment of this object. Were the plan of the convention adverse to the public happiness, my voice would be, Reject the plan. Were the Union itself inconsistent with the public happiness, it would be, Abolish the Union. In like manner, as far as the sovereignty of the States cannot be reconciled to the happiness of the people, the voice of every good citizen must be, Let the former be sacrificed to the latter. How far the sacrifice is necessary has been shown. How far the unsacrificed residue will be endangered is the question before us.

Several important considerations have been touched in the course of these papers, which discountenance the supposition that the operation of the federal government will by degrees prove fatal to the State governments. The more I revolve the subject, the more fully I am persuaded that the balance is much more likely to be disturbed by the preponderancy of the last than of the first scale.

We have seen, in all the examples of ancient and modern confederacies, the strongest tendency continually betraying itself in the members to despoil the general government of its authorities, with a very ineffectual capacity in the latter to defend itself against the encroachments. Although, in most of these examples, the system has been so dissimilar from that under consideration as greatly to weaken any inference concerning the latter from the fate of the former, yet, as the States will retain under the proposed Constitution a very extensive portion of active sovereignty, the inference ought not to be wholly disregarded. In the [ancient] Achæan league it is probable that the federal head had a degree and species of power which gave it a considerable likeness to the government framed by the convention. The Lycian Confederacy, as far as its principles and form are transmitted, must have borne a still greater analogy to it. Yet history does not inform us that either of them ever degenerated, or tended to degenerate, into one consolidated government. On the contrary, we know that the ruin of one of them proceeded from the incapacity of the federal authority to prevent the dissensions, and finally the disunion, of the subordinate authorities. These cases are the more worthy of our attention as the external causes by which the component parts were pressed together were much more numerous and powerful than in our case; and consequently less powerful ligaments within would be sufficient to bind the members to the head and to each other.

In the feudal system, we have seen a similar propensity exemplified. Notwithstanding the want of proper sympathy in every instance between the local sovereigns and the people, and the sympathy in some instances between the general sovereign and the latter, it usually happened that the local sovereigns prevailed in the rivalship for encroachments. Had no external dangers enforced internal harmony and subordination, and particularly, had the local sovereigns possessed the affections of the people, the great kingdoms in Europe would at this time consist of as many independent princes as there were formerly feudatory barons.

The State governments will have the advantage of the federal government, whether we compare them in respect to the immediate dependence of the one on the other; to the weight of personal influence which each side will possess; to the powers respectively vested in them; to the predilection and probable support of the people; to the disposition and faculty of resisting and frustrating the measures of each other.

The State governments may be regarded as constituent and essential parts of the federal government; whilst the latter is nowise essential to the operation or organization of the former. Without the intervention of the State legislatures, the President of the United States cannot be elected at all. They must in all cases have a great share in his appointment, and will, perhaps, in most cases, of themselves determine it. The Senate will be elected absolutely and exclusively by the State legislatures. Even the House of Representatives, though drawn immediately from the people, will be chosen very much under the influence of that class of men whose influence over the people obtains for themselves an election into the State legislatures. Thus, each of the principal branches of the federal government will owe its existence more or less to the favor of the State governments, and must consequently feel a dependence, which is much more likely to beget a disposition too obsequious than too overbearing towards them. On the other side, the component parts of the State governments will in no instance be indebted for their appointment to the direct agency of the federal government, and very little, if at all, to the local influence of its members.

The number of individuals employed under the Constitution of the United States will be much smaller than the number employed under the particular States. There will consequently be less of personal influence on the side of the former than of the latter. The members of the legislative, executive, and judiciary departments of thirteen and more States, the justices of peace, officers of militia, ministerial officers of justice, with all the county, corporation, and town officers, for three millions and more of people, intermixed and having particular acquaintance with every class and circle of people must exceed, beyond all proportion, both in number and influence, those of every description who will be employed in the administration of the federal system. Compare the members of the three great departments of the thirteen States, excluding from the judiciary department the justices of peace, with the members of the corresponding departments of the single government of the Union; compare the militia officers of three millions of people with the military and marine officers of any establishment which is within the compass of probability, or, I may add, of possibility, and in this view alone, we may pronounce the advantage of the States to be decisive. If the federal government is to have collectors of revenue, the State governments will have theirs also. And as those of the former will be principally on the seacoast, and not very numerous, whilst those of the latter will be spread over the face of the country, and will be very numerous, the advantage in this view also lies on the same side. It is true that the Confederacy is to possess, and may exercise, the power of collecting internal as well as external taxes throughout the States; but it is probable that this power will not be resorted to, except for supplemental purposes of revenue; that an option will then be given to the States to supply their quotas by previous collections of their own; and that the eventual collection, under the immediate authority of the Union, will generally be made by the officers, and according to the rules, appointed by the several States. Indeed it is extremely probable that in other instances, particularly in the organization of the judicial power, the officers of the States will be clothed with the correspondent authority of the Union. Should it happen, however, that separate collectors of internal revenue should be appointed under the federal government, the influence of the whole number would not bear a comparison with that of the multitude of State officers in the opposite scale. Within every district to which a federal collector would be allotted, there would not be less than thirty or forty, or even more, officers of different descriptions, and many of them persons of character and weight whose influence would lie on the side of the State.

The powers delegated by the proposed Constitution to the federal government are few and defined. Those which are to remain in the State governments are numerous and indefinite. The former will be exercised principally on external objects, as war, peace, negotiation, and foreign commerce; with which last the power of taxation will, for the most part, be connected. The powers reserved to the several States will extend to all the objects which, in the ordinary course of affairs, concern the lives, liberties, and properties of the people, and the internal order, improvement, and prosperity of the State.

The operations of the federal government will be most extensive and important in times of war and danger; those of the State governments in times of peace and security. As the former periods will probably bear a small proportion of the latter, the State governments will here enjoy another advantage over the federal government. The more adequate, indeed, the federal powers may be rendered to the national defense, the less frequent will be those scenes of danger which might favor their ascendancy over the governments of the particular States.

If the new Constitution be examined with accuracy and candor, it will be found that the change which it proposes consists much less in the addition of NEW POWERS to the Union than in the invigoration of its ORIGINAL POWERS. The regulation of commerce, it is true, is a new power; but that seems to be an addition which few oppose and from which no apprehensions are entertained. The powers relating to war and peace, armies and fleets, treaties and finance, with the other more considerable powers, are all vested in the existing Congress by the Articles of Confederation. The proposed change does not enlarge these powers; it only substitutes a more effectual mode of administering them. The change relating to taxation may be regarded as the most important; and yet the present Congress have as complete authority to REQUIRE of the States indefinite supplies of money for the common defense and general welfare as the future Congress will have to require them of individual citizens; and the latter will be no more bound than the States themselves have been to pay the quotas respectively taxed on them. Had the States complied punctually with the Articles of Confederation, or could their compliance have been enforced by as peaceable means as may be used with success towards single persons, our past experience is very far from countenancing an opinion that the State governments would have lost their constitutional powers, and have gradually undergone an entire consolidation. To maintain that such an event would have ensued would be to say at once that the existence of the State governments is incompatible with any system whatever that accomplishes the essential purposes of the Union. ■

American Politics Today

While the national government gets most of the headlines, much of the real work of American politics takes place in the states. And although each state—and each state capital—is different, the fifty states share a great deal in common. In this selection, political scientists John Dinan and Dale Krane examine key trends in current state government and politics. Above all, governors and state legislators must deal with a political environment largely shaped by what is happening in Washington, D.C.

Questions

1. What common trends in state politics do the authors identify? How have state political issues been shaped by decisions made at the national level?
2. How does state fiscal (taxing and spending) policy differ from fiscal policy at the national level? What accounts for these critical differences? (For comparison, see the discussion of long-term trends in national fiscal policy in selection 13.2.)

2.3 The State of American Federalism (2006)

John Dinan and Dale Krane

Trends in government and politics within the American states sometimes run counter to trends at the national level, as evidenced by the 2004 election results. Not only did Democrats win governorships in several states carried handily by President Bush, but they also gained control of one or more legislative chambers in some Republican states. These results were surprising given the widely held view that the United States has become increasingly polarized into "Red and Blue" states, as exemplified by the following observations [by journalist E. J. Dionne]:

> Democrats see Republicans as a collection of pampered rich people who selfishly seek to cut their own taxes, allied with religious fundamentalists who want to use government power to impose a narrow brand of Christianity on everyone else.
>
> Republicans see Democrats as godless, overeducated elitists who sip lattes as they look down their noses at the moral values of "real Americans" in "the heartland" and ally themselves with "special interest groups" that benefit from "big government."

Some scholars suggest a "clash of cultures" is the primary cause of these partisan divisions, whereas others point to a long list of social and economic differences among states and their residents, including marriage and fertility rates, religious affiliations and church attendance, urban versus rural lifestyles, and even relative housing prices. The heightened level of polarization has particularly distorted national politics—so much so that [Jacob S.] Hacker and [Paul] Pierson assert that Bush has deliberately followed a governing strategy of moving rightward and away from the normal "center" of American politics. Not only has Bush tacked rightward, but he has done so in the face of prevailing public opinion and a rising dismay about "a sea of partisanship but no results" in Washington.

By contrast, state governors and state governments in general continue to operate in the "center." This is in part because recent state elections have produced "purple" states, where governors belong to the party opposite that of the state's national voting pattern. For example, [as of 2005] Republican governors preside[d] over several blue Democratic states such as Massachusetts, California, and New York, and red Republican states such as Arizona, Kansas, Montana, Oklahoma, and Wyoming ha[d] governors who [were] Democrats. Instead of the hardened partisanship found in the nation's capital, "at the state level," Governor [Mitt] Romney (R-MA) notes, "when the election is over, there's a meeting of minds and a readiness to find solutions." Therefore, part of the explanation for the higher incidence of bipartisan policymaking at the state level is the simple fact of divided government in [multiple] states. Bipartisan action by governors and legislatures is also prompted by (1) court rulings that force the enactment of legislation, (2) constitutional requirements for a balanced budget, (3) economic development competition among the states, and (4) public opinion. Governor Kathleen Sebelius (D-KS) claims that the bipartisan resolution of her state's education funding crisis "came not just from the court ruling but also via public opinion, demanding that 'we have to work together, and it can't be just Republican or Democratic.'" The November 2005 defeat of Governor Arnold Schwarzenegger's (R-CA) package of changes in California state government demonstrates the electorate's power to defend the political "center." Although the national level of American government may be sharply divided and unable to resolve pressing fiscal and policy issues, many state governments are characterized by "savvy politicians who are willing to cut the necessary deals to put the [mix of red and blue] ideas into practice," and, as a consequence, state officials produce a stream of pragmatic policies.

State Policy Actions

A commonly cited reason for national policymaking is the lack of action on a problem by state governments. However, the reverse may also be true; that is, states often act to address problems because Washington has failed to do so. Whereas the president and Congress are gridlocked over global warming, states on both coasts adopted proposals to reduce greenhouse gases such as carbon dioxide emitted from motor vehicles and electric power generators. Under the leadership of Governor George E. Pataki (R-NY) seven states in the northeast (Connecticut, Delaware, Maine, New Hampshire, New Jersey, New York, and Vermont) entered into a cooperative agreement to hold power plant emissions at the current level and to reduce the level by 10 percent by 2020. Labeled the Regional Greenhouse Gas Initiative, the plan creates a market-based system of pollution "allowances" and "offsets" that can be auctioned off or purchased by polluters and will encourage technological innovation and lead to lower levels of emitted pollutants. The plan is similar to the one adopted in the early 1990s to address acid rain. On the West Coast, Oregon and Washington adopted California's tough standards on automobile tailpipe emissions. Late in [2005], New York, Connecticut, Rhode Island, Vermont, Maine, Massachusetts, and New Jersey also adopted the California rule, which takes effect in 2009 and requires a 30 percent reduction in carbon dioxide emitted from cars by 2016. Once again in the environmental policy arena, California, not the national government, is at the forefront, as Oregon's air-quality administrator Andrew Ginsburg observes: "For greenhouse gases, the federal government hasn't taken any action at all, and California has. It's clear the federal government won't do it unless California paves the way and enough other states opt in." The U.S. Conference of Mayors in June 2005 adopted a resolution that national and state governments move to abide by the Kyoto treaty.

While the federal government's attention in health policy was concentrated on untangling the administrative fiascoes caused by the poor design of the Medicare prescription drug benefit, nineteen states considered proposals to expand health-care coverage, compared with twelve states in 2003. The Kaiser Family Foundation reported that forty-six states and the District of Columbia increased Medicaid provider payments, nineteen states plus the District of Columbia expanded Medicaid eligibility, eleven states expanded long-term care coverage, and nine states improved Medicaid benefits. Nevertheless, because of Medicaid's rapidly rising costs, forty-nine states and the District of Columbia made changes in provider payment rates, forty-seven states plus the District of Columbia imposed new controls on pharmacies, twenty-seven states and the District of Columbia took new fraud and abuse containment actions, twenty-five states and the District of Columbia adopted new disease and case management procedures, fourteen states expanded managed care arrangements, eight states made cuts in eligibility, eight states added copayments, and seven states reduced benefits. Twenty states increased children's access to health-care coverage and nine states reversed the cuts in children's health care made as part of the efforts to cope with the 2001–2003 fiscal crisis. Illinois, in a bold move, approved low-cost health insurance for all of the state's children to begin July 2006. Another bold move was made by the California attorney general in August 2005 when he sued thirty-nine drug companies for defrauding the state's Medicaid system (Medi-Cal) by charging as much as ten times the price offered to other purchasers.

State governments also took the lead in labor issues, with seven states raising their minimum wages above the federal minimum wage of US$5.15 per hour. [From] 1997, when the national government last boosted the federal minimum wage [through 2005], seventeen states and the District of Columbia . . . increased their wage, and it is likely that several more states will do so. . . . These wage increases have not been enacted only by states with Democratic governors or legislatures; to the contrary, most of the recent rises in state minimum wages have been in states with Republican governors and/or Republican legislatures. It is worth noting that about half of the U.S. workforce lives in states where the minimum wage is above the federal minimum. Eleven states also passed improvements in unemployment insurance coverage.

The National Association of State Public Interest Research Groups reported data-breach laws were introduced in thirty-five state legislatures during the first half of 2005, and at least fifteen states passed some form of identify theft protection. Six states acted to prohibit racial profiling, five states added new laws on nondiscrimination, three states approved criminal penalties for human trafficking, and three more states expanded their hate crimes law.

Of course, some state policy activity occurs as a reaction to policy emanating from the national capital. For instance, states have made strong appeals for more federal dollars to pay for administration of the new Medicare prescription drug benefit. Another example of states going in a direction opposite to or opposing actions taken by the federal government is the estate tax. Although the federal estate tax is scheduled to disappear in 2010, legislators in twenty states worked on plans to uncouple their state's levy from the federal tax, and at least seventeen states plus the District of Columbia have started the process of creating their own estate tax.

State officials also formulate policy independent of federal policy activity, typically in response to conditions or issues unique to the state, such as California's new law restricting the activity of photographers who chase or stalk celebrities. Reminiscent of the mid- to late 1800s, local communities in Kansas and Nebraska offer free land to persons willing to settle in small towns. Kansas continues to be an important battleground in the "culture wars" over evolution. In November 2005 the state Board of Education voted six–four to redefine science and to mandate science curricula that recommend teaching specific doubts about evolution. This past year six states (Georgia, Montana, North Dakota, Rhode Island, Vermont, and Washington) established bans on indoor smoking, and at least 159 cities did as well. Idaho, one of six states without a governor's mansion, decided to offer naming rights to rooms and gardens as a means of attracting private donors to help pay for the conversion of a donated home into the official gubernatorial residence.

Are "Happy Days" Here Again for State Budgets?

. . . [S]tate governments survived one of their worst fiscal periods ever [at the beginning of the decade]. Compared with FY2002, when forty-five states reported revenue shortfalls, FY2005 revenues exceeded projections in forty-five states and were on target in the other five states. Instead of a US$50 billion deficit (FY2002), state total balances for FY2005 came in at US$38.5 billion, and since FY2001 states have reduced aggregate red ink by US$263.8 billion. This reversal in fiscal fortunes is due to (1) actions state governments took to cope with the precipitous decline in revenues that began in 2001 with the collapse of the dot.com economy and the terrorist attacks of September 11, (2) a reinvigorated national economy and the concomitant rise in tax receipts, and (3) the recent increases in federal aid to state and local governments. . . .

These "happy days are here again" numbers do not mean that the future fiscal situation of the American states is sound. As Scott Pattison, executive director of the National Association of State Budget Officers, explains,

> The general picture is that revenue is coming in better than expected for quite a few states. The problem is that the states are like the guy who had been laid off and his income went way down, and now he's got a job again. But in the meantime, he put a lot of expenses on his credit card, his kids' tuition went up and he tapped into his retirement fund. That's exactly what a lot of states did.

Pattison's observation reflects the budget pressures states face even with the return of rising revenues. States attempted to cope with the 2001 fiscal crisis first by draining reserves by an aggregate of more than US$20 billion and then by cutting annual expenditures by more than US$64 billion, while also raising fees and user charges by more than US$25 billion. Not only have state officials had to replace these funds, but they also have had to address the constantly rising costs in Medicaid, K–12 education, and corrections, which together constitute 61 percent of state general fund expenditures. These three policy areas, individually and collectively, drive state spending relentlessly upward. . . .

"States have climbed out of their budget deficits," notes Bill Pound, NCSL [National Conference of State Legislatures] executive director, "and now they're working on the service deficits." For example, funding for public education struggles in many states to enhance teacher salaries, cover health insurance and pensions, and upgrade equipment and facilities, and legislatures also must find funds to comply with court rulings or avoid court orders to provide an "adequate" education. In addition, corrections costs are increasing due to the "graying" of the inmate population, thus pushing up health expenditures at double-digit rates in some states, and also because of the epidemic of methamphetamine production and usage, which has forced a number of states to build more prisons, offer earlier parole, adopt community-based corrections programs, or establish drug courts and mental health courts.

These policy areas illustrate how state officials need to use the new revenue prosperity to fulfill old obligations and meet new expectations, while being mindful that state finances are fragile and can be disrupted by unforeseen events such as Hurricane Katrina, a spike in energy prices, or an economic downturn. State officials now face the constituents of programs (e.g., higher education, local governments) sacrificed during the lean years who are pressuring them to repair the damage. The upswing in state revenues in FY2005 has returned to a rate of increase similar to that in the 1990s, but state total balances have yet to return to levels common before the 2001 downturn. . . .

[This] positive inflow of funds has stanched the fiscal bleeding but has done little to remedy the long-term structural problems in state finances. A structural deficit in state finances occurs when a state's "normal growth of revenues is insufficient to finance the normal growth of expenditures year after year . . . [and] as a result the state faces gaps between estimated revenues and expenditures." More simply, structural deficits are caused by a "persistent mismatch between growth rates in revenues and spending." The Center on Budget and Policy Priorities (CBPP) analysis of state structural budget problems lists ten risk factors that contribute to structural deficits: (1) lack of services in the sales tax base, (2) corporate income tax weakness, (3) untaxed e-commerce, (4) extensive tax preferences for the elderly, (5) limited progressivity of the personal income tax, (6) tax policy mix and choices that worsen structural gaps, (7) growth of expenditure needs for state residents, (8) process barriers such as tax and expenditure limitations, (9) failure to detach from federal policies that reduce state revenue, and (10) presence of structural gaps found by other studies. The more these factors characterize a state's tax policies, the more likely it is that the state experiences (or will experience) a structural deficit. The CBPP's analysis finds 11 states exhibit nine to ten of these factors, and only 11 states exhibit five or fewer of these ten factors. State governments typically address a shortfall in revenues by ad hoc solutions such as a temporary increase in the sales tax rate. However, several trends in the economy, in state and federal policies, and in the larger society make piecemeal measures increasingly ineffective. The current boom in state revenues may yield sufficient funds to recoup previous levels of services, but the long-term mismatch between revenues and necessary expenditures can be resolved only by modernization of a state's tax regime. Failure to align revenues with expenditures will leave state budgets with gaps such as those projected for FY2007 in Kentucky (12.5 percent), New York (13 percent), and New Hampshire (8 percent). It should be noted that Congress has used "unfunded mandates and other cost shifts" to export the national government's burgeoning deficit to the states and that this transfer of the federal structural deficit to the states only compounds state efforts to reduce their own structural gaps. Instead of "happy days," lack of action to modernize state tax codes will leave states in [a] permanent fiscal crisis. . . . ■

Issue and Controversy

A decade ago, the U.S. Supreme Court seemed poised to inaugurate a new era of constitutional federalism. For the first time in sixty years, the justices appeared willing to restrict the powers of the national government in key areas of economic and social policy. The first signs were admittedly modest—a 1994 decision invalidating a federal law aimed at prohibiting the possession of firearms in school zones and a 2000 case striking down a provision of the Violence Against Women Act, which gave alleged victims of gender-based violence the right to sue their alleged attackers in federal court. Proponents of state power hoped—and advocates of national power feared—that these decisions were just the leading edge of a federalism revolution.

Less than ten years later, the revolution does not seem to have materialized. Conservative journalist Ramesh Ponnuru (selection 2.4) assesses the Court's limited record in advancing the cause of states' rights and draws the conclusion that the "Court cannot impose federalism over the objections of the other branches of the government." By contrast, law professor David J. Barron (selection 2.5) argues that "Rehnquist federalism"—so-called after the late Chief Justice, who long advocated limits on national power—has had real effects, and that progressives should not turn their backs on the states.

Questions

1. How significant were the Rehnquist Court's decisions in limiting the power of Washington and increasing the autonomy of the states?
2. What does Ponnuru mean by "symbolic federalism"? By "moral federalism"? What suggestions does he have for conservatives who have been disappointed by the Court's federalism decisions?
3. What does Barron mean by "Rehnquist federalism"? What, in his view, would a "progressive federalism" look like?

2.4 The End of the Federalism Revolution (2005)

Ramesh Ponnuru

The Supreme Court's decision in the medical-marijuana case is being taken as the end of the "federalism revolution" that began under Chief Justice Rehnquist. The Court held that the feds could outlaw the medicinal use of marijuana, whatever California's government (and voters) preferred. Six justices

---

Ramesh Ponnuru, "The End of the Federalism Revolution," *National Review* 57 (July 4, 2005), pp. 33–35. © 2005 by National Review, Inc. 215 Lexington Avenue, New York, NY 10016. Reprinted by permission.

of the Court ruled that the feds could prohibit medical marijuana because the Constitution gave Congress the power to regulate interstate commerce. Justice Clarence Thomas, one of the three dissenters, said that if Congress could use the Commerce Clause to regulate sick people's personal use of marijuana, "then it can regulate virtually anything—and the Federal Government is no longer one of limited and enumerated powers."

This case does not, however, represent the first rumor of the federalism revolution's death. Two years ago, the Court ruled—again with the support of six justices—that Congress could subject state governments to lawsuits under the Family and Medical Leave Act. Many legal commentators thought that this decision, like the medical-marijuana decision, was hard to square with the Court's previous pro-federalism decisions. Justice Ruth Bader Ginsburg, who had dissented from those pro-federalism decisions, crowed, "Federalism this term was the dog that did not bark."

So is the federalism revolution over? No: For the revolution to be over it would have had to begin. The truth is that there never was a federalism revolution.

The most striking thing about the Court's "revolutionary" decisions—which inspired some reporters and commentators to talk as though the Articles of Confederation were making a comeback—is how very limited they were. The "landmark" cases of the revolution struck down the Gun-Free Schools Act and provisions of the Violence Against Women Act on grounds that Congress was acting beyond its Commerce Clause authority. But there were many ways for Congress to get around those decisions. Indeed, Congress enacted a modified Gun-Free Schools Act and the courts left it alone. Justice Stephen Breyer's dissent in the Violence Against Women Act even outlined a variety of ways the Congress could circumvent the Court's ruling.

The Gun-Free Schools Act case provided two other pieces of evidence that the Court's federalism was unserious. The first was that two of the five justices in the majority—Sandra Day O'Connor and Anthony Kennedy—included, among the reasons to strike down the act, that most states had already banned guns in the school. The country was agreed as to ends, and disagreed only as to means. The implication here is that a federal law might have been justifiable if the states were split evenly on the issue. It was, in other words, a vote for federalism because national uniformity already existed.

The second piece of evidence came in the form of judicial silences. Neither the federalist justices nor the centralizing justices have been willing to admit that modern government has strayed far away from the Founders' federalism. Justice Thomas's opinion in the case argued that the Constitution, as originally understood, strictly limits congressional power. But he was unwilling to take the obvious next step with this argument, and declare that much of modern government is unconstitutional. Indeed, he denied any need for a "wholesale abandonment" of the Court's post–New Deal jurisprudence in these matters.

Symbolic Federalism

Many times over the last 15 years it has been said that the Rehnquist Court was getting ready to attack the "core" of the modern regulatory state. Yet the Supreme

Court was never likely to pose any threat to the New Deal or to civil-rights statutes. It may very well have been wise for the justices not to have threatened too much of modern government, for it is hard to see how a judicial campaign to undo the New Deal could have been sustained politically. What that has left us with, as Orin Kerr, a law professor at George Washington University, has written, is a "symbolic federalism." The Court insists on federalism when doing so would not make much practical difference.

The Court's federalism is limited in another way. The justices have tended to think about federalism in terms of the "status," "interests," and "dignity" of state governments. That isn't the only possible conception of federalism. Michael Greve, who runs the Federalism Project at the American Enterprise Institute, argues that many provisions of the Constitution are better understood as limiting the state governments by promoting competition among them. The . . . Court has not shown much interest in reviving these features of the Constitution's federalist architecture.

The medical-marijuana case demonstrated some of the conceptual problems created by a view of federalism that centers on state governments. Either the Commerce Clause authorizes the federal government to prohibit the medicinal use of marijuana, or it does not. But nothing should turn on what the government of California wants. If the federal government has the power to prohibit medical marijuana, then it can do so over the state's objections. If it does not have that power, it does not have that power anywhere. It does not have it in states that agree with it any more than in states that object.

There is a final, and too often neglected, limit on the Court's federalism. The Court has been willing to impose extremely modest restraints on Congress. It has not been willing to impose restraints on itself—and it is, after all, an important part of the federal government. The landmark cases of the Warren and Burger Courts discovered, or, as critics had it, invented, new individual rights, and correspondingly limited state autonomy. The . . . Court has reversed none of those landmark decisions. It has merely slowed down the pace of rights creation. In recent years, it has announced that states may no longer execute murderers who were minors at the time of their crimes, prohibit sodomy, or punish partial-birth abortion.

It has also displayed a marked intolerance for disagreement, as Robert Nagel powerfully demonstrated in *The Implosion of American Federalism* by analyzing the Court's decisions on abortion, gay rights, and term limits. When the Court reaffirmed *Roe* v. *Wade* in 1992, for example, it began its opinion by noting the scandal of disagreement. "Liberty finds no refuge in a jurisprudence of doubt. Yet, 19 years after our holding that the Constitution protects a woman's right to terminate her pregnancy in its early stages, . . . that definition of liberty is still questioned." The Court argued that *Roe*'s supporters had faced "criticism," "ostracism," and even "violence." It "call[ed on] the contending sides of a national controversy to end their national division by accepting" the Court's decisions on abortion. In other words, it invited *Roe*'s opponents to dissolve their movement.

Nagel makes the simple point that fear of national division and conflict is not a promising mindset for the agents of a federalist revolution to have. Nor is an overwrought sense of the fragility of the national union. Yet in 1995—the same year the Gun-Free Schools Act went down—the Court treated the prospect of state-imposed term limits on congressmen as an assault on the idea of America as a nation. The Court frequently finds state laws to lack a "legitimate" purpose or to be "irrational." How much power is a Court that holds such views likely to cede to state legislatures and state electorates? A case can be made that the Court's federalism, viewed in a broader light, has been about aggrandizing itself as the arbiter of national policy as much as it has been about empowering the states to set their own policies.

When the country enjoys a consensus on an issue, such as guns in school or violence against women, the Court may indulge in federalist gestures. When the country is emotionally divided on an issue—as on abortion, gay rights, or, to a lesser extent, medical marijuana—it will impose a national policy to end the possibility of conflict. (Or try to: Sometimes it brings those conflicts into being, and then cites the result to justify more intervention. That's the "implosive cycle" to which Nagel's title refers.)

Moral Federalism

Supporters of the Court's federalist turn have tended to be relatively uninterested in, or even supportive of, the Court's social-issues decisions. (Libertarians have been especially likely to hold these attitudes.) But this is a big mistake. For much of American history we had a federal government that was much more limited than the current one. The principal reason for the older limits was not that we had a federal judiciary that insisted on imposing them. It is that we had a broader political culture that insisted on those limits.

For a lot of reasons—the decline in the cost of transportation and communication not least among them—federalism has lost a lot of its sentimental basis and therefore its political power over the years. When political and legal debate turns to federalism these days, the discussion concerns matters that are of interest chiefly to lawyers. We talk about statutory preemption (when federal laws should be read to override state laws) or sovereign immunity (under what circumstances and in what venues state governments can be sued).

People do care, however, about social issues. People have been known to move from community to community in part because they prefer to live in places whose inhabitants share their values. This migration has helped to produce the division between "red" and "blue" states, in which political and cultural divisions literally map each other. Moral federalism—letting states go their own way on contested social issues—could renew the political basis of federalism. But it is the very robustness of moral federalism, its capacity to generate strong emotions, that leads the Supreme Court to suppress it.

Two decades ago, the dominant assumption among constitutional lawyers was that the courts did not need to protect federalism, since the political process would take care of it. Conservatives mounted a powerful challenge to this idea: There was no reason to expect the political process to get federalism right. By now it should be obvious that there is no reason to expect the courts to get it right, either. One has to ask, at this point, what conservatives have gained by attempting to get the courts to impose limits on congressional authority. While there may be places the Supreme Court could make a salutary difference, it will not, cannot, and probably should not substantially reduce the scope of congressional power. By refusing to face this truth, conservatives have muddied what could otherwise have been a clean fight between judicial activism and restraint.

The Court cannot impose federalism over the objections of the other branches of the government. That project was never likely to succeed and is now over. What the Court can and should do is to stop eroding federalism itself. ∎

2.5 Reclaiming Federalism (2005)

David J. Barron

The revival of states' rights may be the most substantial accomplishment of the Rehnquist Court's conservative majority. . . . What may be called "Rehnquist Federalism" has not yet made a revolution, and defections occur in federalism cases, too. But Rehnquist Federalism has changed the legal landscape by limiting congressional efforts to provide everything from effective remedies against discrimination to enforcement of federal statutory guarantees of overtime pay—all in the name of "state sovereignty" and despite the arguments of the four liberals on the Court.

Progressives used to know what to think about states' rights. The idea was so thoroughly associated with opposition to the civil rights movement and resistance to the New Deal that it seemed to go hand in hand with conservatism. But since the "federalism" revival began in 1992, with a decision curtailing federal authority over hazardous-waste facilities, . . . progressives have begun to wonder whether federalism might be useful after all.

Salon magazine reports the emergence of why-go-to-Canada-when-you-have-federalism discussions within lefty circles. Progressive icons from U.S. representative Barney Frank to the San Francisco city government use states' rights' rhetoric to oppose a federal ban on gay marriage. Look for progressive policy making at the present moment and you are much more likely to find it in a city hall or a state capitol than in a federal agency or a Senate cloakroom. Is there something in a revival of federalism, then, that even a liberal could love? The short answer is, "The revival of federalism? Yes. Rehnquist Federalism? No." Let me explain.

There is no such thing as "federalism." There are only "federalisms," fashioned at specific times and for specific reasons, each necessarily reflecting the particular political vision of its authors. Rehnquist Federalism is not the same as alternative federalisms that prevailed at other times in our history. Some of the framers of the Constitution, for example, favored limiting federal power in order to preserve liberty. They believed that the limited scope of Congress's "enumerated" (that is, explicitly stated) powers made a separate bill of rights unnecessary. The conservative justices on the present Court construe Congress's enumerated powers very narrowly, thus limiting the federal government's ability to give life to those same liberties. These justices have done so (they say) to preserve states' rights.

From David J. Barron, "Reclaiming Federalism," *Dissent* 52 (Spring 2005), pp. 64–68. Reprinted by permission.

Limiting Federal Power

Before progressives address Rehnquist Federalism, they need to understand its implications. A key dimension of the new federalism involves limiting national power in order to expand state and local authority. This entails three distinct lines of doctrine:

◆ The first concerns Congress's enumerated powers. Article I of the Constitution grants Congress the power to regulate "Commerce . . . among the several States" and the Fourteenth Amendment empowers Congress to "enforce" the constitutional guarantee of equal protection of the laws and other basic rights against state infringement. By the end of the 1960s, the Supreme Court had construed these powers to give Congress a great deal of authority and, in doing so, confirmed the legal foundations of both the New Deal and the civil rights era. Now, thanks to the [Supreme] Court's conservatives, Congress has much less power under the Commerce Clause to regulate matters that are not in some sense "economic" (even if they could be shown to have real impact on the national economy). And Congress has only limited power under Section 5 of the Fourteenth Amendment because the Court has taken a very narrow view of the legislature's power to "enforce" constitutional guarantees such as the right to the equal protection of the laws. For example, while the [Supreme] Court continues to permit Congress to prohibit race and sex discrimination, it holds that Section 5 does not give Congress the same power to prohibit state discrimination based on disability or age.

◆ The second line invokes vague principles of "federalism" in order to prohibit Congress from ordering states to implement federal regulatory programs. Congress may preempt state and local actions by passing contrary federal laws, but it may not require state and local governments to become regulators.

◆ The third line protects "sovereign immunity," the right of a government to refuse to respond to a suit brought by a private party. It traces back to the idea that the king can do no wrong. Not surprisingly, no reference to such an immunity is set forth in the Constitution. The [Supreme] Court, however, calls it a "postulate" of our federal system. The practical result is that even when states clearly violate federal statutes, the Court says that they cannot be made to pay damages for the harm they cause.

Congress still has the ability to regulate. Many matters are directly economic, after all, and even if Congress cannot commandeer states, it can (at least for now) get them to do what it wants in other ways. It can, for example, threaten to take away their federal grants. But the real-world consequences of Rehnquist Federalism should not be understated. Here are some examples:

◆ It led to the invalidation of portions of the Violence Against Women Act, which enabled women alleging harms from gender-based violence to seek civil redress in federal court;

◆ It struck down parts of the Brady Act, which required local law enforcement actors to perform background checks on gun purchasers;

◆ It undermined numerous statutes authorizing damages actions against state governments, ranging from the Fair Labor Standards Act to the Americans With Disabilities Act.

Some Limits on States

In each of these instances, the Court's solicitude for the "dignity" of states trumped congressional attempts to protect the dignity of individuals. But these cases tell only half the story—the half that concerns what the Court thinks Congress cannot do and what is reserved to the states. The other half concerns what the federal government should do, and what states and local governments should not. In other words, Rehnquist Federalism also limits state and local power in certain ways in order to expand national authority.

For example, the same Court that waxes eloquent about the need to restrain national power in order to protect state dignity routinely interprets ambiguous federal statutes broadly in order to preempt state regulation of private business. Even without a new federal statute mandating tort reform, the Court's conservatives have engaged in a kind of ad hoc tort reform project of their own. It has displaced significant swaths of state consumer protection law, including some measures that would permit state residents to sue health maintenance organizations. Similarly, some of the Court's leading federalism proponents turn out to be great fans of the so-called "Dormant Commerce Clause." This is a judge-made doctrine that prohibits states and local governments from regulating in ways that might interfere with the free flow of commerce nationwide. For example, Justices Sandra Day O'Connor and Anthony Kennedy helped to forge majorities to invalidate local business regulations on the grounds that they are unconstitutionally protectionist or obstructive of national markets.

Finally, Rehnquist Federalism has expanded the Constitution's "Takings Clause." Historically, that clause required the government to compensate private owners when it seized their land, but not when it merely regulated how they could develop it. Over the last decade or so, the Court has treated more and more land-use regulations—such as restrictions on beachfront development or requirements that developers take steps to limit the costs imposed on the public by new construction—as if they were outright land grabs. As a result, the government increasingly risks multimillion-dollar claims by developers. By changing constitutional doctrine in this way, the Court departs from its view of states and localities as autonomous sovereigns entitled to respect. Instead, it intimates at times that they are nothing more than petty extortionists seeking to rob private businesses.

Viewed as a whole, then, the current "federalism" revival does not simply protect states' rights. It reallocates powers between the federal government and state and local ones, simultaneously limiting and extending the scope of each. And it does so in a politically ingenious way. Rehnquist Federalism synthesizes the social-conservative, small-government, and pro-business philosophies of the Republican Party. . . .

Which Federalism?

The overlap between the Court's decisions and conservative ideology is not perfect, and one cannot prove that it is intentional. The notion that there might be some federalism-based limits on national power, after all, is not senseless. But there is precious little in the Constitution's text or the history of its adoption that compels the particular conservative allocation of national and local powers favored by the Rehnquist Court.

That Rehnquist Federalism promotes a substantively conservative political philosophy should not be surprising. Nor should it be surprising that Rehnquist Federalism limits state power even as it protects it. No one who believes in states' rights believes in unlimited states' rights. Federalism presumes that states exist within a larger nation. Each form of "federalism," therefore, rests on a view of what it is that states should and should not be doing. Some constitutional lawyers say that the allocation between the federal and state levels can be made "neutrally." That is, one can try to discern what the Framers would have wanted or one can make technical judgments about the likely geographic impacts of a government's decision. But neither of these approaches is helpful. What the Framers wanted is arguable, and it is difficult to determine the "local" or "national" effects of state policies. When the highest court in Massachusetts ruled on same-sex marriage, its decision applied only to the state's residents. Yet some analysts think that decision also helped to decide the national presidential election. Thus, cultural, ideological, and social forces that are contemporary and political, rather than timeless or technical, are bound to shape judgments about whether an issue is "national" or "local." In other words, what is "truly local" or "truly national"—as the Rehnquist Court . . . famously described the two domains—is truly political.

To say that Rehnquist Federalism has a strong conservative flavor is not to say that it lacks conceptual integrity as a form of federalism. Roughly speaking, it allocates social regulation to the states and market regulation to the federal government. The . . . Court's conservative majority seems committed to maintaining this boundary even though it may limit the ability of Congress to advance conservative policies in particular cases. Take same-sex marriage. Even though it is an A-list issue for social conservatives, the Court expressly identified marriage (in a recent Commerce Clause case) as a matter of "truly local" concern and not at all "economic." There is little reason to think the Court will back off on this, even if confronted by a federal statute banning same-sex marriage. The [Supreme] Court's federalism, then, is conservative without always generating a conservative outcome.

Federalism and Conservative Interests

Now that we have a better fix on what the new federalism is about, we can return to our initial question of how progressives should think about it. Clearly, there is a lot not to like, beginning with an allocation of national and local powers that promotes the interests of contemporary conservatism so well. In addition, Rehnquist Federalism seems to assume a zero-sum battle for power between national and local governments that is not justified. National legislation can enhance the ability of state and local governments to cope with very local problems. That's why some local officials filed briefs opposing the invalidation (on "federalism" grounds) of both the Brady Act and the Violence Against Women Act referred to earlier.

At the same time, progressives know well the virtues of local power and decentralization. Just ask Eliot Spitzer, New York State's activist attorney general [and current governor], if he would favor congressional action to preempt state business regulation. Thus, the standard progressive approach to federalism—that national governmental institutions must be free to act as they wish and when they wish on any matter of their choosing—seems problematic. The Constitution separates powers not only horizontally among the three branches of the federal government, but also vertically between national and state and local institutions. It's time for a progressive vision that imagines all levels to be important actors and not just the national government.

Of course, securing that vision in constitutional terms is not easy. There are problems with judges' drawing lines between local and national authority. But there are also problems with judges' leaving it to Congress to decide the limits of national authority. With no constitutional limits on congressional power, a majority party can act without constraint. For example, the conventional progressive view of the power of Congress under the Constitution's Commerce Clause—that it covers almost any matter one can think of—would clearly authorize federal legislation banning same-sex marriage or state death-with-dignity laws. So there is, ironically, something attractive for progressives about the [Supreme] Court's defense of judicially enforceable limits on national power. There is also something admirable about its apparent willingness to accept some outcomes that are hardly conservative. This Court is not prone to the case-by-case, nuanced assessment of what makes "good" policy that progressives often favor but that makes them vulnerable to the criticisms that they have positions and no principles. Perhaps progressives should bite some bullets of their own.

For a Progressive Federalism

What would a progressive federalism look like? It might well be a mirror image of Rehnquist Federalism. It would give states and local governments much greater room to regulate the private market. This would check national and multinational business influence as Louis Brandeis and earlier progressives once imagined. It would also give the national government much more power to regulate nonmarket social relations. This would give Congress the power to protect basic Fourteenth Amendment rights.

To expand the ability of states and local governments to regulate private business, progressive federalism would permit federal statutes to trump state regulations only when they were in clear conflict. In other words, states would get the benefit of the doubt in this area. A progressive federalism would also interpret the Takings Clause to give more deference to local efforts to make developers assume the costs of their development. And rather than characterizing state and local regulations as protectionist or as obstructive of the national market, as the Court often does in its Dormant Commerce Clause decisions, progressive federalism would permit sensible attempts by state and local governments to protect their communities from the harsh and dislocating effects of larger economic forces.

But progressive federalism would do more than free states from the limits imposed by Rehnquist Federalism. It would promote a different view of Congress's enumerated powers. It would reinforce Congress's Fourteenth Amendment power to "enforce" basic constitutional rights and thereby protect the prerogatives of national citizenship from threats posed by local prejudices. Among the highest priorities of progressive federalism would be to reverse the [Supreme] Court's unwarranted curtailing of this vital power.

Progressive federalism would not, however, view congressional power as unlimited. Consider Congress's power to grant copyrights. The Constitution authorizes Congress to give "exclusive Right[s]" to "authors" for "limited Times" in order to "promote the Progress of Science and useful Arts." But that grant of power was not intended to turn Congress into a lackey of the national entertainment industry. The [Supreme] Court recently upheld a federal statute—thanks to aggressive industry lobbying—that retroactively extends federal copyrights in creative works for life plus seventy years. This was a legislative giveaway to the Walt Disney Company and other large, national companies, and it hardly promotes the arts. Nor does it comply with the requirement that creative works can be locked up only for a "limited time." A narrower view of Congress's copyright power, therefore, might be quite progressive. It would respond to the concern that the national legislature is unusually likely to be captured by the national entertainment industry.

A progressive federalism might also embrace the Rehnquist Court's limited view of Congress's Commerce Clause power. Congress would retain its ability to regulate economic activity. It would not, however, possess a general power to regulate any matter chosen by a majority of its members.

Such a limit on the Commerce Clause power, moreover, would not prevent Congress from enforcing an inclusive vision of national citizenship. Congress could still act forcefully against discrimination by invoking its Fourteenth Amendment authority to protect rights to equality.

Some legal scholars would say, no doubt, that progressive federalism is "political" rather than constitutional. But it is no more political than Rehnquist Federalism, and it is just as defensible in legal terms. Progressive federalism would not guarantee a liberal outcome in every case any more than Rehnquist Federalism guarantees a conservative one. For instance, progressive federalism might permit some local anti–affirmative-action measures that would otherwise be deemed inconsistent with federal statutory requirements. And a requirement that Commerce Clause legislation target economic activity could jeopardize some applications of environmental regulations, notably to local wetlands. But progressive federalism would promote national/local relations consistent with a broader liberal political vision. That vision has a constitutional pedigree that is at least as legitimate as the conservative one it would displace. Progressive federalism, then, would have just as much—or as little—integrity as today's conservative federalism.

Progressives for too long have been strikingly unimaginative when it comes to federalism. They speak only in a national key. But it is clear that their faith in unlimited national authority was the contingent product of liberal control of national institutions. Circumstances have changed. We should now look at the Constitution's federalism with fresh eyes. Doing so would cast some much needed doubt on the stereotype that progressives love big government. If progressive federalism results in judicial decisions that limit national power too much, there would still be recourse to constitutional amendments. Fighting for an amendment to authorize Congress to protect the environment might, for example, be quite good for a broader liberal agenda.

So, the next time you read a progressive trashing of the [Supreme] Court, resist the impulse to applaud the national government as our sole hope and savior. Federalism is what we make of it. [The Court's conservatives] have been making the most of it for more than a decade. It's time for progressives to do the same. ■

View from the Inside

The devastation wrought by Hurricane Katrina in September 2005 overwhelmed local, state, and national government authorities. The response to Katrina was marked by delays, infighting, miscommunication, and the "blame game." These problems were made worse by the division of responsibility that lies at the heart of American federalism.

In this selection, noted federalism scholar Deil S. Wright analyzes the response to Katrina and concludes that "[t]he breaks in the levees around New Orleans were literal as well as figurative 'cracks' in intergovernmental relations."

Questions

1. What does the author identify as the most serious problems in the intergovernmental response to Katrina? How might these problems have been avoided or lessened if one governmental entity was unambiguously in charge?
2. What lessons might the local, state, and national governments learn from Katrina and its aftermath?

2.6 How Did Intergovernmental Relations Fail in the USA After Hurricane Katrina? (2005)

Deil S. Wright

On August 29, 2005, Louisiana Governor Kathleen Blanco and Michael Brown, head of the Federal Emergency Management Agency (FEMA), stood side-by-side at a press conference shortly after Hurricane Katrina made landfall on the Gulf Coast of Louisiana and Mississippi. They praised and complimented each other for intergovernmental co-operation in responding to the massive storm.

Twenty-four hours later, most of New Orleans was flooded with three to four meters of water and 80 percent of the city's population had evacuated. There were 100,000 people without transportation left in the city, and thousands—nearly all African-Americans—were in the city's Convention Center and Superdome, and looting and violence had started.

Deil S. Wright, "How Did Intergovernmental Relations Fail in the USA After Hurricane Katrina?" Reprinted with the permission of the Forum of Federations, an international network on federalism (www.forumfed.org). Original article appears in *Federations* Magazine, Volume 5, Number 1, November 2005.

From Harmony to Discord

New Orleans Mayor Ray Nagin and Governor Blanco were now criticizing, even cursing, not only FEMA but the Department of Homeland Security and President Bush. They blasted the delays and disorganization of FEMA, Homeland Security and others for failure to aid beleaguered citizens and state/local personnel in New Orleans and the Gulf Coast.

What explains this sudden reversal in intergovernmental relations? Why the dramatic turnabout from commendations to condemnations in the span of one day? The exploding scope of the disaster pushed citizens' and officials' frayed nerves beyond limits. But a host of other factors—political, social, racial, economic, administrative and especially intergovernmental—sent intergovernmental relations on the Gulf Coast into a downward spiral of recriminations and helped turn a disaster into a catastrophe.

The Scale of the Catastrophe

To the one million displaced and dispersed Gulf Coast residents, as well as to millions of others aiding recovery efforts, Hurricane Katrina was a catastrophe. Catastrophes reveal the worst and best of human nature. Some people loot while others lend support, and both of these took place in New Orleans. Some lean toward despair fostering anarchy while others respond to challenges with creativity. In the midst of this, the mayor's core group of 15 people had to relocate to a Hyatt Hotel and scavenge makeshift communications systems after their land lines, cell phones, and police radios all failed. Hurricane Katrina unleashed a catastrophe of unprecedented proportions.

How did local, state and national officials respond? In the nation's capital, on Thursday, September 1, 2005, FEMA Director Brown claimed to be unaware of TV broadcasts showing thousands massed in the Convention Center. While Houston, Texas, took half of the evacuees, cities and states all across the nation offered to host evacuees. More than 500 miles northward, Iowa, for example, set up a shelter for 1,000 persons. The response from different levels of government was mixed. Their responses (and non-responses) turned a manageable disaster into a catastrophe.

Intergovernmental Relations in the USA

It is premature to pass final judgment on the leaders of local, state and national agencies. A search for "guilty" officials is itself a highly contentious issue. We cannot capture the full array of events, actions and communications that occurred—or lapsed—among officials in positions of authority before, during and after Katrina. We gain a better understanding, however, of the Gulf Shore's catastrophe by stating a fundamental proposition of how intergovernmental relations work in America. These relations produce complexities and autonomy that tilt the American system of governance toward devolution, deference and delay. In emergencies, local officials are first responders and state actors are secondary, while national agencies provide "last resort" resources. Public officials favor caution over action.

Politicians and career administrators live with risk and uncertainty rather than actively searching for certainty.

There are more than 87,000 units of local governments in the USA plus 50 state governments and the national government. Virtually all have significant powers to tax and spend almost as they wish. More importantly, there are nearly 500,000 popularly elected local and state officials possessing authority to advocate on behalf of "their citizens." Is it any wonder that the American intergovernmental relations are often described as operating under "mild chaos"? The tragedy of the Katrina catastrophe is that political will and managerial skill failed to overcome the bias that intergovernmental relations have toward chaos.

FEMA was intended to be a disaster-response arrangement that would bypass the "mild chaos" tendency of American intergovernmental relations. But that did not happen. Disaster-response arrangements require unified authority or tight co-ordination. Such tight co-ordination can provide energetic, focused, timely action, and a marshaling of all available resources for the job at hand. This was not the response that was made to Katrina. Was it a flaw in the structures or failure of individual politicians and civil servants that caused this breakdown?

With important exceptions, elected officials at all levels let their "public human nature" run its course of belated and modest responses. But a federal system poses an extra risk. In a book on homeland security and American politics, Donald Kettl observes that "the richly textured system of federalism contains powerful incentives for fragmentation and in the absence of an overpowering force to bridge the cracks in the intergovernmental system those cracks . . . [could] undermine the nation's emergency preparedness." The breaks in the levees around New Orleans were literal as well as figurative "cracks" in intergovernmental relations.

Breakdowns on the Path to Catastrophe

Why did the virtual cracks in American intergovernmental relations go unrepaired in the spiral from a clear hurricane threat to the impending disaster and resulting catastrophe? The fundamental features and numerous nuances of relations among governments in the USA are only the necessary conditions, not the sufficient causes of the Gulf Coast chaos.

Most of the time, governments co-operate haltingly but effectively in the provision of public goods and services to nearly 300 million American "customers." Why the faulty and fatal breakdown with Katrina?

In the absence of an official report similar to the *9/11 Commission Report*, definitive causes are tentative and speculative. And like the 9/11 Commission itself, creating an investigative entity is controversial. It is possible, however, to draw on the 9/11 Commission's analysis to identify the leading factors contributing to the Gulf Coast chaos and catastrophe. The Commission identified these as

1. lack of imagination
2. misplaced policy priorities
3. inadequate capacity
4. ineffective management

A PhD thesis could be written about each of these topics. We are restricted to one or two explanatory sentences.

Imagination involves the likelihood and the gravity of the threat in terms of security. Prior intense hurricanes and floods had occurred and, despite the Katrina warning, too many officials in too many formal positions paid too little attention to imagining that chaos and catastrophe could ensue.

Policy can be represented by one example—FEMA. FEMA was absorbed in the Department of Homeland Security and downgraded in status and resources; it operated in the policy shadows of an anti-terrorism policy emphasis. Its leader lacked any semblance of disaster management experience, and has recently resigned. Were there also, as most African-Americans and a number of other critics believe, misguided policy priorities because of racial and economic factors? Did the fact that most of the remaining residents trapped in the city were poor and African-American contribute to the slow evacuation and rescue efforts?

Capacity, in a few words, reflects the ability to fulfill a mission. The 9/11 Commission's assertions about capacity apply equally well to Katrina and its consequences. "Government agencies . . . are too often passive, accepting what are viewed as givens, including efforts to identify and fix glaring vulnerabilities and dangerous threats that would be too costly, too controversial, and too disruptive." Organizational capacity was woefully short among most if not all of the 75 to 100 local, state, and national agencies tasked with responding to Katrina along the Gulf Coast.

Management covers a wide swath that includes but transcends effective communication within and across governmental jurisdictions. Agencies operating in the American intergovernmental system are much like medical specialists, each doing diagnoses, ordering tests and issuing prescriptions. Conspicuously absent from the myriad of specialists is the attending physician, whose primary task is to see that the specialists work as a team to assure the health of the patient. Effective intergovernmental relations in the USA depend on the presence of many "attending physicians." In the case of the Katrina catastrophe, they were in short or nonexistent supply.

Hindsight and Foresight

The Katrina catastrophe generated economic costs in the billions of dollars. Already a target figure of $200 billion has been set as the national reconstruction contribution alone, plus billions of additional state and local funds. A realistic account has to add to that the loss of between 1,000 and 2,000 lives, rising consumer gas and oil costs and reduced economic growth of between one-half to one percent. Not even a comprehensive national commission study is likely to compute accurately the full costs and consequences of Katrina's Gulf Coast visit.

One fact does seem clear, however. The Katrina drama was played out on a stage defined by the complexities and mild chaos of intergovernmental relations. Preventing another Katrina-like natural or terrorist catastrophe will require public leaders with political wills and experienced administrators with management skills—and the structures and the organization to translate this will and these skills into action. Those qualities are required to span the jurisdictional boundaries confronting every official operating in American intergovernmental relations. Imaginative and collaborative leadership is crucial in preventing or mitigating future national emergencies. ■

Chapter 3

Civil Liberties

The American commitment to individual rights and liberties is one of the distinguishing characteristics of our political system. Even more striking is the fact that we have a written Bill of Rights and that we rely to a great extent on the judicial system to define and defend the rights enumerated there.

Originally, the Bill of Rights applied only to the federal government. The First Amendment, for example, states explicitly that "*Congress* shall make no law . . . abridging the freedom of speech." An 1833 case, *Barron* v. *Baltimore*, made it clear that the restrictions of the first eight amendments were not intended to interfere with laws passed by the states. Over the course of the twentieth century, however, the Supreme Court applied the various provisions of the Bill of Rights, one by one, to the states.

The emphasis in American politics on individual rights raises two sorts of problems. The first involves balancing competing rights. The publication of the name of a rape victim, for example, might violate the victim's right to privacy; but punishing such publication might interfere with a newspaper's right to free speech. Such problems can be extremely troubling, but even more serious are problems that pit the interests of an individual against those of society. How far can society go in limiting the civil liberties of individuals in order to protect itself? Might the police be justified, for example, in torturing suspects in order to prevent a catastrophic terrorist attack?

The selections in this chapter examine these questions from a variety of different viewpoints. Selection 3.1, from John Stuart Mill's *On Liberty*, presents the classic liberal argument for individuality. In selection 3.2, law professor Jeffrey Rosen speculates on the state of abortion rights—and American politics—on the (hypothetical) day after the Supreme Court overturns its decision establishing a constitutional right to abortion. In selection 3.3, legal scholar Michael J. Glennon examines the extremely difficult question of finding an appropriate balance between protecting civil liberties and waging the war on terrorism. Finally, selection 3.4 examines whether the criminal trial is really a search for truth, from the perspective of Alan Dershowitz, who served on the legal team that defended O. J. Simpson in his celebrated 1997 murder trial.

Chapter Questions

1. What are "civil liberties"? Why are they important in a society that values freedom? Why is freedom of thought and expression particularly important?
2. How are individual rights defined and balanced against the rights of other citizens and against the interests of society at large? What factors work to tip such a balancing process in favor of society? In favor of individual rights?

 Foundations

One of the greatest advocates of civil liberties was English philosopher John Stuart Mill. Published in 1859, Mill's *On Liberty* is perhaps the most important statement of the "importance of freedom for the discovery of truth and for the full development of individuality."* Although written in England, Mill's argument found a more receptive audience in the United States; his ideas greatly influenced the United States Supreme Court in later years, especially the opinions of Justices Oliver Wendell Holmes, who served on the Court from 1902 to 1932, and Louis Brandeis, who served from 1916 to 1939.

Mill was a utilitarian; he believed that all arguments had to be grounded in practical reason and justified with reference to the social good that would be brought about or the social evils that would be prevented. Therefore, his argument for allowing the individual the maximum freedom to decide how to live stresses the reasons that such freedom ultimately is good for society, even if the opinions expressed are clearly wrong. Note that his argument—unlike American constitutional arguments—is not based on claims of individual rights. Still, Mill's reasoning lies behind American liberal arguments as to the importance of protecting liberty under the Bill of Rights.

Questions

1. How does Mill justify the protection of individuality even when an individual's actions are clearly detrimental to that person's own well-being?
2. What does Mill mean by the "despotism of custom"? How does it operate? What effect does it have? Is Mill's characterization of his society applicable as well to our own? Why or why not?

---

*David Spitz, Preface to John Stuart Mill, *On Liberty* (New York: W. W. Norton and Co., 1975), p. vii.

3.1 On Liberty (1859)

John Stuart Mill

We have now recognised the necessity to the mental well-being of mankind (on which all their other well-being depends) of freedom of opinion, and freedom of the expression of opinion, on four distinct grounds; which we will now briefly recapitulate.

First, if any opinion is compelled to silence, that opinion may, for aught we can certainly know, be true. To deny this is to assume our own infallibility.

Secondly, though the silenced opinion be an error, it may, and very commonly does, contain a portion of truth; and since the general or prevailing opinion on any subject is rarely or never the whole truth, it is only by the collision of adverse opinions that the remainder of the truth has any chance of being supplied.

Thirdly, even if the received opinion be not only true, but the whole truth; unless it is suffered to be, and actually is, vigorously and earnestly contested, it will, by most of those who receive it, be held in the manner of a prejudice, with little comprehension or feeling of its rational grounds. And not only this, but, fourthly, the meaning of the doctrine itself will be in danger of being lost, or enfeebled, and deprived of its vital effect on the character and conduct; the dogma becoming a mere formal profession, inefficacious for good, but cumbering the ground, and preventing the growth of any real and heartfelt conviction from reason or personal experience.

• • •

Such being the reasons which make it imperative that human beings should be free to form opinions, and to express their opinions without reserve; and such the baneful consequences to the intellectual, and through that to the moral nature of man, unless this liberty is either conceded, or asserted in spite of prohibition; let us next examine whether the same reasons do not require that men should be free to act upon their opinions—to carry these out in their lives, without hindrance, either physical or moral, from their fellow-men, so long as it is at their own risk and peril. This last proviso is of course indispensable. No one pretends that actions should be as free as opinions. On the contrary, even opinions lose their immunity when the circumstances in which they are expressed are such as to constitute their expression a positive instigation to some mischievous act. An opinion that corn-dealers are starvers of the poor, or that private property is robbery, ought to be unmolested when simply circulated through the press, but may justly incur punishment when delivered orally to an excited mob assembled before the house of a corn-dealer, or when handed about among the same mob in the form of a placard. Acts, of whatever kind, which, without justifiable cause, do harm to others, may be, and in the more important cases absolutely require to be, controlled by the un-

John Stuart Mill, *On Liberty* (London: J. W. Parker and Son, 1859).

favourable sentiments, and, when needful, by the active interference of mankind. The liberty of the individual must be thus far limited; he must not make himself a nuisance to other people. But if he refrains from molesting others in what concerns them, and merely acts according to his own inclination and judgment in things which concern himself, the same reasons which show that opinion should be free, prove also that he should be allowed, without molestation, to carry his opinions into practice at his own cost. That mankind are not infallible; that their truths, for the most part, are only half-truths; that unity of opinion, unless resulting from the fullest and freest comparison of opposite opinions, is not desirable, and diversity not an evil, but a good, until mankind are much more capable than at present of recognising all sides of the truth, are principles applicable to men's modes of action, not less than to their opinions. As it is useful that while mankind are imperfect there should be different opinions, so it is that there should be different experiments of living; that free scope should be given to varieties of character, short of injury to others; and that the worth of different modes of life should be proved practically, when any one thinks fit to try them. It is desirable, in short, that in things which do not primarily concern others, individuality should assert itself. Where, not the person's own character, but the traditions or customs of other people are the rule of conduct, there is wanting one of the principal ingredients of human happiness, and quite the chief ingredient of individual and social progress.

In maintaining this principle, the greatest difficulty to be encountered does not lie in the appreciation of means towards an acknowledged end, but in the indifference of persons in general to the end itself. If it were felt that the free development of individuality is one of the leading essentials of well-being; that it is not only a coordinate element with all that is designated by the terms civilisation, instruction, education, culture, but is itself a necessary part and condition of all those things; there would be no danger that liberty should be undervalued, and the adjustment of the boundaries between it and social control would present no extraordinary difficulty. But the evil is, that individual spontaneity is hardly recognised by the common modes of thinking as having any intrinsic worth, or deserving any regard on its own account. The majority, being satisfied with the ways of mankind as they now are (for it is they who make them what they are), cannot comprehend why those ways should not be good enough for everybody; and what is more, spontaneity forms no part of the ideal of the majority of moral and social reformers, but is rather looked on with jealousy, as a troublesome and perhaps rebellious obstruction to the general acceptance of what these reformers, in their own judgment, think would be best for mankind. Few persons, out of Germany, even comprehend the meaning of the doctrine which Wilhelm von Humboldt, so eminent both as a *savant* and as a politician, made the text of a treatise—that "the end of man, or that which is prescribed by the eternal or immutable dictates of reason, and not suggested by vague and transient desires, is the highest and most harmonious development of his powers to a complete and consistent whole"; that, therefore, the object "towards which every human being must ceaselessly direct his efforts, and on which especially those who design to influence their fellow-men must ever keep their eyes, is the individuality of power and development"; that for this there are two requisites, "freedom, and variety of situations"; and that from the union of these arise "individual vigour and manifold diversity," which combine themselves in "originality."

Little, however, as people are accustomed to a doctrine like that of von Humboldt, and surprising as it may be to them to find so high a value attached to individuality, the question, one must nevertheless think, can only be one of degree. No one's idea of excellence in conduct is that people should do absolutely nothing but copy one another. No one would assert that people ought not to put into their mode of life, and into the conduct of their concerns, any impress whatever of their own judgment, or of their own individual character. On the other hand, it would be absurd to pretend that people ought to live as if nothing whatever had been known in the world before they came into it; as if experience had as yet done nothing towards showing that one mode of existence, or of conduct, is preferable to another. Nobody denies that people should be so taught and trained in youth as to know and benefit by the ascertained results of human experience. But it is the privilege and proper condition of a human being, arrived at the maturity of his faculties, to use and interpret experience in his own way. It is for him to find out what part of recorded experience is properly applicable to his own circumstances and character. The traditions and customs of other people are, to a certain extent, evidence of what their experience has taught *them*; presumptive evidence, and as such, have a claim to his deference: but, in the first place, their experience may be too narrow; or they may not have interpreted it rightly. Secondly, their interpretation of experience may be correct, but unsuitable to him. Customs are made for customary circumstances and customary characters; and his circumstances or his character may be uncustomary. Thirdly, though the customs be both good as customs, and suitable to him, yet to conform to custom, merely *as* custom, does not educate or develop in him any of the qualities which are the distinctive endowment of a human being. The human faculties of perception, judgment, discriminative feeling, mental activity, and even moral preference, are exercised only in making a choice. He who does anything because it is the custom makes no choice. He gains no practice either in discerning or in desiring what is best. The mental and moral, like the muscular powers, are improved only by being used. The faculties are called into no exercise by doing a thing merely because others do it, no more than by believing a thing only because others believe it. If the grounds of an opinion are not conclusive to the person's own reason, his reason cannot be strengthened, but is likely to be weakened, by his adopting it: and if the inducements to an act are not such as are consentaneous to his own feelings and character (where affection, or the rights of others, are not concerned) it is so much done towards rendering his feelings and character inert and torpid, instead of active and energetic.

He who lets the world, or his own portion of it, choose his plan of life for him, has no need of any other faculty than the ape-like one of imitation. He who chooses his plan for himself, employs all his faculties. He must use observation to see, reasoning and judgment to foresee, activity to gather materials for decision, discrimination to decide, and when he has decided, firmness and self-control to hold to his deliberate decision. And these qualities he requires and exercises exactly in proportion as the part of his conduct which he determines according to his own judgment and feelings is a large one. It is possible that he might be guided in some good path, and kept out of harm's way, without any of these things. But what will be his comparative worth as a human being? It really is of importance, not only what men do, but also what manner of men they are that do it. Among the works of man, which human life is rightly employed in perfecting and beautifying, the first in importance surely is man himself. Supposing it were possible to get houses built, corn grown, battles fought, causes tried, and even churches erected and prayers said, by machinery—by automatons in human form—it would be a considerable loss to exchange for these automatons even the men and women who at present inhabit the more civilised parts of the world, and who assuredly are but starved specimens of what nature can and will produce. Human nature is not a machine to be built after a model, and set to do exactly the work prescribed for it, but a tree, which requires to grow and develop itself on all sides, according to the tendency of the inward forces which make it a living thing.

It will probably be conceded that it is desirable people should exercise their understandings, and that an intelligent following of custom, or even occasionally an intelligent deviation from custom, is better than a blind and simply mechanical adhesion to it. To a certain extent it is admitted that our understanding should be our own: but there is not the same willingness to admit that our desires and impulses should be our own likewise; or that to possess impulses of our own, and of any strength, is anything but a peril and a snare. Yet desires and impulses are as much a part of a perfect human being as beliefs and restraints: and strong impulses are only perilous when not properly balanced; when one set of aims and inclinations is developed into strength, while others, which ought to co-exist with them, remain weak and inactive. It is not because men's desires are strong that they act ill; it is because their consciences are weak. There is no natural connection between strong impulses and a weak conscience. The natural connection is the other way. To say that one person's desires and feelings are stronger and more various than those of another, is merely to say that he has more of the raw material of human nature, and is therefore capable, perhaps of more evil, but certainly of more good. Strong impulses are but another name for energy. Energy may be turned to bad uses; but more good may always be made of an energetic nature, than of an indolent and impassive one. Those who have most natural feeling, are always those whose cultivated feelings may be made the strongest. The same strong susceptibilities which make the personal impulses vivid and powerful, are also the source from whence are generated the most passionate love of virtue, and the sternest self-control. It is through the cultivation of these that society both does its duty and protects its interests: not by rejecting the stuff of which heroes are made, because it knows not how to make them. A person whose desires and impulses are his own—are the expression of his own nature, as it has been developed and modified by his own culture—is said to have a character. One whose desires and impulses are not his own, has no character, no more than a steam-engine has a character. If, in addition to being his own, his impulses are strong, and are under the government of a strong will, he has an energetic character. Whoever thinks that individuality of desires and impulses should not be encouraged to unfold itself, must maintain that society has no need of strong natures—is not the better for containing many persons who have much character—and that a high general average of energy is not desirable.

In some early states of society, these forces might be, and were, too much ahead of the power which society then possessed of disciplining and controlling them. There has been a time when the element of spontaneity and individuality was in excess, and the social principle had a hard struggle with it. The difficulty then was to induce men of strong bodies or minds to pay obedience to any rules which required them to control their impulses. To overcome this difficulty, law and discipline, like the Popes struggling against the Emperors, asserted a power over the whole man, claiming to control all his life in order to control his character— which society had not found any other sufficient means of binding. But society has now fairly got the better of individuality; and the danger which threatens human nature is not the excess, but the deficiency, of personal impulses and preferences. Things are vastly changed since the passions of those who were strong by station or by personal endowment were in a state of habitual rebellion against laws and ordinances, and required to be rigorously chained up to enable the persons within their reach to enjoy any particle of security. In our times, from the highest class of society down to the lowest, every one lives as under the eye of a hostile and dreaded censorship. Not only in what concerns others, but in what concerns only themselves, the individual or the family do not ask themselves—what do I prefer? or, what would suit my character and disposition? or, what would allow the best and highest in me to have fair play, and enable it to grow and thrive? They ask themselves, what is suitable to my position? what is usually done by persons of my station and pecuniary circumstances? or (worse still) what is usually done by persons of a station and circumstances superior to mine? I do not mean that they choose what is customary in preference to what suits their own inclination. It does not occur to them to have any inclination, except for what is customary. Thus the mind itself is bowed to the yoke: even in what people do for pleasure, conformity is the first thing thought of; they like in crowds; they exercise choice only among things commonly done: peculiarity of taste, eccentricity of conduct, are shunned equally with crimes: until by dint of not following their own nature they have no nature to follow: their human capacities are withered and starved: they become incapable of any strong wishes or native pleasures, and are generally without either opinions or feelings of home growth, or properly their own.

● ● ●

It is not by wearing down into uniformity all that is individual in themselves, but by cultivating it, and calling it forth, within the limits imposed by the rights and interests of others, that human beings become a noble and beautiful object of contemplation; and as the works partake the character of those who do them, by the same process human life also becomes rich, diversified, and animating, furnishing more abundant aliment to high thoughts and elevating feelings, and strengthening the tie which binds every individual to the race, by making the race infinitely better worth belonging to. In proportion to the development of his individuality, each person becomes more valuable to himself, and is therefore capable of being more valuable to others. There is a greater fulness of life about his own existence, and when there is more life in the units there is more in the mass which is composed of them. As much compression as is necessary to prevent the stronger specimens of human nature from encroaching on the rights of others, cannot be dispensed with;

but for this there is ample compensation even in the point of view of human development. The means of development which the individual loses by being prevented from gratifying his inclinations to the injury of others, are chiefly obtained at the expense of the development of other people. And even to himself there is a full equivalent in the better development of the social part of his nature, rendered possible by the restraint put upon the selfish part. To be held to rigid rules of justice for the sake of others, develops the feelings and capacities which have the good of others for their object. But to be restrained in things not affecting their good, by their mere displeasure, develops nothing valuable, except such force of character as may unfold itself in resisting the restraint. If acquiesced in, it dulls and blunts the whole nature. To give any fair play to the nature of each, it is essential that different persons should be allowed to lead different lives. In proportion as this latitude has been exercised in any age, has that age been noteworthy to posterity. Even despotism does not produce its worst effects, so long as individuality exists under it; and whatever crushes individuality is despotism, by whatever name it may be called, and whether it professes to be enforcing the will of God or the injunctions of men.

Having said that the individuality is the same thing with development, and that it is only the cultivation of individuality which produces, or can produce, well-developed human beings, I might here close the argument: for what more or better can be said of any condition of human affairs than that it brings human beings themselves nearer to the best things they can be? or what worse can be said of any obstruction to good than that it prevents this? Doubtless, however, these considerations will not suffice to convince those who most need convincing; and it is necessary further to show, that these developed human beings are of some use to the undeveloped—to point out to those who do not desire liberty, and would not avail themselves of it, that they may be in some intelligible manner rewarded for allowing other people to make use of it without hindrance.

In the first place, then, I would suggest that they might possibly learn something from them. It will not be denied by anybody, that originality is a valuable element in human affairs. There is always need of persons not only to discover new truths, and point out when what were once truths are true no longer, but also to commence new practices, and set the example of more enlightened conduct, and better taste and sense in human life. This cannot well be gainsaid by anybody who does not believe that the world has already attained perfection in all its ways and practices. It is true that this benefit is not capable of being rendered by everybody alike: there are but few persons, in comparison with the whole of mankind, whose experiments, if adopted by others, would be likely to be any improvement on established practice. But these few are the salt of the earth; without them, human life would become a stagnant pool. Not only is it they who introduce good things which did not before exist; it is they who keep the life in those which already exist. If there were nothing new to be done, would human intellect cease to be necessary? Would it be a reason why those who do the old things should forget why they are done, and do them like cattle, not like human beings? There is only too great a tendency in the best beliefs and practices to degenerate into the mechanical; and unless there were a succession of persons whose ever-recurring originality prevents the grounds of those beliefs and practices from becoming merely traditional, such dead matter would not resist the smaller shock from anything really alive, and there would be no reason why civilisation should not die out, as in the Byzantine Empire. Persons of genius, it is true, are, and are always likely to be, a small minority; but in order to have them, it is necessary to preserve the soil in which they grow. Genius can only breathe freely in an *atmosphere* of freedom. Persons of genius are, *ex vi termini*, more individual than any other people—less capable, consequently, of fitting themselves, without hurtful compression, into any of the small number of moulds which society provides in order to save its members the trouble of forming their own character. If from timidity they consent to be forced into one of these moulds, and to let all that part of themselves which cannot expand under the pressure remain unexpanded, society will be little the better for their genius. If they are of a strong character, and break their fetters, they become a mark for the society which has not succeeded in reducing them to commonplace, to point out with solemn warning as "wild," "erratic," and the like; much as if one should complain of the Niagara river for not flowing smoothly between its banks like a Dutch canal.

I insist thus emphatically on the importance of genius, and the necessity of allowing it to unfold itself freely both in thought and in practice, being well aware that no one will deny the position in theory, but knowing also that almost every one, in reality, is totally indifferent to it. People think genius a fine thing if it enables a man to write an exciting poem, or paint a picture. But in its true sense, that of originality in thought and action, though no one says that it is not a thing to be admired, nearly all, at heart, think that they can do very well without it. Unhappily this is too natural to be wondered at. Originality is the one thing which unoriginal minds cannot feel the use of. They cannot see what it is to do for them: how should they? If they could see what it would do for them, it would not be originality. The first service which originality has to render them, is that of opening their eyes: which being once fully done, they would have a chance of being themselves original. Meanwhile, recollecting that nothing was ever yet done which some one was not the first to do, and that all good things which exist are the fruits of originality, let them be modest enough to believe that there is something still left for it to accomplish, and assure themselves that they are more in need of originality, the less they are conscious of the want. . . .

The despotism of custom is everywhere the standing hindrance to human advancement, being in unceasing antagonism to that disposition to aim at something better than customary, which is called, according to circumstances, the spirit of liberty, or that of progress or improvement. . . .

[I]t is not easy to see how [individuality] can stand its ground [against the despotism of custom and other influences that stand against it]. It will do so with increasing difficulty, unless the intelligent part of the public can be made to feel its value—to see that it is good there should be differences, even though not for the better, even though, as it may appear to them, some should be for the worse. If the claims of individuality are ever to be asserted, the time is now, while much is still wanting to complete the enforced assimilation. It is only in the earlier stages that any stand can be successfully made against the encroachment. The demand that all other people shall resemble ourselves grows by what it feeds on. If resistance waits till life is reduced *nearly* to one uniform type, all deviations from that type will come to be considered impious, immoral, even monstrous and contrary to nature. Mankind speedily become unable to conceive diversity, when they have been for some time unaccustomed to see it. ■

American Politics Today

Roe v. *Wade*—the Supreme Court's 1973 decision establishing a woman's constitutional right to obtain an abortion—produced a political backlash of extraordinary proportions. Acting primarily through religious organizations and the Republican party, the "pro-life" movement quickly organized itself and launched a many-pronged attack on *Roe*. It waged a powerful public relations campaign designed to persuade Americans to oppose abortion, either absolutely or under some circumstances. It convinced state and federal lawmakers to restrict access to abortion, for example by requiring parental or spousal consent, imposing mandatory waiting periods, or outlawing certain types of abortion procedures. Above all, it worked to elect presidents and members of Congress who were committed to appointing new Supreme Court justices likely to overturn *Roe* and declare that the right to an abortion was not protected by the Constitution.

Roe's defenders did not sit idly by while all of this was happening. Where possible, "pro-choice" groups blocked legislative attempts to limit abortion rights. When necessary, they went to court, urging state and federal judges to uphold *Roe* and to block attempts to limit its scope. During the Clinton presidency, they urged the appointment of pro-choice judges; during Republican presidencies, they vigorously opposed the nomination of those seen to be hostile to abortion rights.

For decades, both sides have envisioned the possibility that *Roe* might someday be overturned—supporters of abortion rights with dread, critics with great anticipation. President George W. Bush's recent appointments of new (and presumably conservative) justices—especially the 2006 appointment of Justice Samuel Alito to replace Justice Sandra Day O'Connor, who supported abortion rights—have added more urgency to the debate. But what would really happen on the day after *Roe*? In this provocative article, legal scholar Jeffrey Rosen speculates on the legal and political fallout of a Supreme Court decision overturning the abortion decision.

Questions

1. What would be the likely legal impact of a Supreme Court decision overturning *Roe* v. *Wade*? Would decisions on abortion rights fall to Congress? To state legislators? To state judges?
2. What would be the likely political impact of such a decision? How would it affect politics at the national level? At the state level? How would the balance between Republicans and Democrats likely be affected?

3.2 The Day After *Roe* (2006)

Jeffrey Rosen

The day after *Roe*, the handful of state abortion bans that were passed before *Roe* but never formally repealed would arguably spring back to life. According to Clarke Forsythe of Americans United for Life, there are eleven state laws already on the books that would ban abortion throughout pregnancy without making exceptions for threats to a woman's health. (Most have narrow exceptions allowing abortion in cases where the life of the mother is seriously threatened; some also include exceptions for rape or incest.) In at least seven of these eleven states (Arkansas, Louisiana, Michigan, Oklahoma, South Dakota, Texas, and Wisconsin), the draconian abortion bans have never been blocked by state courts as violations of state constitutional rights, and therefore could, in theory, be immediately enforced. If the governor or attorney general in any of these states announced an intention to support these miraculously rejuvenated abortion bans, and if state courts agreed that the bans hadn't been implicitly repealed, abortions might indeed be outlawed in most circumstances.

Even in the most conservative states, however, the overturning of *Roe* would put any pro-life governor or attorney general in a tight spot. For the truth is that draconian state bans on abortion that failed to provide widely supported exceptions would likely be unpopular with majorities in all the states in question. According to Clyde Wilcox, a Georgetown University professor who has studied public opinion on abortion, there would be majority opposition to any law that failed to include these exceptions, even in the most conservative states. "My guess is that any state that has a total prohibition on abortion—that can't stand," Wilcox told me. "If you look at the polls, you'll never get more than 15 or 20 percent that would ban all abortions. Across the board, around 75 percent are in favor of exceptions for rape, incest, and fetal defect, as well as the life and health of the mother. Even in the most conservative states, that will be over 50 percent." In other words, there's less variation among states when it comes to public attitudes about abortion than you might expect. In national Gallup Polls, over the last thirty years, two-thirds of Americans have consistently said that abortion should be legal in the first trimester of pregnancy, although in the second trimester, the number plummets to 25 percent, and in the third trimester it falls further, to 10 percent. And since 1973, according to polls conducted by the National Opinion Research Center, overwhelming majorities—between 80 and 90 percent—have said that abortion should be available to a woman if her health is seriously endangered by the pregnancy, or in cases of rape or risk of serious fetal defects. Whether in conservative states like Texas, swing states like Ohio and Pennsylvania, or liberal states like California, public support for access to abortion in cases of rape, fetal defect, and

From Jeffrey Rosen, "The Day After *Roe*," *Atlantic Monthly* 297 (June 2006), pp. 56–66.

threats to a woman's health, as well as for restrictions on abortion generally, is overwhelming. . . .

The day after *Roe* v. *Wade* falls, members of the pro-life movement will face a choice: Will they . . . include at least a physical-health exception in any abortion law, or will they doom themselves to political defeat? This choice could split the movement in two, and legislatures in some pro-life states might prefer principled failure to pragmatic accommodation. Not all of the seven states where the pre-*Roe* abortion bans are lurking have a popular-recall procedure. This means there might be some states where most citizens would oppose the rejuvenated abortion ban but a defiant state legislature would refuse to repeal it. This is a recipe for voter revolt. In other states—such as Michigan and Arkansas—pro-life legislators could try to head off a recall referendum by modifying the resurrected abortion bans to reflect the will of the voters. . . .

In short, the overturning of *Roe* would put pro-life legislators in an agonizing position: many are inalterably opposed to including an exception for threats to women's health; they argue that these exceptions have been broadly interpreted by doctors and courts in the past to include psychological as well as physical health, in effect subverting the bans and making abortions available throughout pregnancy. "People in the pro-life movement are opposed to health exceptions in any form," the pro-life scholar Paul Linton told me. "On the other hand, people will have to consider whether a narrow physical health exception might be a political necessity." If any of these states now pondering extreme bills did, in fact, pass broad bans without a health exception, they should expect voter insurrections similar to the one now taking shape in South Dakota [which passed such a law in 2006]. By contrast, if health exceptions were included, although abortions might be formally restricted in some states from the beginning of pregnancy—a significant change in the law—elective abortions might, in practice, remain widely available for those who were willing to negotiate the procedural hurdles involved in proving a threat to their mental or physical health.

The day after *Roe*, of course, there would be just as much mobilization in blue states to protect abortion as there would be in red states to restrict it. Even without *Roe* v. *Wade*, according to the Center for Reproductive Rights, a woman's right to choose would be secure in about twenty-three states. Six of these (California, Connecticut, Maine, Maryland, Nevada, and Washington) already have laws on the books protecting choice throughout pregnancy. In ten others (Alaska, California, Florida, Massachusetts, Minnesota, Montana, New Jersey, New Mexico, Tennessee, and West Virginia), state courts have ruled that their state constitutions protect abortion rights broadly throughout pregnancy. And in seven more (Hawaii, Iowa, New Hampshire, New York, Oregon, Vermont, and Wyoming), the political climate is sympathetic to choice, and citizens are likely to demand strong new laws protecting abortion.

The day after *Roe*, pro-choice activists in the most liberal states would have to be careful not to overreach, to avoid duplicating the errors of their pro-life counterparts in the most conservative states. If, for example, pro-choice activists make clear to state legislators in Iowa that they won't accept any state law that imposes restrictions on late-term, partial-birth abortions, which are intensely unpopular throughout the country, they may alienate the moderate middle of the electorate. But regardless of potential self-inflicted wounds by Democratic activists, the right to choose in the twenty-three bedrock pro-choice states is likely to remain broadly available throughout pregnancy.

It's conceivable that a year or two after *Roe*, as many as a dozen red states would adopt draconian restrictions on abortions throughout pregnancy, while a larger group of more populous blue states would offer the same access to abortion as they do now. What effect would this have on the national abortion rate? "My guess is that no more than a dozen states could sustain a total abortion ban, and these are principally states where virtually no legal abortions are performed today," says Gerald Rosenberg, a University of Chicago professor who has studied the effects of *Roe* on abortion rates. "That doesn't mean that individual lives wouldn't be severely impacted, but in terms of national numbers, the effect would be small." For example, if the South Dakota ban survived the overturning of *Roe*, the national impact would be negligible. In 2000, fewer than 1,000 women obtained abortions in South Dakota, representing one-tenth of 1 percent of all the abortions performed in the United States. That year, there were only two abortion providers in the state, and about 30 percent of South Dakota residents who sought abortions traveled to other states, such as Colorado and Nebraska. If the South Dakota abortion ban took effect, that percentage would certainly rise. But while women in the most conservative states would increasingly travel for abortions in a post-*Roe* world, the fact is they have been traveling for abortions throughout the three decades *Roe* has been on the books. In 2000, according to a report by the Guttmacher Institute, a pro-choice research organization, 87 percent of all counties in the United States had no abortion providers, one-third of all American women lived in these counties, and 25 percent of all the women who obtained abortions traveled at least fifty miles to do so. "In the past, the impact of some state restrictions that tried to limit access to abortion was primarily to delay rather than prevent abortions, because women can travel to another state," Lawrence B. Finer of the Guttmacher Institute told me. "But if more and more states pass such restrictions, it becomes harder to travel, which could have a disproportionate impact on poorer women."

A dozen state abortion bans might not dramatically change the national abortion rate, but they would dramatically change state and national politics. After *Roe*, women with disposable incomes would still be able to travel to have an abortion. Poor women, on the other hand, might be forced to seek abortions from illegal local providers. If television footage began to show arrests of illegal abortion doctors, the political framework for the abortion debate would almost certainly be transformed. "With *Roe* on the books, the focus of the abortion debate has tended to be on issues like partial-birth abortion, which is a huge political winner for Republicans," says Michael Klarman of the University of Virginia, a scholar of the Court and public opinion. "If you take *Roe* off the books, the focus will be on poor women in a handful of states trying to get illegal abortions, and these highly salient examples are going to benefit the other side." . . .

As the state electoral maps were thrown into chaos, Congress would come under increasing pressure to intervene. In the late 1960s, as Bill Stuntz of Harvard Law School notes, national opinion shifted after sensationalistic articles appeared in *Newsweek* and *The Saturday Evening Post* exaggerating, by at least a factor of ten, the number of deaths from botched illegal abortions. A year or two after *Roe*, a similarly galvanizing television image might mobilize women in swing states to take to the streets on behalf of the right to choose. "If a young woman who is raped gets pregnant and goes to a downscale abortion provider and dies from the infection, that becomes a huge story," says Stuntz.

It's hard to know precisely how soon after the fall of *Roe* a story about a botched abortion might capture the national imagination. But the moment pro-choice and swing voters perceived that their own right to choose was threatened, there would be increasingly urgent demands for a federal bill protecting the early-term choice that two-thirds of the country supports. If congressional Republicans failed to respond, or insisted on trying to ban early-term abortions instead, their intransigence could set in motion a national backlash that would make the response to *Roe* v. *Wade* itself look tame.

• • •

Once *Roe* is gone, one argument goes, each state would be free to reflect the wishes of local majorities, and the country would quickly reach a democratic equilibrium. But that assumption, as we've seen, may be too optimistic. Since the abortion battle will be fought out in the states and in Congress, rather than settled by a national referendum, it's possible that pro-life and pro-choice extremists could thwart the moderate compromises that national majorities have long supported.

The courts might further complicate the political dynamic in unexpected ways. The day after *Roe*, activists on both sides would rush to court to challenge state abortion laws, claiming that they violated the state and federal constitutions. It's not hard to imagine that a rogue judge (in the spirit of Roy Moore, who was unseated as chief justice of Alabama after he defied a federal court order and refused to remove a monument to the Ten Commandments he had installed in the rotunda of the state judicial building) might overturn a state law protecting abortion. A battleground state like Illinois might provide the stage for a memorable act of pro-life judicial activism. The Illinois state legislature declared in 1975 that an "unborn child is a human being from the time of conception," and it's easy to envision a conservative Illinois judge invoking this pronouncement as he overthrows an Illinois law protecting early-term abortions.

If a Democratic Congress managed to pass a federal law guaranteeing early-term abortions, and a President Hillary Clinton signed it, it's possible that conservative activists on the Supreme Court might further inflame national opinion by striking the law down. Those justices who are most intensely committed to federalism believe that Congress, under the Constitution, has limited authority to regulate interstate commerce; they might decide that because abortion is a medical activity rather than a commercial one, Congress has no authority to prevent states from banning it. This would be a brazen act of judicial activism—no less anti-democratic than *Roe* itself. But the only way to reverse a Supreme Court decision like this would be to ratify a federal constitutional amendment protecting abortion. If the House and Senate were Democratic, it would be very difficult, but perhaps not impossible, to get two-thirds of each chamber to propose a pro-choice constitutional amendment. But persuading three-fourths of the state legislatures to ratify the amendment could take years. As time passed, the frustration of a highly mobilized, pro-choice majority would dramatically increase as it found itself repeatedly thwarted from enacting its wishes into law. "I can imagine a fifty-front war going on for the next thirty years," says Nancy Northup of the Center for Reproductive Rights. "Be careful what you wish for."

Nevertheless, at some point after *Roe* fell, the country would reach some kind of political equipoise on abortion. It's difficult, in America, to deny the wishes of majorities for too long, and whether it takes years or decades, the state legislatures and Congress will eventually come to reflect the popular will. When the dust settles, most of the state laws may look a lot like the compromise that the Supreme Court finally settled on in the 1992 *Casey* decision: protecting early-term abortions and restricting late-term ones. If *Roe* v. *Wade* hadn't short-circuited the national political debate about abortion, the state legislatures might have arrived at this compromise on their own more than a decade earlier. But in light of the polarizing backlash that *Roe* provoked, the Supreme Court today might well move more quickly than our elected representatives to mirror the constitutional views of the moderate majority of Americans. If the Court remains sensitive to the people's constitutional views, as it has been for most of its history, it may be more than a little hesitant to overturn the core of *Roe* in the first place.

In the twentieth century, judicial encounters with laws concerning mandatory sterilization and contraception have confirmed the limited ability of courts to challenge deeply felt currents of public opinion. During the first half of the twentieth century, compulsory sterilization of the "mentally defective" was extremely popular, encouraged by the Progressive political and religious leaders of the American eugenics movement. In response to this public enthusiasm, legislatures in sixteen states passed laws, between 1907 and 1913, authorizing the sterilization of "idiots" and "imbeciles." When lower courts struck down seven of these laws, their decisions had little practical impact, and states passed even more sterilization laws. The Supreme Court upheld these laws in a notorious 1927 opinion by the enthusiastic eugenicist Justice Oliver Wendell Homes Jr. Despite a 1942 Supreme Court opinion questioning mandatory sterilization, sterilization laws remained on the books through the 1960s, and as recently as 1985 the sterilization of the mentally retarded was allowed in at least nineteen states. In the end, American support for sterilization cooled not because of the courts but because of public antipathy to Hitler's eugenics policies and, later, accusations during the civil-rights movement that blacks were disproportionately targets of mandatory sterilization. The judicial response to laws restricting contraception followed a similar pattern. In 1965, the Supreme Court, in *Griswold* v. *Connecticut*, forced the last holdout state to comply with an overwhelming national consensus when it struck down Connecticut's law banning the use of contraceptives by married couples, the only law of its kind in the nation still on the books. Because popular support for banning contraception had eroded, the *Griswold* decision was embraced by Congress, the White House, and the country as a whole.

The great question of American politics is whether this historical pattern of judicial sensitivity to the constitutional views of majorities will continue to hold in the future. In the 1980s and 1990s, partly in response to *Roe* v. *Wade*, interest groups arose on the right and left that urged judges to ignore the views of national majorities as a sign of their constitutional virtue. For more than two decades. Republican presidents have looked for Supreme Court nominees who appeared to be pro-life—and then have prayed that they wouldn't actually overturn *Roe*. But at some point, it's possible that the GOP's luck might run out: Republicans might get too many Court appointment opportunities to prolong this exquisite balancing act, and *Roe* could indeed fall. At that point, it's not clear who would represent the views of the moderate majority that the Supreme Court has tried—and often failed—to capture in its abortion cases. But whatever party or movement managed to seize the vital center in a post-*Roe* world would be likely to dominate American politics for a generation to come. ■

Issue and Controversy

Times of war are never kind to civil liberties, and the war against terrorism has been no exception. With the safety of the nation and its citizens at stake, the U.S. government has moved vigorously to investigate and disrupt suspected and potential terrorists, often at the expense of civil liberties. The government has detained an unspecified number of individuals as "material witnesses"; held suspects—including at least one American citizen—in military custody without access to a lawyer; and expanded its legal authority to place wiretaps on terrorism suspects and to investigate alleged terrorist groups.

Both critics and defenders of the government's policies have been quick to weigh in with their opinions. On one side are those who argue that such tactics undermine the very Constitution that the government is trying to protect, damaging democracy and thus handing a kind of victory to the terrorists. On the other are those who assert that the government's first duty is the protection of the people, and that security is worth some cost in diminished liberty.

In this selection, law professor Michael J. Glennon aims to find a balance between these two positions.

Questions

1. What competing values are at stake in the argument between those who would tilt the balance between civil liberties and the war against terrorism in one direction or the other? How would each side answer the "ticking time bomb" hypothetical described in this selection?
2. What are the implications of Glennon's argument for American policy in the war against terrorism?

3.3 Terrorism and the Limits of Law (2002)

Michael J. Glennon

Cries of outrage erupted around the world this past January when the Pentagon released pictures of Taliban and Al Qaeda prisoners shackled, blindfolded by strange-looking goggles, and forced to kneel during their captivity at the U.S. military base at Guantánamo Bay in Cuba. Secretary of Defense Donald H. Rumsfeld's explanation that such methods were not inhumane and were used only when the men—dangerous terrorist suspects, after all—were moved from place to place did little to still the protests. But millions of Americans, and doubtless many abroad, thought to themselves: So what? It is likely, in fact, that many thought the prisoners deserved far worse. A CNN/USA *Today*/Gallup poll in early October revealed that 45 percent of those surveyed would approve the torture of captured terrorists who knew details of future attacks in the United States. One prominent American law professor has even suggested that judges be empowered to issue "torture warrants."

There is no evidence that the roughly 300 men held at Guantánamo have been tortured, but there is no question that America since September 11 has experienced a sharp clash of values, pitting freedom against security, and law against politics. Yet the months since terrorists brought down the World Trade towers also show how the United States has come to balance competing constitutional values, and—perhaps paradoxically—the way it has come to recognize the limits of the law as a tool for striking that balance.

Why not torture the terrorists? The answer is not as obvious as it may seem—and some of the most obvious answers don't hold up under scrutiny. In 20 years of teaching constitutional law, I have found that considering hypothetical cases can be a useful way to get at bigger truths. Many of these "hypos," as they are called in law schools, are simply outlandish, but one has turned out, alas, to be a lot less improbable than it seemed before September 11. That is the famous, or infamous, "ticking time bomb" hypo:

> Assume that the police capture a terrorist whom they know has planted a nuclear bomb somewhere in New York City. The police know that the bomb will explode very soon; the city cannot possibly be evacuated. The terrorist refuses to talk. Question: Should the police torture him?

Some students always answer with a flat no: Torture, they argue, can never be conducted under any circumstances. They usually give two kinds of reasons, one practical, the other theoretical. On the practical side, students cite the familiar "slippery slope" argument: Once we accept the permissibility of torture under any circumstances, we will end up torturing under many circumstances. The theoreti-

From Michael J. Glennon, "Terrorism and the Limits of Law," *Wilson Quarterly* 22 (Spring 2002), pp. 12–19. Reprinted by permission of the author.

cal reason can best be described as a natural rights argument—it is an almost instinctive American response. It holds that human beings have certain rights that no government can take away, and that one of those rights is the right not to be tortured. Some natural rights proponents would add that it is impermissible to do evil even if good may come of it, or that the end can never justify the means.

Each of these arguments has flaws. The answer to the "slippery slope" view is simply that we have not yet reached the bottom of the slope, indeed, that we are far from it, and that long before we do reach the bottom we will stop. We can torture terrorists without opening the way to the torture of, say, car thieves. It is irrational not to act where we must act just because, some day, we may act where we ought not act.

The answer to the theoretical, natural rights argument is complex, as is the natural rights argument itself. At bottom, though, the response is that the natural rights argument is not really an argument at all, but rather an assertion—an assertion that is as unproved as it is unprovable. It hinges on a set of presuppositions. The most prominent of these is the assumption of eternal right and wrong, of an overarching morality contingent upon neither circumstance nor culture, a "truth" that all rational people everywhere—all persons of "right reason"—must accept. . . .

On the other side of the debate over our hypothetical are students—most students, these days—who respond that of course we should torture the terrorist. Many of these students believe that this is simply a practical argument. They justify torturing, or even killing, the terrorist by relying on simple arithmetic: The lives of eight million are worth more than the life of one. No great philosophical inquiry is needed. Unlike natural rights, utilitarianism is modern and seemingly scientific—"empirical." So it's no big deal, these students believe, to fall back upon the same utilitarian philosophy in deciding to torture the terrorist.

But a vast body of philosophy does underlie the supposition that "simple arithmetic" is the proper focal point. That philosophy is utilitarianism, the notion of the greatest good for the greatest number. It is true that much of Western social policy today is built upon utilitarian scaffolding. The justification for the principle of redistributing wealth that animates many government programs, from graduated income taxes to historic preservation, is the idea that the number of people who will benefit is greater than the number of people who will be harmed.

But utilitarianism, like the natural rights approach, has its difficulties. Utilitarianism can lead to horrific social policies. A majority may somehow be "happier" if all men are required to wear crew cuts, or if all women are required to wear burkas, or if all "infidels" are put to death. How do we answer that majority?

Moreover, "empirical" though it may be, utilitarianism is not without its own presuppositions. Central among them is precisely the same assumption of the moral bindingness of logic that occurs in the natural rights argument. Why ought we give the greatest good to the greatest number? . . .

So the easy answers to the hypothetical are too easy. Each approach, in the end, opens the door to precisely the evils that it seeks to preclude. Each ultimately is arbitrary in that it relies upon premises that cannot be rationally proven but must, rather, be assumed. Each leaves us looking further.

Some years ago, Justice Hugo Black (1886–1971) reportedly gave an intriguing answer to the ticking time bomb hypothetical. There's a particular reason to be interested in Black. He was one of the leading liberals of the Warren Court. Appointed by President Franklin D. Roosevelt, he had a strong commitment to civil liberties and individual freedom. Black was also the quintessential constitutional "absolutist." He liked "bright line" tests—legal standards that were easy to apply and that admitted of no exceptions. When Black read the words, "Congress shall make no law . . ." in the First Amendment, he read them to mean that Congress shall make no law—not some law, not a few laws, but *no* law.

Black disdained "balancing tests"—standards that permitted judges to weigh competing interests case by case to reach different outcomes in different circumstances. Balancing tests, he believed, gave judges too much discretion, allowing them to substitute their own judgment for that of legislators. The job of judges, Black knew, is to interpret the law, not to make the law. Balancing tests reduce the law to mashed potatoes, to be shaped into anything any judge wants it to be, able to support any conclusion the judge desires. Black was the perfect person to whom the hypothetical could be addressed: How would the ultimate no-nonsense, "no exceptions" jurist who had an abiding respect for the dignity of the individual apply a rule that seemed to cry out for an exception? Should we torture the terrorist?

Black's reported answer was, "Yes—but we could never say that."

It is hard to resist reveling in the pithy wisdom of these words. In one sentence, Black reconciles down-home common sense with a profound recognition of the limits of the law—I should say, with a recognition of the limits of human cognitive and linguistic capacity.

Common sense kept Black, in the end, from being a true absolutist, at least within the realm of morality, if not law. By a true absolutist I mean one who refuses to balance competing values. An absolutist would say that a certain act is always, in every situation, wrong. Killing, lying, stealing, assassination—and, of course, torture—are examples of the kinds of acts some absolutists believe are always wrong, regardless of "exigent" circumstances. In his answer to the ticking time bomb hypothetical, Black reveals that he is willing to balance one value against another, weighing the evil of torture against the preservation of human life. So in a moral sense, the hypothetical seemed to have its intended purpose of "smoking him out," of showing that even the most dedicated constitutional absolutist could, under the right conditions, be forced to jump ship.

But Black does not jump ship in the legal realm. *We could never say that.* He is unwilling to allow the law to reflect his moral judgment. It is one thing to acknowledge the moral propriety of torturing the terrorist, but quite another to conclude that such an admission should be acted upon by a court (or, presumably, by a legislature). Why? We can only speculate, but Black might have responded that courts and legislatures, unlike the police, speak with words, not deeds. Don't spell it out in a rule—don't even try to spell it out—just do it. Because the human mind simply is not capable of finding words precise enough to eliminate all unwanted discretion. Because words are too slippery to be entrusted with the responsibility of staying out when strange new facts shake them around. Because any rule that would let us torture a terrorist, however carefully drafted, would inevitably be embraced by corrupt police officers or soldiers or prison guards somewhere as justification for doing what our society finds repugnant.

This answer, however, has an obvious shortcoming. It seems to assume that no legal norm is established if one simply intends not to establish a norm. Black's answer brings to mind Abraham Lincoln's quip: How many legs does a dog have if you call a tail a leg? Four; calling a tail a leg does not make it a leg. Calling a precedent a non-precedent does not make it so. Action counts. Intent is expressed in deeds as well as words. And deeds that are allowed to stand are likely to be repeated by others. Even if those deeds are not repeated, it is possible that the police officer who did the torturing could later be hauled into court for the act. What then? Turning a blind eye to manifest illegality could taint the entire legal system—though the law may have enough give at the joints to limit torture's corrupting influence. (Those found guilty of torture where mitigating circumstances exist could be given suspended sentences, for example.)

Despite its flaws, "not saying that" is sometimes our best option. The courts have various ways of "not saying that." One is encapsulated in Justice Oliver Wendell Holmes, Jr.'s famous dictum that hard cases make bad law. To avoid bad law, avoid hard cases; avoid resolving a conflict when two fundamental values clash. To resolve such a case is to risk establishing a formal legal precedent that will require a future case to be decided in a bad way. This is why the Supreme Court, when confronted with a hard case, is inclined to underscore that its decision is restricted to the precise facts of the case before it.

The ticking time bomb hypothetical is, to be sure, a hard and essentially implausible case. Yet it can be made even harder. Assume that the person who knows the location of the bomb is not a terrorist—or even a wrongdoer. Assume that he happens to know where the bomb is located but, acting upon some perverse principle, refuses to answer the authorities' questions. Suppose, for example, that the police know that the bomb is hidden in his mother's house, unknown to her, and that they don't know her address. Suppose that he declines to cooperate out of fear that the police will hurt his mother. Is it permissible to torture a wholly innocent bystander to spare the lives of eight million people?

One might say that the person is a wrongdoer for the simple reason that it is wrong not to reveal the whereabouts of the bomb. But I am aware of no crime that would be committed by his remaining silent. He is not legally a wrongdoer. Morally, one might think otherwise. But one could also argue that choosing one's own mother's life over the lives of strangers is no moral wrong.

Remember, this person, unlike the terrorist, has not chosen to act outside the law. He has every reason to believe that he is protected from community-sponsored violence. After all, he did what the community told him to do in the only way it could communicate authoritatively with him—through the law. If we are to permit the law's guardians to engage in an improvised and unauthorized utilitarian calculus that trumps the law here, why not elsewhere? And if "elsewhere" can be decided by the law's guardians to be anyplace the guardians wish, what has become of the law?

Since September 11 we have often heard potential departures from the legal order defended with the argument that the "Constitution is not a suicide pact." No one can quarrel with these words (Justice Arthur Goldberg's words, actually).

Survival is the ultimate right, for societies as well as for individuals. But the proposition has come to be relied upon too often, in contexts in which societal survival is not at stake. The statement has come to be shorthand for the idea that whenever the Constitution seems to be at odds with some transient utilitarian calculus, the Constitution must give way.

In its strong form, this argument is not just a case for occasionally violating the Constitution. It is an objection to the very idea of the rule of law. The rule of law substitutes for the series of utilitarian calculations that would otherwise occur in a lawless "state of nature." It says that we agree not to weigh costs against benefits where a specific rule of law applies. We do not permit a bank robber to excuse himself with the defense that the bank charged the community unconscionable interest rates, or a murderer to excuse himself with the defense that the deceased was a congenital bully. No: If the law provides the answer as to how certain wrongs are to be righted, then the law's answer controls. We do not set the law aside because the benefits of doing so seem to outweigh the costs.

I say "seem to outweigh the costs" because our assessment of costs can vary under different conditions. Recall Homer's story of the Sirens, the sea nymphs whose hypnotic singing lured sailors to crash their ships onto the rocks. And recall Odysseus's solution: Knowing that he would surely succumb to the Sirens' song (yet desperately wanting to hear it), he had himself bound to the ship's mast and told his crew to plug their ears. He ordered them to ignore his pleas to be untied, no matter how forceful. Knowing in calmer times, in other words, that he would assess the cost of succumbing to the Sirens differently than he would in a moment of great stress, Odysseus set down a rule that was not to be superseded by a later rule formulated in distress.

Society is like Odysseus. When it formulates constitutional limits, society says to itself: "When confronted with temptation, we may scream to be untied—untied to censor unwanted speech, to ban unwanted religion, to impose cruel and unusual punishments—but do not untie us! We know the true costs of these actions, and those costs are too great!"

So I am not making a roundabout case for the use of torture as an interrogation tool. To the contrary: The captives in Guantánamo Bay do not pose anywhere near as clear and present a danger as the ticking time bomb terrorist. As far as we know, no single, identifiable prisoner possesses information that could save thousands of lives. Torturing prisoners absent such exigent circumstances would represent a momentous and irreversible step backward toward war as it was fought centuries ago, war with no rules, war with no safe havens, war with no limits. No civilized nation can embark upon such a course unless it has decided to write off its future.

My case can be summed up in two words: *balance* and *limits*. The ticking time bomb hypothetical is a useful analytic tool not only for thinking about terrorism but for thinking about thinking. It makes us ponder whether any one value, however central to our culture, can ever be given overriding, controlling weight in any and all circumstances. The hypothetical shows how sticking to any absolute, inflexible principle come hell or high water can ultimately undermine the purposes that principle is intended to vindicate. It reveals the need to balance competing values, to reconcile countervailing ideals, pragmatically, with an eye to real-world consequences, not abstract theory. . . . ■

View from the Inside

The right to "due process of law" is one of the fundamental protections of the United States Constitution. Due process rights are particularly important in the context of criminal proceedings, where a defendant's property, liberty, or even life may be at stake. Among the constitutional rights guaranteed to criminal defendants are the right to remain silent, the right to an attorney, the right to trial by jury, and the right to be free from unreasonable searches and seizures.

Also high on the list of due process protections for criminal defendants is the right not to be convicted of a crime except upon proof "beyond a reasonable doubt." This traditional formula, as attorney Alan Dershowitz argues, serves vitally important values beyond the "search for truth" in any particular case. Dershowitz's discussion of this critical issue draws heavily on his experience as a defense attorney in the 1997 O. J. Simpson murder case.

Questions

1. What, in Dershowitz's view, is the purpose of a criminal trial? Why is it not, in simple terms at least, a "search for truth"?
2. What values are served by the legal system's insistence on the "reasonable doubt" standard? What values would be served by lowering the burden of proof in criminal cases? What would be the advantages and disadvantages of abandoning the reasonable doubt standard in criminal cases?

3.4 Is the Criminal Trial a Search for Truth? (1997)

Alan Dershowitz

The term "search for truth" was repeatedly invoked by both sides of the Simpson case. A review of the trial transcript reveals that this phrase was used more than seventy times. The prosecutors claimed that they were searching for truth and that the defense was deliberately obscuring it. Where it was in their interest to have the jury hear evidence that would hurt Simpson— such as the details of arguments between him and his former wife—the prosecutors argued that the search for truth required the *inclusion* of such evidence, despite its marginal relevance. On other occasions, they argued that the search for truth

---

required the *exclusion* of evidence that demonstrated that one of their key witnesses, Los Angeles Police Detective Mark Fuhrman, had not told the truth at the trial. The defense also claimed the mantle of truth and accused the prosecution of placing barriers in its path. And throughout the trial, the pundits observed that neither side was really interested in truth, only in winning. They were right—and wrong.

In observing this controversy, I was reminded of the story of the old rabbi who, after listening to a husband complaining bitterly about his wife, replied, "You are right, my son." Then, after listening to a litany of similar complaints from the wife, he responded, "You are right, my daughter." The rabbi's young student then remarked, "But they can't both be right"—to which the rabbi replied, "You are right, my son." So too, in the context of a criminal case, the prosecution is right when it says it is searching for truth—a certain kind of truth. The defense is also searching for a certain kind of truth. Yet both are often seeking to obscure the truth for which their opponent is searching. In arguing to exclude evidence that Fuhrman had perjured himself when he denied using the "N" word, Marcia Clark said just that:

> *This is a search for the truth,* but it's a search for the truth of who committed these murders, your Honor. Not who Mark Fuhrman is. That truth will be sought out in another forum. We have to search for this truth now, and I beg the court to keep us on track and to allow the jury to pursue that search for the truth based on evidence that is properly admissible in this case and relevant to that determination.

The truth is that most criminal defendants are, in fact, guilty. Prosecutors, therefore, generally have the *ultimate* truth on their side. But since prosecution witnesses often lie about some facts, defense attorneys frequently have *intermediate* truth on their side. Not surprisingly, both sides emphasize the kind of truth that they have more of. To understand this multilayered process, and the complex role "truth" plays in it, it is important to know the difference between a criminal trial and other more single-minded searches for truth.

What is a criminal trial? And how does it differ from a historical or scientific inquiry? These are among the questions posed in a university-wide course I teach at Harvard, along with Professors Robert Nozick, a philosopher, and Stephen J. Gould, a paleontologist. The course, entitled "Thinking About Thinking," explores how differently scientists, philosophers, historians, lawyers, and theologians think about and search for truth. The goal of the historian and scientist, at least in theory, is the uncovering or discovery of truth. The historian seeks to determine what actually happened in the recent or distant past by interviewing witnesses, examining documents, and piecing together fragmentary records. The paleontologist searches for even more distant truths by analyzing fossils, geological shifts, dust and DNA. Since what's past is prologue, for both the historian and the scientist, efforts are often made to extrapolate from what did occur to what will occur, and generalizations—historical or scientific rules—are proposed and tested.

Although there are ethical limits on historical and scientific inquiry, the ultimate test of a given result in these disciplines is its truth or falsity. Consider the following hypothetical situation. An evil scientist (or historian) beats or bribes some important truth out of a vulnerable source. That truth is then independently tested and confirmed. The evil scientist might be denied his Nobel Prize for ethical reasons, but the truth he discovered is no less the truth because of the improper means he employed to arrive at it. Scientists condemn "scientific fraud" precisely because it risks producing falsity rather than truth. But if a fraudulent experiment happened to produce a truth that could be replicated in a nonfraudulent experiment, that truth would ultimately become accepted.

Put another way, there are no "exclusionary rules" in history or science, as there are in law. Historical and scientific inquiry is supposed to be neutral as to truth that is uncovered. Historians should not favor a truth that is "politically," "patriotically," "sexually," or "religiously" correct. In practice, of course, some historians and scientists may very well skew their research to avoid certain truths—as Trofim Lysenko did in the interests of Stalinism, or as certain racial theorists did in the interests of Hitlerism. But in doing so, they would be acting as policy-makers rather than as historians or scientists.

The discovery of historical and scientific truths is not entrusted to a jury of lay people selected randomly from the population on the basis of their ignorance of the underlying facts. The task of discovering such truths is entrusted largely to trained experts who have studied the subject for years and are intimately familiar with the relevant facts and theories.

Historical and scientific inquiries do not require that fact-finders necessarily be representative of the general population, in race, gender, religion, or anything else—as jurors must be. To be sure, a discipline that discriminates runs the risk of producing falsehood, since truth is not the domain of any particular group. But again, historical and scientific truths may be just as valid if arrived at by segregationists as if by integrationists. In history and science, truth achieved by unfair means is preferred to falsity achieved by fair means.

Nor are historical and scientific truths determined on the basis of adversarial contests in which advocates—with varying skills, resources, and styles—argue for different results. Although the quest for peer approval—tenure, prizes, book contracts, and so on—may become competitive, the historical or scientific method is not premised on the view that the search for truth is best conducted through adversarial conflict.

Finally, all "truths" discovered by science or history are always subject to reconsideration based on new evidence. There are no prohibitions against "double jeopardy." Nor is there any deference to considerations of "finality"; nor are there statutes of limitations. In sum, the historical and scientific inquiry is basically a search for objective truth. Perhaps it is not always an untrammeled search for truth. Perhaps the ends of truth do not justify all ignoble means. But the goal is clear: objective truths as validated by accepted, verifiable, and, if possible, replicable historical and scientific tests.

The criminal trial is quite different in several important respects. Truth, although *one* important goal of the criminal trial, is not its *only* goal. If it were, judges would not instruct jurors to acquit a defendant whom they believe "probably" did it, as they are supposed to do in criminal cases. The requirement is that guilt must be proved "beyond a reasonable doubt." But that is inconsistent with the quest for objective truth, because it explicitly prefers one kind of truth to another. The preferred truth is that the defendant did *not* do it, and we demand that the jurors err on the side of that truth, even in cases where it is probable that he did do it. Justice John Harlan said in the 1970 Supreme Court *Winship* decision that, "I view the requirement of proof beyond a reasonable doubt in a criminal case as bottomed on a fundamental value that it is far worse to convict an innocent man than to let a guilty man go free." As one early-nineteenth-century scholar explained, "The maxim of the law . . . is that it is better that ninety-nine . . . offenders shall escape than that one innocent man be condemned." More typically, the ratio is put at ten to one.

In a criminal trial, we are generally dealing with a decision that must be made under conditions of uncertainty. We will never know with absolute certainty whether Sacco and Vanzetti killed the paymaster and guard at the shoe factory, whether Bruno Hauptmann kidnapped and murdered the Lindbergh baby, or whether Jeffrey MacDonald bludgeoned his wife and children to death. In each of these controversial cases, the legal system was certain enough to convict—and in two of them, to execute. But doubts persist, even decades later.

Those who believe that O. J. Simpson did murder Nicole Brown and Ronald Goldman must acknowledge that they cannot know that "truth" with absolute certainty. They were not there when the crimes occurred or when the evidence was collected and tested. They must rely on the work and word of people they do not know. The jurors in the Simpson case were not asked to vote on whether they believed "he did it." They were asked *whether the prosecution's evidence proved beyond a reasonable doubt that he did it.* Juror number three, a sixty-one-year-old white woman named Anise Aschenbach, indicated that she believed that Simpson was probably guilty "but the law wouldn't allow a guilty verdict." Had the Simpson trial been purely a search for truth, this juror would have been instructed to vote for conviction, since in her view that was more likely the "truth" than that he didn't do it. But she was instructed to arrive at a "false" verdict, namely that although in her view he probably committed the crimes, yet as a matter of law he did not.

This anomaly has led some reformers to propose the adoption of the old Scottish verdict "not proven" instead of the Anglo-American verdict of "not guilty." Even the words "not guilty" do not quite convey the sense of "innocent," although acquitted defendants are always quick to claim that they have been found "innocent." Some commentators have suggested that alternative verdicts—"guilty," "innocent," and "not proven"—be available so that when jurors believe that the defendant did not do it, they can reward him with an affirmative declaration of innocence rather than merely a negative conclusion that his guilt has not been satisfactorily proved.

● ● ●

If the only goal of the adversary system were to find "the truth" in every case, then it would be relatively simple to achieve. Suspects could be tortured, their families threatened, homes randomly searched, and lie detector tests routinely administered. Indeed, in order to facilitate this search for truth, we could all be subjected to a regimen of random blood and urine tests, and every public building and workplace could be outfitted with surveillance cameras. If these methods—common in totalitarian countries—are objected to on the ground that torture and threats sometimes produce false accusations, that objection could be overcome by requiring that all confessions induced by torture or threats must be independently corroborated. We would still never tolerate such a single-minded search for truth, nor would our constitution, because we believe that the ends—even an end as noble as truth—do not justify every possible means. Our system of justice thus reflects a balance among often inconsistent goals, which include truth, privacy, fairness, finality, and equality.

Even "truth" is a far more complex goal than may appear at first blush. There are different kinds of truth at work in our adversary system. At the most basic level, there is the ultimate truth involved in the particular case: "Did he do it?" Then there is the truth produced by cases over time, which may be in sharp conflict. For example, the lawyer-client privilege—which shields certain confidential communications from being disclosed—may generate more truth over the long run by encouraging clients to be candid with their lawyers. But in any given case, this same privilege may thwart the ultimate truth—as in the rare case where a defendant confides in his lawyer that he did it. The same is true of other privileges, ranging from the privilege against self-incrimination to rape shield laws, which prevent an accused rapist from introducing the prior sexual history of his accuser.

Even in an individual case, there are different types—or layers—of truth. The defendant may have done it—ultimate truth—but the police may have lied in securing the search warrant. Or the police may even have planted evidence against guilty defendants, as New York state troopers were recently convicted of doing, and as some jurors believed the police did in the Simpson case.

The Anglo-American criminal trial employs the adversary system to resolve disputes. This system, under which each side tries to win by all legal and ethical means, may be conducive to truth in the long run, but it does not always produce truth in a given case. Nor is it widely understood or accepted by the public.

One night, during the middle of the Simpson trial, my wife and I were attending a concert at Boston Symphony Hall. When it was over a woman ran down the center aisle. We thought she was headed toward the stage to get a close look at Midori, who was taking bows. But the woman stopped at our row and started shouting at me: "You don't deserve to listen to music. You don't care about justice. All you care about is winning." I responded, "You're half right. When I am representing a criminal defendant, I do care about winning—by all fair, lawful, and ethical means. That's how we try to achieve justice in this country—by each side seeking to win. It's called the adversary system."

I did not try to persuade my critic, since I have had little success persuading even my closest friends of the morality of the Vince Lombardi dictum as it applies to the role of defense counsel in criminal cases: "Winning isn't everything. It's the only thing."

There are several reasons why it is so difficult to explain this attitude to the public. First, hardly anybody ever admits publicly that winning is their goal. Even the most zealous defense lawyers proclaim they are involved in a search for truth. Such posturing is part of the quest for victory, since lawyers who candidly admit they are interested in the truth are more likely to win than lawyers who say they are out to win. Second, although defense attorneys are supposed to want to win—regardless of what they say in public—prosecutors are, at least in theory, supposed to want justice. Indeed, the motto of the U.S. Justice Department is "The Government wins when Justice is done." That is the theory. In practice, however, each side wants to win as badly as the other. Does anyone really doubt that Marcia Clark wanted to win as much as Johnnie Cochran did? She told the jury during her closing argument that she had stopped being a defense attorney and became a prosecutor so that she could have the luxury of looking at herself in the mirror every morning and knowing that she always told juries the truth, and that she would only ask for a conviction where she could prove that the defendant was, in fact, guilty. But notwithstanding these assertions, Clark and other prosecutors put Mark Fuhrman on the stand after having been informed that he was a racist, a liar, and a person capable of planting evidence even before they called him as a trial witness. An assistant district attorney, among others, warned the Simpson prosecutors about Fuhrman. The prosecutors also saw his psychological reports, in which he admitted his racist attitudes and actions. The only thing they didn't know was that Fuhrman—and they—would be caught by the tape-recorded interviews that Fuhrman gave an aspiring screenwriter, Laura Hart McKinny. If the tapes had not surfaced, the prosecutors would have attempted to destroy the credibility of the truthful good Samaritan witnesses who came forward to testify about Fuhrman's racism. Only the tapes stopped them from doing that.

Clark behaved similarly with regard to Detective Philip Vannatter. Any reasonable prosecutor should have been suspicious of Vannatter's testimony that when he went to the O. J. Simpson estate in the hours following the discovery of the double murder, he no more suspected Simpson of the killings than he did Robert Shapiro. That testimony had all the indicia of a cover story, and yet Clark allowed it to stand uncorrected.

In practice, the adversary system leads both sides to do everything in their power—as long as it is lawful and ethical—to win. Since most defendants are guilty, it follows that the defense will more often be in the position of advocating ultimate falsity than will the prosecution. But since the prosecution always puts on a case—often relying on police testimony—whereas the defense rarely puts on any affirmative case, it follows that the prosecution will more often be in the position of using false testimony in an effort to produce its ultimately true result.

Outrage at Simpson's acquittal is understandable in those who firmly believe that he did it. No one wants to see a guilty murderer go free, or an innocent defendant go to prison. But our system is judged not only by the accuracy of its results, but also by *the fairness of the process*. Indeed, the Supreme Court has said that our system must tolerate the occasional conviction, imprisonment, *and even execution* of a possibly innocent defendant because of considerations of finality, federalism, and deference to the jury. The United States Supreme Court recently recognized that "our judicial system, like the human beings who administer it, is fallible" and that innocent defendants have at times been wrongfully convicted. The Court concluded that some wrongful convictions and even executions of innocent defendants must be tolerated "because of the very disruptive effect that entertaining claims of actual innocence would have on the need for finality in capital cases, and the enormous burden that having to retry cases based on often stale evidence would place on the States."

While reasonable people may, and do, disagree with that conclusion, it surely must follow from our willingness to tolerate some innocents being wrongly executed by our less than perfect system that we must be prepared to tolerate the occasional freeing of defendants who are perceived to be guilty. This is a Rubicon we, as a society, crossed long before the Simpson verdict—although one might not know it from the ferocity of the reaction to that verdict. As I mentioned earlier, the exclusionary rule is based on our willingness to free some guilty defendants in order to serve values often unrelated to truth. It is interesting to contrast the public reaction to the *jury's* acquittal with what would have happened if Simpson had gone free as a result of the *judge's* application of the exclusionary rule.

What would the public reaction have been if the trial judge had ruled that the original search of Simpson's estate had been unconstitutional and all its fruits had to be suppressed? Such a ruling might have wounded the prosecution's case—although perhaps not mortally. It would have excluded from evidence the bloody glove found behind Simpson's house, the socks found in his bedroom, the blood found in the driveway. It might also have tainted the warrants, which were based, at least in part, on the evidence observed during the initial search. These warrants produced a considerable amount of evidence which might also have had to be suppressed. Indeed, had the search of Simpson's estate been declared unconstitutional, virtually everything found in and around the estate might have been subject to exclusion.

That would still have left the other half of the prosecution's case—everything found at the crime scene—since no probable cause or warrant was required for searches and seizures at Nicole Brown's condominium. But the quantity of the prosecution's evidence against Simpson would have been considerably reduced if the evidence seized at the Simpson estate had been suppressed as the fruits of an unconstitutional search.

Had the trial judge suppressed all the Simpson estate evidence, there would have been a massive public outcry against the judge, the exclusionary rule, the Constitution, and the system. This outcry would have increased in intensity if this suppression had led—either directly or indirectly—to the acquittal of the defendant. "Guilty Murderer Is Freed Because of Legal Technicality," the headlines would have shouted. Conservatives would have demanded abolition of the exclusionary rule. But many liberals and civil libertarians who today rail against the jury verdict in the Simpson case would have defended the decision as the price we pay for preserving our constitutional rights.

This is all, of course, in the realm of the hypothetical, since it is unlikely that any judge—certainly any elected judge with higher aspirations—would have had the courage to find the search unconstitutional and thus endanger the prosecution's case. Recently, I had lunch with a former student who was seeking to be appointed to the California Superior Court. I asked her how she would answer the following question if it were put to her by the judicial nominating committee: "Would you have ruled the search unconstitutional if you believed the police were lying about why they went to Simpson's house, climbed the gate, and entered?" Without a moment's hesitation she responded: "No way. No judge would—are you kidding?"

I think my former student overstated the case in saying that *no* judge would have had the guts to find the police were lying in the Simpson case, but I believe that most judges would do what the two trial judges almost certainly did here: assume a variation of the position of the three monkeys, hearing no lies and seeing no lies. And judges speak the lie of pretending to believe witnesses who they must know are not telling the truth. What does it say about our system of justice that so many judges would pretend to believe policemen they know are lying, rather than follow the unpopular law excluding evidence obtained in violation of the Constitution? I am not alone in believing that the judges in the Simpson case could not really have believed what they said they believed. As Scott Turow argued in a perceptive op-ed piece the day after the verdict:

> The detectives' explanation as to why they were at the house is hard to believe. . . . Four police detectives were not needed to carry a message about Nicole Simpson's death. These officers undoubtedly knew what Justice Department statistics indicate: that half of the women murdered in the United States are killed by their husbands or boyfriends. Simple probabilities made Mr. Simpson a suspect. . . . Also, Mark Fuhrman had been called to the Simpson residence years earlier when Mr. Simpson was abusing his wife. . . .

The fact that the district attorney's office put these officers on the witness stand to tell this story and that the [judge] accepted it is scandalous. It is also routine. . . . Turow then went on to blame the prosecutor and the judges:

> To lambaste only Detectives Fuhrman and Vannatter misses the point. . . . It was the Los Angeles District Attorney's Office that put them on the stand. It was Judge Kennedy-Powell [the judge who presided at the preliminary hearing] who took their testimony at face value rather than stir controversy by suppressing the most damning evidence in the case of the century. And it was Judge Lance Ito who refused to reverse her decision. . . .

Neither the prosecutors nor the judges were searching very hard for the truth of why the detectives went to the Simpson residence. They apparently thought that the disclosure of that truth would make the proving of what they believed was a more important truth—that the defendant was guilty—more difficult. Thus, some people believe that the search for one truth in a criminal case can be served by tolerating other half-truths and even lies. But I believe the prosecution's decision to call Detectives Vannatter and Fuhrman to the witness stand may have been the final nail in a coffin that had been built even earlier by the police. That costly decision was thoughtlessly made by prosecutors who have become so accustomed to police perjury about searches and seizures that they did not even pause to consider its possible impact on this jury. ■

Chapter 4

Civil Rights

The civil rights movement was one of the central forces in American politics in the second half of the twentieth century. Nearly one hundred years after Abraham Lincoln's Emancipation Proclamation freed the slaves, the United States at last began to address the gross disparities between the promise of racial equality and the reality of racial discrimination.

The legal struggle for racial equality began in the 1930s, continued through the 1940s, and led ultimately to the landmark school desegregation case, *Brown* v. *Board of Education*, decided in 1954. *Brown* (along with its companion case, *Bolling* v. *Sharpe*) overturned the Supreme Court's 1896 decision in *Plessy* v. *Ferguson*, which had upheld "separate but equal" facilities as constitutional. (*Plessy* is selection 4.1; *Brown* and *Bolling* are selections 4.2 and 4.3.)

During the same period, the struggle for racial equality moved to the political arena. The adoption of a civil rights plank in the Democratic party's 1948 platform led thirty-five southern delegates to walk out of the convention, and later six thousand southerners met in a separate convention to nominate J. Strom Thurmond of South Carolina on the so-called Dixiecrat ticket. Also in 1948, President Harry Truman ordered the desegregation of the U.S. armed forces.

The political branches did not really move forward on civil rights until the 1960s. In 1963, President John F. Kennedy proposed major civil rights legislation, although Congress did not act. A series of events in 1963, including police violence in Birmingham, Alabama, and a major march on Washington, D.C., greatly raised the visibility of the movement. The following year, after Kennedy's assassination, President Lyndon B. Johnson pushed through the most important civil rights legislation since the 1860s, the Civil Rights Act of 1964. A year later Congress added the Voting Rights Act of 1965, which at last secured for minorities a meaningful right to vote.

Recent years have seen controversy and divisiveness on civil rights issues. One major area of controversy is affirmative action, which involves race-conscious and race-specific remedies to problems of past and present discrimination. Aspects of the affirmative action debate are discussed in selection 4.4, which presents a rare attempt to find a compromise on the issue.

The civil rights movement gave rise to a number of similar attempts to secure equality to other victims of legal and societal discrimination. One offshoot was the women's rights movement, which successfully persuaded the Supreme Court to extend the equal protection of the law to women. But other minority groups continue to struggle for even the basic protections of the law. Gays and lesbians, for example, still face widespread discrimination, but have had recent success in protecting their rights in court. In 2003, for example, the United States Supreme Court overturned state laws criminalizing homosexual activity, and the following year the Massachusetts Supreme Court struck down state laws banning same-sex marriage. The same-sex marriage issue (selection 4.6) has been particularly controversial, as have questions regarding the appropriate policies to apply to illegal aliens (selection 4.5).

Chapter Questions

1. At the heart of any discussion of civil rights is the meaning of equality. What alternative views on equality are illustrated in the selections in this chapter? How has the meaning of equality changed over the past two hundred years?
2. How have legal conceptions of civil rights changed over the past century? Consider *Plessy*, *Brown*, and the affirmative action controversy.
3. Consider the new questions and problems faced by advocates of civil rights in the 1990s, among them the extension of civil rights to previously unprotected groups, including gays and lesbians and illegal aliens. How do these new struggles compare to the goals and purposes of the original civil rights movement?

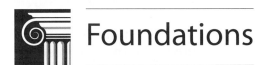 # Foundations

Any discussion of civil rights in the modern era must start with *Brown* v. *Board of Education* (selection 4.2), the 1954 school desegregation case. The impact of *Brown* on race and politics in the United States has been immense. Although *Brown* itself had little effect on school segregation in the Deep South, it set in motion a process that led to the civil rights movement, the Civil Rights Act of 1964, and a host of federal and state programs designed to eliminate and address the effects of racial discrimination.

Brown reversed *Plessy* v. *Ferguson* (selection 4.1), an 1896 case that upheld the segregation of railroad cars in Louisiana. *Brown* based its rejection of *Plessy* on narrow grounds relating to the dangers of segregation in the educational process. In practice, however, the elimination of segregation in public schools led quickly to judicial determinations that virtually all state-sponsored segregation was unconstitutional.

Chief Justice Earl Warren, who wrote the *Brown* opinion, avoided a direct attack on segregation in general; note specifically how his 1954 argument differs from the 1896 dissent of Justice John Marshall Harlan in *Plessy*. Warren's concern was twofold: he sought to ensure that the Court would speak with one voice, believing that an approach such as Harlan's might alienate one or more members of the Court, and he wanted to avoid giving potential critics of the decision a broad target to aim at. His opinion, though criticized by some as insufficiently high-minded, got the job done.

The decision in *Brown* was accompanied by a parallel decision in *Bolling* v. *Sharpe* (selection 4.3), which dealt with segregation in the District of Columbia. Because the

Equal Protection Clause applies to the states and not to the federal government, the Court used the Due Process Clause to strike down segregation in the District.

The first *Brown* decision simply announced that segregated schools were unconstitutional. Implementation of that decision was postponed one year, until 1955, when the Court ordered the federal district courts to implement *Brown* "with all deliberate speed."

Questions

1. Why, in Chief Justice Earl Warren's view, are "separate educational facilities inherently unequal"?
2. Does Justice Harlan's dissent in *Plessy* provide an alternative approach to deciding *Brown*? What are the advantages and disadvantages of this approach?

4.1 *Plessy* v. *Ferguson* (1896)

Justice Henry B. Brown
Justice John Marshall Harlan, dissenting

This case turns upon the constitutionality of an act of the General Assembly of the State of Louisiana, passed in 1890, providing for separate railway carriages for the white and colored races.

• • •

The constitutionality of this act is attacked upon the ground that it conflicts with the Thirteenth Amendment of the Constitution, abolishing slavery, and the Fourteenth Amendment, which prohibits certain restrictive legislation on the part of the States.

1. That it does not conflict with the Thirteenth Amendment, which abolished slavery and involuntary servitude, except as a punishment for crime, is too clear for argument. Slavery implies involuntary servitude—a state of bondage; the ownership of mankind as a chattel, or at least the control of the labor and services of one man for the benefit of another, and the absence of a legal right to the disposal of his own person, property and services. This amendment was said in the *Slaughter-house cases* to have been intended primarily to abolish slavery, as it had been previously known in this country, and that it equally forbade Mexican peonage or the Chinese coolie trade, when they amounted to slavery or involuntary servitude, and that the use of the word "servitude" was intended to prohibit the use of all forms of involuntary slavery, of whatever class or nature. It was intimated, however, in that case that this amendment was regarded by the statesmen of that day as insufficient to protect the colored race from certain laws which had been enacted in the Southern States, imposing upon the colored race onerous disabilities and burdens, and curtailing their rights in the pursuit of life, liberty and

---

163 U.S. 537 (1896).

property to such an extent that their freedom was of little value; and that the Fourteenth Amendment was devised to meet this exigency.

So, too, in the *Civil Rights cases* it was said that the act of a mere individual, the owner of an inn, a public conveyance or place of amusement, refusing accommodations to colored people, cannot be justly regarded as imposing any badge of slavery or servitude upon the applicant, but only as involving an ordinary civil injury, properly cognizable by the laws of the State, and presumably subject to redress by those laws until the contrary appears. "It would be running the slavery argument into the ground," said Mr. Justice Bradley, "to make it apply to every act of discrimination which a person may see fit to make as to the guests he will entertain, or as to the people he will take into his coach or cab or car, or admit to his concert or theatre, or deal with in other matters of intercourse or business."

A statute which implies merely a legal distinction between the white and colored races—a distinction which is founded in the color of the two races, and which must always exist so long as white men are distinguished from the other race by color—has no tendency to destroy the legal equality of the two races, or reestablish a state of involuntary servitude. Indeed, we do not understand that the Thirteenth Amendment is strenuously relied upon by the plaintiff in error in this connection.

2. By the Fourteenth Amendment, all persons born or naturalized in the United States, and subject to the jurisdiction thereof, are made citizens of the United States and of the State wherein they reside; and the States are forbidden from making or enforcing any law which shall abridge the privileges or immunities of citizens of the United States, or shall deprive any person of life, liberty or property without due process of law, or deny to any person within their jurisdiction the equal protection of the laws.

The proper construction of this amendment was first called to the attention of this court in the *Slaughter-house cases*, which involved, however, not a question of race, but one of exclusive privileges. The case did not call for any expression of opinion as to the exact rights it was intended to secure to the colored race, but it was said generally that its main purpose was to establish the citizenship of the negro; to give definitions of citizenship of the United States and of the States, and to protect from the hostile legislation of the States the privileges and immunities of citizens of the United States, as distinguished from those of citizens of the States.

The object of the amendment was undoubtedly to enforce the absolute equality of the two races before the law but in the nature of things it could not have been intended to abolish distinctions based upon color, or to enforce social, as distinguished from political equality, or a commingling of the two races upon terms unsatisfactory to either. Laws permitting, and even requiring, their separation in places where they are liable to be brought into contact do not necessarily imply the inferiority of either race to the other, and have been generally, if not universally, recognized as within the competency of the state legislatures in the exercise of their police power. The most common instance of this is connected with the establishment of separate schools for white and colored children, which has been held to be a valid exercise of the legislative power even by courts of States where the political rights of the colored race have been longest and most earnestly enforced.

• • •

So far, then, as a conflict with the Fourteenth Amendment is concerned, the case reduces itself to the question whether the statute of Louisiana is a reasonable regulation, and with respect to this there must necessarily be a large discretion on the part of the legislature. In determining the question of reasonableness it is at liberty to act with reference to the established usages, customs and traditions of the people, and with a view to the promotion of their comfort, and the preservation of the public peace and good order. Gauged by this standard, we cannot say that a law which authorizes or even requires the separation of the two races in public conveyances is unreasonable, or more obnoxious to the Fourteenth Amendment than the acts of Congress requiring separate schools for colored children in the District of Columbia, the constitutionality of which does not seem to have been questioned, or the corresponding acts of state legislatures.

We consider the underlying fallacy of the plaintiff's argument to consist in the assumption that the enforced separation of the two races stamps the colored race with a badge of inferiority. If this be so, it is not by reason of anything found in the act, but solely because the colored race chooses to put the construction upon it. The argument necessarily assumes that if, as has been more than once the case, and is not unlikely to be so again, the colored race should become the dominant power in the state legislature, and should enact a law in precisely similar terms, it would thereby relegate the white race to an inferior position. We imagine that the white race, at least, would not acquiesce in this assumption. The argument also assumes that social prejudices may be overcome by legislation, and that equal rights cannot be secured to the negro except by an enforced commingling of the two races. We cannot accept this proposition. If the two races are to meet upon terms of social equality, it must be the result of natural affinities, a mutual appreciation of each other's merits and a voluntary consent of individuals. As was said by the Court of Appeals of New York in *People* v. *Gallagher*, "this end can neither be accomplished nor promoted by laws which conflict with the general sentiment of the community upon whom they are designed to operate. When the government, therefore, has secured to each of its citizens equal rights before the law and equal opportunities for improvement and progress, it has accomplished the end for which it was organized and performed all of the functions respecting social advantages with which it is endowed." Legislation is powerless to eradicate racial instincts or to abolish distinctions based upon physical differences, and the attempt to do so can only result in accentuating the difficulties of the present situation. If the civil and political rights of both races be equal one cannot be inferior to the other civilly or politically. If one race be inferior to the other socially, the Constitution of the United States cannot put them upon the same place.

• • •

Mr. Justice Harlan dissenting.

By the Louisiana statute, the validity of which is here involved, all railway companies (other than street railroad companies) carrying passengers in that State are required to have separate but equal accommodations for white and colored persons, "by providing two or more passenger coaches for each passenger train, *or* by dividing the passenger coaches by a *partition* so as to secure separate accommodations." Under this statute, no colored person is permitted to occupy a seat in a coach assigned to white persons; nor any white person, to occupy a seat in a coach assigned to colored persons. The managers of the railroad are not allowed to exercise any discretion in the premises, but are required to assign each passenger to some coach or compartment set apart for the exclusive use of his race. If a passenger insists upon going into a coach or compartment not set apart for persons of his race, he is subject to be fined, or to be imprisoned in the parish jail. Penalties are prescribed for the refusal or neglect of the officers, directors, conductors and employees of railroad companies to comply with the provisions of the act.

• • •

In respect of civil rights, common to all citizens, the Constitution of the United States does not, I think, permit any public authority to know the race of those entitled to be protected in the enjoyment of such rights. Every true man has pride of race, and under appropriate circumstances when the rights of others, his equals before the law, are not to be affected, it is his privilege to express such pride and to take such action based upon it as to him seems proper. But I deny that any legislative body or judicial tribunal may have regard to the race of citizens when the civil rights of those citizens are involved. Indeed, such legislation, as that here in question, is inconsistent not only with that equality of rights which pertains to citizenship, National and State, but with the personal liberty enjoyed by every one within the United States.

• • •

The white race deems itself to be the dominant race in this country. And so it is, in prestige, in achievements, in education, in wealth and power. So, I doubt not, it will continue to be for all time, if it remains true to its great heritage and holds fast in the principles of constitutional liberty. But in view of the Constitution, in the eye of the law, there is in this country no superior, dominant, ruling class of citizens. There is no caste here. Our Constitution is color-blind, and neither knows nor tolerates classes among citizens. In respect of civil rights, all citizens are equal before the law. The humblest is the peer of the most powerful. The law regards man as man, and takes no account of his surroundings or of his color when his civil rights as guaranteed by the supreme law of the land are involved. It is, therefore, to be regretted that this high tribunal, the final expositor of the fundamental law of the land, has reached the conclusion that it is competent for a State to regulate the enjoyment by citizens of their civil rights solely upon the basis of race. ■

4.2 *Brown v. Board of Education* (1954)

Chief Justice Earl Warren

M r. Chief Justice Warren delivered the opinion of the Court.
These cases come to us from the States of Kansas, South Carolina, Virginia, and Delaware. They are premised on different facts and different local conditions, but a common legal question justifies their consideration together in this consolidated opinion.

In each of the cases, minors of the Negro race, through their legal representatives, seek the aid of the courts in obtaining admission to the public schools of the community on a nonsegregated basis. In each instance, they had been denied admission to schools attended by white children under laws requiring or permitting segregation according to race. This segregation was alleged to deprive the plaintiffs of the equal protection of the laws under the Fourteenth Amendment. In each of the cases other than the Delaware case, a three-judge federal district court denied relief to the plaintiffs on the so-called "separate but equal" doctrine announced by this Court in *Plessy* v. *Ferguson*. Under that doctrine, equality of treatment is accorded when the races are provided substantially equal facilities, even though these facilities be separate. In the Delaware case, the Supreme Court of Delaware adhered to that doctrine, but ordered that the plaintiffs be admitted to the white schools because of their superiority to the Negro schools.

The plaintiffs contend that segregated public schools are not "equal" and cannot be made "equal," and that hence they are deprived of the equal protection of the laws. Because of the obvious importance of the question presented, the Court took jurisdiction. Argument was heard in the 1952 Term, and reargument was heard this Term on certain questions propounded by the Court.

Reargument was largely devoted to the circumstances surrounding the adoption of the Fourteenth Amendment in 1868. It covered exhaustively consideration of the Amendment in Congress, ratification by the states, then existing practices in racial segregation, and the views of proponents and opponents of the Amendment. This discussion and our own investigation convince us that, although these sources cast some light, it is not enough to resolve the problem with which we are faced. At best, they are inconclusive. The most avid proponents of the post-War Amendments undoubtedly intended them to remove all legal distinctions among "all persons born or naturalized in the United States." Their opponents, just as certainly, were antagonistic to both the letter and the spirit of the Amendments and wished them to have the most limited effect. What others in Congress and the state legislatures had in mind cannot be determined with any degree of certainty.

An additional reason for the inconclusive nature of the Amendment's history, with respect to segregated schools, is the status of public education at that time. In the South, the movement toward free common schools, supported by general

347 U.S. 483 (1954).

taxation, had not yet taken hold. Education of white children was largely in the hands of private groups. Education of Negroes was almost nonexistent, and practically all of the race were illiterate. In fact, any education of Negroes was forbidden by law in some states. Today, in contrast, many Negroes have achieved outstanding success in the arts and sciences as well as in the business and professional world. It is true that public school education at the time of the Amendment had advanced further in the North, but the effect of the Amendment on Northern States was generally ignored in the congressional debates. Even in the North, the conditions of public education did not approximate those existing today. The curriculum was usually rudimentary; ungraded schools were common in rural areas; the school term was but three months a year in many states; and compulsory school attendance was virtually unknown. As a consequence, it is not surprising that there should be so little in the history of the Fourteenth Amendment relating to its intended effect on public education.

In the first cases in this Court construing the Fourteenth Amendment, decided shortly after its adoption, the Court interpreted it as proscribing all state-imposed discriminations against the Negro race. The doctrine of "separate but equal" did not make its appearance in this Court until 1896 in the case of *Plessy* v. *Ferguson*, involving not education but transportation. American courts have since labored with the doctrine for over half a century. In this Court, there have been six cases involving the "separate but equal" doctrine in the field of public education. In *Cumming* v. *County Board of Education* and *Gong Lum* v. *Rice* the validity of the doctrine itself was not challenged. In more recent cases, all on the graduate school level, inequality was found in that specific benefits enjoyed by white students were denied to Negro students of the same educational qualifications. In none of these cases was it necessary to re-examine the doctrine to grant relief to the Negro plaintiff. And in *Sweatt* v. *Painter*, the Court expressly reserved decision on the question whether *Plessy* v. *Ferguson* should be held inapplicable to public education.

In the instant cases, that question is directly presented. Here, unlike *Sweatt* v. *Painter*, there are findings below that the Negro and white schools involved have been equalized, or are being equalized, with respect to buildings, curricula, qualifications and salaries of teachers, and other "tangible" factors. Our decision, therefore, cannot turn on merely a comparison of these tangible factors in the Negro and white schools involved in each of the cases. We must look instead to the effect of segregation itself on public education.

In approaching this problem, we cannot turn the clock back to 1868 when the Amendment was adopted, or even to 1896 when *Plessy* v. *Ferguson* was written. We must consider public education in the light of its full development and its present place in American life throughout the Nation. Only in this way can it be determined if segregation in public schools deprives these plaintiffs of the equal protection of the laws.

Today, education is perhaps the most important function of state and local governments. Compulsory school attendance laws and the great expenditures for education both demonstrate our recognition of the importance of education to our democratic society. It is required in the performance of our most basic public responsibilities, even service in the armed forces. It is the very foundation of good citizenship. Today it is a principal instrument in awakening the child to cultural values, in preparing him for later professional training, and in helping him to adjust normally to his environment. In these days, it is doubtful that any child may reasonably be expected to succeed in life if he is denied the opportunity of an education. Such an opportunity, where the state has undertaken to provide it, is a right which must be made available to all on equal terms.

We come then to the question presented: Does segregation of children in public schools solely on the basis of race, even though the physical facilities and other "tangible" factors may be equal, deprive the children of the minority group of equal educational opportunities? We believe that it does.

In *Sweatt* v. *Painter*, in finding that a segregated law school for Negroes could not provide them equal educational opportunities, this Court relied in large part on "those qualities which are incapable of objective measurement but which make for greatness in a law school." In *McLaurin* v. *Oklahoma State Regents*, the Court, in requiring that a Negro admitted to a white graduate school be treated like all other students, again resorted to intangible considerations: ". . . his ability to study, to engage in discussions and exchange views with other students, and, in general, to learn his profession." Such considerations apply with added force to children in grade and high schools. To separate them from others of similar age and qualifications solely because of their race generates a feeling of inferiority as to their status in the community that may affect their hearts and minds in a way unlikely ever to be undone. The effect of this separation on their educational opportunities was well stated by a finding in the Kansas case by a court which nevertheless felt compelled to rule against the Negro plaintiffs:

> Segregation of white and colored children in public schools has a detrimental effect upon the colored children. The impact is greater when it has the sanction of the law; for the policy of separating the races is usually interpreted as denoting the inferiority of the negro group. A sense of inferiority affects the motivation of a child to learn. Segregation with the sanction of law, therefore, has a tendency to [retard] the educational and mental development of negro children and to deprive them of some of the benefits they would receive in a racial[ly] integrated school system.

Whatever may have been the extent of psychological knowledge at the time of *Plessy* v. *Ferguson*, this finding is amply supported by modern authority.* Any language in *Plessy* v. *Ferguson* contrary to this finding is rejected.

We conclude that in the field of public education the doctrine of "separate but equal" has no place. Separate educational facilities are inherently unequal. Therefore, we hold that the plaintiffs and others similarly situated for whom the actions have been brought are, by reason of the segregation complained of, deprived of the equal protection of the laws guaranteed by the Fourteenth Amendment. This

---

*[This footnote, number 11 in the original, has become famous. It is frequently referred to simply as "footnote 11."] K. B. Clark, Effect of Prejudice and Discrimination on Personality Development (Midcentury White House Conference on Children and Youth, 1950); Witmer and Kotinsky, Personality in the Making (1952), c. VI; Deutscher and Chein, The Psychological Effects of Enforced Segregation: A Survey of Social Science Opinion, 26 J. Psychol 259 (1948); Chein, What Are the Psychological Effects of Segregation Under Conditions of Equal Facilities?, 3 Int. J. Opinion and Attitude Res. 229 (1949); Brameld, Educational Costs, in Discrimination and National Welfare (MacIver, ed., 1949), 44–48; Frazier, The Negro in the United States (1949), 674–681. And see generally Myrdal, An American Dilemma (1944).

disposition makes unnecessary any discussion whether such segregation also violates the Due Process Clause of the Fourteenth Amendment.

Because these are class actions, because of the wide applicability of this decision, and because of the great variety of local conditions, the formulation of decrees in these cases presents problems of considerable complexity. On reargument, the consideration of appropriate relief was necessarily subordinated to the primary question—the constitutionality of segregation in public education. We have now announced that such segregation is a denial of the equal protection of the laws. In order that we may have the full assistance of the parties in formulating decrees, the cases will be restored to the docket, and the parties are requested to present further argument on Questions 4 and 5 previously propounded by the Court for the reargument this Term. The Attorney General of the United States is again invited to participate. The Attorneys General of the states requiring or permitting segregation in public education will also be permitted to appear as *amici curiae* upon request to do so by September 15, 1954, and submission of briefs by October 1, 1954.

It is so ordered. ∎

4.3 *Bolling* v. *Sharpe* (1954)

Chief Justice Earl Warren

M r. Chief Justice Warren delivered the opinion of the Court.
This case challenges the validity of segregation in the public schools of the District of Columbia. The petitioners, minors of the Negro race, allege that such segregation deprives them of due process of law under the Fifth Amendment. They were refused admission to a public school attended by white children solely because of their race. They sought the aid of the District Court for the District of Columbia in obtaining admission. That court dismissed their complaint. The Court granted a writ of certiorari before judgment in the Court of Appeals because of the importance of the constitutional question presented.

We have this day held that the Equal Protection Clause of the Fourteenth Amendment prohibits the states from maintaining racially segregated public schools. The legal problem in the District of Columbia is somewhat different, however. The Fifth Amendment, which is applicable in the District of Columbia, does not contain an equal protection clause as does the Fourteenth Amendment which applies only to the states. But the concepts of equal protection and due process, both stemming from our American ideal of fairness, are not mutually exclusive. The "equal protection of the laws" is a more explicit safeguard of prohibited unfairness than "due process of law," and, therefore, we do not imply that the two are always interchangeable phrases. But, as this Court has recognized, discrimination may be so unjustifiable as to be violative of due process.

Classifications based solely upon race must be scrutinized with particular care, since they are contrary to our traditions and hence constitutionally suspect. As

347 U.S. 497 (1954).

long ago as 1896, this Court declared the principle "that the Constitution of the United States, in its present form, forbids, so far as civil and political rights are concerned, discrimination by the General Government, or by the States, against any citizen because of his race." And in *Buchanan* v. *Warley*, the Court held that a statute which limited the right of a property owner to convey his property to a person of another race was, as an unreasonable discrimination, a denial of due process of law.

Although the Court has not assumed to define "liberty" with any great precision, that term is not confined to mere freedom from bodily restraint. Liberty under law extends to the full range of conduct which the individual is free to pursue, and it cannot be restricted except for a proper governmental objective. Segregation in public education is not reasonably related to any proper governmental objective, and thus it imposes on Negro children of the District of Columbia a burden that constitutes an arbitrary deprivation of their liberty in violation of the Due Process Clause.

In view of our decision that the Constitution prohibits the states from maintaining racially segregated public schools, it would be unthinkable that the same Constitution would impose a lesser duty on the Federal Government. We hold that racial segregation in the public schools of the District of Columbia is a denial of the due process of law guaranteed by the Fifth Amendment to the Constitution.

It is so ordered. ■

 # American Politics Today

Few areas of law and social policy have been as controversial in recent years as that of affirmative action. Such programs give preferences to women or members of minority groups in competition for jobs, education, or other valuable resources. Defenders of affirmative action claim that only such preferences can compensate for past discrimination, ensure diversity in the classroom and the workplace, and ensure a level playing field for current and future generations. Opponents object to affirmative action because it allows or requires individuals to be judged on the basis of characteristics such as race or gender instead of on their merits as individuals.

Neither side, as political scientist Peter H. Schuck suggests in this selection, has a monopoly on the truth. So rather than choose between them, Schuck suggests a compromise. Under his proposal, the government would not participate in affirmative action programs, but it would allow private corporations or universities to do so. Such an approach would recognize the need for government neutrality while allowing private actors the freedom to act as they see fit.

Question

1. Why, in Schuck's view, should the government be held to a different standard than private actors when it comes to affirmative action? Is his distinction between public and private affirmative action convincing?

4.4 Affirmative Action: Don't Mend or End It—Bend It (2002)

Peter H. Schuck

Affirmative action policy—by which I mean ethnoracial preferences in the allocation of socially valuable resources—is even more divisive and unsettled today than at its inception more than 30 years ago.

Affirmative action's policy context has changed dramatically since 1970. One change is legal. Since the Supreme Court's 1978 Bakke decision, when Justice Lewis Powell's pivotal fifth vote endorsed certain "diversity"-based preferences in higher education, the Court has made it increasingly difficult for affirmative action plans to pass constitutional muster unless they are carefully designed to remedy specific past acts of discrimination. Four other changes [provide evidence of] the triumph of the nondiscrimination principle: blacks' large social gains; evidence on the size, beneficiaries, and consequences of preferences; and new demographic realities—persuade me that affirmative action as we know it should be abandoned even if it is held to be constitutional.

"As we know it" is the essential qualifier in that sentence. I propose neither a wholesale ban on affirmative action ("ending" it) nor tweaks in its administration ("mending" it). Rather, I would make two structural changes to curtail existing preferences while strengthening the remaining ones' claim to justice. First, affirmative action would be banned in the public sector but allowed in the private sector. Second, private-sector institutions that use preferences would be required to disclose how and why they do so. These reforms would allow the use of preferences by private institutions that believe in them enough to disclose and defend them, while doing away with the obfuscation, duplicity, and lack of accountability that too often accompany preferences. Affirmative action could thus be localized and customized to suit the varying requirements of particular contexts and sponsors.

This is excerpted and adapted from Peter H. Schuck, *Diversity in America: Keeping Government at a Safe Distance* (Harvard University Press, 2003), chap. 5. Reprinted by permission of the author.

Triumph of the Nondiscrimination Principle

Why is change necessary? To explain, one must at the outset distinguish affirmative action entailing preferences from nondiscrimination, a principle that simply requires one to refrain from treating people differently because of their race, ethnicity, or other protected characteristics. Although this distinction can blur at the edges, it is clear and vital both in politics and in principle.

When affirmative action became federal policy in the late 1960s, the nondiscrimination principle, though fragile, was gaining strength. Preferences, by contrast, were flatly rejected by civil rights leaders like Hubert Humphrey, Ted Kennedy, and Martin Luther King, Jr. In the three decades that followed, more and more Americans came to embrace nondiscrimination and to oppose affirmative action, yet as John Skrentny shows in his *Ironies of Affirmative Action*, federal bureaucrats extended affirmative action with little public notice or debate. Today, nondiscrimination, or equal opportunity, is a principle questioned by only a few bigots and extreme libertarians, and civil rights law is far-reaching and remedially robust. In contrast, affirmative action is widely seen as a demand for favoritism or even equal outcomes.

Social Gains by Blacks

Blacks, the intended beneficiaries of affirmative action, are no longer the insular minority they were in the 1960s. Harvard sociologist Orlando Patterson shows their "astonishing" progress on almost every front. "A mere 13% of the population," he notes, "Afro-Americans dominate the nation's popular culture. . . . [A]t least 35 percent of Afro-American adult, male workers are solidly middle class." The income of young, intact black families approaches that of demographically similar whites. On almost every other social index (residential integration is a laggard), the black-white gap is narrowing significantly; indeed, the income gap for young black women has disappeared.

Even these comparisons understate black progress. Much of racism's cruel legacy is permanently impounded in the low education and income levels of older blacks who grew up under Jim Crow; their economic disadvantages pull down the averages, obscuring the gains of their far better-educated children and grandchildren. These gains, moreover, have coincided with the arrival of record numbers of immigrants who are competing with blacks. To ignore this factor, economist Robert Lerner says, is like analyzing inequality trends in Germany since 1990 without noting that it had absorbed an entire impoverished country, East Germany. In addition, comparisons that fail to age-adjust social statistics obscure the fact that blacks, whose average age is much lower than that of whites, are less likely to have reached their peak earning years.

My point, emphatically, is not that blacks have achieved social equality—far from it—but that the situation facing them today is altogether different than it was when affirmative action was adopted. Advocates, of course, say that this progress just proves that affirmative action is effective; hence it should be continued or even increased. But this post hoc ergo propter hoc reasoning is fallacious and ignores the policy's growing incoherence and injustice.

Size, Beneficiaries, and Consequences of Preferences

When we weigh competing claims for scarce resources—jobs, admission to higher education, public and private contracts, broadcast or other spectrum licenses, credit, housing, and the like—how heavy is the thumb that affirmative action places on the scales? This is a crucial question. The larger the preference, the more it conflicts with competing interests and values, especially the ideal of merit—almost regardless of how one defines merit.

The best data concern higher education admissions where (for better or for worse) schools commonly use standardized test scores as a proxy for aptitude, preparation, and achievement. William Bowen and Derek Bok, the former presidents of Princeton and Harvard, published a study in 1999 based largely on the academic records of more than 80,000 students who entered 28 highly selective institutions in three different years. Affirmative action, they claimed, only applies to these institutions, although a more recent study suggests that the practice now extends to some second- and even third-tier schools.

Selective institutions, of course, take other factors into account besides race. Indeed, some whites who are admitted have worse academic credentials than the blacks admitted under preferences. Still, Bowen and Bok find a difference of almost 200 points in the average SAT scores of the black and white applicants, and even this understates the group difference. First, the deficit for black applicants' high school grade point average (GPA), the other main admission criterion, is even larger. Thomas Kane finds that black applicants to selective schools "enjoy an advantage equivalent to an increase of two thirds of a point in [GPA]—on a four-point scale—or [the equivalent of] 400 points on the SAT." Second, although the SAT is often criticized as culturally biased against blacks, SAT (and GPA) scores at every level actually overpredict their college performance. Third, the odds were approximately even that black applicants with scores between 1100 and 1199 would be admitted, whereas the odds for whites did not reach that level until they had scores in the 1450–1499 range. With a score of 1500 or above, more than a third of whites were rejected while every single black gained admission. The University of Michigan, whose affirmative action program is detailed in a pending lawsuit, weighs race even more heavily than the average school in the Bowen and Bok sample. At Michigan, being black, Hispanic, or Native American gives one the equivalent of a full point of GPA; minority status can override any SAT score deficit. And a recent study of 47 public institutions found that the odds of a black student being admitted compared to a white student with the same SAT and GPA were 173 to 1 at Michigan and 177 to 1 at North Carolina State.

These preferences, then, are not merely tie-breakers; they are huge—and they continue at the graduate and professional school levels. It is encouraging that an identical share (56 percent) of black and white graduates of the institutions in the Bowen and Bok sample earned graduate degrees; the share of blacks earning professional or doctoral degrees was actually slightly higher than for whites (40 percent vs. 37 percent). But black students' college grades and postgraduate test scores are so much lower on average that their admission to these programs, disproportionately at top-tier institutions, also depends on affirmative action. In the early 1990s, for example, only a few dozen of the 420 blacks admitted to the 18 most selective law schools would have been admitted absent affirmative action. A high percentage of these schools' black graduates eventually pass the bar examination, but some 22 percent of blacks from these schools who take the exam never pass it (compared with 3 percent of whites), and only 61 percent of blacks pass it the first time compared with 92 percent of whites. Blacks who enter the professions do enjoy solid status, income, civic participation and leadership, and career satisfaction. But this hardly makes the case for affirmative action, for the higher-scoring applicants whom they displaced would presumably have done at least as well.

How much of blacks' impressive gains is due to reduced discrimination resulting from changing white attitudes and civil rights enforcement, as distinct from preferences? How would they have fared had they attended the somewhat less prestigious schools they could have attended without preferences? What would the demographics of higher education be without those preferences? We cannot answer these vital questions conclusively. We know that black gains were substantial even before preferences were adopted, that preference beneficiaries are overwhelmingly from middle- and upper-class families, and that most black leaders in all walks of life did not go to elite universities. We also know that many institutions are so committed to affirmative action that they will find ways to prefer favored groups—minorities, legacies, athletes, and others—no matter what the formal rules say. Although California voters banned affirmative action in state programs, their politicians press the university system to jigger the admission criteria until it finds a formula that can skirt the ban and produce the "correct" number of the favored minorities (excluding Asians, who are thought not to need the help).

New Demographic Realities

The moral case for affirmative action rests on the bitter legacy of black slavery, Jim Crow, and the violent dispossession of Native Americans. Yet the descendants of slaves and Native Americans constitute a shrinking share of affirmative action's beneficiaries. Political logrolling has extended preferential treatment to the largest immigrant group, Hispanics, as well as to blacks from Africa, the Caribbean, and elsewhere, Asians and Pacific Islanders, and in some programs to women, a majority group.

Some affirmative action advocates acknowledge this problem and want to fix it. Orlando Patterson, for example, would exclude "first-generation persons of African ancestry" but not "their children and later generations . . . in light of the persistence of racist discrimination in America." He would also exclude all Hispanics except for Puerto Ricans and Mexican Americans of second or later generations and would exclude "all Asians except Chinese-Americans descended from pre-1923 immigrants. . . ." With due respect for Patterson's path-breaking work on race, his formula resembles a tax code provision governing depreciation expenses more than a workable formula for promoting social justice.

Centuries of immigration and intermarriage have rendered the conventional racial categories ever more meaningless. The number of Americans who consider themselves multiracial and who wish to be identified as such (if they must be racially identified at all) was 7 million in the 2000 census, including nearly 2 million blacks

(5 percent of the black population) and 37 percent of all Native Americans. This is why advocacy groups who are desperate to retain the demographic status quo lobbied furiously to preempt a multiracial category.

In perhaps the most grimly ironic aspect of the new demographic dispensation, the government adopted something like the one-drop rule that helped enslave mulattos and self-identifying whites before Emancipation. Under OMB's [Office of Management and Budget] rules, any response combining one minority race and the white race must be allocated to the minority race. This, although 25 percent of those in the United States who describe themselves as both black and white consider themselves white, as do almost half of Asian-white people and more than 80 percent of Indian-white people. The lesson is clear: making our social policy pivot on the standard racial categories is both illogical and politically unsustainable.

Alternatives

Even a remote possibility that eliminating affirmative action would resegregate our society deeply distresses almost all Americans. Nothing else can explain the persistence of a policy that, contrary to basic American values, distributes valuable social resources according to skin color and surname. But to say that we must choose between perpetuating affirmative action and eliminating it entirely is false. To be sure, most suggested reforms—using social class or economic disadvantage rather than race, choosing among minimally qualified students by lottery, and making preferences temporary—are impracticable or would make matters worse. Limiting affirmative action to the descendants of slaves and Native Americans would minimize some objections to the policy but, as Patterson's proposal suggests, would be tricky to implement and would still violate the nondiscrimination and merit principles.

Most Americans who favor affirmative action would probably concede that it fails to treat the underlying problem. Black applicants will continue to have worse academic credentials until they can attend better primary and secondary schools and receive the remediation they need. A root cause of their disadvantage is inferior schooling, and affirmative action is simply a poultice. We must often deal with symptoms rather than root causes because we do not know how to eliminate them, or consider it too costly to do so, or cannot muster the necessary political will. If we know which social or educational reforms can substantially improve low-income children's academic performance, then we should by all means adopt them. But this does not mean that we should preserve affirmative action until we can eliminate the root causes of inequality.

I propose instead that we treat governmental, legally mandated preferences differently than private, voluntary ones. While prohibiting the former (except in the narrow remedial context approved by the Supreme Court), I would permit the latter—but only under certain conditions discussed below. A liberal society committed to freedom and private autonomy has good reasons to maintain this difference; racial preferences imposed by law are pernicious in ways that private ones are not. To affirmative action advocates, it is a Catch-22 to bar the benign use of race now after having used it against minorities for centuries. But to most Americans (including many minorities), affirmative action is not benign. It is not [a] Catch-22 to recognize what history teaches—that race is perhaps the worst imaginable category around which to organize political and social relations. The social changes I have described only reinforce this lesson. A public law that affirms our common values should renounce the distributive use of race, not perpetuate it.

There are other differences between public and private affirmative action. A private preference speaks for and binds only those who adopt it and only for as long as they retain it. It does not serve, as public law should, as a social ideal. As I explained in *The Limits of Law: Essays on Democratic Governance* (2000), legal rules tend to be cruder, more simplistic, slower to develop, and less contextualized than voluntary ones, which are tailored to more specific needs and situations. Legal rules reflect interest group politics or the vagaries of judicial decision; voluntary ones reflect the chooser's own assessment of private benefits and costs. Legal rules are more difficult to reform, abandon, or escape. Voluntary ones can assume more diverse forms than mandated ones, a diversity that facilitates social learning and problem solving.

Still, many who believe in nondiscrimination and merit and who conscientiously weigh the competing values still support affirmative action. If a private university chooses to sacrifice some level of academic performance to gain greater racial diversity and whatever educational or other values it thinks diversity will bring, I cannot say—nor should the law say—that its choice is impermissible. Because even private affirmative action violates the nondiscrimination principle, however, I would permit it only on two conditions: transparency and protection of minorities. First, the preference—its criteria, weights, and reasons—must be fully disclosed. If it cannot withstand public criticism, it should be scrapped. The goal is to discipline preferences by forcing institutions to reveal their value choices. This will trigger market, reputational, and other informal mechanisms that make them bear more of the policy's costs rather than just shifting them surreptitiously to non-preferred applicants, as they do now. Second, private affirmative action must not disadvantage a group to which the Constitution affords heightened protection. A preference favoring whites, for example, would violate this condition.

The Commitment to Legal Equality

For better and for worse, American culture remains highly individualistic in its values and premises, even at some sacrifice (where sacrifice is necessary) to its goal of substantive equality. The illiberal strands in our tangled history that enslaved, excluded, and subordinated individuals as members of racial groups should chasten our efforts to use race as a distributive criterion. Affirmative action in its current form, however well-intended, violates the distinctive, deeply engrained cultural and moral commitments to legal equality, private autonomy, and enhanced opportunity that have served Americans well—even though they have not yet served all of us equally well. ■

Issue and Controversy

The immigration issue has generated controversy in the United States for nearly two centuries. Prejudice against Irish immigrants in the 1840s and 1850s, for example, led to the rise of the "Know-Nothing" party, a short-lived political movement fueled by religious and ethnic prejudice. In the 1880s, federal law suspended immigration from China, and in the 1920s Congress put sweeping restrictions on the number of new immigrants who could be admitted to the United States.

Despite these periodic episodes, America has long been a nation of immigrants. Millions of Americans take pride in their ethnic heritage and in their immigrant ancestors. The museum at Ellis Island in New York harbor—where over 12 million new immigrants first arrived in the United States—has become a major tourist attraction.

In the past few years, controversy over immigration has centered on two issues: the influx of illegal immigrants, especially from Mexico and Latin America, and the problem of border security, especially in the post-9/11 era. Concern over both economic competition and potential terrorist threats has fueled a new wave of anti-immigration sentiment and led to fierce debates over both state and federal policy. President George W. Bush's effort to provide legal status to millions of undocumented aliens created deep splits both within the Republican party and between Republicans and Democrats.

In this selection, reporter John B. Judis visits America's southern border to report on the meaning and impact of the new immigration controversy.

Questions

1. "Among many Arizonans," writes Judis—and presumably for many other Americans concerned about the immigration issue—"the most important issues are cultural." What is the nature of these cultural issues? What are the implications of this cultural side of the immigration debate?
2. Does the civil rights movement provide lessons or guidance that could be helpful in resolving the immigration debate? Why or why not?

4.5 Border War (2006)

John B. Judis

A battered yellow school bus rumbles up a bumpy dirt road on the outskirts of Sasabe, a small Mexican town just over the border from Arizona. At the top of the hill, the bus winds around brick and mud huts. Ragged children stand in the doorways, and emaciated dogs forage for scraps. The bus passes

From John B. Judis, "Border War," *The New Republic* 234 (January 16, 2006), pp. 15–19. Reprinted by permission of *The New Republic,* © 2006, The New Republic, LLC.

dented pickups and old cars without wheels and stops in a dusty clearing, where it disgorges about 40 teenagers dressed in blue jeans and carrying small knapsacks. One boy's T-shirt features a picture of Che Guevara. A girl's pale blue top says ADORABLE in sequined letters. They are subdued, almost expressionless. They mill around, waiting for the *coyotes*, or smugglers, who, for a hefty fee, will take them in pickup trucks to the border.

There, they will climb through holes in the barbed wire fence separating Mexico from the United States. Some will not make it through the 100-plus-degree Arizona desert on the other side (from October 2004 to October 2005, 261 would-be migrants died in the desert before reaching Tucson or Phoenix) and about one-third of them will be apprehended by the U.S. Border Patrol. But, over the course of a year, almost two million will make it, sometimes after several tries, and enter the underworld of undocumented migrants: working on farms, as day-laborers in construction, as servants and maids, or in sweatshops and meatpacking plants. Unable to protest mistreatment, they will be subject to abuse and exploitation, but most of them will still fare better than if they had stayed in their native villages.

This influx of migrants into Arizona—and the fact that many stay in the state rather than moving north or west—has created a political explosion. In November 2004, anti-immigration activists won a bruising campaign to pass Proposition 200, which denies "public benefits" to people who can't prove their citizenship, despite the opposition of the state's congressional delegation, including Republican Senators John McCain and Jon Kyl; Democratic Governor Janet Napolitano; and major business groups and labor unions. Last spring, the Minuteman Project, which George W. Bush wrote off as a group of "vigilantes," set up shop in Tombstone, near the border, to dramatize the failure of the Border Patrol to prevent "illegals" from getting through. Republican state legislators, equally hostile to McCain and Napolitano, are trying to expand Proposition 200 and plan to make illegal immigration the focus of the 2006 elections. "We are ground zero" in the battle over immigration, warns former Arizona House Majority Whip Randy Graf, who spearheaded the campaign for Proposition 200 and is now running for the Tucson area House seat to be vacated by Representative Jim Kolbe.

The furor over illegal immigration is sweeping the country—from California and Washington to Virginia and Tennessee, and even up to Vermont, New Hampshire, and Minnesota—but Arizona is indeed ground zero, having surpassed neighboring states as the principal gateway to the United States for illegal immigrants from Mexico and Central America. Beltway politicians who want to clamp down on the border claim this furor is the result, as Colorado Republican Representative Tom Tancredo has suggested, of immigrants "taking jobs that Americans could take." And many Americans far from the Arizona border certainly believe that— in low-immigration West Virginia, for example, 60 percent of respondents in a recent poll agreed that "immigrants take jobs away from Americans." But that's not what's happening in Arizona's citrus groves or hotels or restaurants. And, in Arizona, those who are most up in arms over illegal immigration are far more concerned with its sociocultural than its economic effects. They are worried about what is commonly called the "Mexicanization" of Arizona. That kind of cultural concern extends to legal as well as illegal immigrants—and it can't be easily fixed by legislation.

Mexicans began crossing the border to Arizona in the early twentieth century to work in "the five Cs"—construction, copper, citrus, cattle, and cotton—but, until recently, the great majority of illegal immigrants came through California and Texas. In 1990, for example, about 90 percent entered through those two states, while only about 5 percent came through Arizona. But, as the uproar over "illegals" grew—in 1994, for example, California passed Proposition 187, denying public benefits to undocumented workers—the Border Patrol instituted Operation Gatekeeper in California and Operation Hold-the-Line in Texas. These programs reduced illegal immigration to those states, but not overall. Instead, illegal immigrants were simply diverted to Arizona's desert border, and, between October 2004 and October 2005, about half of the four million illegal immigrants who entered the United States came through Arizona. According to Princeton University sociologist Douglas Massey, about 1.5 million of them crossed the eastern part of the Arizona border, south of Tucson, and about 470,000 entered through the area around Yuma, near the California border.

Going through the desert is far more dangerous than walking over a bridge into a Texas or California border town or even fording the Rio Grande. And it's more expensive, too. But Mexicans and other Latinos are willing to pay the *coyotes*, because they hope to find well-paying jobs in the United States. And, relative to where they came from, they will. In 2000, according to the U.S. Department of Agriculture (USDA), a farm worker in Mexico could expect to make $3.60 in an eight-hour day, while his counterpart in the United States made $66.32 in the same period. The discrepancy has increased since the North American Free Trade Agreement (NAFTA) went into effect in 1994, removing tariff barriers on the importation of U.S. farm products and decimating small farmers in Mexico. Says Sandra Polaski, a trade expert at the Carnegie Endowment for International Peace, "Small farmers who produced for subsistence but also for the market lost their market access." According to the USDA, Mexican farm income fell 4.3 percent per year during the 1990s. Young men and women left in search of work, and, while some of them found jobs in U.S. factories on the border (*maquiladoras*), many of them crossed the border in search of better-paying jobs.

Most of those who make it do find jobs—92 percent of males, according to one estimate. And, with undocumented workers adding to the normal population increase, Arizona's Latino population has ballooned, going from 19 percent in 1990 to 25 percent in 2000. Phoenix, which was once a primarily Anglo town, has gone from 20 percent to about 34 percent Latino. Says former Arizona Attorney General Grant Woods, one of the state's prominent Republicans, "When I was in the first grade in 1960, Phoenix was the same distance from the border. Phoenix now feels much more like a border town than it did even ten years ago. Billboards in Spanish, a lot of people speaking Spanish. Most of us think this is great, but a lot don't." This transformation in Arizona society and culture, along with the disorder created by the dramatic rise in border-crossings, has made immigration the biggest issue in Arizona politics.

• • •

"Instead of asking what are the top three issues, . . . [says Wes Gullett, a political consultant and a key adviser to John McCain], we have to ask what are the top four, because the first three are immigration. You have to ask, 'What do you care about other than immigration?' It's crazy down there."

But what, exactly, is this craziness about? In Washington, politicians and political organizations regularly attribute the obsession with immigration to illegal migrants taking the jobs of native-born Americans. Tancredo makes that claim, and so do the two leading groups advocating restrictions on immigration, the Federation for American Immigration Reform (FAIR), which bankrolled Proposition 200, and the Center for Immigration Studies. That did happen in Midwestern meatpacking plants several decades ago, and it may still be happening in some parts of the country, but it does not seem to be the case in Arizona, where unemployment hovers below 5 percent and where construction, agriculture, and tourism are plagued by acute labor shortages. Illegal immigration doesn't even seem to be having a dramatic effect on wages, with pay for unskilled work in Arizona regularly exceeding the minimum wage.

Unskilled workers currently make up 32 percent of Arizona's labor force, and they are constantly in demand. Tom Nassif of Western Growers, a trade association, recently complained that the construction industry was "siphoning off" the migrant workers that growers needed in the field. "Farms will not have enough workers to harvest their crops," he warned. Meanwhile, Arizona's tourist industry says it can't find enough workers for its hotels and restaurants. Bobby Surber, the vice president of Sedona Center, who runs three restaurants, two shopping plazas, and a resort, and employs 200 people, says, "Even though we pay larger than average, and full medical and dental, we cannot find enough employees."

Of course, Arizonans could still believe, just as Americans in West Virginia do, that illegal immigrants threaten their jobs. And pollsters invite this response by always asking about the economic effect of immigration and refraining from raising uncomfortable cultural concerns. But, in interviewing Arizonans, one rarely encounters complaints about illegal immigrants taking jobs away. One does hear about the cost of state services for illegal immigrants. Indeed, even the Latinos who voted for Proposition 200 were worried about the burden that illegal immigrants were placing on schools and hospitals. And, in border towns, crime and disorder are pressing issues. (Some of the *coyotes* double as drug smugglers, and the migrants traipse through farms and ranches.) But, among many Arizonans, the most important issues are cultural. They fret about "Mexicanization"—about Arizona becoming a "Third World country" or "the next Mexifornia."

In interviews I conducted last fall, leaders of the movement to restrict immigration usually began by expressing concerns that illegal immigration was undermining the rule of law and allowing terrorists to sneak across the border—concerns they seem to believe are most likely to win over a national audience. But they invariably became most animated, and most candid, when talking about what they see as the unwillingness of Mexican immigrants—legal or illegal—to assimilate into American culture.

Connie, who doesn't want her last name used for fear of retaliation from immigration advocates, was one of the first members of the Minutemen. She lives in Sierra Vista, a small retirement town near the border. Barely five feet tall, with short, graying hair, she prides herself on her feistiness. She is now in charge of patrolling the Nacos area near the border. She says that, at night, she and her husband station themselves on a hill in view of the fence and watch for "illegals." She says that she became interested in the Minutemen because the organization was upholding the rule of law and keeping out terrorists. "We have many apprehensions of Pakistanis and Iraqis on the border. They are coming in disguised as Hispanics and blending in," she says. (When I ask a human rights worker in Sasabe if he had heard of Iraqis entering the United States disguised as Latinos, he laughs. "The [Mexican] army is very watchful about that kind of thing," he says.)

Connie insists that the Minutemen are neither "extremist" nor "racist," but, as we ride along the border in her Ford Navigator, Connie voices distinctly cultural and racial concerns. She says that the illegals she sees coming across the border are the "darker" Mexicans. Mexican President Vicente Fox, she says, "doesn't want them in the country." She speculates that Mexicans might want to take over Arizona: "In Mexico, they are taught this land was taken from them. They are not taught they were paid tons of money for it. There is a belief they want this back." (After defeating the Mexican army in 1848, the United States bought all of California and the Southwest from Mexico for $15 million.) When I comment that California has remained in good shape despite massive immigration, she takes exception. "California is not a shining example," she says. "You have the Chinese, the Vietnamese, the Russians, all these people immigrating. How many languages do you have to have on the ballot?" Asked if she would support McCain's proposal to allow Mexicans to enter the country legally as guest workers, Connie demurs. "Who is going to pay for it?" she asks. "When my grandmother came from Czechoslovakia, one thing she did was assimilate. She was proud to be an American. Their attitude is, 'We won't assimilate.'"

That's what bothers Graf as well. "We are talking about assimilation," says the congressional candidate, as we sit in his East Tucson campaign headquarters. "I don't have any problem about anyone who wants to salute our flag and learn our language and be a citizen. What got me into the whole issue was that I was standing in line in a Safeway, and this woman was ahead of me, and she had an infant, and was pregnant, and her mother was with her. She was paying for groceries in food stamps. And, when the clerk asked for her signature, she acted like she didn't understand English, and neither did her mother. I found it odd that an entire family could be here on welfare and not speak any English. On welfare!"

Graf's chief ally is Pearce, who lives in the Phoenix suburb of Mesa. Last fall, he complained to a reporter from *Stateline.org* about his hometown: "It's not the Mesa I was raised in. They have turned it into a Third World country," he said. By "they," Pearce means Latinos in general. On his website, he warns, "Over 800,000 Americans fled California last year because LA became a clone of Mexico City." Pearce, like Connie and Graf, envisages a cultural conflict between the white America he grew up in and an invading army of dark-skinned, Spanish-speaking immigrants from south of the border.

Ray Borane, the longtime Democratic mayor of Douglas, a border town in Cochise County, laments that Graf "represents the majority opinion" in the state. That may be an exaggeration, given Napolitano's and McCain's continued popularity, but Graf and his angry allies do represent a significant segment of voters—perhaps one-third or more—who are up in arms. And longtime observers of Arizona politics confirm that a concern with Mexicanization lies at the heart of their opposition to illegal immigration. "Nobody is afraid of jobs," says Gullett, the Mc-Cain adviser. "We have got labor demand. That's not a problem. There is no feeling that people are losing their jobs. There is a tremendous fear that our community and our way of life is changing." Dave Wagner, the former political editor of *The Arizona Republic*, who is writing a book about Arizona politics, says that, in Phoenix, "Mexicans and Mexican-Americans have their own culture and stores. It is possible if you are Spanish-speaking to disappear into that culture. That scares the hell out of some people." Says Woods: "Arizona has changed dramatically in the last 20 years, and a lot of people are uncomfortable with that."

• • •

Arizonans on both sides of the controversy are looking to Washington for solutions. They know that states can't pass their own guest-worker programs; nor can they police their own borders. But there is little chance that the Bush administration and Republicans in Congress—sharply divided between social conservatives and business interests—will be able to pass legislation. . . . And, even if the House, the Senate, and the White House could agree on an approach, it would not end the furor over immigration.

[In 2006], conservatives in the House, led by Tancredo and Wisconsin Representative James Sensenbrenner, passed a punitive bill that would erect new walls along the border, make illegal immigration a felony, and require employers to weed out illegal workers by checking their immigration status against a national database. In the Senate, McCain and Massachusetts Democrat Edward Kennedy introduced a bill that is backed by business and by some labor groups. It would let migrant workers obtain renewable three-year visas and allow undocumented workers already in the country to stay provided they pay a fine. McCain and Kennedy probably can't get their bill through the Senate—too many Republicans fear being tagged as proponents of "amnesty" for illegal immigrants—but they could certainly muster enough votes to prevent the Senate from passing a version of the House bill.

In the past, Bush has leaned toward McCain's approach—the president encouraged McCain after the 2004 election to seek Kennedy's support for a bill—but he has recently attempted to appease social conservatives, praising the House's measures to "protect our borders and crack down on the illegal entry into the United States." Bush holds out hope for a Senate bill that would somehow combine McCain's approach with Tancredo's. But that's unlikely to happen.

Even if Congress were to adopt one of these approaches—or a combination of the two—it would not quiet the controversy. Punitive approaches have either had unintended consequences (for instance, encouraging illegal immigrants to stay in the United States rather than return to Mexico) or have proved unenforceable. Border Patrol spending has increased over 1,000 percent since 1986 without reducing border-crossings. McCain and Kennedy's approach is far better, acknowledging the inescapable reality of Latino immigration and its net benefit to the U.S. economy. But granting amnesty to undocumented workers, and inviting new workers in, will not satisfy Americans who are offended by the growing presence—legal or illegal—of Latinos in their midst. And combining the two proposals would more or less reproduce the Immigration Reform and Control Act of 1986, which

hiked border spending, threatened employer penalties, granted amnesty to undocumented workers, *and* led to almost two decades of clamor over immigration.

That furor will not abate until at least one of two conditions is met. The first is a
dramatic generational change in the cultural attitudes of non-Latino Americans—
meaning the acceptance of biculturalism in large parts of the United States, including Arizona. Frank Pierson, the supervising organizer of Arizona's Valley In-
terfaith Network, a coalition of church and labor groups that promotes cultural
integration, wants Arizonans to adopt the biblical tradition of showing "love for
the stranger." But non-Latino Americans probably have to reach a point where
they no longer see immigrants from south of the border as strangers at all.

The other condition is a change in the unequal economic relationship between
the United States and its neighbors to the south, which would reduce the supply of
unskilled laborers seeking jobs in the United States. Such a change could probably
only occur if the United States were to assume the same responsibility toward
Mexico and Central America that the more prosperous nations of Western Europe
did toward Spain, Greece, and Portugal when they wanted to enter the European
Union—granting them aid, along with protection of their industries and agriculture, over a transitional period.

But neither condition is likely to be met in the near future. Americans are not
ready to embrace the teenagers who gathered in Sasabe as their own, and U.S.
business is not ready to see Mexico and Central America as anything other than a
platform for exports and investment. As a result, the conflict over Latino immigration will continue. And, if what's happening on the Arizona border is any gauge,
that's not something to look forward to. ■

 # View from the Inside

Over the past two decades, issues involving gay and lesbian rights have moved to the
forefront of the civil rights struggle. In the early 1990s, controversy focused on the question of gays in the military; the result was a compromise—known as "Don't Ask, Don't
Tell"—which seemed to please neither side. In 2003, gay and lesbian rights groups
scored a major victory when they persuaded the United States Supreme Court to invalidate state laws criminalizing private, consensual homosexual activity. Such laws, concluded Justice Anthony Kennedy for a narrow majority, further "no legitimate state interest which can justify" the state's "intrusion into the personal and private life of the
individual." *

In the late 1990s, attention turned briefly to so-called civil unions, which formalize
the relationship between two men or two women but which do not constitute a legal
marriage. Vermont enacted legislation recognizing such unions in 2000, but the movement never gathered strength. Instead, it was eclipsed by the much more controversial
question of same-sex marriage.

Lawrence v. Texas, 539 U.S. 558 (2003), at 578.

The same-sex marriage issue gained national attention in 2003, when the Massachusetts Supreme Judicial Court ruled in *Goodridge* v. *Department of Public Health* that same-sex marriages were permitted under the state constitution. *Goodridge* produced an immediate backlash; same-sex marriage became a contentious issue in the 2004 elections, and many states passed laws reaffirming the traditional definition of marriage as between a man and a woman.

The following selection examines the same-sex marriage issue from the perspective of those most directly involved—clergy, gay rights activists, and the couples themselves. Ironically, Hillary and Julie Goodridge, who were among the first gay couples to be married in Massachusetts in 2004—and who lent their name to the landmark case—separated in 2006.*

Questions

1. How did the *Goodridge* case impact the debate over gay and lesbian rights? In what ways did the decision advance the cause of gay and lesbian rights? In what ways did it hurt the cause?
2. One journalist interviewed in this selection suggests that "any group that is fighting for its own rights will win in the end." Do you agree or disagree? Why or why not?

4.6 "We Do" (2004)

Neil Miller

W hen Hillary Goodridge was a student at Dartmouth College in the 1970s and first "coming out" as a lesbian, the last thing she thought about was same-sex marriage. She saw herself as a lesbian separatist and an enemy of anything that smacked of traditional institutions. Back then, the issues that engaged her were the anti-nuclear and anti-apartheid movements. At one political rally, a 20-year-old Goodridge got up and shouted fiercely, "Marriage is a patriarchal institution!"

But as the years passed, Goodridge's life underwent significant changes. She became involved in a long-term relationship with Julie, her partner for the past seventeen years. She left New Hampshire and eventually moved to Boston, where she currently serves as program director of the Unitarian Universalist Funding Panel. Eight years ago, Julie gave birth to their daughter Annie. (Hillary, Julie, and Annie share the same surname, which they adopted just before Annie was born.)

*Katie Zezima, "Same Sex Marriage Plaintiffs Separate," *New York Times* (July 22, 2006): 11.

Originally published as "We Do" by Neil Miller, *UU World* 18:3 (May/June 2004). Abridged and reprinted with the permission of the author and *UU World*, the magazine of the Unitarian Universalist Association, www. uuworld.org.

Annie's birth provided them with their first real encounter with the consequences of not being legally married. After problems developed following a planned Caesarian birth, Annie was rushed to the neonatal intensive-care ward. But when Hillary tried to see her, she was told she wasn't allowed. Hospital staff also barred her from visiting Julie in the post-op room. That wouldn't have been the case if they had been legal spouses. "It was really jarring," she recalls.

Three years ago, Hillary and then-five-year-old Annie were discussing love and were naming various couples they knew who were married. Annie asked why she and Julie weren't married. "You don't love each other," Annie said. "If you loved each other, you'd be married!"

Since then, both her mothers have been working hard to remedy the situation. In March 2001, they marched into Boston City Hall to apply for a marriage license.

"Where's the groom?" the clerk asked.

"We're two brides," replied the Goodridges, glowingly, although they knew the outcome from the start.

The clerk told them they needed two grooms.

But the two women were determined to keep faith with Annie. The following month, they took the issue to court, joining six other couples as plaintiffs in the landmark case *Goodridge v. Massachusetts Department of Public Health* challenging Massachusetts laws restricting same-sex couples from marrying. . . . On November 18, 2003, the state's highest court ruled by a 4–3 majority that "barring a person from the protections, benefits, and obligations of civil marriage solely because that person would marry a person of the same sex violates the Massachusetts constitution.". . .

The decision made Massachusetts the first state in the union to grant gays and lesbians full-fledged marriage rights, joining the Netherlands, Belgium, and the Canadian provinces of Ontario and British Columbia. In the months that followed, same-sex marriage seemed to be sweeping like a brushfire across the country. Gay and lesbian couples were camping out overnight and lining up in the rain in front of San Francisco City Hall for marriage licenses. A tiny county north of Albuquerque, New Mexico, handed out twenty-six same-sex marriage licenses before the state invalidated them. The mayor of New Paltz, New York, began officiating same-sex weddings without issuing licenses and faces nineteen misdemeanor charges as a result.

At the same time, the sudden possibility of same-sex marriage created a formidable backlash. Massachusetts legislators narrowly gave preliminary approval to a state constitutional amendment that would allow civil union status for same-sex couples but deny them the right to marry. . . . Ohio's governor signed a bill banning same-sex unions in his state, making Ohio the thirty-eighth state that explicitly bans same-sex marriage. In March [2004], President George W. Bush announced he favored amending the United States Constitution to ban same-sex marriage. Some Republican political strategists sensed a "wedge" issue with which to attack Democrats in the November election. And the religious right saw a crusade against same-sex marriage as a way to revive its political fortunes.

Yet a renewed culture war pitting conservative Christians against the aspirations of same-sex couples appears unlikely to reverse a very real march of progress. Even though same-sex marriage isn't on the legal horizon in most states anytime soon, American culture has come a very long way since the Stonewall riots that launched the gay movement thirty-five years ago.

The current cultural moment has not emerged from a vacuum. The attention of most heterosexual Americans—with perhaps the exception of the religious right—was focused on other matters. But notable shifts within the lives of people like Hillary Goodridge, within the lesbian, gay, bisexual, and transgender (LGBT) community, and within the larger society have prepared the way for the national focus on same-sex marriage. . . . Within the LGBT population, the transformation can be seen as the personal and political maturing of an entire community. At the same time, the larger society has shown increased toleration, if not acceptance, of gays and lesbians. As the two trends have come together, much of the country has witnessed the growing visibility and mainstreaming of the gay and lesbian community, an assimilation into the very core of American life that parallels the path of various ethnic minorities.

The growing acceptance of gays and lesbians in mainstream culture seemed particularly evident [in the] summer and fall [of 2003]. During a period of a few months, the U.S. Supreme Court overturned state sodomy laws, the Canadian province of Ontario granted marriage rights to same-sex couples, the Episcopal Church elected the Rev. V. Gene Robinson as its first openly gay bishop, and millions of Americans were glued to TV shows like *Queer Eye for the Straight Guy*. In the wake of all this came the Massachusetts court decision. For advocates for gay rights, 2003 indeed seemed like a breakthrough year.

"Four years in the gay movement is like twenty-eight years in the rest of society," says E. J. Graff, author of the Beacon Press book *What Is Marriage For?* "We're living in dog time."

In the early years of the gay rights movement, sexual liberation was the dominant concern for many gay men; at the same time, large numbers of lesbians, strongly influenced by the women's movement, focused on building their own community around feminist and anti-patriarchal values. For most gay men, marriage wasn't on their radar screen; for most lesbians, like Hillary Goodridge, marriage seemed inimical to the egalitarian new world they were trying to create.

But as the generation that came of age in the tumultuous and heady years of the 1960s got older, it found itself with radically changing needs. By the mid-to-late 1980s, AIDS was ravaging the gay male community, undercutting the sexual liberation ethos that had sustained many gay men; as a result, many men began focusing on long-term relationships. Among lesbians in the late 1980s, as the separatist ideology lost much of its power and women felt they had more personal and economic choices—and, in many cases, were approaching the end of their childbearing years—a "baby boom" emerged. More and more, gays and lesbians were living lives very much like their heterosexual neighbors. Truth be told, many had always been doing so.

"The main factors that have led us where we are today are AIDS and the maturation of the core population of LGBT people who are politically attuned and motivated," says Sue Hyde, New England field organizer for the National Gay and Lesbian Task Force. "Our needs for equality have changed as we become older and more settled and become parents." Hyde notes that, of the 594,000 cohabiting same-sex couples who identified as such on the 2000 United States census, 34 percent of lesbian and 22 percent of gay male couples had children under 18 at home.

Hyde says that activists now in their forties and fifties remain at the forefront of the gay rights movement today. So, not surprisingly, *their* issues—focused on relationships, family issues, and children—have taken center stage. Hillary Goodridge, now 47, says, "Having kids gives you a fierce, very primal feeling around protection of your family that I didn't realize before. I feel protective about my partner Julie, but it is my daughter Annie who brings out a ferocity."

"The formation of families is so different today than in the '60s and '70s," says Rob Compton, who, along with his partner, was one of the plaintiffs in the Massachusetts case. "At that time, if you wanted to have kids, the only option was a traditional family. Many gay people ignored their gay side for that reason. But in the past few years, so many of our gay friends have adopted children. It is really amazing." Compton himself was married to a woman for many years in order to have the kind of family he wanted. Compton, 54, and his partner, David Wilson, 59, have been together for seven years. Between them, they have five children from previous heterosexual marriages, and six grandchildren.

As the gay and lesbian communities came to look more and more like mainstream America, society also began seeing homosexuality in a new light. Although many early responses to the AIDS epidemic portrayed gay men as sources of contagion, the epidemic also prompted a much wider and more compassionate depiction of homosexuality in the media. More gay men and lesbians came out of the closet, organizing community-based AIDS service organizations and agitating for greater government action. The AIDS Quilt was first displayed at the second gay and lesbian march on Washington, D.C., in 1987 and generated tremendous sympathy and support. "The quilt was a significant turning point," Hyde says. It changed the "you got what you deserved" approach to AIDS to a more sympathetic view of gay people, emphasizing the grief of an entire community.

At the same time, gay and lesbian family issues were gaining attention politically. Various cities passed domestic partnership ordinances that offered health and insurance benefits to partners of gay and lesbian municipal employees. In 1992, Vermont became the first state in the union to approve domestic partnership benefits for same-sex partners of state workers. A variety of companies, notably in the health-care and high-tech industries, began to include same-sex partners in their benefits packages. The decisions of Vermont and Massachusetts courts to legalize second-parent and step-parent adoption by a same-sex partner helped lay the legal groundwork for the later civil union and same-sex marriage decisions in those states.

Despite these shifts, it took time for the idea of same-sex marriage to take hold, especially in urban gay communities. When I traveled around the country researching my book *In Search of Gay America*, published in 1989, I was surprised at the number of gay and lesbian couples I met who had been "married" or "joined in holy union"—sometimes in Unitarian Universalist congregations but primarily in churches that ministered specifically to the gay community, like the Metropolitan Community Church. Same-sex marriage, I wrote, was "a phenomenon rarely found in larger cities, perhaps because the pressure to fit in is not as strong there."

It was the election of Bill Clinton as president in 1992 that marked the first major social shift on gay issues, ushering in a period E. J. Graff calls the "big thaw." Promising "I have a vision and you're part of it," the Arkansas governor actively sought the gay vote in his campaign for president. Once elected, Clinton announced he would issue an executive order ending the U.S. military's ban on gays and lesbians serving in the military. After an intense national debate the Clinton administration retreated, instituting the "Don't Ask, Don't Tell" policy.

Despite the outcome, the discussion focused attention on gay issues as never before. Gay subjects emerged dramatically in literature, theater, and movies, culminating in Tom Hanks' Oscar for his role as a gay lawyer with AIDS in the film *Philadelphia*. Unprecedented visibility humanized a previously ignored and despised group of people. On April 25,1993, hundreds of thousands of gays and lesbians came to the District of Columbia for the Third Lesbian and Gay March on Washington.

Not surprisingly, gays in the military was the major issue of that April 1993 march. But the march marked the first time that same-sex marriage gained some notice, as well. On the day before the march, the Rev. Troy Perry, founder of the Metropolitan Community Church, married 2,000 gay couples in a ceremony on the steps of the Internal Revenue Service building. Although the event was largely obscured by the march itself, for those who participated it was a transforming occasion.

"I remember going down the escalators to catch the Metro to the IRS," recalls Aleta Fenceroy of Omaha, who married her partner Jean Mayberry at that ceremony, "and the whole subway tunnel burst out with people singing 'Going to the Chapel.' It was one of those moments that still gives me goose bumps when I think of it." Later that day, she and Mayberry walked around Dupont Circle with wreaths of flowers in their hair, receiving the congratulations of strangers.

That year, same-sex marriage became a public issue for the first time—and provoked a major public backlash. The Hawaii Supreme Court ruled that the denial of marriage licenses to three same-sex couples represented discrimination on the basis of sex. The state legislature moved quickly to define marriage as only between a man and a woman; five years later, in a hard-fought referendum, almost 70 percent of Hawaii voters passed a constitutional amendment ratifying the legislature's decision. In the years following the Hawaii ruling, thirty-eight states and the federal government passed legislation defining marriage exclusively as a heterosexual province.

For gay activists, Hawaii was a crushing defeat, but for a brief, shining moment, same-sex marriage suddenly seemed possible to millions of gay Americans. Gradually, a subject that had been near the bottom of the gay agenda began to move towards the top. And, E. J. Graff says, in the period following "the big thaw" the "silent majority" of gay people in much of the country were finally able to be more public about their sexual orientation without fear of losing jobs and family.

"They are the ones who were raising kids, who were taking care of their elderly mom upstairs," Graff says. "They are no longer making the 'devil's bargain'—'I live like I'm gay but I don't say it.' They suddenly had a voice. They want to get married, and they want to get married for the same reason their brothers and sisters do." Although division still exists within the gay and lesbian communities over the push for marriage—with some still expressing reservations about having the state define their relationships—same-sex marriage became a grass-roots issue, one that directly touched the lives of gay people, as few issues had before.

And then in 1999 came an event more momentous in terms of the legal recognition of gay couples than anything that had occurred before. In December of that year, the Vermont Supreme Court ruled that the exclusion of same-sex couples from the benefits granted to married people violated the state constitution. A year later, after a highly contentious political debate, Vermont adopted the nation's first civil unions law, granting same-sex couples the same state rights as married couples in terms of probate, medical benefits, child custody, and inheritance. Civil unions might have been "separate but equal" but they were a giant step forward.

The outcome spurred Hillary and Julie Goodridge, Rob Compton and David Wilson, and five other couples into action in Massachusetts, along with the Boston-based legal organization, Gay and Lesbian Advocates and Defenders, which had played a key role in the Vermont decision. If they could say "I do" in Vermont, why not in Massachusetts? And, this time, they were determined, full-fledged same-sex marriage would be the result.

• • •

If you look at American society today, you see a landscape unimaginable twenty-five or even ten years ago—a country where network and cable TV shows feature witty and appealing gay and lesbian characters (Ellen DeGeneres, the openly lesbian comic whose sitcom character came out to much controversy in 1998, has reinvented herself as one of the most popular daytime TV talk show hosts), where thousands of same-sex couples walk around with marriage licenses authorized by the city of San Francisco and by Multnomah County, Oregon, and where thousands of others in Massachusetts plan their weddings.

But the social and political landscape is complicated as well, with wide differences in attitudes towards homosexuality among regions, generations, religious groups, and urban and rural areas. Reality TV shows or sitcoms like *Will and Grace* that depict gays and lesbians in a positive light may open people's eyes a bit, but not everyone has been watching—or marching in lockstep. As political organizer Hyde points out, "To imagine [that] *Queer Eye for the Straight Guy* or a show about finding a boyfriend will generate fundamental political change is magical thinking."

And, in every poll, Americans remain solidly opposed to the legalization of same-sex marriage, in some cases by two-to-one majorities. The numbers of support have moved only slightly in the past ten years, often falling during periods of backlash. Even a *New York Times*/CBS poll last July, which showed that 54 percent of Americans favored legalizing "homosexual relations," revealed strong opposition to same-sex marriage.

Alan Wolfe, director of the Boisi Center for Religion and Public Life at Boston College, argues that while society is increasingly tolerant towards gays and lesbians, tolerance only goes so far. "Americans support the right to privacy," he says. "They will look the other way. But if it is a public phenomenon, which marriage is, people see it as 'in your face.' They don't like the idea, in spite of the overwhelming acceptance of homosexuality." He adds that "the sea change in our culture—at least on TV—hasn't extended to same-sex marriage. Marriage is still viewed as a sacred event that has to do with raising children."

Since the Massachusetts court decision, civil unions—once a radical position that nearly caused the state of Vermont to explode into civil strife—emerged as a "moderate" compromise for many voters and politicians in that state. All the Democratic candidates in the 2004 presidential race supported civil unions, and former senator Carol Mosely Braun, Rep. Dennis Kucinich, and the Rev. Al Sharpton endorsed full same-sex marriage rights.

Chris Bull, who has been covering politics for the past ten years as Washington correspondent for the gay biweekly newsmagazine *The Advocate*, is equally doubtful that the Massachusetts court decision represents where the rest of the country is going—at least right now. In Massachusetts, Bull says, many years of activism and social change laid the groundwork on gay and lesbian issues. The state enacted a gay antidiscrimination law in 1989 (the third in the country after Wisconsin and New Hampshire) and under the liberal Republican Governor William Weld enacted legislation protecting the rights of gay high school students, a national first. A later court decision allowed second-parent adoption by same-sex partners.

"Massachusetts is more like Canada than it is like the rest of the country," Bull says. "The state has a liberal population, the once-powerful Catholic church is under siege, there is no religious right to speak of. Those conditions have hardly been created in few other states. They haven't filtered down to the rest of the electorate."

He suspects what we'll see in the rest of the country is a "patchwork approach," with a few liberal-minded states perhaps legalizing same-sex marriage, and some states banning it outright. Bull argues that various states have to go through battles over gay nondiscrimination bills first, and undergo a ten-year cycle of "desensitization" on a variety of gay issues before they can cope with such a difficult issue as same-sex marriage. "Those states who have gone through the cycle already are ready for it," he believes.

In some places the national controversy over same-sex marriage can make it harder to take those initial steps, as recent events bear out in Sioux City, Iowa, a town of 70,000 in the northwest part of the state. Six years ago the city council narrowly defeated an effort to add "sexual orientation" to the city's civil rights ordinance. This year, the Human Rights Commission proposed that the council take up the issue again. Some local gays and lesbians worried that the controversy over same-sex marriage would make it harder to change the city ordinance. "Everything that is happening in San Francisco could hurt our effort here," cautioned Connie Jones, a Sioux City lesbian. "This marriage thing is coming so quickly. I'm afraid that people will be more reactive." She was right. In late February, the city council rejected gay employment and housing protections by a 4–1 vote, with same-sex marriage a heated subject of discussion.

In Omaha, the nearest major urban area, the view is a little different, at least within the gay and lesbian community. Aleta Fenceroy, who was married at the March on Washington in 1993, sees a "pent-up euphoria" among gays and lesbians there, even though the state's constitution bars the recognition of same-sex marriages. "The reality of what nonrecognition means will happen at a later date," says Fenceroy. "Right now people are caught up in me euphoria."

Fenceroy seems to have caught the wave herself: She admits that she and her partner "considered hopping on a plane" to go to San Francisco to get a marriage license. But they thought better of it, especially since they already consider themselves married. "It would be fun to do a legal ceremony," she says. "But unless it is recognized in Nebraska, it isn't essential."

Despite the current backlash, journalist Bull believes that in the long run acceptance of same-sex marriage nationwide is simply inevitable. There may be a lag time, but it will happen eventually, as indicated by polls that show younger voters generally in favor of extending marriage rights. "People dip their foot into the water [of equality] and pull it out," Bull says. "Then they go back into the water. Maybe they are in the process of pulling it out now. But they'll go back again." More importantly, he argues, any group that is fighting for its own rights will win in the end. "They will be more vigilant than those against."

In the end, beyond politics, beyond social changes and social movements, a greater force may help to transform the landscape. "The real push towards marriage isn't financial or legal," says author Graff. "That is the easiest way to argue it, of course. But the ordinary Jane and Joe Homo, the 'silent majority,' they want to do this because they fall in love and marriage is an expression of love. The real oomph of the movement comes from this—people fall in love and want to get married!" And love may just be unstoppable. ■

Chapter 5

Political Culture and Public Opinion

Political culture and public opinion are closely interrelated. Both refer to the beliefs, values, and ideas held by the people of a nation. But there is a key difference: political culture involves beliefs, values, and ideas that are deeply held and widely shared, whereas public opinion focuses on the people's views on a wide range of issues and controversies. Thus public opinion may change from moment to moment, while a nation's political culture may remain remarkably stable over time—even over many generations.

In modern times, public opinion is weighed and measured on an ongoing basis, primarily through the use of public opinion polls. Many such polls are conducted by news organizations; others are carried out by academic researchers, commercial polling firms, or political organizations and campaigns. Polls can be manipulated or mismanaged, of course, but on the whole they provide an accurate snapshot of Americans' views on a variety of subjects.

By contrast, American political culture is notoriously difficult to measure. Pronouncements on the subject are likely to be filled with assumptions and overgeneralizations, and often neglect minority viewpoints and subcultures. Used judiciously, however, political culture is an important concept that can provide keen insights into the nature of American society and politics.

Because we are immersed in our own political culture, Americans may have difficulty even seeing that we have an identifiable and common set of beliefs about government and politics. Perhaps the best way to understand American political culture, therefore, is to see ourselves through the eyes of people from other cultures.

The most noteworthy foreign observer of American politics in our history was Alexis de Tocqueville (selection 5.1). Tocqueville visited the United States in the 1830s and, like many other observers of the American scene, was struck by the American commitment to equality, liberty, participation in politics, and religion. To this day, visitors to the United States often remark on the informal, easy manner in which Americans relate to one another, on our deep-seated religiosity, and—at least until recently—on our passion for politics. We are, in a word, a *democratic* society—not only in politics but also in our attitudes toward public and private life. Our underlying belief in democracy and all it connotes forms an essential part of the American polity.

This chapter examines several different aspects of political culture and public opinion in the United States. In addition to an excerpt from Tocqueville, the chapter presents a challenge to the common assumption that America is divided by a "culture war" (selection 5.2); a study that subdivides the American public into twelve different cultural and political groups (selection 5.3); an analysis of the advantages and disadvantages of public opinion polls (selection 5.4); and a look at how the Bush administration uses public opinion polling data (selection 5.5). Throughout this chapter, the common theme is to explore the underlying beliefs and values upon which the American political system rests.

Chapter Questions

1. What attitudes and assumptions about politics are distinctly "American"—that is, seem to be widely held by most Americans no matter what their background or political affiliation? How do these attitudes and assumptions differ from those of other nations?
2. How have American political culture and Americans' political beliefs changed since Tocqueville visited 170 years ago? Since the 1960s? Since the early 1990s? Are these changes permanent and fundamental, or fleeting and insignificant? Why do you think so?

 # Foundations

Alexis de Tocqueville, a French nobleman, traveled to the United States in 1831 to study and report back to the French government on the American prison system. As a result of his nine-month trip, he produced not only a report on the prison system but also *Democracy in America*, which, published in 1835, was immediately hailed as a masterpiece of political and social commentary. It remains one of the most important books ever written about American political life. (Tocqueville, incidentally, was accompanied on his trip by his friend Gustave de Beaumont, who also wrote a book on America. It was a novel about a slave woman in Baltimore, titled *Marie*, or *Slavery in the United States*.)

Although he wrote more than 170 years ago, Tocqueville's keen observations of life in the United States offer insights into American political culture that are still valid. The following excerpt highlights the nature of American democracy and the centrality of equality to Americans' understanding of politics.

Questions

1. To what extent is American politics today still based on the idea of equality? Consider not only questions of legal or political equality but also questions of social equality.
2. What examples from modern life support Tocqueville's views on the nature of American democracy? What examples contradict his analysis?

5.1 Democracy in America (1835)

Alexis de Tocqueville

Social Condition of the Anglo-Americans

A social condition is commonly the result of circumstances, sometimes of laws, oftener still of these two causes united; but wherever it exists, it may justly be considered as the source of almost all the laws, the usages, and the ideas, which regulate the conduct of nations: whatever it does not produce, it modifies.

It is, therefore, necessary, if we would become acquainted with the legislation and the manners of a nation, to begin by the study of its social condition.

The Striking Characteristic of the Social Condition of the Anglo-Americans Is Its Essential Democracy

Many important observations suggest themselves upon the social condition of the Anglo-Americans; but there is one which takes precedence of all the rest. The social condition of the Americans is eminently democratic; this was its character at the foundation of the colonies, and is still more strongly marked at the present day.

[Great] equality existed among the emigrants who settled on the shores of New England. The germ of aristocracy was never planted in that part of the Union. The only influence which obtained there was that of intellect; the people were used to reverence certain names as the emblems of knowledge and virtue. Some of their fellow-citizens acquired a power over the rest which might truly have been called aristocratic, if it had been capable of invariable transmission from father to son.

This was the state of things to the east of the Hudson: to the southwest of that river, and in the direction of the Floridas, the case was different. In most of the states situated to the southwest of the Hudson some great English proprietors had settled, who had imported with them aristocratic principles and the English law of descent. I have explained the reasons why it was impossible ever to establish a powerful aristocracy in America; these reasons existed with less force to the southwest of the Hudson. In the south, one man, aided by slaves, could cultivate a great extent of country: it was therefore common to see rich landed proprietors. But their influence was not altogether aristocratic as that term is understood in Europe, since they possessed no privileges; and the cultivation of their estates being carried on by slaves, they had no tenants depending on them, and consequently no patronage. Still, the great proprietors south of the Hudson constituted a superior class, having ideas and tastes of its own, and forming the center of political action. This kind of aristocracy sympathized with the body of the people, whose passions and interests it easily embraced; but it was too weak and too short-lived to excite either love or hatred for itself. This was the class which headed the insurrection in the south, and furnished the best leaders of the American revolution.

At the period of which we are now speaking, society was shaken to its center: the people, in whose name the struggle had taken place, conceived the desire of exercising the authority which it had acquired; its democratic tendencies were awakened; and having thrown off the yoke of the mother-country, it aspired to independence of every kind. The influence of individuals gradually ceased to be felt, and custom and law united together to produce the same result.

But the law of descent was the last step to equality. I am surprised that ancient and modern jurists have not attributed to this law a greater influence on human affairs. It is true that these laws belong to civil affairs: but they ought nevertheless to be placed at the head of all political institutions; for, while political laws are only the symbol of a nation's condition, they exercise an incredible influence upon its social state. They have, moreover, a sure and uniform manner of operating upon society, affecting, as it were, generations yet unborn.

Through their means man acquires a kind of preternatural power over the future lot of his fellow-creatures. When the legislator has once regulated the law of inheritance, he may rest from his labor. The machine once put in motion will go on for ages, and advance, as if self-guided, toward a given point. When framed in a particular manner, this law unites, draws together, and vests property and power in a few hands: its tendency is clearly aristocratic. On opposite principles its action is still more rapid; it divides, distributes, and disperses both property and power. Alarmed by the rapidity of its progress, those who despair of arresting its motion endeavor to obstruct by difficulties and impediments; they vainly seek to counteract its effect by contrary efforts: but it gradually reduces or destroys every obstacle, until by its incessant activity the bulwarks of the influence of wealth are ground down to the fine and shifting sand which is the basis of democracy. When the law of inheritance permits, still more when it decrees, the equal division of a father's property among all his children, its effects are of two kinds: it is important to distinguish them from each other, although they tend to the same end.

In virtue of the law of partible inheritance, the death of every proprietor brings about a kind of revolution in property: not only do his possessions change hands, but their very nature is altered; since they are parcelled into shares, which become smaller and smaller at each division. This is the direct, and, as it were, the physical effect of the law. It follows, then, that in countries where equality of inheritance is established by law, property, and especially landed property, must have a tendency to perpetual diminution. The effects, however, of such legislation would only be perceptible after a lapse of time, if the law was abandoned to its own working; for supposing a family to consist of two children (and in a country peopled as France is, the average number is not above three), these children, sharing among them the fortune of both parents, would not be poorer than their father or mother.

But the law of equal division exercises its influence not merely upon the property itself, but it affects the minds of the heirs, and brings their passions into play. These indirect consequences tend powerfully to the destruction of large fortunes, and especially of large domains.

Among the nations whose law of descent is founded upon the right of primogeniture, landed estates often pass from generation to generation without undergoing division. The consequence of which is, that family feeling is to a certain degree incorporated with the estate. The family represents the estate, the estate the family; whose name, together with its origin, its glory, its power, and its virtues, is thus perpetuated in an imperishable memorial of the past, and a sure pledge of the future.

When the equal partition of property is established by law, the intimate connection is destroyed between family feeling and the preservation of the paternal estate; the property ceases to represent the family; for, as it must inevitably be divided after one or two generations, it has evidently a constant tendency to diminish, and must in the end be completely dispersed. The sons of the great landed proprietor, if they are few in number, or if fortune befriend them, may indeed entertain the hope of being as wealthy as their father, but not that of possessing the same property as he did; their riches must necessarily be composed of elements different from his.

Now, from the moment when you divest the land-owner of that interest in the preservation of his estate which he derives from association, from tradition, and from family pride, you may be certain that sooner or later he will dispose of it; for there is a strong pecuniary interest in favor of selling, as floating capital produces higher interest than real property, and is more readily available to gratify the passions of the moment.

Great landed estates which have once been divided, never come together again; for the small proprietor draws from his land a better revenue in proportion, than the large owner does from his; and of course he sells it at a higher rate. The calculations of gain, therefore, which decided the rich man to sell his domain, will still more powerfully influence him against buying small estates to unite them into a large one.

What is called family pride is often founded upon an illusion of self-love. A man wishes to perpetuate and immortalize himself, as it were, in his great-grandchildren. Where the *esprit de famille* ceases to act, individual selfishness comes into play. When the idea of family becomes vague, indeterminate, and uncertain, a man thinks of his present convenience; he provides for the establishment of the succeeding generation, and no more.

Either a man gives up the idea of perpetuating his family, or at any rate he seeks to accomplish it by other means than that of a landed estate.

Thus not only does the law of partible inheritance render it difficult for families to preserve their ancestral domains entire, but it deprives them of the inclination to attempt it, and compels them in some measure to cooperate with the law in their own extinction.

The law of equal distribution proceeds by two methods: by acting upon things, it acts upon persons; by influencing persons, it affects things. By these means the law succeeds in striking at the root of landed property, and dispersing rapidly both families and fortunes.

Most certainly it is not for us, Frenchmen of the nineteenth century, who daily behold the political and social changes which the law of partition is bringing to pass, to question its influence. It is perpetually conspicuous in our country, overthrowing the walls of our dwellings and removing the landmarks of our fields. But although it has produced great effects in France, much still remains for it to do. Our recollections, opinions, and habits, present powerful obstacles to its progress.

In the United States it has nearly completed its work of destruction, and there we can best study its results. The English laws concerning the transmission of property were abolished in almost all the states at the time of the revolution. The law of entail was so modified as not to interrupt the free circulation of property.

The first having passed away, estates began to be parcelled out; and the change became more and more rapid with the progress of time. At this moment, after a lapse of little more than sixty years, the aspect of society is totally altered; the families of the great landed proprietors are almost all commingled with the general mass. In the state of New York, which formerly contained many of these, there are but two who still keep their heads above the stream; and they must shortly disappear. The sons of these opulent citizens have become merchants, lawyers, or physicians. Most of them have lapsed into obscurity. The last trace of hereditary ranks and distinctions is destroyed—the law of partition has reduced all to one level.

I do not mean that there is any deficiency of wealthy individuals in the United States; I know of no country, indeed, where the love of money has taken stronger hold on the affections of men, and where a profounder contempt is expressed for the theory of the permanent equality of property. But wealth circulates with inconceivable rapidity, and experience shows that it is rare to find two succeeding generations in the full enjoyment of it.

This picture, which may perhaps be thought overcharged, still gives a very imperfect idea of what is taking place in the new states of the west and southwest. At the end of the last century a few bold adventurers began to penetrate into the valleys of the Mississippi, and the mass of the population very soon began to move in that direction: communities unheard of till then were seen to emerge from their wilds: states, whose names were not in existence a few years before, claimed their place in the American Union; and in the western settlements we may behold democracy arrived at its utmost extreme. In these states, founded off hand, and as it were by chance, the inhabitants are but of yesterday. Scarcely known to one another, the nearest neighbors are ignorant of each other's history. In this part of the American continent, therefore, the population has not experienced the influence of great names and great wealth, nor even that of the natural aristocracy of knowledge and virtue. None are there to wield that respectable power which men willingly grant to the remembrance of a life spent in doing good before their eyes. The new states of the west are already inhabited; but society has no existence among them.

It is not only the fortunes of men which are equal in America; even their acquirements partake in some degree of the same uniformity. I do not believe there is a country in the world where, in proportion to the population, there are so few uninstructed, and at the same time so few learned individuals. Primary instruction is within the reach of everybody; superior instruction is scarcely to be obtained by any. This is not surprising; it is in fact the necessary consequence of what we have advanced above. Almost all the Americans are in easy circumstances, and can therefore obtain the first elements of human knowledge.

In America there are comparatively few who are rich enough to live without a profession. Every profession requires an apprenticeship, which limits the time of instruction to the early years of life. At fifteen they enter upon their calling, and thus their education ends at the age when ours begins. Whatever is done afterward, is with a view to some special and lucrative object; a science is taken up as a matter of business, and the only branch of it which is attended to is such as admits of an immediate practical application.

In America most of the rich men were formerly poor: most of those who now enjoy leisure were absorbed in business during their youth; the consequence of which is, that when they might have had a taste for study they had no time for it, and when the time is at their disposal they have no longer the inclination.

There is no class, then, in America in which the taste for intellectual pleasures is transmitted with hereditary fortune and leisure, and by which the labors of the intellect are held in honor. Accordingly there is an equal want of the desire and the power of application to these objects.

A middling standard is fixed in America for human knowledge. All approach as near to it as they can; some as they rise, others as they descend. Of course, an immense multitude of persons are to be found who entertain the same number of ideas on religion, history, science, political economy, legislation, and government. The gifts of intellect proceed directly from God, and man cannot prevent their unequal distribution. But in consequence of the state of things which we have here represented, it happens, that although the capacities of men are widely different, as the Creator has doubtless intended they should be, they are submitted to the same method of treatment.

In America the aristocratic element has always been feeble from its birth; and if at the present day it is not actually destroyed, it is at any rate so completely disabled that we can scarcely assign to it any degree of influence in the course of affairs.

The democratic principle, on the contrary, has gained so much strength by time, by events, and by legislation, as to have become not only predominant but all-powerful. There is no family or corporate authority, and it is rare to find even the influence of individual character enjoy any durability.

America, then, exhibits in her social state a most extraordinary phenomenon. Men are there seen on a greater equality in point of fortune and intellect, or in other words, more equal in their strength, than in any other country of the world, or, in any age of which history has preserved the remembrance.

Political Consequences of the Social Condition of the Anglo-Americans

The political consequences of such a social condition as this are easily deductible.

It is impossible to believe that equality will not everywhere find its way into the political world as it does everywhere else. To conceive of men remaining for ever unequal upon one single point, yet equal on all others, is impossible; they must come in the end to be equal upon all.

Now I know of only two methods of establishing equality in the political world: every citizen must be put in possession of his rights, or rights must be granted to no one. For nations which have arrived at the same stage of social existence as the Anglo-Americans, it is therefore very difficult to discover a medium between the sovereignty of all and the absolute power of one man: and it would be vain to deny that the social condition which I have been describing is equally liable to each of these consequences.

There is, in fact, a manly and lawful passion for equality, which excites men to wish all to be powerful and honored. This passion tends to elevate the humble to the rank of the great; but there exists also in the human heart a depraved taste for equality, which impels the weak to attempt to lower the powerful to their own level, and reduces men to prefer equality in slavery to inequality with freedom. Not that those nations whose social condition is democratic naturally despise liberty; on the contrary, they have an instinctive love of it. But liberty is not the chief and constant object of their desire; equality is their idol: they make rapid and sudden efforts to obtain liberty, and if they miss their aim, resign themselves to their disappointment; but nothing can satisfy them except equality, and rather than lose it they resolve to perish.

On the other hand, in a state where the citizens are nearly on an equality, it becomes difficult for them to preserve their independence against the aggressions of power. No one among them being strong enough to engage singly in the struggle with advantage, nothing but a general combination can protect their liberty: and such a union is not always to be found.

From the same social position, then, nations may derive one or the other of two great political results; these results are extremely different from each other, but they may both proceed from the same cause.

The Anglo-Americans are the first who, having been exposed to this formidable alternative, have been happy enough to escape the dominion of absolute power. They have been allowed by their circumstances, their origin, their intelligence, and especially by their moral feeling, to establish and maintain the sovereignty of the people.

• • •

Political Associations in the United States

In no country in the world has the principle of association been more successfully used, or more unsparingly applied to a multitude of different objects, than in America. Beside the permanent associations which are established by law under the names of townships, cities, and counties, a vast number of others are formed and maintained by the agency of private individuals.

The citizen of the United States is taught from his earliest infancy to rely upon his own exertions, in order to resist the evils and the difficulties of life; he looks upon the social authority with an eye of mistrust and anxiety, and he only claims its assistance when he is quite unable to shift without it. This habit may even be traced in the schools of the rising generation, where the children in their games are wont to submit to rules which they have themselves established, and to punish misdemeanors which they have themselves defined. The same spirit pervades every act of social life. If a stoppage occurs in a thoroughfare, and the circulation of the public is hindered, the neighbors immediately constitute a deliberative body; and this extemporaneous assembly gives rise to an executive power, which remedies the inconvenience, before anybody has thought of recurring to an authority superior to that of the persons immediately concerned. If the public pleasures are concerned, an association is formed to provide for the splendor and the regularity of the entertainment. Societies are formed to resist enemies which are exclusively of a moral nature, and to diminish the vice of intemperance: in the United States associations are established to promote public order, commerce, industry, morality, and religion; for there is no end which the human will, seconded by the collective exertions of individuals, despairs of attaining.

I shall hereafter have occasion to show the effects of association upon the course of society, and I must confine myself for the present to the political world. When once the right of association is recognized, the citizens may employ it in several different ways.

An association consists simply in the public assent which a number of individuals give to certain doctrines; and in the engagement which they contract to promote the spread of those doctrines by their exertions. The right of associating with these views is very analogous to the liberty of unlicensed writing; but societies thus formed possess more authority than the press. When an opinion is represented by a society, it necessarily assumes a more exact and explicit form. It numbers its partisans, and compromises their welfare in its cause; they, on the other hand, become acquainted with each other, and their zeal is increased by their number. An association unites the efforts of minds which have a tendency to diverge, in one single channel, and urges them vigorously toward one single end which it points out.

The second degree in the right of association is the power of meeting. When an association is allowed to establish centers of action at certain important points in the country, its activity is increased, and its influence extended. Men have the opportunity of seeing each other; means of execution are more readily combined; and opinions are maintained with a degree of warmth and energy which written language cannot approach. . . .

Why Democratic Nations Show a More Ardent and Enduring Love of Equality Than of Liberty

The first and most intense passion which is engendered by the equality of conditions is, I need hardly say, the love of that same equality. My readers will therefore not be surprised that I speak of it before all others.

Everybody has remarked, that in our time, and especially in France, this passion for equality is every day gaining ground in the human heart. It has been said a hundred times that our contemporaries are far more ardently and tenaciously attached to equality than to freedom; but, as I do not find that the causes of the fact have been sufficiently analyzed, I shall endeavor to point them out.

It is possible to imagine an extreme point at which freedom and equality would meet and be confounded together. Let us suppose that all the members of the community take a part in the government, and that each one of them has an equal right to take a part in it. As none is different from his fellows, none can exercise a tyrannical power: men will be perfectly free, because they will all be entirely equal; and they will all be perfectly equal, because they will be entirely free. To this ideal state democratic nations tend. Such is the completest form that equality can assume upon earth; but there are a thousand others which, without being equally perfect, are not less cherished by those nations.

The principle of equality may be established in civil society, without prevailing in the political world. Equal rights may exist of indulging in the same pleasures, of entering the same professions, of frequenting the same places—in a word, of living in the same manner and seeking wealth by the same means, although all men do not take an equal share in the government.

A kind of equality may even be established in the political world, though there should be no political freedom there. A man may be the equal of all his countrymen save one, who is the master of all without distinction, and who selects equally from among them all the agents of his power.

Several other combinations might be easily imagined, by which very great equality would be united to institutions more or less free, or even to institutions wholly without freedom.

Although men cannot become absolutely equal unless they be entirely free, and consequently equality, pushed to its furthest extent, may be confounded with freedom, yet there is good reason for distinguishing the one from the other. The taste which men have for liberty, and that which they feel for equality, are, in fact, two different things; and I am not afraid to add, that, among democratic nations, they are two unequal things.

Upon close inspection, it will be seen that there is in every age some peculiar and preponderating fact with which all others are connected; this fact almost always gives birth to some pregnant idea or some ruling passion, which attracts to itself, and bears away in its course, all the feelings and opinions of the time: it is like a great stream, toward which each of the surrounding rivulets seem to flow.

Freedom has appeared in the world at different times and under various forms; it has not been exclusively bound to any social condition, and it is not confined to democracies. Freedom cannot, therefore, form the distinguishing characteristic of democratic ages. The peculiar and preponderating fact which marks those ages as its own is the equality of conditions; the ruling passion of men in those periods is the love of this equality. Ask not what singular charm the men of democratic ages find in being equal, or what special reasons they may have for clinging so tenaciously to equality rather than to the other advantages which society holds out to them: equality is the distinguishing characteristic of the age they live in; that, of itself, is enough to explain that they prefer it to all the rest.

But independently of this reason there are several others, which will at all times habitually lead men to prefer equality to freedom.

If a people could ever succeed in destroying, or even in diminishing, the equality which prevails in its own body, this could only be accomplished by long and laborious efforts. Its social condition must be modified, its laws abolished, its opinions superseded, its habits changed, its manners corrupted. But political liberty is more easily lost; to neglect to hold it fast, is to allow it to escape.

Men therefore not only cling to equality because it is dear to them; they also adhere to it because they think it will last for ever.

That political freedom may compromise in its excesses the tranquillity, the property, the lives of individuals, is obvious to the narrowest and most unthinking minds. But, on the contrary, none but attentive and clear-sighted men perceive the perils with which equality threatens us, and they commonly avoid pointing them out. They know that the calamities they apprehend are remote, and flatter themselves that they will only fall upon future generations, for which the present generation takes but little thought. The evils which freedom sometimes brings with it are immediate; they are apparent to all, and all are more or less affected by them. The evils which extreme equality may produce are slowly disclosed; they creep gradually into the social frame; they are only seen at intervals, and at the moment at which they become most violent, habit already causes them to be no longer felt.

The advantages which freedom brings are only shown by length of time; and it is always easy to mistake the cause in which they originate. The advantages of equality are instantaneous, and they may constantly be traced from their source.

Political liberty bestows exalted pleasures, from time to time, upon a certain number of citizens. Equality every day confers a number of small enjoyments on every man. The charms of equality are every instant felt, and are within the reach of all: the noblest hearts are not insensible to them, and the most vulgar souls exult in them. The passion which equality engenders must therefore be at once strong and general. Men cannot enjoy political liberty unless it has been purchased by some sacrifices, and they never obtain it without great exertions. But the pleasures of equality are self-proffered: each of the petty incidents of life seems to occasion them, and in order to taste them nothing is required but to live.

Democratic nations are at all times fond of equality, but there are certain epochs at which the passion they entertain for it swells to the height of fury. This occurs at the moment when the old social system, long menaced, completes its own destruction after a last intestine struggle, and when the barriers of rank are at length thrown down. At such times men pounce upon equality as their booty, and they cling to it as to some precious treasure which they fear to lose. The passion for equality penetrates on every side into men's hearts, expands there, and fills them entirely. Tell them not that by this blind surrender of themselves to an exclusive passion, they risk their dearest interests: they are deaf. Show them not freedom escaping from their grasp, while they are looking another way: they are blind—or rather, they can discern but one sole object to be desired in the universe.

What I have said is applicable to all democratic nations: what I am about to say concerns the French alone. Among most modern nations, and especially among all those of the continent of Europe, the taste and the idea of freedom only began to exist and to extend itself at the time when social conditions were tending to equality, and as a consequence of that very equality. Absolute kings were the most efficient levellers of ranks among their subjects. Among these nations equality preceded freedom: equality was therefore a fact of some standing, when freedom was still a novelty: the one had already created customs, opinions, and laws belonging to it, when the other, alone and for the first time, came into actual existence. Thus the latter was still only an affair of opinion and of taste, while the former had already crept into the habits of the people, possessed itself of their manners, and given a particular turn to the smallest actions in their lives. Can it be wondered that the men of our own time prefer the one to the other?

I think that democratic communities have a natural taste for freedom: left to themselves, they will seek it, cherish it, and view any privation of it with regret. But for equality, their passion is ardent, insatiable, incessant, invincible: they call for equality in freedom; if they cannot obtain that, they still call for equality in slavery. They will endure poverty, servitude, barbarism—but they will not endure aristocracy.

This is true at all times, and especially true in our own. All men and all powers seeking to cope with this irresistible passion, will be overthrown and destroyed by it. In our age, freedom cannot be established without it, and despotism itself cannot reign without its support. ■

American Politics Today

Politics in the modern era hardly seems to support the idea that Americans are united in a common political culture. Instead, politics today seems to emphasize a wide range of conflicts over fundamental values. Some Americans have even proclaimed the existence of a "culture war" starkly dividing the nation as never before.

Never is this cultural divide more readily apparent than on the night of a presidential election. As the networks tally the state-by-state vote for president, they color in a wall map of the United States—red for the Republicans, blue for the Democrats. In 2000 and 2004, most of America—geographically speaking, at least—was covered in a red swath that blanketed the South, the heartland of the Midwest, and the states of the Rocky Mountains. Small dots of blue could be seen mostly in the populous (but physically small) states of the Northeast and along the Atlantic coast, and in a narrow strip alongside the Pacific Ocean.

The two selections in this section take different approaches to examining the state of public opinion in the United States. In selection 5.2, journalist David Brooks ventures out from "Blue" America to see what "Red" America is like. In selection 5.3, political scientists Steven Waldman and John C. Green go beyond the simple red/blue division and instead break down the American people into twelve political and culture groups, or "tribes." Together, these two selections provide a clear and insightful view of American public opinion today.

Questions

1. According to the authors of these studies, in what ways are the "red" and "blue" states different? In what ways are they similar?
2. What values do Red and Blue America share? On what values do they disagree?
3. What accounts for the overwhelming assumption that Americans are divided by a culture war? What are the consequences of this assumption for American political life?

5.2 One Nation, Slightly Divisible (2001)

David Brooks

• • •

Montgomery County is one of the steaming-hot centers of the great espresso machine that is Blue America. It is just over the border from northwestern Washington, D.C., and it is full of upper-middle-class

David Brooks, "One Nation, Slightly Divisible," *Atlantic Monthly* 288 (December 2001), pp. 53–65. © 2001 David Brooks. First published in *Atlantic Monthly*. Reprinted by permission of the author.

towns inhabited by lawyers, doctors, stockbrokers, and establishment journalists like me—towns like Chevy Chase, Potomac, and Bethesda (where I live). Its central artery is a burgeoning high-tech corridor with a multitude of sparkling new office parks housing technology companies such as United Information Systems and Sybase, and pioneering biotech firms such as Celera Genomics and Human Genome Sciences. . . .

Franklin County is Red America. It's a rural county, about twenty-five miles west of Gettysburg, and it includes the towns of Waynesboro, Chambersburg, and Mercersburg. It was originally settled by the Scotch-Irish, and it has plenty of Brethren and Mennonites along with a fast-growing population of evangelicals. The joke that Pennsylvanians tell about their state is that it has Philadelphia on one end, Pittsburgh on the other, and Alabama in the middle. Franklin County is in the Alabama part. It strikes me as I drive there that even though I am going north across the Mason-Dixon line, I feel as if I were going south. The local culture owes more to Nashville, Houston, and Daytona than to Washington, Philadelphia, or New York. . . .

Some of the biggest differences between Red and Blue America show up on statistical tables. Ethnic diversity is one. In Montgomery County 60 percent of the population is white, 15 percent is black, 12 percent is Hispanic, and 11 percent is Asian. In Franklin County 95 percent of the population is white. White people work the gas-station pumps and the 7-Eleven counters. (This is something one doesn't often see in my part of the country.) Although the nation is growing more diverse, it's doing so only in certain spots. According to an analysis of the 2000 census by Bill Frey, a demographer at the Milken Institute, well over half the counties in America are still at least 85 percent white.

Another big thing is that, according to 1990 census data, in Franklin County only 12 percent of the adults have college degrees and only 69 percent have high school diplomas. In Montgomery County 50 percent of the adults have college degrees and 91 percent have high school diplomas. The education gap extends to the children. At Walt Whitman High School, a public school in Bethesda, the average SAT scores are 601 verbal and 622 math, whereas the national average is 506 verbal and 514 math. In Franklin County, where people are quite proud of their schools, the average SAT scores at, for example, the Waynesboro area high school are 495 verbal and 480 math. More and more kids in Franklin County are going on to college, but it is hard to believe that their prospects will be as bright as those of the kids in Montgomery County and the rest of upscale Blue America.

Because the information age rewards education with money, it's not surprising that Montgomery County is much richer than Franklin County. According to some estimates, in Montgomery County 51 percent of households have annual incomes above $75,000, and the average household income is $100,365. In Franklin County only 16 percent of households have incomes above $75,000, and the average is $51,872.

A major employer in Montgomery County is the National Institutes of Health, which grows like a scientific boomtown in Bethesda. A major economic engine in Franklin County is the interstate highway Route 81. Trucking companies have gotten sick of fighting the congestion on Route 95, which runs up the Blue corridor along the northeast coast, so they move their stuff along 81, farther inland.

Several new distribution centers have been built along 81 in Franklin County, and some of the workers who were laid off when their factories closed, several years ago, are now settling for $8.00 or $9.00 an hour loading boxes.

The two counties vote differently, of course—the differences, on a nationwide scale, were what led to those red-and-blue maps. Like upscale areas everywhere, from Silicon Valley to Chicago's North Shore to suburban Connecticut, Montgomery County supported the Democratic ticket in last year's presidential election, by a margin of 63 percent to 34 percent. Meanwhile, like almost all of rural America, Franklin County went Republican, by 67 percent to 30 percent.

However, other voting patterns sometimes obscure the Red-Blue cultural divide. For example, minority voters all over the country overwhelmingly supported the Democratic ticket last November. But—in many respects, at least—blacks and Hispanics in Red America are more traditionalist than blacks and Hispanics in Blue America, just as their white counterparts are. For example, the Pew Research Center for the People and the Press, in Washington, D.C., recently found that 45 percent of minority members in Red states agree with the statement "AIDS might be God's punishment for immoral sexual behavior," but only 31 percent of minority members in Blue states do. Similarly, 40 percent of minorities in Red states believe that school boards should have the right to fire homosexual teachers, but only 21 percent of minorities in Blue states do.

· · ·

"The People Versus the Powerful"

There are a couple of long-standing theories about why America is divided. One of the main ones holds that the division is along class lines, between the haves and the have-nots. This theory is popular chiefly on the left, and can be found in the pages of *The American Prospect* and other liberal magazines; in news reports by liberal journalists such as Donald L. Barlett and James B. Steele, of *Time*; and in books such as *Middle Class Dreams* (1995), by the Clinton and Gore pollster Stanley Greenberg, and *America's Forgotten Majority: Why the White Working Class Still Matters* (2000), by the demographer Ruy Teixeira and the social scientist Joel Rogers.

According to this theory, during most of the twentieth century gaps in income between the rich and the poor in America gradually shrank. Then came the information age. The rich started getting spectacularly richer, the poor started getting poorer, and wages for the middle class stagnated, at best. Over the previous decade, these writers emphasized, remuneration for top-level executives had skyrocketed: now the average CEO made 116 times as much as the average rank-and-file worker. Assembly-line workers found themselves competing for jobs against Third World workers who earned less than a dollar an hour. Those who had once labored at well-paying blue-collar jobs were forced to settle for poorly paying service-economy jobs without benefits. . . .

Driving from Bethesda to Franklin County, one can see that the theory of a divide between the classes has a certain plausibility. In Montgomery County we have Saks Fifth Avenue, Cartier, Anthropologie, Brooks Brothers. In Franklin County they have Dollar General and Value City, along with a plethora of second-hand stores. It's as if Franklin County has only forty-five coffee tables, which are sold again and again.

When the locals are asked about their economy, they tell a story very similar to the one that Greenberg, Teixeira, Rogers, and the rest of the wage-stagnation liberals recount. There used to be plenty of good factory jobs in Franklin County, and people could work at those factories for life. But some of the businesses, including the textile company J. Schoeneman, once Franklin County's largest manufacturer, have closed. Others have moved offshore. The remaining manufacturers, such as Grove Worldwide and JLG Industries, which both make cranes and aerial platforms, have laid off workers. The local Army depot, Letterkenny, has radically shrunk its work force. The new jobs are in distribution centers or nursing homes. People tend to repeat the same phrase: "We've taken some hits."

And yet when they are asked about the broader theory, whether there is class conflict between the educated affluents and the stagnant middles, they stare blankly as if suddenly the interview were being conducted in Aramaic. I kept asking, Do you feel that the highly educated people around, say, New York and Washington are getting all the goodies? Do you think there is resentment toward all the latte sippers who shop at Nieman Marcus? Do you see a gulf between high-income people in the big cities and middle-income people here? I got only polite, fumbling answers as people tried to figure out what the hell I was talking about.

When I rephrased the question in more-general terms, as Do you believe the country is divided between the haves and the have-nots?, everyone responded decisively: yes. But as the conversation continued, it became clear that the people saying yes did not consider themselves to be among the have-nots. Even people with incomes well below the median thought of themselves as haves. . . .

Hanging around Franklin County, one begins to understand some of the reasons that people there don't spend much time worrying about economic class lines. The first and most obvious one is that although the incomes in Franklin County are lower than those in Montgomery County, living expenses are also lower—very much so. Driving from Montgomery County to Franklin County is like driving through an invisible deflation machine. Gas is thirty, forty, or even fifty cents a gallon cheaper in Franklin County. I parked at meters that accepted only pennies and nickels. When I got a parking ticket in Chambersburg, the fine was $3.00. At the department store in Greencastle there were racks and racks of blouses for $9.99. . . .

Another thing I found is that most people don't think sociologically. They don't compare themselves with faraway millionaires who appear on their TV screens. They compare themselves with their neighbors. "One of the challenges we face is that it is hard to get people to look beyond the four-state region," Lynne Woehrle, a sociologist at Wilson College, in Chambersburg, told me, referring to the cultural zone composed of the nearby rural areas in Pennsylvania, West Virginia, Maryland, and Virginia. Many of the people in Franklin County view the lifestyles of the upper class in California or Seattle much the way we in Blue America might view the lifestyle of someone in Eritrea or Mongolia—or, for that matter, Butte, Montana. Such ways of life are distant and basically irrelevant, except as a source of academic interest or titillation. One man in Mercersburg, Pennsylvania, told me about a friend who had recently bought a car. "He paid twenty-five thousand dollars for that car!" he exclaimed, his eyes wide with amazement. "He got it fully loaded." I didn't tell him that in Bethesda almost no one but a college kid pays as little as $25,000 for a car.

Franklin County is a world in which there is little obvious inequality, and the standard of living is reasonably comfortable. Youth-soccer teams are able to raise money for a summer trip to England; the Lowe's hardware superstore carries Laura Ashley carpets; many people have pools, although they are almost always above ground; the planning commission has to cope with an increasing number of cars in the county every year, even though the population is growing only gradually. But the sort of high-end experiences that are everywhere in Montgomery County are entirely missing here. . . .

No wonder people in Franklin County have no class resentment or class consciousness; where they live, they can afford just about anything that is for sale. (In Montgomery County, however—and this is one of the most striking contrasts between the two counties—almost nobody can say that. In Blue America, unless you are very, very rich, there is always, all around you, stuff for sale that you cannot afford.) And if they sought to improve their situation, they would look only to themselves. If a person wants to make more money, the feeling goes, he or she had better work hard and think like an entrepreneur. . . .

Ted Hale, a Presbyterian minister in the western part of the county, spoke of the matter this way: "There's nowhere near as much resentment as you would expect. People have come to understand that they will struggle financially. It's part of their identity. But the economy is not their god. That's the thing some others don't understand. People value a sense of community far more than they do their portfolio." Hale, who worked at a church in East Hampton, New York, before coming to Franklin County, said that he saw a lot more economic resentment in New York.

Hale's observations are supported by nationwide polling data. Pew has conducted a broad survey of the differences between Red and Blue states. The survey found that views on economic issues do not explain the different voting habits in the two regions. There simply isn't much of the sort of economic dissatisfaction that could drive a class-based political movement. Eighty-five percent of Americans with an annual household income between $30,000 and $50,000 are satisfied with their housing. Nearly 70 percent are satisfied with the kind of car they can afford. Roughly two thirds are satisfied with their furniture and their ability to afford a night out. These levels of satisfaction are not very different from those found in upper-middle-class America.

The Pew researchers found this sort of trend in question after question. Part of the draft of their report is titled "Economic Divide Dissolves."

A Lot of Religion But Few Crusaders

This leaves us with the second major hypothesis about the nature of the divide between Red and Blue America, which comes mainly from conservatives: America is divided between two moral systems. Red America is traditional, religious, self-disciplined, and patriotic. Blue America is modern, secular, self-expressive, and discomfited by blatant displays of patriotism. Proponents of this hypothesis in its most radical form contend that America is in the midst of a culture war, with two opposing armies fighting on behalf of their views. The historian Gertrude Himmelfarb offered a more moderate picture in *One Nation, Two Cultures* (1999), in which she argued that although America is not fatally split, it is deeply divided, between a heartland conservative population that adheres to a strict morality and a liberal population that lives by a loose one. The political journalist Michael Barone put it this way in a recent essay in *National Journal*: "The two Americas apparent in the 48 percent to 48 percent 2000 election are two nations of different faiths. One is observant, tradition-minded, moralistic. The other is unobservant, liberation-minded, relativistic."

The values-divide school has a fair bit of statistical evidence on its side. Whereas income is a poor predictor of voting patterns, church attendance—as Barone points out—is a pretty good one. Of those who attend religious services weekly (42 percent of the electorate), 59 percent voted for Bush, 39 percent for Gore. Of those who seldom or never attend religious services (another 42 percent), 56 percent voted for Gore, 39 percent for Bush.

The Pew data reveal significant divides on at least a few values issues. Take, for example, the statement "We will all be called before God on Judgment Day to answer for our sins." In Red states 70 percent of the people believe that statement. In Blue states only 50 percent do.

One can feel the religiosity in Franklin County after a single day's visit. It's on the bumper stickers: WARNING: IN CASE OF RAPTURE THIS VEHICLE WILL BE UNMANNED. REAL TRUCKERS TALK ABOUT JESUS ON CHANNEL 10. It's on the radio. The airwaves are filled not with the usual mixture of hit tunes but with evangelicals preaching the gospel. The book section of Wal-Mart features titles such as *The Beginner's Guide to Fasting, Deepen Your Conversation with God,* and *Are We Living in the End Times?* Some general stores carry the "Heroes of the Faith" series, which consists of small biographies of William Carey, George Müller, and other notable missionaries, ministers, and theologians—notable in Red America, that is, but largely unknown where I live. . . .

Franklin County is probably a bit more wholesome than most suburbs in Blue America. (The notion that deviance and corruption lie underneath the seeming conformism of suburban middle-class life, popular in Hollywood and in creative-writing workshops, is largely nonsense.) But it has most of the problems that afflict other parts of the country: heroin addiction, teen pregnancy, and so on. Nobody I spoke to felt part of a pristine culture that is exempt from the problems of the big cities. There are even enough spectacular crimes in Franklin County to make a devoted *New York Post* reader happy. During one of my visits the front pages of the local papers were ablaze with the tale of a young woman arrested for assault and homicide after shooting her way through a Veterans of the Vietnam War post. It was reported that she had intended to rob the post for money to run away with her lesbian girlfriend.

If the problems are the same as in the rest of America, so are many of the solutions. Franklin County residents who find themselves in trouble go to their clergy first, but they are often referred to psychologists and therapists as part of their recovery process. Prozac is a part of life.

Almost nobody I spoke with understood, let alone embraced, the concept of a culture war. Few could see themselves as fighting such a war, in part because few have any idea where the boundary between the two sides lies. People in Franklin County may have a clear sense of what constitutes good or evil (many people in Blue America have trouble with the very concept of evil), but they will say that good and evil are in all neighborhoods, as they are in all of us. People take the Scriptures seriously but have no interest in imposing them on others. One finds little crusader zeal in Franklin County. For one thing, people in small towns don't want to offend people whom they'll be encountering on the street for the next fifty years. Potentially controversial subjects are often played down. "We would never take a stance on gun control or abortion," Sue Hadden, the editor of the Waynesboro paper, told me. Whenever I asked what the local view of abortion was, I got the same response: "We don't talk about it much," or "We try to avoid that subject." Bill Pukmel, the former Chambersburg newspaper editor, says, "A majority would be opposed to abortion around here, but it wouldn't be a big majority." It would simply be uncivil to thrust such a raw disagreement in people's faces. . . .

Certainly Red and Blue America disagree strongly on some issues, such as homosexuality and abortion. But for the most part the disagreements are not large. For example, the Pew researchers asked Americans to respond to the statement "There are clear guidelines about what's good or evil that apply to everyone regardless of their situation." Forty-three percent of people in Blue states and 49 percent of people in Red states agreed. Forty-seven percent of Blue America and 55 percent of Red America agreed with the statement "I have old-fashioned values about family and marriage." Seventy percent of the people in Blue states and 77 percent of the people in Red states agreed that "too many children are being raised in day-care centers these days." These are small gaps. And, the Pew researchers found, there is no culture gap at all among suburban voters. In a Red state like Arizona suburban voters' opinions are not much different from those in a Blue state like Connecticut. The starkest differences that exist are between people in cities and people in rural areas, especially rural areas in the South.

The conservatism I found in Franklin County is not an ideological or a reactionary conservatism. It is a temperamental conservatism. People place tremendous value on being agreeable, civil, and kind. They are happy to sit quietly with one another. They are hesitant to stir one another's passions. They appreciate what they have. They value continuity and revere the past. They work hard to reinforce community bonds. Their newspapers are filled with items about fundraising drives, car washes, bake sales, penny-collection efforts, and auxiliary thrift shops. Their streets are lined with lodges: VFW, Rotarians, Elks, Moose. Luncheons go on everywhere. Retired federal employees will be holding their weekly luncheon at one restaurant, Harley riders at another. I became fascinated by a group called the Tuscarora Longbeards, a local chapter of something called the National Wild Turkey Federation. The Longbeards go around to schools distributing Wild About Turkey Education boxes, which contain posters, lesson plans, and CD-ROMs on turkey preservation.

These are the sorts of things that really mobilize people in Franklin County. Building community and preserving local ways are far more important to them than any culture war.

The Ego Curtain

The best explanation of the differences between people in Montgomery and Franklin Counties has to do with sensibility, not class or culture. If I had to describe the differences between the two sensibilities in a single phrase, it would be conception of the self. In Red America the self is small. People declare in a million ways, "I am normal. Nobody is better, nobody is worse. I am humble before God." In Blue America the self is more commonly large. People say in a million ways, "I am special. I have carved out my own unique way of life. I am independent. I make up my own mind."

In Red America there is very little one-upmanship. Nobody tries to be avant-garde in choosing a wardrobe. The chocolate-brown suits and baggy denim dresses hanging in local department stores aren't there by accident; people conspicuously want to be seen as not trying to dress to impress.

For a person in Blue America the blandness in Red America can be a little oppressive. But it's hard not to be struck by the enormous social pressure not to put on airs. If a Franklin County resident drove up to church one day in a shiny new Lexus, he would face huge waves of disapproval. If one hired a nanny, people would wonder who died and made her queen.

In Franklin County people don't go looking for obscure beers to demonstrate their connoisseurship. They wear T-shirts and caps with big-brand names on them—Coke, McDonald's, Chevrolet. In Bethesda people prefer cognoscenti brands—the Black Dog restaurant, or the independent bookstore Politics and Prose. In Franklin County it would be an affront to the egalitarian ethos to put a Princeton sticker on the rear window of one's car. In Montgomery County some proud parents can barely see through their back windows for all the Ivy League stickers. People in Franklin County say they felt comfortable voting for Bush, because if he came to town he wouldn't act superior to anybody else; he could settle into a barber's chair and fit right in. They couldn't stand Al Gore, because they thought he'd always be trying to awe everyone with his accomplishments. People in Montgomery County tended to admire Gore's accomplishments. They were leery of Bush, because for most of his life he seemed not to have achieved anything. . . .

A Cafeteria Nation

These differences in sensibility don't in themselves mean that America has become a fundamentally divided nation. As the sociologist Seymour Martin Lipset pointed out in *The First New Nation* (1963), achievement and equality are the two rival themes running throughout American history. Most people, most places, and most epochs have tried to intertwine them in some way.

Moreover, after bouncing between Montgomery and Franklin Counties, I became convinced that a lot of our fear that America is split into rival camps arises from mistaken notions of how society is shaped. Some of us still carry the old Marxist categories in our heads. We think that society is like a layer cake, with the upper class on top. And, like Marx, we tend to assume that wherever there is class division there is conflict. Or else we have a sort of *Crossfire* model in our heads: where would people we meet sit if they were guests on that show?

But traveling back and forth between the two counties was not like crossing from one rival camp to another. It was like crossing a high school cafeteria. Remember high school? There were nerds, jocks, punks, bikers, techies, druggies, God Squadders, drama geeks, poets, and Dungeons & Dragons weirdoes. All these cliques were part of the same school: they had different sensibilities; sometimes they knew very little about the people in the other cliques; but the jocks knew there would always be nerds, and the nerds knew there would always be jocks. That's just the way life is.

And that's the way America is. We are not a divided nation. We are a cafeteria nation. We form cliques (call them communities, or market segments, or whatever), and when they get too big, we form subcliques. Some people even get together in churches that are "nondenominational" or in political groups that are "independent." These are cliques built around the supposed rejection of cliques.

We live our lives by migrating through the many different cliques associated with the activities we enjoy and the goals we have set for ourselves. Our freedom comes in the interstices; we can choose which set of standards to live by, and when.

We should remember that there is generally some distance between cliques—a buffer zone that separates one set of aspirations from another. People who are happy within their cliques feel no great compulsion to go out and reform other cliques. The jocks don't try to change the nerds. David Rawley, the Greencastle minister who felt he was clinging to a rock, has been to New York City only once in his life. "I was happy to get back home," he told me. "It's a planet I'm a little scared of. I have no desire to go back."

What unites the two Americas, then, is our mutual commitment to this way of life—to the idea that a person is not bound by his class, or by the religion of his fathers, but is free to build a plurality of connections for himself. We are participants in the same striving process, the same experimental journey. . . . ■

5.3 The Twelve Tribes of American Politics (2006)

Steven Waldman and John C. Green

Many Americans, when they think about values and politics, focus on the "religious right"—conservatives led by James Dobson, Jerry Falwell, and Pat Robertson, and interested mostly in cultural issues, such as abortion and same-sex marriage. So on election night in 2004, when exit polls found that the No. 1 priority cited by voters was "moral values," many jumped to the conclu-

From Steven Waldman and John C. Green, "Tribal Relations," *Atlantic Monthly* 297 (January/February 2006), pp. 136–142. © 2006 Steven Waldman and John C. Green. First published in *Atlantic Monthly*. Reprinted by permission of the authors.

sion that these voters and their agenda had propelled George W. Bush back into the White House.

Soon it became clear that the "values vote" had been exaggerated. Only one fifth of the respondents listed moral values as the primary basis for their vote. Nearly four out of five listed one of several foreign-policy, economic, or other domestic concerns. And the same polls showed Americans to have social views that would make conservative Christians weep: 60 percent said gays should be allowed either to legally marry or to form civil unions, and 55 percent believed that abortion should be legal in all or most cases.

Religion and values undoubtedly play a large role in our politics. But their impact is often misunderstood. In the most simplistic renderings values come in only two varieties: those held by the religious right and those held by everybody else. During the 2004 campaign we began to map out a very different topology of religion, values, and politics in America, based on survey data gathered by the Ray C. Bliss Institute at the University of Akron in collaboration with the Pew Forum on Religion & Public Life. We combined measures of religious affiliation, behavior, and belief to see how values cluster within the voting public. The resulting picture . . . reveals not two monolithic and mutually antagonistic camps but, rather, twelve coherent blocs with overlapping interests and values. We call these groups the twelve tribes of American politics.

. . . [The twelve tribes can be characterized by their] positions on cultural and economic issues. The cultural issues include abortion, stem-cell research, and gay rights. The economic issues include social-welfare programs and the scope to the federal government. . . . [W]e will mention [foreign-policy issues] where relevant.

A brief review of the political habits and migratory patterns of the twelve tribes shows both the complex relationship between values and voting in the United States and the striking degree of compatibility in the values of most Americans. It reveals the role actually played by moral values in the 2004 election, and helps illuminate how the clash of values is likely to influence politics and law in the future.

The Republican Tribes

The fervor and coherence of the Republican base, especially the base of social conservatives, attracted a lot of attention in 2004—and compared with the Democratic base, it is cohesive on moral issues. But it's not monolithic. The Republican base sorts into three related tribes that agree on many issues but place different emphasis on each.

The **religious right**, consisting of traditional evangelical Protestants, accounted for 12.6 percent of the electorate and the core of the moral-values voters in 2004. Almost 90 percent of these voted for Bush. This cohort is as Republican as Republican gets: no group is more conservative on moral values, economic issues, or foreign policy. Contrary to popular belief, the religious right is not growing quickly; its size barely changed from 2000 to 2004.

Heartland culture warriors stand arm-in-arm with the religious right on most moral issues and are nearly as numerous (11.4 percent of the electorate). They are traditional Christians outside the evangelical community, the most prominent being Bush (a traditional United Methodist). Cultural warriors are neither as religiously orthodox nor as politically conservative as the religious right, but they were nonetheless energized by same-sex marriage and other high-profile moral issues in 2004. Seventy-two percent voted for Bush in that election.

Heartland culture warriors did not exist as a distinct political group twenty years ago. They are the product of a convulsive theological restructuring—one that has pushed moral values further into the political limelight. Whereas denomination used to predict political affiliation (Catholics were Democrats; Episcopalians were Republicans), religious beliefs and practices are now more important. Congregations and denominations have split over issues such as the inerrancy of the Bible, the role of women, and sexual morality. In recent decades theological conservatives from different denominations—Catholic, Protestant, Mormon—have found one another. In some cases they've formed caucuses within their churches. In others they've switched to more-congenial congregations. One consequence is that they've coalesced on Election Day, voting for candidates who fit their beliefs rather than their churches' historic loyalties.

Moderate evangelicals (10.8 percent of the electorate) make up the final solidly Republican tribe. The less traditional members of evangelical churches, they are culturally conservative but moderate on economic issues, favoring a larger government and aid to the poor. Bush received 64 percent of this tribe's vote, up from 60 percent in 2000.

Moderate evangelicals are much less absolutist than their religious-right cousins: for example, they favor restricting rather than banning abortion, and support some gay rights but not same-sex marriage. As much as anything, they liked Bush's personal faith. . . .

The three [Republican] tribes make up about 35 percent of the electorate, and although their members don't vote exclusively on the basis of cultural issues, values are certainly a key ingredient in the glue that holds the three together. Most of these voters desire a measure of religious expression in public life and a person of faith in the White House. But their positions on such hot-button issues as abortion, gay rights, and stem-cell research are not uniform. Should a future presidential election offer two obviously pious candidates, the Republican "values" base may show itself to be less cohesive than it now appears—and moderate evangelicals in particular could conceivably begin to defect.

The Democratic Tribes

While much hay was made of the "religion gap" in 2004—the tendency of weekly worship attendees to vote Republican—Democrats have religious constituencies too. Indeed, though Democrats may attend church less frequently, many have rich devotional lives, and a surprising number hold conservative cultural views.

A [deeply Democratic] **religious left** is almost exactly the same size as the religious right but receives much less attention. John Kerry is perhaps one representative of this group, which draws members from many Christian denominations and is a product of the same theological restructuring that created the heartland culture warriors. Members of the religious left espouse a progressive theology (agreeing, for instance, that "all the world's great religions are equally true") and are very liberal on cultural issues such as abortion and gay marriage. About a quarter attend church weekly. The religious left is somewhat liberal on economic policy and decidedly to the left on foreign policy. Its stances on both moral values and the Iraq War—but especially the latter—have pushed it further into the Democratic camp. Seventy percent backed Kerry in 2004; 51 percent had backed Gore in 2000. The religious left was the largest—and the fastest-growing—single tribe in the Kerry coalition.

Spiritual but not religious voters, who made up 5.3 percent of the electorate in 2004, are also increasing in number. These are people with no religious affiliation who nonetheless believe in God or the soul. It might be tempting to imagine the members of this tribe as aging flower children or their cultural heirs—and indeed, these voters are liberal on both economic issues and foreign policy. But they actually lean slightly to the right on abortion and gay rights. In 2004 their votes were based on economics and the war, so Kerry won more than three fifths of them.

Black Protestants (9.6 percent of the electorate) are the most traditionally religious of the Democrats tribes, and the most culturally conservative as well—in fact, on moral-values issues they are remarkably similar to the hard-right heartland culture warriors. Whereas many Democrats worried about the intermingling of Bush's faith and his politics, 50 percent of African Americans said his faith had too little impact on his policymaking. Bush made modest gains among black Protestants in Ohio and other battleground states, and those gains contributed to his re-election. But this tribe was also the most liberal on economic and foreign-policy issues, and more than four fifths voted for Kerry.

Jews and **Muslims and Others** make up a small part of the electorate—1.9 percent and 2.7 percent, respectively—but the latter group is growing. Members of non-Christian faiths tend to be liberal on cultural issues, and moral values may have helped Kerry a bit with these constituencies, but . . . they favor the Democratic Party mostly because of its economic and foreign-policy stances.

Non-religious Americans, or **seculars** (10.7 percent of the electorate), are largely responsible for the common view that Democrats are less religious than Republicans—and deeply divided from them on most cultural issues. Seculars are the most culturally liberal of the twelve tribes, and also liberal on economics and foreign policy. Many seculars are especially irritated by Bush's religious expression, and most dislike any commingling of religion and public life. Seculars pose a political dilemma for the Democratic Party: Attempts to energize them based on moral issues would antagonize not only the [Republican] tribes and many swing voters but also many [Democratic] tribes. Yet attempts to play to more-mainstream American views may turn them off, depressing their turnout.

Indeed, while the [Democratic] tribes are fairly well united on economic and foreign-policy issues, they're all over the map on cultural issues. Because the Democratic coalition includes highly religious tribes, non-religious tribes, and everything in between, talking about values can be perilous. Go strongly pro-gay, and one will alienate black Protestants and the spiritual but not religious. Go anti-abortion, and one will lose seculars and the religious left. So Democrats tend to elevate one particular moral value—tolerance—above all others. The merits of tolerance aside, it is part of what keeps the coalition together. But it leaves the Democrats open to attack for lacking a strong moral identity.

The Swing Tribes

Three tribes were up for grabs in 2004 and are still on the move politically. Bush won two of them, and could not have been re-elected without them.

White-bread Protestants (8.1 percent of the electorate) are the most Republican of the [swing] tribes. They come from the once dominant mainstream Protestant churches that were the backbone of the Republican coalition from William McKinley to Gerald Ford. By now their more traditional co-religionists have joined the heartland culture warriors, and their most liberal brethren the religious left.

In 2004 Bush won just under three fifths of this tribe. He held those voters because of his views on tax cuts (they tend to be affluent and laissez-faire) and terrorism. But white-bread Protestants are closer to the Democrats on moral issues: for instance, a majority are pro-choice. From a historical perspective Kerry did well among this group—perhaps a harbinger of further Democratic gains.

Convertible Catholics (7 percent of the electorate) are the more moderate remnant of the non-Latino Catholic vote. Bush won 55 percent of them in 2004. If Kerry, who is Catholic, had done as well with them as the Southern Baptist Al Gore did in 2000, he probably would have won Ohio and the national election.

Convertible Catholics are true moderates. Both the Democrat Maria Shriver and her Republican husband Arnold Schwarzenegger are good examples. Few believe in papal infallibility, but they are less likely than liberals to say that "all the world's great religions are equally true." They are conflicted on abortion and the scope of government, but strongly favor increased spending to help the poor. Many favor a multilateral foreign policy—except when it comes to the war on terrorism, about which they agree with the president. Scholars describe them as "cross-pressured"—in other words, squishy. They feel that neither party represents them well.

Bush pursued convertible Catholics aggressively in 2004 with shrewd appeals to social stability (backing traditional marriage), concern for the poor (faith-based initiatives), and toughness on terrorism. Al-Qaeda was more important than abortion to his success with this tribe.

Latino Christians are the final swing tribe. They went 55 percent for Kerry in 2004, but Bush made large inroads: he'd won only 28 percent of them in 2000. Values played a large part in this swing—but not primarily because of any Latino Catholic affinity for Republican stances on hot-button cultural issues. Latino Catholics, although they tend to be pro-life, voted for Kerry by more than two to one, largely because of their liberal economic views. Bush did best among Latino Protestants, many of whom come from a Pentecostal tradition that stresses conservative values and an emotional, spirit-filled worship experience. Bush's personal history was appealing to them, as were his efforts to reach out to evangelical churches and religious voters.

As one might expect, the [swing] tribes lean in different directions on different issues. But where they lean least—or more precisely, where they vote their leanings least—is on moral issues. They are generally religious, but care little for the culture wars. Their values are largely in line with the legal status quo, and they usually vote based on economic and foreign-policy concerns—at least so long as they don't see either party as seeking a revolution (one way or the other) in personal freedom or the separation of church and state. . . . ■

Issue and Controversy

Public opinion polls are everywhere—reported in the media, analyzed by political experts, poured over by campaign strategists and political operatives. Americans can find out on a daily basis how we regard the president, how we feel about critical public issues, and who we are likely to vote for at election time. The prevalence of public opinion polls, and their increasing sophistication, can tell us more about the state of public opinion than we could ever have known before the modern era.

But are public opinion polls good or bad for democracy? Do they increase or decrease our tendency to participate in politics? Do they improve or damage our public policies? Do they enhance or impoverish our political debates? In this selection, political scientist Herbert B. Asher examines the impact of public opinion polls on American democracy.

Questions

1. In what ways is American democracy improved and enhanced by the prevalence of public opinion polling? In what ways is American democracy harmed or weakened?
2. On balance, do you think public opinion polling is good or bad for American democracy? Why?

5.4 Polling and Democracy (2004)

Herbert B. Asher

• • •

Polls and Their Effect on the Political System

Do polls promote or hinder citizens' influence in their society? Is the overall effect of polls on the political system positive or negative? These questions continue to be vigorously debated. Writing in 1940, [Paul T.] Cherington argued that polls

---

From Herbert B. Asher, *Polling and the Public: What Every Citizen Should Know*, pp. 193–200. Copyright © CQ Press, a division of Congressional Quarterly, Inc. Reprinted by permission of the publisher, CQ Press.

enhanced the public's influence because they provide a way for the voices of a representative cross-section of Americans to be heard; no longer would the views of a tiny segment of the population be the only ones to gain prominence. [Eugene] Meyer argued further that polls provide information about the preferences of the citizenry that enable political leaders to resist the pressures of narrow groups pushing their own agendas in the name of the broader public.

These arguments are still true today, yet the limitations inherent in polls as a mode of citizen influence must be recognized. First, . . . the United States is a representative democracy that comprises, in addition to elected representatives, a wide variety of organized groups trying to promote their own interests. Any assumption that the results of public opinion polls can be translated directly into public policy is naive. It might not be desirable for public opinion polls to be routinely translated into public policy. Polls at times may tap only the most ephemeral and transitory of opinions. Little deliberation and thought may have gone into the responses the public offered. And certainly the rich complexities of issues can never be captured in a public opinion poll as effectively as they are in a legislative debate or a committee hearing.

Second, even if the public's views as reflected in the polls are well formed, polling often demonstrates that there is no majority view on an issue; opinion may be split in many different ways. Moreover, automatically opting for the majority or plurality position would call into question such cherished values as the protection of minority rights. One can envisage situations in which the unqualified use of public opinion polls might threaten rather than enhance representative democracy and related values.

Third, a focus on poll results ignores the processes by which the public's opinions are formed and modified. For example, one factor that shapes popular opinion is the behavior of political elites. When the White House orchestrates a massive public relations campaign, with a nationally televised presidential address, highly publicized presidential travels, and the submission of a legislative package to Congress, it is not surprising to see public opinion shift in the direction the White House intends. Public opinion is not always an independent expression of the public's views; it can be an opinion that has been manipulated, at least in part, by elites.

Sometimes, the president may take the lead on an unpopular issue, as typically occurs during an international crisis. After the president delivers a major address to the nation, public opinion polls usually indicate an upsurge of support for the president's actions, emerging from feelings of patriotism and a desire for national unity in times of crisis. Such was the case with the Persian Gulf crisis that arose in 1990, the terrorist attacks on American soil in 2001, and the war with Iraq in 2003.

Other times, the president may scramble to catch up with and then shape public opinion. That happened in summer and fall 1986 in response to Americans' heightened concern about the drug abuse problem. After the tragic deaths of famous athletes and increased media coverage of the drug crisis, a plurality of Americans cited drugs as the nation's most important problem in a CBS News/*New York Times* poll conducted in August 1986. Congress, particularly House Democrats, trying to get out in front on this issue, proposed a major antidrug offensive. The White

House responded by taking the initiative from Congress: President Ronald Reagan offered his own proposals, and he and the first lady gave an unprecedented joint address on national television. Major new legislation was passed to address the drug problem. In 1989 President George Bush declared a war on drugs and named a drug "czar" to coordinate federal initiatives. The president announced many antidrug proposals, which, according to the polls, were supported overwhelmingly by Americans even though they felt strongly that Bush's plan did not go far enough.

What do these examples say about citizen influence? Certainly, the drug example suggests the potency of popular opinion on issues that arouse the public. But even there the salience of the issue was very much a function of the behavior of the news media and the political elites who brought it to the fore; the public responded to the issue but did not create it. The adoption of antidrug measures into law suggests that aroused public opinion spurs government policy initiatives. But when the media and political leaders stop talking about an issue, it becomes less salient and recedes from popular consciousness, and citizens may have a misguided feeling that somehow the problem has been resolved.

Sometimes political elites may misinterpret (deliberately or unintentionally) what the polls are actually saying. Unfortunately, political leaders sometimes fail to recognize the limitations and circumstances of poll responses and automatically construe supportive poll results as ringing endorsements of a broad policy agenda. The tendency of Americans to rally around the leadership of the president during an international crisis should not be blindly interpreted as a popular mandate for particular policies.

[Benjamin] Ginsberg has argued that polling weakens the influence of public opinion in a democratic society. He asserts that there are many ways besides participating in a poll for citizens to express their opinions, such as demonstrations and protests, letter-writing campaigns, and interest group activities. But because polling is deemed to be scientific and representative of the broad public, it has dominated the other types of expression.

According to Ginsberg, four fundamental changes in the nature of public opinion are attributable to the increased frequency of polling: First, responding to a public opinion survey is an easier form of expression than writing a letter or participating in a protest—activities usually undertaken by citizens who are intensely committed to their positions. Anyone can respond to a poll question, whether or not the feelings about an issue are strong. Thus in a public opinion poll the intense opinions of a small minority can be submerged by the indifferent views of the sizable majority. Indeed, government leaders may try to dismiss the views of dissidents by citing polls that indicate that most Americans do not support the dissidents' position.

Second, polling changes public opinion from a behavior, such as letter writing or demonstrating, to an *attitude*, as revealed in a verbal response to a poll question. Ginsberg argues that public opinion expressed through polls is less threatening to political elites than are opinions expressed through behavioral mechanisms. Moreover, polls can inform leaders about dissidents' attitudes before they become behaviors. The information on attitudes gives government a kind of early warning as well as an opportunity to change attitudes either by seeking remedies to problems or by relying on public relations techniques to manipulate opinions.

Third, polls convert public opinion from a characteristic of groups to an attribute of individuals. This factor enables public officials to ignore group leaders and instead attend directly to the opinions of citizens. Unfortunately, this attention may effectively weaken individuals' political power because organized activity, not individual activity, is the key to citizen influence in the United States. If government leaders are able to use the polls as an excuse to ignore group preferences, then citizen influence will be lessened.

Finally, polling reduces citizens' opportunities to set the political agenda. The topics of public opinion polls are those selected by the polls' sponsors rather than by the citizenry. Therefore, citizens lose control over the agenda of issues, and the agenda as revealed through the polls may differ in major ways from the issues that really matter to people.

Ginsberg's conclusion is that polling makes public opinion safer and less threatening for government. Opinions expressed through the polls place fewer demands and constraints on decision makers and [according to Ginsberg] provide political leaders with an enhanced ability "to anticipate, regulate, and manipulate popular attitudes." In short, Ginsberg's thesis is that the advent and growth of public opinion polling have been detrimental to citizen influence.

Ginsberg has raised some important issues about the dangers inherent in the proliferation of public opinion polls, even if one does not agree with all of his conclusions. Clearly, citizens must be on guard against allowing public opinion to become synonymous with the results of public opinion polls. Public opinion manifests itself in many ways, including those Ginsberg mentioned—protests, letter-writing campaigns, direct personal contact with decision makers, and many others. Political elites recognize the potential costs of ignoring these alternative forms of political expression, but it is critical that the media also recognize that polls are not the only legitimate expression of public opinion. Citizens, too, must avoid allowing a passive activity such as responding to a poll to replace more active modes of political participation.

Although there is evidence that direct electoral participation has declined in the United States, other group-based activities are on the rise. And if groups have the resources, they can use polls to promote their agenda when it differs from that of the political elites. Contrary to Ginsberg's assertion, polls need not make public opinion a property of individuals rather than groups. Polls can identify clusters of citizens (often defined by demographic characteristics) who do not share the prevailing views of the citizenry at large. For example, public opinion polls on the ultimate outcome of the 2000 presidential election campaign showed sharp differences between white and black Americans on the perceived legitimacy of the Bush victory and the overall fairness of the legal and election process. Whether Ginsberg's concerns are overstated or not, the polls are playing a growing role in American political life, in campaigns, in governance, and in popular discourse.

[Larry M.] Bartels takes a different view of the role of public opinion polls in democratic governance. He argues that public opinion polls do not and cannot provide political leaders with directions about what policy options to pursue because, while the polls measure citizens' attitudes, they do not measure the public's preferences on issues of public policy. Bartels argues that responses to policy questions in a poll can vary so dramatically, depending on the wording of the questions, the context in which they are placed, and the choices that are offered, that they provide leaders with little real guidance about how they should govern.

Observers have been concerned about the effect of polls not only on citizens' political clout but also on the performance of elected officeholders. More than fifty-five years ago [Edward L.] Bernays warned that polls would dominate the political leadership and that decision makers would slavishly follow the polls to please the people and maintain popularity. The polls might even paralyze political leaders, preventing them from taking unpopular positions and from trying to educate the public on controversial issues. Political observers like Bernays still contemptuously deride politicians who figuratively always keep the polls in their pockets, lacking the courage to act on their own convictions no matter what the polls say.

Some officeholders do blindly follow the polls, but today those who abuse, manipulate, and misinterpret polls are of greater concern. In particular, presidents have increasingly tried to manage public opinion. For example, [Bruce E.] Altschuler describes how President Lyndon Johnson tried to take the offensive when his poll ratings began to decline. To convince key elites that he was still strong, Johnson attacked the public polls, selectively leaked private polls, and tried to influence poll results and poll reporting by cultivating the acquaintance of the pollsters. Likewise, the Nixon administration tried to manipulate the Gallup and Harris polling organizations by influencing how they carried out and reported their national polls.

In-house polling was a central part of the skillful public relations efforts of the Reagan presidency. Writing about the Reagan administration, [Richard S.] Beal and [Ronald H.] Hinckley argued that polls became more important after the presidential election than before it; indeed, polls were a much more important tool of governing than was commonly recognized. Likewise, polling was central to the operation of the Clinton White House and prominent in the second Bush White House. [Lawrence R.] Jacobs and [Robert Y.] Shapiro have shown how the polling operations of the Kennedy, Johnson, and especially the Nixon presidencies served as precursors for the contemporary White House use of polls. Certainly no one would deny the president and other elected officials their pollsters. But the measure of an incumbent's performance should not simply be the degree of success achieved in shaping public opinion in particular ways.

One final effect of polls on the political system merits consideration: their contribution to political discourse. Because they often are cited as evidence in support of particular positions, polls have become a central part of political discussion. But polls have more subtle effects; in particular, Americans' awareness of the attitudes of their fellow citizens, learned through the polls, may alter their opinions and subsequent behaviors. This phenomenon has been explained in terms of the theories of the spiral of silence and pluralistic ignorance.

The spiral of silence thesis, developed by [Elisabeth] Noelle-Neumann, argues that individuals desire to be respected and popular. To accomplish this, they become sensitive to prevailing opinions and how they are changing. If, on the one hand, individuals observe that their opinions seem to be in the minority and are losing support, they are less likely to express them publicly. Consequently, such opinions will seem to the individuals who hold them to be weaker than they actually are. On the other hand, if people perceive that their views are popular and on the ascendant, they are more likely to discuss them openly. Such opinions then gain more adherents and seem stronger than they actually are. Thus one opinion becomes established as dominant, while the other recedes to the background. "Pluralistic ignorance" refers to people's misperceptions of what other individuals and groups believe. Those misperceptions affect their own views and their willingness to express them. [Kurt] Lang and [Gladys Engel] Lang linked the notions of pluralistic ignorance and the spiral of silence in a discussion of American racial attitudes of twenty years ago:

> Typical of pluralistic ignorance has been the unwillingness of many whites to acknowledge their own antiblack prejudice, which they believe to contradict an accepted cultural ideal. As a way of justifying their own behavior, these whites often attribute such prejudice to other whites by saying "I wouldn't mind having a black neighbor except that my neighbors wouldn't stand for it."
>
> But what if such fears about their neighbors' reactions proved unjustified? What if polls showed an expressed readiness for a range of desegregation measures that these whites do not believe others are prepared to accept? Such a finding contrary to prevailing belief would be controversial. Where the real opinion lies may be less important than the change in perception of the climate of opinion. A definitive poll finding can destroy the premise that underlies the justification for behavior clearly at variance with professed ideals. In these circumstances a spiral of silence about the real opinion fosters a climate inhospitable to segregationist sentiment and drives it underground.

As this example illustrates, public opinion polls provide citizens with a mechanism for knowing what their fellow citizens think and believe. This is especially important for people who interact mostly with like-minded individuals and may therefore have little sense of the diversity of opinion that may exist on an issue. If the polls can accurately measure the underlying beliefs and values of the citizenry, then people no longer have to be at the mercy of unrepresentative views that they mistakenly believe are those of the majority. The polls can tell people a lot about themselves as part of American society, and that self-knowledge may foster a healthier and more open political debate. That being said, it also is possible that what they learn from polls about the views of their fellow citizens may surprise, shock, offend, and even divide them. Certainly it was shocking to learn from public opinion polls that substantial numbers of Americans believed that weapons of mass destruction had been found in Iraq after the war, when they had not; that weapons of mass destruction had been used against American soldiers during the war with Iraq, when they had not; and that Iraq and Saddam Hussein had worked with al Qaeda on the September 11 terrorist attacks, when no proof of such a link had yet been found. . . . But learning about [these beliefs] from public opinion polls helps us better understand the preferences that Americans did hold regarding various aspects of U.S. policy toward Iraq. ∎

View from the Inside

As selection 5.4 suggests, the use of pollsters by presidents and other politicians has become the source of some controversy. Critics point out that the overuse of public opinion polls tends to turn leaders into followers and also encourages politicians to tell the public only what it wants to hear—a practice that can lead to erratic public policy, a dangerous short-term point of view, and a loss of critically needed perspective. Paradoxically, critics suggest, politicians who rely too much on public opinion polls may end up losing touch with the people; they would be better off relying instead on their own political instincts and leadership abilities.

The Clinton administration was well known for its almost obsessive use of polling. Bill Clinton's critics accused him of using polls to shape public policy, in effect following the public instead of leading it. Such claims eventually became part of George W. Bush's presidential campaign, and the new Bush administration soon cultivated the image that it governed, as Joshua Green writes in this selection, "based upon principle and not polls and focus groups."

In fact, Green argues, the Bush administration has not abandoned polls and focus groups. Although Bush remains as reliant on pollsters as any modern president, his pollsters have been banished to the back room and kept out of sight, allowing the administration to benefit from the best techniques of market research while maintaining an anti-polling image.

Questions

1. What advantages do polls and focus groups bring to the president? What dangers do they present? In answering, consider especially the experiences of the Clinton and Bush presidencies.
2. Consider the role of the political pollster in American governance in light of the arguments concerning democracy presented by James Madison in *Federalist* No. 10 (selection 1.1). Do public opinion polls increase the possibility that majority factions will exert an overpowering influence at the national level?

5.5 The Other War Room (2002)

Joshua Green

On a Friday afternoon late last year [2001], press secretaries from every recent administration gathered in the War Room of the White House at the invitation of Ari Fleischer, press secretary to President Bush. There was no agenda. It was just one of those unexpectedly nice things that seemed to transpire during the brief period after September 11 when people thought of themselves as Americans first and Democrats and Republicans second. Over a lunch of crab cakes and steak, Republicans such as Fleischer and Marlin Fitzwater traded war stories with Joe Lockhart, Mike McCurry, and assorted other Democrats. Halfway through lunch, President Bush dropped by unexpectedly and launched into an impromptu briefing of his own, ticking off the items on his agenda until he arrived at the question of whether it was preferable to issue vague warnings of possible terrorist threats or to stay quietly vigilant so as not to alarm people. At this point, former Clinton press secretary Dee Dee Myers piped up, "What do the poll numbers say?" All eyes turned to Bush. Without missing a beat, the famous Bush smirk crossed the president's face and he replied, "In this White House, Dee Dee, we don't poll on something as important as national security."

This wasn't a stray comment, but a glimpse of a larger strategy that has served Bush extremely well since he first launched his campaign for president—the myth that his administration doesn't use polling. As Bush endlessly insisted on the campaign trail, he governs "based upon principle and not polls and focus groups."

It's not hard to understand the appeal of this tactic. Ever since the Clinton administration's well-noted excesses—calling on pollsters to help determine vacation spots and family pets—polling has become a kind of shorthand for everything people dislike about Washington politics. "Pollsters have developed a reputation as Machiavellian plotters whose job it is to think up ways to exploit the public," says Andrew Kohut, director of the Pew Research Center for the People and the Press. Announcing that one ignores polls, then, is an easy way of conveying an impression of leadership, judgment, and substance. No one has recognized and used this to such calculated effect as Bush. When he announced he would "bring a new tone to Washington," he just as easily could have said he'd banish pollsters from the White House without any loss of effect. One of the most dependable poll results is that people don't like polling.

But in fact, the Bush administration is a frequent consumer of polls, though it takes extraordinary measures to appear that it isn't. This administration, unlike Clinton's, rarely uses poll results to ply reporters or congressional leaders for sup-

Joshua Green, "The Other War Room: President Bush Doesn't Believe in Polling—Just Ask His Pollsters," *Washington Monthly* 34 (April 2002), pp. 11–16. Reprinted with permission from *The Washington Monthly*. Copyright by Washington Monthly Publishing, LLC, 733 15th St. NW, Suite 520, Washington, D.C. 20005. (202) 393-5155. Web site: www.washingtonmonthly.com.

port. "It's rare to even hear talk of it unless you give a Bush guy a couple of drinks," says one White House reporter. But Republican National Committee filings show that Bush actually uses polls much more than he lets on, in ways both similar and dissimilar to Clinton. Like Clinton, Bush is most inclined to use polls when he's struggling. It's no coincidence that the administration did its heaviest polling last summer [2001], after the poorly received rollout of its energy plan, and amid much talk of the "smallness" of the presidency. A *Washington Monthly* analysis of Republican National Committee disbursement filings revealed that Bush's principal pollsters received $346,000 in direct payments in 2001. Add to that the multiple boutique polling firms the administration regularly employs for specialized and targeted polls and the figure is closer to $1 million. That's about half the amount Clinton spent during his first year; but while Clinton used polling to craft popular policies, Bush uses polling to spin unpopular ones—arguably a much more cynical undertaking.

Bush's principal pollster, Jan van Lohuizen, and his focus-group guru, Fred Steeper, are the best-kept secrets in Washington. Both are respected but low-key, proficient but tight-lipped, and, unlike such larger-than-life Clinton pollsters as Dick Morris and Mark Penn, happy to remain anonymous. They toil in the background, poll-testing the words and phrases the president uses to sell his policies to an often-skeptical public; they're the Bush administration's Cinderella. "In terms of the modern presidency," says Ron Faucheux, editor of *Campaigns & Elections*, "van Lohuizen is the lowest-profile pollster we've ever had." But as Bush shifts his focus back toward a domestic agenda, he'll be relying on his pollsters more than ever.

Bush's Brain

On the last day of February [2002], the Bush administration kicked off its renewed initiative to privatize Social Security in a speech before the National Summit on Retirement Savings in Washington, D.C. Rather than address "Social Security," Bush opted to speak about "retirement security." And during the brief speech he repeated the words "choice" (three times), "compound interest" (four times), "opportunity" (nine times) and "savings" (18 times). These words were not chosen lightly. The repetition was prompted by polls and focus groups. During the campaign, Steeper honed and refined Bush's message on Social Security (with key words such as "choice," "control," and "higher returns"), measuring it against Al Gore's attack through polls and focus groups ("Wall Street roulette," "bankruptcy" and "break the contract"). Steeper discovered that respondents preferred Bush's position by 50 percent to 38 percent, despite the conventional wisdom that tampering with Social Security is political suicide. He learned, as he explained to an academic conference last February, that "there's a great deal of cynicism about the federal government being able to do anything right, which translated to the federal government not having the ability to properly invest people's Social Security dollars." By couching Bush's rhetoric in poll-tested phrases that reinforced this notion, and adding others that stress the benefits of privatization, he was able to capitalize on what most observers had considered to be a significant political disadvantage. (Independent polls generally find that when fully apprised of Bush's plan, including the risks, most voters don't support it.)

This is typical of how the Bush administration uses polls: policies are chosen beforehand, polls used to spin them. Because many of Bush's policies aren't necessarily popular with a majority of voters, Steeper and van Lohuizen's job essentially consists of finding words to sell them to the public. Take, for instance, the Bush energy plan. When administration officials unveiled it last May [2001], they repeatedly described it as "balanced" and "comprehensive," and stressed Bush's "leadership" and use of "modern" methods to prevent environmental damage. As *Time* magazine's Jay Carney and John Dickerson revealed, van Lohuizen had poll-tested pitch phrases for weeks before arriving at these as the most likely to conciliate a skeptical public. (Again, independent polls showed weak voter support for the Bush plan.) And the "education recession" Bush trumpeted throughout the campaign? Another triumph of opinion research. Same with "school choice," [and] the "death tax." . . . Even the much-lauded national service initiative Bush proposed in his State of the Union address was the product of focus grouping. Though publicly Bush prides himself on never looking in the mirror (that's "leadership"), privately, he's not quite so secure. His pollsters have even conducted favorability ratings on Ari Fleischer and [Bush adviser] Karen Hughes.

• • •

Poll Vault

The practice of presidents poll-testing their message dates back to John F. Kennedy, who wished to pursue a civil rights agenda but knew that he would have to articulate it in words that the American public in the 1960s would accept. Alarm about being known to use polls is just as old. Kennedy was so afraid of being discovered that he kept the polling data locked in a safe in the office of his brother, the attorney general. Lyndon Johnson polled more heavily than Kennedy did and learned, through polling, that allowing Vietnam to become an issue in 1964 could cost him re-election. Richard Nixon brought polling—and paranoia over polling—to a new level, believing that his appeal to voters was his reputation as a skilled policymaker, and that if people discovered the extent to which he was polling, they would view him as "slick" and desert him. So he kept his poll data in a safe in his home. But though presidents considered it shameful, polling became an important tool for governing well. Nixon was smart enough to make good use of his polls, once opting to ban oil drilling off the California coast after polling revealed it to be highly unpopular with voters. Jimmy Carter's pollster, Pat Caddell, was the first rock-star pollster, partying with celebrities and cultivating a high-profile image as the president's Svengali (an image considerably tarnished when Caddell's polling for another client, Coca-Cola, became the rationale for the disastrous "New Coke" campaign in the 1980s).

Ronald Reagan polled obsessively throughout his presidency. His pollster, Richard Wirthlin, went so far as to conduct them "before Reagan was inaugurated, while he was being inaugurated, and the day after he was inaugurated," says an administration veteran. He was the first to use polls to sell a right-wing agenda to the country, but he knew enough to retreat when polls indicated that he couldn't win a fight. (Wirthlin's polls convinced Reagan not to cut Social Security, as he'd planned.) By contrast, his successor, George H. W. Bush, practically eschewed polls altogether. "There was a reaction against using polls because they reacted against everything Reagan," says Ron Hinckley, a Bush pollster. "They wanted to put their own name on everything. But their efforts to not be like Reagan took them into a framework of dealing with things that ultimately proved fatal." Indeed, in his first two years in office, Bush is said to have conducted just two polls. Even at Bush's highest point—after the Gulf War, when his approval rating stood at 88 percent—Hinckley says that his economic numbers were in the 40s. "We were in a hell of a lot of trouble," he says, "and nobody wanted to listen."

Bill Clinton, of course, polled like no other president. In addition to polling more often and in greater detail than his predecessors, he put unprecedented faith in his pollsters, elevating them to the status of senior advisers. His tendency to obsess over polls disconcerted even those closest to him, and his over-reliance on polls led to some devastating errors, such as following a Morris poll showing that voters wouldn't accept a candid acknowledgment of his relationship with Monica Lewinsky. . . .

"The Circle Is Tight"

When George W. Bush launched his campaign for president, he did so with two prevailing thoughts in mind: to avoid his father's mistakes and to distinguish himself from Bill Clinton. To satisfy the first, Bush needed a tax cut to rival the one being offered by Steve Forbes, at the time considered Bush's most formidable rival for the GOP nomination. But to satisfy the second, Bush needed to engage in some tricky maneuvering. A van Lohuizen poll conducted in late 1998 showed tax cuts to be "the least popular choice" on his agenda among swing voters. So Bush faced a dilemma: He had to sell Americans a tax cut most didn't want, using a poll-crafted sales pitch he didn't want them to know about. In speeches, Bush started listing the tax cut after more popular items like saving Social Security and education. In March 2001, with support still flagging, he began pitching "tax cuts and debt relief" rather than just tax cuts—his polling showed that the public was much more interested in the latter. After plenty of creative math and more poll-tested phrases, Bush's tax cut finally won passage (a larger one, in fact, than he'd been offering in '98).

In a way, Bush's approach to polling is the opposite of Clinton's. He uses polls but conceals that fact, and, instead of polling to ensure that new policies have broad public support, takes policies favored by his conservative base and polls on how to make them seem palatable to mainstream voters. This pattern extends to the entire administration. Whereas Clinton's polling data were regularly circulated among the staff, Bush limits his to . . . [a] handful of senior advisers. . . . According to White House aides, the subject is rarely broached with the president or at other senior staff meetings. "The circle is tight," Matthew Dowd, Bush's chief of polling, testifies. "Very tight." As with Kennedy and Nixon, the Bush administration keeps its polling data under lock and key. Reagan circulated favorable polling data widely among congressional Republicans in an effort to build support. Clinton did likewise and extended this tactic to the media, using polls as political currency to persuade reporters that he was on the right side of an issue. "You don't see it like you did in the Dick Wirthlin days," says a top Republican congressman.

"The White House pollster won't meet with the caucus to go through poll data. It just doesn't happen." Says a White House reporter, "The Clinton folks couldn't wait to call you up and share polling data, and Democratic pollsters who worked for the White House were always calling you to talk about it. But there's a general dictate under Bush that they don't use polls to tell them what to think." This policy extends to the president's pollsters, who are discouraged from identifying themselves as such. The strategy seems to be working. A brief, unscientific survey of White House reporters revealed that most couldn't name van Lohuizen as the Bush's primary pollster (most guessed Dowd, who doesn't actually poll). For his part, van Lohuizen sounded genuinely alarmed when I contacted him.

Crafted Talk

It's no mystery why the Bush administration keeps its polling operation in a secure, undisclosed location. Survey after survey shows that voters don't want a president slavishly following polls—they want "leadership" (another word that crops up in Bush's speeches with suspicious frequency). So it's with undisguised relish that Dowd tells me, "It was true during the campaign, it's true now: We don't poll policy positions. Ever."

But voters don't like a president to ignore their desires either. One of the abiding tensions in any democracy is between the need for leaders to respond to public opinion but also to be willing to act in ways that run counter to it. Good presidents strike the right balance. And polls, rightly used, help them do it. . . .

Presidents, of course, must occasionally break with public opinion. But there's a thin line between being principled and being elitist. For many years, Democrats hurt themselves and the country by presuming they knew better than voters when it came to things like welfare, crime, and tax increases. Clinton used polling to help Democrats break this habit. Bush is more intent on using it to facilitate the GOP's own peculiar political elitism—the conviction that coddling corporations and cutting taxes for the rich will help the count, regardless of the fact that a majority of voters disagree.

Bush's attempt to slip a conservative agenda past a moderate public could come back to hurt him, especially now that his high approval ratings might tempt him to overreach. Recent history shows that poll-tested messages are often easy to parry. During the debate over Clinton's healthcare plan, for instance, Republican opponents launched their own poll-tested counterattack, the famous "Harry and Louise" ads, which were broadcast mainly on airport cable networks such as "CNN Airport" where well-traveled congressmen would be sure to spot them and assume they were ubiquitous. Because lawmakers and voters never fully bought Clinton's policy, it couldn't withstand the carefully tested GOP rebuttal. . . .

A similar fate befell the GOP when it took over Congress in 1995, after campaigning on a list of promises dubbed the "Contract With America." As several pollsters and political scientists have since pointed out, the Contract's policies were heavily geared toward the party's conservative base but didn't register with voters—things like corporate tax cuts and limiting the right to sue. The GOP's strategy was to win over the press and the public with poll-tested "power phrases." Education vouchers, for instance, were promoted as a way of "strengthening rights of parents in their children's education," and Republicans were instructed by RNC chairman Haley Barbour to repeat such phrases "until you vomit." But when it came to proposals such as cutting Medicare, Republicans discovered that their confidence in being able to move public opinion—"preserving" and "protecting" Medicare—was misplaced. Clinton successfully branded them as "extremists," and this proposal, along with many of the Contract's provisions, never made it beyond the House.

Like so many other Republican ideas, Barbour's has been reborn under Bush. "What's happened over time is that there's a lot more polling on spin," says [political scientist Lawrence R.] Jacobs. "That's exactly where Bush is right now. He's not polling to find out issues that the public supports so that he can respond to their substantive interests. He's polling on presentation. To those of us who study it, most of his major policy statements come off as completely poll concocted." Should this continue, the administration that condemns polling so righteously may not like what the polls wind up saying. ■

Chapter 6

Interest Groups

Interest groups play a vital role in American politics. Along with political parties, they are the most important way that Americans organize to express their views and make their demands on government. Interest groups play key roles in the electoral arena and in government policy making. They are active in all three branches of the federal government and in the states.

Interest groups are by no means free of controversy. Government responsiveness to interest groups, if carried too far, can lead to the triumph of special interests at the expense of the public interest. Group involvement in support of particular candidates can be a legitimate way for citizens to advance their interests, but such activity can all too easily cross the line into influence peddling and vote buying.

Above all, the controversy over interest groups rests on a critical debate in modern political science: whether the clash of group interests, if fought on a level playing field where all groups are represented fairly and equitably, will inevitably or even generally result in the victory of the public interest. Those who believe that the public interest is, in effect, the sum of the private interests advocate a large number of effective interest groups. Those on the other side look for ways to limit the power and influence of interest groups in order to allow the public interest to emerge.

This chapter examines the roles played by interest groups in American politics, with particular attention to the dramatic changes in interest group activity over recent decades. Selection 6.1 presents a classic analysis of interest groups by the political scientist E. E. Schattschneider. Selection 6.2 provides an up-to-date account of the roles played by interest groups written by political scientists Paul S. Herrnson, Ronald G. Shaiko, and Clyde Wilcox; they argue that interest groups are sophisticated and flexible, and able to adapt quickly to changing circumstances. Selection 6.3 examines the ongoing controversy over the influence of Washington lobbyists, particularly in light of recent scandals involving prominent members of Congress. Finally, selection 6.4 puts the spotlight on how Microsoft Corporation and other high-tech firms learned to play the Washington lobbying game.

Chapter Questions

1. Is a system of interest group politics consistent with the idea of democracy? Reread Madison's *Federalist* No. 10 and *Federalist* No. 51 (selections 1.1 and 1.4) as you consider your answer.
2. Why are interest groups important in the American political system? What roles do they play? How have the roles of interest groups changed in the past several decades?

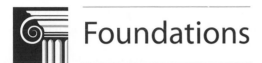 # Foundations

What exactly is an interest group? What is a public interest group, and what distinguishes it from a special interest group? Before examining interest groups in any detail, we need to have an accurate understanding of the meaning of these terms and the nature of interest group politics.

The following selection presents a classic explanation and description of interest group politics. Central to political scientist E. E. Schattschneider's understanding of interest groups are their size and their narrow focus. Interest groups, by definition, are small and specialized. As such, they can be distinguished from political parties, which, to be effective, must be both large and broad-based. A political system that encourages the formation of interest groups, and responds to their arguments, demands, and pressures, will of necessity differ from one in which citizens express their views and make their demands felt primarily through political parties.

Since Schattschneider's book was published in 1961, American politics has, if anything, become even more focused around interest groups. The role of parties as effective mechanisms for transmitting the demands of citizens to their elected representatives has correspondingly diminished.

Schattschneider's analysis, though more than a generation old, remains an excellent introduction to the theoretical underpinnings of interest group politics.

Questions

1. What characteristics distinguish a special interest group from a public interest group? Is this distinction meaningful, in Schattschneider's view?
2. What would one expect to be the logical result of a political system in which small interest groups dominate? What are the implications of such a system for the role of political parties? For the structure of government institutions? For the nature of public policy?

6.1 The Scope and Bias of the Pressure System (1961)

E. E. Schattschneider

Pressure groups have played a remarkable role in American politics, but they have played an even more remarkable role in American political theory. Considering the political condition of the country in the first third of the twentieth century, it was probably inevitable that the discussion of special-interest pressure groups should lead to development of "group" theories of politics in which an attempt is made to explain everything in terms of group activity, i.e., an attempt to formulate a universal group theory. Since one of the best ways to test an idea is to ride it into the ground, political theory has unquestionably been improved by the heroic attempt to create a political universe revolving about the group. Now that we have a number of drastic statements of the group theory of politics pushed to a great extreme, we ought to be able to see what the limitations of the idea are. . . .

We might begin to break the problem into its component parts by exploring the distinction between public and private interests. If we can validate this distinction, we shall have established one of the boundaries of the subject.

As a matter of fact, the distinction between *public* and *private* interests is a thoroughly respectable one; it is one of the oldest known to political theory. In the literature of the subject, the public interest refers to general or common interests shared by all or by substantially all members of the community. Presumably no community exists unless there is some kind of community of interests, just as there is no nation without some notion of national interests. If it is really impossible to distinguish between private and public interests, the group theorists have produced a revolution in political thought so great that it is impossible to foresee its consequences. For this reason the distinction ought to be explored with great care.

At a time when nationalism is described as one of the most dynamic forces in the world, it should not be difficult to understand that national interests actually do exist. It is necessary only to consider the proportion of the American budget devoted to national defense to realize that the common interest in national survival is a great one. Measured in dollars this interest is one of the biggest things in the world. Moreover, it is difficult to describe this interest as special. The diet on which the American leviathan feeds is something more than a jungle of disparate special interests. In the literature of democratic theory the body of common agreement found in the community is known as the "consensus," without which it is believed that no democratic system can survive.

From *Semi-Sovereign People: A Realist's View of Democracy in America*, pp. 21–35. First edition by E. E. Schattschneider, copyright © 1961. Reprinted with permission of Wadsworth, a division of Thomson Learning: www.thomsonrights.com. Fax 800 730-2215.

The reality of the common interest is suggested by demonstrated capacity of the community to survive. There must be something that holds people together.

In contrast with the common interests are the special interests. The implication of this term is that these are interests shared by only a few people or a fraction of the community; they *exclude* others and may be *adverse* to them. A special interest is exclusive in about the same way as private property is exclusive. In a complex society it is not surprising that there are some interests that are shared by all or substantially all members of the community and some interests that are not shared so widely. The distinction is useful precisely because conflicting claims are made by people about the nature of their interests in controversial matters.

Perfect agreement within the community is not always possible, but an interest may be said to have become public when it is shared so widely as to be substantially universal. Thus, the difference between 99 percent agreement and perfect agreement is not so great that it becomes necessary to argue that all interests are special, that the interests of the 99 percent are as special as the interests of the 1 percent. For example, the law is probably doing an adequate job of defining the public interest in domestic tranquility despite the fact that there is nearly always one dissenter at every hanging. That is, the law defines the public interest in spite of the fact that there may be some outlaws.

Since one function of theory is to explain reality, it is reasonable to add that it is a good deal easier to explain what is going on in politics by making a distinction between public and private interests than it is to attempt to explain *everything* in terms of special interests. The attempt to prove that all interests are special forces us into circumlocutions such as those involved in the argument that people have special interests in the common good. The argument can be made, but it seems a long way around to avoid a useful distinction.

What is to be said about the argument that the distinction between public and special interests is "subjective" and is therefore "unscientific"?

All discussions of interests, special as well as general, refer to the motives, desires, and intentions of people. In this sense the whole discussion of interests is subjective. We have made progress in the study of politics because people have observed some kind of relation between the political behavior of people and certain wholly impersonal data concerning their ownership of property, income, economic status, professions, and the like. All that we know about interests, private as well as public, is based on inferences of this sort. Whether the distinction in any given case is valid depends on the evidence and on the kinds of inferences drawn from the evidence.

The only meaningful way we can speak of the interests of an association like the National Association of Manufacturers is to draw inferences from the fact that the membership is a select group to which only manufacturers may belong and to try to relate that datum to what the association does. The implications, logic, and deductions are persuasive only if they furnish reasonable explanations of the facts. That is all that any theory about interests can do. It has seemed persuasive to students of politics to suppose that manufacturers do not join an association to which only manufacturers may belong merely to promote philanthropic or cultural or religious interests, for example. The basis of selection of the membership creates an inference about the organization's concerns. The conclusions drawn from this datum seem to fit what we know about the policies promoted by the association; i.e., the policies seem to reflect the exclusive interests of manufacturers. The method is not foolproof, but it works better than many other kinds of analysis and is useful precisely because special-interest groups often tend to rationalize their special interests as public interests.

Is it possible to distinguish between the "interests" of the members of the National Association of Manufacturers and the members of the American League to Abolish Capital Punishment? The facts in the two cases are not identical. First, *the members of the A.L.A.C.P. obviously do not expect to be hanged.* The membership of the A.L.A.C.P. is not restricted to persons under indictment for murder or in jeopardy of the extreme penalty. *Anybody* can join A.L.A.C.P. Its members oppose capital punishment, although they are not personally likely to benefit by the policy they advocate. The inference is therefore that the interest of the A.L.A.C.P. is not adverse, exclusive, or special. It is not like the interest of the Petroleum Institute in depletion allowances. . . .

. . . The question here is not whether the distinction can be made but whether or not it is worth making. Organization has been described as "merely a stage or degree of interaction" in the development of a group.

The proposition is a good one, but what conclusions do we draw from it? We do not dispose of the matter by calling the distinction between organized and unorganized groups a "mere" difference of degree because some of the greatest differences in the world are differences of degree. As far as special-interest politics is concerned the implication to be avoided is that a few workmen who habitually stop at a corner saloon for a glass of beer are essentially the same as the United States Army because the difference between them is merely one of degree. At this point we have distinction that makes a difference. The distinction between organized and unorganized groups is worth making because it ought to alert us against an analysis which begins as a general group theory of politics but ends with a defense of pressure politics as inherent, universal, permanent, and inevitable. This kind of confusion comes from the loosening of categories involved in the universalization of group concepts.

Since the beginning of intellectual history, scholars have sought to make progress in their work by distinguishing between things that are unlike and by dividing their subject matter into categories to examine them more intelligently. It is something of a novelty, therefore, when group theorists reverse this process by discussing their subject in terms so universal that they wipe out all categories, because this is the dimension in which it is least possible to understand anything.

If we are able, therefore, to distinguish between public and private interests and between organized and unorganized groups we have marked out the major boundaries of the subject; *we have given the subject shape and scope.* We are now in a position to attempt to define the area we want to explore. Having cut the pie into four pieces, we can now appropriate the piece we want and leave the rest to someone else. For a multitude of reasons *the most likely field of study is that of the organized, special-interest groups.* The advantage of concentrating on organized groups is that they are known, identifiable, and recognizable. The advantage of concentrating on special-interest groups is that they have one important characteristic in common; they are all exclusive. This piece of the pie (the organized special-interest groups) we shall call the *pressure system*. The pressure system has boundaries we can define; we can fix its scope and make an attempt to estimate its bias.

It may be assumed at the outset that all organized special-interest groups have some kind of impact on politics. A sample survey of organizations made by the Trade Associations Division of the United States Department of Commerce in 1942 concluded that "From 70 to 100 percent (of these associations) are planning activities in the field of government relations, trade promotion, trade practices, public relations, annual conventions, cooperation with other organizations, and information services."

The subject of our analysis can be reduced to manageable proportions and brought under control if we restrict ourselves to the groups whose interests in politics are sufficient to have led them to unite in formal organizations having memberships, bylaws, and officers. A further advantage of this kind of definition is, we may assume, that the organized special-interest groups are the most self-conscious, best developed, most intense and active groups. Whatever claims can be made for a group theory of politics ought to be sustained by the evidence concerning these groups, if the claims have any validity at all.

The organized groups listed in the various directories (such as *National Associations of the United States*, published at intervals by the United States Department of Commerce) and specialty yearbooks, registers, etc. and the *Lobby Index*, published by the United States House of Representatives, probably include the bulk of the organizations in the pressure system. All compilations are incomplete, but these are extensive enough to provide us with some basis for estimating the scope of the system.

By the time a group has developed the kind of interest that leads it to organize, it may be assumed that it has also developed some kind of political bias because *organization is itself a mobilization of bias in preparation for action*. Since these groups can be identified and since they have memberships (i.e., they include and exclude people), it is possible to think of the *scope* of the system.

When lists of these organizations are examined, the fact that strikes the student most forcibly is that *the system is very small*. The range of organized, identifiable, known groups is amazingly narrow; there is nothing remotely universal about it. There is a tendency on the part of the publishers of directories of associations to place an undue emphasis on business organizations, an emphasis that is almost inevitable because the business community is by a wide margin the most highly organized segment of society. Publishers doubtless tend also to reflect public demand for information. Nevertheless, the dominance of business groups in the pressure system is so marked that it probably cannot be explained away as an accident of the publishing industry.

The business character of the pressure system is shown by almost every list available. *National Associations of the United States* lists 1,860 business associations out of a total of 4,000 in the volume, though it refers without listing (p. VII) to 16,000 organizations of businessmen. One cannot be certain what the total content of the unknown associational universe may be, but, taken with the evidence found in other compilations, it is obvious that business is remarkably well represented. Some evidence of the over-all scope of the system is to be seen in the estimate that 15,000 national trade associations have a gross membership of about one million business firms. The data are incomplete, but even if we do not have a detailed map this is the shore dimly seen.

Much more directly related to pressure politics is the *Lobby Index, 1946–1949* (an index of organizations and individuals registering or filing quarterly reports under the Federal Lobbying Act), published as a report of the House Select Committee on Lobbying Activities. In this compilation, 825 out of a total of 1,247 entries (exclusive of individuals and Indian tribes) represented business. A selected list of the most important of the groups listed in the *Index* (the groups spending the largest sums of money on lobbying) published in the *Congressional Quarterly Log* shows 149 business organizations in a total of 265 listed.

The business or upper-class bias of the pressure system shows up everywhere. Businessmen are four or five times as likely to write to their congressmen as manual laborers are. College graduates are far more apt to write to their congressmen than people in the lowest educational category are.

The limited scope of the business pressure system is indicated by all available statistics. Among business organizations, the National Association of Manufacturers (with about 20,000 corporate members) and the Chamber of Commerce of the United States (about as large as the N.A.M.) are giants. Usually business associations are much smaller. Of 421 trade associations in the metal-products industry listed in *National Associations of the United States*, 153 have a membership of less than 20. The median membership was somewhere between 24 and 50. Approximately the same scale of memberships is to be found in the lumber, furniture, and paper industries where 37.3 percent of the associations listed had a membership of less than 20 and the median membership was in the 25 to 50 range.

The statistics in these cases are representative of nearly all other classifications of industry.

Data drawn from other sources support this thesis. Broadly, the pressure system has an upper-class bias. There is overwhelming evidence that participation in voluntary organizations is related to upper social and economic status; the rate of participation is much higher in the upper strata than it is elsewhere. The general proposition is well stated by [Paul F.] Lazarsfeld:

> People on the lower SES levels are less likely to belong to any organizations than the people on high SES (Social and Economic Status) levels. (On an A and B level, we find 72 percent of these respondents who belong to one or more organizations. The proportion of respondents who are members of formal organizations decreases steadily as SES level descends until, on the D level only 35 percent of the respondents belong to any associations.)

The bias of the system is shown by the fact that *even nonbusiness organizations reflect an upper-class tendency.*

Lazarsfeld's generalization seems to apply equally well to urban and rural populations. The obverse side of the coin is that large areas of the population appear to be wholly outside the system of private organization. A study made by Ira Reid of a Philadelphia area showed that in a sample of 963 persons, 85 percent belonged to no civic or charitable organization and 74 percent belonged to no occupational, business, or professional associations, while another Philadelphia study of 1,154 women showed that 55 percent belonged to no associations of any kind.

A *Fortune* farm poll taken some years ago found that 70.5 percent of farmers belonged to no agricultural organizations. A similar conclusion was reached by two Gallup polls showing that perhaps no more than one third of the farmers of the country belonged to farm organizations, while another *Fortune* poll showed that 86.8 percent of the low-income farmers belonged to no farm organizations. All available data support the generalization that the farmers who do not participate in rural organizations are largely the poorer ones.

A substantial amount of research done by other rural sociologists points to the same conclusion. [A. R.] Mangus and [H. R.] Cottam say, on the basis of a study of 556 heads of Ohio farm families and their wives:

> The present study indicates that comparatively few of those who ranked low on the scale of living took any active part in community organizations as members, attendants, contributors, or leaders. On the other hand, those families that ranked high on the scale of living comprised the vast majority of the highly active participants in formal group activities. . . . Fully two-thirds of those in the lower class as defined in this study were non-participants as compared with only one-tenth of those in the upper class and one-fourth of those in the middle class. . . . When families were classified by the general level-of-living index, 16 times as large a proportion of those in the upper classes as of those in the lower class were active participants. . . .

Along the same line [P. D.] Richardson and [Ward W.] Bauder observe, "Socio-economic status was directly related to participation." In still another study it was found that "a highly significant relationship existed between income and formal participation." It was found that persons with more than four years of college education held twenty times as many memberships (per one hundred persons) as did those with less than a fourth-grade education and were forty times as likely to hold office in nonchurch organizations, while persons with an income over $5,000 hold ninety-four times as many offices as persons with incomes less than $250.

D. E. Lindstrom found that 72 percent of farm laborers belonged to no organizations whatever.

There is a great wealth of data supporting the proposition that participation in private associations exhibits a class bias.

The class bias of associational activity gives meaning to the limited scope of the pressure system, because *scope and bias are aspects of the same tendency.* The data raise a serious question about the validity of the proposition that special-interest groups are a universal form of political organization reflecting *all* interests. As a matter of fact, to suppose that everyone participates in pressure-group activity and that all interests get themselves organized in the pressure system is to destroy the meaning of this form of politics. The pressure system makes sense only as the political instrument of a segment of the community. It gets results by being selective and biased; *if everybody got into the act, the unique advantages of this form of organization would be destroyed, for it is possible that if all interests could be mobilized the result would be a stalemate.*

Special-interest organizations are most easily formed when they deal with small numbers of individuals who are acutely aware of their exclusive interests. To describe the conditions of pressure-group organization in this way is, however, to say that it is primarily a business phenomenon. Aside from a few very large organizations (the churches, organized labor, farm organizations, and veterans' organizations) the residue is a small segment of the population. *Pressure politics is essentially the politics of small groups.*

The vice of the groupist theory is that it conceals the most significant aspects of the system. The flaw in the pluralist heaven is that the heavenly chorus sings with a strong upper-class accent. Probably about 90 percent of the people cannot get into the pressure system.

The notion that the pressure system is automatically representative of the whole community is a myth fostered by the universalizing tendency of modern group theories. *Pressure politics is a selective process* ill designed to serve diffuse interests. The system is skewed, loaded, and unbalanced in favor of a fraction of a minority.

On the other hand, pressure tactics are not remarkably successful in mobilizing general interests. When pressure-group organizations attempt to represent the interests of large numbers of people, they are usually able to reach only a small segment of their constituencies. Only a chemical trace of the fifteen million Negroes in the United States belong to the National Association for the Advancement of Colored People. Only one five hundredths of 1 percent of American women belong to the League of Women Voters, only one sixteen hundredths of 1 percent of the consumers belong to the National Consumers' League, and only 6 percent of American automobile drivers belong to the American Automobile Association, while about 15 percent of the veterans belong to the American Legion.

The competing claims of pressure groups and political parties for the loyalty of the American public revolve about the difference between the results likely to be achieved by small-scale and large-scale political organization. Inevitably, the outcome of pressure politics and party politics will be vastly different. ■

 ## American Politics Today

Interest groups exert their influence throughout the American system of government. They lobby Congress, the White House, and executive agencies; are active in Washington and in the state capitals; and file lawsuits and briefs in both state and federal courts. The conventional wisdom suggests that all of this activity is a bad thing—that interest groups exert undue influence on the political system and tilt it to the advantage of the rich and well connected.

Political scientists Paul S. Herrnson, Ronald G. Shaiko, and Clyde Wilcox acknowledge these criticisms. But they also point to the benefits of the interest group system. By "connecting individuals to government and by allowing a diversity of views to be expressed in the public arena," they conclude, the interest group system "helps to protect some of Americans' most fundamental values—the rights of individuals to liberty, equality, and the pursuit of happiness."

Questions

1. What strategies do organized interest groups use in their attempts to influence officials in the three branches of government? Why do different groups employ different strategies?
2. What are the disadvantages and weaknesses of the interest group system? According to the authors, what are its countervailing strengths and advantages?

6.2 Interest Group Connections in Changing Political Environments (2005)

Paul S. Herrnson, Ronald G. Shaiko, and Clyde Wilcox

. . . [Many] connections exist between interest groups and government, between interest groups and political parties, and among interest groups. These connections, which are myriad and complex, are influenced by the rules and norms of the political process, including those applying to both lobbying and electoral politics. In carrying out their goals, interest groups have adopted a broad array of organizational arrangements, relationships, and activities. Indeed, some of the leading members of the interest group universe are quite sophisticated. They are able to change strategies and tactics in response to political reform, partisan shifts in political power, economic trends, developments in foreign policy, and other important events.

Interest Group Connections

Some lessons about interest group politics have emerged. . . . First, interests participate in virtually every arena of American politics. Groups are active in many aspects of the electoral process, and they seek to influence the executive, legislative, and judicial branches of government. Second, the institutional and political environments in which interests operate influence how they organize and the activities they carry out. When groups move from the legislative arena to try to influence the bureaucracy, for example, they must rely on different resources and use different tactics. And groups that specialize in judicial politics are organized in ways that are quite different from those that specialize in legislative politics. Third, most groups—whether they are organized as PACs, 501(c)s, 527s, corporate public relations offices, grassroots organizations, or other forms—use multifaceted strategies, adapting their tactics to suit new objectives and political circumstances. Groups forge, strengthen, and dissolve connections with various public officials, political institutions, and constituencies in order to pursue their goals most effectively. Combined, these conclusions suggest considerable fluidity in the interest group universe.

From Paul S. Herrnson, Ronald G. Shaiko, and Clyde Wilcox, eds., *The Interest Group Connection: Electioneering, Lobbying, and Policymaking in Washington*, pp. 385–393. Copyright © 2005 CQ Press, a division of Congressional Quarterly, Inc. Reprinted by permission of the publisher, CQ Press.

The Electoral Connection

In the electoral arena, groups forge connections with policymakers by helping with their campaigns for office. The U.S. system of candidate-centered elections creates considerable uncertainty for candidates, who must assemble their own coalitions, raise their own money, and reach out to diverse groups of voters. . . . [G]roups assist candidates' primary and general election campaigns by providing contributions, fundraising assistance, and volunteers. They directly influence voters by endorsing candidates, making personal contact with voters, and conducting television, radio, mail, and e-mail campaigns. By helping candidates, these groups gain access to key members of Congress, including party leaders, committee chairs and ranking members, and influential policy entrepreneurs. Even though groups' access to presidents and presidential candidates is more limited, they do have ready access to the party officials out of government, who tend to be grateful for the support they give party committees and candidates.

Corporations, trade associations, and labor unions are highly skilled at adapting their lobbying strategies to the changing political conditions they encounter. During the 1980s, many business groups decided that Republicans, with whom they agreed on most taxation and regulatory issues, would probably remain the minority party in the House for the foreseeable future. Most corporate and trade association political action committees (PACs) therefore switched from a pro-Republican pattern of contributions, designed to elect a free market–oriented Congress, to an incumbent-oriented pattern intended to give them access to powerful House Democrats. The lobbyists associated with these PACs had learned that they could accomplish some of their goals by working with House Democratic leaders and the officials in a GOP-led executive branch.

Once the 1992 election led to the installation of a Democratic president, some business leaders found themselves shut out of the White House, and more than a few doubled their congressional lobbying efforts. The 1994 GOP takeover of Congress created new incentives for business-oriented PACs to switch their contributions to favor leaders of the newly installed Republican-led Congress. Even some labor groups, which traditionally have given the vast majority of their contributions to Democratic candidates, redirected some of their PAC money toward Republicans. Nevertheless, PACs did not completely abandon House Democrats, because they recognized the possibility that Democratic leadership could return to Congress and wanted to continue to curry favor with the Democratic-led administration.

The 2000 election brought in its wake Republican occupancy of the White House, and the 2002 elections solidified GOP control over both houses of Congress. This turn of events further strengthened business leaders' inclinations to support Republicans.

The Congressional Connection

. . . [T]he relationship between members of Congress and lobbyists relies on an exchange: lobbyists provide members with valuable technical and political information on specific issues, and members may fulfill interest groups' objectives by enacting their preferred policies.

From the 1980s through the early 1990s, most liberal organizations enjoyed easy access to powerful congressional leaders, but they were shut out of the decision making that took place in the higher echelons of the Republican-dominated executive branch. Most conservative groups had to contend with the opposite situation: they were warmly received by the Ronald Reagan and George Bush White Houses, but had only limited clout with congressional Democrats. After the 1994 midterm elections, the situation was reversed. Conservative groups became the new congressional insiders, and liberal groups found that they were more likely to get a warm reception from the chief executive (then Democrat Bill Clinton), members of the cabinet, and other executive branch officials. The first two elections of the new millennium introduced a new set of realities for both parties. Conservative groups saw their power substantially enhanced after the establishment of Republican control over both the executive and legislative branches of the federal government. Liberal groups, by contrast, saw their influence in the nation's capital plummet.

To approach Congress more effectively, groups form connections with other groups. These coalitions are even extremely important in the Republican-controlled Congress, because the GOP has centralized power, limited the access of interest groups, and even sought to limit the resources and actions of lobbyists for certain groups. Coalitions are now more important and more difficult to assemble because of the constraints of policymaking in the context of zero-sum budgetary politics. Under the Republican regime, groups that once could "logroll" to win support for additional spending must now work with allies to protect some sectors of the budget while also competing with these same allies for their slice of the budgetary pie.

Some of the interest groups' strategic responses to the current political circumstances are apparent through their campaign contributions to committee chairs, their participation in the appropriations process, and the decisions they make about coalition partners in Washington and their use of grassroots lobbying. The approaches used by the religious right, labor unions, and even physicians and scientists stand in stark contrast to one another, reflecting the types of receptions they anticipate and receive in the Republican-controlled Congress and the White House.

Regardless of the recent changing partisan tides, the leaders of most of the largest interest groups combine the electoral connection and the legislative connection to influence Congress. For example, many of the same lobbyists who routinely try to influence the policymaking activities of members of Congress use their position to influence the flow of their group's PAC contributions and to help candidates raise money from individuals and other PACs. And members of Congress are no less active in tying together the two connections for their own political gain—that is, they are not shy about soliciting lobbyists who seek policy favors for individual and PAC contributions and assistance with fund-raising.

The Executive Connection

The strategies that help groups form connections in the Congress are less effective in the executive branch. Technical information is a valuable resource in lobbying Congress, but it is far less useful in approaching the executive, which can draw on the expertise of the bureaucracy. The bureaucracy interacts with interest groups, but it does not accept campaign contributions. Many groups care deeply about the rules that are created by administrative agencies, but lack the ability to influence the decision directly. In the GOP Congress, these groups have appealed to the legislature to overturn the rules or limit the ability of the bureaucracy to enforce them.

Presidents are not subjected to the narrow, particularistic lobbying that occurs in Congress, but they do need interest group support to get reelected and to enact their policies. Presidents seeking reelection rely on groups to mobilize voters in their behalf. Before the 2004 elections, they also relied on the soft money generated by interest groups to help finance party efforts to bolster their campaigns. Since 1996 presidential elections have continued to be influenced by group-sponsored issue advocacy advertisements.

Finally, any president seeking to pass key legislation needs groups to mobilize their members and lobbyists behind the administration's proposals in order to help win the support of key legislators. In the absence of lobbyists' direct ties to key White House operatives, the White House Office of Public Liaison is an important generic nexus for presidents and the interest group community.

The Judicial Connection

Interest group connections with the judiciary are very different from those with the legislative and executive branches. Lobbyists are not allowed to communicate directly with Supreme Court justices; they must instead resort to test cases and amicus curiae briefs to influence judicial opinions. As such, many of the key resources of groups—especially membership and lobbying skills—are useless when approaching the courts. But money is useful, because judicial politics are quite expensive. Repeat players, such as corporations and groups that specialize in legal action, are advantaged, for they are able to litigate to affect the rules in areas such as standing. Yet judicial reforms and developments in recent decades, such as fee shifting and class action suits, have served to level the judicial playing field and lessen the advantages of repeat players. Public interest law firms representing interests across the ideological spectrum have also opened up the judicial arena to those interests previously underrepresented in the courts. As the federal court system continues to play an important role in public policymaking, organized interests will remain focused on this branch of government.

Interest Groups and Political Reform

Political reform has had a major impact on interest group politics. Long gone are the days when industrialists and other interest group leaders handed members of Congress bags full of cash in return for casting congressional votes to turn over mining rights on huge tracts of mineral-rich land, grant corporate tax breaks and subsidies, or support some other form of legislation from which a business, labor, or some other group would gain significant benefit. Even legendary icons such as Daniel Webster wrote on Senate stationery to the president of the Second Bank of the United States asking for his "usual retainers" to ensure his support. Mark Twain, in his fictional account of members of Congress, typified the conventional wisdom when he wrote: "A Congressional appropriation costs money. . . . A majority of the

House committee, say $10,000 apiece—$40,000. A majority of the Senate committee, the same each, say $40,000; a little extra to one or two chairmen of one or two such committees, say $10,000 each. There's $100,000 gone to begin with."

By contrast, the scandals of the 1990s involved smaller sums, and in many cases did not even involve violations of law. The "book deal" that led to the resignation of House Speaker James C. Wright Jr., D-TX, in 1989 and the check bouncing scandal at the House bank that resulted in the early retirements and defeats of numerous congressmen in 1992 are cases in point. The Webster example contrasts even more sharply with allegations that PAC contributions of $5,000 or less are used to "buy" members' votes. Political reforms have reduced the level of corruption in American politics, including the level of bribery, quid pro quos, and special payoffs that involve special interests.

Nevertheless, reforms have not, probably cannot, and definitely should not eliminate the influence of organized interests. Reform must be an ongoing process if it is to keep corruption at a minimum, limit the avenues that organized interests can use to influence the political process, and weaken the nexus between campaign contributions and policymaking. Individuals, politicians, and organized interests have time and time again proven themselves capable of adapting to institutional reform and structural changes in government. Problems arise when a small number of groups are able to dominate the political system.

The Federal Election Campaign Act of 1974 (FECA), the gift ban, lobby reform, and the movement toward centralization of power in Congress all demonstrated that interest groups are adept at altering the methods they use to participate in the political process. The FECA, for example, prohibited corporations, trade associations, unions, and other groups from contributing treasury monies to federal candidates, but it laid the groundwork for the skyrocketing number of PACs that were formed in the late 1970s and 1980s. Moreover, the law was eviscerated in 1996 by court rulings that allow groups to use their treasury funds to carry out issue advocacy campaigns. As a result, a small sector of society that represents a limited number of viewpoints is the source of a disproportionate amount of the money spent in election campaigns. The enactment of the Bipartisan Campaign Reform Act of 2002 (BCRA) has done little to reduce the influence of political elites. Indeed, the rise of the multimillion-dollar contributions to 527 groups with close ties to each of the two major parties promises .to undermine one of the major goals of the reformers: the reduction of the influence of wealthy individuals and groups on election outcomes.

Similarly, the Lobbying Disclosure Act of 1995 introduced major improvements in the disclosure and reporting of interest group lobbying activities, and the gift ban, also passed in 1995, curbed the practice of using expensive meals, vacations, and gifts to gain access to federal lawmakers. Yet less than one year after their passage, these reforms were already being legally sidestepped by some lobbyists and lawmakers. Interest group representatives learned to work around the gift ban's prohibitions against lobbyists wining and dining members by reporting their epicurean encounters as campaign contributions.

Apparently, then, the creativity and pragmatism of politicians and lobbyists limit the possibilities for major political reform. When old routes of political influence are shut down, they often blaze new ones. Sometimes, they benefit from assistance from the courts. The connections between government officials and group representatives thus seem impossible to sever. Political reforms typically reroute streams of influence rather than dry them up. Journalists, scholars, reformers, and ordinary citizens must continually be vigilant to prevent a small portion of society from amassing too much political clout.

As demonstrated by the lengthy battles over the BCRA, various dynamics make it difficult for Congress to reform the laws that govern campaign finance. Philosophical disagreements over federal funding, contribution limits, and campaign expenditure ceilings reflect broader tensions over the roles that money and the government should play in politics and society and are a major stumbling block. Partisan concerns, some based on disagreements in philosophy and some based on considerations of electoral expedience, make it difficult for Democrats and Republicans to agree on the kinds of reforms that should be enacted. Differences in the financing of House and Senate campaigns typically lead to disagreements between the chambers. These are frequently exacerbated by the threat of a presidential veto or more subtle forms of White House involvement. The efforts of Common Cause and other so-called public interest groups that whip up popular opposition to incremental change in favor of "all or nothing" reforms make it difficult for members of Congress to back modest improvements and give them excuses for opposing most any kind of campaign finance legislation.

Perhaps the biggest obstacle to campaign finance reform is that those who enact the reforms know they will have to live under them. With the exception of the few legislators who are appointed to fill out a predecessor's term, every member of Congress has some claim of expertise on campaign finance. Members arrive in the House or Senate by way of elections, and fund-raising was a major component of virtually all their campaigns. In the face of their own expertise, experiences, and obvious self-interest, legislators find it extremely difficult to agree on a reform program. Even though many would like to improve the campaign finance system, their notions of what constitutes improvement incorporates both their political experiences and their calculations about how change will influence their future campaigns. Yet ultimately Congress did pass the BCRA, and interest groups immediately began to adapt. In the 2004 presidential campaign, labor unions, environmental and feminist groups, and other liberals formed 527 committees to run issue ads that helped John Kerry match President George W. Bush's phenomenal fund-raising. Some Republican-leaning groups responded by forming their own 527s to support Bush. These new committees were formalized variants on earlier coalitions, but they were able to raise money in large contributions from committed donors.

Similar calculations influence lawmakers' and lobbyists' thinking about other areas of political reform. Proposals to change the way interest groups and politicians approach one another, exchange information, and mobilize legislative and public support for their preferred projects and career aspirations always seem to benefit some participants to the detriment of others. Whatever the case, these proposals almost always result in some unanticipated outcomes that influence both the relationships between those in power and ways of doing things. Successful politicians—that is, those who are in power—and successful lobbyists—that is, those who have risen high enough in the ranks of their firms to form ties with successful politicians—have strong motivations to resist the efforts of reformers.

The result is that political reforms are enacted infrequently and usually in response to widespread public outrage. In the early twentieth century, campaign finance reforms prohibiting banks and corporations from making contributions to federal candidates and imposing ceilings and disclosure requirements on other contributions were passed in response to progressive era protests against the power of big business. In 1974 the FECA was passed after Watergate investigations revealed many improprieties in the financing of President Richard Nixon's 1972 reelection campaign. The 1995 Lobbying Disclosure Act and the gift ban were passed in the wake of the "Keating Five" scandal in the Senate, the post office and banking scandals in the House, and record levels of public hostility and anger at Congress. In 2002 the BCRA was enacted after Sen. John McCain, R-AZ, raised the issue's profile during his unsuccessful 2000 presidential nomination campaign and after the Enron scandal, which encouraged citizens to perceive a link between soft money contributions and corporate corruption. It is unlikely that a legislative coalition in favor of reform can be built in the absence of a major showing of public displeasure. Without public sentiment threatening the electoral security of those who fail to support reform, politicians are unlikely to approve fundamental changes in the campaign finance system. The gulf that separates legislators on reform issues is too wide, because their sense of self-interest is too strong.

Moreover, should Congress and the president succeed in enacting further political reform, interest groups seeking to influence elections and the policymaking process and politicians in need of campaign contributions and technical or political information will undoubtedly find ways to work around the reform's intent without violating the law. As long as interest group representatives wish to influence the regulations, budgetary appropriations, courtroom decisions, public decrees, and other outputs of Congress, the president, the executive branch, and the courts, they will search for ways to present their cases to the government. As long as politicians rely on interest groups for technical expertise and assistance with building legislative coalitions and developing electoral support, they will find more or less convenient ways for lobbyists to state their views. As regulatory regimes mature, those who operate under them test them, overturning some statutes in the courts and unearthing loopholes that enable them to work around the intent of others. What at first appear to be small leaks in a regulatory structure can turn into a flood of activity that may eventually call into question the legitimacy of the framework itself

Interest Groups, Reform, and American Democracy

The general unwillingness and practical inability of reformers to construct regulatory regimes that shut out organized interests from the political process were anticipated by the framers of the Constitution. When they created a decentralized government that featured many points of access and embraced the property values associated with capitalism, they laid the foundation for a political system that rewards the individuals and groups able to mobilize people and money. The framers recognized that because groups would vary in their numbers and financial resources, they would likewise vary in the representation of their views. But the only way to completely prevent this outcome would be to deprive individuals of the freedom to use their talents to advance their interests and express their views—an approach that was repugnant to the framers' notions of liberty.

So, rather than attempt to constrain individual liberty, the framers constructed a political system that utilized a series of checks and balances to prevent any one group from tyrannizing others. The chartering of a national bank, the Louisiana Purchase, and the other early decisions that put the nation on the road toward a large commercial republic also encouraged the development of a diverse population made up of individuals who had overlapping interests. The framers believed that overlapping interests and group memberships would force individuals and organized groups to cooperate with each other in pursuit of their common goals, to respect each others' rights and liberties, and to understand that mutual cooperation and respect were needed to maintain the political system that defended those rights and liberties. The current interest group system is far from perfect—favoring the well-off and the well organized over the less privileged. But, by connecting individuals to government and by allowing a diversity of views to be expressed in the public arena, it helps to protect some of Americans' most fundamental values—the rights of individuals to liberty, equality, and the pursuit of happiness. Interest group connections to the federal government fall short of the high standards set by reformers, but by facilitating representation and participation, the interest group connection makes an important contribution to contemporary American democracy. ■

Issue and Controversy

Scandals involving lawmakers and lobbyists are nothing new, and their existence should surprise no one. The system brings together lawmakers—who have power but need money—with lobbyists—who have money and seek to influence the exercise of power. The possibilities for abuse are endless, and ongoing.

The latest in a long series of scandals centered around the lobbyist Jack Abramoff, an extraordinarily well-connected Washington power player who eventually pleaded guilty to federal criminal charges involving fraud and corruption. Abramoff was sentenced to almost six years in prison, after agreeing to cooperate with federal prosecutors in their investigations of possible wrong-doing by other Washington insiders.

In this selection, Washington reporters Bara Vaida, Eliza Newlin Carney, and Lisa Caruso examine "an industry under duress" in the wake of the Abramoff case.

Questions

1. What characteristics of the lobbying system make it susceptible to scandals like the Abramoff affair?
2. What, if anything, should be done to reform the lobbying system to lessen the likelihood of future scandals? Are such reforms likely to be effective?

6.3 Potholes on K Street (2006)

Bara Vaida, Eliza Newlin Carney, and Lisa Caruso

In one of his regularly televised messages for constituents in 1963, Senate Republican Leader Everett Dirksen tried to explain to voters back in Illinois about a strange "creature" in the nation's capital—the Washington lobbyist.

"Now there has grown a particular sinister connotation about that word 'lobbyist,'" Dirksen intoned. "You think of him as some sinister, skulking creature who is sneaking through the corridors of Congress. . . . There have been a lot of tall tales about parties on an excursion boat going down the Potomac, where there was plenty of food, plenty of liquor, and probably some unattached ladies aboard. And they would give this party for the legislators in order to get a chance to talk to them."

The scratchy, black-and-white film of Dirksen's comments was shown at a National Press Foundation awards dinner in Washington recently. Laughter filled the room when Dirksen's granddaughter, Cissy Baker, played the film clip and noted that not much had changed in the past 43 years.

For the thousands of lobbyists who today make up the vast K Street community, the caricature still stings. In serving their clients, many see themselves as the very embodiment of the First Amendment—the right of the people to petition their government. So the public stereotype of lobbyists—that the K Street crowd is undermining the Republic through slimy behavior and greed—rankles them.

And ever since January 3 [2006], when former lobbyist Jack Abramoff pleaded guilty to conspiracy, fraud, and tax-evasion charges, many who work on K Street have been fielding calls from relatives arid friends asking the same question: "What kind of business are you in?"

Abramoff's plea came about a month after former Rep. Randy (Duke) Cunningham, R-Calif., pleaded guilty to taking bribes from a defense contractor who had lobbied him for business. On Capitol Hill, Democratic and Republican leaders are scrambling to pin the blame on one another—and especially on K Street. "It's like, 'Jack's bad and what Duke did is bad, and so therefore all lobbyists are bad,'" said Dan Danner, executive vice president of public policy for the National Federation of Independent Business.

Even before the Abramoff mess, many Washington lobbyists were struggling to keep up with the changes that have buffeted their industry over the past decade. Lobbying is now a $2 billion-plus annual business in Washington—and that's just the amount that can be tracked through official lobbying filings. Billions more are spent on public-relations, grassroots, and other advocacy efforts that don't have to be disclosed but are increasingly a key part of the influence industry.

Interviews with dozens of lobbyists suggest that five key factors are shaping the lobbying world today:

- **Competition.** Although precise figures are hard to come by, the number of lobbyists vying for the attention of lawmakers and their aides has shot up in recent years, as has the amount of money pouring into the industry.
- **Time.** Members of Congress are spending less time on the Hill than ever before, and more time racing around to fundraisers. The tighter congressional schedule makes it harder for lobbyists to cut through the political noise.
- **Complexity.** Lobbying today is akin to running a sophisticated and expensive political campaign, demanding a multitude of strategic and intellectual skills, and adeptness at tactics and communications.
- **Gridlock.** The closely divided Congress and the partisan atmosphere on the Hill have made the legislative process less open and participatory.
- **Money.** Lawmakers desperate for campaign cash constantly have their hands out to K Street, seeking more dollars for more accounts, including member-run political action committees. Yet when things go wrong, it's the lobbyists who get the blame.

Add to all this the fallout from the Abramoff and Cunningham scandals, and the upshot is an industry under duress. Some on K Street have chosen to lay low and keep their mouths shut, declining interviews with the media and waiting for the whole nasty business to blow over. Others see an opportunity for self-correction. Although Abramoff is universally reviled, some admit that the profession has grown sloppy in recent years and could use more discipline.

Anne Wexler, a longtime lobbyist and former Carter White House aide who founded the firm that is now Wexler & Walker Public Policy Associates, is philosophical. "You try every way you can to correct the distortions, because the essential process is an important one. I just want everyone to understand that it is a profession that brings value to the table."

Then and Now

Lobbying has been around as long as the United States itself, and so have scandals. In 1852, the House passed legislation meant to rein in lobbying, and various efforts have continued ever since.

A congressional investigation in 1913 uncovered evidence that the National Association of Manufacturers had controlled congressional committee appointments, paid the chief page of the House to eavesdrop and report on members' conversations on the floor, and maintained its own office in the Capitol. A now-familiar pattern ensued: Lawmakers expressed indignation and vowed to clamp down on lobbying, but little changed.

Congress has passed several watershed reforms since then: the 1946 Federal Regulation of Lobbying Act, which for the first time required basic reporting and disclosure; the post-Watergate campaign finance reforms of the 1970s, which banned direct corporate and labor contributions and ushered in political action committees; and the Lobbying Disclosure Act of 1995, which grew out of the Koreagate, Abscam, and Keating Five affairs of the 1970s and '80s.

Each new law has widened the public window on the lobbying world, and industry veterans argue that things are actually far cleaner and more ethical today, than before. Still, the absence of any real enforcement mechanism has made the rules easy to break.

"The LDA is a joke in some ways, because no one looks at those filings and there has been no enforcement," said a Republican lobbyist, who didn't want to be named. The clerk of the House and the secretary of the Senate employ a handful of staff members to process between 46,000 and 55,000 LDA filings annually, and it takes months for data to be made public. The Justice Department has investigated a mere 13 violations in the past 10 years, resulting in only three civil settlements and fines, according to a department spokesman.

Sheer competition may drive some on K Street to push the envelope. The number of registered lobbyists has shot up since 1995, though no one is sure exactly how many there are.

In 1998, the General Accounting Office (now called the Government Accountability Office) estimated that in calendar year 1996, the first year the LDA was in effect, 11,325 individuals were listed as lobbyists in Washington. Current estimates on the number of registered lobbyists range from 11,500 to nearly 28,000. But because registered lobbyists represent only a portion of the people trying to influence the policy process in Washington, "well over 100,000" people should be considered lobbyists, says James Thurber, an American University political scientist and director of the school's Center for Congressional and Presidential Studies.

"This profession has exploded," says lobbyist John Buscher of Holland & Knight. "There are more people going into the same number of [congressional] offices every day. On almost every issue, you've got somebody who has been hired on both sides coming in."

Even as the number of people in the industry has grown, the amount of time members spend in Washington has dwindled. Congress rarely goes more than six weeks without a recess, and most legislative and committee action occurs from Tuesday to Thursday.

Lawmakers "have a thousand little kids jumping up and down in front of them raising their hands," notes Rich Gold, head of the public policy and regulation practice group at Holland & Knight. "How do you get called on by the teacher?"

Often, the answer is, host a fundraiser—or at least show up at one. A lobbyist so inclined could eat nearly every meal of the week at fundraising breakfasts, lunches, and dinners booked at such restaurants as the Capital Grille, and at the swank offices of law and lobbying firms and trade groups overlooking Pennsylvania Avenue, the Capitol dome, or the Potomac River.

The more time members spend raising money, the less time lobbyists have to meet with them face-to-face—except at fundraisers.

At the same time, lobbyists' job description has changed. A few decades ago, trade groups such as the U.S. Chamber of Commerce, the AFL-CIO, and the American Medical Association conducted most lobbying, recalls Gary Andres, vice chairman of research and policy at Dutko Worldwide.

As the government has grown, "you've gone from this association-based lobbying to a very individualized lobbying" by corporations and issue-oriented groups, as well as lobbying-only firms, says Andres, whose 20-year career includes stints as a Hill staff member, consultant, corporate-affairs lobbyist, and legislative-affairs aide to Presidents Bush I and II.

To successfully work the Hill today, lobbyists need to be substantive policy experts and communications strategists able to run lobbying efforts like a sophisticated political campaign. The tools of the modern lobbyist's trade, Thurber says, include grassroots advocacy; coalition-building and maintenance; TV and print ads; direct mail; and Web sites and blogs.

Congressional staff have noticed the trend. A survey of 113 Hill staff conducted in March by *National Journal*'s Policy Council, a research group separate from the magazine, found that 77 percent of 89 staffers believe there are "a lot more" ad hoc coalitions promoting a common agenda "than ever before," and 67 percent said these coalitions are "very effective because they present a unified front."

"In the old days," Thurber recalls, "it was, hire [legendary lobbyist] Charlie Walker, and Charlie would walk in and see the chairman of the Ways and Means Committee, and they'd sit around, and maybe they'd even have a drink. And Charlie would say: 'Can't you fix this for me?' And that would happen."

Dysfunction

Lobbyists must also navigate a political battlefield marked by deeply partisan warfare. For some lobbyists, recent scandals have heightened their sense that life inside the Beltway has become dysfunctional and that a herculean effort is needed to get any action at all, no matter what the issue.

"The exceptionally partisan, poisonous atmosphere in Washington keeps anything from working," says W. Bowman (Bo) Cutter, a deputy assistant for economic policy under President Clinton and now co-chairman of the Committee for Economic Development, a nonpartisan business group. "It relegates all action to the realm of the extremely tactical and the extremely political."

Lobbyists surveyed by the Policy Council overwhelmingly shared this view. Of 115 lobbyists surveyed by the council, 90 percent said they think partisanship in Washington is greater than it has ever been, and 72 percent thought the partisanship makes it harder to achieve their objectives.

With both the House and the Senate closely divided, notes Chuck Brain, another Clinton administration veteran, lawmakers are always assessing how an action might affect the balance of power in either chamber. "That adds another level of complexity that you have to address, in addition to the merits and demerits of the issue," says Brain, president of Capitol Hill Strategies.

Lobbyists must also contend with the larger role that Republican leaders play in the legislative process. Congressional leaders regularly rewrite bills or throw in last-minute provisions to secure wavering members' votes, while staff—not members—do most of the heavy lifting in committee, many lobbyists lamented. "If you [once had] 67 markup sessions, now you're lucky to have 67 minutes of markup on a bill," because so many decisions have been made in advance, often by party leaders behind closed doors, says H. Stewart Van Scoyoc, president of Van Scoyoc Associates, a 32-year industry veteran.

Particularly in the House, "you've got to be dialed in to the top," says one Democratic lobbyist, who asked not to be identified. "Unless you have an in with leadership or individual chairmen of committees, it's hard to get things done."

This increasingly closed system creates more points where a hard-fought win could be reversed. At one time, notes Dutko's Andres, decisions made in committee usually held through conference. Now, he says, "you have to remain vigilant a little bit longer through the process because people can swoop in at any time, whether from the outside or from the inside of the process, to change a decision that was made."

Procedural shifts have fueled the trend toward "boutique" lobbying firms that specialize in providing entrée to powerful lawmakers. So-called "access lobbyists" can ply their trade out of both small shops and large, well-established firms. Either way, these lobbyists have ratcheted up the intensity on K Street while earning the disdain of some of their colleagues.

The Abramoff investigation has turned the spotlight on a number of aggressive staffers-turned-lobbyists, such as Ed Buckham and Tony Rudy, the former top aides to Rep. Tom DeLay, R-Texas, who formed the Alexander Strategy Group and marketed their access to their former boss. The firm closed down months ago in the wake of the Abramoff scandal.

One former Hill aide who is now a lobbyist criticized "the overly pushy and aggressive access lobbyist. They think they're entitled; they think they know it all; they think they've got the system down—'I get you access; I get you projects; and you give me a lot of money' is their approach to business."

Because K Street salaries are much fatter and rise more quickly than on the Hill, the "revolving door" spins fast. Some newly minted lobbyists undoubtedly welcome that trend, but more-senior industry pros say it has created problems. They cite short-term Hill staffers whose knowledge base is shallow, forcing them to rely on lobbyists for information. Some lobbyists complain about staffers who are arrogant and demanding. Asked how he'd describe staff he works with, one lobbyist exclaimed: "Rude! Really, really rude!"

Lobbyist Pete Rose, a former congressional aide who is a principal in the Franklin Partnership, talks about a "broken" system on the Hill. "I mourn the loss of institutional knowledge, and as a result of high staff turnover and lack of knowledge on issues there is often a lack of responsiveness."

Some lobbyists told stories of staff members who seemed to take for granted meals at such popular watering holes as Charlie Palmer Steak and the Palm. Under ethics rules, staffers must report the value of meals and tickets they accept from lobbyists. Gifts, including meals, may cost no more than $50, and aides may not accept more than $100 in gifts from one source annually. They are also barred from soliciting a meal or gift. But some can't resist the temptation.

"A lot of staff on the Hill take a look at the lobbying community and see supplemental activities," says Gregg Hartley, COO of lobbying giant Cassidy & Associates. "They call up a lobbyist and hint that they'd be willing to go out for a beer or dinner when no business will be discussed."

One Democratic lobbyist, who didn't want to be named, said he was sitting at the Capital Grille bar with a fellow lobbyist who's a Republican, when an aide to a

Republican leader walked over to them and pointed to a table where some of the aide's friends were seated. "I want you to pay for their dinner," said the aide, according to the lobbyist telling the story. The GOP lobbyist "was so terrified of [the aide] that he complied," the Democrat recounted.

A lobbyist for a well-known corporation says that a senior aide on one House committee called a member of his staff to "let him know it was his birthday and [he] would be expecting a party for him," to be paid for by the company. Yet another lobbyist with a trade association said: "I've gotten calls from staffers who are at a bar at midnight and want to know if I can cover their bar tab."

The stories don't surprise Brett Kappel, counsel in the government-relations and lobbying practice group at Vorys, Sater, Seymour and Pease. "A whole generation of people came to town thinking that this was the way things were done with meals and tickets, and they were supposed to be catered to," Kappel said.

Fundraising, Fundraising, Fundraising

Lawmakers have their hands out, too. They invite lobbyists to fundraising birthday parties; they attend conventions in tropical locales like Hawaii and Jamaica courtesy of trade associations and other groups; they hop on the private jets of corporations based in their states or districts; and they flood lobbyists with invitations to fundraisers, morning, noon, and night.

To many lobbyists, the money chase has become an increasingly time-consuming—and sometimes onerous—part of the job. For all the debate on Capitol Hill over how to restrict meals, gifts, and travel, the proposed changes ignore the real controversy at the heart of lawmaker-lobbyist relationships: campaign money. The campaign dollars that lobbyists raise for members are a far more valuable gift than any meal or plane ride they could offer. "To me, the lobbying crisis centers around three concepts: fundraising, fundraising, and fundraising," said Bert J. Levine, a former lobbyist who now teaches political science at Colgate University.

Wexler agrees. "You have a situation where [lawmakers] aren't here as much," she says. "They spend more time raising money, and they put tremendous pressure on lobbyists to raise money early to protect their incumbency." She adds that at election time, "candidates run against special interests. But it's rhetorical . . . because when they get re-elected they return to office, and right away they call those special interests and ask them for money."

To be sure, the brash trade-offs at the heart of the Abramoff and Cunningham scandals strike most lobbyists as extreme. "It's so alien to my daily way of doing things [to think] that if you take somebody out to dinner and offer to raise $50,000, that they're going to do something for you," says Gold, of Holland & Knight.

What lobbyists hope to get in exchange for raising money is not votes, Gold insists. "What you get is frankness. What you get is communication, discourse. You don't get a change in position. You don't get federal funding for a federal project that is meritless."

Indeed, staffers confirmed that PAC contributions aren't an important factor in determining whether a lobbyist will gain access to their boss. Of 99 staffers who responded to a Policy Council question about access, 13 percent rated PAC support for the member as a determining factor and just 1 percent deemed it the most important. What was most important, according to 56 percent of the respondents, was whether the lobbyist's client is influential in the lawmaker's state or district.

Many lobbyists have started to rankle at a fundraising system that consumes their time and money, and then often gives them a black eye. The campaign season is perpetually in full swing. Member-run political action committees have proliferated, meaning that lawmakers now have yet another pocket in which to stash checks. They can then donate that PAC money to other members, winning their loyalty in the bargain.

Even the ban on unlimited soft-money contributions has put fresh pressure on lobbyists. That's because lawmakers and party leaders who once could count on a single donor for a six-figure check now must raise the same amount in smaller increments from a larger number of sources. This latest "reform" puts a premium on lobbyists with fat Rolodexes who can round up clients for fundraising events.

Indeed, the real leverage point for lobbyists is not the checks that they write, but the ones that they bundle for members of Congress. Lobbyists who host well-attended events can wield tremendous influence—yet they have no obligation to report how much they raise, and for whom. Some argue that the vast sums that lobbyists pull in for lawmakers, particularly for member-run "leadership" PACs, is a kind of "soft" money—ill-regulated and undisclosed.

Many lobbyists counter that bundling and campaign contributions are only part of a successful strategy.

"I think that money, and raising money, gets you access, no question about that," says one lobbyist who asked not to be named. "It gets your phone calls returned. It gets you meetings, it gets you and your client the chance to make your case. But that's it."

The problem is not that money buys votes, says Levine, of Colgate University. The problem is that money influences what he describes as "unrecorded legislative activity," such as amendments written into or left out of a bill in advance. "There is no question that, to the extent that contributions buy access, they do help slant the playing field," Levine maintains.

Even lobbyists who defend their right to raise money concede that it's begun to consume an almost absurd amount of time. Lobbyists are bombarded daily with e-mails, faxes, and glossy brochures enticing them to join members at meals, rock concerts, and ball games and to go on trips. Some describe deleting such e-mails en masse, or tossing wads of invitations into the round file. One lobbyist told of a friend who filled an entire bathtub with his fundraising invitations.

"I think most lobbyists would be perfectly content to not be in the fundraising business," says one well-established lobbyist who asked not to be named. "It's a pain in the ass. Do you want to spend the money you earn making contributions to people? Do you want to spend your time soliciting your clients, soliciting your friends? It's time taken away from the work we actually do."

Lobbyists say that turning down a lawmaker's request for a contribution can be awkward and that uncomfortable situations do arise. There's been a generational shift, says Kappel and other pros in the advocacy industry, that's spawned behavior that once would have been considered taboo.

Some lobbyists fresh off the Hill "have no understanding, nor do they want to have any understanding, either about the rules of ethics, the rules of campaign finance, or the traditions of lobbying," Kappel says. "They will go and ask for things as they hand [a member] the check. I've seen that. That's appalling."

Particularly controversial is the proliferation of lobbyists who actually serve as treasurer of a lawmaker's campaign committee or leadership PAC. By some estimates, more than 70 lobbyists have doubled as treasurers for campaign or leadership committees. Such data can be misleading, experts caution, because the person listed as "treasurer" in public records is sometimes more of a figurehead than the official who actually raises money.

Still, the trend troubles established lobbyists. "I wouldn't be comfortable with our folks doing that," says Gold, of Holland & Knight. Serving as a campaign or leadership PAC treasurer, he adds, "appears to be much closer to purchasing access. You're really involved in a member's business enterprise in a way that you're not when you're an outsider."

A surprising number of lobbyists admit flat-out that they hate the system as it is, and would even endorse a complete campaign finance overhaul. The only effective way to change Washington's culture, they say, would be to use public dollars to pay for all federal campaigns—not that any of them expects Congress to embrace public financing anytime soon.

"It was my No. 1 hope that they would pass something that said lobbyists cannot raise money," says Joel Jankowsky, a partner at Akin Gump Strauss Hauer & Feld. "That would be wonderful." But he quickly adds: "Just kidding." Like many lobbyists, Jankowsky is reluctant to prescribe what, if any, changes Congress should impose on the lobbying industry. . . .

Lobbyist T. J. Petrizzo points out the irony of lawmakers pushing for change without examining themselves. "Some of these same members that are calling for lobbying reform are still making phone calls asking for money," says Petrizzo, who was chief of staff to then-Rep. Jennifer Dunn, R-Wash., and is now president and CEO of Petrizzo Strategic Consulting.

And even more galling to lobbyists is that K Street is getting most of the blame for recent abuses. "I am angry because I love my work and my profession," Van Scoyoc says. "It hurts me deeply that Abramoff is showing up on the front of *Time* magazine—that people are thinking this is a crooked business."

Adds another prominent GOP lobbyist: "It's had a psychological impact on us in that people that go into this business usually go into it with their eyes open and say, 'So what if some people think you are a dirtbag?' But what Abramoff did was so outlandish, and the reporting of what he did is so ubiquitous, that it's embarrassing and depressing, and you kind of want it to all go away."

At the same time, lobbyists as a group have been reluctant to defend themselves. "Personally, I don't think it's appropriate for us to argue with the public or their elected representatives on what kind of restrictions or disclosures should be put in place, because we are interested parties," says Mark Irion, CEO of Dutko Worldwide. "And anything that increases the level of public trust in the system is good for the country and good for us, so we'll live with whatever is put in place."

Others would like to see the industry do more to defend itself. "If we just sit silent, it's going to be guilt by association," says Gary J. LaPaille, president of mCapitol Management.

But for the most part, lobbyists insist that they have no problem with proposed reforms, which include more frequent and extensive disclosure of their activities; restrictions on earmarks; new limits on meals, gifts, and travel; and tighter rules for lawmakers and aides who become lobbyists.

• • •

If history is any guide, lawmakers, aides, and lobbyists will find a way around whatever new rules Congress imposes. That's because, complain as they will, they are comfortable with the system the way it is. Lawmakers, in particular, like the status quo because it so reliably protects incumbents.

"It's a pervasive and inundating system as currently formulated," concludes Akin Gump's Jankowsky. "It takes a lot of time, and it's not perfect. And yet, there's no alternative that's in operation." ■

 # View from the Inside

In the early days of the high-tech industry, entrepreneurs like Microsoft's Bill Gates largely ignored Washington. The industry was focused almost entirely on technological and business issues, and had little need or desire to engage in politics. But the growing importance of the industry in every aspect of life made engagement with Washington inevitable. After a shaky start, the industry found its footing and adapted to the new realities.

As political scientist David M. Hart points out, Microsoft did not even have a Washington office until 1995. But within just a few years, Microsoft and its chairman have become important figures in Washington power circles.

Questions

1. What factors made it possible for Gates and Microsoft to ignore public policy issues in the early years of the high-tech industry? What factors made it necessary and desirable for the company to engage in the Washington power game?
2. What strategies did Microsoft pursue to increase its influence in Washington? Why were these strategies effective?

6.4 High-Tech Learns to Play the Washington Game (2002)

David M. Hart

On March 3, 1998, William H. Gates III, founder and chief executive officer (CEO) of Microsoft, testified for the first time before a congressional committee. Gates's appearance garnered much media attention, including front page coverage in the national press. [According to *Congressional Quarterly Weekly Report*,] Sens. Slade Gorton, R-Wash., and Patty Murray, D-Wash., "struggled to keep up with the Microsoft chief as camera crews and a crowd of onlookers followed him out of the Hart Building." Inside the hearing room Gates sparred with Senate Judiciary Chairman Orrin Hatch, R-Utah, about whether Microsoft had violated the Sherman Antitrust Act. Two of Gates's fiercest rivals and most ardent critics, Scott McNealy, CEO of Sun Microsystems, and James Barksdale, CEO of Netscape Communications, were next to him at the witness table and joined in Hatch's attack. Though undoubtedly good theater, the hearing (like many on Capitol Hill) yielded no new legislation. Nonetheless, it served an important political purpose. It provided Joel Klein, the assistant attorney general in charge of the Justice Department's Antitrust Division, with (as he put it) "a real sense of comfort" in his dogged pursuit of Microsoft, which culminated in the filing of a major lawsuit against the firm two months later.

This brief episode, like many political events, can be understood in two seemingly contradictory ways. From one vantage point—the one that dominated press coverage—Gates's testimony was the result of personal ambitions and rivalries (verging on a crusade on the part of Microsoft's enemies in the eyes of some), tactical maneuvering, and matters of chance. Hatch just happened to represent a state in which two of Microsoft's lesser-known rivals, Novell and WordPerfect, were headquartered. In addition, Hatch was soon to declare his abortive candidacy for the 2000 Republican presidential nomination and was seeking headlines to advance that quest. Gates, for his part, was a computer nerd whose lack of political savvy was the flip side of his technical virtuosity and single-minded dedication to his firm. The world's richest man had once stood aloof from the messy business of politics, but well-connected competitors forced him to get his hands dirty.

From another vantage point, the one favored by most social scientists, Gates's testimony epitomized the inevitable encounter between the high-technology industry and the federal government. Gates personified Microsoft, one of the best-known and fastest-growing firms in an industry that was transforming American society. High-tech products, especially Microsoft's market leading Windows operating system and Office productivity suite for personal computers (PCs), permeated everyday life so deeply that they were bound to make some people and organizations uneasy about a Microsoft-led information revolution. These people and organizations, in turn, were bound to petition their government to take action against the perceived malefactors. And some elements of the government (in this case the Senate Judiciary Committee and the Antitrust Division) were bound to be responsive to these petitions.

The apparent contradiction between the two perspectives lies in the way they relate particular events to larger processes of policymaking and political development. An extreme version of the first perspective would claim that if things hadn't happened just the way they did, everything would be different. That is, if the chairman of the Senate Judiciary Committee were from a different state, the Microsoft suit would never have been filed, and high-tech's most powerful firm would not have evolved into a Washington powerhouse. An equally extreme version of the second perspective would say that this hearing didn't matter, and that the collision between government and the high-tech industry was inevitable.

Less extreme and more measured versions of the two perspectives can be reconciled. It *was* inevitable that the high-tech industry and its leading firm would become important players in policymaking and politics at some point. But the particularities of the testimony placed their stamp on the outcome, too. Gates's combative attitude toward the threat of government action set in motion processes not easily stopped and catalyzed alignments not easily undone. The events of March 3, 1998, will shape the still-unfolding experience of the high-tech industry on the Washington scene.

This [selection] tells the story of [Microsoft's] entry into interest group politics. . . . [It] illustrates broad social processes that were bound in some way to shape that entry. [It] also illustrates how unpredictable and seemingly trivial matters of personality and timing had significant long-term consequences.

• • •

Resistance Is Futile: Microsoft Adapts to Washington

At the beginning of the 1990s high-tech was a discernible presence in American interest group politics. IBM's public policy office had a staff that could handle almost any issue, and a growing array of high-tech firms like Apple and Oracle had opened their own smaller Washington shops. The list of high-tech trade associations was growing, but many in the high-tech policy community doubted that the industry's representation was keeping pace with its growing importance in the economy. The late Eben Tisdale, who ran Hewlett-Packard's Washington office, famously quipped that the industry had "deep pockets and short arms."

Microsoft, for example, did not open a Washington office until 1995 despite surpassing its rivals in the PC software business and joining the ranks of the Fortune 500 in 1988. Even then Microsoft's interest in Washington lagged far behind Washington's interest in Microsoft. Not until about the time of Bill Gates's appearance before Orrin Hatch, some seven years after Gates learned that antitrust prosecutors were investigating his firm, did Microsoft become serious, perhaps too serious, about making its mark in the capital. The lag between the external threat to the firm and its exaggerated reaction reflects the barriers to political involvement that face any entrepreneurial firm but also the particularities of Gates and the firm he built.

The most common barrier to a typical start-up's involvement in Washington is the collective action problem. Any small, young firm has little chance of determining a policy debate or an election, so the firm has little incentive to take political action on its own. Not surprising, Microsoft's initial forays into public policy . . . came through trade associations that mustered industrywide campaigns on vital issues. In 1988, for example, just thirteen years after Microsoft was established and only two years after its initial public offering (IPO) of stock, Microsoft helped to found the Business Software Association (BSA) to combat software piracy, a problem that hit its bottom line directly.

Another barrier confronting start-ups thinking about entering the political marketplace is the fixed cost of Washington representation. A firm that wants a representative independent of trade associations must hire and support professional staff or cover the retainer for an outside lobbying firm. Although a modest $100,000 government affairs budget might plant a firm's flag in the capital and lie unnoticed on the firm's balance sheet, such an investment is unlikely to yield benefits beyond keeping corporate leadership apprised of current events. A million-dollar Washington office, on the other hand, would produce much greater visibility within the Beltway, but at the same time might be perceived at headquarters as a significant cost for a firm with sales of $100 million a year in a highly competitive industry. Microsoft surpassed $100 million in sales before its 1986 IPO and reached $1 billion by 1990. Cost alone seems unlikely to have stood in the way had the firm wanted independent representation in Washington before the late 1990s.

A bigger obstacle for Microsoft might have been a lack of executive attention to politics and policy. Entrepreneurs may fail to engage in public policy debates not because they think the costs of such engagement exceed the benefits, but because they are busy tending their businesses. Gates's single-minded focus on building Microsoft is legendary. *Star Trek* fans among his adversaries portray Microsoft as the Borg, assimilating everything in its path. Washington was for a long while just one of many potential distractions that Gates ignored while he laid waste to his corporate competition. At the time that his firm first came under antitrust investigation in 1991, for example, Gates viewed Apple's lawsuit alleging that Windows infringed on the Mac OS copyright as a much more serious external threat. Microsoft won that case, relegated Apple to the margins of the high-tech industry, and continued its extraordinary growth in the following decade, surpassing $5 billion in sales in 1995 on the way to more than $20 billion in 2000.

To say that Gates ignored public policy for many years is not to say that he was ignorant of it. His parents were involved in public causes, and Gates served as a U.S. Senate page as a teenager. As policy issues increasingly intruded on Gates's growing business during the 1990s, he displayed a willingness to lend his name and his firm's name to efforts to address them. Gates and Microsoft took an interest in government control of encryption software as early as 1991, for example, and in the privatization of the Internet two years later. He made personal contacts at the highest levels of the federal government during the Clinton administration, including the president himself, Vice President Al Gore, and Speaker of the House Newt Gingrich.

Yet like IBM's Tom Watson Jr. before him, Gates chose not to build much of an organizational structure to manage government affairs for Microsoft. As late as

October 1997, *Roll Call*, the Capitol Hill newspaper, reported that "Gates still remains virtually invisible in Washington." With only a tiny office in the capital to focus and amplify Gates's modest personal involvement in the policy process—and to attend to the myriad details below Gates's job description—Microsoft remained a "Washington wimp." The decision to minimize Microsoft's Washington involvement (which Gates referred to as "some overhead" in a 1995 interview) was based at least in part on his interpretation of IBM's experience under Watson's successors. In Gates's view IBM had paid too much attention to Washington and not enough to the fast-moving business it was in. The effort that made the "Incredible Bunch of Morons" (as Microsoftees nicknamed IBM) successful in Washington, Gates thought, contributed to its demise as the high-tech industry's dominant business.

To many policymakers, though, [including Senate Commerce Committee policy director Mark Buse] Microsoft's aloofness implied that the firm "held Washington in disdain." Microsoft's competitors worked hard to deepen this perception. Fear and loathing of Microsoft and Gates convinced high-tech entrepreneurs like Sun's Scott McNealy and Oracle's Larry Ellison of the wisdom of investing in a Washington presence. They hired high-profile figures not previously associated with the high-tech industry, such as Supreme Court nominee Robert Bork and former Senate minority leader Robert Dole, to spread their message. Oracle even hired an investigator to go through the trash of Microsoft-friendly groups in 1999.

This campaign made it more likely that powerful decisionmakers would endorse Assistant Attorney General Joel Klein's professional judgment about prosecuting Microsoft. From the perspective of Microsoft's critics and competitors, government investigations and filings in the early and mid-1990s had produced meager results. The suit lodged in May 1998 represented a major expansion of the scope and objectives of the federal case, alleging a pattern of illegal practices aimed at maintaining and extending Microsoft's monopoly in PC operating systems.

In late 1997 and early 1998, with the threat of another antitrust case looming, Gates joined the political arms race with his competitors in earnest. Microsoft separated its public policy office from its Washington sales office in March 1998 and increased its professional staff from two in 1997 to at least ten by early 1999. The firm dramatically expanded its list of consultants, thereby building its connections to both parties and most of the major presidential candidates. Reported lobbying expenditures rose from $2 million in 1997 to nearly $4 million in 1998 and $5 million in 1999. Contributions to candidates by Microsoft's political action committee quadrupled between 1995 and 1998 and then again in 1999–2000. Soft money contributions from company funds zoomed from $80,000 to $800,000 to more than $900,000. Microsoft pushed its policy proposals with advertising, supported existing interest groups and helped create new ones, conducted polls, made politically significant charitable contributions, and otherwise deployed the full panoply of instruments available to the sophisticated and well-funded Washington corporate player.

The return that Microsoft received on this investment remains hotly debated. Some of the firm's most heavy-handed moves backfired. The firm lobbied to cut the Antitrust Division's appropriation and reaped criticism even from its allies. "'That might have been the dumbest political move of the year,' said a senior [congressional] leadership aide." Members of prominent Republican Ralph Reed's political consulting firm lobbied Republican presidential candidate George W. Bush on Microsoft's behalf, forcing Reed, who consulted for Bush as well as Microsoft, to make a highly public statement of regret about the apparent conflict of interest. Blasted for arrogance when it had appeared to ignore Washington, Microsoft went so far in the other direction that it was blasted again. Among candidates and consultants, the firm was said to be something of a cash cow that heedlessly dumped money into the capital.

Slowly, though, the tenor of the discussion began to change. In April 2000 the *New York Times* reported that Gates was "treated . . . as a national treasure" in his meetings with the leadership of both parties in Congress and the president. Microsoft was increasingly viewed as an upstanding corporate citizen taking its rightful place in policy discussions relevant to the high-tech industry, such as education and the digital divide. The election in 2000 of a new administration not wedded to the 1998 antitrust case raised the prospect that Microsoft might receive the biggest payoff of all: settlement of the case on lenient terms and without a breakup of the firm. Such an outcome would not be a result of Microsoft "assimilating" Washington as it had its adversaries in the business world. The reverse was closer to the truth: Bill Gates and his crew had adapted to Washington. ■

Chapter 7

The Media

A free and unbridled press is one of the safeguards of American liberty. The United States, as Supreme Court Justice William Brennan wrote in 1964, has maintained a "profound national commitment to the principle that debate on public issues should be uninhibited, robust, and wide-open."* The press plays a critical role in promoting democracy by exposing official mismanagement and corruption, providing information that citizens need to make key decisions, giving people a window on the activities of their government, and providing the government with feedback on the opinions and viewpoints of the people.

The role of the media in the United States today, however, is not so simple. The media not only report the news; they also decide what is and what is not news. They not only report on public opinion; they also play a vital role in shaping public opinion. In theory, the media may be free and unencumbered, but journalists live and work in a complex environment, and their employers are typically large corporations, which depend on other larger corporations for necessary advertising revenue. Reporters and editors have their own agendas to pursue, both professionally and, some would say, ideologically. They must both entertain and inform, especially on television and radio; are easily manipulated and used by government officials and candidates; must cope with short deadlines and often with limited information; and must continually try to fight off boredom, bias, and a pack mentality.

All of this is complicated by television and the "new media." More Americans get their news on television than in any other form. Campaigns are waged and the country is governed through media performances, sound bites, and photo opportunities, increasingly on a multitude of twenty-four-hour cable news and talk networks. Candidates and government officials who learn how to use television to their advantage prosper; those who do not flounder. But television is facing increasing competition in recent years from a wide variety of new media sources—including websites, weblogs, and talk radio. These new forms of media have greatly multiplied both the number of news sources available to the American public and the speed at which news stories are transmitted around the globe.

This chapter examines politics and the media from four vantage points. Selection 7.1 examines the constitutional commitment to freedom of the press through the prism of *New York Times Co.* v. *United States*, a 1971 Supreme Court decision that refused to allow

---

New York Times v. Sullivan, 376 U.S. 254 (1964), at 270.

government censorship of the media, even when national security was arguably at stake. Selection 7.2 analyzes the exciting but also problematic world of the new media, with an emphasis on the Internet. Selections 7.3 and 7.4 investigate the question of whether, as is commonly charged, the media are biased. Finally, selection 7.5 presents a firsthand account of the ongoing conflict between law enforcement and the media over the protection of confidential news sources.

Chapter Questions

1. What roles do the media play in American politics? How do these roles conflict with one another; with the economic, personal, or professional interests of journalists; and with the interests of the corporations for which most journalists work?
2. What influences the media's decisions on what news to report and how to report it? To what extent do the media control the agenda in American politics? To what extent are the media manipulated by politicians and government officials?
3. What are the implications of the proliferation of the "new media," including the Internet and other forms of electronic communication?

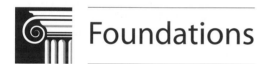 Foundations

The media's critical role in the American political system is grounded in the First Amendment to the United States Constitution, which protects both freedom of speech and freedom of the press. The American commitment to a free press can be traced back as far as 1735, when the printer John Peter Zenger was acquitted by a New York jury even though he admitted to violating the law by publishing criticisms of the colonial government. It was not until the twentieth century, however, that the Supreme Court translated that commitment into legally enforceable doctrine.

The media are not at liberty to publish or broadcast anything they want, of course. Newspapers can still be sued for libel, which involves the publication of false statements damaging to the reputation of an individual or organization, although the rules laid down by the Supreme Court make it difficult for public officials and public figures to win such suits. The broadcast media are more heavily regulated, with television and radio stations subject to licensing requirements and to rules prohibiting or limiting certain kinds of speech, including sexually explicit materials. In general, however, the American press remains remarkably free from governmental control or interference.

One of the Supreme Court's landmark decisions on press freedom was the 1971 case of *New York Times Co. v. United States*. The case arose when the *Times* began to publish the so-called Pentagon Papers, a series of secret documents concerning the Vietnam War. Citing national security considerations, the Nixon administration immediately went to court, asking a federal judge for an injunction (or order) forcing the newspaper to cease publication of the papers. The judge agreed, at least until the issue could be resolved by the courts. Meanwhile, several other newspapers—including the *Washington Post*—began publishing the papers and joined the lawsuit. Within a matter of weeks, the controversy was argued before the Supreme Court, which threw out the lower court order by a vote of six to three, clearing the way for publication.

There was no majority opinion in the case. Instead, eight justices submitted separate opinions. The opinion of Justice Hugo L. Black, which was joined by Justice William O. Douglas, is a passionate and eloquent statement by one of the First Amendment's strongest supporters. Black's opinion underscores the importance of a free press in any democratic society.

Questions

1. What was the purpose of the First Amendment, according to Black? Why is a free press, in his view, essential to the creation and maintenance of a free society?
2. Why does Black reject the Nixon administration's argument that the injunctions in this case were justified by considerations of national security?
3. Should Justice Black's argument be reevaluated in light of the war on terror? Why or why not?

7.1 *New York Times Co. v. United States* (1971)

Justice Hugo L. Black

I adhere to the view that the Government's case against the Washington Post should have been dismissed and that the injunction against the New York Times should have been vacated without oral argument when the cases were first presented to this Court. I believe that every moment's continuance of the injunctions against these newspapers amounts to a flagrant, indefensible, and continuing violation of the First Amendment. . . . In my view it is unfortunate that some of my Brethren are apparently willing to hold that the publication of news may sometimes be enjoined. Such a holding would make a shambles of the First Amendment.

Our Government was launched in 1789 with the adoption of the Constitution. The Bill of Rights, including the First Amendment, followed in 1791. Now, for the first time in the 182 years since the founding of the Republic, the federal courts are asked to hold that the First Amendment does not mean what it says, but rather means that the Government can halt the publication of current news of vital importance to the people of this country.

In seeking injunctions against these newspapers and in its presentation to the Court, the Executive Branch seems to have forgotten the essential purpose and history of the First Amendment. When the Constitution was adopted, many people

---

403 U.S. 713 (1971).

strongly opposed it because the document contained no Bill of Rights to safeguard certain basic freedoms. They especially feared that the new powers granted to a central government might be interpreted to permit the government to curtail freedom of religion, press, assembly, and speech. In response to an overwhelming public clamor, James Madison offered a series of amendments to satisfy citizens that these great liberties would remain safe and beyond the power of government to abridge. Madison proposed what later became the First Amendment in three parts, two of which are set out below, and one of which proclaimed: "The people shall not be deprived or abridged of their right to speak, to write, or to publish their sentiments; and the freedom of the press, as one of the great bulwarks of liberty, shall be inviolable." The amendments were offered to curtail and restrict the general powers granted to the Executive, Legislative, and Judicial Branches two years before in the original Constitution. The Bill of Rights changed the original Constitution into a new charter under which no branch of government could abridge the people's freedoms of press, speech, religion, and assembly. . . . Madison and the other Framers of the First Amendment, able men that they were, wrote in language they earnestly believed could never be misunderstood: "Congress shall make no law . . . abridging the freedom . . . of the press. . . ." Both the history and language of the First Amendment support the view that the press must be left free to publish news, whatever the source, without censorship, injunctions, or prior restraints.

In the First Amendment the Founding Fathers gave the free press the protection it must have to fulfill its essential role in our democracy. The press was to serve the governed, not the governors. The Government's power to censor the press was abolished so that the press would remain forever free to censure the Government. The press was protected so that it could bare the secrets of government and inform the people. Only a free and unrestrained press can effectively expose deception in government. And paramount among the responsibilities of a free press is the duty to prevent any part of the government from deceiving the people and sending them off to distant lands to die of foreign fevers and foreign shot and shell. In my view, far from deserving condemnation for their courageous reporting, the New York Times, the Washington Post, and other newspapers should be commended for serving the purpose that the Founding Fathers saw so clearly. In revealing the workings of government that led to the Vietnam war, the newspapers nobly did precisely that which the Founders hoped and trusted they would do.

The Government's case here is based on premises entirely different from those that guided the Framers of the First Amendment. The Solicitor General [on behalf of the U.S. government] has carefully and emphatically stated:

> Now, Mr. Justice [BLACK], your construction of . . . [the First Amendment] is well known, and I certainly respect it. You say that no law means no law, and that should be obvious. I can only say, Mr. Justice, that to me it is equally obvious that "no law" does not mean "no law," and I would seek to persuade the Court that is true. . . . [T]here are other parts of the Constitution that grant powers and responsibilities to the Executive, and . . . the First Amendment was not intended to make it impossible for the Executive to function or to protect the security of the United States.

And the Government argues in its brief that in spite of the First Amendment, "[t]he authority of the Executive Department to protect the nation against publication of information whose disclosure would endanger the national security stems from two interrelated sources: the constitutional power of the President over the conduct of foreign affairs and his authority as Commander-in-Chief."

In other words, we are asked to hold that despite the First Amendment's emphatic command, the Executive Branch, the Congress, and the Judiciary can make laws enjoining publication of current news and abridging freedom of the press in the name of "national security." The Government does not even attempt to rely on any act of Congress. Instead it makes the bold and dangerously far-reaching contention that the courts should take it upon themselves to "make" a law abridging freedom of the press in the name of equity, presidential power and national security, even when the representatives of the people in Congress have adhered to the command of the First Amendment and refused to make such a law. To find that the President has "inherent power" to halt the publication of news by resort to the courts would wipe out the First Amendment and destroy the fundamental liberty and security of the very people the Government hopes to make "secure." No one can read the history of the adoption of the First Amendment without being convinced beyond any doubt that it was injunctions like those sought here that Madison and his collaborators intended to outlaw in this Nation for all time.

The word "security" is a broad, vague generality whose contours should not be invoked to abrogate the fundamental law embodied in the First Amendment. The guarding of military and diplomatic secrets at the expense of informed representative government provides no real security for our Republic. The Framers of the First Amendment, fully aware of both the need to defend a new nation and the abuses of the English and Colonial governments, sought to give this new society strength and security by providing that freedom of speech, press, religion, and assembly should not be abridged. This thought was eloquently expressed in 1937 by Mr. Chief Justice Hughes—great man and great Chief Justice that he was—when the Court held a man could not be punished for attending a meeting run by Communists.

> The greater the importance of safeguarding the community from incitements to the overthrow of our institutions by force and violence, the more imperative is the need to preserve inviolate the constitutional rights of free speech, free press and free assembly in order to maintain the opportunity for free political discussion, to the end that government may be responsive to the will of the people and that changes, if desired, may be obtained by peaceful means. Therein lies the security of the Republic, the very foundation of constitutional government. ■

American Politics Today

As recently as the mid-1990s, the Internet was a minor factor in American life and politics—the domain of a relative handful of academics, scientists, and other specialists. Today, over 70 percent of American adults are on-line (among young adults, the number is even higher, approaching 90 percent).* Americans can now get their news instantly and any time they want it. They can effortlessly read newspapers and magazines from across the country and around the world. They can access news sources as old and established as the *Times* of London, or as new and unknown as an anonymous blogger.

If information is power, the American people are more powerful than ever. But as Jeremy D. Mayer and Michael Cornfield suggest, the growth of the Internet has been something of a mixed blessing. Mayer and Cornfield praise the Internet for promoting interactivity, independence, and the depth of news coverage, but they warn that the Internet is not available to everyone, that it often subjects Americans to an unmanageable overload of unfiltered information, and that it may promote "a sense of hyper-individualism."

Questions

1. In what ways has the Internet improved the American political system? Conversely, what problems has the Internet failed to solve or even made worse?
2. What advice would you give to Americans to help them use the Internet more effectively as a source of news and information about politics?

7.2 The New Media (2003)

Jeremy D. Mayer and Michael Cornfield

The Promise of the Internet: Interactivity, Independence, and Depth

Each method of communication has properties that confer advantages on its users. The rise of the Internet as a major force in the American media offers three promising changes in politics: interactivity, independence, and depth.

Interactivity   When television broadcast news is the main source of political information, and when Americans learn about politicians and their stances through televised presidential debates and campaign ads, there is little opportunity

---

*Mary Madden, "Internet Penetration and Impact: April 2006," *Pew Internet and American Life Project*, http://www.pewinternet.org/pdfs/PIP_Internet_Impact.pdf.

From Jeremy D. Mayer and Michael Cornfield, "The New Media," in Mark J. Rozell, ed., *Media Power, Media Politics*, 2003, ch. 13. Reprinted by permission of Rowman & Littlefield.

for individual citizens to feel involved in the process. As anticipated by critical theo-
rist Walter Benjamin, the viewers of video discourse are removed from the immediacy of politics, and their attitudes towards politics are also changed. As with art and
religion, politics experienced through the chilly refraction of a camera eye will never
be the same as politics live. The New England town hall democracy and the classic
democracy of the Greek city-states allowed for more interactivity between governed
and governors. The citizens could guide the discussion towards matters of concern
through questions and speeches. Television does not directly allow for any interactivity between the viewers and the viewed, the citizens and their leaders. This empowers the gatekeepers of the media, who are given the power to set the nation's
agenda by what they cover, and perhaps more importantly, what they do not cover.

Now, two-and-a-half millennia after Pericles, some feel that technology will
allow us to have an interactive exchange with our leaders. While reading a story
on the Internet, or watching a streaming video of an interview with a journalist or
a politician, a citizen can shoot an e-mail off to a federal agency, or make a contribution directly to the politician. Newspapers and broadcast stations conduct online political polls at their websites, and report the unscientific results. Media
companies like online polls even though they are of dubious accuracy, because
they are amazingly cheap. Interactivity between journalists and consumers becomes far easier. Consider the ease and immediacy of shooting an e-mail off to Bill
O'Reilly at Fox News versus writing a letter to Walter Cronkite in 1974. Media
companies even monitor from day to day which pages of their websites are looked
at, and by how many people. The consumers of online journalism vote with every
mouse click and download about what issues they want the media to cover. While
newspapers and television stations conducted market research and polling before
the Internet, these did not approach the amount of information given by online
monitoring of media consumption.

The Internet may also bring about higher levels of interactivity between citizens
and the government itself. Arizona and other states are exploring voting online.
Enthusiasm for computer voting went even higher after the debacle in Florida during the election of 2000, in which 19th-century voting technology was exposed as
deeply flawed and widely utilized. All 50 state governments and many localities
distribute information on the Web, and every month more government services
are available online, from paying parking tickets to applying for government contracts. A website and e-mail network made it possible for presidential candidate
and maverick Republican John McCain to raise and spend more than $6 million
in hard money donations in the early months of 2002, enabling him to stay in the
race for the Republican nomination a few extra weeks.

Interest groups, new and old, have rushed to exploit the possibilities of the Internet. In the classic model of pluralism, power in America is distributed un-
equally, with groups that are able to organize more effectively wielding disproportionate power. The ability to organize was previously highly correlated with
income, education, and political efficacy (the sense that your views mattered).
The Internet allows far-flung individuals with little political experience to coa-
lesce around a cause with remarkably little financial outlay. For example, in 1998,
a husband-and-wife team formed moveon.org, a political action committee that
capitalized on citizen outrage with both President Clinton's dissembling about his

affair with Monica Lewinsky and those House Republicans who tried to impeach him for the offense. Moveon.org exists solely online, yet it attracted hundreds of thousands of members, who signed petitions and spent millions of dollars to defeat Republican members of the House Judiciary Committee. The interactivity offered by the Internet will, in the view of some, ameliorate one of the chronic problems in American politics during this century: low levels of citizen participation, particularly in voting. By making information more readily available, by lowering barriers to citizen input and interaction, and by making voting and donating easier, cyberpolitics may enhance citizen interest, influence, and participation.

Independence   The Internet may also weaken the media's control over what citizens learn about politics. Citizens are more independent of the power of media gatekeepers in the age of the Internet. Compare a daily newspaper to a 30-minute evening news broadcast to a CNN website. The 100,000 words of text available in the newspaper represent the editors' view of what an educated citizen should know about current events that day. There is some degree of independence; for example, a committed Republican could choose not to read any reports about Bush's stock dealings in the oil business. By contrast, in watching an anchor deliver the few thousand words of a typical news program, the viewer is passive; he cannot dart ahead, or jump back in the newscast to follow his interest. But the Internet consumer of news is in control. She may click only on the stories that interest her, and can even arrange a website to show her only stories on topics of concern.

Independence also applies to the number of media outlets available today. Throughout this century, concern among political scientists and media analysts has grown about the concentration of media power in fewer and fewer hands. By some estimates, ten multinational corporations control the most influential media outlets in the country. The Internet may well change that. While the most popular sites on the Web are often those affiliated with major media corporations (CNN, MSNBC, Yahoo, AOL, etc.), some of the most influential websites, such as the Drudge Report, are run by individuals. Anyone with a computer and Internet access can set up a website with his or her own political views. "Blogs" or "weblogs" are sites set up by individuals to publicize their experiences and their opinions. They are often vulgar, unsourced, and by definition nonauthoritative. However, one of the leading public intellectuals of the day, Andrew Sullivan, has set up his own website, where his thoughts and essays are available to readers without the filter of editors or the delay of publishing. As Dan Gilmour, a newspaper editor, sees it, some day news coverage itself will be shaped by the reaction of thousands of "bloggers":

> I think we've moved profoundly from the older period in which news was a lecture. Now the job is that we tell you what we have learned, you tell us if you think we are correct, then we all discuss it.

The Internet may also contribute to nonconformist thought in politics. During the height of television's media dominance, some feared that the media were contributing to a "spiral of silence." Because those with minority views would see no support for their opinions in the media, which emphasized conformist and majoritarian views, they would keep silent for fear of social ostracism. Today, thanks to the Internet, almost no opinion (or fetish or preference, for that matter) is so isolated that it cannot find at least one kindred spirit somewhere on the Web. The Internet exceeds the connective power of any other medium, because strangers who share political ideas can use it to find and contact each other. . . .

Clearly, the Internet has expanded the boundaries of the playing fields of politics. That is not the same as leveling the field: wealthy and official voices still hold advantages. But marginal presence on the new field confers an extra shot at influence previously unimaginable for many aspiring players.

Depth   Political scientist Lance Bennett identifies fragmentation and personalization as two of the key defects in modern political coverage. Journalists present issues episodically, without context, and often in a simplistic manner that ignores historical and institutional forces. This is particularly true of televised news. Bennett believes these institutional biases in the way information is presented are a threat to the health of our democracy. The Internet, however, has the potential to redress at least certain aspects of these ills.

For example, even if the streaming videos available on the Web reproduce the fragmented and personalized coverage of televised journalism, the Internet adds depth in two ways: access and context. First, voters can now determine the shallowness (or substance) of a 30-second radio or television spot much more easily because the Internet archives those spots. Second, sustained examinations of the history of many issues and candidates referenced in "drive-by" ads are now only a click away on many news and even some campaign websites. These websites, along with such civic nonpartisan websites as www.vote-smart.org (Project Vote Smart) and www.dnet.org (Democracy Net), often contain thousands of words on issues, transcripts of debates, and links to legislation.

Thus, consumers of politics on the Web may be initially presented with a fragmented and incomplete picture of an event or a candidate, but they are given the tools to put the issue into a deeper context. Whether they choose to do so or not is their decision. Of course, one might note the same about an article in *Time* magazine or a story on the CBS news. It was never impossible for a consumer of the news, intrigued by a particular issue, to become educated on it, through a trip to the library if nothing else. What the Internet changes is the ease with which depth is available. Context is just a click away.

The Defects of the Internet for Media Politics: Access, Overload, Filterlessness, and Cocooning

Each of the positive changes wrought by the introduction of the Internet can be subjected to cross-examination. Not only may the Internet fail to rectify existing problems in American media politics, it may create new ones.

Access   The digital divide is real, and it limits the Internet's effects and leads to greater inequality in our society. The term became fashionable during the mid-1990s to describe the unequal access to the Internet that was emerging. From its birth until this moment, the Internet has been a medium far more often used by the wealthy, the educated, the male, and the white citizens of this country than by others. The skew in usage on each of those factors has lessened since 1996, but has not vanished. Similarly, the first schools to get wired were the wealthier ones, and this remains true today.

One could complacently observe that similar patterns were evident at the dawn of radio and television, and those "electronic divides" rapidly disappeared. The digital divide is certainly getting smaller. According to a Pew Center poll, home computer ownership went from 36% to 59% and venturing online at least occasionally went from 21% to 54% in just the four years from 1996 to 2000. Unequal access may also not be as large a problem, or at least as new a problem, as some see it. Even newspapers in the colonial era were not equally distributed, with many in the lower classes lacking either the literacy to appreciate papers or money to buy them. As compared to the early days of the Republic, when the government did not even attempt to teach the poor how to read, the government is taking steps to address the digital divide. State and federal programs are in place to make computers more available to public school children.

However, there is reason to think that this divide will be more resilient than previous ones. First, many of the educated and wealthy who frequently use the Web do so from their workplaces. It is unlikely that autoworkers, butchers, bus drivers, and plumbers will soon be granted worksite access to the Internet. (And persons accessing the Internet for politics from the workplace must consider the possibility that their movements, words, and activities will be monitored by their employers, if not the government. This could deter workplace use of the Internet for politics.) Second, the cost of access is continually changing, and while basic access (cost of a computer plus cost of an Internet service provider) may have declined in price, the cost for DSL or broadband access is much greater. Many features on the Internet are increasingly geared towards those who can download large amounts of data quickly. The divide in access to that quality of service is very great. In terms of access, the Internet is more akin to cable television than to broadcast television, and even today, millions of Americans cannot afford or choose not to pay a monthly fee for television. Third, even with more Americans learning how to use computers with each passing moment, there remains a generational gap in Internet usage. A 65-year-old in 1960 had little difficulty plugging in a television and watching the Kennedy-Nixon debates. But many senior citizens today still find computers daunting and confusing. For these reasons, if the Internet becomes the most important form of political discourse, it will be a conversation that leaves millions of Americans out of earshot for years to come.

Overload   The media are commonly referred to in government textbooks as a "mediating institution" between the governed and the governors. Among the many functions the media performed in this role were informing citizens of government actions, and informing elites of the public's reactions and desires. The media told citizens what was important in the political world, and told elites what the public felt was important. If the "gatekeeping" or "agenda-setting" power of the media has been reduced, this may actually serve to lessen citizen influence on elites. When there were only three television news networks, and only a few leading nationally influential newspapers, the major media outlets had tremendous power to focus the attention of citizens and elites on a given topic. Today, with so many diverse outlets, there may be far less of a sense of a unified national agenda to which politicians have to react and the public has to pay attention. The citizen, presented with the chaotic, shifting, and massive amount of political information available on the Web, may simply retreat from the overload of data.

The overload of data also comes at Americans at an increasingly dizzying pace, making politics rapid and dynamic. Because the Internet conveys information almost without discernible delay, there are, in hotly competitive political, media, and media/political situations, more cycles of action-reaction communication. This affects political elites as well as ordinary citizens. To illustrate: On September 17, 2000, the Bush and Gore campaigns for president strafed the reporters on their press e-mail lists (consisting of 2,000 and 1,200 names, respectively) with 56 e-mails. Most of these concerned a 16-page "Blueprint for the Middle Class" issued by the Republican nominee. The Democrat's pre-buttal (for it was released prior to the Bush document) was 24 pages long. The 56 e-mails spun, re-spun, and meta-spun (if that is a word adequate to describe commenting with intent to persuade on another's efforts at commenting with intent to persuade) around the topic of which candidate had the better economic plan for America.

Many refer to this phenomenon as the "24-hour news cycle," but that is something of a misnomer. While an action-mediation-reaction cycle can occur at any hour of the day, not just during working hours in one time zone, the phrase can also be interpreted as implying that it takes 24 hours for reactions to an action to register in public. That was in the old days. "Real time" is a much better phrase at conveying the current compression of the interval between action and reaction.

Not all politics and mediation occurs in real time, nor is that likely to develop. But thanks to the Internet, more segments of the mediated politics world can speed up to occur in real time for a while. . . . When real-time political moments crystallize in the digital age, the increase of cycles comes with more players, more messages, and also, note well, less time for any single person to digest all that is being said, and shown, and perhaps substantiated. . . . [The] response of the citizen to this rapid overload of competing claims may well be exhaustion and even alienation.

The overload may also expose interactivity with government officials as a sham and a false hope. See what ensues when you send an e-mail to a public official you've watched at C-SPAN.org, for instance. (Hint: not much.) Perhaps in 1992, when Ross Perot advocated an "electronic town hall" in which all of America would debate and then vote on the issues of the day, Americans might have imagined that technology could take us back to New England town hall democracy. But the overload problem with regard to interactivity is even greater than it is with regard to information; there are too many of us for government to process our inputs on issues beyond the shallowest up or down opinions. The dream of a restoration of a direct democracy is not new in American public life; pollster George Gallup imagined in 1939 that public opinion polling would lead to a responsive and participatory democracy, and that certainly has not occurred. Cyberpolitics has not magically erased the classic problem of the "one and the many"; the overloaded circuits of the Internet may have actually exacerbated it.

Filterlessness   If the Internet grants us independence from the centralized power of the mass media, this independence is inextricably tied to the problem of filterlessness. Political, civic, and media institutions use filters to improve the quality of the information they depend on and release to the public. They check facts, revise sentences, rearrange photos, and so forth. The Internet's virtue of no authoritative control permits dissidents and eccentrics to promulgate their views to the world, but this quality is also a significant weakness. A book that was released by a reputable academic press could be expected to have undergone lengthy peer review by knowledgeable experts. A story printed in the *New York Times* underwent careful and redundant fact checking. As the anecdote has it, a reporter should not print a story about how much his mother loves him unless he can verify it with two independent sources. The rapid pace of the media in the era of cyberpolitics has removed much of the filtering process; rumor, falsehood, and innuendo quickly move into public discourse. Matters about the private sex lives of public officials that would never have been printed in previous eras are now fodder for Web gossips like Matt Drudge.

One can point to examples of the media's abusing its gatekeeping authority in the past, such as its refusal to inform the nation of philandering presidents whose preoccupation with illicit sex arguably raised questions about national security and judgment. However, the loss of gatekeeping power by the mass media has made politics a less appetizing field of endeavor, both for citizens and politicians. . . .

The permeability and universality of the Internet raises questions about the nature of truth itself, in a way that postmodernists may welcome, but that poses challenges to more traditional researchers. Who is an authority, and how do we know? Professors across the country lament that students conducting research for term papers often mistake cranks and kooks for reputable scholars, based on the professional presentation of their thoughts on a website. A colleague of one of the authors received a paper that cited the website of a Holocaust denier as a source on Nazism and its goals. Of course, fringe groups who deny the Holocaust or assert anti-Semitic canards as fact have been publishing books and magazines for centuries. However, librarians had acted as a filter to most of these materials, separating out legitimate challengers to conventional wisdom from irrational ideologues. . . .

Cocooning   The growth of technology's role in American life may contribute to a sense of hyper-individualism, as we all cocoon ourselves away from not only politics but real-world human connections. While champions of the Internet's possibility rave about the potential for spacially separated individuals to form interest groups through the Web, perhaps such groups fail to provide community, solidarity, and other group benefits that are necessary to civil society. Consider the difference between a union hall gathering of workers in 1950 and an Internet chat room on politics today. The union hall meeting requires physical presence, and interactions beyond the level of typing and reading. Those present see each other as complete beings, who have left their private domains to enter into public discourse. The patterns of listening and speaking, of debate and discussion, probably would not be unfamiliar to a colonial Virginian or an ancient Greek. By contrast, the denizens of a chat room or the readers of a bulletin board may hide behind pseudonyms; they may misrepresent their true selves or opinions with careless abandon. Most importantly, they may not feel the same sense of connection to each other as do people who meet in the flesh.

Thinkers as diverse as Tocqueville in the 19th century and political scientist Robert Putnam in the late 20th century have emphasized that America's civil society rests on the health of voluntary associations among citizens. Civic activities that build up "social capital" have been declining rapidly in the last forty years, and this troubles many scholars, politicians, and citizens. One of Putnam's more intriguing findings in his influential 2001 book, *Bowling Alone*, was that for every hour of newspaper reading, civic engagement increased, while for every hour of television watching, it decreased. While comparable data are not yet available for Internet usage, it seems plausible that local "real" activities decline as Internet usage expands. Thus, it becomes important to find out whether the "communal" activities on the Web can produce the same connectedness that characterized traditional groups. As one recent article asked: "When it comes to . . . building community, is the Internet more like a Girl Scout troop or a television set?" Unfortunately, given current patterns of usage, it seems that the Internet is far more similar to the dreaded idiot box than to a meeting with other citizens.

Thus, "cocooning" may represent the most subtle and insidious danger in cyberpolitics. Even before the Internet, many worried that Americans were increasingly unconnected to each other. More and more of the upper classes live in gated communities, send their children to private schools, and fail to interact in any meaningful way with less wealthy Americans. Demonstrations and marches and rallies declined in effectiveness, as Americans ceased congregating in public spaces, replacing downtowns with privately owned malls. With the dawn of Internet shopping, telecommuting, and Web-based entertainment, leaving home becomes almost superfluous. Perhaps the new media possibilities of the Web will provide Americans with access to new and unfiltered information about politics. But if we do not have a sense of community, of shared obligation and values, will we care about political news from home or abroad? Instead of "Thinking globally and acting locally" will we now "Entertain individually and disappear locally"? . . . ■

Issue and Controversy

Critics on both sides of the American political debate have accused the media of bias. Liberals argue that the media are dominated by large corporations, which are themselves dependent on other corporations for advertising revenue. They also point to the conservatives' dominance of the radio talk show circuit and to the influence of allegedly conservative-leaning networks such as Fox News. Conservatives emphasize the liberal orientation of most reporters and editors, and argue that their side rarely gets a fair shake from the major television networks or from newspapers like the *New York Times* or the *Washington Post*.

The debate over media bias has been raging on and off for several decades, but the rhetoric heated up in 2002 with the publication of *Bias*, a self-proclaimed exposé of the media's liberal bias by former CBS journalist Bernard Goldberg. An excerpt from Goldberg's book is followed by a brief rebuttal to Goldberg by journalist Jonathan Chait.

Questions

1. On what basis does Bernard Goldberg argue that the media are biased toward the liberal side of the political spectrum? How does Jonathan Chait counter Goldberg's argument?
2. What factors other than alleged bias might influence the behavior of reporters and editors?

7.3 Bias (2002)

Bernard Goldberg

On December 6, 1998, on a *Meet the Press* segment about Bill Clinton and his relationship with the Washington news corps, one of the capital's media stars, the *Washington Post*'s Sally Quinn, felt she needed to state what to her was the obvious.

The Washington press corps, she insisted, was not some "monolith." "We all work for different organizations," she said, "we all think differently."

Not really, Sally.

Two years earlier, in 1996, the Freedom Forum and the Roper Center released the results of a now famous survey of 139 Washington bureau chiefs and congressional correspondents. The results make you wonder what in the world Sally Quinn was talking about.

The Freedom Forum is an independent foundation that examines issues that involve the media. The Roper Center is an opinion research firm, also with a solid reputation. "No way that the data are the fruit of right-wing press bashers," as the journalist Ben Wattenberg put it.

What these two groups found was that Washington journalists are far more liberal and far more Democratic than the typical American voter:

♦ 89 percent of the journalists said they voted for Bill Clinton in 1992, compared with just 43 percent of the nonjournalist voters.
♦ 7 percent of the journalists voted for George Bush; 37 percent of the voters did.
♦ 2 percent of the news people voted for Ross Perot while 19 percent of the electorate did.

Eighty-nine percent voted for Bill Clinton. This is incredible when you think about it. There's hardly a candidate in the entire United States of America who carries his or her district with 89 percent of the vote. This is way beyond mere

---

landslide numbers. The only politicians who get numbers like that are called Fidel Castro or Saddam Hussein. The same journalists that Sally Quinn tells us do not constitute a "monolith" certainly vote like one.

Sally says they "all think differently." About what? Picking the best appetizer at the Ethiopian restaurant in Georgetown?

What party do journalists identify with?

♦ 50 percent said they were Democrats.
♦ *4 percent* said they were Republicans.

When they were asked, "How do you characterize your political orientation?" 61 percent said "liberal" or "moderate to liberal." Only 9 percent said they were "conservative" or "moderate to conservative."

In the world of media elites, Democrats outnumber Republicans by twelve to one and liberals outnumber conservatives by seven to one. Yet Dan Rather believes that "most reporters don't know whether they're Republican or Democrat, and vote every which way." In your dreams, Dan.

After the survey came out, the *Washington Post* media writer, Howard Kurtz, said on *Fox News Sunday*, "Clearly anybody looking at those numbers, if they're even close to accurate, would conclude that there is a diversity problem in the news business, and it's not just the kind of diversity we usually talk about, which is not getting enough minorities in the news business, but political diversity, as well. Anybody who doesn't see that is just in denial."

James Glassman put it this way in the *Washington Post*: "The people who report the stories are liberal Democrats. This is the shameful open secret of American journalism. That the press itself . . . chooses to gloss over it is conclusive evidence of how pernicious the bias is."

Tom Rosenstiel, the director of the Project for Excellence in Journalism, says, "Bias is the elephant in the living room. We're in denial about it and don't want to admit it's there. We think it's less of a problem than the public does, and we just don't want to get into it."

Even *Newsweek*'s Evan Thomas (the one who thought Ronald Reagan had "a kind of intuitive idiot genius") has said, "There is a liberal bias. It's demonstrable. You look at some statistics. About 85 percent of the reporters who cover the White House vote Democratic; they have for a long time. There is a, particularly at the networks, at the lower levels, among the editors and the so-called infrastructure, there is a liberal bias."

Nonsense!

That's the response from Elaine Povich, who wrote the Freedom Forum report. No way, she said, that the survey confirms any liberal bias in the media.

"One of the things about being a professional," she said, "is that you attempt to leave your personal feelings aside as you do your work," she told the *Washington Times*.

"More people who are of a liberal persuasion go into reporting because they believe in the ethics and the ideals," she continued. "A lot of conservatives go into the private sector, go into Wall Street, go into banking. You find people who are idealistic tending toward the reporting end."

"Right," says Ben Wattenberg in his syndicated column. "These ethical, idealistic journalists left their personal feelings aside to this extent: When queried [in the Freedom Foundation/Roper poll in 1996] whether the 1994 Contract with America was an 'election-year campaign ploy' rather than 'a serious reform proposal,' 59 percent said 'ploy' and only 3 percent said 'serious.'"

It's true that only 139 Washington journalists were polled, but there's no reason to think the results were a fluke. Because this wasn't the first survey that showed how liberal so many journalists are.

A poll back in 1972 showed that of those reporters who voted, 70 percent went for McGovern, the most liberal presidential nominee in recent memory, while 25 percent went for Nixon—the same Richard Nixon who carried every single state in the union except Massachusetts.

In 1985 the *Los Angeles Times* conducted a nationwide survey of about three thousand journalists and the same number of people in the general public to see how each group felt about the major issues of the day:

♦ 23 percent of the public said they were liberal; 55 percent of the journalists described themselves as liberal.
♦ 56 percent of the public favored Ronald Reagan; 30 percent of the journalists favored Reagan.
♦ 49 percent of the public was for a woman's right to have an abortion; 82 percent of the journalists were pro-choice.
♦ 74 percent of the public was for prayer in public schools; 25 percent of the journalists surveyed were for prayer in the public schools.
♦ 56 percent of the nonjournalists were for affirmative action; 81 percent of the journalists were for affirmative action.
♦ 75 percent of the public was for the death penalty in murder cases; 47 percent of the journalists were for the death penalty.
♦ Half the public was for stricter handgun controls; 78 percent of the journalists were for tougher gun controls.

A more recent study, released in March 2000, also came to the conclusion that journalists are different from most of the people they cover. Peter Brown, an editor at the *Orlando Sentinel* in Florida, did a mini-census of 3,400 journalists and found that they are less likely to get married and have children, less likely to do volunteer community service, less likely to own homes, and less likely to go to church than others who live in the communities where they work.

"How many members of the *Los Angeles Times* and the *St. Louis Post-Dispatch*," he asks, "belong to the American Legion or the Kiwanis or go to prayer breakfasts?"

But it's not just that so many journalists are so different from mainstream America. It's that some are downright hostile to what many Americans hold sacred.

On April 14, 1999, I sat in on a *CBS Weekend News* conference call from a speakerphone in the Miami bureau. It's usually a routine call with CBS News producers all over the country taking part, telling the show producers in New York about the stories coming up in their territories that weekend. Roxanne Russell, a longtime producer out of the Washington bureau, was telling about an event that Gary Bauer would be attending. Bauer was the conservative, family-values activist who seven days later would announce his candidacy for the Republican nomination for president.

Bauer was no favorite of the cultural Left, who saw him as an annoying right-wing moralist. Anna Quindlen, the annoying left-wing moralist and columnist who writes for *Newsweek*, once called him "a man best known for trying to build a bridge to the 19th century."

So maybe I shouldn't have been surprised by what I heard next, but I was. Without a trace of timidity, without any apparent concern for potential consequences, Roxanne Russell, sitting at a desk inside the CBS News Washington bureau, nonchalantly referred to this conservative activist as "Gary Bauer, the little nut from the Christian group."

The little nut from the Christian group!

Those were her exact words, uttered at exactly 12:36 P.M. If any of the CBS News producers on the conference call were shocked, not one of them gave a clue. Roxanne Russell had just called Gary Bauer, the head of a major group of American Christians, "the little nut from the Christian group" and merrily went on with the rest of her list of events CBS News in Washington would be covering.

What struck me was not the obvious disrespect for Bauer. Journalists, being as terribly witty and sophisticated as we are, are always putting someone down. Religious people are especially juicy targets. In a lot of newsrooms, they're seen as odd and viewed with suspicion because their lives are shaped by faith and devotion to God and an adherence to rigid principles—opposition to abortion, for one—that seem archaic and closed-minded to a lot of journalists who, survey after survey suggests, are not especially religious themselves.

So it wasn't the hostility to Bauer in and of itself that threw me. It was the lack of concern of any kind in showing that disrespect *so openly*. Producers from CBS News bureaus all over the country were on the phone. And who knows who else was listening, just as I was.

So I wondered: would a network news producer ever make such a disparaging remark, so openly, about the head of a Jewish group? Or a gay group? Or a black group? . . . ■

7.4 Victim Politics (2002)

Jonathan Chait

• • •

When [former CBS journalist Bernard] Goldberg goes beyond his first-person observations at CBS, . . . he does little more than recycle long-standing conservative complaints. He notes, for instance, that news accounts describe Republicans as "right-wing" far more than they call Democrats

Jonathan Chait, "Victim Politics," *The New Republic*, March 18, 2002, pp. 22–25. Reprinted by permission of *The New Republic*, © 2002, The New Republic, LLC.

"left-wing." This may sound like a perfectly impartial objection—mustn't there be as many left-wingers in American politics as right-wingers? If you consider Clinton a leftist, as many conservatives do, then the answer is yes. But the center of American politics has moved rightward over the last 25 years. By historical standards—not to mention the standards of other democracies—American liberals today are rather conservative. Clinton was probably further to the right on domestic policy than Richard Nixon, and he was almost certainly further to the right than European conservatives such as Helmut Kohl and Jacques Chirac. So from these broader perspectives, it's entirely natural that reporters would label more contemporary American politicians "right-wing" than "left-wing."

This same rightward drift has made liberalism less fashionable. So, over the last decade, major newspapers have used the pejorative phrase "unreconstructed liberal" more than five times as often as they've used "unreconstructed conservative." Why isn't this disparity evidence of anti-liberal bias? For basically the same reason Goldberg's example isn't. Reporters are more likely to call liberals "unreconstructed" not because they consider liberalism out of date, but because in recent years liberals have indeed felt the need to reconstruct themselves more than conservatives have.   .   .   .

Another bias that Goldberg repeatedly notes stems from the crass imperative for commercial success. Ratings, he writes—again, apparently without recognition that he is undermining his thesis—are "the reason television people do almost everything." But if networks care only about ratings, why do they risk their profits by offending the political views of their audience? Indeed, in a free market, how could an overwhelmingly liberal media even exist? Even though the conservative FOX NEWS network has increased its share in recent years, "liberal" networks like ABC, CBS, CNN, and NBC still control the bulk of the TV news market and "liberal" newspapers the bulk of the newspaper market. If you believe that the media tilt left, then you must either believe that the public has no objection to this slant, or that the news business is unaffected by the forces of supply and demand.

To avoid such sticky questions, most conservatives ignore the political inclinations of both media owners and media consumers, and concentrate instead on the biases of reporters and editors. And here the right has its strongest case. Reporters, as numerous studies have established, overwhelmingly vote for Democrats. The most famous survey, taken after the 1992 elections, found that 89 percent of Washington journalists had voted for Clinton, 7 percent for Bush père, and only 2 percent for Ross Perot (as compared with 43, 37, and 19 percent, respectively, for the voters at large).

But this doesn't prove quite as much as one might suspect. Reporters may hold liberal views, but not on everything. Fairness and Accuracy in Reporting, a left-wing media watchdog, polled Washington journalists and compared the results with those of the public. It found that, while reporters generally hold more liberal views on social issues, they often take more conservative stances on economic questions. The public was far more likely than were media elites to think that Clinton's tax hike for the wealthy didn't go far enough and that the government should guarantee medical care. Reporters were far more inclined to support free trade and cutting entitlement programs.

This should come as no surprise. The views of the Beltway press reflect the ideology of the socioeconomic stratum in which they reside: secular, educated, urban or suburban, liberal on the environment and social issues, moderately conservative on economics. Indeed, the greatest statistical discrepancy in the 1992 voting pattern is not Washington reporters' lack of support for Bush, but their lack of support for Perot—they were one-fifth as likely as the public to cast a ballot for the GOP candidate, but only one-tenth as likely to support the Texas billionaire. Perot, of course, appealed to the disaffected working class, railing against free trade and immigration. Naturally, this brand of populism held little appeal for the media elite. . . .

On the whole, this set of biases disproportionately benefits Democrats and liberals. The media's aversion to the cultural right is more pronounced than its aversion to the economic left, and, since reporters tend to label politicians according to their social views, they're more apt to consider Democrats moderate. This is the kernel of truth underlying Goldberg's hyperbolic screed.

But there are two important caveats. First, the professional constraints and institutional tendencies of political journalism—which value neutrality, tend to follow compelling story lines, and place a premium on maintaining good sources within both parties—often overwhelm reporters' ideological predilections. Second, conservative Republicans who understand these predilections can turn them to their own advantage. The recent revelation that the 2000 Bush presidential campaign kept Ralph Reed off its payroll is instructive: The reason, according to the *Times*, was that associating Bush too publicly with a former director of the Christian Coalition would complicate his efforts to portray himself as a "compassionate conservative." Bush's advisers understood that reporters would gauge his moderation largely by his distance from social conservatives. (They also no doubt understood that retaining Larry Lindsey, a fervent supply-sider, as his main economic adviser would set off no such alarms in the press.)

Bush outlined his plan to handle the press in a 1999 interview with *National Review*. "I do think [the media] are biased against conservative thought," he said in a forum that received little attention outside the right. "And the reason is that they think conservative thinkers are not compassionate people. And that's one of the reasons I've attached a moniker to the philosophy that I espouse, because I want people to hear a different message." As the Bush campaign understood, reporters are predisposed to seeing conservatives as temperamentally mean-spirited—an idiotic notion (think of Ronald Reagan or Jack Kemp), but a deeply rooted one nonetheless. Therefore, they viewed Bush's cheerful demeanor and apparent affinity for the poor as evidence that he was not all that conservative, and this conclusion permeated coverage of the entire campaign. . . .

It is ironic, then, that at this moment in history, a book alleging liberal media bias would top the best-seller list. And more ironic still that Bush would give it his tacit endorsement. Conservatives like Goldberg may believe that he overcame the systematic liberal bias of a hostile media, but Bush, surely, knows better. ■

View from the Inside

Anonymous sources are the bread and butter of Washington journalism. Hardly a major news story is written without input from key insiders who talk only on condition that their identities remain a secret. Such sources might be identified by vague descriptions, such as "senior administration officials" or "sources close to the Pentagon," or they might be left out of the story altogether, used only as "deep background." The anonymous source system works well for both reporters and Washington insiders—the reporters get access to breaking news and classified information, while their sources get to tell their stories—and, often, to advance their own agendas—without fear of repercussions or reprisal.

For most reporters, maintaining the anonymity of confidential sources is a sacred obligation, both because they have made promises to remain silent and because their future effectiveness depends on their reputation for doing so. But reporters have no legal right to withhold information from federal prosecutors or law enforcement officials. Reporters who refuse to cooperate with federal officials risk large fines and even jail sentences for contempt of court.

The federal investigation of what became known as the Valerie Plame affair led to numerous clashes between reporters and federal prosecutors. One reporter—Judith Miller of the *New York Times*—served jail time for refusing to divulge her sources, and another agreed to cooperate with federal officials only at the very last minute.

The Plame affair grew out of the 2003 battle over whether Iraq possessed nuclear weapons. Plame's husband, former ambassador Joseph C. Wilson 4th, publicly accused the Bush administration of twisting "intelligence related to Iraq's nuclear weapons program . . . to exaggerate the Iraqi threat."[*] Plame was caught in the ensuing controversy when her identity as a CIA "operative" was revealed by Washington journalist Robert D. Novak.[†]

In this selection, *Newsday* reporter Timothy M. Phelps tells of his own involvement in the Plame affair, and argues for the importance of adopting a federal rule allowing journalists to protect their confidential sources.

Questions

1. How do government officials and politicians benefit from the anonymous source system? How do journalists benefit? What are the advantages and disadvantages of the system for the American people?
2. Should the federal government recognize a journalist's right to refuse to reveal the name of a confidential source to prosecutors or law enforcement officials? Why or why not?

---

[*]Joseph C. Wilson 4th, "What I Didn't Find in Africa," *New York Times*, July 6, 2003, p. 9.
[†]Robert D. Novak, "Mission to Africa," *Washington Post*, July 14, 2003, p. A21.

7.5 My Plame Problem—and Yours (2006)

Timothy M. Phelps

The forces unleashed by Robert Novak's column unveiling the secret agent Valerie Plame have shaken the White House, helped destroy any pretense of a reporter's privilege in federal criminal cases, and obliged at least ten Washington journalists, including me, to confront a new, insidious tactic that has altered the balance of power between journalist and leak investigator. But it is interesting to remember that when Novak's column came out in July 2003, it failed to create much of a stir in the equatorial-strength humidity of a Washington summer.

Perhaps it was because Novak mentioned Plame only in passing in the sixth paragraph. Perhaps the aging warrior of the Right just does not have the impact he used to. But if the aim was to discredit Plame's husband, former ambassador Joseph C. Wilson, or, as Wilson alleges, intimidate others from calling attention to government misstatements, as Wilson had in a July 6 op-ed in *The New York Times*, the arrow fell short. . . .

Other than *Time*, which ran a piece on its Website three days later by its new White House correspondent, Matthew Cooper, that said its own "government officials" (now known to be Karl Rove and I. Lewis "Scooter" Libby) had talked to the magazine about Plame, it was primarily liberal Bush administration critics like David Corn of *The Nation* and Paul Krugman of *The New York Times* who raised questions about the outing of a CIA agent.

In his *Times* op-ed, Wilson said the Bush administration had "twisted" information from his 2002 trip to Niger in order to exaggerate Iraq's nuclear threat. Novak's column said, "according to administration officials," that the Niger trip had been set in motion by Wilson's wife, a CIA "Agency operative." When I read the column I wondered whether Plame was working undercover. So, along with *Newsday*'s Knut Royce, known for his sources in the intelligence community, I started making inquiries.

A week later we wrote a story quoting "intelligence officials" as saying that Plame did indeed work undercover at the CIA, on weapons of mass destruction, raising the possibility that the disclosure to Novak broke the law. Novak himself volunteered something interesting when we reached him. "I didn't dig it out, it was given to me." His sources, he said, "thought it was significant; they gave me the name and I used it."

Our story was the first to establish that Plame was undercover. In fact not only was she working for the secret "D. O." or Directorate of Operations at agency headquarters in Langley, Virginia, but she was also still in transition from an even deeper underground mission as a "NOC" for Nonofficial Cover, posing as a businesswoman during agency-sponsored trips to Europe. The day after our story there were calls for an investigation by Democrats, and White House press secretary Scott McClellan vigorously asserted that "That is not the way this White House operates." But the matter still was not on most editors' agendas.

In late September MSNBC and CBS reported that the CIA had asked the Justice Department to investigate the security breach. Such requests are routine and almost never lead to serious investigations. In a front-page story on Sunday, September 28, *The Washington Post* led with the preliminary Justice Department inquiry. But the real news was down in the fifth paragraph:

> Yesterday, a senior administration official said that before Novak's column ran, two top White House officials called at least six Washington journalists and disclosed the identity and occupation of Wilson's wife. . . .
>   "Clearly, it was meant purely and simply for revenge," the senior official said of the alleged leak.

This story finally set off the furor that led Attorney General John Ashcroft to recuse himself and his deputy, James Comey, and to appoint the tough-minded Patrick Fitzgerald to investigate the leak. Two days after the *Post* story, the Justice Department told the White House that it was conducting a full formal investigation of the Plame outing, and ordered that all White House staff members preserve documents relating to conversations with Novak, Royce, and me. (Sources told us that the CIA had referred not only Novak's column but our *Newsday* story to the Justice Department for investigation because we, too, had revealed new classified information—that Plame was working undercover.) Subsequently the document requests relating to the three of us were sent to the CIA and top officials at the Pentagon, as well as hundreds of senior officials at the State Department, where I cover Middle East policy. This would certainly improve my name recognition, but it was also rather chilling to sources I already had.

Newsday decided that Royce and I should no longer cover the story, since we were now part of it. I play a dual role as reporter and editor, and I had to withdraw from any editing involvement as well. So Royce and I could no longer work the story we had been among the first to recognize. We were thus left to watch from the sidelines as the story grew, and to reflect on what it tells us about the sobering changes over the last decade in the standing of the press in America.

Roughly two months after he empaneled a grand jury in Washington in December 2003, Patrick Fitzgerald called *Newsday* saying he wanted to talk to us. So far as I know, we were the first reporters he contacted, with the possible exception of Novak, whose interactions with Fitzgerald are still unknown.

Don't worry, Fitzgerald assured us, he was not asking us to name our sources. He simply wanted some information about our discussions with the sources. Oh.

When it was announced in January that Fitzgerald would ask officials who could have talked to reporters to sign documents waiving their right to confidentiality, I scoffed. Surely no reporter would take such a document seriously. It seemed clear that these waivers were coerced, that they would not have been signed freely. The whole thing seemed like a joke.

But not to our lawyers. Fitzgerald's call and subsequent follow-ups set off an anguished conversation within the paper about our rights under the First Amendment versus our responsibilities in a criminal case involving national security and the White House. Raymond Jansen, then *Newsday*'s publisher, wanted us to do our best to cooperate without violating fundamental principles.

In our case, Fitzgerald intimated that he might have a waiver from one or more of our sources. These exploratory conversations between a prosecutor and news organization usually involve quite a bit of shadow boxing. Neither side wants to give too much away, so things tend to be discussed in theoretical terms. But my impression was that Fitzgerald may have talked to or planned to talk to someone who had admitted talking to us. It seemed likely to us, however, that that person would deny having disclosed that Plame was undercover.

What Fitzgerald wanted us to do, among other things, was to differentiate between Source A, B, or C. Without giving up any names, would we simply outline which source had said what in our story?

To Royce and me, who have sixty-six years of journalism experience between us, this was out of the question. For one thing, it seemed that the waivers were not freely given and were therefore worthless. It was clear that a refusal to sign would lead to dismissal. "We would have to talk personally to our sources and have them assure us convincingly they wanted us to talk. But more fundamentally, why would we want to do anything to help anyone track down our sources? Even if Source A did want us to talk, would not our participation help lead Fitzgerald to Source B? And finally, to ask a source to release us from a promise of anonymity may be, in a leak investigation, to ask for a favor he or she can't refuse. A negative answer might be construed as an obstruction of justice.

The fact that this affair was not so simple to everyone involved, including Fitzgerald, was a testament of how much things have changed since the last time I was the subject of a leak investigation. In 1991 I was the first to report, followed closely by Nina Totenberg of National Public Radio, that Anita Hill had accused the Supreme Court nominee Clarence Thomas of sexual harassment, creating a whirlwind. The Senate voted to confirm Thomas and then to hire a special counsel, Peter Fleming, to investigate who in the Senate gave confidential information to Totenberg and me.

We were subpoenaed to appear before the special counsel, and *Newsday* and NPR were separately subpoenaed to produce notes and other documents. My lawyers at the time, Robert Warren and Theodore Olson, took an uncompromising stand. I knew I would not name any names, but I worried that if I testified about, say, the timeline of my reporting, I might give the special counsel some crucial information.

We decided that I would testify to affirm the truth of what I had written and said later in public, but nothing more. For four hours I kept repeating my assertion that the First Amendment protected me from divulging even the most ridiculously petty details. Totenberg would take a similar stance.

During this time, newspapers across the country championed our First Amendment cause in editorials and news stories. The television networks interviewed us sympathetically. The issue became a First Amendment cause célèbre. Eventually, the Senate could not take the heat and refused to enforce its own subpoenas. My source testified that he or she had not been the one to tell me or Totenberg about Anita Hill, and later discreetly thanked me for my protection.

Like every other reporter's-privilege battle in federal courts, our brief in the Anita Hill case relied on *Branzburg* v. *Hayes*, the now thirty-four-year-old Supreme Court case, which actually was decided against the three reporters involved by a vote of five to four. But one of the justices in the majority, Lewis Powell, wrote a separate concurring opinion saying vaguely that *he* thought there were some limitations on when a reporter could be forced to testify. Since then, countless legal briefs have rested on the minority in the case and on Powell's opinion.

But in the twelve years between the Anita Hill case and Plame, the press's convenient theory that Justice Powell's concurrence granted us some rights has lost considerable ground. We were mindful of this slippage as we debated what to do about Fitzgerald. But Royce and I told our editors at *Newsday* that we would become pariahs in Washington if we agreed to testify—that no other Washington reporter would ever do so. *Newsday* backed us up, and told Fitzgerald in mid-April that we would not help in any way. He threatened a subpoena that for some reason never came.

Of course, we were dead wrong about what the other reporters would do. But each reporter who has testified in the case has faced different circumstances.

Glenn Kessler, a State Department reporter for *The Washington Post* (and a friend of mine), agreed to be interviewed by Fitzgerald last June about conversations he had with Libby the previous July. Kessler said in a statement that he testified because Libby wanted him to, and that he told Fitzgerald that Libby had not mentioned Wilson or Plame.

With somewhat more difficulty Kessler's colleague, Walter Pincus, eventually reached a deal with Fitzgerald. (His source did not release Pincus from his promise of confidentiality, but eventually revealed himself to Fitzgerald.) Tim Russert of NBC reached a deal that limited the scope of the questions.

That left Cooper, the primary author of *Time*'s online follow-up to Novak's column, and Judith Miller of *The New York Times*, who clearly attracted Fitzgerald's interest when he learned of meetings between Miller and Libby around the time of the leak.

We are all too familiar with what happened next. In February a three-judge-panel of the U.S. Court of Appeals for the District of Columbia Circuit ruled unanimously that *Branzburg* did not protect Cooper and Miller in a criminal case, another nail in the coffin for reporters' rights in federal courts. On June 30, *Time* magazine did what until that point was unthinkable, handing over Cooper's notes and e-mails to Fitzgerald, over Cooper's objection. Fitzgerald now knew that Cooper's source was none other than Karl Rove. Cooper agreed to testify a week later after a last-minute call from his source freeing him. That left Judy Miller.

I was reporting in southern Iraq in July and largely out of touch with what was happening in Washington, though I knew that Miller went to jail on July 6. Even though her source—now known to be Libby—had signed a waiver, she said that she was not convinced that he had done so freely. Miller and the *Times* had taken *exactly* the same stand that Royce and I and, ultimately, *Newsday* had taken the previous year.

When I returned from Iraq in early August I was dumbfounded at the lack of attention she was getting. A national reporter was in jail for the first time in years, and, apart from the occasional editorial in the *Times* and a persistent cry for help from Lou Dobbs of CNN, there was almost nothing in the press.

Where was the outrage? What happened to the First Amendment lobby, so active in the Anita Hill case? What had changed?

Branzburg has been slipping away as an underpinning for our constitutional claim, of course. And underneath the legal argument is a familiar litany of economic, cultural, and political factors that have eroded the standing of the press perhaps more than we realize.

But I think the biggest difference in this case may be in who Miller is, and who her sources are. And I think that's a shame.

The journalistic community confused its understandable concern about Miller's reporting and methods with her First Amendment cause. Not only do we not get to pick our standard bearer in a court of law, but we cannot distinguish between sources we like and those we do not. Some complained that Miller's sources weren't "whistleblowers"; they were wrongdoers who ratted out Valerie Plame. And did it perhaps matter that they were Republicans, the dreaded neocons no less?

I asked Floyd Abrams, who represented Miller, the *Times*, and, initially, *Time* magazine, why the atmosphere is so different now than during the Anita Hill investigation, in which he also fought. Abrams has a dog in this fight, of course, but he is still the dean of the First Amendment lawyers. He spoke of a press that has lost some of its sense of mission. And he spoke of politics. "Some journalists think the wrong people are getting protection," he said. "That's the most dangerous thing of all. Worse than changes in the law, worse than grand juries going after journalists, is the image of some journalists making such decisions based on a political rather than a journalistic basis. Certainly a lot of the criticism of Judy Miller within the journalistic community is at its core political. There is an extraordinary animus. It's very hard for me to believe that animus would exist if she were protecting different people in a different administration with different views of the war in Iraq."

So how badly has what we might now call the Judy Miller case damaged the First Amendment? For one thing, there is now no protection for journalists in federal criminal cases in Washington and many other areas of the country. In civil cases, where the balancing act of constitutional needs is different because lawsuits are considered less compelling than law enforcement, rulings in federal courts have been less stacked against the press. Yet the same federal appeals court that ruled against Miller and Cooper refused in November to block a court order that four journalists must testify in the Wen Ho Lee civil case. (Lee, who was suspected of stealing nuclear secrets for China but later largely exonerated, is suing government agencies for allegedly leaking fake information about him. The four reporters, James Risen of *The New York Times*, Robert Drogin of the *Los Angeles Times*, H. Joseph Hebert of The Associated Press and Pierre Thomas of ABC, as well as a fifth, Walter Pincus of the *Post*, have been held in contempt of court and seem headed for the same anguished decision made by Cooper and Miller.)

In a rare though not yet final victory for the press, a federal district court judge in New York ruled last February 24 that there *is* a limited reporter's privilege in criminal cases. The legal combatants were none other than Judy Miller and Patrick Fitzgerald. In his more normal role as U.S. attorney in Chicago, Fitzgerald is investigating with another grand jury who in the government may have told Miller about impending government actions against two Islamic charities in Chicago. Judge Robert Sweet blocked his attempt to obtain Miller's phone records.

But meanwhile, even the original case involving Wilson and Plame is still fraught with danger for the press, as Fitzgerald continues to plough through the ranks of Washington journalists, now including Bob Woodward of *The Washington Post* and Viveca Novak of *Time*. All of the journalists who have testified—mostly under agreements restricting their testimony to very specific issues—are still in jeopardy. If the Libby case goes to trial, Libby's lawyers are not bound by such agreements.

The prosecutor seems to have had the last word about the First Amendment, at least for now. "Journalists are not entitled to promise complete confidentiality—no one in America is," he told Thomas F. Hogan, chief judge of the U.S. District Court for the District of Columbia. Hogan agreed. Of course, we never did have the right to offer complete confidentiality in every circumstance. But as a result of this case and others in the pipeline, the question now is, Can we honestly promise our sources anything? ■

[Editor's note: In March 2007, Libby was convicted of four counts of perjury, obstruction of justice, and lying to federal officials.]

Chapter 8

Parties and Elections

Elections are a central part of any democratic political system. They provide the clearest and most important opportunity for citizens to participate in self-government. They help ensure that the government respects the will of the people, at least in a general way. And by providing a mechanism to demonstrate "the consent of the governed," elections help ensure that governments are—and appear to be—legitimate.

In the modern world, elections are typically fought not just by candidates but also by political parties. Political parties help organize political life, making it easier for voters to make choices and to effect results, and easier for public officials to organize governing majorities. In the United States, parties also form a bridge between the legislative and executive branches by providing natural allies (and, for that matter, opponents) for the president in both houses of Congress.

Parties and elections, however, raise profound questions about the nature and efficacy of democratic politics. American parties, in particular, have historically been notoriously weak; members of the same political party may have little in common with one another, and even one-party control of both branches of government is no guarantee of success in policy making. Moreover, American elections are strongly influenced by special interest groups, most importantly through the campaign finance system, and by the media, which influence the process and which, in turn, are easily manipulated by candidates and public officials.

The selections in this chapter explore a variety of themes. In selection 8.1, political scientist John H. Aldrich presents a theoretical account of why politicians "form . . . exploit . . . or ignore" political parties; he suggests the simple reason that it is in their interest to do so. Selection 8.2 attempts to make sense of the 2006 midterm elections, while selection 8.3 looks at the shifting party loyalties of voters in the Rocky Mountain states—a region that may hold the balance of power in future election cycles. Selection 8.4 examines the ongoing controversy over the Electoral College, while selection 8.5 presents an inside account of how the major networks' coverage of election night 2004 drew upon the painful lessons they learned in 2000.

Chapter Questions

1. "Parties are—or should be—integral parts of all political life," writes John H. Aldrich, "from structuring the reasoning and choice of the electorate, through all facets of campaigns and seemingly all facets of the government, to the very possibility of effective governance in a democracy." What roles do American political parties in fact play? How well do they play those roles? Would replacing our two-party system with a multiparty system make matters better or worse? Why or why not?
2. With recent national elections so closely divided, what strategies might the Democratic and Republican parties use to increase their chances of success in future elections?

 # Foundations

The Constitution makes no mention of political parties. Yet parties are so deeply a part of the American political system that it is difficult even to imagine a system without them. Parties help voters make political decisions at election time, help bridge the divides between the legislative and executive branches and between the national government and the states, make it easier for politicians to act collectively, and provide a mechanism whereby voters can hold politicians collectively responsible for what they have or have not done. "Democracy," wrote political scientist E. E. Schattschneider, "is unthinkable save in terms of parties."*

In contrast to most modern democracies, politics in America is dominated by two major political parties. Minor parties exist, and their candidates occasionally mount a presidential campaign and may even win office at the federal, state, or local level. But for the last 150 years, voters have had to choose for the most part between Republicans and Democrats. The origins of the two-party system are rooted in American political culture (see Chapter 5) and in the laws governing elections, which favor candidates who can muster majorities (or at least large pluralities) of the vote. In multiparty systems, a party that can garner 20 percent of the national vote would be entitled to a fifth of the seats in parliament; in America, the same party might not win a single congressional seat.

Political scientists have offered several explanations for the development and persistence of political parties. Some see parties as evolving almost naturally to reflect the policy views of broad coalitions of voters. Others argue that parties should instead be seen as agents of collective action—and thus should offer voters a clear choice on public policies and be held responsible for the success or failure of their policy agendas. (Even proponents of this theory admit that American parties rarely live up to this responsibility.) A third group defines parties as organizations that exist simply to allow politicians to compete for, and hopefully win, elective office.[†]

---

*Quoted in John H. Aldrich, *Why Parties? The Origin and Transformation of Political Parties in America* (Chicago: University of Chicago Press, 1995), p. 3.

[†]Ibid., pp. 7–14.

In this selection, political scientist John H. Aldrich argues that the major political party is "the creature of the politicians, the ambitious office seeker and officeholder." Politicians have "created and maintained, used or abused, reformed or ignored the political party," he concludes, "when doing so has furthered their goals and ambitions."

Questions

1. What objectives do political parties help office seekers and officeholders to achieve? How do parties help these politicians achieve their objectives?
2. What roles do voters play in the American party system, according to Aldrich? In what ways are parties useful to voters? To politicians?
3. "Not all problems are best solved, perhaps even solved at all, by political parties," writes Aldrich. "The party may even be part of the problem." What problems might be better solved by other institutions and actors, such as interest groups? What problems does the American party system create rather than solve?

8.1 Why Parties? (1995)

John H. Aldrich

• • •

. . . [The] political party is—or should be—central to the American political system. Parties are—or should be—integral parts of all political life, from structuring the reasoning and choice of the electorate, through all facets of campaigns and seemingly all facets of the government, to the very possibility of effective governance in a democracy. . . .

Moreover, [parties] are so deeply woven into the fabric of American politics that they cannot be understood apart from either their own historical context and dynamics or those of the political system as a whole. Parties, that is, can be understood only in relation to the polity, to the government and its institutions, and to the historical context of the times.

The study of political parties, second, is necessarily a study of a major pair of political *institutions*. Indeed, the institutions that define the political party are unique, and as it happens they are unique in ways that make an institutional account especially useful. Their establishment and nature are fundamentally extralegal; they are nongovernmental political institutions. Instead of statute, their basis lies in the actions of ambitious politicians that created and maintain them. They are, in the parlance of the new institutionalism, *endogenous institutions*—in fact, the most highly endogenous institutions of any substantial and sustained political importance in American history.

From John H. Aldrich, *Why Parties? The Origin and Transformation of Political Parties in America*, 1995. Reprinted by permission of the publisher, the University of Chicago Press.

By endogenous, I mean it was the actions of political actors that created political parties in the first place, and it is the actions of political actors that have shaped and altered them over time. And political actors have chosen to alter their parties dramatically at several times in our history, reformed them often, and tinkered with them constantly. Of all major political bodies in the United States, the political party is the most variable in its rules, regulations, and procedures—that is to say, in its formal organization—and in its informal methods and traditions. It is often the same set of actors who write the party's rules and then choose the party's outcomes, sometimes at nearly the same time and by the same method. Thus, for example, one night national party conventions debate, consider any proposed amendments, and then adopt their rules by a majority vote of credentialed delegates. The next night these same delegates debate, consider any proposed amendments, and then adopt their platform by majority vote, and they choose their presidential nominee by majority vote the following night.

Who, then, are these critical political actors? Many see the party-in-the-electorate as comprising major actors. To be sure, mobilizing the electorate to capture office is a central task of the political party. But America is a republican democracy. All power flows directly or indirectly from the great body of the people, to paraphrase Madison's definition. The public elects its political leaders, but it is that leadership that legislates, executes, and adjudicates policy. The parties are defined in relation to this republican democracy. Thus it is political leaders, those [Joseph A.] Schlesinger has called "office-seekers"—*those who seek and those who hold elective office*—who are the central actors in the party.

Ambitious office seekers and holders are thus the first and most important actors in the political party. A second set of important figures in party politics comprises those who hold, or have access to, critical resources that office seekers need to realize their ambitions. It is expensive to build and maintain the party and campaign organizations necessary to compete effectively in the electoral arena. Thomas Ferguson, for example, has made an extended argument for the "primary and constitutive role large investors play in American politics." . . . The study of the role of money in congressional elections has also focused in part on concentrations of such sources of funding, such as from political action committees which political parties are coming to take advantage of. Elections are also fought over the flow of information to the public. . . . Today those with specialized knowledge relevant to communication, such as pollsters, media and advertising experts, and computerized fund-raising specialists, enjoy influence in party, campaign, and even government councils that greatly exceeds their mere technical expertise.

In more theoretical terms, this second set of party actors include those Schlesinger has called "benefit seekers," those for whom realization of their goals depends on the party's success in capturing office. Party activists shade from those powerful figures with concentrations of, or access to, money and information described above to the legions of volunteer campaign activists who ring doorbells and stuff envelopes and are, individually and collectively, critical to the first level of the party—its office seekers. All are critical because they command the resources, whether money, expertise, and information or merely time and labor, that office seekers need to realize their ambitions. As a result activists' motivations shape and constrain the behavior of office seekers, as their own roles are, in turn, shaped and constrained by the office seekers. . . .

Voters, however, are neither office seekers nor benefit seekers and thus are not a part of the political party at all, even if they identify strongly with a party and consistently support its candidates. Voters are indeed critical, but they are critical as the targets of party activities. Parties "produce" candidates, platforms, and policies. Voters "consume" by exchanging their votes for the party's product. Some voters, of course, become partisans by becoming activists, whether as occasional volunteers, as sustained contributors, or even as candidates. But until they do so, they may be faithful consumers, "brand name" loyalists as it were, but they are still only the targets of partisans' efforts to sell their wares in the political marketplace.

Why, then, do politicians create and recreate the party, exploit its features, or ignore its dictates? The simple answer is that it has been in their interests to do so. That is, this is a *rational choice* account of the party, an account that presumes that rational, elective office seekers and holders use the party to achieve their ends.

I do not assume that politicians are invariably self-interested in a narrow sense. This is not a theory in which elective office seekers simply maximize their chances of election or reelection, at least not for its own sake. They may well have fundamental values and principles, and they may have preferences over policies as means to those ends. They also care about office, both for its own sake and for the opportunities to achieve other ends that election and reelection make possible. . . . Their ends are simply more numerous, interesting, and political than mere careerism. Just as winning elections is a means to other ends for politicians (whether career or policy ends), so too is the political party a means to these other ends.

Why, then, do politicians turn to create or reform, to use or abuse, partisan institutions? The answer is that parties are designed as attempts to solve problems that current institutional arrangements do not solve and that politicians have come to believe they cannot solve. These problems fall into three general and recurring categories.

The Problem of Ambition and Elective Office Seeking

Elective office seekers, as that label says, want to win election to office. Parties regulate access to those offices. If elective office is indeed valuable, there will be more aspirants than offices, and the political party and the two-party system are means of regulating that competition and channeling those ambitions. Major party nomination is necessary for election, and partisan institutions have been developed—and have been reformed and re-reformed—for regulating competition. Intra-institutional leadership positions are also highly valued and therefore potentially competitive. There is, for example, a fairly well institutionalized path to the office of Speaker of the House. It is, however, a Democratic [or Republican] party institution. Elective politicians, of course, ordinarily desire election more than once. They are typically careerists who want a long and productive career in politics. Schlesinger's ambition theory, developed and extended by others, is precisely about this general problem. Underlying this theory, though typically not fully developed, is a problem. The problem is that if office is desirable, there will be more, usually many more, aspirants than there are offices to go around. When stated in rigorous form, it can be proved that in fact there is no permanent solution to this problem. And it is a problem that can adversely affect the fortunes of a party. In 1912 the Republican vote was split between William Howard Taft and Theodore Roosevelt. This split enabled Woodrow Wilson to win with 42 percent of the popular vote. Not only was Wilson the only break in Republican hegemony of the White House in this period, but in that year Democrats increased their House majority by sixty-five additional seats and captured majority control of the Senate. Thus failure to regulate intraparty competition cost Republicans dearly.

For elective office seekers, regulating conflict over who holds those offices is clearly of major concern. It is ever present. And it is not just a problem of access to government offices but is also a problem internal to each party as soon as the party becomes an important gateway to office.

The Problem of Making Decisions for the Party and for the Polity

Once in office, partisans determine outcomes for the polity. They propose alternatives, shape the agenda, pass (or reject) legislation, and implement what they enact. The policy formation and execution process, that is, is highly partisan. The parties-in-government are more than mere coalitions of like-minded individuals, however; they are enduring institutions. Very few incumbents change their partisan affiliations. Most retain their partisanship throughout their career, even though they often disagree (i.e., are not uniformly like-minded) with some of their partisan peers. When the rare incumbent does change parties, it is invariably to join the party more consonant with that switcher's policy interests. This implies that there are differences between the two parties at some fundamental and enduring level on policy positions, values, and beliefs. Thus, parties are institutions designed to promote the achievement of collective choices—choices on which the parties differ and choices reached by majority rule. . . . [In] a republican democracy politicians may turn to partisan institutions to solve the problem of collective choice. In the language of politics, parties may help achieve the goal of attaining policy majorities in the first place, as well as the often more difficult goal of maintaining such majorities.

The Problem of Collective Action

The third problem is the most pervasive and thus the furthest-ranging in substantive content. The clearest example, however, is also the most important. To win office, candidates need more than a party's nomination. Election requires persuading members of the public to support that candidacy and mobilizing as many of those supporters as possible. This is a problem of collective action. How do candidates get supporters to vote for them—at least in greater numbers than vote for the opposition—as well as get them to provide the cadre of workers and contribute the resources needed to win election? The political party has long been the solution.

As important as wooing and mobilizing supporters are, collective action problems arise in a wide range of circumstances facing elective office seekers. Party action invariably requires the concerted action of many partisans to achieve collectively desirable outcomes. Jimmy Carter was the only president in the 1970s and 1980s to enjoy unified party control of government. Democrats in Congress, it might well be argued, shared an interest in achieving policy outcomes. And yet Carter was all too often unable to get them to act in their shared collective interests. In 1980 not only he but the Democratic congressional parties paid a heavy price for failed cooperation. . . .

The Elective Office Seekers' and Holders' Interests Are to Win

Why should this crucial set of actors, the elective office seekers and officeholders, care about these three classes of problems? The short answer is that these concerns become practical problems to politicians when they adversely affect their chances of winning. Put differently, politicians turn to their political party—that is, use its powers, resources, and institutional forms—when they believe doing so increases their prospects for winning desired outcomes, and they turn from it if it does not.

Ambition theory is about winning per se. The breakdown of orderly access to office risks unfettered and unregulated competition. The inability of a party to develop effective means of nomination and support for election therefore directly influences the chances of victory for the candidates and thus for their parties. The standard example of the problem of social choice theory, the "paradox of voting," is paradoxical precisely because all are voting to win desired outcomes, and yet there is no majority-preferred outcome. Even if there happens to be a majority-preferred policy, the conditions under which it is truly a stable equilibrium are extremely fragile and thus all too amenable to defeat. In other words, majorities in Congress are hard to attain and at least as hard to maintain. And the only reason to employ scarce campaign resources to mobilize supporters is that such mobilization increases the odds of victory. Its opposite, the failure to act when there are broadly shared interests—the problem of collective action—reduces the prospects of victory, whether at the ballot box or in government. Scholars may recognize these as manifestations of theoretical problems and call them "impossibility results" to emphasize their generic importance. Politicians recognize the consequences of these impossibility results by their adverse effects on their chances of winning—of securing what it is in their interests to secure.

So why have politicians so often turned to political parties for solutions to these problems? Their existence creates incentives for their use. It is, for example, incredibly difficult to win election to major office without the backing of a major party. It is only a little less certain that legislators who seek to lead a policy proposal through the congressional labyrinth will first turn to their party for assistance. But such incentives tell us only that an ongoing political institution is used when it is useful. Why form political parties in the first place? . . . A brief statement of three points will give a first look at the argument.

First, parties are institutions. This means, among other things, that they have some durability. They may be endogenous institutions, yet party reforms are meant not as short-term fixes but as alterations to last for years, even decades. Thus, for example, legislators might create a party rather than a temporary majority coalition to increase their chances of winning not just today but into the future. Similarly, a long and successful political career means winning office today, but it also requires winning elections throughout that career. A standing, enduring organization makes that goal more likely.

Second, American democracy chooses by plurality or majority rule. Election to office therefore requires broad-based support wherever and from whomever it can be found. . . . It is in part the need to win vast and diverse support that has led politicians to create political parties.

Third, parties may help officeholders win more, and more often, than alternatives. Consider the usual stylized model of pork barrel politics. All winners get a piece of the pork for their districts. All funded projects are paid for by tax revenues, so each district pays an equal share of the costs of each project adopted, whether or not that district receives a project. Several writers have argued that this kind of legislation leads to "universalism," that is, adoption of a "norm" that every such bill yields a project to every district and thus passes with a "universal" or unanimous coalition. Thus everyone "wins." [Barry R.] Weingast proved the basic theorem. His theorem yields the choice of the rule of universalism over the formation of a simple majority coalition, because in advance each legislator calculates the chances of any simple majority coalition's forming as equal to that of any other. As a result, expecting to win only a bit more than half the time and lose the rest of the time, all legislators prefer consistent use of the norm of universalism. But consider an alternative. Suppose some majority agree to form a more permanent coalition, to control outcomes now and into the future, and develop institutional means to encourage fealty to this agreement. If they successfully accomplish this, they will win regularly. Members of this institutionalized coalition would prefer it to universalism, since they always win a project in either case, but they get their projects at lower cost under the institutionalized majority coalition, which passes fewer projects. Thus, even in this case with no shared substantive interests at all, there are nonetheless incentives to form an enduring voting coalition—to form a political party. And those in the excluded minority have incentives to counterorganize. United, they may be more able to woo defectors to their side. If not, they can campaign to throw those rascals in the majority party out of office.

In sum, these theoretical problems affect elective office seekers and officeholders by reducing their chances of winning. Politicians therefore may turn to political parties as institutions designed to ameliorate them. In solving these theoretical problems, however, from the politicians' perspective parties are affecting who wins and loses and what is won or lost. And it is to parties that politicians often turn, because of their durability as institutionalized solutions, because of the need to orchestrate large and diverse groups of people to form winning majorities, and because often more can be won through parties. Note that this argument rests on the implicit assumption that winning and losing hang in the balance. Politicians may be expected to give up some of their personal autonomy only when they face an imminent threat of defeat without doing so or only when doing so can block opponents' ability to build the strength necessary to win.

This is, of course, the positive case for parties, for it specifies conditions under which politicians find them useful. Not all problems are best solved, perhaps even solved at all, by political parties. Other arrangements, perhaps interest groups, issue networks, or personal electoral coalitions, may be superior at different times and under different conditions. The party may even be part of the problem. In such cases politicians turn elsewhere to seek the means to win. Thus this theory is at base a theory of ambitious politicians seeking to achieve their goals. Often they have done so through the agency of the party, but sometimes, this theory implies, they will seek to realize their goals in other ways.

The political party has regularly proved useful. Their permanence suggests that the appropriate question is not When parties? but How much parties and how much other means? That parties are endogenous implies that there is no single, consistent account of the political party—nor should we expect one. Instead, parties are but a (major) part of the institutional context in which current historical conditions—the problems—are set, and solutions are sought with permanence only by changing that web of institutional arrangements. Of these the political party is by design the most malleable, and thus it is intended to change in important ways and with relatively great frequency. But it changes in ways that have, for most of American history, retained major political parties and, indeed, retained two major parties. ■

 # American Politics Today

After the 2004 election, President George Bush's chief strategist, Karl Rove, summed up his boss's victory this way:

> President Bush received more votes than any other candidate in American history. He's the first President since 1988 to win a majority of the popular vote. He increased his popular vote total by 11.6 million votes since 2000. . . . President Bush improved his percentage in all but three states. He improved his vote in 87 percent of all counties and carried more than 80 percent of the counties—and he won in 97 of the 100 fastest-growing counties and George W. Bush is also the first President since FDR to be re-elected while his party gained seats in the House and Senate—and the first Republican President since 1924 to get re-elected while re-electing Republican House and Senate majorities. And he won with a higher percentage than any Democratic Presidential candidate has received since 1964.

"The political realignment in America," Rove proclaimed, "is moving ahead."*

Two years later, the Republican realignment seemed to take a giant step backward. In the wake of an unpopular war in Iraq, a series of congressional scandals, and persistent feelings of economic unease among middle class Americans, Bush's party took what the president called a "thumping." Republicans lost not just the House, where a Republican defeat was expected, but also the Senate, where pundits had considered a Democratic victory a long shot at best.

---

*"Remarks of Karl Rove at the New York Conservative Party," June 22, 2005, http://www.washingtonpost.com/wp-dyn/content/article/2005/06/24/AR2005062400097.html.

Every election tells its own story, and past performance (as Rove learned) may not predict future results. But elections also reveal shifts in voting patterns over time, which may be significant for years or even decades to come. The two selections presented below look at recent elections from both perspectives. Selection 8.2, by journalist John B. Judis, analyzes the Democrats' victory in 2006 with an eye toward its implications for 2008. Selection 8.3, by political commentator Ryan Sager, looks at longer-term trends, especially in the Rocky Mountain states, that may favor the Democrats in the long run.

Questions

1. What factors led to the Democrats' victory in the 2006 midterm elections? Which of these, if any, are likely to influence elections in 2008 and beyond? Which were short-term factors that are unlikely to play a role in future elections?
2. Why, according to Ryan Sager, are the Rocky Mountain states trending Democratic? What can the Republican party do to stop this trend? What can the Democrats do to accelerate it?

8.2 How the Democrats Won (2006)

John B. Judis

It's about time. After a series of frustrating election nights for Democrats, dating back to the Florida boondoggle in 2000, [the 2006 election was] a clear triumph. But was it, like the Watergate election of 1974, simply the result of correctible mistakes by the opposition? Or [did] the Republican scandals and the Bush administration's misadventure in Iraq [bring] to the surface trends that will lead to a new political majority? It's too early to say for certain, but it seems this election . . . at least provided Democrats with an *opportunity* to build a lasting congressional majority. Whether they succeed in doing so will depend partly on whether they understand what made for their smashing success [in November 2006]. Here's a hint: It had something to do with energizing their own base, but it had much more to do with winning over voters that historically have had a stormy relationship with the Democratic Party.

Some of the Democratic victories occurred in states or congressional districts carried by Al Gore in 2000 and John Kerry in 2004. These districts were going to turn Democratic when their Republican incumbents retired or when the voters in these districts, faced with Republican malfeasance, decided to vote on party lines. That accounts for Ed Perlmutter's victory in suburban Denver and the defeats of GOP moderates like Representative Jim Leach in Iowa and Senator Lincoln Chafee in Rhode Island. These seats should remain Democratic.

From John B. Judis, "Blue's Clues: How the Dems Won," *The New Republic*, November 20, 2006, pp. 18–21. Reprinted by permission of *The New Republic*, © 2006, The New Republic, LLC.

But Democrats also won in a host of districts and states that George W. Bush carried in the last election. In some cases, Democrats won primarily because the seat had been held by a Republican implicated in a personal or political scandal. But, in many others, Democrats benefited from the reemergence of political trends that had been suppressed after September 11—or, even before that, by Bill Clinton's affair with Monica Lewinsky. The most important of these trends involves independents.

There is no dependable measure of independents. Some states don't even allow voters to register as independents. But, when exit polls and the University of Michigan's American National Election Studies have asked voters whether they consider themselves independents, the percentage has grown from roughly one-fifth of the electorate after World War II to over one-third today, making them a larger group nationally than self-identified Democrats or Republicans.

In the South, independents tend to be former Democrats who have begun to vote Republican but are unwilling to describe themselves as Republicans. In the North and West, however, they occupy a much more distinct political niche. They include libertarian-minded professionals and small-business owners—especially in the West—and white working-class voters in the Northeast and Midwest. They are equally uncomfortable with the feminist left and the religious right. What they dislike most is government interference in their personal lives. They see Washington as corrupt and want it reformed. They favor balanced budgets but also Social Security and Medicare. They worry about U.S. companies moving their plants to Mexico and about China exporting underpriced goods to the United States. They favor a strong military, but they want it used strictly against foreign aggression.

In the 1980s, these voters generally supported Ronald Reagan and George H. W. Bush; but, in 1992, many of them abandoned Bush for Ross Perot, who received 18.9 percent of the national vote. Perot did well in the West, Midwest, and Northeast, but not in the Deep South. In 1994, two-thirds of Perot voters, disgusted with what they saw as continuing corruption in Washington, backed the Gingrich revolution, accounting for much of the GOP's success outside the Deep South.

Perot, of course, vanished from the scene after attempting a repeat performance in 1996. But the constituency he had spoken for remained and even grew. In 1996, Clinton and the Democrats won back many of these voters, but, after September 11, they gravitated toward the Republican Party, helping to account for Republican success in 2002 and 2004. In [the 2006] election, however, independents flocked back to the Democrats. Nationally, the Democrats won independents by 57 percent to 39 percent. In the East, the margin was 63 to 33 percent; in the Midwest, 56 to 41 percent; and, in the West, 58 to 35 percent. Democrats also did well in many of those Western and Midwestern states where Perot had won over 20 percent of the vote in 1992: Arizona, Colorado, Kansas (where the Democrats won two of four House seats and the top state offices), Minnesota, Missouri, Montana, Ohio, and Wisconsin.

The Democrats also made gains among a critical subgroup of independents—the white working-class voters known as Reagan Democrats. In the Midwest, Democrats won these voters (most clearly identifiable in the polls as voters with "some college") by 50 to 49 percent. White working-class support accounted, among other things, for Democratic victories over Republican incumbents in three predominately white downscale Indiana congressional districts that had backed Bush in 2000 and 2004.

Prior to the election, much was made of how conservative some of the Democratic candidates were, but the focus on candidates like North Carolina's Heath Shuler (who won) or Kentucky's Ken Lucas (who lost) misses what helped many Democrats in the Midwest and West unseat Republicans. These candidates were not neoconservatives or liberals, but the heirs to Perot's peculiar centrism. They advocated fair trade, not free trade, and promised to reform the North American Free Trade Agreement (NAFTA). They denounced illegal immigration but didn't endorse the punitive House Republican measures. Rather than advocate new spending measures, they called for balanced budgets and reform of Washington politics.

This description fits the rural New York, Colorado, Montana, and Indiana congressional candidates. It even fits Ohio Senate candidate Sherrod Brown, who was sometimes considered a darling of the Democratic left. In his economic appeals, Brown echoed Perot rather than Ted Kennedy. In one typical commercial, he declared, "Before I ask for your vote, I owe it to you to tell you where I stand. I'm for an increase in the minimum wage and against trade agreements that cost Ohio jobs. I support stem-cell research, tighter borders, and a balanced-budget amendment."

Much was also made of how some successful Democrats, such as Pennsylvania Senator-elect Bob Casey and Colorado Governor-elect Bill Ritter, opposed abortion or gun control. They certainly did, and, by doing so, neutralized some of the opposition from the religious right and the National Rifle Association. But, in general, these centrist Democrats kept the focus on the economy and the war in Iraq and away from social issues, except for stem-cell research, which is universally popular outside the Deep South. Without saying it, they managed to convey that they had no intention of pressing their convictions on guns or abortion.

Democrats also won many of the other constituencies that had begun moving their way two decades ago, but whose movement had halted after September 11. For instance, professionals—best identified in exit polls as voters with postgraduate education—backed Democrats by 58 percent to 41 percent in congressional races. (In the East, the margin was a whopping 67 to 32 percent.) These voters played an important role in the defeat of Arizona Republican J. D. Hayworth and in Democratic victories in suburban Connecticut and high-tech Nashua, New Hampshire. The gender gap, which had closed in 2002, opened wide again, accounting for Senate victories by Claire McCaskill in Missouri, Sheldon Whitehouse in Rhode Island, James Webb in Virginia, and Jon Tester in Montana. Latinos, who had been wooed successfully by the Bush administration but were alienated by the House Republicans, backed Democrats in overwhelming numbers. In the West, Latinos, who had supported Democratic candidates by only 59 to 40 percent in 2004, backed them [in 2006] by a landslide of 72 to 27 percent.

One other constituency deserves mention: younger voters. In 2002, voters aged 18 to 29 split evenly between Democrats and Republicans. [In 2006] they backed Democrats by 63 to 33 percent. These voters won't necessarily provide the numbers to win elections for the Democrats, but they can provide energy to revitalize the party. They write blogs, knock on doors, and encourage candidates, such as Montana's Jon Tester or Northern California's Jerry McNerny, neither of whom were initially taken seriously by party officials. They don't necessarily provide solutions to great policy questions; but they can force attention to problems that require solutions, as they did with the Vietnam war in the 1960s and the Iraq war today. As the unions have lost members and clout, their campaign work has been increasingly supplemented by young recruits from organizations like MoveOn.org.

After the 2000 election, it became fashionable to picture Republican and Democratic gains in red and blue on the national maps. Republicans invariably got the better of this visual display because they enjoyed support among the great empty spaces of the West. [The 2006] election not only altered the lineup of constituent groups, but also the map of American politics. The Republicans now increasingly appear to be a regional party confined to the Deep South. While Republican support collapsed in the Northeast and eroded in the West, it remained steady in the South, where a majority of voters approved of the way George W. Bush has handled his presidency and the war in Iraq. In the new national political map—most clearly seen when states are colored according to their governors—the Northeast, Midwest, and Southern border states of Virginia, West Virginia, Tennessee, and Arkansas are overwhelmingly blue. The Plains and Rocky Mountain states are a mixed palette, but more blue than red, with Democratic governors in Oklahoma, Kansas, Arizona, New Mexico, Colorado, and Montana. Alone among these regions, the Deep South from South Carolina to Georgia and across to Mississippi is dark red.

Republican support in the South is due to the high percentage of white evangelicals, the virtual absence of unions, the widespread dependence (in states like Georgia) on military spending, and the lingering legacy of civil rights strife, which divides the parties along racial lines. But, as Thomas Schaller suggests in *Whistling Past Dixie*, the Republicans' success in the South can prove their undoing elsewhere, as voters in the West recoil from the GOP's close identification with the religious right and voters in the Northeast look askance at governors who owe their elections to support for the Confederate flag. In the 1980s, Ronald Reagan was able to establish the Republicans as America's party. But Reagan's party was of the Sun Belt, not of the South. The new party of Bush and Karl Rove is increasingly that of the Southern Bible Belt.

For the Democrats to succeed Republicans as America's party, its leaders must recognize what it took to build this majority. A Democratic majority in this country must include Massachusetts and Colorado, Ohio and Oregon; fervid Democratic partisans, youthful activists who despise Connecticut Senator Joe Lieberman, and political independents alienated from government; suburban professionals who give money to the National Organization for Women and NARAL; and white workers who worry that politicians will take their guns away. In [the 2006 election] the Bush administration's failure in Iraq and the corruption of the Republican Congress allowed this heterogeneous group to find a temporary home in the Democratic Party. But it will take all the ingenuity and craft that Democrats can muster to turn this halfway house into a permanent residence for a long-term Democratic majority. ■

8.3 Purple Mountains (2006)

Ryan Sager

After the 2004 election, plenty of people noted that a shift of 60,000-odd votes in Ohio would have handed the Electoral College to John Kerry. But there was another place—less remarked upon—where a shift of similar magnitude would have done the same trick: the Southwest. Fewer than 70,000 votes among Colorado, Nevada, and New Mexico, with their collective nineteen electoral votes, could have swung the election just as surely as Ohio's 60,000. And with George W. Bush winning by margins of 5 percentage points, 3 points, and 1 point, respectively, these were swing states by any definition of the term.

Those who don't follow politics closely could be forgiven for feeling surprised. In recent years, the political geography of the West has seemed clear and simple; the Pacific Coast states are blue, and the interior West is red. But while the Pacific Coast is likely to stay solidly blue for the foreseeable future, the partisan tilt of the eight states of the interior West—Arizona, Colorado, Idaho, Montana, Nevada, New Mexico, Utah, and Wyoming—is changing. . . . And the region's political hue in 2008 will speak not only to the question of who wins the White House but also to the durability and future character of the Republican coalition.

Signs of a possible Democratic resurgence in the West have been slowly accumulating since 2000. In 2004, Democrats took over both chambers of the Colorado legislature and sent the Democrat Ken Salazar to the U.S. Senate to replace a retiring Republican, Ben Nighthorse Campbell; Salazar's brother John also won the open U.S. House seat in Colorado's Third District, which was vacated by a Republican. (This turned out to be one of only two open Republican seats in the House picked up by Democrats that year.)

That same year, Montana elected its first Democratic governor in two decades: Brian Schweitzer, a rancher who flaunted his love of guns. Democrats won four out of five statewide offices in that election and also took control of Montana's house and senate. Counting Schweitzer, Democrats now hold the governorships of four of the eight states that make up the interior West; in 2000, they held none. New Mexico's Bill Richardson and Wyoming's Dave Freudenthal each replaced two-term Republican governors in 2002, the same year that Janet Napolitano became the first elected Democratic governor of Arizona since the 1980s. While it's possible to read too much into victories at the state level, *something* is happening throughout the West.

What is it? In part, the region's changing demography is changing its political sensibility. It's no secret that the West is becoming more Hispanic, and Hispanics tend to cast their ballots for Democrats. Republicans made a lot of noise after the 2004 election about their inroads with this population, and initial exit polls showed Bush taking 44 percent of the Hispanic vote nationwide. But later, more careful

Ryan Sager, "Purple Mountains," *The Atlantic Monthly* 297 (July/August 2006), pp. 37–41. Copyright © 2006 by Ryan Sager. Reprinted by permission of William Morris Agency, LLC on behalf of the Author.

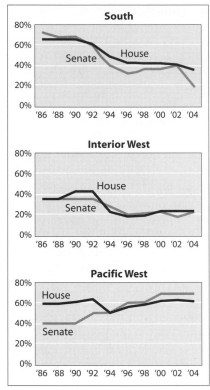

South

Interior West

Pacific West

Figure 1   The Great Realignment
*Democratic Party strength by region
(percentage of seats)*

reviews deflated that figure to 40 percent or less, with much of Bush's support clustered in Texas and Florida. What's more, whatever gains Bush has made among Hispanics seem to begin and end with him. Hispanic party identification consistently registers roughly two to one in favor of the Democrats, and hasn't shown any major swing toward the GOP under Bush. Continuing growth of the Hispanic population in the interior West is bad news for Republicans.

It's not just Hispanics, though. Another politically significant population is also growing quickly throughout the interior West: erstwhile Californians. The congested, generally liberal population centers of California are overflowing—and as they do, it's as if a bucket of blue paint were spilling over the West. More than 400,000 Arizonans and 360,000 Nevadans were born in California. The thinly populated mountain West states are slowly taking on a left-coast character as well: as of the last census, 122,000 native Californians lived in Idaho (total population 1.3 million) while 47,000 lived in Montana (900,000) and 21,000 lived in Wyoming (490,000).

But ultimately, Democratic inroads in the region are less the result of demographic change than of regional discontent with the Republican Party—discontent that has been deepening for quite some time. The story of the Republican Party's march to political dominance over the last five decades has been, at its core, a story about the political realignment of the South, first at the presidential level in 1968 and 1972 and then at the congressional level in 1994. That realignment is by now complete—the GOP could hardly dominate the region more thoroughly. But as the South has become central to Republican Party strategy, its particular flavor of social conservatism, moral certitude, and activist government has infused the national party's character. This is slowly alienating the other major bloc in the Republican coalition: small-government conservatives, especially those who value individual liberty most highly.

While fissures run between these two groups in every state, there is also a larger geography to the modern Republican Party's dilemma. In balancing the religious Right against the libertarian Right, the GOP balances the South against the West. (The Midwest is something of a muddle in between.) Bush-style big-government conservatism has tilted the party's regional balance and put the West in play.

Differences between the West and the South begin with religion. Generally, Republican strongholds have lots of evangelicals, Democratic strongholds have very few, and swing states are in between. By this rule of thumb, the interior Southwest fits neatly into the "swing" category. But so does the interior Northwest, which is typically considered more socially conservative and more solidly Republican. Evangelicals make up between 29 percent and 33 percent of the population in Idaho, Montana, and Wyoming, figures much closer to California's 28 percent or Maine's 26 percent than to Virginia's 41 percent or Texas's 51 percent.

A survey conducted [in 2005] by the Pew Research Center illustrates the cultural gulf between the South and the interior West—where social attitudes often look surprisingly close to those of blue-state northeasterners and Pacific Coasters. For instance, almost twice as many people in the interior West say that religion is "not that important to me" as say the same in the South (30 percent versus 17 percent); both the Pacific Coast and the Northeast also hover at around 30 percent on that question. On gay rights, only 39 percent of southerners think homosexuality "should be accepted by society," while 53 percent in the interior West support tolerance of gays. (That figure bumps up to 60 percent on the Pacific Coast and in the Northeast.) Similarly, 53 percent of southerners think public-school libraries should ban "books that contain dangerous ideas" versus 44 percent in the interior West.

The interior West has a socially libertarian and anti-federal government streak, as long as the Rocky Mountains. Nevada, Colorado, and Montana have laws decriminalizing medical marijuana use, placing those states in the company of some of the bluest in the nation. State legislatures in Colorado, Idaho, and Montana have passed resolutions denouncing the Patriot Act. Colorado and Utah have openly rebelled against No Child Left Behind's federal testing regime by passing laws exempting themselves from it.

Of course, the alienation of western Republicans and independents does not necessarily imply a sudden ardor for all of the Democratic Party's ideals. Westerners are particularly unlikely to be convinced that Wal-Mart, oil companies, and other "bad corporate citizens" are preventing them from getting ahead; the West is about pulling yourself up by your bootstraps. Likewise, Democrats were ruined for a generation in the region by gaining reputations as owl-obsessed gun grabbers—and while environmental protection is now relatively popular there, many Westerners remain wary of Democratic intentions. More generally, *small government* is not a term often associated with the Democratic Party.

Bush's GOP, however, is making a Democratic pitch to libertarian-minded voters more credible. The Republican Party is rapidly losing its identity as the party of fiscal responsibility and small government. And Republican intrusions into private and local affairs—think Terri Schiavo—are making Democrats look comparatively restrained. It's counterintuitive, but the current Republican fixation with social hot buttons could be a boon to Democrats in much of the interior West.

There's widespread agreement among Democrats that Howard Dean's party apparatus "gets" its opportunity out West and is beginning to invest there after years of neglect. Republicans, meanwhile, have had a hard rime adjusting. Colorado's GOP seems to be walking off the same Christian Right cliff that California's did in the 1990s. Republicans lost control of the Colorado legislature in 2004 because they'd spent the previous session on issues like gay marriage, the Pledge of Allegiance,

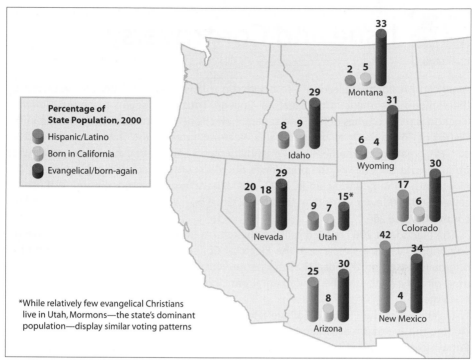

Figure 2   New Settlers of the Old Frontier
Key demographic groups

and the liberal biases of college professors, all while the state faced a monumental fiscal crisis. As the Republican minority leader in the Colorado house said on National Public Radio after the 2004 election, "Our party has basically made the party platform 'guns, God, and gays,' and that wasn't a winning message.'"

• • •

If it seems strange to picture the West losing its reddish cast, well, that's because it *is* strange. In many ways, the interior West represents the Republican Party's classic self-image: dedicated to rugged individualism and old-fashioned leave-me-alone conservatism. And it would seem logical that after so many years of wooing southern voters, the party might now recalibrate, and throw some love at those places and constitutents who've been drifting slowly away from it. That may yet happen. But religious voters tend to be demanding. And party ideology carries a momentum that can be hard to reverse. In . . . 2008, the GOP will be working with Karl Rove's machinery, which is largely built to mobilize churchgoers and rile up socially conservative citizens.

If the political center of the GOP continues to drift southward, the party risks catalyzing another geographic realignment on a par with that which brought it to power—starting up in Montana and running south. Many of the West's mountains are already turning purple. They may yet turn blue. ∎

Issue and Controversy

American presidential elections are decided not by the national popular vote, but by the complex arithmetic of the Electoral College. Thus what seems to be a nationwide election is really a series of fifty-one separate elections (one in each state and one in the District of Columbia). In all but two states, electoral votes are assigned on a winner-take-all basis, creating the mathematical possibility that a candidate can lose the nationwide popular vote but still win the presidency. Such a scenario occurred a few times in the nineteenth century and again in 2000, when then Texas governor George W. Bush received 500,000 fewer votes than Senator Al Gore but won in the Electoral College by a count of 271 to 266.*

The election of 2000 revived calls for the reform or abolition of the Electoral College. The critics' case is a simple one: the Electoral College is a constitutional anachronism originally based on the idea that the people could not be trusted to elect the president directly; it violates the fundamental principles of majority rule and of one person, one vote.

Defenders of the Electoral College point to a variety of pragmatic advantages—including the avoidance of a nationwide repeat of the Florida vote-counting fiasco in 2000. But as political scientist James R. Stoner Jr. makes clear in this selection, the Electoral College can also be defended on the grounds of principle. In his view, the system is neither unfair nor undemocratic—in fact, as Stoner argues, the Electoral College "now functions as a profoundly *democratic* institution," safeguarding democracy "where it is, and can be, most genuinely democratic, namely, in the states."

Questions

1. What are the arguments—both principled and pragmatic—for and against the Electoral College? Which of these arguments do you find most convincing? On balance, should the Electoral College be preserved? Reformed? Eliminated?
2. According to Stoner, how does the Electoral College serve to protect democracy? Is his argument convincing? Why or why not?

---

*One District of Columbia elector, who was expected to cast her electoral vote for Al Gore, abstained to protest the District of Columbia's lack of representation in Congress.

8.4 In Defense of the Electoral College (2001)

James R. Stoner Jr.

One of the most remarkable facts of the remarkable election of 2000 was how readily most Americans acquiesced in the tally of the Electoral College, whereby a man was elected president with a constitutional majority that did not accord with the aggregated popular vote. Go back a mere twenty-five or thirty years ago and read what was written about the Electoral College then, and you will find that the dominant opinion was that Americans would never accept election by the College of anyone other than the winner of the most votes at the polls nationwide. "One person, one vote" remains the constitutional law of legislative reapportionment, but the people seem more loyal to the Constitution than to any simple theory of nationalist majoritarianism.

Perhaps it was that, in the weeks before the election, Democratic commentators had reconciled themselves to the possibility that Al Gore might win the Electoral College but lose in the popular count. Perhaps because all the attention during the post-election campaign was focused on recounts and lawsuits, and all the ire of Democratic partisans after the denouement was directed at the United States Supreme Court, the actual vote in the Electoral College was anti-climactic and complaints against the College for the moment seemed minor or moot. Perhaps enough citizens and opinion leaders have grown to appreciate and even adopt the arguments [in favor of the Electoral College]. Perhaps Americans have, in that mix of good sense and cynicism that seems the spirit of the age, simply acquiesced in "the system," figuring the consequences satisfactory enough and the prospects for reform not worth the effort.

Despite the temporary calm, a principled defense of the Electoral College remains crucial. In the first place, there is the need to support the legitimacy of our institutions: it does the country little good to doubt that the people govern, or to think of the Constitution as an arbitrary set of rules, part of a "system" that does well by those clever enough to master its intricacies but thwarts simple justice. Moreover, anyone who wants to think responsibly about the measures of reform that are sure to be proposed as soon as passage seems politically feasible, or their mere proposal politically useful, will need more than inertia as an argument. To be sure, most commentators quickly notice that the odds are long against passage of an amendment to replace the College with a direct popular vote, since more states stand to lose their relative impact on the election than the thirteen it now takes to block a constitutional amendment. But the scenario suggested by law professor Sanford Levinson, asked by the *Chronicle of Higher Education* to imagine how the

Excerpted from James R. Stoner Jr., "Federalism, the States, and the Electoral College," in Gary L. Gregg, ed., *Securing Democracy: Why We Have an Electoral College*, 2001, pp. 43–54. Reprinted by permission of ISI Books.

case of *Bush* v. *Gore* will appear in fifty years, is more serious than playful: after a few more elections where the popular vote loser wins or nearly wins the electoral vote, a popular president who finally wins will call a constitutional convention that, under pressure, not only scraps the Electoral College in favor of direct election but declares that the ratification of constitutional amendments will henceforth take place by direct popular vote. (After all, Levinson reminds us, the Constitution of 1787, written by the last federal convention, was ratified by its own specified procedure, overriding the legally established process then in place.) That Al Gore's half-million-vote popular plurality would have translated into even fewer electoral votes than he actually received if the redistribution of congressional seats after the 2000 census had taken place before the 2000 election suggests that the Democratic Party might have at least a short-term interest in replacing the College, a point not lost upon several of that party's leading politicians or intellectual friends. And it is inconceivable that Mr. Gore and his backers would have fought for the presidency so fiercely after the election had they not thought themselves on the moral high ground because they had amassed the most popular votes.

Able defenses of the Electoral College have tended to take either a pragmatic or a constitutionalist perspective. The array of alleged pragmatic advantages is impressive, and many are undoubtedly true. Some argue that the Electoral College ensures that small states get noticed in presidential elections; some claim that the winner-take-all choice of electors in the states only magnifies the importance of states containing major centers of population. (Ironically, in the election of 2000, both were true, for George W. Bush needed every three- or four-vote state he got for his victory, while if Al Gore had won a few thousand more votes in Ohio—or of course a few hundred more in Florida—he would have won the College with a commanding lead and no contest.) In addition, the effect of funneling the popular vote through the College often turns relatively weak popular pluralities into decisive electoral victories. (This was the case in both of Bill Clinton's elections, in Woodrow Wilson's first, and Abraham Lincoln's.) The imperatives of the College discourage third parties and their consequent fragmentation of the electorate, frustrating the dream of every radical and stanching the historic blight that clings to many of the failed democracies of the last two hundred years. Since the vote in the College itself is public and certain, with popular balloting conducted state by state, the Electoral College avoids the chaos and danger—now readily imaginable—that would accompany a nationwide recount. And then there is the counsel that recalls the danger of unintended consequences which accompanies any reform.

The constitutionalist defense of the College links it with the other institutional arrangements of the federal government which check and balance the force of national majorities: the separation of powers, bicameralism, equal representation of the states in the Senate, an independent judiciary, the rule of law itself. No one, of course, is an originalist on this point, since the Electoral College quickly ceased to be an assembly of notables choosing the nation's best and became instead a conduit of party competition—though it might be noted that the first architects of the political parties were some of the Founding Fathers themselves. What the constitutionalist perspective clearly highlights is the really misleading character of what has been called for generations the "popular vote": if the popular rather than the constitutional majority had been thought decisive, some voters might well have voted differently, and the candidates surely would have campaigned differently, not ignoring a state, especially a populous state, once they determined the state's vote was committed for or against their campaign, or directing all television advertising to a national audience rather than to media markets in targeted states. Indeed, to alter the College would undoubtedly mandate a change in the whole process of presidential selection, which from the first caucus to the last recount is focused on the individual states precisely because that is where electors are chosen and where they vote.

The Electoral College as a Democratizing Institution

What is usually overlooked in defense of the Electoral College, and what is to my mind decisive, is that the College now functions as a profoundly *democratic* institution: historically it has been the engine that fueled the movement toward democracy on the federal level, while today it safeguards democracy where it is, and can be, most genuinely democratic, namely, in the states.

The historical point is widely known but seldom made. In 1800 . . . only six of the sixteen states chose their electors by a system that included popular voting, most opting instead for a choice by the state legislatures. By 1824, there were twenty-four states, only six of which still allowed their legislatures to choose electors, and within a few years there was only South Carolina, which persisted in this practice until the Civil War. The 1820s also saw the democratization of candidate selection, with the demise of nomination by caucuses in state legislatures and the rise of state nominating conventions. "King Caucus" in Congress likewise fell into disrepute, thanks to the failure of any of its candidates to win an Electoral College victory in 1824 and to Andrew Jackson's successful campaign to discredit the election of his opponent by the House as a "corrupt bargain," catapulting him to a decisive victory in 1828. The first national nominating conventions were held in the early 1830s, in time for Jackson's re-election. Because the Electoral College is chosen by the states, the democratization of the choice of president in the age of Jefferson and Jackson, like the expansion of the franchise and popular election of governors and even judges, resulted entirely from state reforms. As happens so often in American history, the movement was national because the states moved in concert.

At the beginning of the twentieth century, another wave of democratization swept the states, establishing in many of them processes of direct democracy— such as the legislative initiative and referendum—to supplement if not replace representation. When the Seventeenth Amendment, ratified in 1913, took election of United States senators out of the hands of state legislatures and gave it directly to the people of the states, it ratified a practice already more or less developed in some of the states—the famous Lincoln-Douglas campaign for the Senate in 1858 was actually a campaign between two tickets for the Illinois state legislature—though the effect was to divorce state elections from federal politics. While modern expansion of the franchise to blacks, women, and the young has involved amendment to the federal Constitution, even these reforms were pioneered in states. And, embarrassing though it may be to friends of democracy, segregation and the disenfranchisement of blacks in the South in the first half of the twentieth century—two notably anti-democratic developments—took place not in spite of, but as a result of, majority rule.

Still, today the states are more democratic than the federal government. Even leaving aside democratic processes such as the initiative and the election of judges, which are of long standing in the states but unknown at the federal level, government in the states is more immediate and more accessible to the citizens, both voters and candidates for office. Local interests that despair of making their voices heard in Washington can more readily achieve representation in state legislatures and in municipal governments that are the creatures of the states. Political careers get started here, where television is not the only medium of communication and candidates can still campaign door-to-door. New populations get involved in local and state politics long before they make a mark on the national scene. This is no modern accident, but an essential element of the federal system altogether understood at the time of the Founding. Indeed, the most telling Anti-Federalist objection to the Constitution of 1787 was that the representative institutions it established would make impossible the reproduction in miniature of the demographics of the people that was common in the state legislatures.

The States as Political Communities

If state and local governments are necessarily closer and more accessible to the people, the concerns they oversee are often the most immediately important in people's lives: education, security of person and property, keeping the peace, and much else that entails not only the protection of individual liberty but the development of a common life. Of national politics most people are necessarily spectators, and it is no accident that they cluster into ideological coalitions, for their interests are typically distant and abstract. In the states, interests are immediate and concrete, and again it is no accident if the ideological labels that attach to the national parties often fail to predict the policies of their members in local government. It is one thing to be opposed in principle to abortion and quite another to foster the networks of support for family life that make child-bearing honored, attractive, and rewarding. It is one thing to endorse civil rights and quite another to foster genuine peace and and understanding among populations that live side by side in distrust or hostility and form their opinions of one another on the basis of lived experience. It is one thing to be anti-tax or pro-labor, another to figure out how to encourage prosperity and to care for the streets and parks and schools and libraries of the community in which one lives. In the states, in short, one finds the real life of political communities, with all the struggle, disappointment, triumph, and complacency that democratic politics entails.

Some measure of state autonomy is appreciated by observers at the national level. Liberals stress that the states can serve as laboratories to test new legislation; conservatives like the competition between them for investment and even for citizens, thinking this the real test of policy success. But the states are more than useful instruments: they are the political voice of the diverse moral communities bound together in the federal republic. In punishing crime, protecting life and property, promoting education, and fostering morality, the states naturally differ, according to their different circumstances, traditions, populations, and choices;

some are more efficient than others, some more successful, some more just. Of course there are many things they leave for the federal government to do, especially concerning the provision of national defense, the regulation of an increasingly complex and integrated economy, and the protection of those rights that belong to American citizens no matter where they are. As the protection of individual rights abstracted from the particular communities that give them meaning has increasingly become the coin of public discourse in recent years, the federal claim has been expanded, and lest I be misunderstood, I hasten to endorse the value and importance of federal protection for legitimate rights. But community too is a good, and in some ways a very democratic good, and it is the states that remain vibrant self-governing communities, each with its own identity—and true to their diversity, some with a stronger sense of that identity than others. To those of us who do most of our business over the phone or the Internet and have to take a plane to see our friends, the states might seem an annoyance or an amusement, and we move among them indifferently. To the many Americans who do not belong to what might be called the federal class, who live their lives near their families or move somewhere and put down roots and stay, the states are most emphatically home.

By tallying votes for the highest office of the land by state, even giving each state a sort of bonus for being organized as a state, the Electoral College affirms the importance of these self-governing communities and helps secure their interest in self-government. We know this intuitively, as the whole process of presidential selection focuses national attention on the states and their distinctiveness. We are reminded of the tremendous diversity of our country as we watch the candidates move around the country for the caucuses and primaries, and then during the fall campaigns, learning again every four years something new about the coalitions that are patched together to support each set of contenders. Having to go to the people, not as an undifferentiated mass, but in their states, makes candidates aware of, if not always sympathetic to, the whole array of interests articulated principally at the local level but held by people whose votes they need. Of course campaigns for national office ought to focus on national issues and to feature candidates of national stature, and on the whole they do. But to elect the president in a national plebiscite would either suppress what is local or, as has already been the trend, nationalize local concerns, removing their governance away from communities and into the inevitably bureaucratic machinery of a central administration. Much more than did the Seventeenth Amendment, abolishing the Electoral College would diminish the states, treating them as mere vehicles of local administration, not guardians of something as fundamental as self-government. And every diminution of the states in an age of centralization portends further diminution, until equal representation in the Senate and the role of the states in ratifying amendments seem anomalous and indefensible, and the ancient, basic structure of our government is undone. The Electoral College, in other words, for all its uniqueness, in fact plays a critical role in binding together the complex articulation of diverse interests and mixed principles which characterizes, indeed is the glory of, the American constitutional order. Like that order as a whole, it is, in James Madison's words, "partly federal, and partly national," partly concerned with the broadest and most uniform interests of individuals, partly reflective of democratic communities in all their distinctiveness and pride.

To speak well of the states and their traditional place in the American constitutional order is to ensure one will be accused of taking a romantic view of things, out of line with a hard-headed recognition of the globalization of modern life and blind to the patterns of injustice associated in American history with states' rights and local prejudice. Though the romantic label is not one that in every context I would wish to eschew, there need be nothing romantic about drawing attention to the valuable role of the states. As many have noted, ours is an age of the devolution of power as well as globalization; indeed, the processes may go hand in hand, as the ready exchange of information makes knowledge more locally available and as trends towards utilitarian monotony spark an interest in what is independent and distinctive. That the states have been known to work injustice is not in itself an argument against them—so has the federal government, and, besides, the power to do wrong is an unavoidable concomitant of the power to do right. The danger of local prejudice was well known to the Framers of the Constitution, and they succeeded in creating institutions to counter-balance it, not all of them democratic. It is no accident that those who would minimize the place of the states typically make appeal to the least democratic institution of our whole system, the federal courts, and then object most strenuously when those courts protect the states.

In a televised speech to the nation in the midst of the storm of recounts and litigation in late November 2000, Vice President Gore began by saying, "Every four years there is one day when the people have their say." That's not the way it works in my state: We vote several times a year on different propositions, we elect representatives to different levels of government, including the United States Congress, in between the presidential years, and we come across many of them in our communities as we go about our daily lives. That's democracy, and compared to a scenario where all that matters is one vote among a hundred million in a plebiscite for a single ruler in a distant place, I think it's a pretty good thing. It isn't perfect, but neither are the people who run and rule, who pursue their ambitions and their interests, who promote their causes and their friends. Constitutional government and what we now call democracy are not for angels, the Founders of our government famously instructed us, nor did they suppose that we ourselves could live as gods. ■

 # View from the Inside

A close election is the political journalist's dream come true, but for the major television networks election night 2000 seemed like more of a nightmare. All the major networks—ABC, CBS, CNN, Fox News, and NBC—at one point or another mistakenly called Florida (and thus the election) for Al Gore. The networks' errors were largely due to overreliance on polls and other statistical sampling techniques, which (in theory) allowed them to project the winners of the various states before the actual vote totals were available. "In calling winners of individual states based on exit polling and votes from sample precincts," concluded a study commissioned by CNN, "accuracy and completeness of information were sacrificed to the pressures of competition."*

As journalist Rachel Smolkin reports in this selection, the networks learned the lessons of 2000 and applied them in 2004. The result was more responsible—but more boring—journalism.

Questions

1. What lessons did the major networks learn from the 2000 election? How did they apply those lessons in 2004?
2. What recommendations would you make to network executives to improve future coverage of presidential elections? Where would you strike the balance between the networks' responsibility to the public and their need and desire to attract viewers?

8.5 Lesson Learned: A Behind-the-Scenes Look at Election Night Coverage (2004)

Rachel Smolkin

CBS anchor Dan Rather, who had experienced a rough few months, set the tone for election night coverage at 8:22 p.m. with a memorable offering from his stable of trademark axioms. "Beware of certitude," Rather warned his viewers.

Early and misleading exit polls had seeped onto Web sites such as the Drudge Report and Slate and ricocheted through the blogosphere. Left-leaning bloggers were dishing merrily about Kerry's early leads in the pivotal states of Florida and Ohio. Journalists privately pored over those numbers. But the networks, memories of the 2000 election night meltdown all too vivid, avoided them.

"We never reported any of those exit polls here on CNN," anchor Wolf Blitzer piously told President Bush's senior adviser Karen Hughes after midnight, then asked her about the mood at the White House when officials saw the early numbers.

The campaign season had been punctuated by major media missteps (the CBS National Guard story), by reckless replays (the Dean Scream) and by disproportionate attention to unproven allegations (the cable networks' handling of the Swift Boat Veterans for Truth). During the summer, the media fixated relentlessly and depressingly on the candidates' military records from three decades past.

---

*Joan Konner, James Risser, and Ben Wattenberg, "Television's Performance on Election Night 2000: A Report for CNN," *CNN.com* (January 29, 2001), http://archives.cnn.com/2001/ALLPOLITICS/stories/02/02/cnn.report/cnn.pdf.

From Rachel Smolkin, "Lesson Learned: A Behind-the-Scenes Look at Election Night Coverage," *American Journalism Review*, December 2004/January 2005, pp. 44–47. Reprinted from *American Journalism Review*.

But the media also provided serious issues coverage, careful fact-checking and meticulous investigations throughout the campaign. . . . The *Los Angeles Times*, the *New York Times* and other publications helped debunk the Swift Boaters' claims. The *Baltimore Sun's* Susan Baer wrote a prescient page-one article in October about same-sex marriage as the "new front in culture wars." The *L.A. Times'* Ronald Brownstein contributed a late-October story about the Kerry campaign, in a "virtually unprecedented move for a Democrat," all but surrendering the South.

On election night, the media mostly veered toward these loftier instincts. The networks turned suddenly solemn, their coverage restrained. In contrast to the vertigo-inducing debacle of four years ago—when the networks first awarded Florida to Vice President Al Gore, then to George W. Bush, then retracted it again—TV journalists in 2004 heeded Rather's warning. The usual race to scoop competitors became an unlikely contest in most ostentatious show of responsibility.

Such sober coverage doesn't make for riveting television. On November 2, "caution" was the shibboleth of election night analysis. Networks awarded key states to candidates very, very slowly.

New York Times writer Alessandra Stanley characterized their strained efforts to avoid the 2000 blunders as "almost painful," adding it "was the wise, responsible thing to do (quite literally, politically correct), but it left the anchors without much to say."

"Unfortunately," the *San Francisco Chronicle's* Tim Goodman complained in a column, "what we witnessed was a night packed with eggshell walking, overwhelming caution and relatively good manners. Exciting and fun? No. Informative. Not really. A humongous time-killer? Check."

• • •

The National Election Pool—a media-owned consortium that replaced Voter News Service and is composed of the principal TV networks and the Associated Press—sent the first wave of exit-poll data to subscribers around 2 p.m. on November 2. Other media subscribers also pay to see the results, and participants pledge not to publicize or leak the early numbers.

But leak they did. The figures were whizzing through cyberspace by mid-afternoon. Jack Shafer, Slate's media critic and editor at large, explained in his Web post that "Slate believes its readers should know as much about the unfolding election as the anchors and other journalists, so given the proviso that the early numbers are no more conclusive than the midpoint score of a baseball game, we're publishing the exit-poll numbers as we receive them."

The surveys, which created a false impression that Kerry was rolling toward victory, had the "biggest partisan skew since at least 1988," said a November 5 article in the *New York Times*, which had obtained a copy of a report by the system's creators exploring why the exit polls were misleading.

Although those early numbers did not predict final results, Shafer stands by his decision to post them. "The networks were every bit as remiss this year in telegraphing what was in these confidential exit polls that they're not supposed to reveal as in previous years," Shafer says. "They need to be demystified. It's better for my readers to know why a television broadcaster seems to be so up on Kerry at 5 o'clock."

Political bloggers quickly seized on the numbers. In a hip "Marketplace" graphic on November 4, the *Wall Street Journal* interspersed updates from bloggers and network television throughout the afternoon and evening. "PA and Ohio margins widening for Kerry. Florida, Wisconsin tie in early returns," the blog Wonkette.com reported at 9:10 p.m.

As the *Journal* article noted, WSJ.com, the newspaper's Web site, posted a mid-afternoon article saying exit-poll data "purported to give Mr. Kerry an early lead in several key states" and linked to a blog with the numbers. The *Journal's* Web site also questioned their validity.

"I know there'll be a lot of gnashing of incisors tomorrow about blogs leaking leaked exit polls," said a November 2 post by Jeff Jarvis, the blogger behind buzzmachine-com, who also runs online services for Newhouse Newspapers. "To hell with the gnashing. We're all big boys and girls. We can decide whether to (a) believe it and (b) vote on our own. Let information be free. Let us know what big media and big politics know. Transparency, man, transparency."

Jarvis, a former Sunday editor for New York's *Daily News* and former TV critic for *People* and *TV Guide*, argues blogs "were saying what they knew and the journalists were not saying what they knew." He says "big media" should "tell us what they know: 'The exit polls look like Kerry, but boy, they were wrong last time.'"

But Kevin Drum, who blogs for *Washington Monthly*, a small but influential politics and policy magazine, thinks the networks rightly avoided exit polls and the bloggers rightly published them. To me, it's just data," says Drum, who shared early exit-poll data in one post. "If you're interested in looking at it, go ahead and look at it." But the networks are watched by millions of people, and if you're among those viewers, "you're sort of forced to see it."

Jonathan Dube, the managing producer for MSNBC.com and publisher of CyberJournalist.net, notes that Slate and Drudge also published exit polls in 2000. "It's more of a phenomenon that was created by the Internet, and Weblogs are just one way the information is being distributed," Dube says.

But he thought blogs' coverage on election night "got very skewed based on exit polling they were publishing early on." While one of the virtues of bloggers "is that they are independent and will publish what they want, when they want, certain bloggers did a good job of putting certain caveats" on the numbers, Dube says, and "others didn't do quite as good a job."

Network election coverage began at 7 p.m., with each unveiling special sets notable for glitz and excess. NBC coined the silliest set name, dubbing its sky booths outside Rockefeller Center "Democracy Plaza," a phrase which recalled—hopefully inadvertently—administration platitudes such as the "coalition of the willing," "they hate our freedom," and Bush's favorite: "Democracy is on the march."

CNN's set was the most distracting. Not only were video wall graphics and precinct numbers often difficult to see, but the rented Nasdaq site in Times Square looked so much like a running track that it seemed to beckon an earnest Blitzer to relax and take a lap. A "Today" show–style glass window behind the anchors allowed anxious viewers at home to see vapid viewers outside the studio waving to the watchers.

Fox News Channel provided the clearest and most helpful graphics for election night returns with its "Election Ticker," which continuously displayed raw vote numbers, percent of the vote for each candidate and percent of precincts reporting.

Michael Barone, a Fox News contributor and senior writer for *U.S. News & World Report*, analyzed the tabulated vote in swing states such as Florida and Ohio county by county to explain where votes counted so far had originated, why that appeared to benefit Bush and how Kerry still might be able to prevail. Anchor Brit Hume handled questions deftly, keeping Barone's discussion of the numbers accessible to viewers who lack his intimate knowledge of the political landscape.

As Shafer argues, early network coverage did indeed allude obliquely to preliminary exit polls that favored Kerry. Fox News commentators initially looked "stunned and somber as they hinted that early voter surveys showed Mr. Kerry doing better than expected," the *New York Times*' Stanley wrote the next day.

On CNN, "Crossfire" pundits downplayed Bush's chances in Ohio. Conservative cohost Robert Novak announced Republicans in the state were "very pessimistic." They're "looking at the returns; they think it's going to be very tough for Bush" to carry the state, Novak said.

On MSNBC's "Hardball," reporter Lisa Myers enigmatically informed viewers in the 8 o'clock hour that Bush's campaign was finding "that the exit-poll data is significantly underrepresenting the Republican vote."

Despite these veiled hints, the networks held back on risky calls. Linda Mason, the CBS News executive in charge of its "decision desk," characterizes her network's approach as "cautiously aggressive." CBS was the first to call states including South Carolina, Virginia, Mississippi, Pennsylvania, Colorado, Michigan and Minnesota.

CNN Political Director Tom Hannon says he was not monitoring "call sheets" that night tracking what time other networks projected winners. "When the other networks called [a state] was not a factor in decision making," Hannon says.

As midnight neared, the networks offered markedly different approaches to projecting winners in pivotal states.

At 11:39 p.m., ABC called Florida for Bush, followed by CBS. CNN waited until 12:10 a.m., Fox until 12:22. "The race there was very tight," says Mason, who wrote a report for CBS on the 2000 election fiasco. "Of course, Florida holds a certain symbolism for us, so we wanted to he super careful."

Marty Ryan, Fox's executive producer of political programs, says "certainly it was in the back of our mind what happened in 2000," when his network was the first to call Florida for Bush. Ryan says the four-person decision team at Fox wanted to be particularly careful because Florida had extensive early voting. "There was no early gauge to assess how early voting went," he says, and the exit polls became "problematic."

At 12:41 a.m., Fox was the first to call Ohio for Bush, followed by NBC and MSNBC around 1 a.m.

Fox News Senior Vice President John Moody consulted with a pollster and two statisticians hired by the network and decided Bush's more than 100,000-vote lead in Ohio gave him an almost insurmountable edge over Kerry, who would need a huge majority of the as-yet uncounted provisional ballots to triumph. (Provisional ballots are cast by registered voters who have moved but not updated their registration or believe themselves to be eligible but do not appear on the rolls.) "It became a little bit of a math problem" to see how Kerry could prevail, Ryan says.

But ABC, CNN and CBS declined to call Ohio for Bush. At CNN, the decision team was hearing conflicting reports about the number of provisional ballots, with Ohio's secretary of state estimating about 170,000 and Democrats projecting some 250,000. "There was a clear possibility that there could be a dispute over the number of ballots," CNN's Hannon says. "Had we known exactly how many provisional ballots there were with certainty, I think we would have made a call."

CBS declined to call Ohio because Mason and her team believed as many as 250,000 provisional ballots could be outstanding. "In addition to that, there were all those lawyers in Ohio ready to sue on various other counts," Mason says. "It looked like this could be [a repeat of] Florida and be in turmoil for weeks. It would be silly for us not to take all this into account."

But CBS did call Nevada at 3:45 a.m. Before the announcement, Mason told CBS News President Andrew Heyward that her team planned to call Nevada for Bush, and she expected NBC and Fox to follow suit. On those networks, the Nevada call would push Bush over 270 votes in the Electoral College, securing his reelection. Because CBS had not projected a winner in Ohio, it would not be in a position to announce Bush's victory. Does that bother you? she asked Heyward. No, he replied.

ABC called Nevada for Bush about 10 minutes later. Mason expectantly watched NBC and Fox, but neither called Nevada.

"Everybody has a little better knowledge or confidence in different states they look at and concentrate on different things," Fox's Ryan says. The Fox team felt New Mexico, Iowa and Nevada each had "different issues" that precluded projecting a winner. In Nevada, the team was concerned about where the votes were coming from and how that might impact the overall margin.

At about 2:30 a.m., Moody and Ryan went to the studio to explain the situation to Brit Hume and to tell him that unless something occurred to resolve their concerns in the next half hour, they would hold off until morning.

Bush's Electoral College margin on Fox, NBC and MSNBC hovered the rest of the night at 269 votes—a number that would have allowed Kerry to tie, at best, and thrown the election into the GOP-controlled House of Representatives. No network awarded Bush the full 270 votes.

Major newspapers, too, avoided making definitive declarations in their headlines. "Bush nears victory but Ohio count is in dispute," said *USA Today*. "Bush Holds Lead/Kerry Refuses to Concede Tight Race," said the *New York Times*.

Papers around the country echoed those themes. "Down to Ohio" declared the *Akron Beacon Journal*. "WE WAIT/ Bush close to victory, Kerry clings to Ohio," said the *Arizona Republic*. "SQUEAKER!" announced the *Charlotte Observer*.

Like their TV counterparts, many newspaper reporters saw early exit polls, and some crafted preliminary stories relying on those numbers.

Jack Torry, a Washington reporter for Ohio's *Columbus Dispatch*, helped write two different analysis stories on election night. The first, never published, was based on late afternoon exit polls and explored how Kerry won the election, a "referendum on President Bush."

"The more I kept checking with Republican sources who I really do trust, the more I began to wonder: Could those exit polls be right?" Torry says. He and his colleagues scrapped the first piece around 9:30 p.m. Their second analysis, which actually appeared in the paper, examined why the race was so tight.

But not all early misfires based on exit polling stayed out of print. The November 5 story by the *New York Times*' Jim Rutenberg referred to a *Times* snafu. "The *New York Times* removed an analytical piece about the vote based in part on the Election Day survey from its later editions," Rutenberg wrote.

That story, by R. W. Apple and Janet Elder, also appeared in the *International Herald Tribune*. Bush's "bid for reelection was weakened by his failure to compete on even terms with Senator John Kerry among the millions of new voters who cast ballots on Tuesday, preliminary data from exit polling indicated," said the *Herald Tribune* version. The article said "Kerry clung to narrow exit-poll leads" nationally and in Florida, Ohio and Wisconsin. It did not explain that these early surveys might be skewed or misleading.

New York Times Washington Editor Richard L. Berke, who oversaw his paper's election coverage, says the story, which also contained many voter interviews, aimed to give readers a sense of the demographics and voting patterns. "Traditionally, those sorts of things are more reliable in exit polls even if you don't know the outcome," Berke says.

But as the evening progressed, actual vote counts contrasted jarringly with exit-poll results. "It made us nervous, so we pulled the whole story," Berke says. "I wanted to reshape the story to focus on all the [voter] interviews, but we ran out of time, so we pulled the whole thing."

Although Berke "felt OK at the time about using the exit polls for demographic information and not using it to call states or the outcome," he wants to review how they're used on election night in the future. "I'd be lying if I said it didn't affect our thinking and our planning for what the outcome could be," he says. "We have to give second thought to how and if and whether we use the exit polls at all."

The close of an election inevitably, and rightly, ushers in a period of self-examination for political journalists—after they catch up on some much-needed sleep.

"Across the campaign, I thought there was a lot of very good coverage that demonstrated that newspapers and broadcast networks do learn more each cycle about how to cover campaigns," says Doyle McManus, Washington bureau chief of the *Los Angeles Times*. "You got a lot, I thought, of quite impressive coverage on phenomena like fundraising and the use of television commercials, and quite sophisticated demographic analysis by my colleague Ron Brownstein and others."

The media correctly portrayed the race as tight in the campaign's final days. "People were describing Ohio as a critical swing state; they were describing the race as a competition to get out the base vote on each side," McManus says. "In retrospect, all of that looks remarkably accurate."

McManus also credits newspapers with giving "quite full, detailed and sophisticated coverage to all the major issues," despite the usual carping from critics that journalists ignored issues in favor of the horse race. But "we need to find more ways to direct our readers to places on the Internet or elsewhere," McManus says, "so we can escape the trap of having written about Issue X in early September when our readers didn't get interested [until] early October."

Of course, McManus adds, the media did fall "prey to the temptation to chase rabbits," to fixate on what he calls "ephemeral controversies" such as the Swift Boat saga and the missing explosives in Iraq. "But each of those ephemeral controversies was a metaphor for a larger issue," he says. "They weren't trivial, just ephemeral."

Not everyone gives the media such high marks for their performance. *National Journal's* [William] Powers [a columnist who covers media and politics] faults the usual "herd thinking" for chilling more creative political journalism—and he's not talking about the sort of creativity displayed by CBS during the National Guard document fiasco.

Powers says coverage was "way, way too poll driven" and blasts polls as an "addiction" for the media. "It's very hard to come up with something new every day. And these numbers provide newness," Powers says. "It zaps a lot of resources and energy and reduces the campaign to numbers in a way that is not helpful to democracy."

Another Powers peeve: "Every four years, we have this story line about the youth vote—'The youth vote is going to be gigantic.' The story never pans out, but we kind of go through these ridiculous rituals."

And don't get him started on the media's "gigantic obsession" with red and blue states. "The red-blue theme is so overdone and also really reductive," Powers says. "We have this red-blue motif because we have a two-party system in which we go into the booth and are supposed to choose between two parties," not because everyone falls neatly into a red or blue category. "Yet we play this story up because it's sexy; it's easy; it's simple. It was easy to have that map after the 2000 election, but it portrays the country far too simplistically and does a disservice to the public."

The media also would better serve the public—and the English language—by bucking the prevailing clichés of each election season. In 2004, candidates "barnstormed" the country, appealing to one-time "soccer moms" who metamorphosed into "security moms" after the terrorist attacks. Pollsters combed those "red and blue states" to gauge the preferences of a "polarized" and "closely divided" electorate, wondering whether the "youth vote" could tip the election but flummoxed by the "cell-phone generation." In the end, as pollsters and journalists foretold, it all came down to the "ground game" in Ohio, "the Florida of 2004." Sort of.

Fundraising prowess fueled media attention, in some cases leading to sophisticated reporting, such as the *Washington Post's* two-day series in May exploring links between fundraising and access to the administration . . . but often producing a mind-numbing array of horse-race, money-chase dailies.

During the political conventions, the broadcast networks abdicated their civic responsibilities in search of higher ratings from sexier reality shows. The cable networks galloped into the void, but too often padded downtime with shouting heads and insipid spin from party officials.

There was rampant media speculation throughout the campaign: When would a whipped Kerry admit defeat and drop out of the primaries? Whom would a triumphant Kerry tap as his running mate? ("KERRY'S CHOICE: Dem picks Gephardt as VP candidate," blared the *New York Post* in one of the season's more entertaining media meltdowns.) Might Bush drop Dick Cheney from the ticket? When would Kerry sideline Bob Shrum, the famed Democratic adviser and perennial presidential campaign loser? Did a home loss by the Washington Redskins the Sunday before the election presage victory for Kerry?

But the networks pulled themselves together for election night—at least for a few hours.

By 1:26 a.m. on November 3, hours before a victor had been officially declared in the 2004 presidential race, anchors and pundits, perhaps reeling from their night of restraint, already were speculating about Democratic candidates in 2008. On NBC, Washington Bureau Chief and "Meet the Press" host Tim Russert predicted a battle for the "soul of the Democratic Party."

After all, the next presidential election was only 1,462 days away. ■

Chapter 9

The Congress

Over the long term of American history, it is fair to conclude that Congress has lost political power to the executive branch. Since the New Deal, Congress has been forced to delegate more and more power to the federal bureaucracy, which has the expertise and resources to deal with the increasingly complex and diverse roles of the federal government. Since America's rise to power in international affairs after World War II, Congress has also lost power to what has been called the "imperial presidency." The shift in power from Congress to the executive branch seemed to slow or even reverse itself after the Vietnam War, but only temporarily. In the aftermath of the terrorist attacks of September 11, 2001, the Bush administration pressed forward with a new and even more expansive view of executive power. Although he asked for (and received) congressional approval to fight the war on terror and the war in Iraq, Bush did not seek Congress's permission to wiretap American civilians suspected of communicating with terrorists, or (at first) to detain terrorism suspects without trial or carry out military trials of enemy combatants. Some of these policies have been rejected by the courts, but others remain very much in force despite fierce opposition in Congress.

Even so, no president can afford to ignore or slight Congress for very long. Congress remains the focal point of the American national government. Its power in domestic affairs remains paramount, and it has powerful cards to play even in the area of foreign relations. Government agencies are highly dependent on good relations with Congress, and especially with the committees that have jurisdiction over their affairs.

Interest groups direct the lion's share of their energies toward Congress, and the media often take their cues from Congress as to what issues are worth reporting on. The federal courts, whatever else they do, must focus their energies in large part on interpreting congressional statutes. Presidents may propose, as the saying goes, but Congress disposes. Congress retains the power to investigate wrongdoing in the executive branch; has final budgetary and taxing authority; has the power to confirm executive and judicial appointments; and, as Bill Clinton learned, has the power of impeachment as well.

The readings in this chapter revolve around the fundamental question of the nature of representative government in the United States. Although the Framers clearly wanted congressmen to "refine and filter" the public's views (see *Federalist* No. 10, selection 1.1), members of Congress have always considered themselves "local men, locally minded, whose business began and ended with the interests of their constituency."* Congress

---

*Bernard Bailyn, *The Ideological Origins of the American Revolution* (Cambridge, Mass.: Belknap Press of Harvard University Press, 1967), p. 162.

must also balance its role as a democratic institution with the need to provide checks and balances—not only against the executive branch, but also against runaway majorities in its own chambers.

The first two selections in this chapter present classic arguments from the *Federalist Papers* regarding the nature of the legislative branch. Selection 9.3 fast-forwards to a contemporary analysis of how well Congress performs its multifaceted roles in the American political system. Selections 9.4 and 9.5 present a debate over the legitimacy and usefulness of the Senate filibuster, which allows forty-one senators to frustrate the will of the majority on many issues, including the confirmation of judicial nominees. The final selection provides a profile of freshman senator Barack Obama (D-Ill.), one of the rising stars in the Senate and in the Democratic party.

Chapter Questions

1. Review the Federalists' conception of the separation of powers. In what ways does the operation of the modern Congress underscore the Framers' belief that "ambition must be made to counteract ambition"? What evidence is there in the readings in this chapter to suggest that Congress plays an active role in the administrative process and that the president plays an active role in the legislative process? The readings in Chapter 10 ("The Presidency") may cast light on these questions as well.
2. What roles do members of Congress play? How do these roles conflict with one another? How do members of Congress seek to balance their own goals, their constituents' interests, and the public or national interest?

 # Foundations

The Federalists' view of representation was twofold. Representatives were expected not only to represent their constituents' interests but also to "refine and enlarge the public views, by passing them through the medium of a chosen body of citizens, whose wisdom may best discern the true interest of their country and whose patriotism and love of justice will be least likely to sacrifice it to temporary or partial considerations" (see *Federalist* No. 10, selection 1.1). Congress was expected to be a deliberative body that would think about and consider public questions and resolve them in the public interest. Thus the Framers made the connection between members of Congress and their constituents close but not too close: elections were to be held every two years, not every year, despite the popular eighteenth-century slogan that "when annual election ends, tyranny begins." Senators were to be elected every six years, and by the state legislatures, not by the people directly.

The Framers' views on representation and on Congress's role as the primary decision-making body, at least in matters of domestic policy, form the background for this chapter. *Federalist* No. 55, written by James Madison, defends the small size of the original Congress (only sixty-five members) as a way of securing "the benefits of free consultation and discussion." Moreover, the Framers thought, a small House would encourage representatives to think of the national interest instead of the local interest when they voted on public questions. But as *Federalist* No. 57 points out, the Framers believed the members of Congress would still be close to their constituents and would still faithfully represent their interests in the federal capital.

Questions

1. What does Madison mean when he writes, "Had every Athenian citizen been a Socrates, every Athenian assembly would still have been a mob"?
2. How might a member of Congress seek to balance his or her role as the representative of a local district with the sometimes conflicting role of acting in the interest of the entire nation?

9.1 *Federalist* No. 55 (1788)

James Madison

Outline

I. Critics' objections to the relatively small size of the House of Representatives (sixty-five members).
II. Madison's response.
   A. General remarks on the problem of size of legislatures.
   B. Specific remarks on the United States House of Representatives.
      1. Size of House will increase as population increases.
      2. Size of House is not dangerous to the public liberty.

The number of which the House of Representatives is to consist forms another and a very interesting point of view under which this branch of the federal legislature may be contemplated. Scarce any article, indeed, in the whole Constitution seems to be rendered more worthy of attention by the weight of character and the apparent force of argument with which it has been assailed. The charges exhibited against it are, first, that so small a number of representatives will be an unsafe depositary of the public interests; second, that they will not possess a proper knowledge of the local circumstances of their numerous constituents; third, that they will be taken from that class of citizens which will sympathize least with the feelings of the mass of the people and be most likely to aim at a permanent elevation of the few on the depression of the many; fourth, that defective as the number will be in the first instance, it will be more and more disproportionate, by the increase of the people and the obstacles which will prevent a correspondent increase of the representatives.

In general it may be remarked on this subject that no political problem is less susceptible of a precise solution than that which relates to the number most convenient for a representative legislature; nor is there any point on which the policy of the several States is more at variance, whether we compare their legislative assemblies directly with each other, or consider the proportions which they respectively bear to the number of their constituents. Passing over the difference between the smallest and largest States, as Delaware, whose most numerous branch consists of twenty-one representatives, and Massachusetts, where it amounts to between three and four hundred, a very considerable difference is observable among States nearly equal in population. The number of representatives in Pennsylvania is not more than one fifth of that in the State last mentioned. New York, whose population is to that of South Carolina as six to five, has little more than one third of the number of representatives. As great a disparity prevails between the States of Georgia and Delaware or Rhode Island. In Pennsylvania, the representatives do not bear a greater proportion to their constituents than of one for every four or five thousand. In Rhode Island, they bear a proportion of at least one for every thousand. And according to the constitution of Georgia, the proportion may be carried to one to every ten electors; and must unavoidably far exceed the proportion in any of the other states.

Another general remark to be made is that the ratio between the representatives and the people ought not to be the same where the latter are very numerous as where they are very few. Were the representatives in Virginia to be regulated by the standard in Rhode Island, they would, at this time, amount to between four and five hundred; and twenty or thirty years hence, to a thousand. On the other hand, the ratio of Pennsylvania, if applied to the State of Delaware, would reduce the representative assembly of the latter to seven or eight members. Nothing can be more fallacious than to found our political calculations on arithmetical principles. Sixty or seventy men may be more properly trusted with a given degree of power than six or seven. But it does not follow that six or seven hundred would be proportionably a better depositary. And if we carry on the supposition to six or seven thousand, the whole reasoning ought to be reversed. The truth is that in all cases a certain number at least seems to be necessary to secure the benefits of free consultation and discussion, and to guard against too easy a combination for improper purposes; as, on the other hand, the number ought at most to be kept within a certain limit, in order to avoid the confusion and intemperance of a multitude. In all very numerous assemblies, of whatever characters composed, passion never fails to wrest the scepter from reason. Had every Athenian citizen been a Socrates, every Athenian assembly would still have been a mob.

It is necessary also to recollect here the observations which were applied to the case of biennial elections. For the same reason that the limited powers of the Congress, and the control of the State legislatures, justify less frequent election than the public safety might otherwise require, the members of the Congress need be less numerous than if they possessed the whole power of legislation, and were under no other than the ordinary restraints of other legislative bodies.

With these general ideas in our minds, let us weigh the objections which have been stated against the number of members proposed for the House of Representatives. It is said, in the first place, that so small a number cannot be safely trusted with so much power.

The number of which this branch of the legislature is to consist, at the outset of the government, will be sixty-five. Within three years a census is to be taken, when the number may be augmented to one for every thirty thousand inhabitants; and within every successive period of ten years the census is to be renewed, and augmentations may continue to be made under the above limitations. It will not be thought an extravagant conjecture that the first census will, at the rate of one for every thirty thousand, raise the number of representatives to at least one hundred. Estimating the Negroes in the proportion of three fifths, it can scarcely be doubted that the population of the United States will by that time, if it does not already, amount to three millions. At the expiration of twenty-five years, according to the computed rate of increase, the number of representatives will amount to two hundred; and of fifty years, to four hundred. This is a number which, I presume, will put an end to all fears arising from the smallness of the body. I take for granted here what I shall, in answering the fourth objection, hereafter show, that the number of representatives will be augmented from time to time in the manner provided by the Constitution. On a contrary supposition, I should admit the objection to have very great weight indeed.

The true question to be decided, then, is whether the smallness of the number, as a temporary regulation, be dangerous to the public liberty? Whether sixty-five members for a few years, and a hundred or two hundred for a few more, be a safe depositary for a limited and well-guarded power of legislating for the United States? I must own that I could not give a negative answer to this question, without first obliterating every impression which I have received with regard to the present genius of the people of America, the spirit which actuates the State legislatures, and the principles which are incorporated with the political character of every class of citizens. I am unable to conceive that the people of America, in their present temper, or under any circumstances which can speedily happen, will choose, and every second year repeat the choice of, sixty-five or a hundred men who would be disposed to form and pursue a scheme of tyranny or treachery. I am unable to conceive that the State legislatures, which must feel so many motives to watch and which possess so many means of counteracting the federal legislature, would fail either to detect or to defeat a conspiracy of the latter against the liberties of their common constituents. I am equally unable to conceive that there are at this time, or can be in any short time, in the United States, any sixty-five or a hundred men capable of recommending themselves to the choice of the people at large, who would either desire or dare, within the short space of two years, to betray the solemn trust committed to them. What change of circumstances time, and a fuller population of our country may produce requires a prophetic spirit to declare, which makes no part of my pretensions. But judging from the circumstances now before us, and from the probable state of them within a moderate period of time, I must pronounce that the liberties of America cannot be unsafe in the number of hands proposed by the federal Constitution. . . .

As there is a degree of depravity in mankind which requires a certain degree of circumspection and distrust, so there are other qualities in human nature which justify a certain portion of esteem and confidence. Republican government pre-supposes the existence of these qualities in a higher degree than any other form. Were the pictures which have been drawn by the political jealousy of some among us faithful likenesses of the human character, the inference would be that there is not sufficient virtue among men for self-government; and that nothing less than the chains of despotism can restrain them from destroying and devouring one another. ■

9.2 *Federalist* No. 57 (1788)

James Madison

Outline

I. Madison's responses to the charge that the members of the House of Representatives will not have sympathy with the common people.

   A. Members of the House will be elected by the people.

   B. Every citizen of the appropriate age will be eligible for election to the House.

   C. For several reasons, the representatives will remain loyal to their constituents.

      1. In general, representatives will be men of high character.

      2. They will show gratitude and affection for those who elected them.

      3. They will be attached to representative government out of pride and vanity.

      4. They will be subject to frequent elections.

      5. Their constituents will insist they subject themselves to every law they make.

The *third* charge against the House of Representatives is that it will be taken from that class of citizens which will have least sympathy with the mass of the people, and be most likely to aim at an ambitious sacrifice of the many to the aggrandizement of the few.

Of all the objections which have been framed against the federal Constitution, this is perhaps the most extraordinary. Whilst the objection itself is leveled against a pretended oligarchy, the principle of it strikes at the very root of republican government.

The aim of every political constitution is, or ought to be, first to obtain for rulers men who possess most wisdom to discern, and most virtue to pursue, the common good of the society; and in the next place, to take the most effectual precautions for keeping them virtuous whilst they continue to hold their public trust. The elective mode of obtaining rulers is the characteristic policy of republican government. The means relied on in this form of government for preventing their degeneracy are numerous and various. The most effectual one is such a limitation of the term of appointments as will maintain a proper responsibility to the people.

Let me now ask what circumstance there is in the constitution of the House of Representatives that violates the principles of republican government, or favors the elevation of the few on the ruins of the many? Let me ask whether every circumstance is not, on the contrary, strictly conformable to these principles, and scrupulously impartial to the rights and pretensions of every class and description of citizens?

Who are to be the electors of the federal representatives? Not the rich, more than the poor; not the learned, more than the ignorant; not the haughty heirs of distinguished names, more than the humble sons of obscure and unpropitious fortune. The electors are to be the great body of the people of the United States. They are to be the same who exercise the right in every State of electing the corresponding branch of the legislature of the State.

Who are to be the objects of popular choice? Every citizen whose merit may recommend him to the esteem and confidence of his country. No qualification of wealth, of birth, of religious faith, or of civil profession is permitted to fetter the judgment or disappoint the inclination of the people.

If we consider the situation of the men on whom the free suffrages of their fellow-citizens may confer the representative trust, we shall find it involving every security which can be devised or desired for their fidelity to their constituents.

In the first place, as they will have been distinguished by the preference of their fellow citizens, we are to presume that in general they will be somewhat distinguished also by those qualities which entitle them to it, and which promise a sincere and scrupulous regard to the nature of their engagements.

In the second place, they will enter into the public service under circumstances which cannot fail to produce a temporary affection at least to their constituents. There is in every breast a sensibility to marks of honor, of favor, of esteem, and of confidence, which, apart from all considerations of interests, is some pledge for grateful and benevolent returns. Ingratitude is a common topic of declamation against human nature; and it must be confessed that instances of it are but too frequent and flagrant, both in public and in private life. But the universal and extreme indignation which it inspires is itself a proof of the energy and prevalence of the contrary sentiment.

In the third place, those ties which bind the representative to his constituents are strengthened by motives of a more selfish nature. His pride and vanity attach him to a form of government which favors his pretensions and gives him a share in its honors and distinctions. Whatever hopes or projects might be entertained by a few aspiring characters, it must generally happen that a great proportion of the men deriving their advancement from their influence with the people would have more to hope from a preservation of the favor than from innovations in the government subversive of the authority of the people.

All these securities, however, would be found very insufficient without the restraint of frequent elections. Hence, in the fourth place, the House of Representatives is so constituted as to support in the members an habitual recollection of their dependence on the people. Before the sentiments impressed on their minds by the mode of their elevation can be effaced by the exercise of power, they will be compelled to anticipate the moment when their power is to cease, when their exercise of it is to be reviewed, and when they must descend to the level from which they were raised; there forever to remain unless a faithful discharge of their trust shall have established their title to a renewal of it.

I will add, as a fifth circumstance in the situation of the House of Representatives, restraining them from oppressive measures, that they can make no law which will not have its full operation on themselves and their friends, as well as on the great mass of the society. This has always been deemed one of the strongest bonds by which human policy can connect the rulers and the people together. It creates between them that communion of interests and sympathy of sentiments of which few governments have furnished examples; but without which every government degenerates into tyranny. If it be asked, what is to restrain the House of Representatives from making legal discriminations in favor of themselves and a particular class of society? I answer: the genius of the whole system; the nature of just and constitutional laws; and, above all, the vigilant and manly spirit which actuates the people of America—a spirit which nourishes freedom, and in return is nourished by it.

If this spirit shall ever be so far debased as to tolerate a law not obligatory on the legislature, as well as on the people, the people will be prepared to tolerate anything but liberty.

Such will be the relation between the House of Representatives and their constituents. Duty, gratitude, interest, ambition itself, are the cords by which they will be bound to fidelity and sympathy with the great mass of the people. It is possible that these may all be insufficient to control the caprice and wickedness of men. But are they not all that government will admit, and that human prudence can devise? Are they not the genuine and the characteristic means by which republican government provides for the liberty and happiness of the people? . . . ■

 # American Politics Today

"[I]f a thoughtful citizen were to take an informed, clear-eyed, and consistent view of Congress," ask political scientists Paul J. Quirk and Sarah A. Binder, "what would it be?" In other words, how well does Congress do its job? In particular, how well does Congress function as an "institution of democracy"? These questions are not simple ones, for Congress has conflicting roles and conflicting priorities. Moreover, as Quirk and Binder point out, "[t]here are sure to be partisan, ideological, and philosophical disagreements about how Congress should work."

To guide their analysis, Quirk and Binder begin by clearly stating their yardsticks for measuring congressional performance. Congress, they believe, should "strike reasonable balances on certain long-term trade-offs, such as that between majority and minority rule." Both the House and the Senate should be open to "the possibility of change," should deliberate intelligently, and should avoid "extreme disharmony," "obvious manipulation," and clear rule violations. In policy terms, they argue, Congress should be fiscally responsible, active and responsive, independent, and willing to stand up to the White House.

Over the long term, Quirk and Binder find that Congress "has been successful and effective in many ways," but they also find "significant failures." In evaluating the contemporary Congress, however, they see considerably more minuses than plusses.

Questions

1. In what ways has the modern Congress failed to live up to the standards laid down by Quirk and Binder? Give examples.
2. Compare and contrast the performance of the contemporary Congress with the expectations of the Framers, as reflected in *Federalist* Nos. 55 and 57. What reforms, if any, might be beneficial in helping Congress to play a more effective role in American democracy?

9.3 Congress and American Democracy: Assessing Performance (2005)

Paul J. Quirk and Sarah A. Binder

• • •

[T]he contemporary Congress presents [considerable] cause for concern. At bottom, many scholars have cast blame toward exceptionally polarized congressional parties—a condition that has deep roots in economic, political, and demographic trends across the country. Rebirth of two-party competition in the South—dormant since the Civil War—has propelled Republicans to the ideological right and Democrats to the left. Old pockets of liberalism in the Republican Party in the Northeast dried up with the south and westward movement of the party. Similarly, the deep conservative southern base of the Democratic Party has all but disappeared, as the party has solidified its base in the urban cities of the east and west coasts.

It may seem odd that many scholars of American politics bemoan the rise of ideologically polarized parties. Strong political parties—cohesive and disciplined across the branches—were after all heralded by party government scholars under the auspices of the American Political Science Association (APSA) in the mid-twentieth century. *Toward a More Responsible Two-Party System*—a 1950 report of the APSA—was the mantra of scholars like E. E. Schattschneider, who had remarked years earlier that "democracy was unthinkable save in terms of parties." Responsible parties were expected to propose programmatic party agendas, enact them under the leadership of a strong president and unified congressional party, and present their collective records to the voters. In short, government would be held accountable to voters through vigorous and contested elections.

The problem is, as Morris Fiorina has observed, today's cohesive and disciplined parties have not ushered in an era of responsible parties. Ideologically polarized parties have more often found themselves mired in gridlock, and have been prone to adopt measures marked by programmatic inefficiencies. Public approval of Congress—never very high—has dipped to record lows, along with the president's standing. In a June 2005 Gallup opinion poll, nearly 60 percent of those polled disapproved of the way Congress was handling its job. Even more troubling is the perception that partisanship so colors elites' views about policy and politics that independent judgment is rare. As the economist Paul Krugman has argued, "we're not living in the America of the past, where even partisans sometimes changed their views when faced with the facts. Instead, we're living in a country in which there is no longer such a thing as nonpolitical truth."

. . . [T]he contemporary environment has had harmful effects on many dimensions of congressional performance. We briefly review the range of forces that have shaped politics in the contemporary Congress, and then consider the profound effects that heightened partisan competition and polarization have had on Congress's capacity for democratic governance.

The Electoral Context

The rise in polarization stems from numerous sources, many related to the contours of contemporary congressional elections. By far the most prevalent explanation is based on the electoral realignments that have occurred in the South and Northeast since the 1960s. As David Rohde has elaborated, the mobilization of African American voters on the heels of pivotal voting rights acts in 1965 and again in 1982 fundamentally altered the partisan landscape of the South. By the 1990s, the solid Democratic South had been converted into Republican territory, with the GOP holding a majority of House districts. As conservative Democrats were replaced by conservative Republicans, the Democratic Party became more liberal. The realignment also reinforced the conservatism of the newly Republican South. Population shifts to the south and west further bolstered the ranks of conservative Republicans, as GOP majorities in those states picked up additional seats after reapportionment following the 1990 and 2000 Censuses. Redistricting after the Census and in subsequent years in Texas also improved Republican control in these regions.

Electoral change in the South had repercussions elsewhere, most pronounced in the North and East, which had been the decades-long base of moderate, even liberal, Republicans. The conservative turn of the Republican Party meant that Northeastern Republicans felt increasingly out of place in the GOP. The result has been the gradual, but marked, disappearance of the Republicans' moderate wing, with just a handful of districts held by moderate Republicans in the Mid-Atlantic and New England and a coterie of moderate Republican senators.

The polarized electoral coalitions we see today extend beyond elites in both parties. Scholars have detected the polarization of the parties' electoral bases in demographic terms as well as policy attitudes. Whether mass polarization drives or is driven by elite polarization is a matter of debate. In Gary Jacobson's view, congressional candidates began to take more extreme positions in the 1990s. In turn, those signals may have moved the electorate to embrace more polarized policy views. As Morris Fiorina has warned, however, when the electorate is given polarized choices, voters may look more polarized even if their views have remained moderate. Indeed, opinion surveys continue to suggest that most Americans hold relatively moderate views on major issues, even on more contentious matters of social policy. Still, Fiorina and others have detected ample evidence that political activists within each party have moved to the right and to the left, ensuring that the bases of the two parties have polarized along with their elected partisans.

The Policy Context

Perhaps most often noted about the contemporary Congress is the pervasiveness of budget issues. As budget deficits grew in the 1980s, almost all aspects of the policy agenda came to be seen through the prism of the budget. Deficits constrained the scope of policy initiatives that could be attempted, forced legislators to consider the impact of new policy proposals on the budget, and more importantly focused attention on the critical issue of whether and how to reduce the size of government. That of course is the central issue defining and dividing the two parties.

The difficulty of resolving budget issues (particularly in periods of divided government in the 1980s and 1990s) brought party leaders to the center of most budget negotiations, moving most committee chairs to the sidelines. As Christopher Deering and Steven Smith have noted, the centrality of budgeting decisions and the difficulty of the votes they required, encouraged leaders to lean more heavily on procedural tactics that would obscure legislators' responsibilities for those tough choices. The rise of thousand-page omnibus bills in the contemporary period—legislative packages rarely read by members before they cast their vote—has been driven in large part by the emergence of budget issues to the forefront of the congressional agenda. The involvement of party leaders in budgeting decisions no doubt reinforces the polarizing character of debates over fiscal policy.

Partisan Competition

Most striking about the partisan landscape since the Republican takeover of Congress in 1994 has been the near parity of the two parties. Republican majorities since 1994 have been consistent, but small, holding on average just over half of House seats. In comparison, Democratic majorities between 1954 and 1994 held on average 60 percent of chamber seats. Senate Republican majorities have been equally slim, averaging just fifty-three seats between the elections in 1994 and 2004—well short of the sixty votes needed to defeat Democratic filibusters. President George W. Bush's electoral margin has also been exceedingly narrow, winning 51.4 percent of the two-party vote in 2004. Given the distribution of the vote across the states, analysts have noted that neither party has an electoral base sufficient to guarantee victory in the next presidential election.

What impact do slim congressional and presidential majorities have on the contemporary Congress? The Republicans' slim hold on majority status reinforces divisions between the two parties: Neither party has an interest in giving the other side a break. The electoral stakes are simply too high to give much ground on political or policy debates. The rise of the so-called permanent campaign—blurring the lines of campaigning and governing—has fueled the parties' incentives to disagree and to reject compromises that might in fact be preferred by the moderate middle. Although the parties have tightly contested both branches since the mid 1990s, the resumption of unified Republican control in 2003 likely accelerated the majority party's "win at all costs" strategies, as Democrats found themselves with fewer tools to block the Republicans' agenda. And as John Hibbing argues . . . the public's dissatisfaction with Congress stems in part from the media's coverage of the body as an institution mired in gridlock and motivated by purely partisan and electoral concerns, when important public problems remain unsolved.

Institutional Context

Heightened partisanship and polarized parties in both the House and Senate raise questions about the impact of chamber rules and practices on the emergence of this partisan state of affairs. Given how differently the two chambers distribute power across their membership, we typically think that the House's concentration of procedural power in the hands of the majority party and its leadership must account for that chamber's heightened partisanship. But as Eric Schickler points out . . . record levels of party voting have occurred in the Senate as well—a chamber in which power is diffused across the membership and the majority leader has few procedural advantages over other senators.

Still, the House and Senate exhibit very different procedural tendencies, and such differences lead them to different policy choices. As Steven Smith observes . . . the Senate's . . . [rules] make unlikely the success of purely partisan strategies, unlike in the House, where institutional reforms in the 1970s detailed by Barbara Sinclair . . . have provided a reservoir of procedural advantages for the majority party and its leadership. In contrast, House majority leaders can use their party's control of the Rules Committee to manipulate the floor agenda and to raise the bar against adoption of proposals preferred by the minority party or even by cross-party coalitions. As Donald Wolfensberger, a former staff director for the House Rules Committee during Republican-led Congresses, has observed, Republican majorities have used restrictive rules during consideration of major measures at a higher rate than their Democratic predecessors. Democrats, to be sure, perfected the art of limiting the minority party's participation in chamber proceedings, but Republicans appear to be taking advantage of these inherited practices to further limit full deliberation and consideration of competing ideas.

Performance as a Democratic Institution

How has this partisan and polarized state of affairs affected Congress's performance as an institution of democracy? . . . Here, we evaluate [the contemporary] Congress on . . . four central criteria of performance.

Constitutional Stability   As the framers made clear in explaining how the branches would be prevented from encroaching on the rights of the others, "the interest of the man must be connected with the constitutional rights of the place." This is where Congress falls short in our estimation: A Republican-controlled Congress has shown extraordinary deference to a Republican president. Charles Shipan notes . . . increased scrutiny of the administration during the period of divided government in the late 1990s, but such oversight dropped off precipitously with the election of a Republican president.

Such deference was widely evidenced in Congress's decision in 2002 to give preemptive authority to the president to go to war in Iraq, and afterwards when it became clear that the rationale for going to war was based on faulty evidence and argument. It is indeed possible that Congress's acquiescence to the president—at least after the war had begun if not before—is partially responsible for the poor trajectory of the war at this writing. Had Congress more vigorously challenged the administration's preference for war, perhaps the administration might have felt compelled to devise an exit strategy before going to war. Nor has Congress asserted its considerable powers of oversight to investigate scandals over the treatment of prisoners abroad. The performance of the military and the administration elicited some attention by the Senate after the events of Abu Ghraib prison were exposed, but Republican leaders essentially quashed any such inquiries in the House of Representatives.

Equally troubling has been recent administrations' extreme reluctance to share information with the Congress. During the George W. Bush administration, only Democrats—with rare exception—have cared enough to seek to assert their institution's right to such information. Such debates have affected the course of confirmation battles and numerous other disputes, with Congress rarely if ever succeeding in extracting information its members deem essential to performing their legislative and oversight responsibilities. Expert assessment is that the reluctance to share information has "become the default position in the post Sept. 11 world." Such a position challenges and weakens Congress's ability to assert its constitutional independence and responsibilities.

Democratic Values   The contemporary Congress has had a notable lack of success in striking appropriate balances on certain conflicts of democratic values, especially those between majority and minority rights, or majoritarian and consensual procedures. Many scholars decried the limitations on minority rights that Democrats placed on Republicans over the latter half of their forty year rule of the House. In our view, today's House majorities outdo the restraints imposed by their Democratic forerunners. They have excluded minority party alternatives during floor debate, limited minority participation in some House committees and conference committees, and bent rules on voting procedures to secure victories on the floor.

Meanwhile, the Senate has had a breakdown in consensus over the rules of the game. The Senate in early 2005 came to the brink of parliamentary warfare over both the rules for consideration of judicial appointments and the legitimate means of changing those rules. Given their sharp differences over the nominees, senators' stands were driven by partisan and policy goals. Lacking amid the acrimony . . .

was any semblance of collective deliberation over the institutional issues at stake. Leadership devolved to an *ad hoc* "Gang of 14"—an informal coalition of moderates and mavericks that came together to pull the Senate back from the brink. Although defusing the immediate crisis, the solution was temporary—shelving for future consideration the constitutional and institutional disputes that led to the crisis in the first place. In short, the Senate has been unable either to deliberate collectively about these major issues of procedure or even to reach a stable resolution.

As the findings of the Annenberg Survey of Congressional Staff reveal . . . Democrats and Republicans are sharply divided in their assessment of the contemporary Congress; Democrats are indeed alienated. Ninety percent of Democratic respondents said that "the majority party makes decisions regardless of the minority's views." Only one-third of Republicans agreed. By the same token, only one-third of Democrats believed that "the decision making process faithfully follows established procedures," a view endorsed by 79 percent of Republicans.

As suggested above, . . . the contemporary Congress's commitment to ensuring fair and competitive elections is fairly weak. Contested elections have all but disappeared in recent House elections, leaving only two dozen or so truly competitive House elections. Most other districts are reliably Democratic or Republican, raising doubts about the degree to which elections still provide a mechanism for holding legislators accountable for their performance in office. To be sure, the absence of turnover may represent the hypersensitivity of legislators to the views of their constituencies. Competitive elections may still be sending highly responsive representatives to Washington. In our view, highly responsive representation is more likely when legislators must retain their seats in competitive elections. It seems hard to evaluate Congress's performance on democratic values very highly so long as the life-blood of democracy—free and competitive elections—are too often missing.

Policymaking . . . Although we cannot take the space for thorough discussion, expert commentary points to a variety of problematic tendencies in policymaking. Today's highly partisan state of affairs has left moderate, responsible policy choices in short supply and has done little to temper Congress's appetite for catering to parochial and narrow interests. Ideologically driven parties seem to produce extreme policies, with decisions greased by parochial bargains to buy wavering votes.

Tax cuts in 2001 and 2003 were heavily skewed to upper income taxpayers; energy reform in 2005 created additional tax cuts for innumerable industries; and a landmark expansion of Medicare was enacted in 2003, laden with giveaways to the pharmaceutical industry and other special interests. A farm bill was enacted in 2002, reversing reforms enacted in 1996 that had been heralded as a positive step towards reducing inefficient agricultural subsidies. And just as the Clinton administration had bought critical votes for its North American Free Trade Agreement in 1993 by doling out particularized benefits for hard-hit interests, the Bush administration in 2005 rounded up votes for a Central American pact by doling out parochial favors.

On social policy, congressional Republicans proposed and voted on, with the president's support, a constitutional amendment to ban gay marriage—even though it was given little chance of mustering the necessary two-thirds majority. Congress also devoted time to intervening in end of life decisions for an incapacitated

Florida woman. On economic and social policy, majority party leaders cater to the activist base of the party rather than risking a full airing of policy alternatives that might pull public policy back to the center.

Any evaluation of Congress's recent performance must include its degree of fiscal responsibility, and on this dimension the contemporary Congress scores quite poorly. In nominal terms, the fiscal 2005 budget deficit appears at this writing to be the third largest in the history of the United States. Highly charged ideological divisions between the parties have made it harder for Congress to agree on the budgeting tools required to address today's fiscal challenges and those of the future. Add in Republicans' fervent commitment to tax cuts, and the resulting equation portends ill for fiscal solvency in the years to come. Presidents of both political parties likely will continue to exploit earlier centralizing reforms in the budget process to control outcomes at the expense of Congress's power of the purse.

The contemporary Congress's deficiencies in policymaking are apparent to congressional insiders. In response to the Annenberg Survey, only 39 percent of congressional staff members said that Congress performs well in policymaking. Three-quarters judged that congressional policy decisions are distorted by pressure from special interests. And most Democrats and even some Republicans denied that policies are made through careful discussion and deliberation. Unfortunately, in their view, the truncated deliberation is not yielding efficient action: 91 percent of the respondents agreed that significant policy change is very difficult.

Adaptation and Reform   What can we conclude from recent Congresses about the institution's contemporary capacity to adapt effectively to social and political change, as well as scandal and calls for reform? How, if at all, has the rise of polarized parties affected the institution's capacity to police itself and to respond to external demands? To take just one example, the uproar over the ethics of House leaders at the start of the 109th Congress in 2005 suggests that partisan and electoral pressures continue to hamper Congress's reform capacities.

The debacle over ethics started in the fall of 2004 when the House Republican Caucus agreed—before reversing itself when confronted with internal dissent and public disgust—that indicted party leaders would not have to step down from their leadership posts. When the House convened to organize in January, a standoff over the chamber's ethics panel ensued. Ignoring the practice of involving the minority party when considering changes to the bipartisan panel, Republicans adopted on a party-line vote three changes to the structure of the ethics panel that would have made it easier for the majority party to limit minority party influence over investigations of member misconduct. Stymied by their inability to organize the panel, Republicans eventually gave in to most of the elements of a compromise floated by Democrats. Still, despite reports of alleged violations of the chamber's ethics standards regarding privately funded travel (by both Democrats and Republicans), there has of this writing been little progress in reviewing these charges and standards. Partisan disputes over the procedures for judging the ethical standards of their colleagues do not bode well for the chamber's ability to respond to demands for improving congressional integrity.

As suggested above . . . , neither the House nor Senate seems capable of debating institutional reforms in an open and deliberative manner. That is, legislators rarely consider the broader repercussions for Congress's institutional capacities when arguing over the rules of the game. As C. Lawrence Evans observes . . . , this is nothing new: partisan, policy, and electoral motives have been central to episodes of institutional change across history. Unfortunately, the heightened partisan state of affairs has made deliberation over the rules of the game even more contentious, meaning that bipartisan agreement is even less likely. In the case of the [2005 controversy over] judicial filibusters . . . Republicans made little effort to educate the public on why change was good for the institution, moving promptly instead to a partisan strategy of whipping up organized interests for a fight over the rules. Would Democrats have done the same, if the tides were turned? Probably so. We are pessimistic because the Congress has yet to develop the incentive or means to consider reforms in light of their impact on critical democratic values.

• • •

The Future and Reform

We have reached several conclusions about Congress. First, Congress has always had considerable weaknesses, as well as strengths, as an institution of democracy. Second, as a result of historically rare levels of partisan and ideological conflict, along with other developments in American politics, its performance has been on a downward trajectory, with important institutional norms and working arrangements in virtual collapse. And third—unfortunately, under the circumstances—it has very limited capabilities for broadly based deliberation about institutional matters or for institutional reform. Congress, in a word, is in trouble. In this section, we briefly discuss what the future of Congress may hold, and what, if anything, congressional leaders, reformers, or others might usefully attempt to do about it.

Although scholars cannot predict the future, nothing visible on the horizon indicates an impending reversal or even an approaching limit of the trend toward increasing ideological polarization. Historically, party conflict is moderated primarily by the arrival of important issues that cut across party lines. In fact, some of this moderating already occurs in contemporary American politics, as both parties seek support from economically conservative but socially liberal suburbanites, on the one hand, and from economically liberal but socially conservative working-class families, on the other. If either economic or social issues subside in importance in coming years, party polarization will probably become even more severe.

One potential result is increasingly conflictual, unproductive bouts of divided party control of government. With the relative strength of the two parties quite comparable, divided control—especially with a Democratic president and a Republican Congress—is highly likely. In the most recent period of divided control, from 1995 to 2000, President Bill Clinton and the Republican Congress fought a vicious battle over health care reform, ending in stalemate; allowed the federal government to be shut down for several days in a budget impasse; and spent a full year contesting a doomed Republican effort to remove Clinton from office through impeachment. The next round of divided party control . . . could witness even more destructive conflict. Projecting present trends into the future, American government may lurch from periods of ill-deliberated, ideologically extreme policy, with Congress acting as a rubber stamp for the president, to periods of profound disagreement and acrimony between the branches, with severe gridlock in policymaking.

Promising strategies for reducing polarization are in short supply. As a long-shot strategy, political reformers should look for viable ways to reduce political party and incumbent-politician control of state redistricting processes. Redistricting reform will certainly encounter powerful resistance. Moreover, it may not be possible, even through a nonpartisan process, to design House districts that produce large numbers of competitive seats. To a great extent, large party majorities reflect the increasing economic and social segregation of the society. And in any case, polarization in the Senate is not affected by redistricting. But politicians should not be permitted to design districts to prevent competition, and even a small increase in competitive seats would make Congress more responsive to national trends.

Another possible strategy is to encourage state parties to adopt open primaries—with voters allowed to participate in either party primary regardless of their party registration. If some Democrats vote in a Republican primary election for Congress, a moderate Republican has a better chance of winning. Finally, any method of increasing voter turnout in general elections and especially in primaries will likely raise the proportion of moderate voters. In the end, however, the prospect of adopting reforms that significantly increase the number of moderates in Congress is fairly remote.

The alternative, more realistic approach is to accept that Congress will be deeply partisan for the foreseeable future and seek to improve the functioning of party government. Above all, the two parties need to work out viable understandings on the structural and procedural issues that have produced extraordinary rancor in recent Congresses. For example, they should seek some agreement to limit the majority's use of restrictive rules in House floor action and the minority's use of filibusters and holds in the Senate. Reform of judicial selection procedures, along the lines suggested by Forrest Maltzman, . . . might also improve the Senate. Unfortunately, neither the House majority nor the Senate minority has much incentive to give up their respective advantages. As the parties continue to become more centralized, it might eventually be possible to negotiate a single agreement to moderate the practices in both chambers.

But another sort of accommodation is more likely: Congress may have to simply recognize that bipartisan cooperation will be minimal, and avoid procedural practices and expectations that require much of it. Members would understand that the mainstream of the majority party will pass its bills in the House, without much real discussion; that sixty senators will be required to pass bills in the Senate; and that business can proceed without comity. Such a Congress would need to look for ways to substitute for some of its traditional capabilities. With committee and floor deliberative processes compromised, the parties would need to strengthen their internal deliberative processes. They should develop larger, more specialized and expert staff, and create more formal and elaborate arrangements for deliberation within the party. Ideally they should expose party deliberations to more publicity and external criticism.

In addition, if a thoroughly partisan Congress is to continue to play its central and constitutional role in what David Mayhew . . . calls "the public sphere"— shaping the broader political discourse of the nation—it will have to rely increasingly on the types of actions that individual members or the minority party can take outside of formal congressional processes. For example, if a rubber-stamp majority party refuses to investigate the executive branch, the minority party may have to run its own, unofficial investigations—as it has occasionally done in recent years. Unless a highly partisan Congress can develop new capabilities and restore its constitutionally mandated independence through some of these means, American government and the nation will be diminished.

American citizens have good reason to be proud of Congress, notwithstanding its weaknesses. But they should recognize that a transformation of Congress has been underway for at least two decades. Anyone who is proud of Congress's past performance also has good reason to be concerned about its future. In our view, American leaders and citizens should place high priority on finding workable ways to restore Congress's capacity for democratic governance. ■

 # Issue and Controversy

The Senate has never pretended to be a fully democratic institution. Until 1913, senators were appointed by the state legislatures; only after the ratification of the Seventeenth Amendment did the Constitution require their direct election by the people. Even so, the Senate (with two seats for each state) remains the only legislative body in the United States elected without regard to population—meaning that the smallest states have as much clout as big states such as California, Texas, New York, or Florida.

But the Senate's non-democratic character goes beyond simple arithmetic and is deeply impressed into the culture of the institution itself. Senators have always fancied themselves as a check on the more directly democratic House of Representatives. A well-known story has Thomas Jefferson asking George Washington why the Constitution created a Senate. "'Why did you pour that coffee into your saucer?' asked Washington. 'To cool it,' said Jefferson. 'Even so,' responded Washington, 'we pour legislation into the senatorial saucer to cool it.'"*

The Senate's role in checking the majority is nowhere more clearly illustrated than with the filibuster, which for more than a century has been used by Senate minorities to block legislation and, later, judicial nominees. The filibuster derives from the Senate's tradition of allowing unlimited debate. Taking advantage of this rule, a small number of senators could kill legislation simply by refusing to stop talking about it. Senate rules eventually permitted such debates to be ended by a two-thirds vote; later the requirement was reduced to three-fifths. In the old days, filibusters were literally nonstop marathons (Senator Strom Thurmond, then a Democrat from South Carolina, once spoke for over twenty-four hours). Today, they are largely symbolic affairs, which allow the Senate to conduct other business while waiting for negotiations to permit a vote on the issue in question.

---

*Quoted in "Senate Legislative Process," United States Senate, http://www.senate.gov/legislative/common/briefing/Senate_legislative_process.htm.

In recent years, the filibuster has been generally accepted when applied to legislation, but has generated considerable controversy when used to block floor votes on judicial nominees. The following two selections present the two sides of the filibuster debate.

Questions

1. What are the advantages and disadvantages of the Senate filibuster? In general, does the filibuster advance or hinder the goals of American democracy? Explain.
2. Evaluate the filibuster in terms of the political philosophies of the Federalists and Antifederalists (see Chapter 1 as well as selections 9.1 and 9.2). Is the filibuster consistent with the views of one side or the other? Neither? Both?

9.4 Slaying the Dinosaur: The Case for Reforming the Senate Filibuster (1995)

Sarah A. Binder and Thomas E. Mann

• • •

[No] one disputes that the incidence of filibusters has increased exponentially. . . . Although it is often thought that the early filibusters were exclusively sectional in nature (as senators aligned on a regional basis to fight legislation favored by northern and western senators), partisanship often pervaded early obstructionism as well. Democrats fighting Whig expansionism before the Civil War, as well as Democrats fighting Republican efforts to protect blacks in the postbellum period, availed themselves of the filibuster to block legislation their parties opposed.

The explosion in the number of filibusters began after the 1950s. Where the 1950s averaged one filibuster per Congress, the 1970s averaged 11 and the 1980s, 19. At the same time, the average number of cloture votes [cutting off debate and allowing a floor vote] rose from fewer than 1 per Congress in the 1950s to 27 per Congress in the 1980s. Not only did the sheer number of filibusters and cloture votes climb, but the targets of filibustering senators expanded as well. In the 1950s, the filibuster was used almost exclusively by a coalition of conservative Republicans and southern Democrats to thwart civil rights legislation. . . . So long as a supermajority of senators was required to alter chamber rules, opponents of civil rights legislation could prevent changes in the Senate cloture rule that would have otherwise made it easier for a majority to act. But by the end of the 1970s the filibuster was no longer the preserve of conservatives. Liberals discovered that the filibuster could block policy initiatives and court nominations of the Nixon administration. . . .

From Sarah A. Binder and Thomas E. Mann, "Slaying the Dinosaur: The Case for Reforming the Senate Filibuster," *The Brookings Review*, Summer 1995, pp. 43–46. Reprinted by permission.

Senators have turned increasingly to the filibuster to block Senate action because there are few incentives not to. As crystallized by political scientist Richard F. Fenno, Jr., the Senate's shift from a communitarian body in the 1950s to an individualistic one after 1970 has meant the demise of the old Senate—where incentives and norms encouraged quiet apprenticeship and deference to committee and chamber elders. In today's Senate, senators are encouraged to be more responsive to their own personal agendas than to the needs of their colleagues and party leaders. Explosions in interest group pressures, media attention, campaign costs, and constituency obligations have all combined to give senators an overwhelming incentive to exploit their procedural rights. And when party leaders in the 1970s began to adjust to this new style of Senate activism, their decision to "track" filibusters by setting contested bills aside and moving onto other pressing legislation only increased further the use of the filibuster.

As a result, holds by individual senators—in effect a threat to filibuster—have proliferated and filibusters and cloture votes have grown apace. Not only have senators been more willing to filibuster measures they oppose, they have also exploited their procedural prerogatives to filibuster bills at multiple stages—on the motion to proceed to their consideration, on amendments to the bill, and at all three steps of the otherwise pro forma motions to agree to go to conference with the House. Because Senate leaders depend on gaining unanimous consent to structure the floor agenda (unless they can easily muster 60 votes to invoke cloture—a rare feat for recent majority parties), a single senator's pet objections can throw off the entire Senate agenda. Given increases in legislative demands and senators' conflicting schedules, party leaders can ill afford to call the bluff of senators threatening to filibuster or to force senators to hold the floor continuously during a filibuster. Instead, the mere threat to filibuster is enough to block action on legislation potentially favored by a sizable majority. As one senator has put it colorfully, "You have to think of the Senate as if it were 100 different nations and each one had the atomic bomb and at any moment any one of you could blow up the place. So that no matter how long you've been here or how short you've been here, you always know you have the capacity to go to the leader and threaten to blow up the entire institution. And, naturally, he'll deal with you."

Filibusters and Popular Majorities

The most common defense of the filibuster is that legislation favored by a popular majority has never been killed by extended debate. Senators, so the argument goes, will be unable to sustain a filibuster if they lack broad support within and outside the chamber. But it is wildly unrealistic to imagine that a largely apolitical public can serve as a watchdog on the dozens of filibusters waged each year. Indeed, the routinization of the filibuster, and the information overload associated with it, effectively eliminates any meaningful role for public opinion in disciplining the behavior of minority factions in the Senate. Even on broadly salient issues Senate obstructionism has surely killed measures that would otherwise have passed. The 40-year journey for civil rights legislation starting with anti-lynching bills in the 1920s is strong evidence that the filibuster permits a minority of the Senate to bottle up measures enjoying majority support.

• • •

Perhaps the strongest argument in favor of reform is that senators themselves have been quite willing to limit the right to filibuster when such limits serve their immediate policy interests. In more than three dozen instances in recent decades, Congress has placed into statute strict limits on debate and amending activity on House and Senate floors. These antifilibuster provisions, generally known as "expedited procedures," have been used to ensure that a vote can be taken on a resolution either approving or disapproving some action proposed by the president or other executive branch official. If the law requires that Congress formally approve some action by the executive branch before it can be implemented, filibustering the resolution of approval can kill the initiative. Conversely, if the law mandates that Congress must formally disapprove an executive branch initiative in order to kill it, a filibuster against the resolution of disapproval can protect the initiative. When senators have had a policy interest in voting on the proposed delegation of power to the executive branch, they have pointedly banned the filibuster on the relevant resolution.

"Fast-track" procedures often used to guarantee a final vote on trade packages negotiated by the president are probably the best known expedited procedures. A strict 30-hour debate limit with no chance for amendment in the past has been imposed during consideration of nontariff trade packages on the Senate floor, although legislation extending fast-track authority can be filibustered. Similarly, the 1974 Budget Act imposed a 20-hour debate limit for consideration of budget reconciliation bills. When such expedited procedures are in place, senators opposed to some provision in the package cannot filibuster a bill to kill the offending provision.

But expedited procedures are not reserved for simply the most politically salient legislation. Senate majorities have banned the filibuster across a host of issues that involve delegation of authority to the executive branch, including foreign assistance, arms control, and energy and environmental regulations . . . Statutory debate limits have been included in legislation regulating unfunded mandates and in a bill to permit Congress to review newly issued agency regulations. Although senators tend to claim a principled commitment to preserving Senate tradition, they are quite willing to foreclose their rights to filibuster when such limits serve more immediate political and policy interests.

Proposals for Reform

To limit the harm done by the filibuster, the Senate should consider three approaches to reform. The first would limit the ability of senators to filibuster presidential nominations for executive and judicial branch positions. . . . "The Constitution grants the Senate the power to advise and consent . . ." argued [Robert] Pastor in the *Washington Post*, "not to delay and obstruct." Just as senators have been willing to impose statutory limits on debate on trade, budget, and other issues, they should also consider expedited procedures for consideration of nominations. Such a move would protect the full Senate's power to advise and consent on nominations.

A second reform approach, advocated . . . by then Senate Majority Leader George Mitchell (D-Maine), would limit the number of stages at which a measure can be filibustered. Rule 22 provides six opportunities to filibuster a bill before the vote on final passage—including on the motion to proceed to consideration of a bill and on the three votes related to going to conference. In recent years, senators have increasingly been prone to target the motion to proceed. By launching a fili-buster on the procedural motion, a senator can prevent the chamber from even taking up legislation he or she opposes. The mere threat of a filibuster in the form of registering a hold on the bill has been enough to convince Senate leaders to shelve the motion to proceed and with it the bill. Although senators often lift many such holds, a threat to filibuster the motion to proceed delays the Senate and confounds party leaders' ability to set the chamber's schedule.

Under the Mitchell proposals, debate on the motion to proceed would be lim-ited to two hours, a move that would guarantee the majority a debate (if not a vote) on bills high on the Senate's agenda. Moreover, by limiting individual sena-tors' right to obstruct the motion, the majority leader would no longer be forced to engage in extended negotiations over even the most routine bills on the Senate's agenda. Senators of both political parties, including Senator Robert Byrd (D-West Virginia), perhaps the Senate's greatest champion of the filibuster, have at times endorsed such a limit on the motion to proceed.

The Mitchell proposals would also consolidate into a single motion the three votes necessary to go to conference with the House. The filibuster would be per-mitted only during consideration of a measure, on the single motion to proceed to conference, and on the conference report itself. Although these reforms would not temper the incentive of senators to exploit their procedural prerogatives, they would make it easier for the majority leader to organize the Senate schedule, lend some predictability to the consideration of legislation on the Senate floor, and force opponents of bills to focus extended debate on the measure itself rather than the preceding procedural motion.

The third approach to reform, advocated by Senators Tom Harkin (D-Iowa) and Joseph Lieberman (D-Connecticut), would ratchet down over several days the number of senators required to invoke cloture. [In 1995] the Senate rejected Harkin and Lieberman's proposed reform of Rule 22 that would have set a four-vote procedure to attain cloture, with the requisite number of votes for cloture declining with each vote. The initial 60-vote requirement would be lowered to 57, 54, and 51 votes on the following three votes. Under this proposal, a large mi-nority could delay consideration of a bill by extended debate over a minimum of eight days and more likely several weeks, but would eventually have to give way to a simple majority seeking to cast a vote on the measure. Ratcheting down the number of votes required to invoke cloture would both preserve the minority's right to be heard while boosting Senate leaders' ability to move forward on favored legislation.

The Filibuster and the Character of the Senate

Whenever proponents of Senate reform have sought limits on extended debate, defenders of the filibuster have accused them of trying to undermine the unique-ness of the Senate, particularly its original role as a moderating force on intemper-ate majorities in the House. But the filibuster can be reformed without imperiling

the inherent distinctness of the Senate or the Madisonian system of separated institutions competing for shared power. Its members will still serve six-year terms,
allowing them to take a more measured approach than House members under the
perpetual gun of a reelection campaign. Only a third of the Senate will still be up
for reelection in any given year, diluting the impact of strong electoral waves. . . .
And senators from large and small states alike will still be given an equal vote, retaining the overweighting of rural interests in the Senate. The trick, of course, in
any set of reforms is to balance two goals: protecting the right of individuals and
minorities to be heard and ensuring the right of the majority to act. The use of the
filibuster in today's Senate serves the interests of the minority at the expense of
the majority. Far from preserving the Senate's role as a deliberative assembly, the
filibuster today encourages rampant individualism and obstructionism, endless delays and unfocused discussion, hardly conducive to the thoughtful consideration of
measures to solve vexing problems of public policy. ■

9.5 Defending the Dinosaur: The Case for Not Fixing the Filibuster (1995)

Bill Frenzel

D efending the filibuster may not be quite as nasty as taking candy from a
baby, but neither is it a good route to popular acclaim. Few kind words are
ever spoken in defense of filibusters. Conventional wisdom and political
correctness have pronounced them to be pernicious. The very word is pejorative,
evoking ugly images of antidemocratic activities.

During the last biennium, filibusters became so unlovable that a group, including former senators, formed "Action, Not Gridlock!" to try to stamp them out.
The public, which had tested both gridlock and action, seemed to prefer the former. The organization disappeared.

As that public reaction suggests, political correctness is a sometime thing and
conventional wisdom oft goes astray. The American public may not be rushing to
embrace the filibuster, but neither has it shown any inclination to root it out. The
Senate's overwhelming vote earlier this year [1995] against changing the filibuster
means that the practice won't go away soon, so it is worth examining. Despite its
bad press, the story of the modern filibuster is not one-sided.

Filibusters, the Constitution, and the Framers

Filibuster haters claim they are contrary to the spirit of the Constitution because
they require extraordinary majorities. The rationale is that the Framers, who created a majority system and rejected supermajorities, would be horrified by filibusters.

From Bill Frenzel, "Defending the Dinosaur: The Case for Not Fixing the Filibuster," *The Brookings Review*, Summer 1995, pp. 47–49. Reprinted by permission.

Perhaps, but don't be too sure. Remember that no one has dug up a Framer lately to testify to the accuracy of this theory.

The Framers created our system based on their profound distrust of government. They loaded the system with checks and balances to make it work very slowly and with great difficulty. Their intention was to prevent swift enactment of laws and to avoid satisfying the popular whimsy of each willful majority. Maybe they would trade popular election for a filibuster rule.

Without any live Framers, we can only speculate about their feelings. However, it is hard to believe that, having designed an extremely balky system, they would want to speed it up today. More likely, they would merely remind us that for more than 200 years major American policymaking has been based on "concurrent majorities" anyway.

Parliamentary Comparisons

Most of the parliaments of the world are copies, or variants, of [England's "Westminster" system]. With only one strong house and no separated executive branch, they can usually deliver laws swiftly. But when their actions affront public opinion, there is a political price to be paid, often very quickly. The government that offends the people soon becomes the opposition.

In our regional system, our majorities, assisted by a wide range of taxpayer-paid perks, do not usually pay any price. Our members of Congress are unbeatable. . . . Our majorities are not eternal, but they are long-lived. . . .

The Filibuster and the Popular Will

The filibuster has been often indicted for denying the popular will, but over recent history, that point is hard to demonstrate. In the first place, it is not easy to get, and hold, 41 votes in the Senate under any circumstances. It is practically impossible to do so against a popular proposal. Filibusters simply do not succeed *unless* they have popular support or unless there is a lack of enthusiasm for the proposal being filibustered. . . .

If the public wants a vote, it tells its representatives. . . . If any proposal has substantial public support, a couple of cloture votes will kill the filibuster. The political reality is: frivolous filibusters do not succeed. The modern filibuster can gridlock ideas that are not popular, but it has not gridlocked the people.

The Bicameral System

In our unique system, the two houses of Congress have developed similar, but not identical, personalities and processes. The House of Representatives, with 440 orators, is harder to manage and has therefore created a set of rules to limit debate. In recent years, its majority has handled bills under rules that permitted few, if any, amendments and only an hour or two of debate.

The Senate, with only 100 orators, has stayed with free debate and an open amendment system. That is not a bad division of process. One house has been too closed, the other too open. The House operates with the relentlessness of Westminster majority, and the Senate has more time to examine, to delay, to amend, and, if necessary, to kill. All are vital functions of any legislature. . . .

There is still a relatively open pipeline for bills flowing from the House. . . . Following the Framers' wisdom, it is prudent to have a sieve in the Senate to compete with that open pipe in the House. At least some of the worst legislative lumps may be smoothed out in the finer mesh. Only if unlimited debate and amendments were guaranteed for all House bills would it make sense to kill the Senate filibuster.

Key to Compromise

Many filibusters are not filibusters at all, but merely threats. Most are undertaken to notify the managers of the proposal that problems exist. They are a signal from a minority to a majority that negotiations are in order. Sometimes the majority tries a cloture vote or two before negotiating. Sometimes it negotiates. Sometimes it does not. Most of these procedures end in a modified bill, not a dead bill. . . .

The filibuster surely gives a minority a little more clout, but it does not prevent a majority from passing reasonably popular proposals. It gives a minority the opportunity to negotiate what it believes is an intolerable proposal into one it can live with. That compromise may serve the needs of the majority tolerably well too.

No Need for a Heavy Hand

One political reality test for the filibuster is the congressional ingenuity in finding ways to avoid it when necessary. Trade and Reconciliation bills are considered under laws that obviate filibusters. When there is a good reason to finesse the filibuster, the Senate always seems to get the job done.

Many other Senate rules, only dimly understood by common folks, reduce the legislative pace. I do not mean to bless multiple efforts to filibuster the same proposal. Once on the bill and once on the conference report is enough. Unlimited amendment after cloture is also too much opportunity for mischief.

Former Senate Majority Leader Mitchell has left constructive proposals to speed the work of the Senate without damaging the filibuster. They ought to be considered. The minority needs rights for protection. The majority needs the ability to move its program. Both needs can be well served by the modern 60-vote cloture rule. It should not be changed.

Keep the Filibuster

The test of the filibuster ought to be whether it is fair, appropriate, and constructive. It may have been a killer in the old days, when it slew civil rights bills, but under the new 60-vote system, it is difficult to recall a filibustered proposition that stayed dead if it was popular.

Most antifilibuster noise comes from advocates of ideas that were going to fail anyway. It is not essential for every idea that comes bouncing up or down Pennsylvania Avenue to become law. The filibuster is a useful legislative tool, consistent with the goals of the Framers, that keeps whimsical, immature, and ultimately unpopular bills out of the statute books. . . . ■

View from the Inside

Senators have always been major players in American politics. Whereas members of the House of Representatives are typically unknown outside their home districts or official Washington, many Senators are high-profile media stars. They appear frequently on television talk shows, make highly publicized visits to foreign capitals, and attract large crowds at political speeches and fund-raising events. Senators also figure prominently in presidential campaign politics. Senators or former senators, for example, led a major party presidential ticket in 1996, 2000, and 2004 (curiously, the senator or former senator lost each time, to a governor or former governor).

When a young, charismatic, well-spoken, and dynamic new senator is elected, therefore, he or she naturally attracts a great deal of media attention. Such was the case with Barack Obama, who was elected as a freshman senator from Illinois in 2004. That Obama is an African American—only the third African American to be popularly elected to the Senate in American history—only increased the public's interest and attention. Almost before he took his seat, Obama was talked about as a possible presidential or vice-presidential candidate in 2008.

This selection presents a report on Obama's early days in the United States Senate.

Questions

1. How did Obama's high public profile affect his adjustment to the United States Senate? How was his experience different from those of his lesser-known colleagues?
2. According to this article, what are Obama's long-term goals? How do his conflicting roles as U.S. senator, Democratic party leader, and potential presidential or vice-presidential candidate affect his strategy for achieving those goals? His chances of achieving them?

9.6 Great Expectations (2006)

Jodi Enda

By 30 minutes and several days, Barack Obama is running late. He is supposed to be at his grandmother's in Hawaii—his wife and daughters already are there—but the Senate is still voting on some fairly significant legislation. So here he is, stuck in Washington nine days before Christmas. Illinois' junior senator just came from the Senate floor, where he and his fellow Democrats scored big by blocking a Republican drive to reauthorize the USA PATRIOT Act. He appears at once exhausted and energetic as he carefully places his finely tailored, charcoal-gray suit jacket on the back of a chair and centers his long, lean frame on the sofa beneath a large oil painting of an Illinois cornfield. Some of his heroes stare down at him from his office walls: Abraham Lincoln, JFK, and Mahatma Gandhi to his left; Martin Luther King, Jr., Thurgood Marshall, and Nelson Mandella across the room. A White Sox cap lies atop his desk, a symbol of triumph secured after years in the wilderness.

Obama closes his eyes and turns his youthful, angular face upward, as if he is contemplating all the world's problems from a place deep inside himself. His head rests against the back of the gold couch; his left fingertips touch his forehead. His right leg, long and crooked at the knee, is stretched across a coffee table. He speaks softly and slowly, pausing frequently to choose just . . . the right . . . words.

The question on the table—and the reason for the pause—is the future of the Democratic Party. It's not an easy question for anyone these days, and it's not a question that is normally asked of a first-term senator with only one year's experience. But Obama is not a normal first-termer—not after the slew of national magazine profiles that ran before he was even elected (and while he was still a state senator), and definitely not after The Speech, his electric keynote address at the 2004 Democratic Convention, which catapulted him from obscurity (people sometimes called him "Alabama") to the national A-list. These days, people want to know what Obama thinks about everything, from baseball to foreign affairs.

His party, it's worth remembering, didn't even want him to get to the Senate—Illinois' historically muscular Democratic machine backed a party insider in the primary. But Obama blew away that opponent, and five others, winning an outright majority of 53 percent of the vote. Now, at 44, Obama embraces his role with confidence, a great deal of pleasure—and no small amount of care. Speculation swirls about his becoming America's first black president (he is the biracial son of a black, Kenyan father and a white, Kansan mother). . . .

Obama is coy about that. But he has little doubt about what he views as the role he should play in the Senate, within his party, and even as a force in shaping the nation's future. He wants to change things, and he envisions himself doing so. There is about him a sense of, well, destiny; his background, his charm, his intellect, and his way with words have marked him as someone special. Obama is aware of this, and every so often, he will say something that tacitly acknowledges as much. But usually he manages himself well, upward and downward, mindful to show the proper respect for his colleagues, some of whom have been in the Senate for most of his life, and for the voters who sent him to Washington with extraordinarily high expectations. He tells me he was happy to have made it through his first Senate year without falling "flat on my face."

That he has not pushed through major legislation matters hardly at all, not to him, not to supporters. He is a fledgling in the minority party and, during his first year, 99th in seniority. No matter. Obama has bigger ideas.

Back to the Democrats. The first part of his answer involves some boilerplate about the usual list of issues—education, health care, energy independence—peppered with deferential language about wanting to "be a part of the process." Then, he gets to the business about what makes him different: "Where I probably can make a unique contribution is in helping to bring people together and bridging what I call the 'empathy deficit,' helping to explain the disparate factions in this country and to show them how we're joined together, helping bridge divides between black and white, rich and poor, even conservative and liberal." Later, in a similar vein: "The story that I'm interested in telling is how we can restore that sense of commitment to each other in a way that doesn't inhibit our individual freedoms, doesn't diminish individual responsibility, but does promote collective responsibility."

Obama wants nothing less than to redefine progressive values, make them more universal, and unite the country around them. His staggering 72 percent approval rating in Illinois—a number that reflects strong support not only in and around Democratic Chicago, but from Republican downstate as well—shows he may be figuring out how to do that. His first year in the Senate suggests a man on a long, ambitious, and intricate journey. It's not too much to say that the future of the Democratic Party, and maybe even the country, could be profoundly affected by where that journey ends.

Like any freshman, Obama didn't know exactly how to get around in the Senate. But unlike any freshman, save Hillary Clinton in 2001, he came to town with a national platform. All eyes were on him, and hopes, particularly among liberals, ran high. Obama took things slowly at first. He didn't want to arrive in Washington looking "too big for his britches," says his communications director, Robert Gibbs. So he turned down repeated invitations to appear on national talk shows (and most of the 300 or so solicitations he received each week) and focused instead on such issues as veterans' disability pay and money for locks and dams back home. He wanted to demonstrate to the people of Illinois that he was working for them, and to his fellow senators that he was "not just a show horse," said his political consultant, David Axelrod.

He surrounded himself with people experienced in Senate protocol and procedure. He hired as his chief of staff Pete Rouse, who for years held the same position for former Senate Democratic Leader Tom Daschle. He took the unusual step of hiring a policy adviser, nabbing Karen Kornbluh, who had been deputy chief of staff to Treasury Secretary Robert Rubin. But even with a star staff, Obama has moved slowly; one senior aide told me that if Obama has one regret about his first year in office, it is that he occasionally has been "late to pull the trigger." A case in point is an immigration bill sponsored by Edward M. Kennedy and John McCain. The two Senate titans asked Obama early in his term if he wanted to sign on to the bill as a cosponsor. Brushing aside the advice of his staff, he declined, saying he hadn't had a hand in crafting the bill. It was only in December, after it became clear that immigration would be a hot topic in 2006, that he attached his name to the legislation. At the same time, he told Kennedy he would like to strengthen the section on border security by adding some measures from a Republican bill.

His concern about border security shows a side of Obama that occasionally has taken some liberals by surprise. It would be far too strong to say that he's been heterodox—after all, he has voted for the liberal position the vast majority of the time, and the initiatives and bills he has emphasized in his year have been solidly progressive. But he has thrown enough curves to keep people guessing.

When George W. Bush nominated Condoleeza Rice as secretary of state last January, Obama resisted pressure from liberal groups and civil rights advocates and voted for her confirmation. In that case, he was with most of his fellow Democrats in backing Rice. But two weeks later, when the Senate voted on a Republican bill to limit class-action lawsuits, Obama was one of 17 Democrats to oppose the trial lawyers—who contributed more than any other special interest to his 2004 campaign—and support the bill. He said at the time that he remained a "strong believer" in class-action lawsuits, and he briefly explained why he supported a bill that would move more of the suits from state to federal court. "When multimillion-dollar settlements are handed down and all the victims get are coupons for a free product, justice is not being served," he said in a statement. "And when cases are tried in counties only because it's known that those judges will award big payoffs, you get quick settlements without ever finding out who's right and who's wrong."

Obama sided against many of his natural allies on that vote, including labor, consumer and civil-rights groups, and environmentalists. Yet, the fallout (or lack of it) demonstrates that he has a way of communicating with people so that these breaches never grow into outright rifts. Todd Smith, immediate past president of the Association of Trial Lawyers of America (ATLA) and a Chicago lawyer, paid a visit to Obama shortly after the Senate passed the bill. Smith told Obama how disappointed he was that Obama voted for legislation the trial lawyers considered to be bad for "regular Americans." Obama told Smith he was unhappy with mailers the group distributed throughout Illinois saying he was "depriving poor people of the right to go to court," according to one of his senior aides.

"It was quite open," Smith recalled. "He said, 'Todd, go right ahead, speak your mind.' And I did. He believed there needed to be changes and, on balance, he felt it was the right way to go." Smith, who chairs the Board of Trustees of ATLA's political action committee, said he intends to continue to back Obama with campaign contributions. "I don't think your support for somebody rises or falls on a single issue. He will be there for regular people and their rights the vast majority of the time and when he's not, it's going to be, at least in his mind I'm certain, for solid reasons," Smith told me. "He's an outstanding U.S. senator already."

Obama almost goes out of his way sometimes to challenge members of his own party and their loyalists. In a move that was highly unusual for a sitting senator, he took to the blogosphere last fall to confront progressives who criticized two other Democrats for voting to confirm John Roberts as chief justice of the Supreme Court. Although Obama opposed Roberts, he defended his colleagues, Patrick Leahy of Vermont and Russ Feingold of Wisconsin, during a frank exchange on Daily Kos—the largest liberal Web site and home to the ferocious "Kossacks," who usually lambaste politicians who deviate from the accepted line.

What Obama wrote speaks volumes about his political philosophy and independent streak: ". . . to the degree that we brook no dissent within the Democratic Party, and demand fealty to the one, 'true' progressive vision for the country, we risk the very thoughtfulness and openness to new ideas that are required to move this country forward. When we lash out at those who share our fundamental values because they have not met the criteria of every single item on our progressive 'checklist,' then we are essentially preventing them from thinking in new ways about problems. We are tying them up in a straightjacket and forcing them into a conversation only with the converted. Beyond that, by applying such tests, we are hamstringing our ability to build a majority. We won't be able to transform the country with such a polarized electorate."

Markos Moulitsas Zúniga, the site's proprietor—sounding not unlike the ATLA's Smith—said the main reaction among site visitors was one of "gratitude." "He didn't come to pander, but to take a stand that might not have been all that popular with a certain segment of the community," Moulitsas says. "That showed a level of leadership that is oftentimes missing in a party more afraid to offend than in taking principled stands on issues."

These deviations from the script have caused some concern. One leader of the progressive wing of the Democratic Party said he thought Obama was demonstrating a "Clinton sensibility" by standing up to liberals. The leader, who asked not to be identified because of his relationship with the senator, said Obama did not take on centrists when they wanted to purge the party of anti-war liberals. "That's defining himself as Hillary Clinton defines herself—as needing to get to the center—which I think is a mistake in strategy, but one that he is flirting with," the leader said. Obama ran as an anti-war candidate. [In] November [2005], after a small number of his colleagues had begun calling for a quick withdrawal, he told the Chicago Council on Foreign Relations that "U.S. forces are still a part of the solution in Iraq" and came out for a phased withdrawal. He reiterated the message from Iraq in January [2006].

Obama told me he viewed the give-and-take on Daily Kos as a "teachable moment" and rebuffed the notion that he was trying to score political points. "What I want to be able to do if possible, and it's not always possible, is to engage people who disagree with me in a dialogue," he said. "One of the assumptions I think that a lot of progressives in a sort of knee-jerk way make is that if you stray from the progressive orthodoxy then you automatically must be doing it for political reasons—that you must either be getting campaign contributions from somebody, or you're positioning for national office, or you're a wimp, right? They never assume that you just don't agree with them on something. And so part of what I like to do is at least try to dispel that cynicism about motives."

• • •

It may be that the very universality of his personal appeal prevents Obama from appearing, or wanting to be, overtly ideological—as if his life story and his gift for connecting with people are too large to be categorized. He clearly wants to be thought of differently, as too complex to be encompassed by one label. When I ask if he's liberal, progressive, or centrist, he says: "I like to think I'm above it. Only in the sense that I just don't like how the categories are set up." He describes two common Democratic caricatures: the "DLC-centrist-Joe Lieberman–Al From types" and the "old-time-religion-Ted Kennedy-die-hard-liberal types."

"There are dangers in both camps," he continues. "Sometimes the DLC camp seems to want to run to the center no matter how far right the Republican Party has moved the debate—that sense of 'let's cut a deal no matter what the deal is.' The old-time-religion school sometimes seems unreflective and is unwilling to experiment or update old programs to meet new challenges.

"And the way I would describe myself is I think that my values are deeply rooted in the progressive tradition, the values of equal opportunity, civil rights, fighting for working families, a foreign policy that is mindful of human rights, a strong belief in civil liberties, wanting to be a good steward for the environment, a sense that the government has an important role to play, that opportunity is open to all people and that the powerful don't trample on the less powerful . . . I share all the aims of a Paul Wellstone or a Ted Kennedy when it comes to the end result. But I'm much more agnostic, much more flexible on how we achieve those ends."

And yet, for all these demurrals, when he finally did decide to occupy the spotlight last year [2005], it was on a tried-and-true liberal issue. After Hurricane Katrina hit in August [2005], Obama decided that it was time to speak out. As the Senate's only African American and as someone who had worked on poverty issues, he knew people would be looking to him for leadership. He traveled to Houston with former Presidents George H. W. Bush and Clinton. He went on ABC's *This Week*. "Whoever was in charge of planning was so detached from the realities of inner-city life in New Orleans . . . that they couldn't conceive of the notion that [residents] couldn't load up their SUVs, put $100 worth of gas in there, put some sparkling water, and drive off to a hotel and check in with a credit card," he snapped. But he later said Democrats must accept some of the blame because they, too, had downplayed poverty as a national issue. . . .

On other issues, too, Obama has stuck close to the traditional liberal line. Just two months into his term, he became the first senator to speak out on avian flu, spearheading an effort to spend $25 million to prevent a pandemic. In November [2005], he introduced a bill that would help underwrite health-care costs for automakers that produce fuel-efficient cars. And, invoking a pragmatic political strategy, he has repeatedly teamed up with Republicans to accomplish worthwhile goals. He has worked with the ultraconservative Tom Coburn of Oklahoma to stop the Bush administration from awarding no-bid contracts for post-Katrina reconstruction projects. Most notably, Obama has developed a particularly close relationship with Indiana's Richard Lugar, the well-regarded chairman of the Foreign Relations Committee. The two inspected nuclear and biological weapons sites in the former Soviet Union [in] August [2005], then cosponsored a bill to reduce stockpiles of conventional weapons.

Obama thinks Democrats need to talk more concretely about health care, energy, globalization, and education. . . . Beyond that, he says, they need to address the values problem.

"I do think that there's a strain of the Democratic Party—it's not uniform—that is somewhat patronizing towards people who go to church," says Obama, who attends the Trinity United Church of Christ in Chicago, which is Congregationalist, and keeps a Bible in his car. "If you go to a black evangelical church, there may be traditions that secular humanists might be uncomfortable with—hoopin' and hollerin', wavin' and dancin,'" he says, purposefully slipping into the vernacular. But, he says, the preachers and the parishioners are talking about the same things that Democratic leaders are: "They're talking about health care and looking after our seniors and trying to salvage young men from going into the prison system. So there's nothing alien about it. And yet sometimes, the Democratic Party, I think, just assumes that as long as people are in church that somehow we can't reach them, that we have nothing in common. That's simply not true and certainly hasn't been true historically."

There is also a strain of the Democratic Party—and a broad one—that is promoting Obama as the party's savior. "He represents the future of the party for a lot of people, which is good because a lot of people question whether we have a future as a party," said strategist Jenny Backus.

Harold Ickes, a high-ranking White House aide under President Clinton and 2000 campaign adviser to Hillary Clinton, said Obama is poised to speak to issues that "have gotten short shrift in the past two decades among progressive Democrats," like poverty and income distribution. "He's a powerful spokesman and he comes into Washington fresh, not encumbered by Washington mentality," Ickes said. "He certainly has the capacity to speak out on issues and get attention. And that's no small accomplishment. . . . I personally have high hopes for him."

Senator Dick Durbin, Obama's Illinois partner and the second-ranking Democrat in the Senate, has no doubt about the future of his state's most popular politician. "He's an odds-on favorite to run for higher office," Durbin predicts. "If you are a personal investment banker, you certainly want to invest in the Barack Obama IPO. . . . It is a solid investment in the American political scene."

It's ironic, all this talk, given that his party didn't even want him in the first place. . . . In any case, his party can't get enough of him now. Obama has bolstered his status within his party by raising huge amounts of cash for his colleagues' campaigns. His political action committee, Hopefund, raised an estimated $1.8 million in 2005. That doesn't count the millions he has raised for and donated to the Democratic Senatorial Campaign Committee and to individual candidates. In one night alone last fall [2005], he raised $1 million for the Arizona Democratic Party by drawing 1,400 people to a dinner. And with one e-mail, Obama raised $800,000 for Senator Robert Byrd of West Virginia, a powerhouse who first was elected to the Senate nearly three years before Obama was born. ■

[Obama declared his candidacy for the 2008 Democratic presidential nomination in February 2007.]

Chapter 10

The Presidency

At first glance, the American presidency is the most powerful office in the world. To the president's vast formal powers are added extraordinary informal powers: to lead Congress, to cope with emergency situations, to take charge of world affairs. The president's constitutional authority, broad and expansive, is supplemented by huge delegations of power from Congress and by the power that comes from the prestige of the office itself.

Yet for all his powers, the president is boxed in by limitations of every kind. He must share his constitutional authority with Congress, with which he must continually negotiate and bargain, and with the federal courts, which he can influence only uncertainly and, usually, only in the long run. His own cabinet officials often have their own political bases and their own agendas, and even his personal staff may become ambitious and unreliable. He must spend much of his first term preparing for reelection, and all of his second term, if he has one, with the knowledge that the Constitution forbids him from running again.

Both the extent and limits of presidential power were amply displayed in the aftermath of the terrorist attacks of September 11, 2001. In the hours and days after the event, as David Frum describes in selection 10.6, millions in America and around the world turned to George W. Bush for leadership and reassurance. Acting both on his own authority and by providing decisive leadership to Congress, Bush waged war in Afghanistan, rounded up thousands of terrorist suspects, and conducted clandestine operations against terrorist operations across the globe. He set forth a bold agenda in both foreign and domestic policy, and watched as his public approval rating soared toward 90 percent.

But as the months and years passed, the limits of Bush's power began to show. In 2005 and 2006, the Supreme Court ruled against Bush's policies regarding the legal status of enemy combatants, holding that detainees were entitled to certain rights under law. Congress likewise woke from its slumber, raising concerns about the administration's attitude toward the Geneva Convention and toward harsh treatment (or torture) of terrorism suspects. As the war in Iraq dragged on, Bush's approval ratings fell dramatically, and his party was soundly defeated in the 2006 midterm elections.

The readings in this chapter share a common theme: they present the paradox of a president whose immense resources are not always sufficient to perform the tasks expected of him by the American people and the world. Selection 10.1, which is drawn from the *Federalist Papers*, provides the classic justification for a strong and unitary presidency. Selection 10.2, by political scientist Richard Neustadt, argues that the informal powers of the presidency are as important to consider as are his formal powers. In selection 10.3, political scientist Jeffrey Tulis examines the tension between the president's relatively narrow legal powers and the vast powers he can exercise by leveraging his informal powers. Selections 10.4 and 10.5 examine the controversy over presidential signing statements, while selection 10.6 presents an inside account of life in the White House on the day of the terrorist attacks on America.

Chapter Questions

1. What are the sources of the president's formal authority? His informal authority?
2. Consider Richard Neustadt's argument (in selection 10.2) that a president's real power comes from his ability to bargain and persuade effectively. What examples of bargaining and persuading can be found in this chapter? Consider the president's foreign affairs power, his dealings with Congress, and his relationship with his own staff, for starters.
3. The presidency, some suggest, is an eighteenth-century office forced to function in a twentieth-first-century world. How has the presidency adjusted to the extraordinary political, social, and technological changes of the past two hundred years? Has this adaptation been successful? Explain.

 Foundations

The Framers of the Constitution recognized the importance of a unitary executive. Legislative bodies could deliberate and plan policy in the long run, perhaps, but only a unitary executive could act with the speed, decisiveness, and, when appropriate, secretiveness necessary for effective leadership. These qualities were especially important, the Framers believed, in matters of foreign and military policy.

Americans are so used to a strong presidency that it is easy to forget how much opposition there was in the beginning to such an office. The opponents of the Constitution feared that the presidency would quickly be transformed into an oppressive monarchy (the Articles of Confederation, remember, had no federal executive). They feared the Constitution's broad grants of legislative power to the president (especially the veto power and the power to make treaties), the commander-in-chief clause, and the president's power to appoint the federal judiciary.

Alexander Hamilton's strong defense of presidential power in *Federalist* No. 70 is a clear indication that the Framers favored both efficiency and liberty, and indeed believed that one was impossible without the other. In *Federalist* No. 68, for example, Hamilton defends the mode of appointment of the president; he suggests that the indirect scheme the Framers designed would ensure to a "moral certainty that the office of

President will seldom fall to the lot of any man who is not in an eminent degree endowed with the requisite qualifications."*

Yet the Antifederalists' fears were not wholly unfounded. Maintaining the balance between a presidency strong enough to do what is required yet constrained enough to be controlled by the people remains a difficult, and daunting, task. The president's only hope of governing under such circumstances, as political scientist Richard Neustadt suggests, is to rely not only on his formal powers, but also on his informal powers—especially his power to bargain with and persuade his friends, his opponents, and the American people.

Questions

1. Why is a unitary executive necessary, according to Hamilton? What characteristics does a single individual possess that a body of individuals—Congress, for example—lacks?
2. Have Hamilton's arguments become stronger or weaker over the past two hundred years? Has the modern presidency borne out his views or those of his opponents?
3. What advantages does a president have in the bargaining process, according to Richard Neustadt? Does he have any significant advantages or disadvantages in dealing with Congress? With the bureaucracy? With the American people?

10.1 *Federalist* No. 70 (1788)

Alexander Hamilton

Outline

I. The importance and components of strength and energy in the executive branch.
   A. A strong and energetic executive branch requires unity, duration in office, adequate resources, and sufficient powers.
II. Defense of a unitary (one-person) executive rather than a council.
   A. Importance of limiting dissension and disagreement with the executive branch.
   B. Importance of being able to fix responsibility within the executive branch.

There is an idea, which is not without its advocates, that a vigorous executive is inconsistent with the genius of republican government. The enlightened well-wishers to this species of government must at least hope that the supposition is destitute of foundation; since they can never admit its

*Alexander Hamilton, *Federalist* No. 68.

truth, without at the same time admitting the condemnation of their own principles. Energy in the executive is a leading character in the definition of good government. It is essential to the protection of the community against foreign attacks; it is not less essential to the steady administration of the laws; to the protection of property against those irregular and high-handed combinations which sometimes interrupt the ordinary course of justice; to the security of liberty against the enterprises and assaults of ambition, of faction, and of anarchy. Every man the least conversant in Roman history knows how often that republic was obliged to take refuge in the absolute power of a single man, under the formidable title of dictator, as well against the intrigues of ambitious individuals who aspired to the tyranny, and the seditions of whole classes of the community whose conduct threatened the existence of all government, as against the invasions of external enemies who menaced the conquest and destruction of Rome.

There can be no need, however, to multiply arguments or examples on this head. A feeble executive implies a feeble execution of the government. A feeble execution is but another phrase for a bad execution; and a government ill executed, whatever it may be in theory, must be, in practice, a bad government.

Taking it for granted, therefore, that all men of sense will agree in the necessity of an energetic executive, it will only remain to inquire, what are the ingredients which constitute this energy? How far can they be combined with those other ingredients which constitute safety in the republican sense? And how far does this combination characterize the plan which has been reported by the convention?

The ingredients which constitute energy in the executive are unity; duration; an adequate provision for its support; and competent powers.

The ingredients which constitute safety in the republican sense are a due dependence on the people and a due responsibility.

Those politicians and statesmen who have been the most celebrated for the soundness of their principles and for the justness of their views have declared in favor of a single executive and a numerous legislature. They have, with great propriety, considered energy as the most necessary qualification of the former, and have regarded this as most applicable to power in a single hand; while they have, with equal propriety, considered the latter as best adapted to deliberation and wisdom, and best calculated to conciliate the confidence of the people and to secure their privileges and interests.

That unity is conducive to energy will not be disputed. Decision, activity, secrecy, and dispatch will generally characterize the proceedings of one man in a much more eminent degree than the proceedings of any greater number; and in proportion as the number is increased, these qualities will be diminished.

• • •

Whenever two or more persons are engaged in any common enterprise or pursuit, there is always danger of difference of opinion. If it be a public trust or office in which they are clothed with equal dignity and authority, there is peculiar danger of personal emulation and even animosity. From either, and especially from all these causes, the most bitter dissensions are apt to spring. Whenever these happen, they lessen the respectability, weaken the authority, and distract the plans and operations of those whom they divide. If they should unfortunately assail the supreme executive magistracy of a country, consisting of a plurality of persons, they might impede or frustrate the most important measures of the government in the most critical emergencies of the state. And what is still worse, they might split the community into the most violent and irreconcilable factions, adhering differently to the different individuals who composed the magistracy.

Men often oppose a thing merely because they have had no agency in planning it, or because it may have been planned by those whom they dislike. But if they have been consulted, and have happened to disapprove, opposition then becomes, in their estimation, an indispensable duty of self-love. They seem to think themselves bound in honor, and by all the motives of personal infallibility, to defeat the success of what has been resolved upon contrary to their sentiments. Men of upright, benevolent tempers have too many opportunities of remarking, with horror, to what desperate lengths this disposition is sometimes carried, and how often the great interests of society are sacrificed to the vanity, to the conceit, and to the obstinacy of individuals, who have credit enough to make their passions and their caprices interesting to mankind. Perhaps the question now before the public may, in its consequences, afford melancholy proofs of the effects of this despicable frailty, or rather detestable vice, in the human character.

Upon the principles of a free government, inconveniences from the source just mentioned must necessarily be submitted to in the formation of the legislature; but it is unnecessary, and therefore unwise, to introduce them into the constitution of the executive. It is here too that they may be most pernicious. In the legislature, promptitude of decision is oftener an evil than a benefit. The differences of opinion, and the jarring of parties in that department of the government, though they may sometimes obstruct salutary plans, yet often promote deliberation and circumspection, and serve to check excesses in the majority. When a resolution too is once taken, the opposition must be at an end. That resolution is a law, and resistance to it punishable. But no favorable circumstances palliate or atone for the disadvantages of dissension in the executive department. Here they are pure and unmixed. There is no point at which they cease to operate. They serve to embarrass and weaken the execution of the plan or measure to which they relate, from the first step to the final conclusion of it. They constantly counteract those qualities in the executive which are the most necessary ingredients in its composition—vigor and expedition, and this without any counterbalancing good. In the conduct of war, in which the energy of the executive is the bulwark of the national security, everything would be to be apprehended from its plurality. . . .

But one of the weightiest objections to a plurality in the executive, and which lies as much against the last as the first plan is that it tends to conceal faults and destroy responsibility. Responsibility is of two kinds—to censure and to punishment. The first is the more important of the two, especially in an elective office. Men in public trust will much oftener act in such a manner as to render them unworthy of being any longer trusted, than in such a manner as to make them obnoxious to legal punishment. But the multiplication of the executive adds to the difficulty of detection in either case. It often becomes impossible, amidst mutual accusations, to determine on whom the blame or the punishment of a pernicious measure, or series of pernicious measures, ought really to fall. It is shifted from one to another with so much dexterity, and under such plausible appearances, that the public opinion is left in suspense about the real author. The circumstances which may have led to any national miscarriage or misfortune are sometimes so complicated that where there are a number of actors who may have had different degrees and kinds of agency, though we may clearly see upon the whole that there has been mismanagement, yet it may be impracticable to pronounce to whose account the evil which may have been incurred is truly chargeable. . . . ■

10.2 Presidential Power (1960)

Richard E. Neustadt

The separateness of institutions and the sharing of authority prescribe the terms on which a President persuades. When one man shares authority with another, but does not gain or lose his job upon the other's whim, his willingness to act upon the urging of the other turns on whether he conceives the action right for him. The essence of a President's persuasive task is to convince such men that what the White House wants of them is what they ought to do for their sake and on their authority.

Persuasive power, thus defined, amounts to more than charm or reasoned argument. These have their uses for a President, but these are not the whole of his resources. For the men he would induce to do what he wants done on their own responsibility will need or fear some acts by him on his responsibility. If they share his authority, he has some share in theirs. Presidential "powers" may be inconclusive when a President commands, but always remain relevant as he persuades. The status and authority inherent in his office reinforce his logic and his charm.

Status adds something to persuasiveness; authority adds still more. When Truman urged wage changes on his Secretary of Commerce while the latter was administering the steel mills, he and Secretary Sawyer were not just two men reasoning with one another. Had they been so, Sawyer probably would never have agreed to act. Truman's status gave him special claims to Sawyer's loyalty, or at least attention. In Walter Bagehot's charming phrase "no man can *argue* on his knees." Although there is no kneeling in this country, few men—and exceedingly few Cabinet officers—are immune to the impulse to say "yes" to the President of the United States. It grows harder to say "no" when they are seated in his oval office at the White House, or in his study on the second floor, where almost tangibly he partakes of the aura of his physical surroundings. In Sawyer's case, moreover, the President possessed formal authority to intervene in many matters of concern to the Secretary of Commerce. These matters ranged from jurisdictional disputes among the defense agencies to legislation pending before Congress and, ultimately, to the tenure of the Secretary, himself. There is nothing in the record to suggest that Truman voiced specific threats when they negotiated over wage increases. But given his *formal* powers and their relevance to Sawyer's other interests, it is safe to assume that Truman's very advocacy of wage action conveyed an implicit threat.

A President's authority and status give him great advantages in dealing with the men he would persuade. Each "power" is a vantage point for him in the degree that other men have use for his authority. From the veto to appointments, from publicity to budgeting, and so down a long list, the White House now controls the most encompassing array of vantage points in the American political system. With hardly an exception, the men who share in governing this country are aware that at some time, in some degree, the doing of *their* jobs, the furthering of *their* ambitions, may depend upon the President of the United States. Their need for presidential action, or their fear of it, is bound to be recurrent if not actually continuous. Their need or fear is his advantage.

A President's advantages are greater than mere listing of his "powers" might suggest. The men with whom he deals must deal with him until the last day of his term. Because they have continuing relationships with him, his future, while it lasts, supports his present influence. Even though there is no need or fear of him today, what he could do tomorrow may supply today's advantage. Continuing relationships may convert any "power," any aspect of his status, into vantage points in almost any case. When he induces other men to do what he wants done, a President can trade on their dependence now *and* later.

The President's advantages are checked by the advantages of others. Continuing relationships will pull in both directions. These are relationships of mutual dependence. A President depends upon the men he would persuade; he has to reckon with his need or fear of them. They too will possess status, or authority, or both, else they would be of little use to him. Their vantage points confront his own; their power tempers his.

Persuasion is a two-way street. Sawyer, it will be recalled, did not respond at once to Truman's plan for wage increases at the steel mills. On the contrary, the Secretary hesitated and delayed and only acquiesced when he was satisfied that publicly he would not bear the onus of decision. Sawyer had some points of vantage all his own from which to resist presidential pressure. If he had to reckon with coercive implications in the President's "situations of strength," so had Truman to be mindful of the implications underlying Sawyer's place as a department head, as steel administrator, and as a Cabinet spokesman for business. Loyalty is reciprocal. Having taken on a dirty job in the steel crisis, Sawyer had strong claims to loyal support. Besides, he had authority to do some things that the White House could ill afford. Emulating Wilson, he might have resigned in a huff (the removal power also works two ways). Or emulating Ellis Arnall, he might have declined to sign necessary orders. Or, he might have let it be known publicly that he deplored what he was told to do and protested its doing. By following any of these courses Sawyer almost surely would have strengthened the position of management, weakened the position of the White House, and embittered the union. But the whole purpose of a wage increase was to enhance White House persuasiveness in urging settlement upon union and companies alike. Although Sawyer's status and authority did not give him the power to prevent an increase outright, they gave him capability to undermine its purpose. If his authority over wage rates had been vested by a statute, not by revocable presidential order, his power of prevention might have been complete. So Harold Ickes demonstrated in the famous case of helium sales to Germany before the Second World War.

The power to persuade is the power to bargain. Status and authority yield bargaining advantages. But in a government of "separated institutions sharing powers," they yield them to all sides. With the array of vantage points at his disposal, a President may be far more persuasive than his logic or his charm could make him. But outcomes are not guaranteed by his advantages. ■

 # American Politics Today

Presidential power, according to political scientist Jeffrey K. Tulis, is based on two "constitutions." The first—with a capital "C"—is the Constitution written and ratified in the 1780s. Presidents who govern under this first Constitution can draw on the formal powers of the office, but must share power with Congress and the Supreme Court. The second constitution is informal, and is based on "continuous presidential leadership of public opinion"; its first and foremost advocate was President Woodrow Wilson. Presidential power under the second constitution can be virtually unlimited, especially in times of crisis, but can shrink rapidly if the public mood changes. The first Constitution relies primarily on legal authority, the second on political rhetoric.

Modern presidents can draw on either constitution as they think best. During the Clinton impeachment proceedings, for example, the White House retreated into the comfort of the first Constitution. After September 11, 2001, by contrast, President George W. Bush put his trust in the second constitution. As he built his case for the war in Iraq, Bush reached out for support to the American people. In doing so, Bush was forced to oversimplify, or distort, the case for war. The president's ensuing loss of credibility, Tulis argues, was a "by-product of a second constitution that lives in tension with the first."

Questions

1. What does Tulis mean by the "two constitutional presidencies"? What is the origin and nature of the first constitutional presidency? The second constitutional presidency?
2. What are the strengths and weaknesses of presidential reliance on the first constitutional presidency? The second constitutional presidency? Under what circumstances would the president be well advised to rely on one or the other of the two constitutional presidencies?

10.3 The Two Constitutional Presidencies (2006)

Jeffrey K. Tulis

The modern presidency is buffeted by two "constitutions." Presidential action continues to be constrained, and presidential behavior shaped, by the institutions created by the original Constitution. The core structures established in 1789 and debated during the founding era remain essentially unchanged. For the most part, later amendments to the Constitution have left intact the basic features of the executive, legislative, and judicial branches of government. Great questions, such as the merits of unity or plurality in the executive, have not been seriously reopened. Because most of the structure persists, it seems plausible that the theory on which the presidency was constructed remains relevant to its current functioning.

Presidential and public understanding of the constitutional system and of the president's place in it have changed, however. This new understanding is the "second constitution" under which presidents attempt to govern. Central to this second constitution is a view of statecraft that is in tension with the original Constitution—indeed it is opposed to the Founders' understanding of the presidency's place in the political system. The second constitution, which puts a premium on active and continuous presidential leadership of popular opinion, is buttressed by several institutional, albeit extraconstitutional, developments. These include the proliferation of presidential primaries as a mode of selection and the emergence of the mass media as a pervasive force.

Many of the dilemmas and frustrations of the modern presidency may be traced to the president's ambiguous constitutional station, a vantage place composed of conflicting elements.

• • •

Both constitutions were designed to encourage and support an energetic president, but they differ over the legitimate sources and alleged virtues of popular leadership. For the Founders, presidents draw their energy from their authority. Their authority rests on their independent constitutional position. For Woodrow Wilson and for presidents ever since, power and authority are conferred directly by the people. *The Federalist* and the Constitution proscribe [prohibit] popular leadership. Wilson prescribed it. Indeed, he urged the president to minister continually to the moods of the people as a preparation for action. The Founders' president was to look to the people, but less frequently, and to be judged by them, but usually after acting.

The second constitution gained legitimacy because presidents were thought to lack the resources necessary for the energy promised but not delivered by the first.

From Jeffrey K. Tulis, "The Two Constitutional Presidencies," in Michael Nelson, ed., *The Presidency and the Political System*, 8th ed. Copyright © 2006 CQ Press, a division of Congressional Quarterly, Inc. Reprinted by permission of the publisher, CQ Press.

The second constitution did not replace the first, however. Because many of the founding structures persist, while our understanding of the president's legitimate role has changed, the new view should be thought of as superimposed on the old, altering without obliterating the original structure.

Many commentators have noted the tendency of recent presidents to raise public expectations about what they can achieve. Indeed, public disenchantment with government altogether may stem largely from disappointment in presidential performance, inasmuch as the presidency is the most visible and important American political institution. Yet, rather than being the result of the personality traits of particular presidents, raised expectations are grounded in an institutional dilemma common to all modern presidents. Under the auspices of the second constitution, presidents must continually craft rhetoric that pleases their popular audience. Even though presidents are always in a position to promise more, the only additional resource they have to make good on their promises is public opinion itself. Because Congress retains the independent status conferred on it by the first Constitution, it can resist the president.

Naturally, presidents who are exceptionally popular or gifted as orators can overcome the resistance of the legislature. For the political system as a whole, this possibility is both good and bad. To the extent that the system requires periodic renewal through synoptic [comprehensive] policies that reconstitute the political agenda, it is good. But the very qualities that are necessary to achieve such large-scale change tend to subvert the deliberative process, which makes unwise legislation or incoherent policy more likely.

Ronald Reagan's major political victories as president illustrate both sides of this systemic dilemma. On the one hand, without the second constitution it would be difficult to imagine Reagan's success at winning tax reform legislation. His skillful coordination of a rhetorical and a legislative strategy overcame the resistance of thousands of lobbies that sought to preserve advantageous provisions of the existing tax code. Similarly, Social Security and other large policies that were initiated by Franklin D. Roosevelt during the New Deal may not have been possible without the second constitution.

On the other hand, Reagan's first budget victory in 1981 and the Strategic Defense Initiative (SDI, also known as Star Wars) illustrate how popular leadership can subvert the deliberative process or produce incoherent policy. The budget cuts of 1981 were secured with virtually no congressional debate. Among their effects was the gutting of virtually all of the Great Society programs initiated by Lyndon B. Johnson, which themselves were the product of a popular campaign that circumvented the deliberative process.

When Congress does deliberate, as it has on SDI, the debate is often structured by contradictory forms of rhetoric, the product of the two constitutions. The arguments presidents make to the people are different from those they make to Congress. To the people, President Reagan promised to strive for a new defense technology that would make nuclear deterrence obsolete. But to Congress, his administration argued that SDI was needed to supplement, not supplant, deterrence. Each kind of argument can be used to impeach the other. Jimmy Carter found himself in the same bind on energy policy. When he urged the American people to support his energy plan, Carter contended that it was necessary to remedy an existing crisis. But to Congress he argued that the same policy was necessary to forestall a crisis.

The second constitution promises energy, which is said to be inadequately provided by the first. This suggests that the two constitutions fit together, to form a more complete whole. Unfortunately, over the long run, the tendency of the second constitution to make extraordinary power routine undermines, rather than completes, the logic of the original Constitution. Garry Wills has described how presidents since John F. Kennedy have attempted to pit public opinion against their own executive establishment. Successors to a charismatic leader then inherit "a delegitimated set of procedures" and are themselves compelled "to go outside of procedures—further delegitimating the very office they [hold]." In Reagan's case, this cycle was reinforced by an ideology opposed to big government. "In the present crisis," Reagan said at his first inaugural, "government is not the solution to our problem; government is the problem." Although fiascoes like the Iran-contra affair are not inevitable, they are made more likely by the logic and legitimacy of the second constitution.

It was hard to imagine that any leader would embrace the second constitution more than Reagan did, but Bill Clinton surpassed him. According to George Edwards,

> The Clinton presidency is the ultimate example of the rhetorical presidency—a presidency based on a perpetual campaign to obtain the public's support and fed by public opinion polls, focus groups, and public relations memos. No president ever invested more in measuring, and attempting to mold, public opinion. [This administration] even polled voters on where it was best for the First Family to vacation. This is an administration that spent $18 million on ads in 1995, a nonelection year! And this is an administration that repeatedly interpreted its setbacks, whether in elections or health care reform, in terms of its failure to communicate rather than in terms of the quality of its initiatives or the strategy for governing. Reflecting his orientation in the White House, Bill Clinton declared that "the role of the President of the United States is message."

The Clinton presidency was a roller coaster of political successes and failures. No doubt it will take scholars decades to make sense of Clinton's political choices and the public's reactions to them. No simple explanation is suitable to explain how this president, who was the head of his political party when the Democrats were badly defeated in 1994, rebounded so decisively in 1996, how he came to be impeached by the House in 1998 yet be acquitted by the Senate in 1999. A full analysis of these political undulations and their consequences for the polity would include, at a minimum, accounts of the president's character, his political acumen, the state of the economy and the world, and the actions of the Republican opposition. Without venturing to offer even the beginning of such an analysis, it may be helpful to suggest how the two constitutional presidencies may be a useful backdrop for a fuller narrative. The political dilemmas Clinton faced and the choices he made to contend with them are, at least in part, products of the uneasy conjunction of the two constitutions.

For example, the president's fidelity to the second constitution contributed to the most serious mistake that prompted the impeachment proceeding. Faced with an inquiry into his relationship with Monica Lewinsky, Clinton sought a rhetorical solution to his political difficulty. Oriented to the immediate demands of persuasion in a national plebiscite, Clinton relied on his bully pulpit. On the advice of his former pollster Dick Morris and friend and media adviser Harry Thomason, the president went on national television and forcefully denied that he had "sexual relations" with Lewinsky. That denial, more than the conduct it concealed, fueled congressional opposition and delegitimized his presidency in the eyes of many of his critics and even some of his allies.

Yet presidents are schooled by both constitutions even when they only consciously understand the second. President Carter discovered the Rose Garden strategy of retreating from public view when the demands of foreign policy placed him in a position to see the benefits of a political posture inherent to the first Constitution. Similarly, President Clinton rediscovered the first Constitution as the nation taught itself the constitutional meaning of impeachment.

As the impeachment drama unfolded, Clinton was uncharacteristically mute. He let his lawyers and other surrogates do the talking about impeachment-related matters while he attended to the nation's other business. The nation's resurrection of a nineteenth-century constitutional anachronism, impeachment, placed the president in a position from which he could see the political benefit of acting like a nineteenth-century president. Because the animating charge of the political opposition was that Clinton had disgraced his office—whether through his sexual behavior or his subsequent deceptions and alleged perjury—the president's conduct during the formal proceedings became a rhetorical or dramaturgical refutation of the main charge against him. The one exception to this presidential style, so characteristic of the first Constitution, seemed to prove its significance. When the president emerged from the White House to lead congressional allies in a show of support immediately following the House vote, he was severely criticized for politicizing a constitutional process. Clinton's conscious and seemingly instinctive understanding of leadership conflicted with the model of statesmanship inherent to the constitutional order. After that misstep, the president attempted to recapture the advantages that the dignity of the office provided him.

Although political circumstance encouraged President Clinton to rediscover the first Constitution, political crisis has led President George W. Bush to a more rhetorical presidency than would be his natural inclination. Bush is not a gifted orator. Like his father, he has difficulty expressing himself, is prone to misstatement, and seems unable to master the proper cadences of formal speech. Nevertheless, the terrorist attack on New York and Washington, Bush's response to it in Afghanistan, and his subsequent war against Iraq have required him to lead. In this array of circumstances and responsibilities, one can see both the promise and the pitfall of presidential leadership under the auspices of two constitutions. Bush's response to the 9/11 terrorist attack shows how the president's traditional roles under the Constitution can be enhanced by modern rhetorical practices. His leadership of the nation into the war in Iraq reveals how the second constitution sometimes undermines the first.

In the wake of the terrorist attack on America, Bush found it necessary to deliver a number of speeches to a grieving nation. Because it was proper for the president to do this, even under the first Constitution, his words gained in politically constructed authority what they lacked in natural grace. The Constitution, its norms, institutions, and traditions, elevated an ordinary speaker to a station from which he was able to deliver extraordinarily effective leadership.

By contrast, Bush's case for war in Iraq did not respond to a widely felt crisis. Rather, the president tried to convince the nation that an unseen crisis existed. To do this he developed a public case for war that differed, at least in emphasis, from the real reasons that actually animated decision makers within the administration. The case for war with Iraq that prevailed within the administration stood on three basic grounds: the threat from weapons of mass destruction, Iraq's support of terrorism, and the brutality of Iraq's totalitarian practices on its own people. Taken together, these three reasons were all grounded in the nature of the Iraqi regime type and therefore were thought to necessitate regime change. Although all three were part of the public case for war, the threat of weapons of mass destruction was the one the administration stressed. When it became apparent that there were no such weapons, the president's policy was, in effect, hoisted by its own rhetorical petard. Bush's credibility was undermined by the rhetorical choices he made to speedily gain popular support for the war and to pressure Congress to authorize the use of force. His "deception" was not, as many commentators alleged, an intentional effort to lie to Congress, to the UN, or to the American people. Instead, it was an effort to simplify a complex argument to make it more rhetorically effective. The problem of credibility that now hounds the Bush administration is not his personality or moral character. Rather, it is a by-product of a second constitution that lives in tension with the first. ■

Issue and Controversy

What should the president do when Congress passes a law that he believes to be unconstitutional? In theory, the best response might be a veto, which (unless Congress can muster two-thirds majorities in both houses) would prevent the law from ever going into effect. But the veto is not always a realistic response. The president might object to only one provision in a very long bill, for example, and not want to endanger the whole for the sake of one part. Or the provision in question might be constitutional when applied in some circumstances, but not in others.

When faced with this dilemma, modern presidents have resorted with increasing frequency to the presidential signing statement. Under this approach, the president writes out his constitutional objections to the bill in question, but signs it anyway. The bill becomes law, but the president has laid the groundwork for his later refusal to obey the provision in question, or at least to challenge it in court.

Critics of presidential signing statements, such as legal scholar Neil Kinkopf, object to the procedure on the grounds that the president's refusal to obey the law violates his constitutional responsibility to "take care that the Laws be faithfully executed." When the president combines a refusal to obey the law with a broad interpretation of his own independent powers, Kinkopf argues, the rule of law is quickly eroded. Defenders of presidential signing statements, like Deputy Assistant Attorney General Michelle Boardman, dismiss such concerns. Signing statements, Boardman argues, are "an essential part of the constitutional dialogue between the branches that has been a part of the etiquette of government since the early days of the Republic."

Questions

1. Do presidential signing statements show contempt for the law and the Constitution, as Kinkopf suggests, or do they instead demonstrate a respect for the constitutional balance of power, as Boardman argues? Can these two very different views of signing statements be reconciled?
2. Do signing statements reflect what Jeffrey K. Tulis calls the "first constitutional presidency" or the second (see selection 10.3)? Both? Explain your views.

10.4 The Tension Between Presidential Signing Statements and the Rule of Law (2006)

Neil Kinkopf

Signing statements have been very much in the news lately. But this publicity has been as likely to engender confusion as understanding. In part this is because "signing statement" is used as a short-hand reference for two distinct issues: one issue has to do with whether and when the President may refuse to enforce a law that the President regards as unconstitutional; the other issue is whether the courts should take into account the views of the President when reviewing the legislative history of a statute. I propose to focus on the former issue because the current Bush Administration has so vigorously and frequently asserted the authority to refuse that the issue has taken on an immediate importance. . . .

Historically, signing statements have served a largely innocuous and ceremonial function. They are issued by the President to explain his reasons for signing a bill into law. A signing statement thus serves to promote public awareness and discourse in much the same way as a veto message. Controversy arises when a signing statement is used not to extol the virtues of the bill being signed into law, but to simultaneously condemn a provision of the new law as unconstitutional and announce the President's refusal to enforce the unconstitutional provision. This refusal to enforce laws represents a controversial exercise of presidential power, but it is crucial to keep this controversy distinct from the vehicle by which that power is announced—the signing statement. There is nothing inherently wrong with or controversial about signing statements. Most do not contain an assertion of presi-

---

From Neil Kinkopf, "Signing Statements and the President's Authority to Refuse to Enforce the Law," *American Constitution Society Issue Brief* (June 2006). Reprinted by permission of The American Constitution Society for Law and Policy, and the author.

dential power. For those that do, the signing statement itself ironically serves the laudable function of promoting accountability. Even if one rejects the idea that the President may refuse to enforce a law, at least the President is openly declaring what he plans to do. Put differently, if the President is to sign a bill into law with his fingers crossed, better that they be crossed where we can see them than that they be crossed behind his back. The controversy, then, is not over the use of signing statements but over the assertion of a non-enforcement power that is sometimes declared in signing statements.

The controversy over whether the President has the authority to refuse to enforce laws he views as unconstitutional has been sharpened during the current administration by the frequency with which it has asserted this authority. In a recent and important study, political science Professor Philip Cooper has analyzed the exercise of this non-enforcement power by the Bush Administration. He found that President Bush has deployed the non-enforcement power with unprecedented breadth and frequency—over 500 times during the first term alone. The figures from the study were updated in an excellent article by *Boston Globe* reporter Charlie Savage, which puts the number at over 750, which is more than all of President Bush's predecessors combined. As a result, a front page article in *USA Today* cataloging the ways in which the Bush Administration has sought to expand presidential power listed presidential non-enforcement (using the label "signing statements") first.

The Controversy

The assertion of a presidential power to refuse to enforce a law stands in deep tension with the Constitution. As the Supreme Court has repeatedly recognized, the Take Care Clause—which provides that the President "shall take care that the Laws be faithfully executed"—establishes that the President does not hold the royal prerogative of a dispensing power, which is the power to dispense with or suspend the execution of the laws. The Take Care Clause, then, makes plain that the President is duty-bound to enforce all the laws, whether he agrees with them or not.

A presidential power to refuse to enforce the laws is also inconsistent with the constitutional process for the enactment of legislation. . . . [T]he Constitution provides that a bill cannot become a law unless the President gives his assent. This assent must be given or withheld in whole, as the Supreme Court recently emphasized in striking down a statutory line-item veto. In *The Federalist*, James Madison describes the system of checks-and-balances. The President's principal weapon against legislative encroachments and against improvident legislation is his veto power. Under the Constitution's design, then, if the President regards a provision of a bill to be unconstitutional, the appropriate remedy is a veto.

The case against a presidential power of non-enforcement seems quite powerful. Yet Presidents of both parties have over the course of many years refused to enforce unconstitutional laws, including laws they themselves have signed into existence. How can this be? The explanation has both pragmatic and formal elements. As a practical matter, some legislation cannot be vetoed. Especially as Congress turns more and more to the use of omnibus legislation which encompasses many indispensable provisions—funding for the military, for example—it becomes practically impossible for even the most scrupulous President to veto a bill simply because one minor and obscure provision is unconstitutional. As a formal matter, Presidents do not typically assert the power to refuse to enforce a law. Rather, Presidents note that because the Constitution is also a law, they must enforce the Constitution by refusing to enforce an unconstitutional law. To take an uncontroversial example, the Supreme Court ruled all legislative vetoes unconstitutional in *INS* v. *Chadha* (1983). After the *Chadha* decision, no one has criticized the Presidents (of both parties) who have refused to enforce the thousands of legislative vetoes that remain on the books. Moreover, as Louis Fisher has pointed out, Congress has enacted hundreds of legislative vetoes since *Chadha*, and not even members of Congress expect the President to veto such legislation or to enforce the patently unconstitutional legislative veto provisions. The President complies with, rather than violates, his Take Care Clause duty by adhering to the Constitution's requirements and by refusing to apply the incompatible and unconstitutional law. The principled and fairly consistent (between the political parties) position of the executive branch boils down to this: where a statute is unconstitutional, it is the President's duty to refuse to enforce the unconstitutional statute.

The executive branch's position raises a difficult question: when is a statute unconstitutional? It is surely the case that when a statute is definitively determined to be unconstitutional, such a statute should not be enforced. But there are many occasions where a law's constitutionality is indeterminate. For example, a statute may raise a question that has not been squarely addressed by the courts. Or, if squarely addressed, the President may nevertheless believe that he can convince the court in a subsequent case to draw a distinction or overrule its precedent—as President Franklin Roosevelt did with respect to his New Deal legislation. What is the President to do when he regards a law to be unconstitutional, but for one reason or another, there is no definitive resolution to the question? This is the most difficult aspect of the controversy.

Resolving the Constitutional Tensions

Some commentators take an absolutist position: until a statute's unconstitutionality is definitively established, the President must enforce the statute. The absolutist position is contrary to longstanding and consistent executive branch practice dating at least to 1860. Moreover, the absolutist position fails to account for the complexities of how constitutional meaning is established. For example, the President's determination that he will enforce a law that he regards as unconstitutional will sometimes deprive the judiciary of the opportunity to rule on the question. Imagine, for example, that Congress enacts a statute (overriding the President's veto) that forbids the Justice Department to pursue any investigation or prosecution of [a member of Congress]. The President would almost certainly regard this statute as an unconstitutional encroachment on the prosecutorial discretion of the executive branch, but there is not sufficient precedent on the subject to predict with confidence what the Supreme Court would ultimately say. If the President were to order the Justice Department to comply with the statute and cease prosecution, there would be no occasion for the judiciary to rule on the constitutional question of whether the statute violates the constitutional powers of the executive. Similarly, had President Woodrow Wilson enforced the provisions of the Tenure in Office Act, there would have been no apparent basis for the lawsuit in which the Supreme Court ultimately declared the Act unconstitutional. Thus, the absolutist position can actually lead to a situation in which unconstitutional laws are enforced with no meaningful opportunity for judicial review.

If absolute enforcement is unacceptable, we must determine when it is appropriate for a President to decline to enforce a statute because the President regards the statue as unconstitutional. Walter Dellinger, writing as the head of the Justice Department's Office of Legal Counsel, set forth the classic treatment of this question in a memorandum for then-White House Counsel Abner Mikva. Dellinger concluded that "[a]s a general matter, if the President believes that the Court would sustain a particular provision as constitutional, the President should execute the statute, notwithstanding his own beliefs about the constitutional issue. If, however, the President, exercising his independent judgment, determines both that a provision would violate the Constitution and that it is probable that the Court would agree with him, the President has the authority to decline to execute the statute."

But Dellinger emphasized that this authority does not represent an unbounded discretion. Rather, in determining how to act, the President must pursue the course of action that takes account of and advances all the relevant aspects of constitutional structure. The decision will inevitably be dependent on the context of the specific case. In deciding whether to enforce a statute, the President should be guided by: "a careful weighing of the effect of compliance with the provision on the constitutional rights of affected individuals and on the executive branch's constitutional authority. Also relevant is the likelihood that compliance or noncompliance will permit judicial resolution of the issue." The decision is to be guided by close consideration of the effect of enforcement on individual rights, the constitutional balance of power between the branches, and the Supreme Court's "special role in resolving disputes about the constitutionality of enactments."

So formulated, the President does not enjoy a power to decline to enforce a law whenever he sees fit, or whenever he can articulate a constitutional objection (which practically may amount to the same thing). Take the application of the Dellinger principles in the Clinton Administration. In 1996, Congress passed as part of the annual military appropriation bill a provision requiring the discharge from military service of anyone with human immunodeficiency virus (HIV). The President believed that the HIV provision was unconstitutional but signed the bill into law because he could not deprive the military of the money it needed to operate (this coming on the heels of two government shutdowns). President Clinton decided to follow a two-pronged strategy. He would seek the repeal of the HIV provision and, failing repeal, he would enforce the provision in order to secure a judicial resolution of the controversy. Threatened with the prospect of judicial rebuke, Congress repealed the HIV provision.

Disregard for the Constitution

The Bush Administration's approach is in stark contrast with the Clinton Administration's. Far from a careful, contextual weighing of disparate constitutional factors framed by a respect for the special role of the Supreme Court in resolving constitutional issues, the Bush Administration has operated with a careless disregard for constitutional structure and has asserted its own raw power with contempt for the role of the Supreme Court. This is dramatically illustrated by the frequency with which the Bush Administration has articulated its intention not to enforce laws. The Bush Administration has not fought for the repeal of the more than 700 provisions it has identified as unconstitutional, much less has it carefully weighed the facts and circumstances of each of those instances. Indeed, a review of these objections shows that they are treated in a mechanical fashion, with boilerplate objections phrased over and over again in signing statements.

The contempt of the Bush Administration for constitutional limits on its own power is nowhere more evident than in the statement accompanying the signing of the McCain Amendment. The McCain Amendment forbids United States personnel from engaging in cruel, inhuman, and degrading treatment of detainees, adding these prohibitions to the existing prohibition on the use of torture. Upon signing the McCain Amendment into law, President Bush issued a statement declaring that the executive branch would interpret the McCain Amendment "in a manner consistent with the constitutional authority of the president to supervise the unitary executive branch and as Commander in Chief and consistent with the constitutional limitations on the judicial power. . . ." The President cannot have concluded that his view would likely be vindicated by the Court. The "unitary executive" view of presidential power is an extreme construction that lacks judicial sanction. Moreover, it is precisely this view that supported the Administration's infamous torture memo, which the Bush Administration itself pointedly refused to defend, and ultimately repudiated, after it became public.

It is even more remarkable that the language of the McCain Amendment signing statement is itself boilerplate. This "power to supervise the unitary executive" objection was raised, essentially verbatim, against 82 separate provisions of law during the first term of the Bush Administration alone, according to Professor Philip Cooper's study. This simply cannot be the result of a careful balancing of constitutional considerations. Moreover, the clinching phrase about the constitutional limitations of the judicial power speaks volumes about the Administration's contempt for the judiciary's role in constraining executive power, coming as it did on the heels of the Supreme Court's declaration in *Hamdi* v. *Rumsfeld* (2004) that "a state of war is not a blank check for the President. . . ."

These problems are not limited (if 82-and-counting occurrences can be called limited) to the President's construction of his own power as unitary executive. President Bush's arsenal includes boilerplate language for objecting to laws that he recommend legislation to Congress, that he disclose information to Congress or the public, that set qualifications for federal officeholders, or that so much as mention race. For example, the President signed into law a bill establishing an Institute of Education Sciences. The signing statement pertaining to this law raised a constitutional objection in what seems like a laudable and unobjectionable goal for the new institute: "closing the achievement gap between high-performing and low-performing children, especially achievement gaps between minority and non-minority children and between disadvantaged children and such children's more advantaged peers." The signing statement questions this provision's conformity with "the requirements of equal protection and due process under the Due Process Clause of the Fifth Amendment." There is no judicial precedent that would question the validity of this law under the Fifth—or any other—Amendment. Only under a radical and unsupported reconceptualization of the idea of equality could working to eliminate the achievement gap be considered constitutionally suspect. This is not the Dellinger paradigm of a President wrestling to resolve a conflict between statutory and constitutional law. The posture of the Bush Administration is that of an Administration that is wrestling to create conflicts in order to support the assertion of a power to dispense with the execution of the laws.

Because President Bush has found constitutional problems with statutes so readily and because he takes such a radically expansive view of his own power, President Bush's position amounts to a claim that he is impervious to the laws that Congress enacts. This amounts to the view articulated in President Richard Nixon's notorious dictum, "If the President does it, that means it is not illegal." Precisely to guard against such claims, Congress has enacted a law that requires the Attorney General to "submit to the Congress a report of any instance in which the Attorney General or any officer of the Department of Justice . . . establishes or implements a formal or informal policy to refrain . . . from enforcing, applying, or administering any provision of any Federal statute . . . whose enforcement, application, or administration is within the responsibility of the Attorney General or such officer on the grounds that such provision is unconstitutional." Subsection (e) of that statute extends this reporting obligation to the head of each executive agency or military department that implements such a policy of "constitutional noncompliance." Such a report must be made within 30 days after the policy is implemented, and must "include a complete and detailed statement of the relevant issues and background (including a complete and detailed statement of the reasons for the policy or determination)."

But President Bush apparently regards this reporting requirement, like so many others, to raise serious constitutional concerns. As such, he may be refusing to comply with it. If so, this represents a serious assault on the constitutional system of checks and balances. That system is premised on the idea that the President is not above the law but is, like all other citizens, bound to obey the law. The primary check that Congress has on the President is its power to legislate rules that govern everyone, including the President himself. This is the preeminent power in our constitutional system and explains why James Madison famously regarded Congress to be the most dangerous branch under our Constitution. If the President may dispense with application of laws by concocting a constitutional objection, we will quickly cease to live under the rule of law. ■

10.5 Presidential Signing Statements Maintain the Balance of Power (2006)

Michelle Boardman

. . . Presidents throughout history . . . have issued what may be called "constitutional" signing statements, and it is this use of the signing statement that has recently been the subject of public attention. Presidents are sworn to "preserve, protect, and defend the Constitution," and thus are responsible for ensuring that the manner in which they enforce acts of Congress is consistent with America's founding document. Presidents have long used signing statements for the purpose of "informing Congress and the public that the Executive believes that a particular provision would be unconstitutional in certain of its applications." . . .

. . . [The] practice of issuing signing statements does not mean that a President has acted contrary to law or the Legislative Branch. The practice is consistent with, and derives from, the President's constitutional obligations, and is an ordinary part of a respectful constitutional dialogue between the branches. When Congress passes legislation containing provisions that could be construed or applied in certain cases in a manner contrary to well-settled constitutional principles, the President can and should take steps to ensure that such laws are interpreted and executed in a manner consistent with the Constitution. . . .

The President takes an oath to "preserve, protect and defend the Constitution of the United States." The President has the responsibility and duty also to faithfully execute the laws of the United States. But these duties are not in conflict: the law the President must execute includes the Constitution—the supreme law of the land. Because the Constitution is supreme over all other law, the President must resolve any conflict between statutory law and the Constitution in favor of the Constitution, just as courts must.

This presidential responsibility may arise most sharply when the President is charged with executing a statute, passed by a previous Congress and signed by a prior President, a provision of which . . . he finds unconstitutional under intervening Supreme Court precedent. A President that places the statutory law over the constitutional law in this instance would fail in his duty faithfully to execute the laws. The principle is equally sound where the Supreme Court has yet to rule on an issue, but the President has determined that a statutory law violates the Constitution. To say that the principle is not equally sound in this context is to deny the President's independent responsibility to interpret and uphold the Constitution. It is to leave the defense of the Constitution only to two, not three, of the branches of our government.

From Michelle Boardman, "Presidential Signing Statements," statement to the United States Committee on the Judiciary, June 27, 2006, http://judiciary.senate.gov/testimony.cfm?id=1969&wit_id=5479.

While most will agree with this principle, everyone will disagree with its application some of the time because there is honest disagreement about what the Constitution requires. But whether a particular constitutional objection should be made is a different question from whether constitutional signing statements are an appropriate exercise of every President's power. . . .

To appreciate the value of signing statements, consider the alternatives. As we understand the argument, some critics of presidential signing statements would prefer that a President either reject the legislation outright through veto or remain silent upon signing the legislation. First, it has never been the case that the President's only option when confronting a bill containing a provision that is constitutionally problematic is to veto the bill. Presidents Jefferson (e.g., the Louisiana Purchase), Lincoln, Theodore Roosevelt, Wilson, Franklin Roosevelt, Truman, Eisenhower, Kennedy, Lyndon Johnson, Ford, Carter, as well as George H. W. Bush and Clinton, have signed legislation rather than vetoing it despite concerns that particular aspects of the legislation posed constitutional difficulties. Assistant Attorney General Dellinger explained early during the Clinton Administration: "In light of our constitutional history, we do not believe that the President is under any duty to veto legislation containing a constitutionally infirm provision." To be sure, Presidents have the option of vetoing a bill most of whose provisions are clearly constitutional but that contains a few provisions that may be read to permit certain unconstitutional applications. It is more sensible, however, to accept the bill while giving the problematic provisions a "saving" construction. . . .

As for the second suggested alternative to signing statements—presidential silence—it is not clear what critics of signing statements hope will be gained by such a course. Signing statements have the virtue of making the President's views public. A statement may notify the Congress and the American people of concerns that the President has about the legislation and how the Executive Branch will construe a particular law. Or it may serve only as a reminder to those in the Executive Branch charged with executing a law that the law must be applied within the confines of the Constitution. Neither Congress nor the public would be better served by either of these statements being restricted to an internal Executive Branch audience. Employing signing statements to advise Congress of constitutional objections is more respectful of Congress's role as an equal branch of government than public silence, and promotes a constitutional dialogue that is healthy in a democracy.

The last possible alternative—for the President to remain publicly silent and not to direct subordinate Executive Branch officials to construe the law in a constitutional manner—would flatly contradict the Constitution's requirement that the President "take care that the Laws [are] faithfully executed." Recent administrations, including the Reagan, George H. W. Bush, and Clinton Administrations, consistently have taken the position that "the Constitution provides [the President] with the authority to decline to enforce a clearly unconstitutional law." Indeed, "every President since Eisenhower has issued signing statements in which he stated that he would refuse to execute unconstitutional provisions.". . . Rather than tacitly placing limitations on the enforcement of provisions (or declining to enforce them), as has been done in the past, signing statements promote a constitutional dialogue with Congress by openly stating the interpretation that the President will give certain provisions.

Finally, some have raised the concern that courts will use signing statements to interpret statutes in contravention of the legislative goal. Signing statements, of course, are not binding on the courts; they are principally an exercise of the President's responsibility as head of the Executive Branch to determine the correct interpretation of the law for purposes of executing it faithfully. There must be an authoritative interpretation of the law within the Executive Branch, and it is the President's responsibility as Chief Executive to ensure that the law is authoritatively interpreted consistent with the Constitution. . . . ■

 # View from the Inside

At the White House—as at millions of other workplaces—September 11, 2001, started out as just another Tuesday. But the routine was soon shattered by news of the worst terrorist attacks in U.S. history. In this memoir, White House speechwriter David Frum recalls the events of that long and painful day.

Question

1. Were critics justified in suggesting that Bush could have handled the events of 9/11 more effectively? What might he have done differently?

10.6 September 11, 2001 (2003)

David Frum

Inside the White House, the events of September 11 began just the way they did for everyone else: on television. But for those of us who worked there, the events did not remain on the screen for very long.

I arrived at work late that morning. Washington's highway traffic, never good, was especially horrible that day, and I had to inch my way to the office from my children's school, too irritated even to listen to the radio. I did not pull into the little strip of parking spaces in front of the old Executive Office Building until a few minutes after nine.

My cell phone rang as I reached my desk. It was my wife's gentle voice that first introduced me to the hard facts of our new life: Two hijacked planes had crashed into the World Trade Center. The twin towers were burning. Thousands of people were in danger. The United States had been attacked.

Hours after the bombing of Pearl Harbor, Eleanor Roosevelt declared on the radio that "the moment we all dreaded had arrived." September 11 was a moment that had been dreaded by almost nobody except for a few terrorism experts. A quiet August was slipping unnoticeably into a golden September. Americans felt safe and remote from the troubles of the rest of the globe. The president's long vacation from Washington had ended; the country's long vacation from history had promised to go on and on.

Now history had exploded on us like a bomb, killing God knows how many thousands of people. I rushed to my desk and turned on my television. And there it was: the worst crime ever recorded on videotape.

I suddenly recollected that I was supposed to cross the Potomac River at noon to have lunch with a friend over at the Pentagon. I telephoned his office to cancel: Nobody, I thought unprophetically, would be leaving his or her desk today. My friend's assistant picked up the phone. I began to say that something terrible in New York had happened, we would all be needed at our posts . . . but she cut me off. "They're evacuating this building," she said grimly. "I cannot talk. We must leave."

I turned the television's sound back on. They were reporting that a third plane had struck the Pentagon—a truck bombing was reported at the State Department—fires had been set on the National Mall. My wife called again, her voice taut and strained. "The White House will be next! You have to get out of there—don't wait, please hurry!"

I felt a surge of . . . what? Battle fever? Mulishness? I only remember how hot my ears felt. "No!" I said fiercely. "No! I am not leaving!" I clicked off the phone, ready to . . . well, I don't know what I was ready to do—whatever it is that speechwriters do in times of war. Type, I suppose—but type with renewed patriotism and zeal. And at precisely that blood-boiling moment, a Secret Service agent was pounding on my door, shouting, "Everybody must evacuate this building now—this is an order—everybody must evacuate now!" A face popped through the doorway. "You! Out—now! Now!"

My heroic moment had lasted less than two minutes. I stepped out into the corridor. The tiled hallways of the Executive Office Building are wide enough and high enough for a chariot race. No matter how many people they hold, they always look and sound half-empty . . . . but not that day. Little streams of clicking feet merged into rivers of footsteps, and then into a torrent. "Don't run!" the guards shouted, and the torrent slowed. We poured through the tall, carved oak doors of the building onto the avenue between the Executive Office Building and the West Wing of the White House and were reinforced by another rivulet of secretaries and staffers.

The guards suddenly changed their minds. "Run!" they now shouted. "Ladies—if you can't run in heels, kick off your shoes."

The northwest gate to the White House was thrown open, and out we all raced. More guards waited for us on Lafayette Square. "Keep going!" The offices in the town houses along the west side of the square emptied themselves into the crowd. "Don't stop!"

We ran past the statues of Count Rochambeau, the hero of Yorktown, and General Steuben, who drilled Washington's army. We ran alongside Andrew Jackson astride his horse, Sam Patch. We ran under the windows of the house of Commodore Stephen Decatur ("Our country! . . . . may she always be in the right—but our country, right or wrong!"). We finally halted on the south side of H Street. "Take your badges off!" shouted another guard, and we pulled over our heads the blue or orange plastic cards that might mark us for a sniper. And there we stood: banished from our offices, stripped of our identifiers, helpless and baffled.

During the fighting in Afghanistan, it became popular for White House staffers to wear red, white, and blue plastic cards around their necks with the motto "These colors don't run." But that day they did run, and I ran with them, and I will never fully extract the sting of that memory.

The crowd of staffers milled aimlessly about the streets. Senior directors of the National Security Council, presidential assistants, and officers in uniform stood on the sidewalks, punching again and again at the dial pads of their cell phones, unable to get a signal, unable to keep a signal if they did get it, uncertain of where to go or what to do. The White House's emergency plans dated back to the cold war and were intended to protect the president, the vice president, and a handful of top aides against a nuclear attack. The rest of the staff, it was quietly assumed, would have been vaporized into radioactive dust.

But here we all were, alive but shaken, knowing less about what was going on in the world than a CNN viewer in Tasmania. I spotted John McConnell, the vice president's speechwriter. "We're just a couple of blocks from the American Enterprise Institute," I proposed. "They'll have land lines and television sets. And maybe we'll be able to think of something useful to do." We struck off across Farragut Square—and arrived to the news that the south tower of the World Trade Center had collapsed, killing unknown thousands of people inside.

Chris DeMuth, AEI's president, greeted McConnell and me like sailors hauled in from the water. He offered us offices and telephones, Internet connections and e-mail—"Whatever you need," he said urgently.

McConnell and I had been trying for an hour to reach Michael Gerson by pager, by phone, by e-mail. We would have sent pigeons if we had had them. We finally found him at his home in Alexandria. He had been late to work that morning, too—and had been stuck in a traffic jam underneath the flight path of American Airlines Flight 77 when it crashed into the Pentagon.

Gerson told us that DaimlerChrysler had volunteered its Washington office as an improvised headquarters for the White House staff. We should walk over and get to work at once on a statement the president could issue on his return to Washington. It would be impossible for Gerson to enter the city. He would work from home.

A statement for the president. But what would it say? What *could* it say?

McConnell and I set off again. It was drawing close to noon. A security perimeter was being drawn around the center of Washington, D.C. To reach the DaimlerChrysler building we had to cross a police line, guarded by uniformed Secret Service agents who scrutinized our passes with unusual minuteness.

I had assumed that the federal government had designated these offices in advance for emergency use. In fact, the only reason we were here was that somebody on the White House staff was married to somebody in DaimlerChrysler's management, who offered up the premises in a spontaneous gesture. It was about 11:45. I was pointed to an office and told it was mine for the day. Its regular tenant gave me his long-distance dialing codes, showed me how to work his e-mail, packed his briefcase, and shook my hand on his way through the door.

There's an old political—okay, Republican—joke about the biggest lie in the world being "I'm from the government, and I'm here to help you." The joke didn't seem very funny on September 11. We were from the government, and as far as the people at DaimlerChrysler were concerned, we *were* here to help them—by helping their president defend their country. And they in turn wanted to help us.

Somehow they had contrived to set out trays of sandwiches, bowls of salad, cookies, cake, coffee, and soft drinks before they left. Anxious, weary, and parched, the ravenous White House staffers wolfed down the food and then settled at DaimlerChrysler's computers and telephones.

The White House was now distributed in three principal places, with stragglers spread throughout the capital. The mid-level staff was here at 1401 H Street. The vice president and his chief of staff, Lewis Libby; National Security Adviser Condoleezza Rice; Deputy Chief of Staff Josh Bolten—they were all beneath the White House in a hardened bunker. And the president, Chief of Staff Andy Card, and the top political and communications aides were flying westward on Air Force One.

The president had been reading to the second-grade class at the Emma E. Booker Elementary School in Sarasota, Florida, when Card whispered into his ear the confirmation that the plane crashes in New York City were terrorist attacks. He finished reading and then approached the microphones. Reprising a line of his father's from ten years before, he declared that terrorism against the United States "would not stand."

It is hard to govern during an age of instantaneous broadcast. There were no microphones to preserve every quaver in Abraham Lincoln's voice after the firing on Fort Sumter; we cannot study Franklin Delano Roosevelt's face for traces of uncertainty in the seconds after Pearl Harbor. There would be much criticism of Bush's seeming disorientation and unease in the early hours after the attack. Well, who that day *wasn't* disoriented and uneasy? Yet we do live in an age of instantaneous media and have no choice but to play by its rules—and those rules would treat Bush harshly from his first remarks that morning until he returned to Washington that night.

The president ordered Air Force One to fly back to Washington as swiftly as possible. But as the president's plane approached the capital, the Secret Service received intelligence suggesting that the plane was a terrorist target, too. It would take many days for that intelligence to be proved false. So the big jet was rerouted to Barksdale Air Force Base in Louisiana. The president disembarked there to address a shocked and terrified nation at 12:40 eastern time: "The resolve of our great nation is being tested," he said. "But make no mistake: We will show the world that we will pass this test. God bless."

The words were correct and reassuring. The images were not. Air force bases do not come equipped with television studios, so the president was obliged to record his message in a bare room over a herky-jerky digital connection. He looked and sounded like the hunted, not the hunter. Even such a good friend of the administration as the editorial page of *The Wall Street Journal* cuttingly commented that Bush's flight from air force base to air force base before finally returning to the capital showed that he "could not be frightened away for long, if at all."

With Air Force One apparently a target, and the White House shuttered and largely useless, Bush proceeded to Strategic Command at Offutt Air Force Base in Nebraska. From Offutt the president can command the defense of the nation's airspace, if need be, and teleconference with his National Security Council.

As Bush flew westward, taking phone calls, gathering information, and deciding upon his and the nation's course, his writers were pacing and talking and drafting and redrafting a formal message that the president could deliver to the nation from the Oval Office that evening.

By now, Matthew Scully had made his way to the DaimlerChrysler building, and he, McConnell, and I gathered around a computer screen, with Gerson on the other end of a phone line. When we finished, we fired the text to Gerson's home; he edited it some more and then forwarded it to Hughes.

Our work was interrupted by a terrible bulletin. McConnell had said to me on our walk through the empty city: "There are going to be thousands and thousands of funerals in this country over the next week. Everybody is going to know someone among the dead." Now it was our turn. My wife telephoned into our office. She could barely speak. She had learned that Barbara Olson, wife of Solicitor General Theodore Olson, had been one of the passengers aboard the flight that crashed into the Pentagon. In the confusion and terror of the hijacking, Barbara Olson had somehow found the cool and courage to call her husband on her cell phone. Her call gave the government early notice of the seizure of a third plane. Her last words expressed her infinite faith in Ted: "The pilot is here with me. Tell him what to do."

I keep a transliteration of the Kaddish, the Jewish prayer for the dead, on my PalmPilot. I stepped out of our little office, retreated to the photocopy room, closed the door, and looked around for something with which to cover my head. I could find nothing, so I pulled my arms out of my jacket, pulled it up and over my head like a shawl, recited the ancient words, and mourned my brave and beautiful friend.

The sun was setting. Information circulated that the president would be returning to Washington at about eight o'clock and that the White House would be reopened to staff. McConnell, Scully, and I decided to return to the office in case we were needed for something. We cleared our desks and gathered up our notes and copies of our e-mails for the presidential record keepers. I left a short note of thanks for the man whose desk I had occupied all day, but I have a bad feeling that the record keepers scooped it up, too. We stepped out of the office, into the elevator, and out of the building—into a world transformed.

Washington was empty and silent, save for the screams of sirens far off in the distance and the periodic roar of F-16s overhead. Entire city blocks were cordoned off by yellow police tape. Uniformed guards checked our passes every fifty feet. Black-clad paramilitary agents clutching murderous automatic weapons surveyed us skeptically. Otherwise, there were no people to be seen. A sad and lonely stillness had settled upon the central precinct of American power.

We were all weary from the emotions that had surged through us that day: fear and rage and grief. But we were not depleted. The fear and the rage receded, the grief had to be postponed. What was left was a budding tenderness toward every symbol of this wounded country. The lights that illuminated the monuments of the capital had been defiantly switched on. The evening air was sweet and soft. And we looked with new and more loving eyes at the familiar streets. There! There was the Treasury Department—where they would mobilize the limitless resources of the nation for war. There! There was the East Wing, the office of the First Lady, who had visited Congress that morning—and who could have easily numbered among the dead had the fourth hijacked jet struck the Capitol. And there! There! There was the flag over the White House. Tomorrow it would be lowered to half-staff. Today it flew high, brilliantly lit, in defiance of all terror— still gallantly streaming, just as it had for an imprisoned poet on the deck of an enemy warship two centuries ago.

The day's violence seemed to be over for the moment. The night was quiet. But tomorrow? What would happen tomorrow? And the next day?

McConnell, Scully, and I drew near the black iron fence around the White House. We showed our passes once more, and a guard radioed our names to some authority inside. A long wait—and then one by one we were permitted to step through the gate.

Even on the dullest day, stepping from the outside to the inside of the White House gate feels like crossing into a forbidden city. But never before had the line of separation felt so thick and high. The silent, patrolled city beyond the lush lawn and the still-thick greenery of the trees, beyond the sensors, the fence, and the gates, fell away behind us into remoteness and invisibility as we trudged along West Executive Avenue to the entrance to the West Wing. We stepped under the white canopy that extends from the side doorway to the avenue—and into a building that was humming back to life after the longest session of inactivity perhaps in its existence.

We entered the small basement suite of offices that Gerson and his assistant shared with another senior staffer and his assistant. We turned on the television, sat on a couch, and watched the president walk briskly across the South Lawn to the Oval Office. There was an hour to wait before he would speak to the country.

The screens began to flash images of the White House as the networks readied themselves for the president's message. My mind traveled backward through all the images of this president those same networks had shown the American people since he had emerged on the national scene two years before. Had they seen a man in whom they could place their trust? It was nine o'clock. We were about to learn. ∎

Chapter 11

The Bureaucracy

Bureaucracy is a pervasive and inescapable fact of modern existence. Every large organization in society—not just the government—is managed by a bureaucratic system: tasks are divided among particular experts, and decisions are made and administered according to general rules and regulations. No one who has attended a university, worked for a large corporation, served in the military, or dealt with the government is unfamiliar with the nature of bureaucracies.

Bureaucracies, as sociologist Max Weber observed, are a necessary feature of modern life. When social organizations are small—as in a small business or a small academic department—decisions can be made and programs carried out by a few individuals using informal procedures and with a minimum of red tape and paperwork. As these organizations grow, it becomes increasingly necessary to delegate authority, develop methods of tracking and assessment, and create general rules instead of deciding matters on a case-by-case basis. Suddenly a bureaucracy has arisen.

In the political realm, bureaucracies serve another purpose. Beginning with the Pendleton Act of 1883, civil service reformers sought to insulate routine governmental decisions from the vagaries of partisan politics—to ensure, in other words, that decisions were made on the basis of merit instead of on the basis of party affiliation. The Pendleton Act greatly reduced the number of presidential appointments in such departments as the Customs Service and the Post Office, putting in place an early version of the merit system. As the federal government's responsibilities grew, the need to keep politics out of such functions as tax collection, administration of social security and welfare, and similar programs became even greater.

The bureaucratization of government therefore serves important purposes: increasing efficiency, promoting fairness, ensuring accountability. Yet at the same time, it creates problems of its own. Bureaucracies have a tendency to grow, to become rigid, to become answerable only to themselves, and to create barriers between citizens and the government. These bureaucratic "pathologies" are well known; they are the subject of frequent editorials and commentaries. Politicians can always count on stories about bureaucratic inefficiency and callousness to strike a chord with the voting public.

The selections in this chapter cover the bureaucracy from several different viewpoints. In selection 11.1, sociologist Max Weber provides the classic description of the bureaucratic form of governmental power; in selection 11.2, political scientist James Q. Wilson updates Weber, examining what government agencies do and why they do it.

Selection 11.3 looks at the bureaucratic response—or lack of response—to the warning signs that preceded the 9/11 attacks, while selection 11.4 provides a light-hearted but realistic glimpse into the inner workings of the Washington bureaucracy.

As you read these selections, keep in mind that the alternative to bureaucratic government in the modern world is not some sort of utopian system in which all decisions are fair, all programs efficient, all children above average. Limiting the power of bureaucracies means increasing the power of other institutions: Congress, the presidency, private businesses, or the courts. Reducing the power of the bureaucracy may also create a government that is less fair or less accountable.

Also keep in mind that bureaucrats—like baseball umpires—are most noticeable when they make mistakes. Americans tend to take for granted the extraordinary number of government programs that work well: the letters delivered correctly and on time, the meat inspected properly, the airplanes that land safely. Criticism and evaluation of the bureaucracy must be kept in a reasonable perspective.

Chapter Questions

1. What role does the bureaucracy play in any large social system? What functions does the bureaucracy perform? What are its most significant characteristics?
2. What is the relationship between the bureaucracy and the other political institutions in the United States? What are the alternatives to bureaucratic power? What are the advantages and disadvantages of these other forms of power?

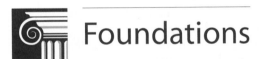 # Foundations

Any discussion about bureaucracy—in the United States or anywhere else—must begin with Max Weber, who is best known for his work laying the intellectual foundation for the study of modern sociology. Weber wrote extensively on modern social and political organization; his works include the unfinished *Wirtschaft und Gesellschaft* [Economy and Society] (1922) and the influential *The Protestant Ethic and the Spirit of Capitalism* (1904–1905).

Weber was born in Thuringia, in what is now eastern Germany, in 1864; he died in 1920. Although his observations on bureaucracy draw on historical and contemporary European examples, they were heavily informed by his experiences in the United States. While traveling in the New World, Weber was struck by the role of bureaucracy in a democratic society. The problem, as he saw it, was that a modern democracy required bureaucratic structures of all kinds in the administration of government and even in the conduct of professional party politics. Handing over the reins to a class of unelected "experts," however, threatened to undermine the very basis of democracy itself. In particular, Weber stressed two problems: the unaccountability of unelected civil servants and the bureaucratic tendency toward inflexibility in the application of rules.

In this brief selection, Weber describes the essential nature of bureaucracy.

Questions

1. What are the characteristics of the bureaucratic form of governmental power? What are bureaucracy's strong points? Weak points?
2. Why are rules so important in a bureaucracy? What are the advantages and disadvantages of making decisions on the basis of general rules, rather than on a case-by-case basis?

11.1 Bureaucracy (1922)

Max Weber

I: Characteristics of Bureaucracy

Modern officialdom functions in the following specific manner:

I. There is the principle of fixed and official jurisdictional areas, which are generally ordered by rules, that is, by laws or administrative regulations.

1. The regular activities required for the purposes of the bureaucratically governed structure are distributed in a fixed way as official duties.

2. The authority to give the commands required for the discharge of these duties is distributed in a stable way and is strictly delimited by rules concerning the coercive means, physical, sacerdotal, or otherwise, which may be placed at the disposal of officials.

3. Methodical provision is made for the regular and continuous fulfillment of these duties and for the execution of the corresponding rights; only persons who have the generally regulated qualifications to serve are employed.

In public and lawful government these three elements constitute "bureaucratic authority." In private economic domination, they constitute bureaucratic "management." Bureaucracy, thus understood, is fully developed in political and ecclesiastical communities only in the modern state, and, in the private economy, only in the most advanced institutions of capitalism. Permanent and public office authority, with fixed jurisdiction, is not the historical rule but rather the exception. This is so even in large political structures such as those of the ancient Orient, the Germanic and Mongolian empires of conquest, or of many feudal structures of state. In all these cases, the ruler executes the most important measures through personal trustees, table-companions, or court-servants. Their commissions and authority are not precisely delimited and are temporarily called into being for each case.

II. The principles of office hierarchy and of levels of graded authority mean a firmly ordered system of super- and subordination in which there is a supervision of the lower offices by the higher ones. Such a system offers the governed the possibility of appealing the decision of a lower office to its higher authority, in a

From *Max Weber: Essays in Sociology*, by Max Weber, edited and translated by H. H. Gerth and C. Wright Mills, 1946, pp. 196–198, 214–216. Used by permission of Oxford University Press, Inc.

definitely regulated manner. With the full development of the bureaucratic type, the office hierarchy is monocratically organized. The principle of hierarchical office authority is found in all bureaucratic structures: in state and ecclesiastical structures as well as in large party organizations and private enterprises. It does not matter for the character of bureaucracy whether its authority is called "private" or "public."

When the principle of jurisdictional "competency" is fully carried through, hierarchical subordination—at least in public office—does not mean that the "higher" authority is simply authorized to take over the business of the "lower." Indeed, the opposite is the rule. Once established and having fulfilled its task, an office tends to continue in existence and be held by another incumbent.

III. The management of the modern office is based upon written documents ("the files"), which are preserved in their original or draught form. There is, therefore, a staff of subaltern officials and scribes of all sorts. The body of officials actively engaged in a "public" office, along with the respective apparatus of material implements and the files, make up a "bureau." In private enterprise, "the bureau" is often called "the office."

In principle, the modern organization of the civil service separates the bureau from the private domicile of the official, and, in general, bureaucracy segregates official activity as something distinct from the sphere of private life. Public monies and equipment are divorced from the private property of the official. This condition is everywhere the product of a long development. Nowadays, it is found in public as well as in private enterprises; in the latter, the principle extends even to the leading entrepreneur. In principle, the executive office is separated from the household, business from private correspondence, and business assets from private fortunes. The more consistently the modern type of business management has been carried through the more are these separations the case. The beginnings of this process are to be found as early as the Middle Ages.

It is the peculiarity of the modern entrepreneur that he conducts himself as the "first official" of his enterprise, in the very same way in which the ruler of a specifically modern bureaucratic state spoke of himself as "the first servant" of the state. The idea that the bureau activities of the state are intrinsically different in character from the management of private economic offices is a continental European notion and, by way of contrast, is totally foreign to the American way.

IV. Office management, at least all specialized office management—and such management is distinctly modern—usually presupposes thorough and expert training. This increasingly holds for the modern executive and employee of private enterprises, in the same manner as it holds for the state official.

V. When the office is fully developed, official activity demands the full working capacity of the official, irrespective of the fact that his obligatory time in the bureau may be firmly delimited. In the normal case, this is only the product of a long development, in the public as well as in the private office. Formerly, in all cases, the normal state of affairs was reversed: official business was discharged as a secondary activity.

VI. The management of the office follows general rules, which are more or less stable, more or less exhaustive, and which can be learned. Knowledge of these rules represents a special technical learning which the officials possess. It involves jurisprudence, or administrative or business management.

The reduction of modern office management to rules is deeply embedded in its very nature. The theory of modern public administration, for instance, assumes that the authority to order certain matters by decree—which has been legally granted to public authorities—does not entitle the bureau to regulate the matter by commands given for each case, but only to regulate the matter abstractly. This stands in extreme contrast to the regulation of all relationships through individual privileges and bestowals of favor, which is absolutely dominant in patrimonialism, at least in so far as such relationships are not fixed by sacred tradition. . . .

Technical Advantages of Bureaucratic Organization

The decisive reason for the advance of bureaucratic organization has always been its purely technical superiority over any other form of organization. The fully developed bureaucratic mechanism compares with other organizations exactly as does the machine with the nonmechanical modes of production.

Precision, speed, unambiguity, knowledge of the files, continuity, discretion, unity, strict subordination, reduction of friction and of material and personal costs—these are raised to the optimum point in the strictly bureaucratic administration, and especially in its monocratic form. As compared with all collegiate, honorific, and avocational forms of administration, trained bureaucracy is superior on all these points. And as far as complicated tasks are concerned, paid bureaucratic work is not only more precise but, in the last analysis, it is often cheaper than even formally unremunerated honorific service.

Honorific arrangements make administrative work an avocation and, for this reason alone, honorific service normally functions more slowly; being less bound to schemata and being more formless. Hence it is less precise and less unified than bureaucratic work because it is less dependent upon superiors and because the establishment and exploitation of the apparatus of subordinate officials and filing services are almost unavoidably less economical. Honorific service is less continuous than bureaucratic and frequently quite expensive. This is especially the case if one thinks not only of the money costs to the public treasury—costs which bureaucratic administration, in comparison with administration by notables, usually substantially increases—but also of the frequent economic losses of the governed caused by delays and lack of precision. The possibility of administration by notables normally and permanently exists only where official management can be satisfactorily discharged as an avocation. With the qualitative increase of tasks the administration has to face, administration by notables reaches its limits—today, even in England. Work organized by collegiate bodies causes friction and delay and requires compromises between colliding interests and views. The administration, therefore, runs less precisely and is more independent of superiors; hence, it is less unified and slower. All advances of the Prussian administrative organization have been and will in the future be advances of the bureaucratic, and especially of the monocratic, principle.

Today, it is primarily the capitalist market economy which demands that the official business of the administration be discharged precisely, unambiguously, continuously, and with as much speed as possible. Normally, the very large, modern capitalist enterprises are themselves unequalled models of strict bureaucratic organization. Business management throughout rests on increasing precision, steadiness, and, above all, the speed of operations. This, in turn, is determined by the peculiar nature of the modern means of communication, including, among other things, the news service of the press. The extraordinary increase in the speed by which public announcements, as well as economic and political facts, are transmitted exerts a steady and sharp pressure in the direction of speeding up the tempo of administrative reaction towards various situations. The optimum of such reaction time is normally attained only by a strictly bureaucratic organization.

Bureaucratization offers above all the optimum possibility for carrying through the principle of specializing administrative functions according to purely objective considerations. Individual performances are allocated to functionaries who have specialized training and who by constant practice learn more and more. The "objective" discharge of business primarily means a discharge of business according to *calculable rules* and "without regard for persons."

"Without regard for persons" is also the watchword of the "market" and, in general, of all pursuits of naked economic interests. A consistent execution of bureaucratic domination means the leveling of status "honor." Hence, if the principle of the free-market is not at the same time restricted, it means the universal domination of the "class situation." That this consequence of bureaucratic domination has not set in everywhere, parallel to the extent of bureaucratization, is due to the differences among possible principles by which polities may meet their demands.

The second element mentioned, "calculable rules," also is of paramount importance for modern bureaucracy. The peculiarity of modern culture, and specifically of its technical and economic basis, demands this very "calculability" of results. . . . [The] specific nature [of bureaucracy], which is welcomed by capitalism, develops the more perfectly the more the bureaucracy is "dehumanized," the more completely it succeeds in eliminating from official business love, hatred, and all purely personal, irrational, and emotional elements which escape calculation. This is the specific nature of bureaucracy and it is appraised as its special virtue.

The more complicated and specialized modern culture becomes, the more its external supporting apparatus demands the personally detached and strictly "objective" *expert*, in lieu of the master of older social structures, who was moved by personal sympathy and favor, by grace and gratitude. Bureaucracy offers the attitudes demanded by the external apparatus of modern culture in the most favorable combination. As a rule, only bureaucracy has established the foundation for the administration of a rational law conceptually systematized on the basis of such enactments as the latter Roman imperial period first created with a high degree of technical perfection. During the Middle Ages, this law was received along with the bureaucratization of legal administration, that is to say, with the displacement of the old trial procedure which was bound to tradition or to irrational presuppositions, by the rationally trained and specialized expert. ∎

American Politics Today

Critics of the American bureaucracy frequently attack the public sector as wasteful, inefficient, and unaccountable to the public. Such criticisms, however, are frequently nothing more than cheap shots, for they ignore the very great differences between the public and private sectors. A fair appraisal of the public bureaucracy must begin with a clear view of what we expect from the public sector and of the constraints under which it must operate.

The government, as political scientist James Q. Wilson points out in the following selection, does indeed compare badly to the private sector when viewed in terms of economic efficiency. The problem, he suggests, is that government is constrained in ways that the private sector is not. And those constraints, he concludes, come from the people themselves. It is the people—expressing themselves individually, by way of interest groups, or through the legislature—who impose the constraints under which the bureaucracy must operate.

Central to Wilson's argument is his attempt to broaden the concept of efficiency to include more than economic efficiency. If we measure governmental action by the simple standard of economic efficiency—that is, the cost per unit output—government compares badly to the private sector. Once we recognize that a true measure of bureaucratic efficiency must take into account *"all* of the valued outputs"—including honesty, accountability, and responsiveness to particular constituents—the equation becomes more complicated, and perhaps more favorable to the government.

Wilson's argument is no whitewash for the government bureaucracy. Even if we allow for all of this, as he points out, government agencies may still be inefficient. Recognizing the multifaceted and complex constraints on government officials will, in any event, provide a reasonable and realistic way to evaluate the bureaucracy.

Questions

1. Wilson suggests that government officials operate under very different constraints from their counterparts in the private sector. What are these differences, and what is their effect? Put another way, why does Wilson assert that "the government can't say 'yes'"?
2. What values other than economic efficiency do we demand of government? Why is the avoidance of arbitrariness so important?

11.2 Bureaucracy: What Government Agencies Do and Why They Do It (1989)

James Q. Wilson

On the morning of May 22, 1986, Donald Trump, the New York real estate developer, called one of his executives, Anthony Gliedman, into his office. They discussed the inability of the City of New York, despite six years of effort and the expenditure of nearly $13 million, to rebuild the ice-skating rink in Central Park. On May 28 Trump offered to take over the rink reconstruction, promising to do the job in less than six months. A week later Mayor Edward Koch accepted the offer and shortly thereafter the city appropriated $3 million on the understanding that Trump would have to pay for any cost overruns out of his own pocket. On October 28, the renovation was complete, over a month ahead of schedule and about $750,000 under budget. Two weeks later, skaters were using it.

For many readers it is obvious that private enterprise is more efficient than are public bureaucracies, and so they would file this story away as simply another illustration of what everyone already knows. But for other readers it is not so obvious what this story means; to them, business is greedy and unless watched like a hawk will fob off shoddy or overpriced goods on the American public, as when it sells the government $435 hammers and $3,000 coffeepots. Trump may have done a good job in this instance, but perhaps there is something about skating rinks or New York City government that gave him a comparative advantage; in any event, no larger lessons should be drawn from it.

Some lessons can be drawn, however, if one looks closely at the incentives and constraints facing Trump and the Department of Parks and Recreation. It becomes apparent that there is not one "bureaucracy problem" but several, and the solution to each in some degree is incompatible with the solution to every other. First there is the problem of accountability—getting agencies to serve agreed-upon goals. Second there is the problem of equity—treating all citizens fairly, which usually means treating them alike on the basis of clear rules known in advance. Third there is the problem of responsiveness—reacting reasonably to the special needs and circumstances of particular people. Fourth there is the problem of efficiency—obtaining the greatest output for a given level of resources. Finally there is the problem of fiscal integrity—assuring that public funds are spent prudently for public purposes. Donald Trump and Mayor Koch were situated differently with respect to most of these matters.

Accountability   The Mayor wanted the old skating rink refurbished, but he also wanted to minimize the cost of the fuel needed to operate the rink (the first effort

---

to rebuild it occurred right after the Arab oil embargo and the attendant increase in energy prices). Trying to achieve both goals led city hall to select a new refrigeration system that as it turned out would not work properly. Trump came on the scene when only one goal dominated: get the rink rebuilt. He felt free to select the most reliable refrigeration system without worrying too much about energy costs.

Equity   The Parks and Recreation Department was required by law to give every contractor an equal chance to do the job. This meant it had to put every part of the job out to bid and to accept the lowest without much regard to the reputation or prior performance of the lowest bidder. Moreover, state law forbade city agencies from hiring a general contractor and letting him select the subcontractors; in fact, the law forbade the city from even discussing the project in advance with a general contractor who might later bid on it—that would have been collusion. Trump, by contrast, was free to locate the rink builder with the best reputation and give him the job.

Fiscal Integrity   To reduce the chance of corruption or sweetheart deals the law required Parks and Recreation to furnish complete, detailed plans to every contractor bidding on the job; any changes after that would require renegotiating the contract. No such law constrained Trump; he was free to give incomplete plans to his chosen contractor, hold him accountable for building a satisfactory rink, but allow him to work out the details as he went along.

Efficiency   When Parks and Recreation spent over six years and $13 million and still could not reopen the rink, there was public criticism but no city official lost money. When Trump accepted a contract to do it, any cost overruns or delays would have come out of his pocket and any savings could have gone into his pocket (in this case, Trump agreed not to take a profit on the job).

Gliedman summarized the differences neatly: "The problem with government is that government can't say, 'yes' . . . there is nobody in government that can do that. There are fifteen or twenty people who have to agree. Government has to be slower. It has to safeguard the process."

Inefficiency

The government can't say "yes." In other words, the government is constrained. Where do the constraints come from? From us.

Herbert Kaufman has explained red tape as being of our own making: "Every restraint and requirement originates in somebody's demand for it." Applied to the Central Park skating rink Kaufman's insight reminds us that civil-service reformers demanded that no city official benefit personally from building a project; that contractors demanded that all be given an equal chance to bid on every job; and that fiscal watchdogs demanded that all contract specifications be as detailed as possible. For each demand a procedure was established; viewed from the outside, those procedures are called red tape. To enforce each procedure a manager was appointed; those managers are called bureaucrats. No organized group demanded that all skating rinks be rebuilt as quickly as possible, no procedure existed to enforce that demand, and no manager was appointed to enforce it. The political process can more easily enforce compliance with constraints than the attainment of goals.

When we denounce bureaucracy for being inefficient we are saying something that is half true. Efficiency is a ratio of valued resources used to valued outputs produced. The smaller that ratio the more efficient the production. If the valued output is a rebuilt skating rink, then whatever process uses the fewest dollars or the least time to produce a satisfactory rink is the most efficient process. By this test Trump was more efficient than the Parks and Recreation Department.

But that is too narrow a view of the matter. The economic definition of efficiency (efficiency in the small, so to speak) assumes that there is only one valued output, the new rink. But government has many valued outputs, including a reputation for integrity, the confidence of the people, and the support of important interest groups. When we complain about skating rinks not being built on time we speak as if all we cared about were skating rinks. But when we complain that contracts were awarded without competitive bidding or in a way that allowed bureaucrats to line their pockets we acknowledge that we care about many things besides skating rinks; we care about the contextual goals—the constraints—that we want government to observe. A government that is slow to build rinks but is honest and accountable in its actions and properly responsive to worthy constituencies may be a very efficient government, *if* we measure efficiency in the large by taking into account *all* of the valued outputs.

Calling a government agency efficient when it is slow, cumbersome, and costly may seem perverse. But that is only because we lack any objective way for deciding how much money or time should be devoted to maintaining honest behavior, producing a fair allocation of benefits, and generating popular support as well as to achieving the main goal of the project. If we could measure these things, and if we agreed as to their value, then we would be in a position to judge the true efficiency of a government agency and decide when it is taking too much time or spending too much money achieving all that we expect of it. But we cannot measure these things nor do we agree about their relative importance, and so government always will appear to be inefficient compared to organizations that have fewer goals.

Put simply, the only way to decide whether an agency is truly inefficient is to decide which of the constraints affecting its action ought to be ignored or discounted. In fact that is what most debates about agency behavior are all about. In fighting crime are the police handcuffed? In educating children are teachers tied down by rules? In launching a space shuttle are we too concerned with safety? In building a dam do we worry excessively about endangered species? In running the Postal Service is it important to have many post offices close to where people live? In the case of the skating rink, was the requirement of competitive bidding for each contract on the basis of detailed specifications a reasonable one? Probably not. But if it were abandoned, the gain (the swifter completion of the rink) would have to be balanced against the costs (complaints from contractors who might lose business and the chance of collusion and corruption in some future projects).

Even allowing for all of these constraints, government agencies may still be inefficient. Indeed, given the fact that bureaucrats cannot (for the most part) benefit monetarily from their agencies' achievements, it would be surprising if they were not inefficient. Efficiency, in the large or the small, doesn't pay.

But some critics of government believe that inefficiency is obvious and vast. Many people remember the 1984 claim of the Grace Commission (officially, the President's Private Sector Survey on Cost Control) that it had identified over $400 billion in savings that could be made if only the federal government were managed properly. Though the commission did not say so, many people inferred that careless bureaucrats were wasting that amount of money. But hardly anybody remembers the study issued jointly by the General Accounting Office and the Congressional Budget Office in February 1984, one month after the Grace Commission report. The GAO and CBO reviewed those Grace recommendations that accounted for about 90 percent of the projected savings, and after eliminating double-counting and recommendations for which no savings could be estimated, and other problems, concluded that the true savings would be less than one-third the claimed amount.

Of course, $100 billion is still a lot of money. But wait. It turns out that about 60 percent of this would require not management improvements but policy changes: for example, taxing welfare benefits, ending certain direct loan programs, adopting new rules to restrict Medicare benefits, restricting eligibility for retirement among federal civilian workers and military personnel, and selling the power produced by government-owned hydroelectric plants at the full market price.

That still leaves roughly $40 billion in management savings. But most of this would require either a new congressional policy (for example, hiring more Internal Revenue Service agents to collect delinquent taxes), some unspecified increase in "worker productivity," or buying more services from private suppliers. Setting aside the desirable goal of increasing productivity (for which no procedures were identified), it turns out that almost all of the projected savings would require Congress to alter the goals and constraints of public agencies. If there is a lot of waste (and it is not clear why the failure to tax welfare benefits or to hire more IRS agents should be called waste), it is congressionally directed waste.

Military procurement, of course, is the biggest source of stories about waste, fraud, and mismanagement. There cannot be a reader of this book who has not heard about the navy paying $435 for a hammer or the air force paying $3,000 for a coffeepot, and nobody, I suspect, believes Defense Department estimates of the cost of a new airplane or missile. If ever one needed evidence that bureaucracy is inefficient, the Pentagon supplies it.

Well, yes. But what kind of inefficiency? And why does it occur? To answer these questions one must approach the problem just as we approached the problem of fixing up a skating rink in New York City: We want to understand why the bureaucrats, all of whom are rational and most of whom want to go [sic] a good job, behave as they do.

To begin, let us forget about $435 hammers. They never existed. A member of Congress who did not understand (or did not want to understand) government accounting rules created a public stir. The $3,000 coffeepot existed, but it is not clear that it was overpriced. But that does not mean there are no problems; in fact, the real problems are far more costly and intractable than inflated price tags on hammers and coffeemakers. They include sticking too long with new weapons of dubious value, taking forever to acquire even good weapons, and not inducing contractors to increase their efficiency. What follows is not a complete explanation of military procurement problems; it is only an analysis of the contribution bureaucratic systems make to those problems.

When the military buys a new weapons system—a bomber, submarine, or tank—it sets in motion a procurement bureaucracy comprised of two key actors, the military program manager and the civilian contract officer, who must cope with the contractor, the Pentagon hierarchy, and Congress. To understand how they behave we must understand how their tasks get defined, what incentives they have, and what constraints they face.

Tasks   The person nominally in charge of buying a major new weapon is the program manager, typically an army or air force colonel or a navy captain. Officially, his job is to design and oversee the acquisition strategy by establishing specifications and schedules and identifying problems and tradeoffs. Unofficially, his task is somewhat different. For one thing he does not have the authority to make many important decisions; those are referred upward to his military superiors, to Defense Department civilians, and to Congress. For another, the program he oversees must constantly be sold and resold to the people who control the resources (mostly, the key congressional committees). And finally, he is surrounded by inspectors and auditors looking for any evidence of waste, fraud, or abuse and by the advocates of all manner of special interests (contractors' representatives, proponents of small and minority business utilization, and so on). As the Packard Commission observed, the program manager, "far from being the manager of the program . . . is merely one of the participants who can influence it."

Under these circumstances the actual task of the program manager tends to be defined as selling the program and staying out of trouble. Harvard Business School professor J. Ronald Fox, who has devoted much of his life to studying and participating in weapons procurement, found that a program manager must spend 30 to 50 percent of his time defending his program inside DOD and to Congress. It is entirely rational for him to do this, for a study by the General Accounting Office showed that weapons programs with effective advocates survived (including some that should have been terminated) and systems without such advocates were more likely to be ended (even some that should have been completed). Just as with the New York City skating rink, in the Pentagon there is no one who can say "yes" and make it stick. The only way to keep winning the support of the countless people who must say "yes" over and over again is to forge ahead at full speed, spending money at a rate high enough to prevent it from being taken away. . . .

Incentives   In theory, military program managers are supposed to win promotions if they have done a good job supervising weapons procurement. In fact, promotions to the rank of general or admiral usually have been made on the basis of their reputation as combat officers and experience as military leaders. According to Fox, being a program manager is often not a useful ticket to get punched if you want to rise to the highest ranks. In 1985, for example, 94 percent of the lieutenant colonels who had commanded a battalion were promoted by the army to the rank of colonel; the promotion rate for lieutenant colonels without that experience was only half as great. The armed services now claim that they do promote procurement officers at a reasonable rate, but Fox, as well as many officers, remain skeptical. The perceived message is clear: Traditional military specialties are a surer route to the top than experience as a program manager. . . .

Civilian contract officers do have a distinct career path, but as yet not one that produces in them much sense of professional pride or organizational mission. Of the more than twenty thousand civilian contract administrators less than half have a college degree and the great majority are in the lower civil-service grades (GS-5 to GS-12). Even the most senior contract officers rarely earn (in 1988) more than $50,000 a year, less than half or even one-third of what their industry counterparts earn. Moreover, all are aware that they work in offices where the top posts usually are held by military officers; in civil-service jargon, the "head room" available for promotions is quite limited. . . .

The best evidence of the weakness of civilian incentives is the high turnover rate. Fox quotes a former commander of the military acquisition program as saying that "good people are leaving in droves" because "there is much less psychic income today" that would make up for the relatively low monetary income. The Packard Commission surveyed civilian procurement personnel and found that over half would leave their jobs if offered comparable jobs elsewhere in the federal government or in private industry.

In short, the incentives facing procurement officials do not reward people for maximizing efficiency. Military officers are rewarded for keeping programs alive and are encouraged to move on to other assignments; civilian personnel have weak inducements to apply a complex array of inconsistent constraints to contract administration.

Constraints   These constraints are not designed to produce efficiency but to reduce costs, avoid waste, fraud, and abuse, achieve a variety of social goals, and maintain the productive capacity of key contractors.

Reducing costs is not the same thing as increasing efficiency. If too little money is spent, the rate of production may be inefficient and the managerial flexibility necessary to cope with unforeseen circumstances may be absent. Congress typically appropriates money one year at a time. If Congress wishes to cut its spending or if DOD is ordered to slash its budget requests, the easiest thing to do is to reduce the number of aircraft, ships, or missiles being purchased in a given year without reducing the total amount purchased. This stretch-out has the effect of increasing the cost of each individual weapon as manufacturers forgo the economies that come from large-scale production. As Fox observes (but as many critics fail to understand), the typical weapons program in any given year is not overfunded, it is *under*funded. Recognizing that, the Packard Commission called for adopting a two-year budget cycle.

Reducing costs and eliminating fraud are not the same as increasing efficiency. There no doubt are excessive costs and there may be fraud in military procurement, but eliminating them makes procurement more efficient only if the costs of eliminating the waste and fraud exceed the savings thereby realized. To my knowledge no one has systematically compared the cost of all the inspectors, rules, and auditors with the savings they have achieved to see if all the checking and reviewing is worth it. Some anecdotal evidence suggests that the checking does not always pay for itself. In one case the army was required to spend $5,400 to obtain fully competitive bids for spare parts that cost $11,000. In exchange for the $5,400 and the 160 days it took to get the bids, the army saved $100. In short, there is an optimal level of "waste" in any organization, public or private: It is that level below which further savings are worth less than the cost of producing them.

The weapons procurement system must serve a number of "social" goals mandated by Congress. It must support small business, provide opportunities for minority-owned businesses, buy American-made products whenever possible, rehabilitate prisoners, provide employment for the handicapped, protect the environment, and maintain "prevailing" wage rates. One could lower the cost of procurement by eliminating some or all of the social goals the process is obliged to honor; that would produce increases in efficiency, narrowly defined. But what interest group is ready to sacrifice its most cherished goal in the name of efficiency? And if none will volunteer, how does one create a congressional majority to compel the sacrifice?

Weapons procurement also is designed to maintain the productive capacity of the major weapons builders. There is no true market in the manufacture of missiles, military aircraft, and naval vessels because typically there is only one buyer (the government) and no alternative uses for the production lines established to supply this buyer. Northrop, Lockheed, Grumman, McDonnell Douglas, the Bath Iron Works, Martin Marietta—these firms and others like them would not exist, or would exist in very different form, if they did not have a continuous flow of military contracts. As a result, each new weapons system becomes a do-or-die proposition for the executives of these firms. Even if the Pentagon cared nothing about their economic well-being it would have to care about the productive capacity that they represent, for if it were ever lost or much diminished the armed services would have nowhere else to turn when the need arose for a new airplane or ship. And if by chance the Pentagon did not care, Congress would; no member believes he or she was elected to preside over the demise of a major employer.

This constraint produces what some scholars have called the "follow-on imperative": the need to give a new contract to each major supplier as work on an old contract winds down. If one understands this it is not necessary to imagine some sinister "military-industrial complex" conspiring to keep new weapons flowing. The armed services want them because they believe, rightly, that their task is to defend the nation against real though hard to define threats; the contractors want them because they believe, rightly, that the nation cannot afford to dismantle its productive capacity; Congress wants them because its members believe, rightly, that they are elected to maintain the prosperity of their states and districts.

When these beliefs encounter the reality of limited resources and the need to make budget choices, almost everyone has an incentive to overstate the benefits and understate the costs of a new weapons system. To do otherwise—to give a cautious estimate of what the weapon will achieve and a candid view of what it will cost—is to invite rejection. And none of the key actors in the process believe they can afford rejection.

The Bottom Line   The incentives and constraints that confront the military procurement bureaucracy push its members to overstate benefits, understate costs, make frequent and detailed changes in specifications, and enforce a bewildering array of rules designed to minimize criticism and stay out of trouble. There are hardly any incentives pushing officials to leave details to manufacturers or delegate authority to strong program managers whose career prospects will depend on their ability to produce good weapons at a reasonable cost.

In view of all this, what is surprising is that the system works as well as it does. In fact, it works better than most people suppose. The Rand Corporation has been studying military procurement for over thirty years. A summary of its findings suggests some encouraging news, most of it ignored amidst the headlines about hammers and coffeepots. There has been steady improvement in the performance of the system. Between the early 1960s and the mid-1980s, cost overruns, schedule slippages, and performance shortfalls have all decreased. Cost overruns of military programs on the average are now no greater than they are for the civil programs of the government such as highway and water projects and public buildings. Moreover, there is evidence that for all its faults the American system seems to work as well or better than that in many European nations.

Improvements can be made but they do not require bright new ideas, more regulations, or the reshuffling of boxes on the organizational chart. The necessary ideas exist in abundance, the top-down reorganizations have been tried without much effect, and the system is drowning in regulations. What is needed are changes in the incentives facing the key members. ∎

 # Issue and Controversy

In the wake of the September 11, 2001, terrorist attacks, Congress established the National Commission on Terrorist Attacks Upon the United States (or 9/11 Commission) and charged it with compiling "a full and complete account of the circumstances surrounding the . . . attacks, including preparedness for and the immediate response to the attacks," and with making "recommendations designed to guard against future attacks." In carrying out its mandate, the Commission interviewed over 1,200 individuals and reviewed 2.5 million pages of documents.*

The Commission's report drew a bleak and stark conclusion. "[O]n that September day we were unprepared," wrote Commission Chairman Thomas H. Kean and Vice Chairman Lee H. Hamilton. "We did not grasp the magnitude of a threat that had been gathering over time."† Although there was plenty of blame to go around, the Commission focused much of it on the federal bureaucracy.

---

*National Commission on Terrorist Attacks Upon the United States, http://www.9-11commission.gov/; Thomas H. Kean and Lee H. Hamilton, "Public Statement: Release of 9/11 Commission Report" (July 22, 2004), p. 5, http://www.9-11commission.gov/report/911Report_Statement.pdf.

†Kean and Hamilton, "Public Statement," p. 1.

Questions

1. To what extent can the government's failure to prevent the 9/11 attacks be attributed to the bureaucracy itself? To the laws and regulations which govern the bureaucracy? To White House and congressional officials who manage and oversee the bureaucracy?
2. Are the problems identified by the 9/11 Commission inherent in any large bureaucracy? (See selections 11.1 and 11.2 as you consider your answer.)

11.3 The 9/11 Commission Report (2004)

National Commission on Terrorist Attacks Upon the United States

We believe the 9/11 attacks revealed four kinds of failures: in imagination, policy, capabilities, and management. . . .

Imagination

. . . Imagination is not a gift usually associated with bureaucracies. For example, before Pearl Harbor the U.S. government had excellent intelligence that a Japanese attack was coming, especially after peace talks stalemated at the end of November 1941. These were days, one historian notes, of "excruciating uncertainty." The most likely targets were judged to be in Southeast Asia. An attack was coming, "but officials were at a loss to know where the blow would fall or what more might be done to prevent it." In retrospect, available intercepts pointed to Japanese examination of Hawaii as a possible target. But, another historian observes, "in the face of a clear warning, alert measures bowed to routine."

It is therefore crucial to find a way of routinizing, even bureaucratizing, the exercise of imagination. Doing so requires more than finding an expert who can imagine that aircraft could be used as weapons. Indeed, since al Qaeda and other groups had already used suicide vehicles, namely truck bombs, the leap to the use of other vehicles such as boats . . . or planes is not far-fetched.

Yet these scenarios were slow to work their way into the thinking of aviation security experts. In 1996, as a result of the TWA Flight 800 crash, President Clinton created a commission under Vice President Al Gore to report on shortcomings in aviation security in the United States. The Gore Commission's report, having thoroughly canvassed available expertise in and outside of government, did not mention suicide hijackings or the use of aircraft as weapons. It focused mainly on

---

Excerpted from National Commission on Terrorist Attacks Upon the United States, "The 9/11 Commission Report," chap. 11, July 22, 2004, http://www.9-11commission.gov/report/index.htm.

the danger of placing bombs onto aircraft. . . . The Gore Commission did call attention, however, to lax screening of passengers and what they carried onto planes. . . .

In late 1998, reports came in of a possible al Qaeda plan to hijack a plane. One, a December 4 Presidential Daily Briefing [PDB] for President Clinton . . . brought the focus back to more traditional hostage taking; it reported Bin Ladin's involvement in planning a hijack operation to free prisoners such as the "Blind Sheikh" Omar Abdel Rahman. Had the contents of this PDB been brought to the attention of a wider group, including key members of Congress, it might have brought much more attention to the need for permanent changes in domestic airport and airline security procedures.

Threat reports also mentioned the possibility of using an aircraft filled with explosives. The most prominent of these mentioned a possible plot to fly an explosives-laden aircraft into a U.S. city. . . .

[Richard] Clarke [the White House staffer long responsible for counterterrorism policy coordination] had been concerned about the danger posed by aircraft since at least the 1996 Atlanta Olympics. There he had tried to create an air defense plan using assets from the Treasury Department, after the Defense Department declined to contribute resources. The Secret Service continued to work on the problem of airborne threats to the Washington region. In 1998, Clarke chaired an exercise designed to highlight the inadequacy of the solution. This paper exercise involved a scenario in which a group of terrorists commandeered a Learjet on the ground in Atlanta, loaded it with explosives, and flew it toward a target in Washington, D.C. Clarke asked officials from the Pentagon, Federal Aviation Administration (FAA), and Secret Service what they could do about the situation. Officials from the Pentagon said they could scramble aircraft from Langley Air Force Base, but they would need to go to the President for rules of engagement, and there was no mechanism to do so. There was no clear resolution of the problem at the exercise.

We can therefore establish that at least some government agencies were concerned about the hijacking danger and had speculated about various scenarios. The challenge was to flesh out and test those scenarios, then figure out a way to turn a scenario into constructive action.

Since the Pearl Harbor attack of 1941, the intelligence community has devoted generations of effort to understanding the problem of forestalling a surprise attack. Rigorous analytic methods were developed, focused in particular on the Soviet Union, and several leading practitioners within the intelligence community discussed them with us. These methods have been articulated in many ways, but almost all seem to have at least four elements in common: (1) think about how surprise attacks might be launched; (2) identify telltale indicators connected to the most dangerous possibilities; (3) where feasible, collect intelligence on these indicators; and (4) adopt defenses to deflect the most dangerous possibilities or at least trigger an earlier warning.

After the end of the Gulf War, concerns about lack of warning led to a major study conducted for DCI [Director of Central Intelligence] Robert Gates in 1992 that proposed several recommendations, among them strengthening the national intelligence officer for warning. We were told that these measures languished under Gates's successors. Responsibility for warning related to a terrorist attack passed from the national intelligence officer for warning to the CTC [the CIA's Counterterrorist Center]. An Intelligence Community Counterterrorism Board had the responsibility to issue threat advisories.

With the important exception of analysis of al Qaeda efforts in chemical, biological, radiological, and nuclear weapons, we did not find evidence that the methods to avoid surprise attack that had been so laboriously developed over the years were regularly applied.

Considering what was not done suggests possible ways to institutionalize imagination. To return to the four elements of analysis just mentioned:

1. The CTC did not analyze how an aircraft, hijacked or explosives-laden, might be used as a weapon. It did not perform this kind of analysis from the enemy's perspective ("red team" analysis), even though suicide terrorism had become a principal tactic of Middle Eastern terrorists. If it had done so, we believe such an analysis would soon have spotlighted a critical constraint for the terrorists—finding a suicide operative able to fly large jet aircraft. They had never done so before 9/11.

2. The CTC did not develop a set of telltale indicators for this method of attack. For example, one such indicator might be the discovery of possible terrorists pursuing flight training to fly large jet aircraft, or seeking to buy advanced flight simulators.

3. The CTC did not propose, and the intelligence community collection management process did not set, requirements to monitor such telltale indicators. Therefore the warning system was not looking for information such as the July 2001 FBI report of potential terrorist interest in various kinds of aircraft training in Arizona, or the August 2001 arrest of Zacarias Moussaoui because of his suspicious behavior in a Minnesota flight school. In late August, the Moussaoui arrest was briefed to the DCI and other top CIA officials under the heading "Islamic Extremist Learns to Fly." Because the system was not tuned to comprehend the potential significance of this information, the news had no effect on warning.

4. Neither the intelligence community nor aviation security experts analyzed systemic defenses within an aircraft or against terrorist-controlled aircraft, suicidal or otherwise. The many threat reports mentioning aircraft were passed to the FAA. While that agency continued to react to specific, credible threats, it did not try to perform the broader warning functions we describe here. No one in the government was taking on that role for domestic vulnerabilities. . . .

The methods for detecting and then warning of surprise attack that the U.S. government had so painstakingly developed in the decades after Pearl Harbor did not fail; instead, they were not really tried. They were not employed to analyze the enemy that, as the twentieth century closed, was most likely to launch a surprise attack directly against the United States. . . .

Policy

The road to 9/11 again illustrates how the large, unwieldy U.S. government tended to underestimate a threat that grew ever greater. The terrorism fostered by Bin Ladin and al Qaeda was different from anything the government had faced before.

The existing mechanisms for handling terrorist acts had been trial and punishment for acts committed by individuals; sanction, reprisal, deterrence, or war for acts by hostile governments. The actions of al Qaeda fit neither category. Its crimes were on a scale approaching acts of war, but they were committed by a loose, far-flung, nebulous conspiracy with no territories or citizens or assets that could be readily threatened, overwhelmed, or destroyed. . . .

The U.S. policy response to al Qaeda before 9/11 was essentially defined following the embassy bombings of August 1998 [in Africa]. . . . It is worth noting that . . . [decisions on how to respond to these attacks] were made by the Clinton administration under extremely difficult domestic political circumstances. Opponents were seeking the President's impeachment. In addition, in 1998–99 President Clinton was preparing the government for possible war against Serbia, and he had authorized major air strikes against Iraq.

The tragedy of the embassy bombings provided an opportunity for a fall examination, across the government, of the national security threat that Bin Ladin posed. Such an examination could have made clear to all that issues were at stake that were much larger than the domestic politics of the moment. But the major policy agencies of the government did not meet the threat.

The diplomatic efforts of the Department of State were largely ineffective. Al Qaeda and terrorism was just one more priority added to already-crowded agendas with countries like Pakistan and Saudi Arabia. After 9/11 that changed.

Policymakers turned principally to the CIA and covert action to implement policy. Before 9/11, no agency had more responsibility—or did more—to attack al Qaeda, working day and night, than the CIA. But there were limits to what the CIA was able to achieve in its energetic worldwide efforts to disrupt terrorist activities or use proxies to try to capture or kill Bin Ladin and his lieutenants. As early as mid-1997, one CIA officer wrote to his supervisor: "All we're doing is holding the ring until the cavalry gets here."

Military measures failed or were not applied. Before 9/11 the Department of Defense was not given the mission of ending al Qaeda's sanctuary in Afghanistan.

Officials in both the Clinton and Bush administrations regarded a full U.S. invasion of Afghanistan as practically inconceivable before 9/11. It was never the subject of formal interagency deliberation.

Lesser forms of intervention could also have been considered. One would have been the deployment of U.S. military or intelligence personnel, or special strike forces, to Afghanistan itself or nearby—openly, clandestinely (secretly), or covertly (with their connection to the United States hidden). Then the United States would no longer have been dependent on proxies to gather actionable intelligence. However, it would have needed to secure basing and overflight support from neighboring countries. A significant political, military, and intelligence effort would have been required, extending over months and perhaps years, with associated costs and risks. Given how hard it has proved to locate Bin Ladin even today when there are substantial ground forces in Afghanistan, its odds of success are hard to calculate. We have found no indication that President Clinton was offered such an intermediate choice, or that this option was given any more consideration than the idea of invasion. . . .

Capabilities

... Before 9/11, the United States tried to solve the al Qaeda problem with the same government institutions and capabilities it had used in the last stages of the Cold War and its immediate aftermath. These capabilities were insufficient, but little was done to expand or reform them.

For covert action, of course, the White House depended on the Counterterrorist Center and the CIA's Directorate of Operations. Though some officers, particularly in the Bin Ladin unit, were eager for the mission, most were not. The higher management of the directorate was unenthusiastic. The CIA's capacity to conduct paramilitary operations with its own personnel was not large, and the Agency did not seek a large-scale general expansion of these capabilities before 9/11. James Pavitt, the head of this directorate, remembered that covert action, promoted by the White House, had gotten the Clandestine Service into trouble in the past. He had no desire to see this happen again. He thought, not unreasonably, that a truly serious counterterrorism campaign against an enemy of this magnitude would be business primarily for the military, not the Clandestine Service.

As for the Department of Defense, some officers in the Joint Staff were keen to help. . . . [But at] no point before 9/11 was the Department of Defense fully engaged in the mission of countering al Qaeda, though this was perhaps the most dangerous foreign enemy then threatening the United States. The Clinton administration effectively relied on the CIA to take the lead in preparing long-term offensive plans against an enemy sanctuary. The Bush administration adopted this approach, although its emerging new strategy envisioned some yet undefined further role for the military in addressing the problem. Within Defense, both [Clinton Defense] Secretary [William] Cohen and [Bush Defense] Secretary Donald Rumsfeld gave their principal attention to other challenges. . . .

The most serious weaknesses in agency capabilities were in the domestic arena. . . . The FBI did not have the capability to link the collective knowledge of agents in the field to national priorities. The acting director of the FBI did not learn of his Bureau's hunt for two possible al Qaeda operatives in the United States or about his Bureau's arrest of an Islamic extremist taking flight training until September 11. The director of central intelligence knew about the FBI's Moussaoui investigation weeks before word of it made its way even to the FBI's own assistant director for counterterrorism.

Other agencies deferred to the FBI. In the August 6 PDB reporting to President Bush of 70 full-field investigations related to al Qaeda, news the President said he found heartening, the CIA had simply restated what the FBI had said. No one looked behind the curtain.

The FAA's capabilities to take aggressive, anticipatory security measures were especially weak. Any serious policy examination of a suicide hijacking scenario, critiquing each of the layers of the security system, could have suggested changes to fix glaring vulnerabilities—expanding no-fly lists, searching passengers identified by . . . [a preflight] screening system, deploying Federal Air Marshals domestically, hardening cockpit doors, alerting air crew to a different kind of hijacking than what they had been trained to expect, or adjusting the training of controllers and managers. . . .

Management

[There were] various missed opportunities to thwart the 9/11 plot. Information was not shared, sometimes inadvertently or because of legal misunderstandings. Analysis was not pooled. Effective operations were not launched. Often the handoffs of information were lost across the divide separating the foreign and domestic agencies of the government.

However the specific problems are labeled, we believe they are symptoms of the government's broader inability to adapt how it manages problems to the new challenges of the twenty-first century. The agencies are like a set of specialists in a hospital, each ordering tests, looking for symptoms, and prescribing medications. What is missing is the attending physician who makes sure they work as a team. . . .

The DCI did not develop a management strategy for a war against Islamist terrorism before 9/11. Such a management strategy would define the capabilities the intelligence community must acquire for such a war—from language training to collection systems to analysts. Such a management strategy would necessarily extend beyond the CTC to the components that feed its expertise and support its operations, linked transparently to counterterrorism objectives. It would then detail the proposed expenditures and organizational changes required to acquire and implement these capabilities.

DCI Tenet and his deputy director for operations told us they did have a management strategy for a war on terrorism. It was to rebuild the CIA. They said the CIA as a whole had been badly damaged by prior budget constraints and that capabilities needed to be restored across the board. Indeed, the CTC budget had not been cut while the budgets had been slashed in many other parts of the Agency. By restoring funding across the CIA, a rising tide would lift all boats. They also stressed the synergy between improvements of every part of the Agency and the capabilities that the CTC or stations overseas could draw on in the war on terror.

As some officials pointed out to us, there is a tradeoff in this management approach. In an attempt to rebuild everything at once, the highest priority efforts might not get the maximum support that they need. Furthermore, this approach attempted to channel relatively strong outside support for combating terrorism into backing for across-the-board funding increases. Proponents of the counterterrorism agenda might respond by being less inclined to loosen the purse strings than they would have been if offered a convincing counterterrorism budget strategy. The DCIs management strategy was also focused mainly on the CIA.

Lacking a management strategy for the war on terrorism or ways to see how funds were being spent across the community, DCI Tenet and his aides found it difficult to develop an overall intelligence community budget for a war on terrorism.

Responsibility for domestic intelligence gathering on terrorism was vested solely in the FBI, yet during almost all of the Clinton administration the relationship between the FBI Director and the President was nearly nonexistent. The FBI Director would not communicate directly with the President. His key personnel shared very little information with the National Security Council and the rest of the national security community. As a consequence, one of the critical working relationships in the counterterrorism effort was broken. . . . ■

View from the Inside

Kenneth Ashworth—currently a public administration professor but once a bureaucrat himself—draws on his experiences in the public sector to dispense wisdom in a series of letters from "Uncle Ken" to his niece Kim, who is interested in a career in public service. In this selection, Uncle Ken dispenses some practical advice on how government officials can succeed in influencing public policy.

Questions

1. What does Ashworth mean by "opportunism"? What characteristics of bureaucracy might discourage officials from acting opportunistically?
2. How might the federal officials involved in counterterrorism before 9/11 (see selection 11.3) have benefited from heeding Ashworth's advice?

11.4 Taking the Initiative, or Risk Taking Inside Government (2001)

Kenneth Ashworth

Dear Kim

You will by now be hearing a lot about theories and models as to how decisions and public policies are made. And you will probably have run across some criticism of these conceptual frameworks, such as that they ignore the role played by opportunity and chance events in how things get done in government. Politicians are forever being criticized for being opportunists. I want to see if I can't defend to you opportunism as an effective approach to promoting government programs and policies.

In the first place, why would we believe that a person who feels strongly about a cause or goal should not eagerly take advantage of circumstances that can advance that cause or goal? Since a primary requirement for moving governments to address public issues is the political will to act and since a responsibility of public executives is to infuse that political will into policymakers, anything that can solidify or influence political will is too good to be ignored or discarded.

In the 1950s it was suddenly discovered that the popular use in Europe of thalidomide to ease sleeping problems of pregnant women was the cause of severe birth defects. With that the mounting criticisms of the Federal Drug Administration (FDA) as being too slow in approving new drugs immediately stopped. Those defending and wishing to reinforce the agency's rigorous review procedures for new drugs seized on the circumstances to strengthen the FDA's legal and regulatory position.

Since opportunities and chance events can have such an impact on policy development, government officials endeavor to find ways to shape and influence events to their advantage, that is, to create "opportunities." Odd as it may seem for a public administrator not to run from criticism, one way to create opportunities is to build opposition to an existing condition. For example, if you are convinced that a change in policy needs to be made, one sure way to get shot down quickly is to propose the change because you personally can look ahead and foresee its need. You can help kill such a good policy change by saying it is your personal sense that it is a good idea. This is particularly true when there is no visible or audible objection to the present situation or existing policy.

Politicians and many policymakers do follow the old adage, "If it ain't broke, don't fix it." And if you alone say something is broke, you are likely to be ignored. It is far better for you to propose a modification to a policy in response to vigorous criticism of the status quo. In other words, it sometimes helps to have countervailing opposition to how you and your agency are doing things at the moment. This may mean that you need to stimulate an opposition group, or even to create one, to attack you for doing nothing about their concerns. This criticism then allows you to modify your rules or to propose to your policymaking body a compromise position that moves away from the old policy. You aren't out on a limb by yourself. Rather you are trying to find a reasonable new policy to accommodate those people who are complaining.

When there was reluctance and hesitancy by the state government to move quickly enough in responding to minority underrepresentation in higher education, I appointed an advisory committee and arranged for the minority co-chairs (Hispanic and African American) to address our board on the committee's findings. They used this meeting as a public forum to present facts and projections that would have drawn yawns or tut-tuts if presented by our own staff. The emotional quality of the reports, presented by minorities, was essential to give the issue personal and human interest for press coverage and visibility. Much of the criticism was directed at our agency and some of it at me personally. This created a situation that demanded a reaction by us and by the legislature. In their zeal, the critics—those I had appointed as co-chairs—moved on in their enthusiasm to visit legislators and other state leaders as well. And in doing so, they were presenting data my own staff had put together. In the meantime we and our board were busy setting new directions and goals in anticipation of coming pressures from the legislature and the governor's office. Even if I were represented as unresponsive and dilatory in not taking action before the report, it was a small price to pay for the progress we were able to make afterward.

When the Federal Fifth Circuit Court ruled in 1996 that Texas could no longer take race into consideration in admissions and financial aid decisions, I appointed a committee of fifteen sociologists, consisting of a majority of minority members. Their task was to study the feasibility of identifying markers and social characteristics that we might use as a surrogate for race. When they reported their findings to our board, the committee told us that they had found that using combinations of all other sociological categories, but not race, would still result in a fifty percent reduction in minority admissions in coming years. But these negative findings were not useless. They were picked up by the legislature in drafting bills to ease the impact of the court ruling. The findings had a particular impact on the conservative legislators, who did not want minority enrollments to decline sharply because they recognized that Texas will soon become "majority minorities." They might object to favoritism of any kind based on race or ethnicity, but as a result of our study they suddenly became very interested in finding other approaches the schools and the legislature could still use to recruit and retain minority students.

I have always thought that Alice Roosevelt Longworth, Theodore Roosevelt's daughter, was talking about this approach to policymaking when she was in her nineties. A reporter asked her if she had developed a philosophy of life from her experience. She replied, "I have. Empty what's full, fill what's empty, and scratch where it itches." I think she believed in this definition of the primary responsibility of the public servant: "Comfort the afflicted and afflict the comfortable." I'll bet she would have been among the first to agree that from time to time you have to introduce a few gnats and fleas to start some itching.

Once when I was addressing an annual meeting of the Mexican American Legal Defense and Education Fund (MALDEF), I was commending them for how effectively we had been working together despite our apparent differences in public. We were getting results even if we were a long way from conspiring. They had been impatiently pushing the state to move off the dime to increase Hispanic enrollments in higher education, and our agency had been progressively making things somewhat better by responding to their pushing. As a metaphor in my talk I used Mark Twain's comment that every dog should have a few fleas; it keeps him from forgetting he's a dog. Several of them apologized later after some of their colleagues had left the meeting to report that the commissioner was now calling Mexican Americans fleas.

This reminds me of a blooper during a campaign for governor. The campaign staff of one candidate tried out the new capacity of computers to use first names in the salutation of letters to voters to personalize the governor's campaign messages. For example, you would have received a "Dear Kim" letter from this candidate whom you did not know at all. A friend from the Mexican American Legal Defense and Education Fund sent me a copy of a note he had written to a colleague with the African American Students Association at a nearby university. My MALDEF friend wrote, "I am enclosing a campaign letter I just received beginning, 'Dear Mexican.' It is with fear and trepidation that I wait to learn how yours was addressed."

The opportunities that come your way may be in small things, not big nation-shaking policies. In 1965, I was working with the U.S. Office of Education (before it became a department), running a grant program of several hundred million dollars for constructing college classrooms and laboratories. At the end of the fiscal year in June we had about $5 million left over that we could not commit because some states had not fully used up their allotted shares. I was in my office over lunch trying to figure out how to allocate these remaining funds among the states.

My division director, Jay du Von, came in and said President [Lyndon] Johnson had just talked with the secretary of Health, Education and Welfare and the secretary had, in turn, called him to say the president wanted all federal agencies to do everything they could to help Topeka, Kansas, and Washburn University. Just the night before the city had been hit by a devastating tornado and the university had been largely destroyed. Jay said to let him know right away if I had any ideas on how we might help.

When he left I turned back to the problem on my desk, how to deal with the $5 million figuratively lying there awaiting my decision. I saw an opportunity and I quickly dashed off a briefing memo which made these points:

We have $5 million for construction grants left for the year.

Our rules say to divide it among states with remaining demand.

All states have received funds under the program.

Congress likes the program so much they have *doubled* our appropriation for next year.

With everybody counting on more money next year and Washburn U so badly hurt, I doubt any state or university president would want to appear a "dog in the manger" and complain if President Johnson were to announce that he has given the $5 million to Washburn University.

No bureaucratic delays here. As I recall, the White House announced the commitment of the funds within the hour. Our offer was the first to reach the president's desk since his directive to the federal agencies and departments. And when my direct boss returned from lunch and found out what we had done, he was livid at our having violated written rules and regulations in such a cavalier manner.

Lessons: (a) Learn to quickly write short and convincing briefing memos, and (b) when the big boss is in the stew with you, you'll probably survive being unorthodox. Incidentally, I will make a note to tell you in a later letter a few things about writing briefing memos.

The greatest fun in being a government executive is the ability from time to time to create a new program. One day I had to go to Corpus Christi to give a commencement talk and as I read over my speech before leaving my office I was not particularly pleased with it. So I grabbed a handful of my business cards. That night, after congratulating the graduates, I said, "But I'm talking to the wrong group here. You are sitting there in your caps and gowns all prepared for success. I want to address the younger people here tonight. To be successful you will need a network of influential people so in a few years you can also be sitting down there in your own caps and gowns. I want to be part of your network to help you get ahead. After the ceremony is over if you young people will come up here on the stage I will give you my business card. I want you to take it home and stick it on your mirror where you'll see it every day to remind you of our deal we are going to make tonight. Our deal is this: You graduate from high school and I will guarantee that you will get the financial aid you need to go to college."

Of course I ran out of cards, but I wrote names and addresses on the back of my speech and the next week we sent those students cards and letters as well. This was no big commitment on my part because the state already guaranteed student financial aid to needy high school graduates. Students and parents just don't always know this. Our agency turned what I did that evening into a statewide program.

Today we still send a newsletter to the eighth grade students across the state as we try to reach the most economically deprived young people. We have received hundreds of letters over the years from students I have promised to help, calling on me to meet my end of our bargain since they have met theirs by graduating from high school. One letter I remember particularly. A thirteen-year-old girl wrote saying, "I have lost the card you gave me. Does that mean I can't go to college?"

The point here is that entrepreneurship is not limited to the business sector. You need to learn to be a risk taker in government too. You must learn to recognize opportunities when they come your way and be prepared to grab them. Often those opportunities are ephemeral and will disappear quickly. "Wild Bill" Donovan, chief spy and director of the OSS [Office of Strategic Services] in World War II, frequently used to say, "The perfect is the enemy of the good." A perfect or better decision or plan of action late by a day or even an hour may prove worthless. A timely but merely good decision or plan of action may serve to seize an opportunity that will otherwise be lost. Of course you must learn to expect the Monday morning quarterbacks who will later criticize you for not having used a more perfect approach to the circumstances you faced at the moment.   .   .   .

I have been telling you about opportunity and the role it plays in government decisions and policies. But there is a corollary and that is patience. When I first took on higher level positions I constantly worried about how to be ready for every problem that I saw coming at me or likely to come. I spent enormous amounts of energy and time trying to develop responses and to be ready for those eventualities. Then in time several things became clear to me. I have gained confidence that I can handle the problems when they actually arrive. Second, I have found that some of the problems never came to full bloom and I was wasting my time planning ahead too far. Third, that the problems, when they do come into full bloom, are so different from what I had imagined and spent time preparing for that an entirely different response is often required. And last, I have found I can be more effective in trying to influence the circumstances and conditions related to the developing problems rather than focusing on the imagined problems to come. I have learned I can sometimes shape the development of the problem more to my liking. I look constantly for opportunities to change the way problems come to me. I have discovered this is a better and more effective use of my time and energy than worrying about detailed solutions and responses for possible use in the future.

Another point about patience. There was a time when I became convinced that I could not survive in my job because the governor wanted me out. The governor had just appointed one-third of my eighteen-member board every two years, and the new governor had just appointed six who seemed committed to questioning my every move and recommendation and to make my job as agency executive miserable. I reasoned that with his next set of six appointees he'd have the two-thirds necessary to have me removed. I considered, metaphorically speaking, turning off my engine when I saw a flat, green pasture ahead and gliding down to an easy landing, that is, taking a job in one of our universities, from whence I had come to this job. But the more I thought about it the more I came to the realization that I had come into the public service to have at least one really good fight someday, and this might be it. I decided, to continue the metaphor, I'd rather be shot down in flames. So I was unremitting in my staff recommendation to the board and refused to quit. Then two years later, when the next six appointees arrived, I found that I had underestimated the educability of the governor's first six appointees. I still had twelve solid supporters on the board, who immediately set out to educate the new, entering freshman class of board members that the governor might be wrong about their executive.

I have had the impression that every new governor wanted me fired. It is not so much that the governors have disliked me—and several of them truly have—but because I have worked for the previous governor and because they would prefer to have their own person in the commissioner's position. There is clearly a good argument to be made for the cabinet form of government, wherein every new governor should be able to appoint his or her own people to all top state agency positions. How else can the new governor carry out policies and be responsive to the voters who elected him or her to do certain things and change government in accordance with the platform if he or she cannot put his or her own appointees into the key jobs?

On the other hand, I can argue, with a strong personal interest, that the higher education commissioner's job should not be politicized and that it should remain nonpartisan. Under a cabinet form of government, the commissioner and other offices filled by a governor become lame duck positions when the governor is in his last term. Moreover, there would be a great loss of continuity and expertise with frequent turnovers in the office. This argument can be made for other specialized fields in government as well, such as health, the public schools, and the state police. The structure wherein governors appoint boards which, in turn, hire and fire commissioners and agency heads seems to me to provide sufficient accountability to the governor and the voters, even if there is a time delay during which the governor is not able to force immediate turnover in all agency executives. In any event, you can see why I like this system better than the cabinet form of state government. This is the principal reason I have survived in my job for over twenty years.

One lesson I learned is to have patience and to keep on working and playing the game. I gained an appreciation for the Arab story about the camel driver caught in the sheik's harem. When he returned to the prison yard from his scheduled execution, everyone was amazed and asked how he had managed to survive. He explained that he had convinced the sheik that he would teach his horse to fly. They all exclaimed this was impossible, why bother to try? To which he replied, "Perhaps. But while I am teaching the horse to fly many things might happen. The sheik might die. The horse might die. I might die. And, who knows, I may teach that horse to fly." Keep your options open. Keep playing the game.

You asked in your last letter for me to write to you about leadership. I have been, haven't you noticed? Everybody wants the formula or the secrets or they want the books and instructional tapes that reveal the formulas and secrets. In any event, I will think on it after I've written you on several other topics I've jotted down—if there's anything special left over to say on the topic.

Your transgressive kinsman,

Uncle Ken ■

Chapter 12

The Judiciary

Nearly fifty years ago, constitutional scholar Robert G. McCloskey surveyed the history of the Supreme Court of the United States and concluded, "Surely the record teaches that no useful purpose is served when the judges seek the hottest political cauldrons of the moment and dive into the middle of them." Instead, "The Court's greatest successes have been achieved when it has operated near the margins of, rather than in the center of, political controversy, when it has nudged and gently tugged the nation, instead of trying to rule it."* Writing after the Court's 1954 school desegregation decision but before the controversies over reapportionment of state legislatures, abortion, busing, and school prayer, McCloskey feared for the Court's future if it did not learn the lessons of its past.

The Court, of course, did not follow McCloskey's advice. Over the past five decades, the Supreme Court has become an increasingly important force in American politics and the subject of intense, and at times bitter, political controversy. In the 1960s and 1970s, the Court's most controversial decisions involved questions of civil rights and civil liberties. Although such cases remain prominent on the Court's agenda, in recent years the justices have also turned their attention to other divisive issues, including those arising from the separation of powers, federalism, economic rights, abortion rights, and the war on terrorism. In 2000, the Court even injected itself into the contentious arena of electoral politics, making a ruling in *Bush* v. *Gore* that, in effect, decided who would be the next president of the United States.

All of this judicial activity has created a highly charged political debate over the proper role of the courts in American society. Every president since Ronald Reagan has endeavored to reshape the Court in his image, with varying degrees of success. Most recently, President George W. Bush had the opportunity to appoint two new justices, to replace Chief Justice William H. Rehnquist and Associate Justice Sandra Day O'Connor. Bush chose two men with impeccable conservative credentials—John G. Roberts Jr. to replace Rehnquist, and Samuel A. Alito Jr. to replace O'Connor. Although it is too early to say for sure, the Roberts and Alito appointments seem likely to move the Court in a more conservative direction.

This chapter surveys the many aspects of the judiciary's role in American politics and society. Selections 12.1 and 12.2 present two classic arguments on behalf of judicial review—the first by Alexander Hamilton, the second by Chief Justice John Marshall.

---

*Robert McCloskey, *The American Supreme Court* (Chicago: University of Chicago Press, 1960), p. 229.

Selection 12.3, by *Baltimore Sun* reporter Lyle Denniston, examines the ongoing transition from the Rehnquist to the Roberts Court. Selection 12.4 spotlights the debate over whether the Constitution should be interpreted according to its original meaning or as a living document, while selection 12.5 tells the story of a man who had the extraordinary experience of arguing his own case before the Supreme Court.

Chapter Questions

1. What are the advantages and disadvantages of leaving political decisions to the courts instead of to the political branches of the federal government or to the states? What qualities do the courts have that make such activism attractive? Unattractive, or even dangerous?
2. What is the relationship between the federal judiciary and the other branches of the federal government? In what ways do the three branches of government work together to make policy? In what ways is the relationship competitive or adversarial?

Foundations

The Supreme Court's power to review acts of Congress and decide whether they are unconstitutional is perhaps the most extraordinary power possessed by any court in the world; the decision of five of nine justices can nullify the expressed will of the people's representatives in Congress. Moreover, the Court can strike down laws passed by state or local officials based on a conflict with federal law. Although Supreme Court decisions striking down major acts of Congress have been relatively infrequent, the Court has frequently nullified unconstitutional measures passed by the states.

Despite the enormity of the Court's power of judicial review, as it is known, this power was not explicitly granted to the Court by the Constitution. The lack of specific language in the Constitution on this point—probably because the delegates could not agree as to whether the state or the federal courts should have the last word—made it necessary for the Supreme Court to claim and defend its power of judicial review later. The justices who were most influential in this struggle were Chief Justice John Marshall and his ally, Justice Joseph Story.

The following two selections trace the highlights of this struggle. The first is Alexander Hamilton's classic defense of judicial review in *Federalist* No. 78. The second is Marshall's 1803 decision in *Marbury* v. *Madison*, in which the Supreme Court first claimed the power of judicial review.

Question

1. Hamilton begins his argument with a defense of the Constitution's provision for life appointment of justices of the Supreme Court. How does this argument relate to his and John Marshall's defense of judicial review?

12.1 *Federalist* No. 78 (1788)

Alexander Hamilton

Outline

I. Mode of appointment of federal judges.

II. Necessity of lifetime appointments for federal judges.

   A. The judiciary is the least dangerous and the weakest branch; life tenure is essential to preserving its independence from the other branches.

   B. Life tenure is particularly important in a system with a limited Constitution, which cannot be preserved in practice except if judges have the authority to strike down laws that are inconsistent with the Constitution (a power known as judicial review).

      1. Defense of judicial review.

         i. Congress merely acts as the agent of the people; the Constitution sets out the terms of agency and must take precedence over acts of Congress.

         ii. The Constitution is a fundamental law; it belongs to the judges to give it meaning and to enforce it in preference to any legislative act.

         iii. The Courts cannot substitute their own judgment for that of the legislature; they must exercise judgment, not will.

         iv. Judges must be independent (and thus hold life tenure) in order to play this role without legislative interference.

      2. An independent judiciary also protects against legislative acts which do not violate the Constitution but do interfere with private rights.

      3. There are a few individuals in society who combine the necessary skill and integrity to be federal judges; life tenure may be necessary to encourage such people to leave the private practice of law for the federal bench.

We proceed now to an examination of the judiciary department of the proposed government.

In unfolding the defects of the existing Confederation, the utility and necessity of a federal judicature have been clearly pointed out. It is the less necessary to recapitulate the considerations there urged, as the propriety of the institution in the abstract is not disputed; the only questions which have been raised being relative to the manner of constituting it, and to its extent. To these points, therefore, our observations shall be confined.

The manner of constituting it seems to embrace these several objects: 1st. The mode of appointing the judges. 2d. The tenure by which they are to hold their places. . . .

First. As to the mode of appointing the judges; this is the same with that of appointing the officers of the Union in general. . . .

Second. As to the tenure by which the judges are to hold their places; this chiefly concerns their duration in office; the provisions for their support; the precautions for their responsibility.

According to the plan of the convention, all judges who may be appointed by the United States are to hold their offices DURING GOOD BEHAVIOR; which is conformable to the most approved of the State constitutions and among the rest, to that of this State. Its propriety having been drawn into question by the adversaries of that plan, is no light symptom of the rage for objection, which disorders their imaginations and judgments. The standard of good behavior for the continuance in office of the judicial magistracy, is certainly one of the most valuable of the modern improvements in the practice of government. In a monarchy it is an excellent barrier to the despotism of the prince; in a republic it is a no less excellent barrier to the encroachments and oppressions of the representative body. And it is the best expedient which can be devised in any government, to secure a steady, upright, and impartial administration of the laws.

Whoever attentively considers the different departments of power must perceive, that, in a government in which they are separated from each other, the judiciary, from the nature of its functions, will always be the least dangerous to the political rights of the Constitution; because it will be least in a capacity to annoy or injure them. The Executive not only dispenses the honors, but holds the sword of the community. The legislature not only commands the purse, but prescribes the rules by which the duties and rights of every citizen are to be regulated. The judiciary, on the contrary, has no influence over either the sword or the purse; no direction either of the strength or of the wealth of the society; and can take no active resolution whatever. It may truly be said to have neither FORCE nor WILL, but merely judgment; and must ultimately depend upon the aid of the executive arm even for the efficacy of its judgments.

This simple view of the matter suggests several important consequences. It proves incontestably, that the judiciary is beyond comparison the weakest of the three departments of power; that it can never attack with success either of the other two; and that all possible care is requisite to enable it to defend itself against their attacks. It equally proves, that though individual oppression may now and then proceed from the courts of justice, the general liberty of the people can never be endangered from that quarter; I mean so long as the judiciary remains truly distinct from both the legislature and the Executive. For I agree, that "there is no liberty, if the power of judging be not separated from the legislative and executive powers." And it proves, in the last place, that as liberty can have nothing to fear from the judiciary alone, but would have every thing to fear from its union with either of the other departments; that as all the effects of such a union must ensue from a dependence of the former on the latter, notwithstanding a nominal and apparent separation; that as, from the natural feebleness of the judiciary, it is in continual jeopardy of being overpowered, awed, or influenced by its coordinate branches; and that as nothing can contribute so much to its firmness and independence as permanency in office, this quality may therefore be justly regarded as an indispensable ingredient in its constitution, and, in a great measure, as the citadel of the public justice and the public security.

The complete independence of the courts of justice is peculiarly essential in a limited Constitution. By a limited Constitution, I understand one which contains certain specified exceptions to the legislative authority; such, for instance, as that it shall pass no bills of attainder, no *ex-post-facto* laws, and the like. Limitations of this kind can be preserved in practice no other way than through the medium of courts of justice, whose duty it must be to declare all acts contrary to the manifest tenor of the Constitution void. Without this, all the reservations of particular rights or privileges would amount to nothing.

Some perplexity respecting the rights of the courts to pronounce legislative acts void, because contrary to the Constitution, has arisen from an imagination that the doctrine would imply a superiority of the judiciary to the legislative power. It is urged that the authority which can declare the acts of another void, must necessarily be superior to the one whose acts may be declared void. As this doctrine is of great importance in all the American constitutions, a brief discussion of the ground on which it rests cannot be unacceptable.

There is no position which depends on clearer principles, than that every act of a delegated authority, contrary to the tenor of the commission under which it is exercised, is void. No legislative act, therefore, contrary to the Constitution, can be valid. To deny this, would be to affirm, that the deputy is greater than his principal; that the servant is above his master; that the representatives of the people are superior to the people themselves; that men acting by virtue of powers, may do not only what their powers do not authorize, but what they forbid.

If it be said that the legislative body are themselves the constitutional judges of their own powers, and that the construction they put upon them is conclusive upon the other departments, it may be answered, that this cannot be the natural presumption, where it is not to be collected from any particular provisions in the Constitution. It is not otherwise to be supposed, that the Constitution could intend to enable the representatives of the people to substitute their WILL to that of their constituents. It is far more rational to suppose, that the courts were designed to be an intermediate body between the people and the legislature, in order, among other things, to keep the latter within the limits assigned to their authority. The interpretation of the laws is the proper and peculiar province of the courts. A constitution is, in fact, and must be regarded by the judges, as a fundamental law. It therefore belongs to them to ascertain its meaning, as well as the meaning of any particular act proceeding from the legislative body. If there should happen to be an irreconcilable variance between the two, that which has the superior obligation and validity ought, of course, to be preferred; or, in other words, the Constitution ought to be preferred to the statute, the intention of the people to the intention of their agents.

Nor does this conclusion by any means suppose a superiority of the judicial to the legislative power. It only supposes that the power of the people is superior to both; and that where the will of the legislature, declared in its statutes, stands in opposition to that of the people, declared in the Constitution, the judges ought to be governed by the latter rather than the former. They ought to regulate their decisions by the fundamental laws, rather than by those which are not fundamental.

This exercise of judicial discretion, in determining between two contradictory laws, is exemplified in a familiar instance. It not uncommonly happens, that there are two statutes existing at one time, clashing in whole or in part with each other, and neither of them containing any repealing clause or expression. In such a case, it is the province of the courts to liquidate and fix their meaning and operation. So far as they can, by any fair construction, be reconciled to each other, reason and law conspire to dictate that this should be done; where this is impracticable, it becomes a matter of necessity to give effect to one, in exclusion of the other. The rule which has obtained in the courts for determining their relative validity is, that the last in order of time shall be preferred to the first. But this is a mere rule of construction, not derived from any positive law, but from the nature and reason of the thing. It is a rule not enjoined upon the courts by legislative provision, but adopted by themselves, as consonant to truth and propriety, for the direction of their conduct as interpreters of the law. They thought it reasonable, that between the interfering acts of an EQUAL authority, that which was the last indication of its will should have the preference.

But in regard to the interfering acts of a superior and subordinate authority, of an original and derivative power, the nature and reason of the thing indicate the converse of that rule as proper to be followed. They teach us that the prior act of a superior ought to be preferred to the subsequent act of an inferior and subordinate authority; and that accordingly, whenever a particular statute contravenes the Constitution, it will be the duty of the judicial tribunals to adhere to the latter and disregard the former.

It can be of no weight to say that the courts, on the pretense of a repugnancy, may substitute their own pleasure to the constitutional intentions of the legislature. This might as well happen in the case of two contradictory statutes; or it might as well happen in every adjudication upon any single statute. The courts must declare the sense of the law; and if they should be disposed to exercise WILL instead of JUDGMENT, the consequence would equally be the substitution of their pleasure to that of the legislative body. The observation, if it prove any thing, would prove that there ought to be no judges distinct from that body.

If, then, the courts of justice are to be considered as the bulwarks of a limited Constitution against legislative encroachments, this consideration will afford a strong argument for the permanent tenure of judicial offices, since nothing will contribute so much as this to that independent spirit in the judges which must be essential to the faithful performance of so arduous a duty.

This independence of the judges is equally requisite to guard the Constitution and the rights of individuals from the effects of those ill humors, which the arts of designing men, or the influence of particular conjunctures, sometimes disseminate among the people themselves, and which, though they speedily give place to better information, and more deliberate reflection, have a tendency, in the meantime, to occasion dangerous innovations in the government, and serious oppressions of the minor party in the community. Though I trust the friends of the proposed Constitution will never concur with its enemies, in questioning that fundamental principle of republican government, which admits the right of the people to alter or abolish the established Constitution, whenever they find it inconsistent with their happiness, yet it is not to be inferred from this principle, that the representatives of the people, whenever a momentary inclination happens to lay hold of a majority of their constituents, incompatible with the provisions in the existing Constitution, would, on that account, be justifiable in a violation of those provisions; or that the courts would be under a greater obligation to connive at infractions in this shape, than when they had proceeded wholly from the cabals of the representative body. Until the people have, by some solemn and authoritative act, annulled or changed the established form, it is binding upon themselves collectively, as well as individually; and no presumption, or even knowledge, of their sentiments, can warrant their representatives in a departure from it, prior to such an act. But it is easy to see, that it would require an uncommon portion of fortitude in the judges to do their duty as faithful guardians of the Constitution, where legislative invasions of it had been instigated by the major voice of the community.

But it is not with a view to infractions of the Constitution only, that the independence of the judges may be an essential safeguard against the effects of occasional ill humors in the society. These sometimes extend no farther than to the injury of the private rights of particular classes of citizens, by unjust and partial laws. Here also the firmness of the judicial magistracy is of vast importance in mitigating the severity and confining the operation of such laws. It not only serves to moderate the immediate mischiefs of those which may have been passed, but it operates as a check upon the legislative body in passing them; who, perceiving that obstacles to the success of iniquitous intention are to be expected from the scruples of the courts, are in a manner compelled, by the very motives of the injustice they meditate, to qualify their attempts. This is a circumstance calculated to have more influence upon the character of our governments, than but few may be aware of. The benefits of the integrity and moderation of the judiciary have already been felt in more States than one; and though they may have displeased those whose sinister expectations they may have disappointed, they must have commanded the esteem and applause of all the virtuous and disinterested. Considerate men, of every description, ought to prize whatever will tend to beget or fortify that temper in the courts: as no man can be sure that he may not be to-morrow the victim of a spirit of injustice, by which he may be a gainer to-day. And every man must now feel, that the inevitable tendency of such a spirit is to sap the foundations of public and private confidence, and to introduce in its stead universal distrust and distress.

That inflexible and uniform adherence to the rights of the Constitution, and of individuals, which we perceive to be indispensable in the courts of justice, can certainly not be expected from judges who hold their offices by a temporary commission. Periodical appointments, however regulated, or by whomsoever made, would, in some way or other, be fatal to their necessary independence. If the power of making them was committed either to the Executive or legislature, there would be danger of an improper complaisance to the branch which possessed it; if to both, there would be an unwillingness to hazard the displeasure of either; if to the people, or the persons chosen by them for the special purpose, there would be too great a disposition to consult popularity, to justify a reliance that nothing would be consulted but the Constitution and the laws.

There is yet a further and a weightier reason for the permanency of the judicial offices, which is deducible from the nature of the qualifications they require. It has been frequently remarked, with great propriety, that a voluminous code of laws is one of the inconveniences necessarily connected with the advantages of a free government. To avoid an arbitrary discretion in the courts, it is indispensable that they should be bound down by strict rules and precedents, which serve to define and point out their duty in every particular case that comes before them; and it will readily be conceived from the variety of controversies which grow out of the folly and wickedness of mankind, that the records of those precedents must unavoidably swell to a very considerable bulk, and must demand long and laborious study to acquire a competent knowledge of them. Hence it is, that there can be but few men in the society who will have sufficient skill in the laws to qualify them for the stations of judges. And making the proper deductions for the ordinary depravity of human nature, the number must be still smaller of those who unite the requisite integrity with the requisite knowledge. These considerations apprise us, that the government can have no great option between fit character; and that a temporary duration in office, which would naturally discourage such characters from quitting a lucrative line of practice to accept a seat on the bench, would have a tendency to throw the administration of justice into hands less able, and less well qualified, to conduct it with utility and dignity. In the present circumstances of this country, and in those in which it is likely to be for a long time to come, the disadvantages on this score would be greater than they may at first sight appear; but it must be confessed, that they are far inferior to those which present themselves under the other aspects of the subject.

Upon the whole, there can be no room to doubt that the convention acted wisely in copying from the models of those constitutions which have established GOOD BEHAVIOR as the tenure of their judicial offices, in point of duration; and that so far from being blamable on this account, their plan would have been inexcusably defective, if it had wanted this important feature of good government. The experience of Great Britain affords an illustrious comment on the excellence of the institution. ■

12.2 *Marbury v. Madison* (1803)

Chief Justice John Marshall

[In 1801, at the very end of his presidential term, John Adams made a number of last-minute judicial appointments, hoping to install members of his own Federalist party in key positions before the Republican president, Thomas Jefferson, took over. One of these appointments was given to William Marbury, who was appointed to be a justice of the peace of the District of Columbia. In the confusion of the last few days of Adams's term, however, Marbury's commission was never delivered to him. When President Jefferson came into the White House, he held up Marbury's commission. Marbury sued in the Supreme Court, asking the Court to order the new secretary of state, James Madison, to deliver the commission to him.

5 U.S. (1 Cranch) 137 (1803).

The legal and political aspects of the case are extremely complex. Chief Justice Marshall, a staunch Federalist, did not want to condone Jefferson's actions, but he also did not want to risk ordering the administration to deliver the commission; he would be a laughingstock if Jefferson and Madison simply ignored him. He solved this dilemma by writing a strong opinion condemning Jefferson's acts as illegal but refusing to issue a compliance order. To do so, Marshall concluded, would be unconstitutional.

In one stroke, Marshall embarrassed Jefferson, protected his own position, and claimed for the first time the power to review acts of Congress as unconstitutional. The part of the argument making the last point follows.]

• • •

The question, whether an act, repugnant to the constitution, can become the law of the land, is a question deeply interesting to the United States; but, happily, not of an intricacy proportioned to its interest. It seems only necessary to recognize certain principles, supposed to have been long and well established, to decide it.

That the people have an original right to establish, for their future government, such principles as, in their opinion, shall most conduce to their own happiness, is the basis on which the whole American fabric has been erected. The exercise of this original right is a very great exertion; nor can it, nor ought it, to be frequently repeated. The principles, therefore, so established, are deemed fundamental. And as the authority from which they proceed, is supreme, and can seldom act, they are designed to be permanent.

This original and supreme will organizes the government, and assigns, to different departments, their respective powers. It may either stop here; or establish certain limits not to be transcended by those departments.

The government of the United States is of the latter description. The powers of the legislature are defined, and limited; and that those limits may not be mistaken, or forgotten, the constitution is written. To what purpose are powers limited, and to what purpose is that limitation committed to writing, if these limits may, at any time, be passed by those intended to be restrained? The distinction, between a government with limited and unlimited powers, is abolished, if those limits do not confine the persons on whom they are imposed, and if acts prohibited and acts allowed, are of equal obligation. It is a proposition too plain to be contested, that the constitution controls any legislative act repugnant to it; or, that the legislature may alter the constitution by an ordinary act.

Between these alternatives there is no middle ground. The constitution is either a superior, paramount law, unchangeable by ordinary means, or it is on a level with ordinary legislative acts, and, like other acts, is alterable when the legislature shall please to alter it.

If the former part of the alternative be true, then a legislative act contrary to the constitution is not law: if the latter part be true, then written constitutions are absurd attempts, on the part of the people, to limit a power, in its own nature illimitable.

Certainly all those who have framed written constitutions contemplate them as forming the fundamental and paramount law of the nation, and consequently the theory of every such government must be, that an act of the legislature, repugnant to the constitution, is void.

This theory is essentially attached to a written constitution, and is, consequently to be considered, by this court, as one of the fundamental principles of our society. It is not therefore to be lost sight of in the future consideration of this subject.

If an act of the legislature, repugnant to the constitution, is void, does it, notwithstanding its invalidity, bind the courts, and oblige them to give it effect? Or, in other words, though it be not law, does it constitute a rule as operative as if it was a law? This would be to overthrow in fact what was established in theory; and would seem, at first view, an absurdity too gross to be insisted on. It shall, however, receive a more attentive consideration.

It is emphatically the province and duty of the judicial department to say what the law is. Those who apply the rule to particular cases, must of necessity expound and interpret that rule. If two laws conflict with each other, the courts must decide on the operation of each.

So if a law be in opposition to the constitution; if both the law and the constitution apply to a particular case, so that the court must either decide that case conformably to the law, disregarding the constitution; or conformably to the constitution, disregarding the law; the court must determine which of these conflicting rules governs the case. This is of the very essence of judicial duty.

If, then, the courts are to regard the constitution; and the constitution is superior to any ordinary act of the legislature; the constitution, and not such ordinary act, must govern the case to which they both apply.

Those then who controvert the principle that the constitution is to be considered, in court, as a paramount law, are reduced to the necessity of maintaining that courts must close their eyes on the constitution, and see only the law.

This doctrine would subvert the very foundation of all written constitutions. It would declare that an act which, according to the principles and theory of our government, is entirely void; is yet, in practice, completely obligatory. It would declare, that if the legislature shall do what is expressly forbidden, such act, notwithstanding the express prohibition, is in reality effectual. It would be giving to the legislature a practical and real omnipotence, with the same breath which professes to restrict their powers within narrow limits. It is prescribing limits, and declaring that those limits may be passed at pleasure.

That it thus reduces to nothing what we have deemed the greatest improvement on political institutions—a written constitution—would of itself be sufficient, in America, where written constitutions have been viewed with so much reverence, for rejecting the construction. But the peculiar expressions of the constitution of the United States furnish additional arguments in favour of its rejection.

The judicial power of the United States is extended to all cases arising under the constitution.

Could it be the intention of those who gave this power, to say that, in using it, the constitution should not be looked into? That a case arising under the constitution should be decided without examining the instrument under which it arises?

This is too extravagant to be maintained.

In some cases, then, the constitution must be looked into by the judges. And if they can open it at all, what part of it are they forbidden to read, or to obey?

There are many other parts of the constitution which serve to illustrate this subject. It is declared that "no tax or duty shall be laid on articles exported from any state." Suppose a duty on the export of cotton, of tobacco, or of flour; and a suit instituted to recover it. Ought judgment to be rendered in such a case? ought the judges to close their eyes on the constitution, and only see the law?

The constitution declares that "no bill of attainder or *ex post facto* law shall be passed."

If, however, such a bill should be passed and a person should be prosecuted under it; must the court condemn to death those victims whom the constitution endeavors to preserve?

"No person," says the constitution, "shall be convicted of treason unless on the testimony of two witnesses to the same overt act, or on confession in open court."

Here the language of the constitution is addressed especially to the courts. It prescribes, directly for them, a rule of evidence not to be departed from. If the legislature should change that rule, and declare one witness, or a confession out of court, sufficient for conviction, must the constitutional principle yield to the legislative act?

From these, and many other selections which might be made, it is apparent, that the framers of the constitution contemplated that instrument, as a rule for the government of *courts*, as well as of the legislature.

Why otherwise does it direct the judges to take an oath to support it? This oath certainly applies, in an especial manner, to their conduct in their official character. How immoral to impose it on them, if they were to be used as the instruments, and the knowing instruments, for violating what they swear to support!

The oath of office, too, imposed by the legislature, is completely demonstrative of the legislative opinion on this subject. It is in these words: "I do solemnly swear that I will administer justice without respect to persons, and do equal right to the poor and to the rich; and that I will faithfully and impartially discharge all the duties incumbent on me as according to the best of my abilities and understanding, agreeably to *the constitution*, and laws of the United States."

Why does a judge swear to discharge his duties agreeably to the constitution of the United States, if that constitution forms no rule for his government? If it is closed upon him, and cannot be inspected by him?

If such be the real state of things, this is worse than solemn mockery. To prescribe, or to take this oath, becomes equally a crime.

It is also not entirely unworthy of observation that in declaring what shall be the *supreme* law of the land, the *constitution* itself is first mentioned; and not the laws of the United States generally, but those only which shall be made in *pursuance* of the constitution, have that rank.

Thus, the particular phraseology of the constitution of the United States confirms and strengthens the principle, supposed to be essential to all written constitutions, that a law repugnant to the constitution is void; and that *courts*, as well as other departments, are bound by that instrument. . . . ∎

American Politics Today

President Bill Clinton had the opportunity to appoint two Supreme Court justices in eight years; President George W. Bush was able to appoint two within six months. Bush's appointments of Chief Justice John G. Roberts Jr. and Associate Justice Samuel A. Alito Jr. may mark a critical turning point in the Court's modern history.

The symbolic significance of a new chief justice may mask the larger importance of the Alito appointment. Roberts replaced Chief Justice William H. Rehnquist, who died in September 2005 after a long illness. Court-watchers note a difference in style between the two chief justices (Roberts, for one thing, is more than thirty years younger than Rehnquist) but ideologically the differences between them seem minor. By all accounts, Roberts shares his predecessor's generally conservative philosophy, and his appointment is thus unlikely to shift the Court's ideological balance of power.

The appointment of Justice Alito to replace Justice Sandra Day O'Connor is a very different matter. O'Connor, who was appointed by President Ronald Reagan as the Court's first female justice, sat squarely in the center of the very divided Rehnquist Court. Although a conservative on many matters, including federalism and criminal law, she cast decisive votes on the liberal side in a number of cases involving social issues—most notably abortion, religion, and affirmative action. Although no one knows for sure how Alito will act in future cases, the early record suggests that his record will be closer to Rehnquist's than to O'Connor's.

With the Rehnquist Court now in the history books and the fledgling Roberts Court just underway, journalist Lyle Denniston examines the state of the current Court. Although a shift to the right is likely, he suggests, the Court remains deeply divided.

Questions

1. What does Denniston mean when he suggests that, in the short term, the Roberts Court is more likely to be a "split-the-difference" Court than a "Reagan revolutionary" Court? On what evidence does he base this prediction?

2. The judiciary, wrote Alexander Hamilton in *Federalist* No. 78 (see selection 12.1), "may truly be said to have neither FORCE nor WILL, but merely judgment." Do analyses like Denniston's—which emphasize the ideological and political nature of the justices' decision-making—undermine Hamilton's claim? Why or why not?

12.3 From Rehnquist to Roberts (2006)

Lyle Denniston

Exactly one week before Chief Justice Warren E. Burger's retirement was publicly announced (the White House knew in advance of his plan), the Supreme Court gave President Reagan and his aides a reminder of what could be at stake in the selection of his successor. More than anything else in its domestic aspirations, the Reagan Administration wanted a more conservative Court, especially to raise the chances for overruling *Roe v. Wade*—that despised legacy of the Burger Court. On June 11, 1986, the Court reaffirmed the right to seek an abortion, but this time it was only by the narrowest of margins—5 to 4. That had never happened before. As important as the vote itself was the fact that four Justices, the dissenters, made it clear they were ready to reconsider *Roe*; thus, a single vote seemed to hold *Roe* in place.

The Reagan Administration, of course, had other ambitions for a more conservative Court. It was eager for a revival of the prerogatives of the states—its "New Federalism" campaign. It wanted to close the widening seperatism on church-state matters. It was troubled by the Burger Court's failure to do much in rolling back the Warren Court's constitutional protections for criminal suspects.

In the mind of President Reagan's advisers, Associate Justice William H. Rehnquist was just the nominee who would advance the Administration's agenda on abortion, federalism, religion, and crime.

● ● ●

[But] because of [Justice Sandra Day] O'Connor, in significant part, the campaign to cast *Roe* aside had not succeeded, despite repeated tries by Reagan Administration lawyers appearing in the Supreme Court. And it was anything but clear that there actually had been a "Reagan Revolution" on the Court, at least not one genuinely deserving of the word "revolution"—again, mostly because the moderate centrism of O'Connor remained a constraint. That goal remained as elusive—and yet as eagerly desired—when Rehnquist died in office on September 3, 2005, as on the day he was elevated to the Chief Justiceship.

True, Rehnquist had succeeded—with significant aid from O'Connor—in the restoration of the concept of "state sovereignty" and a revival of federalism jurisprudence. That, indeed, was Rehnquist's most significant personal contribution to American jurisprudence. But Rehnquist was not able to amass a Court for anything more than an incremental advance of conservative church-state decisions, and it was he who wrote the decision . . . putting the *Miranda v. Arizona* decision on a firm constitutional foundation for the first time, and for no less than a 7-2

Excerpted from Lyle Denniston, "Rehnquist to Roberts: The 'Reagan Revolution' Fulfilled?" *University of Pennsylvania Law Review* 155 (2006), pp. 63–73. http://www.pennumbra.com/issues/articles/154-6/Denniston/pdf. Reprinted by permission of the University of Pennsylvania Law School.

majority—exactly the result against which Reagan's Attorney General, Edwin Meese, had so passionately warred.

Rehnquist was also unable to stop the opening and expansion of a new gay rights jurisprudence, a development that the nation's Christian conservatives (and many Republican officeholders) saw as tearing at the very social fabric of the nation. And he had cast his vote to support the Court's ruling, perhaps the most important in history on women's equality, in the Virginia Military Institute case. . . .

But then there came Justice O'Connor's retirement on July 1, 2005, and a sea change in the Court's modern history seemed ready to begin, especially with President George W. Bush, a deep-dyed conservative, in the White House. A much more politically confident Christian Right was now determined to make over the Supreme Court in its own image.

The "sons of the Reagan Revolution," a cadre of smart, young legal professionals, who had populated the Justice Department under Edwin Meese in the Reagan years (providing it with some of the brashest ideas for changing the law), were now grown-up, accomplished lawyers and judges who—by all appearances—were still true believers in the cause. Their names showed up on every short list for Supreme Court nominations in the Bush II Administration. It was from that list that the President, first and last, was determined to pluck John Glover Roberts, Jr., a freshman federal Circuit Court judge who had been one of the most seasoned and respected advocates at the Supreme Court Bar after his stint lawyering in the Reagan Administration. There was no hesitancy in the White House in putting him forth for O'Connor's seat, because that was the one that was definitely available, and it was seen by insiders as merely a way station en route to his becoming Chief Justice. With Rehnquist's death, Roberts was promptly moved up in an overnight switch.

After the President was rudely reminded of what was demanded of him by his conservative political base in the fiasco over the nomination of White House Counsel Harriet E. Miers to succeed O'Connor, the President reached quite purposefully to the far right of the lower federal bench, and nominated Samuel A. Alito, Jr.—so conservative that the media loved reminding everyone that he had sometimes been called "Scalito," an ideological clone of Justice Antonin Scalia. Alito had been another star in the Reagan Justice Department.

So, there it was: the "Roberts Court," the best and brightest hope of the committed and long-disappointed Reaganites. How soon would great civil rights precedents begin falling? Liberal activist groups like People for the American Way and the Alliance for Justice were persuaded that doomsday was at hand. How long would it be before even *Roe* was overruled? And, if not *Roe* right away, how about *Planned Parenthood* v. *Casey*, the decision partially reaffirming *Roe*'s core holding? That was one of the most important decisions O'Connor had helped fashion, so its fate could be a bellwether of a changed judicial climate.

And what about the Supreme Court's attitude toward the war on terrorism, and its reaction to the breathtaking claims of presidential war powers asserted by President Bush and Vice President Cheney? There was speculation, not easily dismissed, that a "Roberts Court" would fall meekly in line behind the White House, just as Congress had done since 9/11, even though the Rehnquist Court had refused to do so in 2004 in the first test case. Judge Roberts, on the D.C. Circuit, had been part of a majority on that court to uphold the President's power to create "war crimes" tribunals to try war-on-terrorism suspects held at Guantanamo Bay, Cuba. And Alito, as a young lawyer in the Justice Department, had been a hearty supporter of the Edwin Meese project of expanding presidential power—a project that would pale, in its dimensions, to the Executive ambitions of the George W. Bush presidency.

The addition of Roberts and Alito to the Court, to be sure, did not make a new conservative majority a certainty. Reaganites and the Bush political base had long since lost all hope for Justice David H. Souter, put on the Court by George H. W. Bush, and had grown almost equally exasperated with Justice Anthony M. Kennedy, a Reagan appointee. And those two could be found, regularly for Souter, often for Kennedy, making common cause with the liberal bloc: Justices John Paul Stevens (a Gerald Ford nominee), Ruth Bader Ginsburg, and Stephen G. Breyer (both Bill Clinton nominees). If Roberts and Alito were, in fact, as conservative as President Bush yearned for them to be, they could ally with Justice Scalia (a Reagan appointee) and Justice Clarence Thomas (named by Bush I). But that would still only make four.

The most likely prospect, at least in the short term, then, appeared not to be a Reagan revolutionary Court, but more likely a Court that would imitate the latter years of the Rehnquist Court—a "split-the-difference" Court.

Chief Justice Roberts, as a nominee before the Senate Judiciary Committee, had talked of the virtues of judicial modesty. He gave no indication that he would be prepared to lead a wholesale assault on precedent, and only the deepest cynic could suggest that he was dissembling on the point. Those who knew him were certain that he would want to lead the Court more than he would want to fade into irrelevance as a frustrated, yet ideologically pure, dissenter. After all, at age fifty as he began his service, he had time to wait for the Court of the future to unfold, and ample opportunity to shape it. He would be a conservative, no doubt, and the Court he would lead would be more conservative than Rehnquist's had been; O'Connor's departure made sure of that. But would he, and the Court, be what President Bush and his followers had imagined? Would this be the true "Rehnquist Court" (albeit led by a former Rehnquist clerk) that had never quite come into being?

There is the beginning of a record now—more so for Chief Justice Roberts than for Justice Alito, who, although arriving in time to take part in some of its most important decisions, served just a little more than half of the Court's 2005 term.

Figures . . . show that Roberts and Alito "agreed in full in 89% of the cases they both heard." Roberts agreed with Scalia 85% of the time and with Thomas 83%. But he also agreed 81% of the time with Kennedy. Alito, according to the data, agreed in full with Thomas and Kennedy 76% of the time and with Scalia 74%.

In the term's twelve 5-4 splits, . . . Kennedy was in the majority nine times, Roberts and Scalia eight each, and Thomas seven. Alito voted on nine 5-4 splits, and was in the majority six times. None of the Court's more liberal members exceeded six times in a 5-4 majority (Ginsburg was in such a majority six times, Stevens and Souter five, and Breyer four).

That is a statistical portrait of a conservative-leaning Court. Somewhat more revealing are some of the details in particular cases. In them, "fine-shaven outcomes," in Judge [J. Harvie] Wilkinson's phrase, are more evident.

It is possible to argue that this was the pattern in most of the truly major outcomes of the term. . . .

But, this more revealing, close-up portrait is exceptionally vivid in one field of law that is sure to continue to provide a measure of the Roberts Court's conservative tendencies—that is, of course, the issue of abortion, the prime target of the would-have-been "Reagan Revolution."

It is thus worth examining—early though it may be—the new Court's initial responses in that field to test the proposition. There were a few developments, none of which by itself would qualify among the most significant actions of the term, but each telling in its own right. Two were rulings, and one was an order managing the scope of review in a forthcoming case.

The first was the unanimous ruling in *Ayotte* v. *Planned Parenthood*, decided on January 18, 2006 (before Justice Alito joined the Court). This holding was one of the early indications of the new Chief Justice's stated desire to encourage more unanimity on the Court, even in controversial areas of its work. He assigned the opinion to Justice O'Connor, one of the architects of *Casey*, who was then about to conclude her service. Probably with some urging from Roberts, the Court's two implacable foes of abortion rights—Justices Scalia and Thomas—were persuaded not only to remain silent, but to join the opinion. That was somewhat remarkable, especially since the Court declared that it was "established" by precedent that "a State may not restrict access to abortions that are 'necessary, in appropriate medical judgment, for preservation of the life or health of the mother.'"

It is true that the opinion, at the outset, declared that "[w]e do not revisit our abortion precedents today, but rather address a question of remedy." That perhaps was a way to ward off dissents, but it ordinarily would not appear to have been strong enough to do so in this area of law that so bitterly divides the Court.

Perhaps it helped that the decision was confined to the narrowest possible ground, as an exercise in judicial modesty. . . . But the Court had been asked, by the state of New Hampshire, to decide a question the Court has never quite settled: the constitutional standard for judging . . . challenges to abortion restrictions. . . .

A pair of amici ["friends of the Court" briefs], two "individual activists seeking an end to abortion," boldly asked the Court to address whether *Roe* v. *Wade* and its progeny are in fact viable in the face of a growing body of literature that suggests that the court erred." The nation's Catholic bishops also argued in an amicus filing that "we believe *Casey* was wrongly decided."

This is not to suggest that the Court was in any way obliged to address such fundamental issues, but the resistance to temptation, if temptation did exist, may well have been the kind of "judicial modesty" that the new Chief Justice has advocated. Whatever the reason for resisting, the end result was that *Ayotte*, a closely watched new test on abortion rights, created little if any new law.

In a second decision (in which Alito did not participate), the Court swiftly and unanimously put an end to a case that had been the hardest-fought courthouse battle over blockades of abortion clinics—a case lingering in the courts for two decades and twice before decided by the Court. The Court avoided deciding one of the broader issues—whether a private party could sue under the anti-racketeering RICO law for an injunction—and instead resolved . . . [a narrower point]. Crafted as it was, the decision had largely symbolic meaning in closing out an angry chapter of abortion jurisprudence. It was also another exhibition of judicial minimalism.

Finally, in the abortion context, the Court put itself in position—over the objection of the Bush Administration—to decide a major new abortion controversy on narrow grounds, thus perhaps avoiding, at least for some time, a reckoning with one of its more controversial precedents. On April 21, 2006, the Court agreed to rule on the constitutionality of the 2003 federal law banning nationwide the so-called "partial-birth abortion" procedure. The law reflects Congress's determination to override the Supreme Court's 2000 decision striking down a Nebraska "partial-birth abortion" ban and finding that such a ban must have a medical exception; Congress insisted in the 2003 law that there never is a medical necessity for the procedure it banned. . . .

The stage is thus set for a second round of testing the Roberts Court on abortion. No doubt, too much can be read into one part of the Justices' caseload, just as too much emphasis has been placed upon the abortion question in the White House selection and Senate review of Supreme Court nominees. But there is no bellwether like abortion, and conservative theorists keep looking for ways to push the Court to reconsider that question. . . . ■

Issue and Controversy

The provisions of the United States Constitution do not always interpret themselves; determining what they mean and how they apply in particular cases is often difficult, and usually controversial. Over the years, Supreme Court justices and legal scholars have clashed not only on specific constitutional issues, but on the larger question of how the Constitution should be interpreted and applied.

In one camp are those who stress the *original meaning* of the constitutional text. Originalism is most closely associated with the Supreme Court's most conservative justices—especially Antonin Scalia and Clarence Thomas—although originalism need not lead to conservative results. The justices' task, according to the originalist viewpoint, is to determine what the words of the Constitution meant at the time it was adopted, and (in Scalia's words) to construe the original language "reasonably, to contain all that it fairly means."*

In the other camp are those who advance the idea of the "living Constitution." Those who subscribe to this viewpoint see the originalist approach as confining and limiting; the Constitution, they believe, was "intended to endure for ages to come," and needs to evolve to reflect the realities of modern life and society's evolving moral and political standards.†

---

*Antonin Scalia, *A Matter of Interpretation: Federal Courts and the Law* (Princeton, NJ: Princeton University Press, 1997), p. 23.

†*McCulloch v. Maryland*, 17 U.S. 316 (1819), at 415.

The brief excerpt from the case of *Kelo* v. *City of New London* (2005) nicely illustrates these two approaches to constitutional interpretation. *Kelo* involved the Constitution's "Takings" Clause, which provides that private property shall not be taken "for public use, without just compensation." In this case, the city of New London, Connecticut, had seized private property as part of an urban redevelopment project; in effect, private property was taken from some and then sold to others. Although the city offered just compensation, the original property owners sued on the grounds that the redevelopment project did not constitute a "public use."

For Justice John Paul Stevens, who wrote the majority opinion, the meaning of the phrase "public use" had evolved over time, as our understanding of the role of government changed and grew. For Justice Thomas, who dissented, all of this was irrelevant; the case turned instead on the meaning of the phrase "public use" in 1787.

Questions

1. What did the Framers mean by "public use," according to Justice Thomas? How does Justice Stevens's definition reflect a broader interpretation of the phrase?
2. Why does Justice Thomas believe it is inappropriate for the Supreme Court to interpret the phrase "public use" except according to the original meaning? Why does Justice Stevens view the original meaning as inadequate? What are the advantages and disadvantages of the two approaches?

12.4 Should the Constitution Be Interpreted According to Its Original Meaning? (2005)

Justice John Paul Stevens
Justice Clarence Thomas, dissenting

JUSTICE STEVENS delivered the opinion of the Court. . . .

Two polar propositions are perfectly clear. On the one hand, it has long been accepted that the sovereign may not take the property of A for the sole purpose of transferring it to another private party B, even though A is paid just compensation. On the other hand, it is equally clear that a State may transfer property from one private party to another if future "use by the public" is the purpose of the taking; the condemnation of land for a railroad with common carrier duties is a familiar example. Neither of these propositions, however, determines the disposition of this case.

As for the first proposition, the City would no doubt be forbidden from taking petitioners' land for the purpose of conferring a private benefit on a particular pri-

---

Excerpted from *Kelo* v. *City of New London*, No. 04-108 (2005).

vate party. Nor would the City be allowed to take property under the mere pretext of a public purpose, when its actual purpose was to bestow a private benefit. The takings before us, however, would be executed pursuant to a "carefully considered" development plan. . . .

On the other hand, this is not a case in which the City is planning to open the condemned land—at least not in its entirety—to use by the general public. Nor will the private lessees of the land . . . be required to [make] their services available to all comers. But . . . this "Court long ago rejected any literal requirement that condemned property be put into use for the general public." Indeed, while many state courts in the mid-19th century endorsed "use by the public" as the proper definition of public use, that narrow view steadily eroded over time. Not only was the "use by the public" test difficult to administer (e.g., what proportion of the public need have access to the property? at what price?), but it proved to be impractical given the diverse and always evolving needs of society. Accordingly, when this Court began applying the Fifth Amendment to the States at the close of the 19th century, it embraced the broader and more natural interpretation of public use as "public purpose." Thus, in a[n] [1896] case upholding a mining company's use of an aerial bucket line to transport ore over property it did not own, Justice Holmes' opinion for the Court stressed "the inadequacy of use by the general public as a universal test." . . .

The disposition of this case therefore turns on the question whether the City's development plan serves a "public purpose." Without exception, our cases have defined that concept broadly, reflecting our longstanding policy of deference to legislative judgments in this field. . . .

In *Berman v. Parker* (1954), this Court upheld a redevelopment plan targeting a blighted area of Washington, D.C., in which most of the housing for the area's 5,000 inhabitants was beyond repair. Under the plan, the area would be condemned and part of it utilized for the construction of streets, schools, and other public facilities. The remainder of the land would be leased or sold to private parties for the purpose of redevelopment, including the construction of low-cost housing.

The owner of a department store located in the area challenged the condemnation, pointing out that his store was not itself blighted and arguing that the creation of a "better balanced, more attractive community" was not a valid public use. Writing for a unanimous Court, Justice Douglas refused to evaluate this claim in isolation, deferring instead to the legislative and agency judgment that the area "must be planned as a whole" for the plan to be successful. . . . The public use underlying the taking was unequivocally affirmed:

> . . . [T]he concept of the public welfare is broad and inclusive. . . . The values it represents are spiritual as well as physical, aesthetic as well as monetary. It is within the power of the legislature to determine that the community should be beautiful as well as healthy, spacious as well as clean, well balanced as well as carefully patrolled. In the present case, the Congress and its authorized agencies have made determinations that take into account a wide variety of values. It is not for us to reappraise them. If those who govern the District of Columbia decide that the Nation's Capital should be beautiful as well as sanitary, there is nothing in the Fifth Amendment that stands in the way.

. . . Viewed as a whole, our jurisprudence has recognized that the needs of society have varied between different parts of the Nation, just as they have evolved over time in response to changed circumstances. . . . For more than a century, our public use jurisprudence has wisely eschewed rigid formulas and intrusive scrutiny in favor of affording legislatures broad latitude in determining what public needs justify the use of the takings power. . . .

Petitioners contend that using eminent domain for economic development impermissibly blurs the boundary between public and private takings. Again, our cases foreclose this objection. Quite simply, the government's pursuit of a public purpose will often benefit individual private parties. . . . The owner of the department store in *Berman* objected to "taking from one businessman for the benefit of another businessman," referring to the fact that under the redevelopment plan, land would be leased or sold to private developers for redevelopment. Our rejection of that contention has particular relevance to the instant case:

> The public end may be as well or better served through an agency of private enterprise than through a department of government—or so the Congress might conclude. We cannot say that public ownership is the sole method of promoting the public purposes of community redevelopment projects.

. . . Alternatively, petitioners maintain that for takings of this kind we should require a "reasonable certainty" that the expected public benefits will actually accrue. Such a rule, however, would represent an even greater departure from our precedent.

> When the legislature's purpose is legitimate and its means are not irrational, our cases make clear that empirical debates over the wisdom of takings—no less than debates over the wisdom of other kinds of socioeconomic legislation—are not to be carried out in the federal courts.

. . . In affirming the City's authority to take petitioners' properties, we do not minimize the hardship that condemnations may entail, notwithstanding the payment of just compensation. We emphasize that nothing in our opinion precludes any State from placing further restrictions on its exercise of the takings power. Indeed, many States already impose "public use" requirements that are stricter than the federal baseline. Some of these requirements have been established as a matter of state constitutional law, while others are expressed in state eminent domain statutes that carefully limit the grounds upon which takings may be exercised. . . . [T]he necessity and wisdom of using eminent domain to promote economic development are certainly matters of legitimate public debate. This Court's authority, however, extends only to determining whether the City's proposed condemnations are for a "public use" within the meaning of the Fifth Amendment to the Federal Constitution. Because over a century of our case law interpreting that provision dictates an affirmative answer to that question, we may not grant petitioners the relief that they seek. . . .

JUSTICE THOMAS, dissenting.

Long ago, [the Eighteenth-century English legal scholar] William Blackstone wrote that "the law of the land . . . postpone[s] even public necessity to the sacred and inviolable rights of private property." The Framers embodied that principle in the Constitution, allowing the government to take property not for "public necessity," but instead for "public use." Defying this understanding, the Court replaces the Public Use Clause with a "'[P]ublic [P]urpose'" Clause (or perhaps the "Diverse and Always Evolving Needs of Society" Clause), a restriction that is satisfied, the Court instructs, so long as the purpose is "legitimate" and the means "not irrational." This deferential shift in phraseology enables the Court to hold, against all common sense, that a costly urban renewal project whose stated purpose is a vague promise of new jobs and increased tax revenue, but which is also suspiciously agreeable to the Pfizer Corporation, is for a "public use."

I cannot agree. If such "economic development" takings are for a "public use," any taking is, and the Court has erased the Public Use Clause from our Constitution. I do not believe that this Court can eliminate liberties expressly enumerated in the Constitution, and therefore [I dissent]. Regrettably, however, the Court's error runs deeper than this. Today's decision is simply the latest in a string of our cases construing the Public Use Clause to be a virtual nullity, without the slightest nod to its original meaning. In my view, the Public Use Clause, originally understood, is a meaningful limit on the government's eminent domain power. Our cases have strayed from the Clause's original meaning, and I would reconsider them.

I

The Fifth Amendment provides:

> No person shall be held to answer for a capital, or otherwise infamous crime unless on a presentment or indictment of a Grand Jury, except in cases arising in the land or naval forces, or in the Militia, when in actual service in time of War or public danger, nor shall any person be subject for the same offense to be twice put in jeopardy of life or limb, nor shall be compelled in any criminal case to be a witness against himself, nor be deprived of life, liberty, or property, without due process, of law; *nor shall private property be taken for public use, without just compensation.* (Emphasis added.)

It is the last of these liberties, the Takings Clause, that is at issue in this case. In my view, it is "imperative that the Court maintain absolute fidelity to" the Clause's express limit on the power of the government over the individual, no less than with every other liberty expressly enumerated in the Fifth Amendment or the Bill of Rights more generally.

Though one component of the protection provided by the Takings Clause is that the government can take private property only if it provides "just compensation" for the taking, the Takings Clause also prohibits the government from taking property except "for public use." Were it otherwise, the Takings Clause would either be meaningless or empty. If the Public Use Clause served no function other than to state that the government may take property through its eminent domain power—for public or private uses—then it would be surplusage.* Alternatively,

---

*Surplusage: unnecessary, excess language.

the Clause could distinguish those takings that require compensation from those that do not. That interpretation, however, "would permit private property to be taken or appropriated for private use without any compensation whatever." In other words, the Clause would require the government to compensate for takings done "for public use," leaving it free to take property for purely private uses without the payment of compensation. This would contradict a bedrock principle well established by the time of the founding: that all takings required the payment of compensation. The Public Use Clause, like the Just Compensation Clause, is therefore an express limit on the government's power of eminent domain.

The most natural reading of the Clause is that it allows the government to take property only if the government owns, or the public has a legal right to use, the property, as opposed to taking it for any public purpose or necessity whatsoever. At the time of the founding, dictionaries primarily defined the noun "use" as "[t]he act of employing anything to any purpose." The term "use," moreover, "is from the Latin *utor*, which means 'to use, make use of, avail one's self of, employ, apply, enjoy, etc.'" When the government takes property and gives it to a private individual, and the public has no right to use the property, it strains language to say that the public is "employing" the property, regardless of the incidental benefits that might accrue to the public from the private use. The term "public use," then, means that either the government or its citizens as a whole must actually "employ" the taken property.

Granted, another sense of the word "use" was broader in meaning, extending to "[c]onvenience" or "help," or "[q]ualities that make a thing proper for any purpose." Nevertheless, read in context, the term "public use" possesses the narrower meaning. Elsewhere, the Constitution twice employs the word "use," both times in its narrower sense. Article 1, § 10 provides that "the net Produce of all Duties and Imposts, laid by any State on Imports or Exports, shall be for the Use of the Treasury of the United States," meaning the Treasury itself will control the taxes, not use it to any beneficial end. And Article I, § 8 grants Congress power "[t]o raise and support Armies, but no Appropriation of Money to that Use shall be for a longer Term than two Years." Here again, "use" means "employed to raise and support Armies," not anything directed to achieving any military end. The same word in the Public Use Clause should be interpreted to have the same meaning.

Tellingly, the phrase "public use" contrasts with the very different phrase "general Welfare" used elsewhere in the Constitution. ("Congress shall have Power To . . . provide for the common Defense and general Welfare of the United States" . . . Constitution established "to promote the general Welfare.") The Framers would have used some such broader term if they had meant the Public Use Clause to have a similarly sweeping scope. Other founding era documents made the contrast between these two usages still more explicit. The Constitution's text, in short, suggests that the Takings Clause authorizes the taking of property only if the public has a right to employ it, not if the public realizes any conceivable benefit from the taking.

The Constitution's common law background reinforces this understanding. The common law provided an express method of eliminating uses of land that adversely impacted the public welfare: nuisance law. Blackstone and [nineteenth-century American legal scholar James] Kent, for instance, both carefully distinguished the law of nuisance from the power of eminent domain. Blackstone rejected the idea that private property could be taken solely for purposes of any public benefit. "So great . . . is the regard of the law for private property," he explained, "that it will not authorize the least violation of it it—no, not even for the general good of the whole community.". . . When the public took property, in other words, it took it as an individual buying property from another typically would—for one's own use. The Public Use Clause, in short, embodied the Framers' understanding that property is a natural fundamental right, prohibiting the government from "tak[ing] property from A. and giv[ing] it to B."...

[II]

Our current Public Use Clause jurisprudence, as the Court notes, has rejected this natural reading of the Clause. The Court adopted its modern reading blindly, with little discussion of the Clause's history and original meaning, in two distinct lines of cases: first, in cases adopting the "public purpose" interpretation of the Clause, and second, in cases deferring to legislatures' judgments regarding what constitutes a valid public purpose. . . . The weakness of those two lines of cases . . . fatally undermines the doctrinal foundations of the Court's decision. Today's questionable application of these cases is further proof that the "public purpose" standard is not susceptible of principled application. This Court's reliance by rote on this standard is ill advised and should be reconsidered. . . .

[III]

The consequences of today's decision are not difficult to predict, and promise to be harmful. So-called "urban renewal" programs provide some compensation for the properties they take, but no compensation is possible for the subjective value of these lands to the individuals displaced and the indignity inflicted by uprooting them from their homes. Allowing the government to take property solely for public purposes is bad enough, but extending the concept of public purpose to encompass any economically beneficial goal guarantees that these losses will fall disproportionately on poor communities. Those communities are not only systematically less likely to put their lands to the highest and best social use, but are also the least politically powerful. If ever there were justification for intrusive judicial review of constitutional provisions that protect "discrete and insular minorities," surely that principle would apply with great force to the powerless groups and individuals the Public Use Clause protects. The deferential standard this Court has adopted for the Public Use Clause is therefore deeply perverse. It encourages "those citizens with disproportionate influence and power in the political process, including large corporations and development firms," to victimize the weak. . . .

The Court relies almost exclusively on this Court's prior cases to derive today's far-reaching, and dangerous, result. But the principles this Court should employ to dispose of this case are found in the Public Use Clause itself. . . . When faced with a clash of constitutional principle and a line of unreasoned cases wholly divorced from the text, history, and structure of our founding document, we should not hesitate to resolve the tension in favor of the Constitution's original meaning. ■

View from the Inside

As the saying goes, "a lawyer who defends himself has a fool for a client." Yet that did not stop Dr. Michael A. Newdow from taking his own case all the way to the United States Supreme Court.

On behalf of his second-grade daughter, Newdow brought a federal lawsuit challenging the constitutionality of the Pledge of Allegiance. Because the Pledge contains the words "under God," Newdow argued, it violates the First Amendment's prohibition against an "establishment of Religion."

Newdow is a lawyer, but he had never appeared before the Supreme Court. As this selection suggests, the appearance of a novice is atypical; the task of arguing a case before the highest tribunal in the land is normally reserved to a small group of specialists.

Newdow, by the way, did not win his case. The justices ruled that he was not legally entitled to bring the case on his daughter's behalf, and thus declined to rule on the constitutionality of the Pledge of Allegiance.

Questions

1. What is the purpose of oral arguments before the Supreme Court? What role do the lawyers play in helping the justices resolve the case? Why is arguing a case before the Supreme Court different from arguing a case before a jury?
2. What advantages do specialists in Supreme Court litigation have over other lawyers? Would the Court be better served if the system encouraged more non-specialists to appear and argue cases? Why or why not?

12.5 A Novice Confronts the Supreme Court (2004)

Michael McGough

. . . Dr. Michael A. Newdow, an atheist from California who objected when his daughter's second-grade class pledged allegiance to "one nation, under God," [is] personally appear[ing] before the nine justices of the U.S. Supreme Court [to argue] that including the Deity in a public school pledge violates the Constitution's prohibition against the state establishment of religion.

Although Newdow is a lawyer as well as a doctor, in representing himself before the nation's highest court he [is] disregarding the legal adage that "a man who rep-

---

resents himself has a fool for a client." Newdow's refusal to entrust his case to an experienced advocate has attracted almost as much attention among attorneys as the issue at stake, which is one of the battlegrounds in the U.S. culture war.

Although oral arguments are only one factor in how the court rules—along with written briefs and the predilections of the justices—they are important. There is a saying among lawyers that while you can't win a case in oral arguments, you can lose it.

Even experienced lawyers often find oral arguments before the Supreme Court an unfamiliar and disorienting experience. An attorney typically has only 30 minutes to state his or her case and answer sometimes argumentative questions from the bench. And factors that would be to a lawyer's advantage in lower courts—eloquent oratory or a sympathetic client—can be disadvantages in the highest one.

That explains why parties to landmark cases before the Supreme Court, even state governments represented by their attorneys general, often turn to a cadre of experienced high court advocates, most of them based in Washington and several of them alumni of the U.S. Solicitor General's office, which represents the U.S. government in court.

"There's been a growing recognition over the past 20 to 25 years that it is a specialty to argue in the Supreme Court and that there are advantages to having someone who knows how to talk to that court," said Paul M. Smith of the Washington law firm of Jenner & Block.

Smith is one of a dozen or so "name" Supreme Court advocates. He has argued 10 cases before the court, including last year's *Lawrence* v. *Texas*, in which Smith persuaded the justices to reverse a 1986 ruling and hold that laws against same-sex sodomy violate the Constitution.

Smith also represented a group of Pennsylvania Democrats in an argument last December asserting that "partisan gerrymandering" of the state's congressional districts was unconstitutional. . . .

To the extent that Supreme Court advocacy is a specialty, many otherwise accomplished lawyers might not be doing their clients a service by taking their case all the way to the pinnacle of the judicial system. That is especially true, experienced Supreme Court advocates say, of lawyers accustomed to trying cases before a jury. But even lawyers with experience in appellate courts often don't grasp the unique demands of Supreme Court advocacy.

Lawyers often cite this humorous advice to practitioners: "If the law is on your side, pound on the law. If the facts are on your side, pound on the facts. If neither is on your side, pound on the table."

"Pounding on the table will get you attention [from the justices], but not the kind of attention you want," said Kathryn Kolbert, now at the University of Pennsylvania's Annenberg Public Policy Center. Kolbert argued the 1992 case of *Planned Parenthood* v. *Casey* in which the Supreme Court reaffirmed a constitutional right to abortion. "Anything that detracts from your argument is a negative."

Stephen Sachs, a former Maryland attorney general, agrees that "speechmaking and histrionics have no place in an appellate argument." But he wouldn't bar all references to the real-life context of a case. "Judges are human," he said, "and as long as you aren't speechifying, as long as you're within the four corners of the case, it's necessary and helpful to communicate the emotional stakes involved."

Stirring speeches are ill advised for another reason, according to Smith. Despite the popular perception that the Supreme Court exists to right wrongs against individuals, the court's real interest is in broad principles of law.

"The court is extremely used to allowing injustices to go unredressed in a particular case," Smith said, noting that the court is asked to review thousands of cases every year, a "substantial percentage" of which probably involve what the justices would consider unfairness. A lawyer who passionately lectures the justices about how his client has been wronged "is not helping them," Smith said.

"What they need to do is figure out what the rule should be. That is really the mistake—not helping them figure out [what] rule makes sense and will it be applied by the court and how far will it go and what is the limiting principle."

In the sodomy case, for example, Smith prepared a response in case justices asked if striking down sodomy laws would set a precedent that would apply to gay marriage or the U.S. military's policies towards gays and lesbians. "I had a lot of answers ready for them that 'no, you're not resolving those issues today.'"

Preparing for the Arguments

It's easy to see why lawyers arguing before the Supreme Court would make a mistake by pounding the table or, given the court's interest in broad principles, the facts of the specific case. But sometimes, Smith said, it is also a mistake to "pound the law," in the sense of citing what the Supreme Court has said in previous cases. An appeal to precedent, so useful in lower appellate courts, is not so important in the Supreme Court.

"The Supreme Court isn't bound by anything," Smith said. "They can change the law when they want to." That reality, and the fact that an argument must be pitched to nine justices rather that the three judges on a typical federal appeals court, makes for a "different level of challenge."

Not every Supreme Court advocate is up to the challenge. A recurring issue in discussions of advocacy before the high court is whether state attorneys general— often elected officials with aspirations for higher office—should appear on behalf of their states in high-profile cases.

Sachs, who, unlike some of his former colleagues, is an experienced appellate advocate, concedes that there can be a political advantage to arguing a case in the nation's highest court. "There you are on the steps of the Supreme Court with 'Equal Justice Under Law' behind you and the TV cameras rolling."

But Sachs, who argued three cases before the court as attorney general for Maryland, said that what matters is that the lawyer for the state know the case inside and out. "To know what your limitations are is important for an attorney general," he said. "If you have an assistant who worked on the issue and knows it, the impulse is to permit that person to argue the case."

One member of the Supreme Court bar believes that the problem with state attorneys general arguing before the court often is their lack of preparation time rather than a lack of ability.

Maureen Mahoney, of the firm of Latham & Watkins, has won 11 of 12 cases she has argued before the court—including her defense last year of the University of Michigan law school's affirmative action program. Mahoney noted that some oral arguments require 200 hours of preparation.

"Very few elected officials can set aside that sort of time," she said.

What goes on during those 200 hours? Not unlike presidential candidates preparing for a televised debate, Supreme Court advocates rehearse and role-play. "Moot courts" are assembled with a bench consisting of practicing lawyers, law professors and sometimes even a former judge.

"We don't have people play particular justices, "Smith said, "but we have three or four judges up there trying to figure out every question the justices could ask you. I've found that that's absolutely indispensable to understanding a case. I often use the Georgetown [law school] moot court because they bring in really good people from other law firms or faculty people. I did that with *Lawrence* v. *Texas*, with 30 students watching. Everyone had a sense of history being made."

The other pillar of preparation for Supreme Court advocates is their opening statement, which sometimes must be as adjustable as an accordion to accommodate either a barrage of questions from the bench or prolonged silence, which Kolbert endured during one argument for nine minutes.

On the one hand, Sachs pointed out, an advocate "must respond to what is on a judge's mind. The most important part of your anatomy is your ears."

But it is also vital to present his own strongest arguments.

Smith writes out 15 minutes' worth of text that he would deliver if there were no interruptions.

"You're almost always going to be interrupted," Smith said. "The real trick is to get your points across as if you're answering the question but you're really making your points. That's why I spend a lot of time actually phrasing what I will say and then committing it almost to memory."

During preparation, advocates also consult with their clients—which in high-profile cases often have a broader political objective than simply winning the case.

In the election year of 1992, when Kolbert represented Planned Parenthood in its challenge to Pennsylvania's Abortion Control Act, her clients wanted her to focus on the big picture—the continuing viability of *Roe* v. *Wade*—rather than the particular provisions of the law, such as the requirement that married women seeking an abortion notify their husbands.

"In *Planned Parenthood* v. *Casey*, the entire case was litigated on the theory that we were going to lose, and that the issue of reproductive choice would be going back to the political arena," Kolbert said.

Accordingly, in her argument to the court, Kolbert emphasized the importance of preserving abortion as a fundamental right, prompting Justice Sandra Day O'Connor at one point to ask her if she was ever going to discuss the specific provisions of the law.

When the court decided the *Casey* case, it did announce a new standard for evaluating abortion laws—the extent to which they posed an "undue burden" on a woman's right to choose—but also said that it was reaffirming the "essential holding" of *Roe* v. *Wade*. The decision was overwhelmingly interpreted as a victory for the pro-choice movement.

Neophyte Takes Some Comfort

Can a novice Supreme Court advocate like Michael Newdow hope to influence the justices the way Kolbert apparently did in the abortion case?

Reached in Washington, where he was participating in moot court practice . . . Newdow said he hopes for a unanimous decision in his favor in the Pledge of Allegiance case. Asked if he had second thoughts about representing himself, he said, "I always have second thoughts" but added that he was increasingly comfortable with the process.

As well he might be: Not only did Newdow prevail in the 9th Circuit Court of Appeals, which struck down the use of "under God" in the pledge, he also persuaded Justice Antonin Scalia—a likely vote against him—to recuse himself from the case. . . .

Newdow also can take some comfort from this passage in the Guide for Counsel handed out to lawyers by the clerk of the Supreme Court: "Ordinarily the justices will know whether you are making your first argument before the court. Be assured that some first-time arguments have been far superior to presentations from counsel who have argued several times."

Maureen Mahoney agrees that "someone who is well prepared can do well even on their first argument before the court." But Kathryn Kolbert, asked what advice she would give Newdow, replied: "Get a lawyer." ■

Chapter 13

Public Policy

The purpose and function of government is to make and implement policy—that is, to create and administer the rules and programs under which society is to be governed. In a sense, all of the previous chapters have been examining the policy-making process: the institutions that interact to create policy and the constitutional foundation within which they operate, the relationship of policy making to public opinion and the electoral process, and the role of nongovernmental actors—such as the media and interest groups—in policy development. In this chapter, we turn to examining the total picture.

Political scientists typically divide policy into two broad categories—domestic policy and foreign policy. Domestic policy involves a broad range of issues, including health care, education, the economy, and criminal justice. Foreign policy includes not only diplomacy but also military affairs and international economic issues.

Domestic policy making in the United States underwent several transformations in the twentieth century. The New Deal greatly expanded the federal government's role in economic regulation and social policy making. In the 1960s, Lyndon Johnson's Great Society widened the scope of federal welfare programs, a trend continued under President Richard Nixon. In the 1980s, the election of Ronald Reagan initiated a period of struggle for control over the scope and direction of federal social and economic policy. That struggle has grown even more intense in recent years.

At bottom, the debate over social policy in the United States is marked by a contest between those who believe that the national government should take the lead in solving society's social problems and those who believe that state and local governments and the private sector should carry the load. As for foreign policy, Americans tend to agree on the broad goals that the United States should pursue, but frequently disagree—sometimes vehemently—on how best to pursue those goals in a complex and often hostile world.

The selections in this chapter cover a wide range of issues related to public policy. Selection 13.1 introduces the concept of public policy and draws distinctions between different types of policies and among the different stages of policy making. Selection 13.2 examines the long-term consequences of federal spending policy, while selection 13.3 probes the nature of American unilateralism in foreign policy. Finally, selection 13.4 provides an inside look at how policy is made, through the eyes of a member of Congress.

Chapter Questions

1. How have the larger trends and currents in American politics over the past thirty years affected domestic policy? Consider in particular the increasingly bitter conflict between liberal and conservative ideologies.
2. How has American foreign policy changed since the terrorist attacks of September 11, 2001, and the invasion of Iraq in 2003? Have these events changed the goals of American foreign policy? Have they changed America's available options for attempting to achieve these goals?

 Foundations

Government policy is made by all three branches and is heavily influenced and constrained by public opinion and by the electoral process. The Framers designed a system that prevents any one branch from making policy on its own, and to a great extent the system in fact works just that way. Policy making, in general, involves cooperation, negotiation, and, at times, conflict among many different players. Nor is that process completed once a policy is enacted into law. The law must be implemented by the executive branch, under congressional and judicial supervision. When necessary, the program must be modified to fit new or unexpected circumstances. Each year the program must be funded through the congressional budget process, and periodically, it must be reauthorized by Congress as well.

Political scientists have categorized public policy making along several dimensions; for example, one can look at the various stages of the process, at the different types of policy, or at the different political actors involved. The following selection, by two political scientists, examines public policy making from a variety of perspectives.

Questions

1. What are the major stages of public policy making? Which institutions are most effective at each stage? Why?
2. Explain these terms: *distributive policies, regulatory policies,* and *redistributive policies.* What are the defining characteristics of each?

13.1 Domestic Policy Making (1994)

Roger H. Davidson and Walter J. Oleszek

Definitions of Policy

Because policies ultimately are what government is about, it is not surprising that definitions of policy and policy making are diverse and influenced by the beholder's eye. David Easton's celebrated definition of public policy as society's "authoritative allocations" of values or resources is one approach to the question. To put it another way, policies can be regarded as reflecting "who gets what, when, and how" in a society. A more serviceable definition of policy is offered by Randall Ripley and Grace Franklin: policy is what the government says and does about perceived problems. . . .

Stages of Policy Making

Whatever the time frame, policy making normally has four distinct stages: setting the agenda, formulating policy, adopting policy, and implementing policy.

Setting the Agenda   At the initial stage, public problems are spotted and moved onto the national agenda, which can be defined as "the list of subjects to which government officials and those around them are paying serious attention." In a large, pluralistic country like the United States, the national agenda at any given moment is extensive and vigorously debated.

How do problems get placed on the agenda? Some are heralded by a crisis or some other prominent event—the hijacking of a plane by terrorists, the demise of savings and loan associations, or a campaign-funding scandal. Others are occasioned by the gradual accumulation of knowledge—for example, increasing awareness of an environmental hazard like acid rain or ozone depletion. Still other agenda items represent the accumulation of past problems that no longer can be avoided or ignored. Finally, agendas may be set in motion by political processes—election results, turnover in Congress, or shifts in public opinion. The 1994 election results are an example of how the GOP's control of the 104th Congress and its Contract with America drove the national agenda.

Agenda items are pushed by *policy entrepreneurs*, people willing to invest time and energy to promote a particular issue. Numerous Washington "think tanks" and interest groups, especially at the beginning of a new president's term, issue reports that seek to influence the economic, social, or foreign policy agenda of the nation. Usually, however, elected officials and their staffs or appointees are more likely to shape agendas than are career bureaucrats or nongovernmental actors. Notable policy entrepreneurs on Capitol Hill are congressional leaders who push their

Roger H. Davidson and Walter J. Oleszek, *Congress and Its Members*, 6th ed. (Washington DC: CQ Press, 1998), pp. 349–356. Reprinted by permission of Congressional Quarterly.

party's policy initiatives. Speaker Newt Gingrich with his advocacy of a minimalist role for the central government (the "Republican revolution") is a good example.

Lawmakers frequently are policy entrepreneurs because they are expected to voice the concerns of constituents and organized groups and to seek legislative solutions. Politicians generally gravitate toward issues that are visible, salient, and solvable. Tough, arcane, or conflictual problems may be shunned because they offer few payoffs and little hope of success.

Sometimes only a crisis—such as the oil price increases in the 1970s—can force lawmakers to address difficult questions. Yet, despite enactment of legislation designed to ameliorate future energy problems, Americans today are as dependent on imported oil as they were two decades ago. Forecasters predict another energy crisis unless steps are taken to develop alternative fuels, change habits of consumption, and reduce the spiraling demand for oil, especially from the volatile Middle East. This kind of "creeping crisis" is often difficult for members of Congress to grapple with, in part because of the "two Congresses" dilemma. As conscientious lawmakers, members might want to forge long-term solutions. But as representatives of their constituents, they are deterred from acting when most citizens see no problems with the immediate situation.

Formulating Policy   In the second stage of policy making, items on the political agenda are discussed and potential solutions are explored. Members of Congress and their staffs play crucial roles by conducting hearings and writing committee reports. They are aided by policy experts in executive agencies, interest groups, and the private sector.

Another term for this stage is *policy incubation*, which entails "keeping a proposal alive while it picks up support, or waits for a better climate, or while a consensus begins to form that the problem to which it is addressed exists." Sometimes this process takes only a few months; more often it requires years. During Dwight D. Eisenhower's administration, for example, congressional Democrats explored and refined policy options that, while not immediately accepted, were ripe for adoption by the time their party's nominee, John F. Kennedy, was elected president in 1960.

The incubation process not only brings policies to maturity but also refines solutions to the problems. The process may break down if workable solutions are not available. The seeming intractability of many modern issues complicates problem solving. Thomas S. Foley, D-Wash. (Speaker, 1989–1995), held that issues had become far more perplexing since he came to Congress in 1965. At that time "the civil rights issue facing the legislators was whether the right to vote should be federally guaranteed for blacks and Hispanics. Now members are called on to deal with more ambiguous policies like affirmative action and racial quotas."

Solutions to problems normally involve "some fairly simple routines emphasizing the tried and true (or at least not discredited)." A repertoire of proposals exists—for example, blue-ribbon commissions, trust funds, or pilot projects—that can be applied to a variety of unsolved problems. Problem solvers also must guard against recommending solutions that will be viewed as worse than the problem.

Adopting Policy   Laws are ideas whose time has come. The right time for a policy is what scholar John Kingdon calls the *policy window*: the opportunity presented by circumstances and attitudes to enact a policy into law. Policy entrepreneurs must seize the opportunity before the policy window closes and the idea's time has passed.

Once policies are ripe for adoption, they must gain popular acceptance. This is the function of *legitimation*, the process through which policies come to be viewed by the public as right or proper. Inasmuch as citizens are expected to comply with laws or regulations—pay taxes, observe rules, or make sacrifices of one sort or another—the policies themselves must appear to have been properly considered and enacted. A nation whose policies lack legitimacy is in deep trouble.

Symbolic acts, such as members voting on the House or Senate floor or the president signing a bill, signal to everyone that policies have been duly adopted according to traditional forms. Hearings and debates, moreover, serve not only to fine-tune policies but also to cultivate support from affected interests. Responding to critics of Congress's slowness in adopting energy legislation, Sen. Ted Stevens, R-Alaska, asked these questions:

> Would you want an energy bill to flow through the Senate and not have anyone consider the impacts on housing or on the automotive industry or on the energy industries that provide our light and power? Should we ignore the problems of the miner or the producer or the distributor? Our legislative process must reflect all of the problems if the public is to have confidence in the government.

Legitimating, in other words, often demands a measured pace and attention to procedural details. (Another strategy is to move quickly—before opposition forces can mobilize—to enact bold changes and then work to gain the public's acceptance of them.)

Implementing Policy In the final stage, policies shaped by the legislature and the highest executive levels are put into effect, usually by a federal agency. Policies are not self-executing: they must be promulgated and enforced. A law or executive order rarely spells out exactly how a particular policy will be implemented. Congress and the president usually delegate most decisions about implementation to the responsible agencies under broad but stated guidelines. Implementation determines the ultimate effect of policies. Officials of the executive branch can thwart a policy by foot dragging or sheer inefficiency. By the same token, overzealous administrators can push a policy far beyond its creators' intent.

Congress therefore must exercise its oversight role. It may require executive agencies to report or consult with congressional committees or to follow certain formal procedures. Members of Congress get feedback on the operation of federal programs through a variety of channels: media coverage, interest group protests, and even constituent casework. With such information Congress can and often does pass judgment by adjusting funding, introducing amendments, or recasting the basic legislation governing a particular policy.

Types of Domestic Policies

One way to understand public policies is to analyze the nature of the policies themselves. Scholars have classified policies in many different ways. The typology we shall use identifies three types of domestic policies: distributive, regulatory, and redistributive.

Distributive Policies   Distributive policies or programs are government actions that convey tangible benefits to private individuals, groups, or firms. Invariably, they involve subsidies to favored individuals or groups. The benefits are often called "pork" (special-interest spending for projects in members' states or districts), although that appellation is sometimes difficult to define. After all, "one person's pork is another person's steak." The projects come in several different varieties:

> Dams, roads and bridges, known as "green pork," are old hat. These days, there is also "academic pork" in the form of research grants to colleges, "defense pork" in the form of geographically specific military expenditures and lately "high-tech pork," for example the intense fight to authorize research into super computers and high-definition television (HDTV).

The presence of distributive politics—which makes many interests better off and few, if any, visibly worse off—is natural in Congress, which as a nonhierarchical institution must build coalitions in order to function. A textbook example was the $1-billion-plus National Parks and Recreation Act of 1978. Dubbed the "Park Barrel" bill, it created so many parks, historical sites, seashores, wilderness areas, wild and scenic rivers, and national trails that it sailed through the Interior (now Resources) Committee and passed the House by a 341-61 vote. "Notice how quiet we are. We all got something in there," said one House member, after the Rules Committee cleared the bill in five minutes flat. Another member quipped, "If it had a blade of grass and a squirrel, it got in the bill." Distributive politics of this kind throws into sharp relief the "two Congresses" notion: national policy as a mosaic of local interests.

The politics of distribution works best when tax revenues are expanding, fueled by high productivity and economic growth—characteristics of the U.S. economy from the end of World War II through the mid-1970s. When productivity declines or tax cutting squeezes revenues, it becomes difficult to add new benefits or expand old ones. Such was the plight of lawmakers in the 1980s and 1990s. Yet distributive impulses remained strong, adding pressure to wring distributive elements out of tight budgets. Even in the tight-fisted 104th Congress, lawmakers in both parties ensured that money would be spent for particular purposes in their districts or states. As one account noted:

> With Republicans cutting non-military spending but protecting the defense budget from reductions, the huge $243 billion Pentagon spending bill this year has taken the place of pork-barrel public works measures of old. Instead of seeking bridges and roads, members of Congress in both parties have been clamoring for defense contracts to protect home-state jobs and businesses.

House GOP freshman John Ensign of Nevada highlighted both the "two Congresses" and the prevailing legislative sentiments toward distributive policy making when he said, "I hate the idea of pork, but if there's a pot of money, I want to make sure that Nevada gets its fair share."

Regulatory Policies   Regulatory policies are designed to protect the public against harm or abuse that might result from unbridled private activity. For example, the Food and Drug Administration (FDA) monitors standards for foodstuffs and tests drugs for purity, safety, and effectiveness, and the Federal Trade Commission (FTC) guards against illegal business practices, such as deceptive advertising.

Federal regulation against certain abuses dates from the late nineteenth century, when the Interstate Commerce Act and the Sherman Antitrust Act were enacted to protect against transport and monopoly abuses. As the twentieth century dawned, scandalous practices in slaughterhouses and food processing plants, colorfully described by reform-minded muckraking reporters, led to meatpacking, food, and drug regulations. The stock market collapse in 1929 and the Great Depression paved the way for the New Deal legislation that would regulate the banking and securities industries and labor-management relations. Consumer rights and environmental protection came of age in the 1960s and 1970s. Dramatic attacks on unsafe automobiles by Ralph Nader and others led to new laws mandating tougher safety standards. Concern about smog produced by auto exhausts led to the Clean Air Act of 1970. And concern about airline delays, congestion, and safety prompted Congress to consider new regulatory controls for the nation's air traffic system. . . .

Redistributive Policies   Redistribution, which visibly shifts resources from one group to another, is the most difficult of all political feats. Because it is controversial, redistributive policy engages a broad spectrum of political actors—not only in the House and Senate chambers but also in the executive branch and among interest groups and the public at large. Redistributive issues tend to be ideological: they often separate liberals and conservatives because they upset relationships between social and economic classes. Theodore R. Marmor described the thirty-year fight over medical care for the aged as "cast in terms of class conflict":

> The leading adversaries . . . brought into the opposing camps a large number of groups whose interests were not directly affected by the Medicare outcome. . . . [I]deological charges and countercharges dominated public discussion, and each side seemed to regard compromise as unacceptable.

Most of the divisive socioeconomic issues of the past generation—civil rights, affirmative action, school busing, aid to education, homelessness, abortion, tax reform—were redistributive problems. Fiscal policy making has taken on a redistributive character as federal expenditures outpace revenues, and lawmakers are forced to find ways to close the gap. Cutting federal benefits and opening up new revenue sources both involve redistribution because they turn "haves" into "have nots." That is why politicians today find budget and revenue issues so burdensome. "I wasn't here in the glory days, when a guy with a bright idea of a scholarship program or whatever could get a few hundred million dollars to pursue it," lamented Rep. Richard J. Durbin, D-Ill. "Now you've got to take from one to give to the other."

Federal budgeting is marked not only by extreme conflict but also by techniques to disguise the redistributions or make them more palatable. Omnibus budget packages permit legislators to approve cuts *en bloc* rather than one by one, and across-the-board formulas (like "freezes") give the appearance of spreading the misery equally to affected groups. In all such vehicles, distributive elements are added to placate the more vocal opponents of change. Such is the unhappy lot of politicians consigned to lawmaking in a redistributive mode. ■

American Politics Today

Conversations about federal budgetary policy usually cause eyes to glaze over, but few issues are of greater importance, especially in the long run. The most critical problem is the federal budget deficit—the difference between how much the government spends and how much it takes in. The annual federal deficit is currently counted in the hundreds of billions of dollars; given existing spending commitments and projected revenues, the deficit is likely to continue for years to come. Already Washington spends over $400 billion every year just in interest payments.*

   Unless the government cuts spending, raises taxes, or both, the budget deficit is likely to rise to unprecedented levels over the next few decades. The main problems involve spending on Social Security and Medicare, which provide pension payments and health insurance to older Americans. As Americans live longer, and as medical care becomes more expensive, spending on both programs—but especially Medicare—is expected to grow rapidly.

   Something, it seems, will have to give. In this selection, economist David R. Henderson argues that that something is likely to be on the spending side of the equation rather than on the taxing side. In any event, the resolution of the federal government's budgetary problems will have enormous consequences for the daily lives of millions of Americans. Although Henderson talks in the language of numbers, his analysis raises issues of the highest order of importance.

Questions

1. Why does Henderson believe that the federal government will eventually have to limit spending, especially on Medicare? Why does he believe that sufficient tax increases are unlikely?
2. What policy changes will be necessary to rein in spending on Medicare and other government programs? What are the likely political consequences of such changes?

---

*U.S. Treasury Department Office of Public Affairs, "Preliminary Statement of Budget Results for Fiscal Year 2006," October 11, 2006, Table 3, http://www.fms.treas.gov/mts/10-11-06-Budget-Results.pdf.

13.2 Why Spending Has Got to Give (2006)

David R. Henderson

Federal spending rose from about 18.5 percent of gross domestic product (GDP) at the end of the Clinton administration to 20.3 percent by the end of George W. Bush's first term—during the watch, that is, of a Republican president and a Republican Congress. Of course, much of this increase is in defense spending and homeland security. But President Bush has not chosen guns at the expense of butter: He has opted for both. He did not veto even a single spending bill. And real (that is, inflation-adjusted) domestic discretionary spending, not counting homeland security, rose by an annual average of 4.8 percent over his first four years in office. Someone who favors relatively small government could get awfully depressed looking at these numbers.

One does not get less depressed contemplating the spending increases that are projected over the next 45 years. Credible estimates from the Congressional Budget Office and from independent budget analysts show federal spending doubling as a percent of GDP by the middle of the twenty-first century, reaching about 40 percent of GDP (see Figure 1). Yet some historical constants and some facts about Americans' views on taxes incline this observer to believe that federal spending will come nowhere close to 40 percent of GDP by mid-century.

Before we turn to the good news, let us consider the bad news: the news on spending. Defense spending rose by $161 billion between fiscal years 2001 and 2005, an increase of $117 billion in 2001 dollars. This was large, and yet it took defense spending from a postwar low of 3.0 percent of GDP in 2001 (tied with 1999

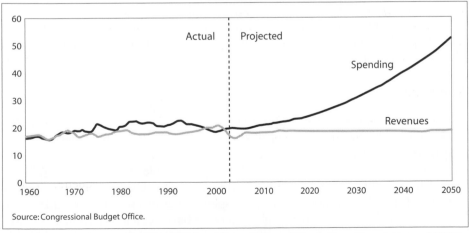

Figure 1   A Scenario for Total Federal Spending and Revenues, Percentage of GDP

From David R. Henderson, "Why Spending Has Got to Give," *Policy Review*, April/May 2006, pp. 3–13. Reprinted by permission.

and 2000) to 3.8 percent of GDP. Even if the U.S. government maintains a strong military presence in the world, which seems likely, it can do so with less than 4 percent of GDP. To see where spending is projected to grow substantially as a percentage of GDP, therefore, we must look elsewhere. The three programs accounting for most of this increase are projected to be Medicare, Medicaid, and Social Security. Medicare and Medicaid spending together are credibly predicted to be about 21 percent of GDP by 2050, and Social Security spending is expected to equal about 6 percent of GDP by 2050. All three are driven by demographics—the aging of the U.S. population—and the first two are also driven, ironically, by improvements in health care.

Consider Social Security first. Social Security spending, which is now about 4.2 percent of GDP, is likely to be 6.2 percent of GDP by the middle of the twenty-first century unless changes are made in the program. This is due to two main factors: 1) the retirement of the baby-boom generation and 2) the increasing life expectancy of the elderly. The two factors together mean that the fraction of people aged 65 or older will rise from 12 percent of the population in 2000 to 19 percent in 2030. The working-age population, by contrast, is projected to fall from 59 percent to 56 percent. Based on this, the Social Security trustees project that the number of workers per Social Security recipient will decline from about 3.3 in the early 2000s to 2.2. in 2030. Of course, substantially increased immigration of younger people or a significant decline in life expectancy of the elderly could slow this trend but absent that, these population numbers are fairly firm. And absent a change in that ratio, absent policy changes in Social Security (more on that later), and absent a substantial increase in the growth of productivity, the increase in Social Security to about 6 percent of GDP is also fairly firm.

The scarier numbers are in Medicare, the federal government's socialized medicine program for the elderly, and Medicaid, the program for the poor and near-poor: Not only is the number of people enrolled in these programs increasing, but spending per person has also increased and will likely continue to do so.

Since 1967, the first full year of Medicare spending, spending has risen from 0.2 percent of GDP to about 2.3 percent in fiscal year 2004. Medicaid spending rose from 0.3 percent of GDP in 1970 to 1.5 percent in 2003, a quintupling of its share of output. Between 1970 and 2003, Medicare spending per person rose annually by 3 percentage points more than the growth of per capita GDP. Over approximately the same period, Medicaid spending per person rose annually by 2.7 percentage points more than the growth of per capita GDP. The spending growth comes from the combination of Medicare and Medicaid beneficiaries spending other people's money plus the incentive thereby created to develop technological improvements allowing doctors and hospitals to do more. The spending is valuable. That's not the problem. The problem is that Medicare and Medicaid recipients are spending other people's money and therefore do not restrain their spending as much as they would if they were spending their own. What would otherwise have been an individual decision by someone trading off between health care and other goods becomes, instead, society's problem because the government has made it into society's problem. And because incremental dollars spent are partly paid for by taxpayers, people trade off at a different point than they would if they were spending their own money. Specifically, they buy medical care that they would not be willing to purchase on their own.

This is not to say that medical spending would not be rising as a percentage of GDP if there were no Medicare or Medicaid. Economists Robert E. Hall and Charles I. Jones argue that because health care adds years to our lives, people will voluntarily spend a higher fraction of their income on health care as their real incomes grow. Hall and Jones project, in fact, that overall health care spending could be as much as 33 percent of GDP by mid-century (up from about 15 percent today) and argue that there is nothing wrong with that. They are right. The problem, as noted above, comes when people spend other people's money.

Based on past growth in spending per person and assuming no changes in policy, the Congressional Budget Office projects that by 2050, Medicare and Medicaid spending could be as much as 21 percent of GDP (see Figure 2). Together with the growth in Social Security spending, and assuming that other spending doesn't fall as a percentage of GDP, this would put federal government spending in 2050 at about 40 percent of GDP, or twice its share of GDP today.

Tax Increases Aren't Enough

That's the bad news. Now the good news. The Congressional Budget Office said it best:

> In the past half-century, total revenues have ranged from 16.1 percent to 20.8 percent of GDP, with no obvious trend over time. On average their share of GDP has hovered around 18.5 percent.

This is about as close to a historical constant as one finds in public-sector economics. U.S. experience differs dramatically from that of other countries. This is probably because of the political equilibrium we have reached in the United States due not only to our particular demographics but also, and more important, to division of powers and a republican rather than a parliamentary political system. Clearly, unless the deficit takes up a lot of the slack (which is highly unlikely . . .), something's gotta give. Which will it be: taxes or government spending? The odds-on favorite is government spending.

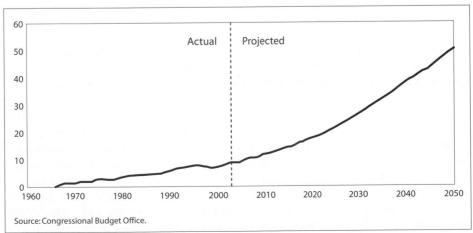

Figure 2 Total Federal Spending for Medicare and Medicaid, Percentage of GDP

It's true that taxes as a share of GDP did rise in the late 1970s from 18 percent in fiscal year 1977 to 19.6 percent in fiscal 1981. But there are three things to note about this. First, the high inflation of the 1970s drove people into higher tax brackets, and the indexing of tax brackets that Ronald Reagan and Congress put into the 1981 tax law, effective in 1985, means that inflation alone can no longer put people into higher tax brackets. Inflation, therefore, cannot be the income-tax-revenue generator for government that it was in the late 1970s. Second, the increase in tax revenue generated by inflation was one of the main factors that led to popular support for Reagan's 1981 cut in income tax rates at all income levels. Third, this increase in tax revenue as a percent of GDP still kept the number within the 20-percent upper limit.

Ample polling data also support the view that Americans, whatever their other positions, are against higher taxes on themselves. Various polling organizations asked Americans their views on taxes in 1938 and in most years since 1947. The percentage who thought their taxes were too low was always between 0 and 2, except for 2003, 2004, and 2005, when the number hit 3 percent. And in every year but 1949 and 2003, the percentage who thought their taxes were too high exceeded the percentage who thought their taxes were about right, usually by a wide margin.

It's not surprising, of course, that people would think their own taxes are too high. But as the following evidence shows, most Americans are even against taxing the highest-income people more and, indeed, favor taxing them less. A Roper Center/*Reader's Digest* poll in October 1995 asked people what they thought was the highest percentage of income governments at all levels should take in taxes of all forms. The higher the hypothetical income, of course, the higher was the percentage people found to be fair. What was striking, though, was how low this percentage was. Even for the highest-income family asked about, one making $200,000 a year, the mean percentage that people found to be fair was 27 and the median percentage found to be fair was 25. To put this in perspective, a real family making $200,000 a year or more at about that time paid about 28.7 percent of its income in federal taxes of all forms. Adding in their state and local taxes would take this number well above 30 percent and close to 35 percent. In other words, high-income people were already paying well above the median level that the Americans surveyed thought fair.

Nor did the Bush tax cuts change this much. A 2002 study by economists William G. Gale and Samara R. Potter found that, taking account of the 2001 Bush tax cut, people in the top 1 percent of the income distribution paid 31.3 percent of their income in taxes of all forms. To add more perspective, consider the fact that left-wing politician Al Sharpton, who advocates higher taxes on "the rich," when asked by ABC News reporter John Stossel what percentage of their income "the rich" should pay in federal income taxes, answered "around fifteen percent." This is well below the approximately 20 percent, in income taxes alone, that they now pay. It's true that Sharpton can get away with advocating tax increases on high-income people because few people know just how much high-income people pay in taxes, but various economists and reporters will certainly get these facts out to the public whenever a tax increase becomes a serious threat.

The bottom line is that it would be extremely difficult for the federal government to raise taxes by more than a few percentage points of GDP. Even if federal taxes were to rise, say, to 25 percent of GDP, this would imply a 35 percent increase in the federal tax share of GDP over its historical average share of 18.5 percent and would still require government spending to "give" much more than taxes.

The implications of these facts about government spending and taxation are huge. First, the dominant problem of domestic economic policy for the next 40 years will be how to rein in the growth of government spending. The president and Congress may have the luxury of escaping it for the next few years, but by sometime in the next decade (and possibly even during this one), reining in spending will be paramount. Second, many of the proposals now being pushed by pro-free-market economists that are not treated seriously by politicians in Washington will be taken very seriously very soon. These include cashing out Medicare by giving every recipient straight cash or a health care voucher, raising the age to receive full Social Security benefits to 70 and then indexing it to life expectancy, raising the age to qualify for Medicare to accord with the age to qualify for Social Security, capping Social Security benefits in real terms so that they no longer grow, requiring Medicare and Medicaid recipients to pay substantial co-payments for medical care, and privatizing the disability insurance component of the Social Security program. All of these, I predict, will be on the bargaining table. They may not yet be politically feasible but will quickly become so once they become politically necessary. . . .

Issue and Controversy

Since at least the Second World War, American foreign policy has rested on a delicate balance between *multilateralism* and *unilateralism*. Under a multilateral approach, the United States works closely with other nations across the globe to develop and implement foreign policy goals. Under a unilateral approach, by contrast, American policy makers are willing, when it is necessary or convenient, to act alone.

Multilateralism relies heavily on international organizations, such as the United Nations and the North Atlantic Treaty Organization (NATO), and on consultation and coordination with our many allies. Multilateralism may often achieve its desired ends, but it will often involve compromises, endless delays, and a good deal of frustration for American officials. Unilateralism, by contrast, holds great attractions. Under a unilateral approach, the United States can pursue the foreign policy goals it believes to be most important, when and how it thinks best.

Although multilateralism remains critically important to American foreign policy, since 2001 the United States has tilted at key moments in a more unilateralist direction. Exhibit number one is clearly Iraq, where the Bush administration—despite emphasizing that the war was fought by a "coalition of the willing"—provided both the impetus and the vast majority of the resources necessary for the invasion and its aftermath. Yet the

United States has also shown a willingness to act in cooperation with its allies on other critical issues, including efforts to stop Iran and North Korea from developing nuclear weapons.

In this selection, law professor Jed Rubenfeld examines the origins and implications of American unilateralism. For Rubenfeld, unilateralism should not be confused with militarism or with a disdain for the opinions of the rest of the world. Nor should unilateralism be justified by crass self-interest. Indeed, Rubenfeld favors international cooperation and mutual respect among nations. What he rejects is the idea that international agencies or organizations should be able to bind individual nations as a matter of *law*. Such interference with the sovereign power of individual nations does not promote democracy, he argues, but undermines it.

Questions

1. What are the origins of American multilateralism? Of American unilateralism? What arguments might justify the multilateral approach? The unilateral approach?
2. Under what circumstances has the United States relied on a multilateral approach to foreign policy? When and why has the United States turned to a more unilateral approach? Give examples of successful and unsuccessful foreign policy experiences under each approach.

13.3 The Two World Orders (2003)

Jed Rubenfeld

What's the source of America's growing unilateralism? The easy answer is self-interest: We act unilaterally to the extent that we see unilateralism as serving our interests. But the answer prompts a more searching question: Why do so many Americans view unilateralism this way, given the hostility it provokes, the costs it imposes, and the considerable risks it entails? Americans sometimes seem unilateralist almost by instinct, as if it were a matter of principle. Might it be?

It will not do to trace contemporary U.S. unilateralism to the 18th-century doctrine of isolationism, for unilateralism is a very different phenomenon. An isolationist country withdraws from the world, even when others call on it to become involved; a unilateralist country feels free to project itself—its power, its economy, its culture—throughout the world, even when others call on it to stop. Although there may still be a thread of isolationism in the United States today, unilateralism, the far more dominant trend, cannot usefully be derived from it.

The search for an explanation should begin instead at the end of World War II. In 1945, when victory was at hand and his own death only days away, Franklin

From Jed Rubenfeld, "The Two World Orders," *Wilson Quarterly*, Autumn 2003, pp. 32–36. Reprinted by permission of the author.

Roosevelt wrote that the world's task was to ensure "the end of the beginning of wars." So Roosevelt called for a new system of international law and multilateral governance that would be designed to stop future wars before they began. Hence, the irony of America's current position: More than any other country, the United States is responsible for the creation of the international law system it now resists.

The decisive period to understand, then, runs roughly from the end of the war to the present, years that witnessed the birth of a new international legal order. . . . America's leadership in the new internationalism was, at the beginning, so strong that one might be tempted to see today's U.S. unilateralism as a stunning about-face, an aberration even, which may yet subside before too much damage is done. But the hope that the United States will rediscover the multilateralism it once championed assumes that America and Europe were engaged in a common internationalist project after World War II. Was that in fact the case?

It's undoubtedly true that, after the war, Americans followed the path Roosevelt had charted and led Europe and the world toward an unprecedented internationalism. We were the driving force behind the United Nations, the primary drafters of the initial international human-rights conventions, the champions of developing an enforceable system of international law. Indeed, America pressed on Europe the very idea of European union (with France the primary locus of resistance). At the same time, America promoted its new constitutionalism throughout Europe and the world, a constitutionalism in which fundamental rights, as well as protections for minorities, were laid down as part of the world's basic law, beyond the reach of ordinary political processes.

How then did the United States move from its postwar position of leadership in the new international order to its present position of outlier?

The Cold War played an essential role in the change, fracturing the new international order before it had taken root. At the same time, the Cold War also had the effect of keeping the Atlantic alliance intact for many decades by suppressing divisions that would show themselves in full force only after 1989. When, in the 1990s, the United States emerged as the last superpower standing, it became much easier for the forces of European union to move ahead and for the buried divisions between America and its European allies to be made apparent. The most fundamental of those divisions had been the most invisible: From the start, the postwar boom in international and constitutional law had had different meanings in America and Europe—because the war itself meant different things in America and Europe.

At the risk of overgeneralization, we might say that for Europeans (that is, for those Europeans not joined to the Axis cause), World War II, in which almost 60 million people perished, exemplified the horrors of *nationalism*. Specifically and significantly, it exemplified the horrors of *popular* nationalism. Nazism and fascism were manifestations, however perverse, of popular sovereignty. Adolf Hitler and Benito Mussolini rose to power initially through elections and democratic processes. Both claimed to speak for the people, not only before they assumed dictatorial powers but afterward, too, and both were broadly popular, as were their nationalism, militarism, repression, and, in Hitler's case, genocidal objectives. From the postwar European point of view, the Allies' victory was a victory *against* nationalism, *against* popular sovereignty, *against* democratic excess.

   The American experience of victory could not have differed more starkly. For Americans, winning the war was a victory *for* nationalism—that is to say, for *our* nation and *our* kind of nationalism. It was a victory *for* popular sovereignty (*our* popular sovereignty) and, most fundamentally, a victory *for* democracy (*our* democracy). Yes, the war held a lesson for Americans about the dangers of democracy, but the lesson was that the nations of continental Europe had proven themselves incapable of handling democracy when left to their own devices. If Europe was to develop democratically, it would need American tutelage. If Europe was to overcome its nationalist pathologies, it might have to become a United States of Europe. Certain European countries might even need to have democratic institutions imposed upon them, although it would be best if they adopted those institutions themselves, or at least persuaded themselves that they had done so.

   These contrasting lessons shaped the divergent European and American experiences of the postwar boom in international political institutions and international law. For Europeans, the fundamental point of international law was to address the catastrophic problem of nationalism—to check national sovereignty, emphatically including national *popular* sovereignty. This remains the dominant European view today. The United Nations, the emerging European Union, and international law in general are expressly understood in Europe as constraints on nationalism and national sovereignty, the perils of which were made plain by the war. They are also understood, although more covertly, as restraints on *democracy*, at least in the sense that they place increasing power in the hands of international actors (bureaucrats, technocrats, diplomats, and judges) at a considerable remove from popular politics and popular will.

   In America, the postwar internationalism had a very different meaning. Here, the point of international law could not ultimately be antidemocratic or antinationalist because the Allies' victory had been a victory for democracy (American democracy) and for the nation (the American nation). America in the postwar period could not embrace an antinationalist, antidemocratic international order as Europe did. It needed a counterstory to tell itself about its role in promoting the new international order.

The counterstory was as follows: When founding the United Nations, writing the first conventions on international rights, creating constitutions for Germany and Japan, and promoting a United States of Europe, Americans were bestowing the gifts of American liberty, prosperity, and law, particularly American constitutional law, on the rest of the world. The "new" international human rights were to be nothing other than the fundamental guarantees made famous by the U.S. Constitution. Wasn't America light-years ahead of continental Europe in the ways of democracy? International law would be, basically, American law made applicable to other nations, and the business of the new internationalism would be to transmit American principles to the rest of the world. So of course America could be the most enthusiastic supporter of the new international order. Why would it not support the project of making the world more American?

   In the American imagination, then, the internationalism and multilateralism we promoted were for the rest of the world, not for us. What Europe would recognize as international law was law we already had. The notion that U.S. practices—such as capital punishment—held constitutional by our courts under our Bill of Rights might be said to violate international law was, from this point of view, not a conceptual possibility. Our willingness to promote and sign on to international law would be second to none—except when it came to any conventions that might require a change in U.S. domestic law or policy. The principal organs of U.S. foreign policy, including the State Department and, famously, the Senate, emphatically resisted the idea that international law could be a means of changing internal U.S. law. In the 1950s, the United States refused to join any of the major human-rights and antigenocide conventions. The rest of the world might need an American-modeled constitution, but we already had one.

In part, this exceptional attitude reflected American triumphalism in the wake of the war; in part, it expressed American know-nothing parochialism; and, in part, it placated southern fears that U.S. participation in international rights agreements could loosen the chokehold in which American blacks were held. But it reflected something more fundamental as well: a conception of constitutional democracy that had been reaffirmed by the war. It was impossible for Americans to see the new international constitutionalism as Europeans saw it—a constraint on democratic nationalism—for that would have contradicted America's basic understanding of constitutional democracy.

• • •

Three specific developments over the past decade helped press the United States toward unilateralism: the 1999 military intervention in Kosovo; a growing skepticism about international law, including the concern that international law might be used as a vehicle for anti-Americanism; and the events of September 11, 2001. Each merits additional consideration.

For many in the United States, the Kosovo intervention stands today as a unilateralist precedent. Because the UN Security Council never approved the use of force in Kosovo, international lawyers regarded the U.S.-led bombing as plainly illegal. But this asserted illegality has not caused Americans to regret the intervention. On the contrary, it has reinforced the view that events in the former Yugoslavia represented an appalling failure on the part of the international law system, the United Nations, and, in particular, the nations of Europe. From the American perspective, if the UN-centered international law system could not bring itself to authorize the use of force in Kosovo, then that system was incapable of discharging the responsibility that is an essential corollary of authority.

The United States had no compelling territorial, imperial, or economic interests in Kosovo. The intervention sought rather, at least in the American account, to prevent manifest, grotesque, genocidal crimes. And if the United Nations did not respond to the most blatant, wanton, and massive of human rights violations in Kosovo, how could it be trusted to respond to less demonstrable but perhaps more dangerous threats elsewhere?

Kosovo is a doubly significant precedent because it illustrates how Americans do not quite recognize the UN Charter as *law*. American society is notorious for turning political questions into legal ones. Yet Americans, including American lawyers, were and are largely uninterested in the Kosovo bombing's asserted illegality under the UN Charter. The same broad indifference would emerge again when internationalists claimed that the war in Iraq was illegal.

To be sure, some American international-law specialists are interested in these issues, but they are often perceived by the rest of the U.S. legal world to be speaking a foreign language, or not so much a language as a kind of gibberish lacking the basic grammar—the grammar of enforceability—that alone gives legal language a claim to meaning. Kosovo symbolizes not merely an exceptional, exigent circumstance in which the United States was justified in going outside the UN framework, but rather an entire attitude about that framework, according to which the UN system, while pretending to be a legal system, isn't really a legal system. And what, in this view, is the United Nations really about? The several possible answers to the question are not attractive: hot air, a corrupt bureaucracy, an institution that acts as if it embodied world democracy when in reality its delegates represent illegitimate and oppressive autocracies, an invidious wonderland where Libya can be elected president of a human-rights commission.

A second spur to U.S. unilateralism has been a growing skepticism about the agenda the "international legal community" has been pursuing. The skepticism is partly due to the proliferation of human rights conventions that are systematically violated by many of the states subscribing to them. A good example is the convention banning discrimination against women, which the United States has been almost alone in refusing to ratify. But what is one to make of the fact that the signatory nations include Saudi Arabia and other states not exactly famous for respecting women's equality?

A deeper reason for the skepticism lies in the indications that international law may be used as a vehicle for anti-American resentments. A case in point is the position taken by the "international community" with respect to the continuing use of capital punishment in some American jurisdictions. Most Americans, whatever their view of capital punishment, can respect the moral arguments that condemn the death penalty. But what many Americans have trouble respecting or understanding is the concerted effort to condemn the United States as a human-rights violator because of the death penalty and to expel the United States from international organizations on that ground. When the international community throws down the gauntlet over the death penalty in America while merely clearing its throat about the slaughter in Yugoslavia, Americans can hardly be blamed if they see a sign that an anti-American agenda can be expected to find expression in international law.

This is not a purely speculative concern. Given that the U.S.-led military interventions in Kosovo and Iraq were probably in violation of international law, might U.S. officers therefore be liable to criminal prosecution in international courts? No, say the international lawyers. Americans need not fear criminal repercussions because international law "clearly" distinguishes between *jus ad bellum*, the law that determines whether the use of military force is legal, and *jus in bello*, the law that determines whether particular acts undertaken during armed hostilities are criminal. But academic certainty about the "clear" meaning of law has never been a reliable predictor of how the law will actually be interpreted by courts. How can Americans be certain that the international law system will not embrace the perfectly reasonable logic under which an *unlawful* bombing becomes a *criminal* act, especially when Americans have acted unilaterally? This possibility may help explain U.S. resistance to the International Criminal Court.

The events of September 11, 2001, had obvious implications for U.S. unilateralism. There was a critical period in the weeks following the massacre when a renewed U.S. multilateralism in the prosecution of the war against terrorism seemed a distinct possibility. Americans were stunned by the prevalence and intensity of anti-American sentiments expressed all over the world. Even Europeans who condemned the attacks frequently suggested, implicitly and explicitly, that the United States had it coming, that the motives behind the attack were understandable, and that the massacre, though reprehensible, might have a salutary effect on U.S. policy. A period of soul-searching followed in the United States. It lasted maybe a month and ended with a characteristically American reaction: to hell with them.

So began the rhetoric that continues to escalate today. The White House took increasingly belligerent positions, which elicited new denunciations of our bullying, and the denunciations spurred Americans to feel more and more that they would have to fight this world war on their own. The fighting in Afghanistan hardened that resolve. For whatever reason, the European nations, with the exception of Great Britain, contributed almost nothing to the war, and instead issued repeated warnings that the war might be illegal, that the bombings could be considered war crimes if too many civilians died, and that the fight, in any case, would be unwinnable once the opposition took to the mountains. Did we win? That remains to be seen. But the American experience of the Afghan campaign was of an overwhelming, unexpectedly swift victory—achieved essentially without the help of the international community. And this made possible the war in Iraq.

Because of that war, U.S. unilateralism is now identified in many people's minds with U.S. military aggression and the occupation of Iraq. I am not arguing here either for or against the Iraq War; the case for U.S. unilateralism does not turn on the justifiability of that war. The fundamental question is this: Which of two visions of world order will the United States use its vast power to advance? Since World War II, much of "old" Europe has been pursuing an antinational, antidemocratic world constitutionalism that, for all its idealism and achievements, is irreconcilable with America's commitment to democratic self-government.

• • •

The justification of unilateralism outlined here is not intended to condone American disdain for the views of other nations. On the contrary, America should always show a decent respect for the opinions of the rest of mankind, and America would be a far safer, healthier place if it could win back some of the support and affection it has lost. Unilateralism does not set its teeth against international cooperation or coalition building. What sets its teeth on edge is the shift that occurs when such cooperation takes the form of binding agreements administered, interpreted, and enforced by multilateral bodies—the shift, in other words, from international *cooperation* to international *law*. America's commitment to democratic self-government gives the United States good reason to be skeptical about—indeed, to resist—international legal regimes structured, as they now are, around antinationalist and antidemocratic principles.

The unilateralism I am defending is not a license for aggressive U.S. militarism. It is commanded by the aspirations of democracy and would violate its own essential principles if it were to become an engine of empire. But the great and unsettling fact of 21st-century global governance is that America is doomed to become something like a world policeman. With the development of small, uncontainable nuclear technologies, and with the inability of the United Nations to do the job, the United States will be in the business of using force abroad against real or feared criminal activity to a far greater extent than ever before.

This new American role will be deeply dangerous, to other nations and to our own, not least because American presidents may be tempted to use the role of world's law enforcer as a justification for a new American militarism that has the United States constantly waging or preparing for war. If the United States is going to act unilaterally abroad, it's imperative that in our domestic politics we retain mechanisms for combating presidential overreaching.

Since September 11, 2001, the White House has flirted with a dangerous *double* unilateralism, joining the president's willingness to act without international consent abroad to an effort to bypass Congress and the judiciary at home. In December 2001, without congressional approval, the president announced the withdrawal of the United States from an important missile treaty with Russia. In early 2002, the White House began claiming a presidential power to deem any individual, including an American citizen arrested on American soil, an "enemy combatant" and on that basis to imprison him indefinitely, with no judicial review. Later that year, the president came close to asserting a power to make war on Iraq without express congressional authorization.

This double unilateralism, which leaves presidential power altogether unchecked, is a great danger. If we are to be unilateralists abroad, we have a special responsibility—to ourselves and to the world—to maintain and reinvigorate the vital checks and balances of American constitutionalism at home. ■

 # View from the Inside

The development and implementation of public policy does not occur spontaneously. Policies must be nurtured and developed by individuals and organizations committed to a cause, and willing to spend the resources—in time and money—to turn their ideas into reality. Such "policy entrepreneurs" can be found in the executive branch, in interest groups, among the general public, and in Congress.*

One such policy entrepreneur is Rep. David E. Price (D-NC), who has served in Congress since 1987. In this selection, Price recalls his successful efforts to gather support for what became the Scientific and Advanced Technology Act of 1992.

---

*See selection 11.4 for additional views on policy entrepreneurship.

Questions

1. What led Price to decide to concentrate his efforts on the Scientific and Advanced Technology bill? What factors contributed to his success in this endeavor? What obstacles did he have to overcome?
2. Would you characterize the Scientific and Advanced Technology Act as a "distributive policy," a "regulatory policy," or a "redistributive policy"? (See selection 13.1.) What lessons might Price's experience teach us about the making of policy in Congress? About policy making in general?

13.4 Policy Entrepreneurship in Congress (2004)

David E. Price

• • •

The issue that comes to me most naturally by virtue of my background and experience is education. My mother was a high school English teacher; I have early memories of former students coming up to her on the street, recounting what she had done for them, and sometimes, to my amazement, thanking her for demanding so much. My father taught biology and served as high school principal until the needs of our growing family forced him to take a job with more adequate pay. Education opened up the wider world to me, and it probably surprised no one that I chose teaching as a career. When I ran for Congress, both my personal credentials and the preoccupations of my district dictated that the need to support and improve education would be a central campaign theme.

From my earliest months in the House, I was looking for a fit between my education interests and my committee assignments. This helped attract me to the Science Committee and to Science, Research, and Technology (SRT) as the subcommittee most attuned to education policy. This in turn led my staff and me to focus on workplace literacy as a concept that tied education to the demands of workplaces that were becoming more and more technologically sophisticated. North Carolina leaders in industry and research continually told me of their need for a trained workforce; the two years beyond high school, provided most often by community colleges, was the level of training increasingly required by most new, good jobs. Yet neither the Department of Education nor the National Science Foundation (NSF), an agency under the Science Committee's jurisdiction, had done much to encourage educational improvements at that level.

Doug Walgren (D-Pennsylvania), chairman of the SRT Subcommittee, was a generous, accommodating colleague who had pushed for years to get NSF to use

---

From *The Congressional Experience* by David E. Price. Reprinted by permission of Westview Press, a member of Perseus Books Group.

methods successfully employed at other educational levels to improve curricula and teaching methods in advanced technology at community colleges. He welcomed my interest and scheduled a subcommittee hearing in [my district] for November 9, 1987, ten months into my first term. This allowed me to assemble a stellar cast of North Carolinians, including the president of the community college system, the general manager of IBM, and other business, education, and civic leaders, for a full day of hearings. I staked out training for the workplace and strengthening community colleges as education issues I intended to pursue. We defined workplace literacy broadly, hearing from organizers of various sorts of literacy programs, but the hearings helped define a focus on the particular challenges of the high-tech workplace that we maintained for the ensuing five years.

One option was to make a renewed push for Walgren's community college proposal. But the bill had encountered resistance from NSF and even his subcommittee's own staff, and a strong community of advocacy had never developed around it. It seemed advisable to open up another arena for considering the issue, exploring alternative approaches and mobilizing additional interest and support. This I was able to do through the Sunbelt Caucus: Rep. Hal Rogers (R-Kentucky) and I cochaired a task force on workplace literacy and commissioned a Sunbelt Institute study that identified functional literacy as "the South's number one competitiveness issue." I then organized a Sunbelt Caucus literacy summit in [my district] early in the 101st Congress, which carried forward some of the interest and enthusiasm generated in our 1987 hearing.

By mid-1989, I was ready to introduce my own bill, the Science and Technological Literacy Act. I retained the basic thrust of Walgren's earlier proposal: individual project grants from NSF to community colleges to support meritorious training programs and the creation of ten "centers of excellence" among these colleges to serve as national clearinghouses for best practices in technical training and/or science and mathematics education. I added sections authorizing a focus, in this and other NSF programs, on curricular revision and the development of innovative instruction technologies. Before introducing the bill on August 3, I carefully assembled a bipartisan group of cosponsors, including Rogers and Sherwood Boehlert (R-New York), ranking Republican on the SRT Subcommittee, as well as Walgren and Robert Roe (D-New Jersey), chair of the full Science Committee.

The SRT hearing on October 31 was an upbeat affair, with a number of members participating and former (and future) North Carolina governor Jim Hunt serving as leadoff witness. But NSF continued to drag its feet. Out of a budget approaching $3 billion, NSF acknowledged spending only $4 million annually on two-year institutions, with most of that going for instrumentation and laboratory equipment. The foundation insisted that it needed no new statutory authority to do what the bill envisioned and that these kinds of training programs would be best handled by the Education and Labor Departments. This attitude changed somewhat in the ensuing months. When NSF Director Erich Bloch made a rare joint appearance with Secretary of Education Lauro Cavazos before our subcommittee on February 28, 1990, he identified "adult science and technical training" as an area that was "falling through the cracks" between the two agencies—an admission I immediately seized on as a demonstration "that strengthening NSF's . . .

support for the development of exemplary technical training programs . . . might not be quite as distant from NSF's mission as some have suggested in the past." We were not able to move the bill in the 101st Congress, a disappointment to me as I prepared to leave the Science Committee for Appropriations. But we had made some headway, not only in softening NSF and Bush administration opposition but also in mobilizing the national community college associations and institutions in the districts of key members. I was determined to press ahead in the 102nd Congress.

Election night 1990 brought unwelcome news of Walgren's defeat and necessitated a fine-tuning of our strategy. His successor as subcommittee chair, Rick Boucher (D-Virginia), was a friend and a sponsor in past years of the Walgren bill. But with the accession of my North Carolina colleague Tim Valentine to the chair of the Subcommittee on Technology and Competitiveness, Valentine and I and our staffs saw an opportunity to give the bill an added boost. On reintroducing the bill (H.R. 2936) on July 17,1991, I sought and received a joint referral to both subcommittees. I had refined the earlier bill considerably and added provisions authorizing grants to community colleges for partnerships with four-year colleges aimed at helping students pursue degree programs in mathematics, science, engineering, or technology. I reenlisted most of my 1989 cosponsors, including George Brown (D-California), the new chair of the full committee; the list eventually grew to sixty-four. Valentine's subcommittee held a hearing and then forwarded the bill to the full committee on October 31. The momentum this created and the continuing efforts of Valentine, ranking Republican Sherwood Boehlert, and their staffs were critically important in pressing Boucher's Science Subcommittee and the full committee to act.

Committee and subcommittee staffs worked on the bill prior to a March 18, 1992, markup, addressing the concerns of NSF and its defenders in various ways. The full committee reported the bill to the House on April 30, but floor consideration was delayed while the staff of the Education and Labor Committee, to whom H.R. 2936 had been jointly referred, scrutinized its provisions. They eventually agreed, after minor changes, to release the bill; the House passed it without dissent on August 10 and sent it to the Senate. This would have been impossibly late in the session had the Senate been required to consider the House bill de novo. Fortunately, however, Senator Barbara Mikulski (D-Maryland) and her staff had been working with community college leaders and my staff on a companion bill (S. 1146) that tracked H.R. 2936 in most respects. House passage of my bill enabled Mikulski to put S. 1146 on a fast track. Senate Labor and Human Resources Committee members, many of them hearing from community college leaders in their own states, agreed to bring the bill more closely into line with the final version of H.R. 2936 and expedite its consideration on the Senate floor. The Senate passed the Mikulski bill by voice vote on October 2, and the next day the House gave its final approval. On October 23, President Bush signed what was now called the Scientific and Advanced-Technology Act of 1992 into law.

The bill as finally approved was more tightly focused than the earlier proposals we fashioned around workplace literacy and fully addressed any lingering concerns about diverting the NSF. Agency reluctance and the multiplicity of committee and subcommittee checkpoints had made for a long and torturous road to passage. By the same token, responsibility for the final product was widely shared—with Doug Walgren, who initially pushed for NSF–community college engagement and provided support for my early efforts; with Valentine, Boehlert, Boucher, and other committee leaders and staff members who persevered after Walgren and I left the Science Committee; with Mikulski, who did a skillful end run around Senate procedures; and with community college leaders who brought home to many members what otherwise might have been an obscure Science Committee initiative. As always, I was indebted to my staff for creative strategizing and repeated reformulations that enabled us to respond to critics while retaining the basic thrust of my bill. . . . ■